Introduction to Political Science

REASON, REFLECTION, AND ANALYSIS

Introduction to Political Science

REASON, REFLECTION, AND ANALYSIS

R. Kenneth Godwin
University of North Texas

John C. Wahlke
University of Arizona

Harcourt Brace College Publishers

Fort Worth   Philadelphia   San Diego   New York   Orlando   Austin   San Antonio
Toronto   Montreal   London   Sydney   Tokyo

Publisher:	Christopher P. Klein
Acquisitions Editor:	David Tatom
Development Editor:	Fritz Schanz, Christopher Nelson
Project Editor:	Matt Ball
Art Director:	Jeanette Barber
Production Manager:	Serena Manning
Product Manager:	Steve Drummond
Copy Editor:	David Talley
Proofreader:	Steven Baker
Indexer:	Leoni McVey

Cover Image: © 1997 Photodisc, Inc.
Text Type: Times Roman

Address for orders:
Harcourt Brace College Publishers
6277 Sea Harbor Drive
Orlando, FL 32887
1-800-782-4479 or 1-800-433-0001 (in Florida)

Address for editorial correspondence:
Harcourt Brace College Publishers
301 Commerce Street, Suite 3700
Fort Worth, TX 76102

Harcourt Brace College Publishers may provide complimentary instructional aids and supplements or supplement packages to those adopters qualified under our adoption policy. Please contact your sales representative for more information. If as an adopter or potential user you receive supplements you do not need, please return them to your sales representative or send them to:

Attn: Returns Department
Troy Warehouse
465 South Lincoln Drive
Troy, MO 63379

ISBN: 0-15-500578-2

Library of Congress Catalog Card Number: 96-78133

Printed in the United States of America

6 7 8 9 0 1 2 3 4 5   067   9 8 7 6 5 4 3 2 1

Preface

Three challenging tasks confront teachers of introductory courses to politics and government: 1) Introduce students to the enduring normative questions of politics and to the great thinkers about them; 2) Provide students with information about political systems and issues from around the world and help them see the relevance of comparative and international issues to their own lives; and 3) Teach them to think critically about politics and to apply logic and empirical analysis to political questions. Despite the immense amount of material that these challenges involve, this text endeavors to accomplish all three.

We had to make several pedagogical choices about how best to meet the above challenges. Most of the students who use this book begin with little knowledge of nations outside of the Anglo-American context. Similarly, many students have had little practice in studying critically normative questions or in applying the scientific method to social science questions. Therefore, we first had to decide how to include complex concepts and ideas from political philosophy and political science while also introducing basic information about a variety of specific governments, political institutions, and political events. Because there are so many new concepts and ideas that beginning students must learn, we begin the book with Western political ideas and examples taken largely from American and British politics and history. With each chapter the emphasis on American politics and Western ideas declines so that the last three chapters deal almost exclusively with countries outside of the United States. The book is not organized around individual countries or particular governments, but around political ideas, institutions, processes and problems. The discussion of these, however, should lead the student to a cumulative, and a comparative, familiarity with specific political systems.

Our second pedagogical task was to choose the approach, or paradigm, through which students could master the most material. We rejected the idea of surveying the "fields of political science" as laid out in the curricula of political science departments. We wanted to focus attention on the world of politics, and not on political science or political scientists. Through a number of trial-and-error attempts while team-teaching the introductory course at the University of Arizona, we found that the rational (or social) choice framework provides a conceptual model that students can understand, and that allows them to identify and analyze both normative and empirical questions. Compared to alternative approaches, students find this perspective easier to apply and to critique. We realize that many political science instructors believe this approach tends to treat all decisions as "economic" decisions, implying that political decisions and choices should be based on reckoning benefits and costs in dollars and cents. Some feel its practitioners tend to be economic conservatives in their personal political ideologies. We do not believe that the social choice paradigm necessarily leads to a conservative or any other particular bias. Nor do we think it eliminates normative considerations from analysis of politics, let alone imply economic benefit-cost analysis. We think it is an effective tool for analyzing the consequences of different choices and decisions, and the different procedures for arriving at them. It can therefore be an effective tool to analyze and critique existing institutions.

Our third pedagogical decision dealt with the extent to which we should integrate empirical and computer exercises into the text. We chose not to integrate them so closely that students must do the assignments to understand the later chapters of the book. We have written the book so the instructor can choose not to use the computer exercises. While we strongly believe that computer literacy is one of the requirements of an educated person in the twenty-first century, the exercises are not essential to the integrity of the text. However, the exercises have helped our own students to understand numerous complex concepts.

An instructor who chooses to cover the entire text and to have students do all assignments will have a difficult time covering all of the material in one semester. For this reason, we have divided the book into sections as well as into chapters. With the exception that all students should read the Introduction and Chapter 1, each section can stand alone. The computer exercises, however, should be done in sequence. Prior assignments are essential to later ones. The assignments teach skills as well as provide students with opportunities to examine logically and empirically concepts covered in the text.

COMPUTER AND STATISTICAL ANALYSES

We chose to include Micro-Crunch rather than more familiar packages, such as SPSS or SAS, because of cost. Micro-Crunch allows students to make copies of the program and put it on their computers. Micro-Crunch is user friendly for a DOS-based, menu-driven package. It does not require punctuation or on-screen editing. Most students doing the exercises and assignments will probably use their college's computer, and all users of Apple computers will work in a Windows environment. We have therefore included SPSS system files for the datasets on the same data disk as the Micro-Crunch datasets and the codebooks. Numerous alternative datasets are available from the University of North Texas, Department of Political Science World Wide Web home page. All datasets are in ASCII format. The Web address is: http:\\www.psci.unt.edu. Each semester we add datasets and they can be downloaded easily from any WWW site. Professors wishing to have the datasets in SPSS or Micro-Crunch formats may send a disk to the first author and indicate the preferred format.

ACKNOWLEDGMENTS

This book represents the efforts of many individuals. Perhaps the most essential were our students in the introduction to politics and introduction to political science classes at Oregon State University, the University of Iowa, the University of Arizona, and the University of North Texas. They were kind, if not always willing, collaborators in the development of the text. Neal Tate and Steve Poe wrote the judicial and international relations chapters respectively. Tony Mugan wrote large portions of Chapters 7 and 8. Bruce Shepard wrote the original versions of many of the questions for analysis. His contributions form the core of the correlation and regression exercises, and he has generously allowed us to use these materials not only in this book, but also in our classes over the last 15 years. Michael Ault wrote the appendix on using SPSS for Windows.

Four teaching assistants played a major role in the development and completion of the text. Two, Drs. Irini Karahalios, currently at the Center for the Study of Multinational Corporations, and Sylvia Pinal, currently at The Monterey Technical Institute, were teaching assistants at the University of Arizona during the period that the authors team-taught this course. Their careful interaction with students helped us identify many early problems with the empirical analysis and computer sections. Two teaching assistants at the University of North Texas, Rafe Major and Michael Ault, tested and retested the final versions of the computer exercises. They also supplied important editorial comments on drafts of various chapters. Two colleagues at the University of North Texas, Steve Forde and Gloria Cox, provided valuable insights into the first four chapters of the book.

A number of reviewers offered thoughtful and constructive suggestions throughout the development of this book. We would like to thank Tim Amen, University of Puget Sound; Charles T. Barber, University of Southern Indiana; Thomas Callaghy, University of Pennsylvania; Vic DeSantis, University of North Texas; Bradley Dyke, Longview Community College; Bert Hanson, Oklahoma State University; David E. Hartsfield, Northeast Missouri State University; Scott P. Hays, Southern Illinois University at Carbondale; Michael A. Krassa, University of Illinois; Aruna N. Michie, Kansas State University; Samuel C. Patterson, Ohio State University; David E. Schmitt, Northeastern University; Steven C. Seyer, Lehigh County Community College; Martin Slann, Clemson University; John W. Smith, Henry Ford Community College; John S. Vanderoef, Florida State University; and Robert A. Wood, North Dakota State University.

The individual without whom the book would not have been possible is Erik Godwin. He tested the first version of every assignment, and he helped rewrite material that was unclear. He also eliminated portions of the book which he judged as uninteresting to anyone other than a professor of political science. Finally, he was the first copy editor of the entire book.

We dedicate this book to the most important teachers in our own lives, Charlie Milford, Avery Leiserson, and Earl Latham. Their contributions improved our understanding, our teaching, and our lives.

Although all of the above people were essential to the writing of this book and to its merits, we take full responsibility for its faults.

Contents

Preface   v

INTRODUCTION: POLITICS AND POLITICAL SCIENCE   1

What Are Your Positions on Important Political Issues?   1

Politics   2

    Government and Luck   2
    Inconsistencies in Political Choices   3

Political Science   4

Can There Be a "Science" of Politics?   4

    Normative versus Empirical Issues   5
    Political Science in a Changing World   5
    Approaches to the Study of Politics   6

Goals and Organization of This Book   7

    Questions and Exercises   8
    Analysis: Connecting Normative and Empirical Statements in Logical Arguments   9
    Summary   11

PART 1: THE SPHERE OF GOVERNMENT   13

CHAPTER 1: JUSTIFICATIONS FOR GOVERNMENT   15

Minimal Government   15

    Protection and Order   16
    Collective Goods and Collective Dilemmas   16
    Negative Externalities   21
    Rights and Duties   22

Beyond Minimal Government   23

    Social Justice   23

Box 1.1: Taken to the Cleaners: My Elderly Mother May Lose Her Security   24

    Economic Efficiency   26
    Government Intervention in the Economy   27
    Government as a Moral Force   28
    Political Socialization   29

How Did Governments Arise?   30

The Development of Law   33

    Beginnings of Law   33
    The Government as Law Maker   34

Some Key Terms   35
    Government   35
    State   36
    Nation   37
    Nation-State   38
Summary   38
Questions and Exercises   38

PART 2: POLITICAL PHILOSOPHY AND FORMS OF GOVERNMENT   41

CHAPTER 2: THE EVOLUTION OF WESTERN LIBERAL THEORY   43

Classical Western Liberalism   43
    The Role of Reason   44
    Thomas Hobbes and the Social Contract   45
    John Locke and Limited Government   47
    Adam Smith and the Natural Laws of Economics   51
The Problems of Natural Law and the Rise of Reform Liberalism   53
Box 2.1: Unearned Rents   55
    Utilitarianism: Jeremy Bentham's Answer to Doom and Gloom   56
    John Stuart Mill: Greatest Liberal or First Socialist?   58
Contemporary Adaptations of Liberalism   62
    Summary of Liberal Theory   62
Constitutionalism   64
    Written Constitutions   65
    Constitutionalism: Basic Principles and Historical Development   65
    Participation to Limit Government   66
    Checks on Majority Rule   68
Summary   69
Questions and Exercises   70

CHAPTER 3: DEMOCRACY, COMMUNITY, AND EQUALITY   75

The Development of Liberal and Constitutional Institutions   75
Jean-Jacques Rousseau and Communitarian Democracy   77
    The General Will   79
    Rousseau and Democracy   81
Box 3.1: Modern Technology for Direct Democracy   82
    Rousseau and Totalitarianism   83
Modern Communitarians   84
Marxian Socialism   86
    Karl Marx and Friedrich Engels   86
    Principal Sources of Marxist Theory   87
    Elements of Marxist Theory   88
Box 3.2: Would You Want to Live in a Communist Society?   91

Democratic Socialism   92
  Fabian Socialism   92
  Contemporary Socialism   94
Summary   94
Questions and Exercises   95

CHAPTER 4: NONCONSTITUTIONAL REGIMES   105

Totalitarianism   106
Totalitarianism in Nazi Germany   106
  Adolph Hitler   107
  Nazi Party Doctrine   108
  The Power of the Leader's Words   109
  The Nazi Regime   110
Communism and Totalitarianism   110
Totalitarianism in Democratic Kampuchea (Cambodia)   111
  Elimination of *Potential* Counterrevolutionaries   111
  The Utopian Vision and the Corruption of Thoughts   112
What Is Totalitarianism?   113
Authoritarianism   114
  Military Rule   115
Box 4.1: A Tale of Two Dictators   116
  Single-Party Civilian Regimes   117
  Kenya and Mexico: Examples of Single-Party Authoritarian Regimes   118
Democratization   119
  Why Did the Soviet Empire Fall?   121
  Can the New Democracies Succeed?   122
  Religious, Ethnic, and Nationalistic Conflicts   123
  Elite Support for Democracy   123
Summary   124
Questions and Exercises   126

PART 3: THE CITIZEN AND THE STATE   135

CHAPTER 5: POLITICAL PARTICIPATION   137

Introduction   137
What Is Political Participation?   138
  Why Study Mass Political Participation?   139
  Categories of Political Participation   139
Why Do People Participate?   140
  The Simple Act of Voting   140
  Testing Alternative Models of Voting   142
Participation beyond Voting   146
  Testing Olson's Model of Collective Action   148
  Unlawful Participation   150

Is Participation Rational?   151

Who Participates?   152
The Paradox of Participation   152
Demographic Influences on Participation   153

Summary   154
Questions and Exercises   155

CHAPTER 6: LINKING CITIZENS TO GOVERNMENT   173

Institutions   174
Institutions and Democracy   175

Ideology   175
Ideological Dimensions   178

Political Parties   182
Can a Strong, Two-Party System Achieve Majority Rule?   183
The Voters' Paradox   184
Aggregation of Citizen Demands   186
Majority Rule in Multiparty Systems   186
Other Functions of Political Parties   188
Summary of Party Linkage   188

Interest Groups and Linkage   189
The Problems of Special Interests   192

Box 6.1: The Great Federal Panty Raid   193
Pluralism: The Ideal World for Interest Groups   195
Why Organized Minorities Defeat Unorganized Majorities   199
Summary of Interest Group Linkage   200

Elections   200
Ethnicity, Religion, and Nationalism: The Dangerous Issues   201
Summary   202
Questions and Exercises   203

PART 4: INSTITUTIONAL ARRANGEMENTS   211

CHAPTER 7: THE FORMS OF GOVERNMENT: PARLIAMENTARY
          AND PRESIDENTIAL SYSTEMS   213

Parliamentary and Presidential Systems   214
Heads of State and Heads of Government: Ceremonies, Symbols, and Power   215
How Governments Are Formed and Dissolved   216
Coalition and Minority Governments   217
Cabinet Responsibility and the Dissolution of Parliament   218

The Institutional Framework   219
Legislative Competence   219
Number of Chambers   220
Rules of Procedure   221
Authority and Leadership Structure   222
Committee Systems   223

Summary for Legislative Institutions   224

The Legislative Process   224
Initiation   224
Deliberation   226
Enactment   227

Legislative Performance   228
Representation   228
Evaluating Legislation and Public Policy   230
Oversight and Control Over the Executive   231
Other Functions   231

Summary   232
Questions and Exercises   233

CHAPTER 8: CHOOSING, MAKING, AND IMPLEMENTING POLICY: THE PROCESS
OF GOVERNMENT   241

The Policy-Making Process   242
Agenda Setting, Formulation, and Legitimation in Different Types of Regimes   244
Nondemocratic Governments   244
Democratic Regimes   247
Summary for Agenda Setting, Policy Formulation, and Legitimation   250

The Bureaucracy and Policy Implementation   251
Making and Implementing Laws through Bureaucracies   251
Key Principles of Bureaucratic Organization and Decision Making   252
Policy Implementation in Democratic Regimes   253

Box 8.1: What's Wrong with Bureaucracy?   254
Managing the Bureaucracy   255
Summary for Policy Implementation   257

Policy Evaluation   257
Summary   258
Questions and Exercises   258

CHAPTER 9: COURTS AND JUDICIAL POLICY MAKING   271

Courts and Judges: What They Are and What They Do   272
Triadic Conflict Resolution   272
Social Control   274
Judging and Administration   275
Lawmaking   276
The Mechanical Conception of the Judicial Process   276
Lawmaking and "Wrong" Judicial Decisions   277
The Rule of Precedent   278
Code Law Decision Making   279
Judicial Discretion and Law Making   279
Scope and Depth of Decision Making   280
Judicial Review   280

Court Hierarchies   281
Trial Courts/Courts of First Instance   282
Appeals and Courts of Appeal   283

Supreme Courts: Final Arbiters   285

The Importance of Legal Policy Making   286

A Global Expansion of Judicial Power?   288

Judicial Power and the Attitudes of Judicial Policy Makers   289

Activism/Restraint and Values   290
Civil Rights and Liberties Issues   290
Economic Issues   290
Activism, Values, and Decision Making   291

Summary   291

Questions and Exercises   292

PART 5: CONTEMPORARY PROBLEMS AND ISSUES   299

CHAPTER 10: ISSUES FACING LESS INDUSTRIALIZED COUNTRIES   301

The Current Situation in Most Third-World Countries   302

Economic Explanations   303

Box 10.1: The Law of Comparative Advantage   304

Dependency Theory   305

Cultural Explanations   308

**Box 10.2: Why the Israelites Worshipped Bael and Why Athletes Wear Dirty
Socks   310**

Political Explanations   311

Government Control over the Economy   312
Government Corruption   314
Government Instability   315

Box 10.3: The Ultimate Kleptocrat: Mobutu Sese Seko   316

Regime Types and Development   317

Totalitarian Governments and Economic Growth   318
Authoritarian Governments and Development   318
Charismatic Leadership   319
Military Regimes   321
Single-Party, Noncommunist Regimes   322
Democratic Regimes   323

Summary   325

Questions and Exercises   326

CHAPTER 11: POLITICS IN MORE INDUSTRIALIZED COUNTRIES   337

Criteria for More Industrialized Countries   342

The Development of the Welfare State   342

Reasons for the Slowdown in Growth among the MICs   346

Economic Inequality   348

Institutions and Ideologies in MICs   350

Institutional Similarities   350
Institutional Differences   351

The Success Records of Alternative Political Systems in MICs   353
    Welfare Expenditures, Poverty, and Inequality   353
    Unemployment, Inflation, and Economic Growth   355

Summary   357
Questions and Exercises   357

CHAPTER 12: GLOBAL POLITICS IN A CHANGING WORLD   365

Improved Technology, Increasing Interactions   366
Box 12.1: The World Politics Experiment   **367**
Realism in World Politics   368
Box 12.2: Do the Ends Justify the Means?   **370**
    Critics of Realism   371
    Realist Failure: Actors Other than Nation-States   372

A Brief Survey of World Problems   374
War   376
    The Costs   376
    Trends in Warfare   377
    Why War?   378

International Wars and Human-Rights Violations   382
    Violence against Fellow Citizens   382
    The Growing Concern for Human Rights   383

Political Science and the Study of Human Rights   383
Box 12.3: Is International Law Really Law?   **384**
    Political Scientists' Studies of Human Rights   385
    Human Rights and National Sovereignty   389

Positive Development in World Politics: A Few Rays of Hope   390
Summary   391
Questions and Exercises   392

CONCLUSION: THE FUNCTIONS OF GOVERNMENT REVISITED   399

Appendix A: Using Micro-Crunch   404
Appendix B: Using SPSS 6.1 for Windows   416
Appendix C: Codebooks for Data Sets   431
Glossary   450
Index   457

Introduction: Politics and Political Science

Key Terms

Politics	**Empirical**	**Political Behavior**
Political Science	**Political Philosophy**	**Public Choice**
Normative		

What Are Your Positions on Important Political Issues?

All readers of this book are citizens of some country. Everyone has lived under the jurisdiction of city, county, state, or provincial governments. Few readers, however, have ever asked the questions: Why do people have governments? What activities are appropriate for government? How do people know if their government is performing well? This book addresses these questions and ways to answer them. Before you begin your search for those answers, take a few moments and write down your responses to the following questions:

1. Should the most important factor in a person's future be her choice of parents?

2. Should owners of property have the right to rent or sell to anyone they choose?

3. Should children who live in wealthy neighborhoods receive better educations than children who live in poor neighborhoods?

4. Should the government put pregnant women in jail if they are alcohol dependent in order to prevent fetal alcohol syndrome?

5. Should people be allowed to exercise free speech at their work places?

6. If an individual believes that a child is being killed inside a private building, should that person trespass to stop the act? Should the government punish the individual for trespassing?

7. If science determines that working with personal computers increases the probability of genetic damage to a male's sperm, should the government enact legislation that would prohibit fertile men from working with personal computers?

8. Should a fundamentalist Christian who rejects the theory of evolution be allowed to teach biology in public high schools?

9. Should people have the right to discriminate on the basis of ethnicity or gender?

10. Should parents be allowed to use their own resources to ensure that their children receive the best possible educational opportunities?

11. Should the government actively prosecute antiabortion demonstrators who enter clinics and urge the women there not to have abortions?

12. Should the government spend more money on education, police, or prisons?

Politics

All societies must answer these questions and a host of others that are equally difficult. Through this process, societies accept the values and interests of some people and reject those of others. When societies make choices, they demonstrate which values have priority. The term **politics** refers to the process of social choice. Politics decide who gets what, when, and how from the government and who pays. This process can be noble or corrupt.

People learn as they decide whether to spend scarce resources on health care, defense, pollution control, or debt reduction. The political process can help us to see the merits of claims that conflict with our own priorities. If your local government must decide whether to reduce the number of police or the number of teachers it hires, participation in this process can educate you about your community and the relative needs of preserving order and educating the young.

GOVERNMENT AND LUCK

As one of their most critical choices, societies must determine how much government will compensate people for bad luck. Look at the oddly phrased first question in the previous list. Children do not choose their parents. Rather, the characteristics of one's parents depend on luck. Therefore, the list might more accurately phrase the question, "Should the most important factor in people's lives be their luck at birth?" Clearly no other incident matters as much as the circumstances of a person's birth. It determines country, gender, and ethnicity. It decides genes that affect health, looks, intelligence, and temperament. It also influences family income, caring or uncaring upbringing, and whether the family can and will invest in their child's future. Consider how a single variable, the ethnicity of a person's parents, affects life chances:

- One in every eight African American babies is born at a dangerously low birth weight.
- In the United States, 18 out of every 1,000 African American newborns die in infancy, more than twice the infant mortality rate of white infants.

- During the first year of life, African American babies die from fires and burns at a rate 450 percent higher than that of white infants.

- Of the children born HIV-positive, 75 percent have been either African American or Hispanic.[1]

The critical role of luck in people's lives affects their answers to the question, "What is the proper role of government?" Some argue that government should ensure that bad luck at birth does not rob people of realistic opportunities to have good lives. Others contend that if government begins compensating people for bad luck, nothing will prevent it from intervening in almost every aspect of citizens' lives. The principle of compensating people for bad luck invites government to take away liberty as well as property.

INCONSISTENCIES IN POLITICAL CHOICES

Like most people, the authors of this book hold inconsistent beliefs about what government should do in various situations. These inconsistencies typically arise from conflicts between important values or from differences in images of the people the government's decisions will affect. Take Questions 2 and 9 from the previous list. People in the United States typically respond "yes" to Question 2 and "no" to Question 9. Yet, if property owners have the right to sell to anyone they choose, then they may choose to discriminate on the basis of ethnicity or gender. The values concerning property rights are at odds with the desire to live in a society that does not discriminate against people because of their ethnicity or gender.

Examine Questions 3 and 10. Many people might answer "no" to Question 3 and "yes" to Question 10. Yet, these answers are fundamentally inconsistent. People may not like the idea that the luck of birth will affect access to education. After all, education strongly influences how well an individual can live and the income the individual will earn. On the other hand, many believe that parents ought to spend their money as they see fit and that society should encourage them to invest in their children's futures.

Did you answer "yes" to Question 4 and "no" to Question 7? Presumably if you were willing to incarcerate a woman because her behavior might harm her offspring, then you should be willing to restrict job opportunities to men who do the same thing. In each case, the value of a person's current liberty conflicts with the value of reducing possible future harm to a potential person and possible future costs to society. Often, preferences on government policy reflect attitudes toward the people that the policy seems likely to affect. Someone may have a negative image of the alcoholic woman and a positive image of the job-seeking man.

How about Questions 6 and 11? Did you answer that the individual should attempt to stop the murder and that the government should not punish the individual for trespassing? Did you also disapprove of active prosecution of antiabortion demonstrators who attempt to enter a clinic to persuade women not to have abortions? The demonstrators may believe that a fetus is a human being and should have all the rights of other humans, so when they discourage someone from having an abortion, they see themselves as attempting to stop a murder.

What about Questions 5 and 8? Do your answers reveal consistent views on freedom of speech? Would you prevent persons from obtaining a job for which they have trained because they *might* teach their beliefs rather than the state-approved curriculum? Is this a restriction of speech at the work place? Is it discrimination based on religious preference?

Politics is the name for the process by which society makes choices about what government should do. The major goal of this book is to teach readers how to reach informed and logical opinions about how much government a society needs and what policies government should pursue. To achieve this goal, the book attempts three tasks:

1. To familiarize you with the choices that great political thinkers have advocated and the reasons for their recommendations

2. To show you how to evaluate logically and empirically the likely consequences of any particular choice

3. To acquaint you with many of the choices that governments in countries around the world currently face

Political Science

Understanding how societies make choices and examining the impacts of those choices are the essential tasks of **political science.** The authors do not expect that this book will make you a political scientist any more than the authors of an introductory textbook in biology or chemistry expect readers to become accomplished biologists or chemists after completing a single book. This book intends primarily to help readers to become informed citizens who have the knowledge and skills they need to think scientifically about politics and political choices.

The word *science* comes from the Latin word *scientia* which means knowledge, as opposed to belief or opinion.[2] Science uses empirical observation, reason, and logic to produce and test hypotheses. Science strives to explain empirical facts in ways that allow us to understand what has happened in the past and to predict what will happen in the future. People expect scientists to pursue knowledge free of value judgments. Physicists do not have preferences about how subatomic particles move and are held together; the job of the physicist is to find out how these particles behave and influence other particles. Medical researchers do not have a preference that guides their study of the relationship of the HIV virus and AIDS. Their job is to discover how the virus lives, spreads, and dies.

To the extent that political scientists act as other scientists, then political science should help people to understand past social choices and allow them to successfully predict future choices.

Can There Be a "Science" of Politics?

Political scientists ask many different types of questions such as: Why do nations go to war? Why do some people participate actively in politics while others do not? Why do some countries have only two major political parties while others have many more? How do interest groups affect public policy? Why do some policies achieve their objectives while others do not? These questions deal with a common theme of how societies choose and the results of those choices.

Although political scientists generally follow the rules of the scientific method in their research, some reasonably argue that there cannot be a "science" of politics. This is a sensible argument for two very important reasons: Political science cannot avoid normative issues, and the relationships among political phenomena appear to change from one place to another and from one point in time to another.

NORMATIVE VERSUS EMPIRICAL ISSUES

The study of politics includes both **normative** and **empirical** statements. Normative statements deal with values and require ethical or moral judgments about what state of affairs a society ought to prefer among various alternatives. As indicated earlier, most science deals with knowledge of empirical phenomena rather than with opinions concerning whether those phenomena are good or bad. However, the questions listed early in this introduction illustrate that politics is a process of choice between competing alternatives. People presumably choose one alternative over another because they prefer it; they believe it is better. Thus, political science often studies how people make normative choices.

Political science is inevitably involved in normative issues for another reason—because the information it discovers often affects normative debates. Suppose that several people in your class answered that the government should incarcerate pregnant women who are alcoholics. Presumably, they favored this choice because they wanted the babies to be born as healthy as possible. This preference is a normative judgment; it identifies one outcome as better than another. The individuals who answered "yes" to Question 4 believe that the incarceration of alcoholic mothers is a worthwhile price to pay for healthier babies.

The empirical information generated by political science might change this policy preference. Suppose an empirical (scientific) study discovered that the incarceration policy would actually lead to more rather than fewer birth defects by discouraging pregnant women who drink from going to doctors for essential prenatal care. The study might discover that these women would avoid prenatal care fearing that doctors would turn them in to the authorities and that the authorities would put them in jail. In the face of this empirical or factual knowledge, the individuals in the class who favored incarceration might change their opinions.

Notice that political science cannot tell whether the cost of the liberty lost when the state incarcerates pregnant women is worth less than the benefits of having fewer children born with birth defects. That is a strictly normative decision. Political science may, however, indicate whether an incarceration policy will bring about the desired goal. It can do this because that is an empirical (factual) question.

POLITICAL SCIENCE IN A CHANGING WORLD

The second reason that some doubt the possibility of a political science results from changes in the causal relationships among variables from one situation to another. For example, the factors that influenced British elections in the 19th century are not the same as those that influenced American elections in the 20th century. In fact, major issues appear to change from one election to the next within a single country. Similarly, the causes of the 1789 revolution in France were probably quite different from the causes of the 1917 revolution in Russia. Certainly, the causes of the Vietnam War as well as its outcomes do not appear similar to the causes of World War I and its outcomes. If the causes of political phenomena continually change, can anyone really practice political science?

Political scientists argue that although people make political choices in changing situations, they make those choices in relatively stable ways. Therefore, the appropriate goal of political science is to understand the decision process and the underlying factors that remain the same. This understanding allows political scientists to explain past events and to predict future events.

To understand this argument, assume that your first job after graduation is in Seattle. You are single, you do not make a great deal of money, and you expect to spend most of your time at work rather than at home. Therefore, you might choose to live in an inexpensive apartment near work. Your choice of housing 10 years later probably will be quite different if you live in Atlanta, have children, and make considerably more money. In this situation, you might buy a house in the suburbs where your children can play in the yard, the schools are good, and your family is safe. Although these situations differ in many ways and you will likely choose quite different housing, your decision process in the two situations is likely to be quite similar. In each case you evaluate your housing goals, the importance of housing to you and those who live with you, and how much you can afford to spend.

APPROACHES TO THE STUDY OF POLITICS

The study of politics has developed several approaches to studying social choice. The oldest approach is **political philosophy,** the study of political ideas. This method of studying politics deals largely with normative questions. It began with Socrates when he asked, "How should humans live?" and "What forms of government encourage them to live this type of life?" Political philosophers from Plato in 400 B.C. to John Rawls, who continues to write today, have asked the questions, "What is justice?" and "What forms of government are most likely to lead to just societies?" Current political philosophers ask and attempt to answer many important questions: What should government do about the luck of birth? What is the relationship between freedom and equality? What are the obligations of the political leader in a democracy? What are the appropriate goals of a country in its dealings with other countries?

Political philosophy highlights the importance of ethics in political choices. Political philosophy also teaches people to use logic to deduce the probable outcomes of a social choice, to reveal inconsistencies among various social choices, and to better anticipate the likely outcomes of social choices. The methodological tools of political philosophy are logic and empirical observation.

A second approach to the study of politics is the study of **political behavior.** This approach is more empirical and less normative than political philosophy. Those who study political behavior are interested not in how citizens and governments should behave, but in how they actually behave. They ask, "What social choices do leaders make? Why do they make these choices? How do citizens attempt to influence those choices?" This approach to political science began with the Greek writer Thucydides, who analyzed the causes, actions, and consequences of the war between Athens and Sparta in the 5th century B.C. Thucydides spent little time discussing the nature of justice or how humans should make political choices; rather he described how they behaved and attempted to say why.

The second great political scientist to follow the behavioral approach to politics was Aristotle (384–322 B.C.). In many respects, Aristotle was the very first true scientist. He searched for systematic relationships among phenomena and attempted to discover the causes of these relationships.

Today, Aristotle's search for relationships and causal models to explain them represents the dominant form of political science. Students of political behavior attempt to explain many questions. Why do some people participate actively in politics while others do not? What are people's opinions on critical issues of the day? How do current economic conditions affect the outcomes of elections? Why do people seek public office and what guides their decisions once they gain office?

Among their major tools, those who study the political behavior of the masses employ extensive survey research and statistical analysis using computers. Survey research allows them to ask thousands of people in many different countries similar questions. This ability, combined with computer analysis of the huge amounts of data, helps them to understand similarities and differences in political behavior in different countries and cultures.

A third approach to the study of politics, **public choice,** relies heavily on two assumptions about politics. First, it assumes that political actors behave as if they weigh the benefits and costs of their actions and then choose the action that leads to the best outcome for themselves. Second, it assumes that the institutional setting within which an individual acts influences those benefits and costs. For example, if people act rationally, then they are more likely to protest government policies when they believe their protests will influence government policy and when the costs of protesting are low. The public-choice approach is characterized by extensive use of abstract models, simplifying assumptions about human behavior, and logical deductions based on those models and assumptions. This method of political science (sometimes called *rational choice* or *social choice*) borrows methods and models from economics and a branch of mathematics called *game theory.*

This book uses all the approaches discussed in this section—political philosophy, political behavior, and public choice—to help you understand how societies make choices. Each approach has strengths and weaknesses, but all help us understand the political world. This discussion has omitted other approaches to the study of politics, such as systems theory, structural-functionalism, and phenomenology. Although we do not rely extensively on these approaches in this book, political science majors will learn about them and how to use them in future courses.

Goals and Organization of This Book

This book does not introduce all of the different subfields of political science. We do not attempt to present all of the questions that political science attempts to answer. You may have noticed (perhaps with some relief) that this book is shorter than introductory texts in other subjects. We chose to write a shorter text because we attribute more importance to learning how to think critically and how to use the scientific method than to knowing what each subfield of political science studies or remembering a lot of political facts.

The book divides its topic into five sections. The first examines how governments first developed, the major objectives that most modern governments attempt to achieve, and how the contemporary ideas of law and legislation developed over time. The second section of the text deals with political philosophy. This section analyzes the major political philosophies in the world today: democratic liberalism and Marxism. We emphasize democratic liberalism because it is the value system that shaped the institutions of government in western democracies, and it was instrumental in the development of constitutional governments. We believe that unless you know the values and assumptions that underlie your political, social, and economic institutions, then it is almost impossible for you to think critically about those institutions or to conduct informed analyses of them. We study Marxism and other nondemocratic forms of government because most of the people in the world live not in liberal democracies but in authoritarian regimes. To understand the politics that affect the majority of the people in the world, you must understand how authoritarian regimes make social choices.

The third section of the book examines the reasons why people participate in politics and the institutions through which democratic governments attempt to link citizen demands to public-policy outcomes. These chapters will help you analyze your own political participation and the roles that political parties and interest groups play in the political process.

The fourth section of the book deals with the basic institutions of government: legislatures, executives, bureaucracies, and courts. This part of the book stresses comparisons among the various forms of government, both democratic and nondemocratic.

The final part of the book looks at the contemporary problems that face governments and people around the world. It begins with the issues that arise in less industrialized countries, moving on to deal with problems in more industrialized countries and finally with war and violence throughout the world. In these final chapters, we ask you to pretend that you live in other countries and to examine the benefits and costs of possible policies that people there might make.

All chapters in the book include exercises. These elements encourage you to reflect on what you have learned, to think logically, and to use empirical data to test theories and hypotheses presented in the chapter text. The exercises also introduce students to the computer and its many uses inside and outside political science.

We hope that you enjoy this book. You can increase that possibility because the learning process centers around your participation. The exercises, including the computer exercises, may frustrate you at first. To provide benefits for your frustration and effort, however, we have tried to ensure that the skills you learn will help you both in your remaining college courses and in your life after you graduate.

QUESTIONS AND EXERCISES

The introduction explained that the study of politics involves both normative and empirical issues. Normative issues arise because politics constitute the process of choosing among competing values. Empirical issues arise because people expect certain policy actions to lead to particular outcomes. Political science must treat normative and empirical statements differently, and therefore it must distinguish clearly between them. This exercise helps to clarify when a statement is normative and when it is empirical. The exercise also shows how to use scientific methods to evaluate normative choices.

Consider two statements:

1. Most adults in Mexico *should* want their government to provide public safety.
2. Most adults in Mexico want their government to provide public safety.

These sentences differ in only one word, but that word changes drastically how political science treats the two statements. The first statement is normative. It is a value statement that some condition (in this case the desire of Mexicans for their government to provide public safety) ought to occur. Value statements declare that conditions are good or bad, or that one condition is better than another. The statement, "Democracy is the best form of government," is a normative statement. No one can test the truth or falsity of this statement by observation. Instead, arguments for the statement's acceptance center on values and logic.

The second statement is empirical. It asserts that most adults in Mexico do, in fact, want their government to provide public safety. A scientific study of the adult population in Mexico could confirm or refute this assertion. Scientists call assertions about the empirical world *hypotheses*. Although Chapter 3 will study hypotheses in greater detail, note now that they have two critical characteristics: Hypotheses are value free, and they can be tested through observation. A value-free statement includes no preference for one outcome over another. The statement, "Most adults in Mexico want their government to provide public safety" meets this condition. Survey research can test whether or not the majority of Mexicans actually agree with the statement, "Government should provide public safety," so the statement also meets the requirement that it can be tested through observation.*

ANALYSIS: CONNECTING NORMATIVE AND EMPIRICAL STATEMENTS IN LOGICAL ARGUMENTS

Politics and political discussion blend normative and empirical statements. For example, suppose that you and a friend are arguing about whether or not the government should put alcohol-dependent women in jail. Assume for a moment that you believe that the government should do this and your friend disagrees. Each of you makes a value judgment. You argue that society would be better if the government did this. Your friend argues that the action would make society worse. Each of you, therefore, is making a value judgment.

Now assume that you and your friend really want to settle this argument. It is likely that your position and your friend's position each depend on two things: A preference for

---

*In science, *observation* does not mean actually seeing something; it means only that the observer can measure it. For example, physicists do not see subatomic particles, but they can indirectly measure whether or not those particles exist. The same is true for attitudes and beliefs in the social sciences. No one can see an attitude, but researchers can measure it indirectly through survey questions.

a particular outcome, and the truth of one or more empirical hypotheses concerning actions necessary to reach that outcome. Both you and your friend probably prefer healthy babies to unhealthy ones. The empirical question that separates you is whether or not a government policy to incarcerate pregnant women who depend on alcohol would increase or reduce the probability of healthy births. You hypothesize that it would, and only if this hypothesis is true do you support the incarceration policy. Three statements, two normative and one empirical, summarize your argument:

1. I prefer healthy babies. (Normative)

2. A policy to incarcerate alcohol-dependent women would increase the probability of healthy babies. (Empirical)

3. Therefore, the government should incarcerate alcohol-dependent women. (Normative policy conclusion based on normative preference and the truth of the empirical statement)

Your friend's similar three-statement argument differs from yours only in the second statement: "A policy to incarcerate alcohol-dependent women would not increase the probability of healthy babies." You and your friend can now settle the argument by comparing the birthrates of healthy babies in states that attempt to incarcerate pregnant women who depend on alcohol with those in states that do not attempt to do this.

Almost all of the questions you answered at the beginning of the Introduction were normative. They asked you what you thought the government *should* do. Many readers based answers on beliefs concerning the expected empirical consequences of government actions. Suppose that you answered "No" to the question, "Should a fundamentalist Christian who rejects the theory of evolution be allowed to teach biology in public high schools?" Presumably, you gave that answer because you hypothesized that a fundamentalist Christian would not effectively teach the theory of evolution to students, and this omission would harm their understanding of biology. In this situation, your three-statement argument might look like this:

1. Students should know the current scientific information concerning how humans evolved. (Normative preference)

2. Students who have Christian fundamentalists as biology teachers will learn less about human evolution than students whose biology teachers are not Christian fundamentalists. (Empirical hypothesis)

3. Therefore, the government should prohibit Christian fundamentalists from teaching high school biology. (Normative policy conclusion based on normative preference and the truth of an empirical statement)

Examine the issue of whether or not national governments should have to balance their budgets. You and your friend might disagree on whether the United States should adopt a constitutional amendment forcing Congress to balance the federal government's budget. Both of you might have the same normative preference for a rapidly growing economy. However, you hypothesize that budget deficits reduce economic growth, while your friend hypothesizes that budget deficits do not negatively affect economic growth. In this situation, your arguments look quite similar. You argue as follows:

1. I prefer rapid economic growth.
2. Budget deficits decrease economic growth.
3. Therefore, the nation should pass a constitutional amendment to force Congress to balance the budget.

   Your friend's argument appears quite similar.

1. I prefer rapid economic growth.
2. Budget deficits do not decrease economic growth.
3. Therefore, the nation should not pass a constitutional amendment to force Congress to balance the budget.

In this situation, you may be able to resolve the argument by agreeing about some empirical test of the second statements in the two logical arguments. For example, the two of you might collect data on the budget deficits, rates of economic growth, and total gross national products of all industrialized countries. Using these data, you could determine whether the economies of countries with larger budget deficits grew more slowly than those of countries with smaller deficits or surpluses. If this analysis revealed that larger deficits lead to lower rates of growth, then you could conclude that your hypothesis was correct and your policy preference was an appropriate conclusion. If, however, your research identified no relationship of deficits to growth or a connection between larger deficits and more rapid growth, then your friend's policy preference would look like the correct conclusion.

Empirical tests cannot resolve all normative issues. For example, you may support food stamp programs because you believe that all children, regardless of the incomes of their parents, should have adequate nutrition. Your friend might oppose all welfare programs, including food stamps, believing that the government commits theft whenever it takes money from some people and gives it to others. Even if you could show that the food stamp program saves lives and leads to healthier children who become more productive adults, this result might be irrelevant to your friend's position. The beneficial consequences still might not justify the perceived theft by the government.

SUMMARY

Normative and empirical statements are fundamentally different, but each is necessary for political discourse. Normative statements describe the types of actions and outcomes that people value. They deal with what is good or bad, what ought to occur, and what ought not occur. Empirical statements describe or predict what actually occurs. Hypotheses make up one important category of empirical statements. A hypothesis is an assertion that empirical evidence can either support or reject.

Questions for Analysis

Using the statements provided, develop a three-sentence logical sequence that states your preference, provides an empirical hypothesis, and then gives the logical policy conclusion. The concluding statement must begin with *Therefore* and include the word *I*.

Example Statement: "The government should actively prosecute antiabortion demonstrators who trespass in clinics to urge women not to have abortions."

Derive a preference statement for this outcome. For example:

1. (Outcome preference) I prefer that women who want abortions have the opportunity to obtain them without interference from antiabortion demonstrators.

Now, what empirical question must you answer to accept the original statement? For example:

2. (Empirical expectation) Women who live in states that actively prosecute protesters who illegally enter abortion clinics are less likely to experience interference from protesters than women who live in states that do not actively prosecute protesters.

If that empirical statement is true, then you can make your logical conclusion.

3. (Logical conclusion) Therefore, the government should actively prosecute antiabortion demonstrators who trespass in clinics to urge women not to have abortions.

Statement 1: The state government should require that all school districts have equal per-pupil budgets.

1. (Outcome preference)

2. (Empirical expectation)

3. (Logical conclusion)

Statement 2: The federal government should cut back on student loan programs.

1. (Outcome preference)

2. (Empirical expectation)

3. (Logical conclusion)

NOTES

[1] *Newsweek,* September 11, 1989.

[2] Herman W. Smith, *Strategies of Social Research,* 3d ed. (Fort Worth, Tex.: Holt, Rinehart and Winston, 1991), p. 4.

PART 1

The Sphere of
Government

1

Justifications for Government

Minimal Government

The introduction to this book examined 12 questions concerning the rights of individuals and the duties of government. The analysis of those questions revealed that most people hold somewhat inconsistent opinions concerning individual rights, and that reasonable people disagree concerning what governments ought to do. In this chapter, we ask you to examine the justifications for government activities and to study three important questions:

1. What minimal tasks do all governments attempt to accomplish?

2. What justifications do governments cite for exceeding these minimal tasks?

3. How did governments first arise?

The final section of the chapter distinguishes among several concepts important to the study of politics.

To begin this discussion, consider what you and all other citizens would want your government to do, regardless of whether it were a democracy or a dictatorship and whether the economy were capitalist, socialist, or somewhere in between. In other words, what tasks are uniquely suited to government rather than to some other institution in society?

PROTECTION AND ORDER

Normally, the first goals of government are the safety of its citizens and the preservation of order. Although most people view the need for institutions to preserve order and safety as obvious, some political philosophers have favored a model for society without such institutions. These individuals advocate **anarchy,** a society without formal government. Anarchists believe that a society without police and military forces would be peaceful and cooperative. They contend that the coercive force of government is morally wrong and that this force actually encourages people to commit violent acts. Peter Kropotkin, a Russian anarchist, argued that people would be good to each other in the absence of government. Kropotkin based this conclusion on his studies of cooperation among animals other than humans.

Most people do not share Kropotkin's optimistic view of human nature. Even those who view humans as basically good cannot see how, without government, society could deal with those who break its rules. If all people were law-abiding, cooperative, and respectful of the rights of others, and if all countries were peaceful, then no society would need an armed force to maintain safety and repel external invasion. However, all people do not respect the rights of others. All countries are not peaceful. For these reasons, most people want institutions to protect public safety and to punish those who break the laws.

But, why must the *government* do this work? Why can't citizens voluntarily contribute money and time to a private organization that will provide police protection and defend the nation? The answer to this question provides insights into the necessary minimal tasks of any government. These tasks share a common attribute: *If individuals act in their rational self-interests, society will suffer*. Notice that this does not say that individuals acting in greedy or criminal ways will make society suffer. If individuals act *rationally,* then in certain situations they will make their society a worse place to live rather than a better one.

COLLECTIVE GOODS AND COLLECTIVE DILEMMAS

Funding for national defense and public safety are almost ideal examples of situations in which people acting in their rational self-interests will harm society. National defense and public safety are examples of **collective goods,** benefits that any member of the community can enjoy only if all members share them. All individuals receive the goods whether or not they contribute to the cost of supplying them. For example, if your neighbor receives protection from foreign invasion, then you share that benefit. The government could not provide your neighbor protection while denying it to you. This is true whether or not you paid taxes to help provide that protection.

To see why voluntary contributions to national defense or public safety would not work, ask yourself, "Would I contribute my full share to the national defense if contributions were totally voluntary?" Most people, or at least the authors of this book, would answer, "No!" At current tax rates, the average U.S. citizen pays approximately $3,000 yearly to fund the nation's military. As the 1995 U.S. defense budget exceeded $300 billion, each citizen might ask whether the level of national defense would be any different with a budget of $299,999,997,000? One person's contribution cannot pay even the salary of one soldier. Certainly, that contribution would not make a difference in the number of ships, planes, tanks, rockets, and bombs that the United States builds and maintains. While the authors' contributions do not affect the level of national defense, an extra $3,000 each year would make a difference in other aspects of their lives.

If we, the authors, were to act rationally and maximize our personal welfare, then we would keep our money and let other citizens pay for the country's defense or the community's police. Individuals who allow others to pay the cost of a collective good and yet enjoy the benefits of that good are known as **free riders.** Of course, the authors would not be the only free riders. Almost everyone would refuse to contribute. Thus, voluntary contributions to the military and police budgets would result in a severely underfunded Department of Defense and local police.* This problem of free riders necessitates some institution to force people to contribute to public safety and national defense. We call such institutions "governments."

The difficulties of voluntary contributions for national defense illustrate a broad category of problems called **collective dilemmas.** Collective dilemmas occur when individual actions to maximize personal self-interest reduce the total benefits to the group below the benefits individuals could enjoy if they did not follow personal self-interest but cooperated for the good of the community. Perhaps the simplest example of a collective dilemma is the problem faced by two prisoners caught by police after robbing a bank and hiding the money. The police do not have sufficient evidence to convict them unless at least one prisoner confesses. The police did, however, catch the bandits with handguns for which they had no permits. The prosecuting attorney is quite confident that she will obtain at least one confession to the bank robbery.

Why is she so certain that at least one prisoner will confess? Assume that you are one of the prisoners and that the prosecutor offers you the following deal. If you confess and your partner does not, you will spend only 6 months in jail while your partner will spend 20 years. On the other hand, if your partner confesses and you do not, then the partner will go to jail for 6 months and you will get 20 years. Not being totally stupid, you ask what will happen if neither partner confesses. The prosecutor tells you that she will send you both to jail for 1 year for carrying weapons without a permit. Now you ask what will happen if both you and your partner confess. The prosecutor answers that you will each serve 10 years.

You face the situation shown in Figure 1.1. *Regardless of what your partner does,* you will serve only half as much time in jail if you confess. If your partner confesses, you will serve 10 years rather than 20. If your partner does not confess, you will serve 6 months rather than 1 year. Being rational, you confess. Of course, if your partner is also acting rationally you will enjoy each other's company in jail for the next 10 years.

In the prisoner's dilemma, the collective good for the robbers is to minimize the total amount of time they spend in jail. Clearly, the prisoners maximize their collective well-being if neither confesses. However, if each acts in individual self-interest, both will

---

*The authors do not claim that no one would contribute or even that no one would contribute a full share. When the national interests of countries have been threatened by military action, millions of persons have volunteered and risked their lives for their countries. Even in these extraordinary times, however, most countries resort to some form of conscription.

FIGURE 1.1

PRISONER'S DILEMMA GAME

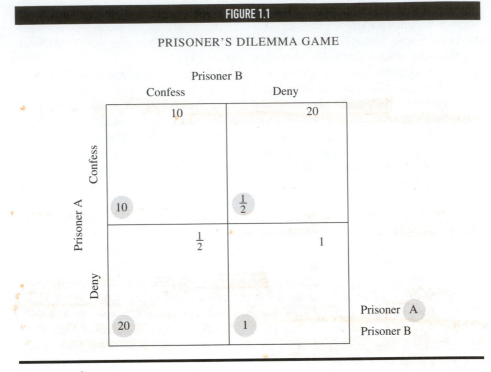

Sentences are in years.

confess and each will spend 10 years in jail. Despite arguments about honor among thieves, prosecutors often get criminals to confess by placing them in this situation.

In a famous article, "The Tragedy of the Commons," biologist Garrett Hardin describes another collective dilemma.[1] He supposes a pasture jointly owned by ten families. Each family may graze as many of its cattle on the pasture as it wishes and the family that owns a particular cow enjoys all the benefits from its use or sale. Hardin argues that such an arrangement may work for a time, but ultimately the total number of cattle grazed on the pasture will surpass the carrying capacity of the land. Adding cattle beyond its carrying capacity damages the land and reduces the amount of grass that will grow there. This, in turn, reduces the number of animals the land can support.

Any rancher knows that a given piece of pasture can feed only a certain number of cattle. Too many animals can destroy the land's ability to grow grass. Carrying capacity measures the maximum number of animals that a given piece of land can support without harming its growing ability.

In Hardin's example, assume that once the herd reaches the carrying capacity of the land, each additional cow creates $500 in damage to the pasture and that the value of a mature cow is only $400. If a single family owned the pasture, it would not add cattle past the carrying capacity because to do so would reduce the family's wealth. This is not true, however, when ten families own the land in common. Hardin argues that families will continue to add cattle beyond the carrying capacity even though the total benefits to the ten families are less than the total costs.

This occurs because all the benefits of an additional animal go to the family that owns it, while all families share the additional cost. The benefit to an individual family of adding a cow would equal the animal's full value, $400. The cost to that family, however, would be $500 divided by 10, or only $50. Thus, adding a cow would earn the family a profit of $350. As all families face the identical situation, all will continue to add cattle until they destroy the pasture. As the families act rationally and maximize their own economic benefits, everyone loses.

Hardin suggests that this "tragedy of the commons" is similar to many current environmental problems such as overfishing the oceans and air pollution. Individuals who fish receive all the benefits of the fish they catch and pay only a fraction of the costs of their actions. Factory owners similarly receive all the benefits of dumping waste into the air and pay only a portion of the costs of damaging the environment. Hardin's analysis highlights a critical point: A voluntary decision by a single family or individual to stop overgrazing, overfishing, or overpolluting would be not only irrational but also completely ineffective. Others would still overgraze the land, overfish the oceans, and overpollute the air. The individuals who voluntarily reduced their grazing, fishing, or dumping would become the first to starve or to go out of business!

Although the tragedy of the commons may resemble many environmental problems, it does not accurately illustrate most problems involving collective goods. In the commons, each member of the community faced the same costs and benefits. In real life, however, some people gain more than others from the resolution of a collective dilemma. This creates additional problems when participants try to decide how much each should pay for the collective good. Take the quite ordinary example of paving a road. Figure 1.2 depicts an unpaved road in Oregon on which a friend, Bruce Shepard, lived for 10 years. In winter the road was muddy and filled with potholes. In summer the road was dusty and filled with potholes. The road ate car suspensions and bicycles without knobby tires. All the people who owned property on the road agreed that they wanted the road paved and that the benefits of paving the road would exceed the cost. In addition, once the road was paved the county would maintain it.

Still, 20 years later, the road remains unpaved because the people who live on it cannot agree how much each property owner should pay. The owners of houses at the top of the circle travel much further along the road than those who live near the highway. For this reason, the people living near the highway believe that the others should pay more. The people who live farther from the highway argue that the county government charges each property owner to pave a road on the basis of the lot's frontage (how many feet of the owner's property the road touches). They contend that the owners along the road should follow the same rule. Similarly, the people who own the lots without houses argue that they should pay less because they are not using the road. The people who already live there maintain that the owners of empty lots should pay as much as anyone else because when they build on their lots, their houses will be worth much more.

The argument over this road resembles most collective goods problems because providing a collective good generally raises strong disagreements about how much different

FIGURE 1.2

BRUCE'S ROAD

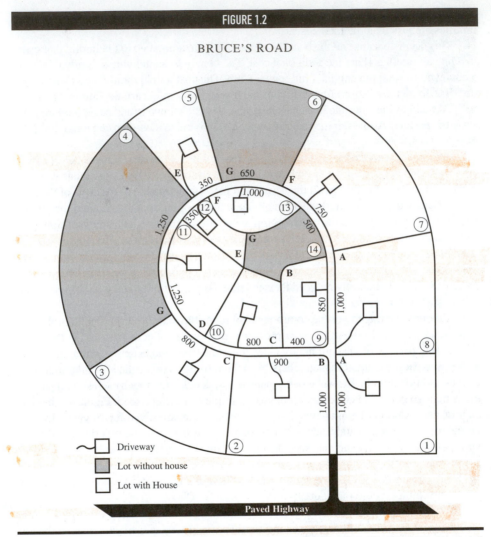

Source: Kenneth Godwin, "Introducing the Enduring Questions of Politics: A Problem-Solving Approach," *Teaching Political Science* (July 1981). Reprinted with permission of the Helen Dwight Reid Educational Foundation. Published by Heldref Publications, 1319 18th St. N.W. Washington, D.C. 20036-1802. Copyright 1981.

sets of people should pay. Should the city downstream pay more to obtain clean water because it currently suffers the most from pollution, or should the city upstream pay more because it is creating the problem? Should the factories in the Midwest pay to clean their emissions, or should the people in the Northeast pay more to avoid the acid rain caused by those emissions? Should wealthy people pay more for police protection, or should people in crime-ridden neighborhoods pay more to reflect the higher probability that they will be robbed?

Governments can resolve some collective dilemmas by changing property rights. In Hardin's tragedy of the commons, property rights were inappropriate because the gains a family received from using the pasture were not tied to the damage the family caused by adding animals to graze on it. If a single family had owned the pasture, however, a problem would not have arisen. The family would not overgraze the land because its own costs of adding an animal would exceed its own benefits. Similarly, if all animals grazing on the pasture were the common property of all the families, this too would prevent overgrazing because all families would share both the benefits and the costs. The community would have every incentive to determine just how many animals it should graze, and it would not graze more than that number.

People cannot so easily solve the overfishing of the oceans. The fish migrate from the territorial waters of one country into those of another or into the open sea. No single government can effectively prevent other countries from harvesting more fish than nature will replace when the fish are outside the country's jurisdiction. In other words, no one has any property rights to the fish because no one can enforce such rights. *Effective property rights require that the owner of a good or a service must be able to prevent others from using it.* For example, if you buy a blouse or shirt, then you have the right to wear it and, if you wish, to exclude others from wearing it. In addition, others cannot wear it while you are wearing it. If you purchase a car, then you have the right to drive it and to prevent others from sharing that right. As with the clothing, if you are driving the car then no one else can do so.

However, if some citizens pay for national defense, they cannot exclude others from enjoying the benefits of their purchase. While they enjoy the protection they buy, free riders will enjoy it as well. If some families were to pave the road in Oregon, they could not prevent other families from driving on it. Because of this inability to exclude free riders or to force them to contribute, the people will purchase less of collective goods than they would buy in the absence of free rider problems. The role of government in providing collective goods is to reduce the number of free riders. In other words, government compels everyone to contribute.

NEGATIVE EXTERNALITIES

Collective dilemmas occur because people acting in their own self-interests destroy their own long-term benefits as well as the benefits of others. **Negative externalities** occur because the behavior of one individual acting in personal self-interest negatively affects other individuals without their permission. The negative externality differs from a collective dilemma because the individual who causes the negative externality benefits from those actions. For example, if you play loud music at 3 o'clock on Thursday morning when your neighbor wants to sleep, you have created a negative externality for your neighbor. If that neighbor then mows her lawn at 7 o'clock on Sunday morning when you want to sleep, you suffer a negative externality. More serious negative externalities are created when factories pollute the air for people who live downwind and when people infected with hepatitis handle food in restaurants.

Negative externalities occur when the actions of some individuals harm others who are not directly involved in the actions. For example, suppose that a farmer relies on a stream to irrigate crops and someone upstream uses so much water that the stream no longer carries enough to irrigate; the farmer has suffered a negative externality. When farmers use pesticides on their crops, some of the chemicals wash into nearby streams and lakes. This runoff may negatively affect the health or the recreation opportunities of others.

Almost all actions generate externalities. Take the simple act of going out to eat. Cigarette smokers in the restaurant inflict passive smoke on others. Noisy children at one table reduce the enjoyment of eating for customers at surrounding tables. The cars in which patrons drive to the restaurant pollute the air along their routes. Producers of negative externalities often ignore the costs they impose on others unless those who suffer the externalities can force them to stop. Government regulations attempt to reduce negative externalities or to make the producers of the externalities reimburse society for the costs that they inflict on others. Examples of such regulations are government bans on smoking on commercial airplane flights and requirements for pollution control equipment in factories and on cars.

Some negative externalities are either too trivial, too difficult, or too costly to benefit from government action. Although the government may require large farms to meet certain standards concerning pesticide use, it may choose not to regulate homeowners who spray weeds in their yards. If your neighbor paints a house an ugly purple, then you suffer a negative externality. It is unlikely, however, that the government will attempt to regulate your neighbor's choice of paint color.

RIGHTS AND DUTIES

To achieve its minimal goals of protection and order, resolutions of collective dilemmas, and reductions in negative externalities, government must do one more thing. It must assign and enforce the rights and duties of citizens. The Declaration of Independence of the United States asserts that all individuals have the "unalienable rights [to] life, liberty, and the pursuit of happiness." Does your right to live include the right not to breathe smoke from other people's cigarettes, to drive on a road free of drunken drivers, to eat seafood unpolluted by pesticides, and to be sure that your medications are safe? Does your right to liberty include the liberty to discriminate against persons whose race, religion, or looks you find disagreeable? Do you have the duty to sell your house to anyone who can pay, regardless of race, religion, or looks? Do auto makers have the right to manufacture automobiles without air bags as standard equipment and thereby charge lower prices to consumers, or do they have the duty to protect drivers by installing air bags? Should women have the right to abort unwanted pregnancies, or do they have the duty to carry fetuses to term? Should all residents of a community or only property owners have the right to vote in local elections? Regardless of your specific answers to these questions, society needs some kinds of answers. Unless government decides who has which rights, it is difficult for people to make informed decisions and to live in peace.

Just as governments must decide rights, they must also decide duties. The saying, "The only sure things in this life are death and taxes," captures at least one of the duties that governments require of their citizens: to pay taxes. Some governments require all citizens over a certain age to vote in national elections. Other governments require people in specific age categories to serve in their armed forces. In many countries, governments determine the duties parents owe to their children, husbands to their wives, and wives to their husbands.

If government did not assign rights and duties, it could not preserve order, resolve collective dilemmas, or reduce negative externalities. The laws of society determine what actions constitute crimes and who pays the costs of maintaining the government. Someone must have the duty to pay the taxes necessary to support the institutions that preserve order, guarantee safety, and defend the country. To resolve the collective dilemma of air pollution, the law determines who has the right to pollute. Box 1.1 provides an example that demonstrates the difficulty of the government's task and how even the best intentions cannot prevent a policy from harming people who are innocent of wrongdoing.

This section has now identified four goals that any government attempts to achieve. First, government must protect the safety of its population and protect itself from internal revolutions and external invasions. Beyond this basic function, government attempts to improve the general welfare of its citizens by resolving collective dilemmas and minimizing negative externalities. To accomplish these tasks, government must specify and enforce the rights and duties of citizens. Government must act in these areas because rational individuals acting independently could not achieve the desired outcomes.

Beyond Minimal Government

Governments often attempt much more than the four goals discussed earlier. Most of the world's governments work to accomplish at least four additional objectives:

1. Increase social justice
2. Improve economic efficiency
3. Encourage morality
4. Socialize citizens to accept obligations appropriate to their roles in the existing regime

SOCIAL JUSTICE

Perhaps the most frequent justification for a larger role for government is the argument that society is unjust without it. Certainly, the desire of citizens to force the government to act in a just manner and to improve the level of social justice in society followed not long after the development of the minimal government. Those who would limit government to its minimal size typically contend that government has no justification for seizing the resources of some people to improve the lives of other people. Those who argue that government should go beyond the minimal functions contend that the government should redistribute resources because the existing distribution of wealth in society is neither fair nor efficient. What are some of the reasons for this opinion?

First, the factor that most influences a person's opportunities in life is the parents to whom he is born. If you want the best possible chance to make lots of money, enjoy all the things that wealth can bring, and live a long and healthy life, then you will need parents who are white or oriental, well-educated, wealthy, tall, and attractive; have long-lived

BOX 1.1

Taken to the Cleaners

My Elderly Mother May Lose Her Security
Because of Changing Community Standards

In June, a few days after her 84th birthday, my mother received a certified letter from the state of Oregon. It wasn't a birthday greeting, but it is likely to change the way she celebrates every birthday from now on. It almost certainly will change her way of life. My mother lives now, as she has for many years, alone and independently in a house on the edge of a small Willamette Valley town. Every spring she plants a garden. Every Saturday from spring until fall she circles her yard clipping flowers to fill two bouquets for her church. She moved to this corner in 1952, 2 years after my father died.

My mother was 38 when my father slipped from a construction scaffold in an accidental fall. I was 7, my brother 5. After his discharge from wartime service in the shipyards of Bremerton, Wash., my father had barely established himself as an electrician. He left $2,100 in death benefits. My mother updated her teaching credentials and found work in a rural school. Then, with $1,500 in hand, she went to the local bank. She wanted a loan to construct a small commercial building on the downtown lot where we then lived. The building, she said, would be her security. It would offer what my father now couldn't—a source of support in her old age.

In 1952, the building opened its doors. On one side of its 40-foot storefront, The Little Charm Shop displayed children's clothing. NuWay Cleaners filled the other side. The two stores served Main Street shoppers for 25 years until the operators of the cleaners retired. A flower shop moved into the space. By that time, the hardships imposed by the building were over. The days of pinching pennies and relying on grocery-store credit to make payments had ended. After more than 20 years of teaching seventh graders in town schools, my mother was looking forward to retirement. The future looked as rosy as the flowers in her tenant's cooler.

All that has changed. The building that once represented security produced a menace with the potential to bankrupt her. The discovery of contamination in city-park well water triggered groundwater tests in the area. Waste products once discarded by dry cleaners were identified as a likely source of contamination. Although a dry cleaner hasn't operated for 20 years on my mother's property, chemicals remain in the soil. Mother knew nothing of this hazard until a letter came from the Oregon Department of Environmental Quality. It said she should decide if she would oversee further testing and cleanup herself or if she would let the state handle it. In either case, my mother would pay the costs.

Property-tax appraisals set the current value of her building at just under $70,000. State employees and independent environmental consultants warn us that $200,000 is a conservative estimate for cleanup costs. My mother's entire estate, including the building, her home, and her savings, wouldn't cover the bill. At 84, she has enough money to live long and comfortably. She has enough savings to preserve her independence. She does not have enough money to bear the enormous costs of changing community standards.

The dry cleaner that operated in her building 40 years ago disposed of chemicals the same way as others did. Water samples show similar chemicals at other dry-cleaner locations in town. None of these businesses was operating in a negligent manner. They followed standards accepted by the community in 1952. Now we are learning that we must live more carefully if we are to survive in a world that is safe and clean.

My question is: Who should be responsible for costs imposed by changing community standards? Does liability stop with the easiest target? Or should the costs be shared by taxpayers and legislators who made the changes? This question, I'm told, worries senators and judges. It's not easily answered. The questions are ethical, political, and economic. The impact is profoundly human.

While the politicians debate, my mother has been gripped by uncertainty and fear. We were advised that she could try to spread the liability. She could take action against the dry cleaner, seek payment from companies that supplied his chemicals. She could attempt to identify insurers of the building before environmental hazards were written out of liability coverage. This is possible, we are told, but she must deal with it. She must pay the attorneys. She must hire the experts. The cost of spreading the burden is her burden. This is because state and federal law make her, the property owner, fully responsible. Even if she succeeded in distributing the burden of environmental cleanup among others, the effort could easily consume her savings.

Reluctantly, my mother humbled herself this summer. She bundled up tax records, savings statements, and retirement-fund reports and applied to the state of Oregon for hardship status. The appeal brought mercy, but not justice. It saved her home and her savings, but not her self-confidence. It appears she will lose the building that has been a symbol of security and prudent investment. The state has reserved the right to take the building in payment for cleanup costs. The law still holds her culpable.

My mother is on her own again. She's alone at the front of an issue that promises to stretch across the nation, touching thousands of small businesses. Dry cleaners, mechanics, print shops—all will face the same questions eventually. Who will pay? Who will be responsible for cleaning up messes made before we knew better?

These costs go beyond the loss of a rental-income building. Instead of facing the remainder of her life confident that she can provide for herself and contribute to her community, my mother is stocking up on shoes and underwear—fearful that she won't be able to afford them in the future.

The crippling realization that she could at any time be stripped of the means to support herself financially seems to have invaded her very cells. Her legs ache. Some days now, she leans on a chrome walker, unable to carry her own weight for the first time in her adult life. Surely this was not what we intended when we assessed the environmental transgressions of our past and set out to clean up the errors we made as a society on our way to the American Dream.

genes; and live in a high-income country. Then you are likely to have these same characteristics. Even if you do not happen to be particularly intelligent, parents with those beneficial attributes still give you a high probability of being wealthy and living a long life. But what if you are less fortunate in your parents? Perhaps your parents are poor and uneducated, have short-lived genes, or live in countries such as Haiti or Bangladesh. Then you have a high probability of living a poor, uneducated, short life.

Because you cannot choose your parents, the most important influence on your chance of living the good life is beyond your control. This fact has led many people to argue that government should redistribute some resources from those with helpful parents to those with less helpful ones. Advocates of such redistribution maintain that everyone in a country as wealthy as Japan, Sweden, or the United States should have a reasonable chance to achieve a good education and get a decent job. To condemn persons to unhealthy, uneducated, and undernourished lives seems unjust when a country has more than enough resources to provide everyone adequate health care, education, and food.

The government of almost every country tries to provide social services to people who cannot provide for themselves. In Sweden, Australia, Germany, and Austria, adults receive public assistance if they work for wages below officially defined poverty levels or are not currently working. Such assistance includes income supplements, subsidized food, and free or subsidized health care. In the United States, physically impaired people who cannot work can receive monthly incomes from the government. In all of the more industrialized countries and many less industrialized ones, when persons reach the age of retirement, they receive government pensions. In some countries, medical care is free to everyone. How do these societies justify these activities? How did they become government activities?

In the United States, government programs such as unemployment insurance, disability payments, old age pensions, and aid to low-income families with children began during the Great Depression. This event included a massive breakdown of the national economy, bank failures that deprived families of their life savings, loss of jobs by 30 percent of the work force, and massive waves of foreclosures by banks that dispossessed people from their houses. The Great Depression taught people that, even though they had worked and saved, they were vulnerable to economic disaster. The government responded by developing programs to help people when disaster struck.

Other countries provide far more public assistance than the United States provides. Some governments provide payments to persons who are not working regardless of the causes of their unemployment. Proponents of such payments often justify them in two ways. First, they say that every human being has a right to a reasonable minimum standard of living. Second, they assert that individuals' current problems were caused not only by themselves, but also by the society and by bad luck in their choice of parents.

ECONOMIC EFFICIENCY

Many proponents of spending government resources to provide citizens with adequate medical care, food, shelter, and education contend that such programs bring other benefits besides improving social justice; promoters claim that the programs also increase economic prosperity. For example, to increase its standard of living, a country must improve the skills of its labor force. This requires education. Basic skills in reading, writing, and math allow people to participate in complex industrial societies like those of Germany, Canada, or Israel. American politicians make frequent calls for better education. The most common justification for government expenditures on education is not to make educated people happier, to increase their understanding of the world around them, or to help them appreciate art or literature. Rather, advocates of greater funding for schools contend that it will increase economic efficiency and the well-being of all in the society. These advocates contend that the United States economy is falling behind that of Japan because Japanese workers are better educated than American workers.

Proponents of government intervention to ensure adequate diets for children make a similar argument. Young children who receive inadequate diets face higher probabilities of becoming mentally handicapped adults. This reduces their economic productivity and increases the likelihood that the government will have to spend tax dollars caring for these individuals rather than receiving taxes from their earnings. Thus, the government increases future economic productivity and decreases the future need for welfare programs by guaranteeing adequate diets for children.

People who believe that the government should provide health care argue that all of society benefits if the government ensures that everyone receives this service. For example, most college students received immunizations before starting kindergarten or the first grade. They were immunized against measles, mumps, polio, diphtheria, and typhoid. Few of these students or their parents had any choice in this matter because the government had decided that the best way to prevent epidemics was to make sure that all students received immunizations. Supporters of the government provision of education, nutrition, and health care can base their support on appeals to both social justice and economic efficiency. If children receive good educations, nutrition, and health care, then they become more productive and all of society benefits. Thus, the consumption of these goods by individuals provides **positive externalities**[†] for society. When the consumption of a good by some individuals improves the welfare of others in society, and society decides to subsidize the consumption of this good, it is a **merit good.** The government's decision to subsidize merit goods implies that if government does not subsidize them, private individuals will not consume levels sufficient to maximize the benefits to society. For example, if the government did not heavily subsidize education, the poor might be unable to afford enough learning to make them productive citizens. The government not only subsidizes many merit goods such as education and immunization, but it also requires people to consume them.

GOVERNMENT INTERVENTION IN THE ECONOMY

Among the most widely debated issues about the appropriate tasks of government is when government should intervene in the national economy. In socialist societies such as

---

[†] A positive externality occurs when the actions of some produce benefits for others. For example, if your neighbors take good care of their homes and yards, then when you are ready to sell your house you are likely to benefit from a higher price and a quicker sale. Externalities can be either positive or negative. For example, if the person sitting next to you is smoking a foul-smelling cigar, you receive a negative externality. On the other hand, if the person next to you is smoking marijuana, you may believe you are receiving a positive externality.

Vietnam, China, and Cuba, the government decides what goods and services the society will produce, how much the society will invest, and what purchases that investment will fund. In capitalist societies such as Japan, Great Britain, and Germany, private individuals make most of these decisions.

The modern bases for these diametrically opposed governmental roles come from the writings of the two most influential economists in history, Adam Smith and Karl Marx.[‡] Advocates of minimalist government agree with Adam Smith's assertion that "little else is requisite to carry a state to the highest degree of opulence from the lowest barbarism, but peace, easy taxes, and a tolerable administration of justice."[2] Smith stated that the *invisible hand* of the market, working through the laws of supply and demand, is the most efficient device for deciding what goods and services society will produce. Therefore, he claimed, the state should have no role in economic decisions aside from defining and protecting property rights, limiting monopolies, providing collective goods, and requiring that the prices of goods include all production costs.

Karl Marx took the opposite perspective. He believed that government and economic decisions are completely intertwined and that government simply enforces the values and protects the interests of the dominant economic class. Followers of Marx contend that the governments in socialist societies should act on behalf of the populations and guide national economies so that those societies produce the goods and services that the people need most. A socialist government should also insure that these goods and services are distributed fairly.

Governments in today's world operate between the extreme positions of Smith and Marx. Just as governments intervene in capitalist economies, the Chinese government currently encourages greater reliance on the market to determine which goods and services to produce.

GOVERNMENT AS A MORAL FORCE

In every society, government supports social norms and standards of morality. Governments accomplish these tasks by passing and enforcing laws that reinforce social norms and religious teachings. Some of these norms protect life and clearly fall within the appropriate jurisdiction of even a minimal government. However, governments seek to enforce religious practices and principles when they enact laws that prohibit sales of alcohol or drugs, ban nudity or appearance in public without a veil, force segregation or integration of races, prohibit prostitution, or censor sexually explicit books. Legislation based on ethical or moral considerations also includes requirements for or prohibitions against prayer in public schools.

Government and religious leaders have a long history of cooperation. The pharaohs, caesars, popes, and emperors all legitimized their power by combining religious and state authority. The doctrine of divine right of kings and the theocracies of Calvinism and the

---

[‡]Karl Marx, the father of modern communism, wrote a number of influential works examining state intervention in the economy and outlining the relationships between politics and economics. The most comprehensive of these works was *Das Kapital*. Volume I of *Das Kapital* was first published in 1883 and the entire work was finally available in 1910. Adam Smith, the father of modern capitalism, wrote his justly famous book, *The Wealth of Nations*, in the previous century with the first publication occurring in 1776.

Puritans did much the same thing. Iran provides the most visible example of this principle today; the Imam is portrayed as a divinely inspired, infallible spiritual leader who also wields supreme civil authority. When the ruler claims to be the messenger of god, the laws of the state become commandments ordained by a higher power. In this way, governments use religion to bolster their rule. In return, the government uses its coercive power to support and maintain the religion and its moral precepts.

Although most governments do not claim divine authority or inspiration, the laws of a nation often express the preferences of the dominant religion. Laws against adultery, homosexuality, polygamy, sterilization, and abortion provide examples of church-inspired legislation concerning sexual and reproductive practices. Less obvious religious prohibitions inspire laws related to so-called *victimless crimes* such as prostitution, gambling, pornography, and drug use. In part, such laws reflect attempts by society to maintain order. They also reflect the desire of government authorities to socialize citizens to appropriate attitudes, values, and behaviors.

Rulers may choose to impose laws to promote moral or ethical behavior. They do this to make the society a better place and to improve the happiness of its citizens. Perhaps the best Western statement of this justification for government action came from Aristotle. He argued that a government that does not improve morality cannot be worthwhile. Because people's actions are often driven by passion rather than reason, Aristotle maintained, government should legislate virtuous behavior. Citizens would then learn virtue by practicing virtuous acts so that they would become habits. Aristotle proposed legal restrictions on speech as well as on behavior. He maintained that these restrictions were necessary to protect young people from corruption.

POLITICAL SOCIALIZATION

No government wants people to obey its laws and support the current rulers only because they fear punishment. A government prefers that people obey laws, vote, sing the national anthem, and pay taxes because they believe that they ought to do so. When citizens believe that they should obey the laws and that the current government and the institutions of the state deserve their loyalty, then the government is *legitimate* in the eyes of its citizens.

Governments work hard to establish legitimacy through **political socialization**, the process by which people acquire views and attitudes about government and politics. Numerous institutions take part in this socialization process, including the family, church, peer group, school, media, and government. For example, Japanese schools teach children that democratic government is good, the prime minister is a legitimate ruler, and citizens ought to participate in the democratic process. Similarly, courses in American schools on American government, American history, and good citizenship are not known for the objective view they develop of American institutions. These schools further aid the socialization process by requiring students to elect class presidents, recite the Pledge of Allegiance, and sing the national anthem.

Political socialization tries to make people feel that their identity is tied to the state. Social institutions teach people to think of themselves as Americans, Canadians, Mexicans, or citizens of other countries. As with religious identification, political identification extends beyond a simple benefit-cost analysis of individual outcomes. Bumper stickers announce "My Country: Right or Wrong!" and "America, Love it or Leave It!" As James Madison pointed out in *Federalist No. 49,* a government is much safer when reason is fortified by the practices and prejudices of public opinion and social institutions:

> A reverence for the laws would be sufficiently inculcated by the voice of enlightened reason. But a nation of philosophers is as little to be expected as the philosophical race of kings wished for by Plato. And in every other nation, the most rational government will not find it a superfluous advantage to have the prejudices of the community on its side.[3]

Aristotle identified political socialization as a regime's most important task. He wrote that the legislator must work for the education of the young above all. A particular regime should educate for the values proper to its characteristics—a democratic character for a democracy, an oligarchic character for an oligarchy. Abraham Lincoln taught respect for the law and the importance of obeying the law, even if it is unjust. Lincoln told students in a young men's school in Illinois that their political institutions and laws were a legacy bequeathed to them from the nation's founders. It was the students' task of gratitude, he said, to faithfully maintain the institutions and to obey the law. Students must respect laws because the only alternative is rule by the mob led by a demagogue.[4]

In many societies, and almost all stable ones, the other institutions of society—the family, the church, and the media—reinforce the teachings of the educational system. If you review your own experiences, you probably will find that your government and your society have spent substantial time socializing you to love your country and its institutions. Most readers learned at an early age that the police officer was part of the government, that the president was a powerful and important person, and that democracy is the best form of government.

Regimes have difficulty when the teachings of other institutions in society deny the government's legitimacy. For example, the Kurdish people live on land controlled by Turkey, Iraq, Iran, and Syria. Most Kurds do not accept these governments as legitimate. Kurdish parents teach their children that these governments have no right to rule Kurdistan. While most Kurds are Sunni Muslims, most of their rulers are not. For this reason, the religious leaders in Kurdistan also argue against the legitimacy of the existing governments. To reduce the ability of the church and other institutions to socialize Kurds against their governments, the schools in Kurdistan teach children using languages other than Kurdish and even prohibit students from speaking Kurdish. Because the governments that rule Kurdistan cannot achieve legitimacy in the eyes of the Kurdish people, these governments must enforce their rule through coercive, often deadly, force.

How Did Governments Arise?

Even accepting the principle that most people desire governments, a question remains about how these governments first arose. Did people living in an area come together and decide that they would all be worse off if they were left to follow their individual rational self-interests? Did they worry that the group would have no defense against external threats? Did these people realize that without clearly specified rights and duties, they would suffer anarchy and violence? Did they realize that they could not solve important collective dilemmas? Based on such reasoning, did people then come together and write a social contract or constitution to create a government? They probably did not.

In a provocative essay, economist Mancur Olson, Jr. has attempted to show that governments arose when humans moved from hunting and gathering societies to communities based on agriculture.[5] Hunting and gathering societies did not need structured governments. These societies had few members, most of them related by kinship. In addition, almost all adults had to cooperate to ensure the continuation of the community. In such a situation, problems with collective goods and free riders rarely arose because self-interest and the collective good were almost identical. Because of this common feeling, hunting and gathering societies could make decisions through voluntary agreements; coercion by a government was unnecessary.

Olson has argued that voluntary agreements began to fail when people changed from hunting and gathering societies to agricultural societies. The development of agriculture created four important social changes. First, people remained in a single location for long periods. Second, the farmers could potentially produce a surplus of food. This surplus allowed some people to pursue activities such as art and religion that were not directly related to food production. Third, it became profitable for one set of people to subjugate another. People who owned slaves could avoid agricultural labor themselves. Fourth, the agricultural nature of the economy made possible larger societies. Taken together, these changes made voluntary agreements less effective.

To see Olson's argument, assume that an agricultural society grew to 1,000 people. Could voluntary agreements maintain order and safety among so many people? Could all agree about who would have rights to grow crops on particular lands, what to do if one person's pig were to eat another person's crops, and who would be obligated to defend the community against attack? Is it probable that all would agree concerning how much each citizen would pay to build a temple, hire a priest, or track down a runaway slave? Olson wrote:

> . . . [W]e should not be surprised that while there have been lots of writings about the desirability of "social contracts" to obtain the benefits of law and order, no one has ever found a large society that obtained a peaceful order or other public goods through [a voluntary] agreement among the individuals in society.[6]

At the very time that larger and more complex societies made voluntary cooperation more difficult, the need for such cooperation increased. Agricultural communities not only stored surplus food, but they also used it to pay artisans, priests, and other individuals not directly involved in growing crops. These developments made it profitable for bandits to join together and raid agricultural communities. Olson argues that governments arose when groups of bandits forcefully subjugated agricultural communities. Early in the development of agriculture, roving bandits went from community to community stealing everything of value they could take with them.[§] Olson hypothesized that at some point, these bandits figured out that pillaging a community and moving on was less efficient

---

[§]Excellent examples of such roving bandits are found in the movies *The Seven Samurai* and *The Magnificent Seven*.

than settling in a community and taking the surplus in the form of regular taxation. Olson argued that the first rulers were simply "stationary bandits."

Interestingly, this change from roving marauders to stationary bandits could benefit both the community and the bandits. A bandit who becomes stationary can maintain income only by protecting the people who pay taxes and guarding against revolt by the citizenry and against external attack by other bandits. This protection from external attacks also protects subjects and increases social order. It allows for increases in productivity because the people have protection for that portion of their surplus that the stationary bandit does not seize as taxes.

If a stationary bandit wishes to gain more wealth, coercive power can increase the wealth of the community by providing collective goods such as protection, order, and clear definitions of rights. For example, if people know that roving bandits will come and take all of their crops, they have little incentive to cooperate on long-term projects. They are unlikely to improve the land or cooperate to build collective goods such as irrigation canals. People gain little from improving the productive capacity of the land if they are likely to lose everything to a roving bandit. On the other hand, if the members of a community know that their stationary bandit will protect them and that they can keep some portion of their increased production, then it becomes rational for them to improve the land and to increase their productivity.

Olson's analysis reasserts the beneficial roles of government. First, even rule by a stationary bandit is preferable to violent anarchy because both the subjects and the bandit live better. If the stationary bandit successfully accomplishes the four minimal tasks of government, then the people's lives improve. If these activities increase the productivity of the people and make their lives better, then the ruler's life also improves by increasing personal wealth through taxes. Therefore, government by a stationary bandit may be bad, but it is better than life under the threat of roving bandits.

Olson may seem too pessimistic in his portrayal of rulers as authoritarian bandits. History is filled with monarchs and other autocrats who improved the long-term wealth of their countries and well-being of their people. Why might a stationary bandit do this? The most straightforward reason is to gain even greater wealth. A wealthier community can provide greater potential wealth for the ruler. The wealth of a society can grow only if the society invests. Rulers who seize all the surplus that citizens create make it impossible for citizens to invest in future productivity. Therefore, a ruler who expects to hold power for a long time will leave subjects a sufficient surplus to encourage economic growth.

The concept of stationary bandits trying to maximize their wealth encourages consideration of reasons why some communities might become more stable and prosperous than others. A critical variable may be the length of time that the ruler expects to rule. If a ruler is weak compared to others in the area, the ruler may not expect to hold power very long. In this situation, the stationary bandit will act very much like a roving bandit, taking as much as possible in a short time and keeping it in a form such as gold (or a Swiss bank account) to grab and carry away in fleeing. Such a strategy discourages economic growth and political stability.

A ruler who is sufficiently strong to discourage attack, however, may expect to hold power for life. A longer expected tenure in power leads the ruler to place more value on the economic growth of the subject lands. Therefore, a ruler who expects a long future is more likely to attempt tasks that increase productivity. This ruler will also more likely leave subjects sufficient surplus to encourage future economic growth.[7] If the ruler's child will probably rule subsequently, and if the ruler cares about the child's well-being, this succession extends the ruler's planning horizon still further. This argument explains, therefore, why both the ruler and the ruled in a society may prefer a hereditary monarchy rather than rule by the most powerful member of the stationary bandit's army.

The Development of Law

Law is the principal instrument by which governments achieve their goals. It provides an orderly process for people to follow in their social relationships and a mechanism to protect citizens from each other. In addition, law can help create a just society. As James Madison wrote, " . . . the ordinary administration of justice [is], of all others, the most powerful, most universal, and most attractive source of popular obedience and attachment."[8] Modern governments formulate laws, implement them with bureaucracies, and interpret them in courts, and they maintain police to apprehend violators. Governments did not always formulate and implement explicit laws. The development of this conception of law took thousands of years.

BEGINNINGS OF LAW

For most of human history, the vast majority of law did not come from formal actions by rulers or legislatures. Rather, law consisted largely of rules developed from customary practices among the members of society. Humans seem to have a natural tendency in societies to produce legal orders that enforce custom-sanctioned rules. Societies also seem universally driven to write down their customary rules. This occurred in every literate society almost as soon as it invented or imported writing.

Publishing and systematically compiling rules of law were the next steps in the development of law. This began with "law givers," learned statesmen who collected and organized established rules. Some also elaborated basic principles they perceived to underlie the laws.[||] One of the best-known examples of an early *codification* is the Code of Hammurabi (Babylon, c. 1792–1750 B.C.) This code was primarily a restatement of accepted principles.

Another critical step in the development of law and government was the shift of responsibility for the enforcement of law from the victims and their families to official government agents. Various administrative officers gradually assumed responsibility for applying laws to settle disputes in particular cases and to punish violators. Central organs of government, such as the Athenian Assembly in the 5th and 4th centuries B.C., also

---

[||] According to the Old Testament, God gave Moses the Mosaic Code (13th century B.C.) during the Israelites' flight from Egypt. Besides the Ten Commandments, it embodied criminal law and religious law. The Bible contains these laws in the books of Exodus, Leviticus, Numbers, and Deuteronomy, all said to have been written by Moses. The folk myths of many early peoples included mythical "law givers" as sources of primitive rules. These rules were invariably said to have been "handed down," that is, transmitted from some higher authority than humans.

interpreted and applied laws in particular cases. None of these agencies "made" law in the modern sense. They did not decide what rules people would have to follow. They limited themselves to converting existing norms and rules into written legal codes. The modern conception of legislation as law-making did not take shape until 15 centuries later.

Roman Law   The *content* of the law of the land in much of today's Western world took shape in Rome. The steady development of Roman law over 13 centuries provided a major step toward the modern concept of law. This step was "enactment." A *lex* (law) was a rule derived from custom along with a declaration that acknowledged its binding character.** The proposal became law when adopted by vote of the Assembly. The practice began about 250 B.C. in response to citizen demands to know in advance what laws the magistrates and assembly might enforce.

The capstone on the monumental Roman legal system was the codification commissioned by, and named for, the Emperor Justinian, the *Corpus Juris Civilis* (535 A.D.). It included the basic civil law in all the major branches recognized today—contracts, torts, property rights, personal rights, etc. So thorough was the code's inclusion of preexisting law that it declared that no laws preceding it could be cited as laws or precedents or in any way referred to in legal documents.

English Common Law   English Common Law is the second great body of law in the Western world. Until the 11th century, law in England was much like that in feudal Europe—local customs administered by the lords of manors or rulers of noble estates. From feudal times on, English kings, like monarchs in Europe, had the right to create their own courts. They created the Court of Common Pleas. The term *common law* arose to distinguish the law applied by the king's courts from the local and manorial law applied by the monarch's vassals in their fiefs. The king's law applied nominally to all the kingdom "in common."

The most distinctive feature of English common law is its focus on *case law*. That is, it is expressed in decisions made by judges in particular cases brought before them. Judges find the rule of law that applies to a particular case in *precedents,* decisions in earlier cases that dealt with the same issues. A related general principle called *stare decisis* holds that precedents embody binding law that courts should follow, although exceptions may occur. Another principle of common law makes higher courts' decisions binding on all lower courts. Commentaries on the law written by legal scholars are important adjuncts to case law. The most famous such scholar was William Blackstone (1723–1780). His opinions remain influential in countries that use English Common Law.

THE GOVERNMENT AS LAW MAKER

Throughout the long process that produced Roman law and English Common Law, government bore responsibility for correctly interpreting and fairly applying the law. These traditions did not assign government the job of *making* law. The rise of monarchs encouraged the development of the modern conception of law and government.

**It belonged to the class of rules that Romans called *Jus,* the root of our word *justice.*

Monarchs fought continually to expand their realms by conquest and by marriages. They centralized power within their kingdoms by force and by creating bureaucracies. By the beginning of the 16th century, a decreasing number of powerful monarchies ruled increasingly large realms across Europe. Rulers justified their rule by appealing to the "divine right of kings." They based this claim on the biblical injunction, "Let every soul be subject unto the higher powers, for the powers that be are ordained of God."[9] One 16th-century advocate of divine-right absolutism described vividly the unlimited power that God granted: "The King is, in this world, without law, and may, at his lust, do right or wrong, and shall give accounts but to God only."[10]

A French political thinker, Jean Bodin, supplied the concept through which rulers could justify such absolute obedience. The concept was **sovereignty.** Bodin saw sovereignty as the characteristic that distinguishes the state from all other social groupings. He defined sovereignty as supreme power over citizens and subjects, *unrestrained by law.* It is unrestrained by law because the sovereign is the source of law. Sovereignty, according to Bodin, is absolute, perpetual, and unlimited power over government by a unitary control through the apparatus of the state. Bodin defined citizenship as subjection to a sovereign and said that this subjection makes people citizens. He argued that customary law applies only if the sovereign's sanction permits it to exist.

This role of the sovereign radically changed the conception of law. Thus: *"Rather than written rules derived from customs, human choices came to specifically shape laws."* Laws resulted from the command of the sovereign. This conception of law led to the concept of the sovereign state and the modern system of international relations. A **sovereign state** is free and independent. It has undivided jurisdiction over all people and property within its territory and claims the right to regulate its economic life without regard for its neighbors. No other nation may rightly interfere in its domestic affairs. In its external affairs, the sovereign state claims the right to enforce its own conception of rights and to declare war.[11]

Some Key Terms

Many terms in political science, journalism, and ordinary political conversations are confusing. In political science, among the most confusing terms are *government, country, state, nation,* and *nation-state.* The confusion arises because people often treat them as interchangeable terms. In the following paragraphs, we briefly define how we use the terms in this book.

GOVERNMENT

We have discussed the goals of government without defining what we mean by that word or examining how government institutions differ from other social institutions. **Government,** as we use the term, refers to political institutions with the authority to make and implement laws. These institutions can have national, regional, or local jurisdictions. Perhaps the most important difference between governments and other social institutions such as churches, families, unions, and universities is that people recognize government rules as more binding. The rules of churches, families, and universities do not legally bind even the members of those institutions unless the government passes laws that allow this. Certainly, the rules of church, family, and university do not obligate people who are not members of these institutions. Finally, if a government's rule conflicts with that of another institution, the government's rule takes precedence unless the government decides otherwise.

The comprehensive nature of government authority shows one more difference between governments and other institutions. Participation in a unit of government is not voluntary in the same sense that church, union, and even family membership are voluntary. Normally, people voluntarily marry, join churches, and become union members. They consciously choose to place themselves under the rules of these institutions. In contrast, people do not normally choose to place themselves under the rule of a government. It happens automatically. If you were born in the United States, you are, with only a few exceptions, a U.S. citizen. Even if you renounce your citizenship, you still must live within the rules of the country unless you leave it and place yourself under the rules of the government of another country. On the other hand, you can leave a labor union, church, or family without placing yourself under the rules of another union, church, or family.

STATE

One of the most difficult terms in political science is *the state*. This abstract concept refers to all of the institutions that participate in making and in enforcing public policy. For example, in a communist country, the state includes not only the institutions of government but also the institutions of the Communist Party and the network of informers paid by the secret police. In Mexico, certain labor and business associations are components of the governing party, the *Partido Revolucionario Institucional* (PRI). These institutions act to control labor and to influence business decisions. They are part of the state, despite the fact that they are not officially part of the government. In its broadest meaning, *the state* includes all citizens and their defined rights and duties. This conception usually underlies statements such as, "It is not in the interests of the United States to become involved in Bosnia."

Clearly, *the state* is a broader term than *government*. A government is the specific individuals who hold public offices and exercise power in the name of the state or the people. Governments change frequently, while the state remains.

As mentioned earlier, one of the characteristics of the state is its sovereignty. Until the fall of the Soviet Union in 1991, Russia had not been a state for over 70 years. Rather, it was one part of the Soviet Union. Today, Russia is once again a state because no higher authority can overrule its decisions. Texas, Scotland, and Ontario are not states. Although their governments make rules that apply to people living within their borders, the governments that govern all of the United States, Great Britain, and Canada can overrule the decisions of Texas, Scotland, and Ontario. If a conflict arises between the government of Ontario and the government of Canada, the institutions of Canada determine the outcome of the conflict.

NATION

If *the state* refers to the common political community of a country and its institutions of government-related coercion, what does *nation* mean? Although writers often use *nation, country,* and *state* as synonyms, we use the term **nation** to mean a sizable group of people united by common bonds of language, culture, traditions, and common aspirations.[12] Although people often use this term interchangeably with *state,* many national groups, such as the Kurds, have not yet achieved independence. In addition, some states, such as India, encompass more than one nation. Instability often results when a state contains more than one nation. The Soviet Union, Czechoslovakia, and Yugoslavia were all states that included two or more nations; this characteristic led each of these states to break up into two or more states. In 1995, the citizens of Quebec voted in a referendum to determine whether the French-speaking province would remain a part of Canada or become a separate state.

When cultures collide within the same nation-state, even the most stable and long-lived states such as Canada can become fragile.

NATION-STATE

Perhaps you can already define the term *nation-state*. Strictly speaking, a nation-state encompasses only one nation in the area covered by the state to include most of the people who consider themselves part of that national culture. Japan, Sweden, Norway, and Argentina are examples of such nation-states. In practice, political scientists tend to refer to any independent state as a *nation-state*. Thus, although India, the United States, Turkey, Canada, South Africa, Nigeria, and Israel do not limit their states to the governance of people who share a common language, ethnic background, culture, or religion, people still refer to them as *nation-states*.

Summary

This chapter introduced many of the activities that governments pursue and the justifications for those actions. The chapter argued that the minimal state would provide protection and order, attempt to resolve collective dilemmas that might harm the society, reduce negative externalities, and define rights and duties. The chapter then examined justifications for government actions beyond those of the minimal state. The modern concept of the state and government as a law maker arose with the development of monarchies and the idea of sovereignty. Finally, the chapter discussed the differences between government and other social institutions as well as the meanings of *sovereignty, state, government,* and *nation*.

QUESTIONS AND EXERCISES

Questions for Reason

1. Give three examples of collective dilemmas not mentioned in this chapter. Is each appropriate for government intervention? Why or why not?
2. Give three examples of free rider problems not mentioned in this chapter. Is each appropriate for government intervention? Why or why not?
3. Give three examples of negative externalities not mentioned in this chapter. Is each appropriate for government intervention? Why or why not?
4. Explain the concept of merit goods.

Questions for Reflection

Government must often resolve conflicts between the goals of social justice and economic efficiency in setting public policy. For example, in 1995 and 1996, the Republican-controlled Congress and President Clinton fought over spending priorities in balancing the budget and how many years it should take to achieve that goal. The Republicans argued that the government must balance its budget in 7 years and that cutting health care protection for the poor was a reasonable step toward a balanced budget. President Clinton argued that it would be better to take 10 years to balance the budget so that the country could continue to provide health care for the poor.

In this debate, the Republicans did not argue that providing medical care for the poor is an unworthy goal or that it is an inappropriate task for government. Similarly, President Clinton did not argue that balancing the budget was a bad idea. He strongly supported that goal. Given that both goals seem worthy, write a short essay discussing how should a government set priorities for them.

Question for Analysis   Using the technique for combining normative and empirical statements you learned in the Introduction, take statements from either the president's most recent State of the Union address or the 1996 Democratic or Republican Party platforms. Choose two policy proposals and break them down into outcome preference, empirical expectation, and logical conclusion.

NOTES

[1] Garrett Hardin, "The Tragedy of the Commons," *Science,* December 13, 1968, pp. 1243–1248.

[2] Adam Smith, The Wealth of Nations. (New York: The Modern Library, 1937), p. 14.

[3] Publius, *The Federalist Papers, No. 49,* ed. by Andrew Hacker (New York: Washington Square, 1964), p. 118. *The Federalist Papers* were written by James Madison, Alexander Hamilton, and John Jay and published under the pseudonym *Publius* from 1787 to 1788. The documents argued for the ratification of the newly drafted Constitution.

[4] Abraham Lincoln, Speech to the Young Men's Lyceum, Springfield, Illinois, January 27, 1837.

[5] Mancur Olson, Jr., "Dictatorship, Democracy, and Development," *American Political Science Review* 87 (1993), pp. 567–568.

[6] Ibid., p. 568.

[7] Ibid., p. 571.

[8] Publius, *The Federalist Papers, No. 17* (New York: Heritage, 1945), p. 106.

[9] Rom. 13:1.

[10] William Tyndale, "Obedience of a Christian Man," ed. by H. Walter (Cambridge: Parker Society, 1843), p. 178.

[11] *New Columbia Encyclopedia*, s.v. "law."

[12] Ibid., p. 24.

Political Philosophy and Forms of Government

John Locke

Adam Smith

2

The Evolution of Western Liberal Theory

Key Terms

State of Nature	Invisible Hand	Economic Efficiency
Social Contract	Laissez-Faire	Veil of Ignorance
Leviathan	Law of Population	Original Position
Natural Law	Utilitarianism	Difference Principle
Natural Right	Unearned Rent	Constitutionalism

Everyone has ideas about what a good society would look like and the role that government would play in that kind of society. Such beliefs and values influence people's evaluations of the events they read about, hear of, or see. As the Introduction revealed, however, few people have organized their ideas, beliefs, and values into coherent and logically consistent frameworks. A normative political theory is such a framework, and political philosophy is the part of political science that develops and evaluates such theories.

Two normative theories currently dominate the ideological premises of many of the world's governments: western liberalism and Marxism-Leninism. These frameworks supply conflicting answers to the questions posed in the Introduction and Chapter 1. Both originated in western Europe, in part in response to the social, political, and economic conditions there; still, they have a tremendous appeal throughout the world. The governments of most industrialized and many less industrialized countries profess to follow the prescriptions of either western liberalism or Marxism-Leninism. In this chapter, we examine the first of these theories.

Classical Western Liberalism

Chapter 1 explained that the development of large nations headed by monarchs gradually began to dominate much of the world by the 16th century, accompanied by the ideas of divine right and sovereignty. Following these ideas, monarchs gradually claimed the right to create laws that took precedence over past laws that had developed through customs being written into rules. The epitome of this kind of government is the reign of Louis XIV in France, who is said to have proclaimed, "I am the state!" In the face of such an absolute interpretation of power, political questions began to focus on, as one medieval writer put it, "how to put a bridle on a king." A theoretical justification for bridling the monarch came from the evolution of a political philosophy called *liberalism.*

Liberalism developed during the 17th and 18th centuries in Europe. This framework is not the same as the principles suggested by the word *liberal* in the contemporary United States. Today's observer would consider the ideas of the earliest liberals as more "conservative" than "liberal." Regardless of whether you consider yourself liberal or conservative, most of the policies you would support derive from the ideology of liberalism. If you live in the United States, western Europe, Canada, Australia, or New Zealand, your government is based on the ideas of western liberalism. What are these ideas?

At the heart of western liberalism are the beliefs that government must acknowledge limits to its authority and that it exists to safeguard the rights and liberties of citizens.[1] Liberalism places its faith in reason and believes that progress is possible through the application of reason and science. Finally, liberalism is antagonistic to hereditary political rank.

Prior to the development of liberalism, people viewed governments as divinely ordained parts of God's plan, and they assumed that the leaders of those governments ruled on the basis of divine right. Simply put, people accepted the claim that God chose the rulers and gave them their powers. Rulers certainly did not get their power from the consent of the governed. The major role of a government based on divine right was to implement the natural order that God had ordained. Monarchs learned what God wanted them to do through meditation, religious training, and revelations. Citizens could not criticize their government or their rulers because such criticisms would effectively attack God's choices. If a country had a bad ruler, people saw their suffering as God's punishment. Ordinary citizens had no role in politics, as they could make no political choices.[2]

Another idea that modern observers often take for granted, the idea of inalienable rights, did not exist in law prior to liberalism. Neither the Romans, Greeks, Chinese, Jews, or any other known ancient society recognized such rights. Even within recent western history, this ideal has been the exception rather than the rule.[3]

THE ROLE OF REASON

The first step away from the idea of divine right came when Martin Luther (1483–1546) and John Calvin (1509–1564) challenged the claim that only those in authority (the clergy and the monarchy) could understand God's plan. Luther and Calvin believed that every individual can have a private relationship with God and that, through this relationship, the individual can understand God's plan. When political philosophers combined the idea that everyone can understand God's natural order with the belief that God gave people reason so that they could understand, they established the legitimacy of all people making political choices. All citizens could legitimately claim to understand God's plan, at least for themselves. Ordinary citizens could then question and criticize their rulers without challenging God and the church. Citizens could participate in political criticism without jeopardizing their souls.

THOMAS HOBBES AND THE SOCIAL CONTRACT

Thomas Hobbes (1588–1679) made the next step leading to the development of liberalism. At the time Hobbes wrote his influential book *Leviathan,* England had just completed one of the most tumultuous periods in its history. First, the people rebelled against the tyrannical rule of Charles I and cut off his head. They replaced Charles not with another monarch but with Oliver Cromwell, a Puritan who ruled as a dictator. When Oliver Cromwell died, his son Richard succeeded him, and another revolt replaced Richard with Charles II, the exiled son of Charles I. The English people ultimately decided not that they preferred dictators to monarchs or monarchs to dictators, but rather that they objected to the idea of rule by divine right. Therefore, they needed a different justification of political authority when they invited Charles II to become king. Thomas Hobbes, a tutor of Charles II, provided this justification.

The experience of the previous civil war and its associated anarchy, death, and disease convinced Hobbes that societies needed strong rulers who could impose order on disorderly mobs. But Hobbes had to justify this authority with some premise other than divine right. He did this through the inventions of a **"state of nature"** and the **"social contract."** Hobbes argued that prior to government, people lived in a chaotic state of nature. The social contract was the agreement through which people overcame the state of nature and its inherent terror.

To justify all-powerful rule by Charles II, Hobbes put forth two major arguments. First, he asserted that the most important task of government is to establish order; but this order need not be "God's order." Second, because the order is not necessarily divinely inspired nor is the ruler divinely chosen, Hobbes claimed, rulers receive their power from another source: the people whom they rule. He explained that rational people confer this power when they come together and form the social contract in order to avoid anarchy. The contract allows the ruled to trade their freedom to a powerful ruler in return for physical safety.

Hobbes did not create the idea that order is the principal aim of government. Almost all political theories assume that government will maintain order; otherwise, neither governments nor citizens could accomplish other goals. For example, the role of the pharaoh in Egypt during the Middle Kingdom was to guide the people of Stemmed so that they might re-create the divine order of the Gods. For Aristotle, the state created an orderly society so that it could create the virtuous citizen. In European political theories prior to Hobbes, governments created order so that people could live in a way that reflected God's plan and led to individual salvation. For Hobbes, however, order was not a means to an end; it was the end itself.

Why was the establishment of order so important for Hobbes? Because he saw humans as inherently greedy, selfish, and violent. He argued that in the absence of a strong government life would simply be, "a time of Warre, where every man is Enemy to every man." In such a situation, Hobbes contended that,

[T]here is no place for Industry; because the fruit thereof is uncertain and consequently no Culture of the Earth; no Navigation . . .; no Knowledge of the face of the Earth; no account of Time; no Arts; no Letters; no Society; and which is worst of all, continual feare, and danger of violent death; And the life of man, solitary, poore, nasty, brutish, and Short.[4]

Hobbes contended that at some point in history, rational human beings who wanted to avoid the horrible situation in which they found themselves came together and agreed to a social contract. This contract bound them to renounce their rights to kill and steal and gave the state the power to enforce this contract. Hobbes argued that the best possible state would be exceptionally strong, its laws pervasive, and its justice stern. Otherwise, because humans are greedy and selfish, disorder would represent a constant threat. In Hobbes's ideal world, an all-powerful ruler who can "suppress dissent with an iron hand" represents the state.[5] Hobbes called this all-powerful sovereign "**Leviathan.**"

Why must the sovereign be all powerful? Because humans are selfish and subject to rule by their passions. Hobbes insisted that concepts such as right and wrong or justice and injustice have little meaning outside of civil society. Other than the right of an individual to self-preservation, any rights come from the Leviathan. For Hobbes, the only injustice is the violation of the government's laws. The idea that people have any right to contradict the government is nonsense. The only limitations on the power of the Leviathan are voluntary and retractable promises, his indifference to certain activities, and his physical or administrative weakness.[6]

This feeding center in Somalia illustrates how harsh life becomes when the state can no longer preserve order. The result is the world that Hobbes feared and shows why he argued for an all-powerful ruler.

The name "Leviathan" clearly illustrates Hobbes's vision of the sovereign's power. The Leviathan was a powerful beast in the book of Job in the Bible. Readers who grew up in a Jewish or Christian tradition may remember the story of Job, who worshiped and loved God, obeying all of God's laws. In a conversation between the devil[7] and God, the devil argues that Job loves God only because Job is rich, healthy, and happy. The devil bets God that if Job were not so blessed, he would not love God nearly so much. God and the devil then test this hypothesis when God allows the devil to take away Job's wealth, kill his family, and destroy his health. Despite all of these afflictions, Job continues to love and worship God. After God proves this point to the devil and reminds Job that it is not his place to question what God does, God makes Job healthy, wealthy, and happy once again.

Why did Hobbes choose to name the sovereign after the beast from the book of Job? First, Hobbes wanted to make clear that the ruler must be strong, though not necessarily nice. In addition, it is difficult to imagine a more terrible treatment of a subject than what Job suffered from the devil with the permission of God. Yet, Job had to continue to worship, obey, and love God. Hobbes argued that citizens have a similar obligation to obey their sovereign. Just as Job had only the rights and justice that God granted him, so too do citizens have only the rights and justice that the sovereign grants them. Just as God reminded Job that he had no authority to question what God did, Hobbes argued that citizens have no right to question the acts of the sovereign. For Hobbes, the only natural right that citizens have is the right to self-preservation.

Obviously Hobbes grounded his view of human nature in his personal experience and the terrifying ordeal of the civil war in England. Hobbes saw a straightforward choice between order and liberty: Order comes first, he asserted, and the state must limit liberty. Although Hobbes's views on human nature and the appropriate role of the state were decidedly illiberal by today's standards, his writings set the stage for the development of liberalism. His social contract changed the source of political power from the divine choice of God to the rational choice of the people. The political theorist discussed in the next section developed a decidedly different governmental system based on this same idea.

JOHN LOCKE AND LIMITED GOVERNMENT

John Locke is the political philosopher most consider to be the originator of western liberalism. Locke replaced Hobbes's Leviathan with a government of limited power and scope. Instead of controlling everything, Locke's ideal government would have sufficient power to protect life and property, but it would not have sufficient power to destroy individual liberty. How did Locke reach this conclusion, and why did it differ so much from the vision of Hobbes?

One major cause of the differences between Hobbes and Locke was the contrast in their relationships with their monarchs. Like Hobbes, Locke was intimately involved with the English civil wars and the debate concerning the rights of the monarch. Whereas Hobbes was a close friend of Charles II, Locke's father had helped to overthrow Charles I, and Locke himself was a close associate of people who attempted to overthrow Charles II. Because of his opinions, and perhaps his actions, Locke fled England and did not return until after the Glorious Revolution, which removed James II, the son of Charles II, and installed King William and Queen Mary in a limited monarchy. Whereas Hobbes attempted to justify an all-powerful ruler, Locke tried to find a basis for challenging that power.

A second reason for the differing views of Hobbes and Locke arose from their varying views of human nature. Hobbes viewed humans as rational, selfish, and evil. Locke saw people as rational and self-interested. Although Locke admitted that some people are evil and degenerate, he believed that most are not. Reason, he asserted, leads people to realize that their individual welfare depends in part on the common good. This realization leads them to maintain civil behavior. Locke's more positive view of human nature and his belief that government did not total power to protect life and liberty allowed him to emphasize liberty rather than order. Locke's more optimistic view of human nature led him to argue that government must be limited to functions necessary to protect the rights of its citizens. This led to a critical question: What are those rights?

The key to Locke's vision of the best government was the idea of **natural law.** Natural law is a universal and unchanging law with authority prior to that of laws put forth by government. It is a law so obvious and true that it is a fundamental part of human nature. This natural law produces **natural rights** for all citizens that government cannot take from them. For Locke, these natural rights were the rights to life, liberty, property, and equality before the law.

The concepts of natural law and natural rights originated in Western philosophy with Stoicism, a Greek school of philosophy founded by Zeno (c. 490–c. 430 B.C.). Thomas Aquinas (1225–1274) incorporated natural law into Christian philosophies, contending that the Greek ideas of Aristotle and the Stoics were compatible with Christian theology. Particularly important were Aquinas's arguments that reason and faith lead to the same laws (God's laws), and that reason alone can deduce them. Locke took the next step and replaced the argument for divine origins of these laws with the idea that people could reasonably deduce them from the natural law of self-preservation.

Locke argued that everyone inherently understands natural law. He claimed that all people enjoyed natural rights and that, in the state of nature, natural law rules all people. In the state of nature, people have the right to protect and enforce these rights. Natural law requires mutual respect, mutual restraint, and secure property rights. Anyone who murders, steals, or restricts the liberty of another person infringes upon that person's natural rights and commits a crime against the entire society:

> Man being born . . . with a title to perfect freedom, and an uncontrolled enjoyment of all the rights and privileges of the law of nature equally with any other man or number of men in the world, hath by nature a power not only to preserve his property—that is, his life, liberty, and estate—against the injuries and attempts of other men, but to judge of and punish the breaches of that law in others as he is persuaded that the offence deserves, even with death itself. . . .[8]

A critical difference between Locke's view of the state of nature and natural rights and the Hobbesian vision centers on property. Locke claimed that any individual has a right to property and that other individuals will respect and enforce that right. Hobbes's state of nature includes only one natural right, the right to self-preservation. In Locke's state of nature, individuals can acquire property by mixing their labor with the natural resource. For example, when a farmer plows land that is not owned by others, this improvement to the land confers rights to it and to its produce. The current value of the land and the food it produces result from the mixture of the farmer's labor with the land. The land and its produce are, therefore, the farmer's "property," and the owner has a right to it. This right to property makes possible a better life for the inhabitants of the state of nature, as they have an incentive to produce new property and to improve existing resources. They will do this because they can keep and enjoy their property.

In the Lockean state of nature, anyone would have the right to kill a murderer or punish a thief. Locke, like Hobbes, used the Bible to support his argument for unmistakable natural rights. Locke found support in the story of Cain killing his brother Abel. After Cain murdered his brother, Cain feared that people would seek him out and kill him because of his behavior: "And Cain was so fully convinced that every one has the right to destroy such a criminal, that after the murder of his brother he cried out, 'Every one that findeth me shall slay me;' so plain was it writ in the hearts of mankind."[9]

Locke believed that every person has a right to her life unless the individual forfeits this right through criminal behavior. Further, in the state of nature, every individual can enforce penalties upon persons who abridge the natural rights of others. Thus, anyone who knew of Cain's actions had the right to kill him.

Despite people's natural laws and natural rights in the state of nature, problems arose. Locke listed three critical deficiencies with the state of nature. First, people may fail to see that the law applies to them. Although, "the law of nature be plain and intelligible to all rational creatures," often an individual's own interests may prevent him from seeing that the law applies to him. Similarly, ignorance may cause failure to see that the law is binding in a particular case. Second, the state of nature lacks an unbiased judge to determine who is in the right when disagreements occur. Locke contended that society needs institutions to resolve disagreements fairly and without violence. Finally, in the state of nature, people may lack sufficient might to enforce the right.[10] Criminals may have more strength or better weapons than those who would enforce the law. Because of these three deficiencies, "Mankind, notwithstanding all the privileges of the state of nature, . . . are quickly driven into society."[11]

Clearly, Locke accepted Hobbes's contention that rational individuals will come together and form a contract that binds members of the society together and creates a government. However, Locke rejected the idea that power should lie in the hands of an all-powerful sovereign. The presence of such a ruler, Locke argued, violates natural law because one purpose of ending the state of nature was to prevent people from judging their own cases. People can correct this defect only if there is "a known authority to which every one of that society may appeal . . . and which every one of the society ought to obey."[12] In other words, Locke believed that natural law required everyone to be subject to the law and equal before it. An all-powerful sovereign would not be equal to others under the law, as the sovereign would be the judge of his own case. Locke concluded, therefore, that such a government would violate natural law and the original purpose of creating a civil government.

What would Locke's ideal government look like, and what would it have the power to do? Most importantly, his government would wield limited authority and the individual's interests would be prior to those of the state. In the state of nature, individuals held all rights; they chose which liberties they would give up in order to protect their natural rights.

If a government wants a particular power, it must demonstrate that it needs this power to protect citizens' natural rights. Through this logic, Locke fundamentally changed the nature of the debate over the rights of the individual and the rights of the state. *Prior to Locke, the individual had to prove that the government should not have a particular power and that the individual was justified in exercising liberty. After Locke, the government had to prove that it needed a particular power to protect individuals' rights.*

What powers would the government need? Locke contended that the social contract would limit government's powers and duties to: (1) protecting citizens' natural rights of life, liberty, and property; (2) punishing people who violate the rights of others; and (3) adjudicating disputes when they occur. These purposes correspond to the three faults that Locke identified within the state of nature. He maintained that rational people would not willingly give up any liberties to government except to redress these three problems.

Locke's ideal government is based originally on majority rule. The principle of political equality necessitates a majoritarian choice of the type of government and the rulers. People may choose a direct democracy, an oligarchy, or a monarchy.* The critical characteristic is the people's choice of their desired form of rule through a majority vote. When the powers of a regime change, the majority of citizens must vote to approve these changes.

Although the idea of popular selection of the government and rulers does not appear revolutionary today, in Locke's time these ideas were truly radical. In addition, Locke not only proposed how people should select governments and rulers; he also indicated the circumstances in which subjects could legitimately overthrow their government. Locke argued that the people have a right to overthrow or dissolve a government and select a new one if rulers exceed the powers delegated to them by the people, if rulers change the rules for passing laws or selecting leaders without the consent of the people, or if rulers destroy or reduce the natural rights of the citizens.

Locke's writings, particularly his *Second Treatise of Civil Government,* express most of the basic tenets of western democracies. These include individualism, limited government, civil liberties, majority decision making, equality under the law, and the sanctity of life and property. This combination of ideas set the stage for the development of modern conservative and liberal ideologies, and it laid the groundwork for modern, liberal states. Perhaps no document summarizes the ideas of John Locke and classical liberalism as clearly as the U.S. Declaration of Independence:

> We hold these truths to be self-evident: That all men are created equal; that they are endowed by their Creator with certain unalienable rights; that among these are life, liberty, and the pursuit of happiness; that to secure these rights, governments are instituted among men, deriving their just powers from the consent of the governed; that whenever any form of government becomes destructive of these ends, it is the right of the people to alter or to abolish it, and to institute a new government, laying its foundation on such principles, and organizing its power in such form, as to them shall seem most likely to effect their safety and happiness.

---

*Locke allowed the possibility of a hereditary monarchy so long as a majority of the citizens selected this type of government at the time of the initial installation of the monarch, and the monarchs did not exceed the powers that the people had allocated to them.

ADAM SMITH AND THE NATURAL LAWS OF ECONOMICS

The ideas of Locke and other liberal political philosophers provided essential fuel for the development of modern, liberal governments. The ideas also encouraged the liberal economic theories of prominent political economists including Adam Smith, Thomas Malthus, David Ricardo, Jeremy Bentham, and John Stuart Mill. Interestingly, as Chapter 3 will explain, Locke's theory of labor value became an important part of Marxism-Leninism, the major ideological competitor to western liberalism.

Two books in economics have had more impact than any others. In one of these, *Das Kapital,* Karl Marx explained why he believed that capitalism must fail and why communism is inevitable. In the other, *An Inquiry into the Nature and Causes of the Wealth of Nations* Adam Smith, explained how capitalism works. These books, along with the Bible, Locke's *Second Treatise,* and Charles Darwin's *Origin of Species,* have had as much or more influence on the western world than any others. Why is Adam Smith's book part of such an illustrious list? What is its contribution to western liberalism?

Perhaps the most important contribution Adam Smith made to the modern world was that he answered two critical questions: How can a society hang together when everyone follows a personal self-interest? Why does the pursuit of economic self-interest lead not to economic and social disintegration, but to economic efficiency and social well-being? Smith answered these questions as he explained the laws of supply and demand. These laws use the **invisible hand** of the market to force the private interests of individuals to the outcome that most benefits the interests of the whole society. Economist Robert Heilbroner has summarized Smith's contribution to understanding the market:

> Adam Smith's laws of the market are basically simple. They tell us that the outcome of a certain kind of behavior in a certain social framework will bring about perfectly definite and foreseeable results. Specifically, they show us how the drive of individual self-interest in an environment of similarly motivated individuals will result in the provision of those goods that society wants, in the quantities that society desires, and at the prices society is prepared to pay.[13]

Adam Smith believed that he had discovered and clarified the natural laws of economics. An example provides the easiest way to explain how these laws of capitalism work. Prior to the development of automobiles and trucks, horse-drawn carriages and trains supplied land transportation for people and goods. Workers found jobs raising and training horses, designing and building carriages, manufacturing the materials necessary to build trains, and building, servicing, and running trains. Investors put their savings into these activities expecting substantial profits.

When Henry Ford began to mass-produce automobiles and trucks, consumers began buying them and traveling in them; consumers bought fewer horses, carriages, and train tickets. Because consumers purchased fewer of these items, producers in these industries cut back production and reduced prices to get rid of existing inventory. Lower sales and prices meant lower profits, and investors began to put their money in other enterprises. The horse-and-carriage and railroad industries needed fewer workers, so people had to find jobs elsewhere.

While these cutbacks occurred in one sector, increases in the demand for cars and trucks boosted profits in auto manufacturing. Investors expected large profits and put their funds into that industry. These investments built more factories and increased the demand for skilled auto workers. The demand increased the wages of these workers and attracted more people to the industry. As production expanded to meet demand, prices for cars and trucks fell and profits in the industry moved downward toward the average profit for all industries. Similarly, wages for auto workers fell to the level of other skilled workers. The major beneficiary of all of this change, the consumer, could then purchase a car or truck at the lowest possible price.

The invisible hand of the market guided all the necessary adjustments of investors, producers, and workers in both declining and growing industries. No ministry of planning forced investors to invest less in carriages or more in automobiles. No central bank demanded that the railroad industry cut back production or forced car and truck producers to increase output. Blacksmiths needed no bureau of labor to tell them to choose another profession, nor did workers need instructions to seek employment in the auto industry. Self-interest and competition among investors, producers, workers, and consumers reallocated investment, production, and labor in exactly the manner required to meet consumer demand and promote technological innovation. Self-interest drove individuals to make economically correct choices, and competition kept prices as low as possible.

All of this may seem rather elementary and obvious. But with only the principles of self-interest and competition, Adam Smith explained: (1) how capitalism keeps prices of goods from ranging arbitrarily away from the actual costs of production, (2) how society can induce producers to provide the commodities it wants, and (3) why high prices and profits are a self-curing disease, because they attract additional production and competition into the industry. In addition, Smith accounted for the similarity of incomes and profits among laborers and investors across industries.[14]

To abandon the discussion of Adam Smith here would treat him unfairly. Contemporary proponents of the free market often forget several other parts of *The Wealth of Nations* worth remembering. Smith wrote of the problem of the poverty and misery of the lower class in England that, "No society can surely be flourishing and happy, of which by far the greater part of the numbers are poor and miserable." Smith wrote of capitalists that because of their greed, they, "neither are, nor ought to be, the rulers of mankind," and that "People of the same trade seldom meet together but that the conversation ends in a conspiracy against the public, or in some diversion to raise prices."[15] Adam Smith saw enemies of **laissez-faire** capitalism besides government interventions through taxes on imports and exports, subsidies and tariffs that shelter businesses, and unproductive government spending; he observed equally important enemies in the form of monopolies and conspiracies of investors, producers, and workers to circumvent the operation of the market. According to Smith, the real beneficiary of the laws of the market was neither the worker nor the capitalist; it was the consumer. Specialization, division of labor, and technological innovation increased efficiency, and through this process capitalism increased the wealth of a nation and made more and better goods available to everyone.

The Problems of Natural Law and the Rise of Reform Liberalism

The liberalism of John Locke and Adam Smith seemed a perfect social system, one that relied on natural laws in economics and politics. The system would succeed when self-interested individuals acted with few government restraints on either their expressions of political ideas or their economic choices. Government needed only to protect order, enforce contracts, and punish those who violated the natural rights of others. Locke and Smith wrote, however, before the industrial revolution. They did not foresee the misery of the sweat shops, child labor under inhumane conditions in mines and textile factories, horrible water and air pollution from factories, and the remaining problems of the early part of the industrial revolution so vividly described in Charles Dickens's *Oliver Twist*. Political economists who have followed Adam Smith have had to deal with the tremendous social, political, and economic consequences of capitalism and the industrial revolution.

Thomas Malthus and David Ricardo made the first suggestions that Smith's invisible hand might really behave like an invisible foot. Rather than bringing about a better world for everyone, they suspected that capitalism would lead to famine and class conflict. Only 22 years after *The Wealth of Nations,* the Reverend Thomas Malthus published a famous treatise, *An Essay on the Principle of Population as It Affects the Future Improvement of Society.* In this short work, Malthus argued that Adam Smith erred in predicting a wonderful world where efficiency and technology improved the lives of all: landowner, farmer, capitalist, and worker. Using Smith's own driving forces, self-interest and competition, Malthus argued that capitalism doomed the laboring class to a hopeless struggle in which famine rather than plenty was the inevitable lot in life.

David Ricardo followed close behind Malthus and showed that competition among capitalists would limit profits to small amounts. Ricardo contended that the real winners from industrial growth were the landowners, people who had often inherited their land and who, through no productive efforts of their own, would reap most of the benefits of the efficient engine of capitalism. Look more closely at the arguments of Malthus and Ricardo.

One of Adam Smith's laws of capitalism was the **Law of Population.** Smith contended that human labor is like any other input into the production process and that the demand for laborers would regulate their production. A labor shortage would increase the wages of the laboring class, and their improved standard of living would lead to an increase in the number of children who would live to working age.[16] This change ultimately would lead to a surplus of labor. This surplus would cause wage rates to fall, in turn reducing the number of children who would survive. Smith argued that although wages would tend toward subsistence levels, they generally would remain above this level. As nations became more wealthy, the lives of people in the laboring class would also improve.

Malthus criticized Smith for excessive optimism. The laboring class, Malthus argued, would always work at or near subsistence wages because any technological increases in productivity that capitalism might bring could not match the biological productivity of the working class. Malthus contended that passion rather than reason determined the sexual behavior of the laboring class, and, for this reason, women in this class would conceive as many children as was biologically possible. Wages of the parents would determine how many children would survive. In a labor shortage, wages would increase and family income would grow. In this situation, more children would survive. Their survival, however, would increase the supply of laborers and wages would once again fall because the supply of labor would exceed demand. This drop in wages would reduce the living standard of the laborers below the level of subsistence, and fewer children would survive to working age. The cycle would then begin anew.

Malthus argued that increases in technology and productivity caused by capitalism would not allow laborers to escape this population cycle because population can increase much more rapidly than the supply of food, shelter, or other goods and services. For example, while agricultural technology might double food production every 10 years, a single couple can double their family's number in half that time. If parents' wages were sufficient to purchase enough food to allow six children to survive, then those six children and their mates could produce 36 children, assuming that their wages permitted the purchase of sufficient food. In other words, two couples with six children each could produce 36 grandchildren in less than 30 years, a 900 percent increase in population. Thus, Malthus argued, population increases would always outstrip increases in the production of goods and services. Malthus believed that only disease and famine could check the population growth of the laboring class. Adam Smith's natural laws of economic efficiency were no match for the natural law of population.

Thomas Malthus's best friend, David Ricardo, articulated even more pessimistic positions. Ricardo argued that the laboring class was not the only class whose standard of living would fail to improve under capitalism. The capitalists—who were the driving force in the creation of new products, new wealth, and greater efficiency—would find themselves in the same sinking boat as the workers.

Ricardo accepted Adam Smith's contention that competition is the driving force of capitalism. This competition would not, however, make capitalists rich, he asserted; instead, it would make them poor. If a capitalist developed a new way of making boots more cheaply, he could sell the boots at a lower price than the competition and, in the short run, make a larger profit. The other boot makers would lose money because they could not sell their goods as cheaply as the innovative boot maker. The innovative capitalist would not continue to make large profits, though. The other boot makers would quickly adopt the innovation and everyone's profit margin would fall to the lowest possible level at which the firm could produce boots and stay in business.

The personal computer industry provides a modern example of this situation. In 1985, the price of a personal computer with a 10-megabyte hard drive and two floppy disks was about $2,500. Now you can purchase a computer that has much greater capability for under $500. Today, manufacturers produce and sell many more computers because more people can afford them. This means that computer companies employ more workers to keep up with demand. But computer manufacturers are not making larger profits. In fact, many have fallen into bankruptcy because they could not produce good computers as cheaply as other producers. Competition forced all producers to sell their computers at the lowest possible prices. According to Ricardo, for both boot makers and computer manufacturers, new technologies and innovations increase long-term productivity, but they do not increase long-term profits.

BOX 2.1

Unearned Rents

Many students do not immediately see why landowners receive unearned rents on more productive land when the price of food is set by costs on less productive lands. Assume that you were an English landowner in Ricardo's day. Your most productive land, the flat area next to the stream, has sufficient water, good top soil, and good drainage. This makes planting and harvesting easy, and crop yields are high. Perhaps it costs you $5 to grow a bushel of corn on this land. So long as the price of corn is greater than $5 per bushel, you will cultivate this good land.

The hilly land farther from the stream requires irrigation. It costs you $8 to grow a bushel of corn on this land.

Because capitalism increases the size of the population, the demand for food increases and the price of corn rises. You will respond by beginning to cultivate your less productive land when the price of corn exceeds $8 per bushel. You certainly will not cultivate this land unless you can get at least as much for your corn as you must spend to produce it.

What would your total profits be if the price of corn were to rise to $9 per bushel? Suppose that you produce 10,000 bushels on the land nearest the stream and 5,000 bushels on the land farther from the stream. Your total profit would equal:

$$(10,000 * \$4) + (5,000 * \$1) = \$45,000$$

Ricardo refers to the profits on the more productive land next to the stream as *unearned rents.* They are unearned because the landowner does no real work to earn them. The landowner might gain a price increase and a resulting windfall, for example, simply by convincing Parliament to enact high tariffs and quotas on imported grains. Such laws would lead to unearned rents and a massive redistribution of income from those who did not own land to those who did.

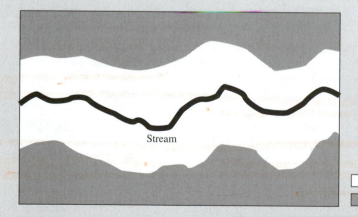

Stream

☐ More productive land
▨ Less productive land

If the laboring class remains poor and capitalists fare little better, who will gain from the tremendous increases in productivity that capitalism creates? Ricardo stated that the true winners in capitalism are the landowners. As the number of jobs increases, the population will increase to meet the demand for labor. To feed this larger population, landowners will cultivate more land. They get wealthy because the additional land that they cultivate is not as productive as the land that was already being farmed. No landowner will farm additional land without expecting to make a profit on *that* land, so the price of the food will be at least as high as the cost of producing crops on the least productive land.

Why does this process build the wealth of landowners? Because the owners of more productive land receive profits equal to the difference between the cost of producing food on the least productive land and the cost of producing food on more productive land. (See Box 2.1.)

Ricardo calls this difference between production costs on the less productive land and costs on the more productive land **"unearned rent."** It is unearned because the landowners do nothing to merit the increase in their profits. They gain through the external impetus of the growth in population caused by the increase in the number of jobs that capitalists created. The greater demand for food increases the value of their land. This result, argued Ricardo, is unjust and will lead to class struggle.

People who labor to make goods and provide services will continue to receive subsistence wages. Wages will rise because labor costs more, but the laborer's life does not improve. The people who invest and risk their money to create inexpensive goods and new wealth, the capitalists, will have to pay higher wages to keep their workers alive, so their profit margins will remain small. Therefore, Ricardo contended, the two productive classes will not prosper. Passion will keep the laborers at subsistence levels and competition will keep profits at a minimum. The only winners are the landowners, most of whom simply inherit their lands and do nothing to merit the wealth that capitalism brings them. In fact, Ricardo refers to them as "a kind of economic parasite."

UTILITARIANISM: JEREMY BENTHAM'S ANSWER TO DOOM AND GLOOM

The discovery that the natural laws of economics might not lead to the happy outcomes expected by Adam Smith sent political and economic thinkers looking for answers to the extreme poverty brought on by the industrial revolution. Jeremy Bentham provided the insights necessary to deal with the natural laws of economics. He did this by rejecting the ideas of natural rights and the social contract.

If a government as limited as that suggested by Locke and Smith leads to bad outcomes, then Bentham proposed the simple solution of increasing the scope of government so that it can pursue policies that lead to better outcomes. What are better outcomes? *Bentham argued that the best society is the one that provides the greatest happiness to the greatest number of people.* Therefore, any policy that increases pleasure or decreases pain is a good policy. Bentham advocated empirical tests to determine which policies will increase pleasure and decrease pain. Suppose, for example, that someone demonstrates less total pleasure in a society in which a few members have most of its wealth and the majority of people live in poverty than in a society in which the wealthy have less but few suffer in poverty; that society may choose to take some of the wealth of the richest members and distribute that wealth to the poor. Suppose, again, that society discovers that the absence of an adequate education for everyone with the capability to learn reduces its net sum of happiness; then society might choose to provide free public education to everyone.

But what about natural rights? Can society so easily dismiss the wealthy person's natural right to property? Is not all of western liberalism founded on the presumption of these rights and the natural laws that go with them? Bentham answered, "No!" Unlike Locke, Bentham denied the validity of natural rights. Rights to life, liberty, and property do not predate society, he asserted; they are possible only because society protects them. If no one has any rights without society, then society may expand or restrict these rights if its action will make more people happier. Bentham maintains that *the rightness or wrongness of an action should be judged by its consequences, not by its intent or by its appeal to some higher authority.* In the modern vernacular, he proposed a principle of, "Whatever works."

Political scientists call Bentham's political philosophy **utilitarianism.** This philosophy had radical implications for a government and society based on natural rights and limited government. Bentham believed that anyone, regardless of income, education, or social class, can feel pleasure and pain and that the pleasure or pain of one person should not count for more than that of another simply because the first is wealthier, better educated, or a member of a higher social class. The combination of this concept of personal equality with the denial of any natural rights leads to an unlimited scope of authority for government and a sweeping ability to redistribute income and rights. This is hardly a liberal outcome, in that it clearly violates the sanctity of property required by classical liberalism! As a student once pointed out, "If Bentham is right, then if I earned $100,000 and nine others didn't work and earned nothing, government could take my money and divide it equally because this would increase the total happiness and decrease the total pain. That's theft!"[†]

To answer this criticism, Bentham would have argued that government would make such a redistribution only if that action would consistently improve total happiness. Bentham would suggest that this result would not occur, because if government pursued such a policy, then people would quit producing because their production would not substantially improve their own positions. Rational individuals would free ride and allow others to work and then ask the government to redistribute the income. Society would have a collective dilemma where all rational individuals would refuse to work and all would starve.

This does not mean that Bentham would reject all redistributions, though. Government policy would leave sufficient rewards to encourage producers to continue producing. Further, he might suggest that government could redistribute enough to less wealthy people to increase their happiness, but not enough to decrease their desire to become wealthier by

---

[†] Some readers may doubt that redistributing income from more wealthy people to less wealthy ones would normally increase the total happiness of society, since the amount of wealth remains the same. The amount of money remains the same, but money, like almost everything else, is subject to the law of diminishing returns. For example, adding $1,000 to the income of someone who makes $10,000 per year probably increases that person's happiness considerably more than adding $1,000 to the income of someone who makes $100,000 per year.

working. Society would determine empirically (through actual experiments) the appropriate distribution that would maximize the long-term happiness of all.[‡]

Two extremely critical changes in liberalism result from Bentham's rejection of natural rights and his emphasis on the total pleasure and pain of all members of society. First, these innovations change government from a largely negative, limiting force to one that can have positive effects. Second, Bentham's utilitarian approach to government and law highlights not only the procedures involved in equality before the law, but also the outcomes created by alternative distributions of rights, duties, and income.

For John Locke and Adam Smith, *freedom* meant the absence of external forces restraining individuals' liberties. Government represented the major restraint on political and economic freedom for Locke and Smith. Locke emphasized the problem of unlimited government and resulting tyranny. Smith focused on the problem of government interference in the free market that would reduce economic efficiency and total economic wealth.

Bentham reacted not to a tyrannical government but to a society dominated by poverty, disease, and the hopelessness of the laboring class in London. While government tyranny did not restrict freedom to act and choose, poverty accomplished a much more severe restriction of freedom. In response to this situation, Bentham argued that natural rights or natural laws of politics or economics could not supply solutions. Solutions had to come from social change. In this situation, government could be a positive force by pursuing policies that would increase the pleasure and minimize the pain of all. Bentham's reformulation of liberalism and his emphasis on improving the happiness of all in society had a profound effect on perhaps the greatest of the reform liberals, John Stuart Mill.

JOHN STUART MILL: GREATEST LIBERAL OR FIRST SOCIALIST?

In his wonderful book, *The Worldly Philosophers,* Robert Heilbroner wrote that, in an age filled with unbelievable characters, John Stuart Mill was the most remarkable of them all:

> John Stuart Mill was born in 1806. In 1809 [at age 3] he began to learn Greek. At age seven he had read most of the dialogues of Plato. The next year he began Latin, having meanwhile digested Herodotus, Xenophon, Diogenes Laertius, and part of Lucian. Between eight and twelve he finished Virgil, Horace, Livy, Sallust, Ovid, Terence, Lucretius, Aristotle, Sophocles, and Aristophanes; mastered geometry, algebra, and the differential calculus; [wrote] a Roman History, an Abridgment of the Ancient Universal History, a History of Holland, and a few verses. "I never composed at all in Greek, even in prose, and but little in Latin," he wrote in his famous *Autobiography.* "Not that my father could be indifferent to the value of this practice . . . but because there really was not the time for it."
>
> At the ripe age of twelve, Mill took up logic and the work of Hobbes. At thirteen he made a complete survey of all there was to be known in the field of political economy.[17]

[‡] Notice that Bentham did not appeal to a natural or moral right of either wealthier or poorer people. Instead, he sought to calculate the total pleasure minus pain of all affected members of society. If modern western society concentrated on outcomes rather than natural rights or moral principles, the resulting social policies might be significantly different from current ones.

Just as John Stuart Mill received education through the great books of western civilization, he left behind several more. *Considerations on Representative Government* explains his arguments for superiority of this form of government.§ *System of Logic* describes the basic rules for scientific thinking. *On Liberty* is the classic plea for the sanctity of individual rights against the power of government. *Utilitarianism* elaborates and elucidates Bentham's ethics. Finally, *Principles of Political Economy,* had it not been written in the same period as *The Wealth of Nations* and *Das Kapital,* would surely have been the most important work in political economy in the 18th and 19th centuries. In addition, Mill co-authored with his wife, Harriet Taylor, an influential treatise on the unethical treatment of women and the necessity of equal rights for both sexes.

Although Mill's contributions to liberalism were many and varied, this chapter will examine only those that flow from *Principles of Political Economy* and *On Liberty.* Persuaded by Bentham's arguments against natural laws and rights in politics, Mill showed in *Principles* that the natural laws of economics are considerably more limited than Smith, Malthus, and Ricardo had suggested. Mill conceded the truth of the natural laws of supply and demand and all of the other natural economic laws that Adam Smith had discovered and explained. *But, he asserted, they were true only in the explanation of the most efficient methods of production.* As Heilbroner states, "this is perhaps the biggest *but* in economics" because Mill argued that the laws of economics have little to do with distribution. Once wealth is produced, he said, society can do what it wishes with the wealth.[18]

This *but* is important because it allows government to redistribute income without reducing efficiency. Mill showed that society can make no "natural" or "correct" distribution. If the "natural" action of the market depresses wages or creates unearned rents, society can use the power of government to subsidize wages and tax rents. This means that government can pursue policies that improve the opportunities of the laboring class without destroying the productive efficiency of the capitalist system!

To Mill, and to modern people, this discovery is critical in that it allows government to take reasonable actions to pass laws and levy taxes for universal public education, adequate health care for everyone, and a minimum income. Mill's argument makes these policies more reasonable because it denies that government actions automatically destroy economic efficiency.[‖] Suddenly, Bentham's goal to maximize pleasure and minimize pain for everyone seemed free of many constraints of the natural laws of economics that Smith, Malthus, and Ricardo had acknowledged.

This point is a difficult one. How can government change the distribution of income without affecting economic efficiency? Because every different distribution of income has a different efficient production. Efficiency requires that society produce at the lowest possible cost the goods that consumers demand and can afford; the total income and its distribution determine what people can afford.

---

§ This assertion provides perhaps the best justification for representative democracy in arguing that such a government is best, not because it will necessarily make the best decision in the short run, but because it will make the best citizens in the long run.

‖ We define *efficiency* as the point at which both producers and buyers of commodities are satisfied with the current combination of goods produced and prices charged and at which the cost of producing this amount of goods is at the minimum necessary to achieve the desired quality.

Look at the effects of two distributions of income on demand. First, imagine a society of 100 families in which the two wealthiest receive $1 million per year and the other 98 families receive only $10,000 each. The demand for automobiles will include only two luxury cars. No one else can afford a car. Now imagine a society in which the two wealthiest families each receive $100,000 and the remaining members of society receive about $28,368. The total wealth of the society is the same—$2,980,000—but the demand for cars shows drastic changes. The two wealthiest families will probably buy very good cars, but not luxury cars; the remaining families have sufficient money to buy subcompacts. Now the efficient production of cars will include two very good cars and 98 small cars. In each case, the market operates efficiently so long as it produces the cars demanded at the lowest possible cost.

Mill argued that the economic laws apply to production and, at least within very broad limits, not to distribution; therefore, he claimed, society has substantial latitude in its policies, and it might change the distribution of the wealth, goods, and services that capitalism produces. Mill's recommendations for government policy reflect the influences of his education, his training in liberal theory, and his exposure to the utilitarian ideas of Bentham. First and most forcefully, Mill argued that everyone deserves an education, for education allows everyone to reason effectively and it reveals the elaborate interrelationships between the long-term interests of individuals and their society. He asserted that government could use education, taxation, and regulation to change social behavior. The working classes, if educated, would understand the need to voluntarily reduce the number of their children. Then, when new industry would bid up the price of labor, no surplus labor would emerge to reduce wages again.

John Stuart Mill did not rely solely on the education of the working classes to improve society. He believed that universal education would lead most people to see the logic of utilitarian ethics and the necessity to serve their long-term rather than their short-term interests. When this occurred, representative governments could pass laws to prevent landlords from receiving unearned rents and to prevent capitalists from exploiting workers, particularly women and children; additional laws could ensure that everyone would have sufficient food, shelter, and education.

The writings of John Stuart Mill provided the basic foundations of the modern welfare state. Contemporary social welfare and civil rights programs such as free public education; unemployment compensation; subsidized food, housing, and medical care for the poor; and regulations to promote worker safety and reduce sexual harassment, all emerge from Mill's policy recommendations. These sweeping government economic policies may tempt some critics to argue that Mill was not a true liberal because such recommendations allow government too much intervention in the lives of individuals and threaten private property. Still, political scientists classify Mill as a liberal because he continued to place the individual's liberty first, to depend upon individuals' capacity to reason, and to argue for private property.

Individual liberty and personal development retained primary roles in Mill's policy recommendations. He saw his recommendations not as reductions of liberty but as expansions of it. By giving government a positive role to improve the conditions of workers, he intended to help society maximize the greatest good for the greatest number. By providing education to everyone, he claimed that the productive capacity of the entire society would increase. Rationality would replace passion in economic decision processes, and all individuals could debate rationally to identify policies that seemed likely to increase long-term happiness.

John Stuart Mill remains a member of the pantheon of liberal theorists for another important reason. His book, *On Liberty,* remains today the best liberal discussion of where the rights of the individual end and the rights of government and society begin. In this short book, Mill took the Lockean position that members of society, either individually or collectively, could justifiably interfere with the liberty of action of any individual only to ensure their own self-protection. People or government can exercise power over individuals against their will only to prevent harm to others. Mill argued that in a society of educated persons, freedom of speech and expression must be absolute. Society, he contended, has a strong tendency to see its customs, religious practices, and dominant prejudices as universal moral principles: "The disposition of mankind, whether as rulers or as fellow-citizens, to impose their own opinions and inclinations as a rule of conduct on others, is so energetically supported by some of the best and by some of the worst feelings incident to human nature, that it is hardly ever kept under restraint by anything but want of power."[19] Mill believed that governments too often succumb to this disposition and curtail liberty. Government should work, not to restrain opinions, but to keep humans from forcing their opinions and beliefs on others.

Finally, Mill contended that no society is free unless all members are free to pursue their own good in their own way so long as they do not harm others. This is true regardless of the form of government. Isaiah Berlin classifies Mill as a liberal because Mill believed in the necessity of an area of personal freedom that must be protected from violation, for overstepping this limit prevents individuals from developing their natural capacities, which allow them to conceive and to pursue their chosen goals.[20] Mill clearly believed in a limited government, fearing the tyranny of majority opinion and social norms, and he argued for a clear line between public authority and private life.

Where, then, do Bentham and Mill take society? What would their most favored society look like and what policies might realize this vision? Briefly, utilitarianism rejects natural law, natural rights, and the absolute sanctity of property. It takes these steps to give everyone in society an opportunity to become happier. Thus, utilitarianism teaches that the accident of birth and the good or bad situations into which individuals are born should not completely determine their opportunities in life. Every citizen should receive an education and the benefits that learning makes possible. In addition, to achieve the greatest long-term happiness for the greatest number of people, utilitarians argue that government must intervene in the economy to the extent necessary to ensure that everyone has certain basic levels of food, clothing, and shelter and to prevent the exploitation of workers by capitalists and landowners.

Although the utilitarians' rejection of the absolute sanctity of property allows government to take a positive role in increasing people's economic life chances, the utilitarianism of Mill prohibits government from enforcing opinions of any one person or group about what is right, moral, or ethical upon other individuals. In particular, it must carefully avoid infringing anyone's freedom of expression. Mill agrees with Locke that the government can restrain individual behavior only when the behavior creates a clear and direct threat of physical harm to other members of society.

Contemporary Adaptations of Liberalism

People in the United States today must resolve substantial confusion over the modern meanings of the words *liberal* and *conservative*. We will attempt to clarify these meanings. In terms of liberalism as we have discussed it in this chapter, both Newt Gingrich and Bill Clinton are essentially liberals. Both believe in limited government, individual rights, and government actions to promote certain democratically chosen goals. However, the media typically classify Gingrich as a conservative and Clinton as a liberal. Why?

Three issues tend to distinguish contemporary liberals and conservatives. First, they disagree about how much redistribution of opportunities and outcomes government should encourage. Liberals tend to favor policies that redistribute wealth and opportunities from more advantaged members of society to less advantaged ones. Conservatives tend to oppose such policies. For example, liberals want government to eliminate the effects of racial, ethnic, and gender prejudice, and they sometimes advocate policies such as affirmative action programs to improve the income and status of ethnic minorities and women.

Second, liberals tend to favor government regulation to protect the environment, improve safety in the work place, and protect consumers. While conservatives do not oppose environmental quality, work-place safety, or consumer protection, they believe that many of the laws intended to achieve these goals violate more fundamental rights to liberty. They also criticize these laws as too costly in relation to their benefits.

The final issues that distinguish modern liberals and conservatives deal with rights and social norms. Liberals tend to support policies that protect the rights of people accused of crimes, promote individual privacy in areas such as sexual preferences and practices, and reject censorship in almost any form. They believe that people should not use government to impose their preferences on another person's behavior or beliefs in matters that do not directly affect others. For example, you may believe that prostitution is morally wrong, but liberals would assert that this belief should not affect public policy so long as the people involved are consenting adults.

In contrast, conservatives tend to support policies that promote their conception of a moral society. Many would allow the state to censor publications, prohibit behaviors that liberals would view as purely private concerns, and promote activities such as school prayer that they believe would increase the morality of citizens.** Perhaps the two best representatives of contemporary conservative and liberal positions are the two political philosophers Robert Nozick and John Rawls. Nozick is a conservative in the contemporary usage of that label, while Rawls is a liberal.

In his book *Anarchy, State, and Utopia* Nozick argues for an ultraminimal state.[21] In Nozick's ideal society, the state may pursue only the four minimal goals set forth in Chapter 1: provide safety and protection, resolve collective dilemmas, reduce externalities, and define and enforce rights and duties. The state may not transfer income, property, or opportunities from one person to another except to correct an unjust transfer. In other

---

** Note that people who call themselves liberals or conservatives need not accept the liberal or conservative positions we have described on all three issues. In fact, few people would probably exactly fit either label. For example, a libertarian might accept the conservative position on the issues of redistribution and regulation, but he would definitely reject the conservative tolerance for censorship.

words, if someone robs you, Nozick asserts that the state has the power and the obligation to take the property from the robber and return it to you.

Other than returning property to its legitimate owner, Nozick would not allow the state to coerce transfers from some people to others. The state could not tax people to provide merit goods such as public education, immunization, and health care. To attempt these tasks, the state would have to seize income, property, and opportunities from some and give these benefits to others. But the people from whom the state would take the resources would not have obtained them unjustly from the people to whom the state would give the resources. Nozick finds this transfer unacceptable. He also denies the possibility of merit goods because such a concept argues that someone knows an ultimate principle of justice or truth that allows individuals' rights to be violated without their consent. Nozick's ideal state cannot use its monopoly on violence to reduce the advantages that luck bestows on some and the misfortune that it bestows on others.

While Nozick represents a conservative voice for modern contractarians, John Rawls's *A Theory of Justice* provides an example of liberalism.[22] Rawls, like Nozick, argues against utilitarian solutions to contemporary problems because those measures can and do violate basic human rights. Beyond that point, however, Nozick and Rawls agree on almost nothing. Rawls contends that society should pursue a goal of establishing justice rather than minimizing coercion by the state. But, what is a just society?

Rawls answers that a just society would include those institutions of government that people would choose if they were ignorant of where, to what parents, and with what talents they would be born. A person in this situation would, Rawls argues, follow three principles in establishing government institutions: (1) greatest equal freedom, (2) fair equality of opportunity, and (3) the "**difference principle**." The difference principle allows only those inequalities that ultimately improve the position of the least advantaged in society. These principles would have serious implications for the state's response to "accidents of birth" and other inequalities caused by luck.

To understand Rawls's proposal, imagine that you have not yet been born; you know only that you will be born in the United States. You do not know whether your parents will be rich or poor, what your racial and ethnic characteristics will be, what your intelligence will be, or what other accidents of birth will come your way. In fact, you do not know whether you will be born now or at some time in the future. In this situation, you are operating behind what Rawls refers to as the **veil of ignorance.** Rawls contends that people in this situation, which he refers to as the **original position**, would choose institutions that would ensure everyone an approximately equal chance in life to get what they think is best.

How would people operating behind this veil of ignorance choose to deal with inequalities? Rawls postulates that rational people would allow inequalities to occur if, and only if, over time those differences would maximize the prospects of the least advantaged members of society. For example, if accumulation of private property by some people leads to inequalities, but this accumulation is necessary for economic growth and greater liberty, people in the original position would choose to allow accumulation that would provide, in the long run, a better life for those who are most disadvantaged.

Rawls further argues that people in the original position would create institutions that would keep people from falling below some minimum threshold of well-being. No one should be so disadvantaged, Rawls contends, that she cannot maintain her self-respect and defend her interests against people with much greater wealth or power. In taking this position, Rawls specifically rejects the utilitarian position of maximizing the greatest good for the greatest number.

To see why, assume that people in the original position can choose between two societies. In one, 900 people of every 1,000 are economically advantaged and happy. The remaining 100 people live in abject poverty and extreme unhappiness. In addition, this arrangement will continue into the future and the children of the 100 less advantaged people will continue to live in poverty and misery. The alternative outcome is a society in which the 900 have fewer advantages than before, but the other 100 are not nearly as disadvantaged. In addition, both groups are equally likely to have children in the more advantaged category.

Rawls contends that rational people would choose the second option. They would be unwilling to allow people to fall into such unhappiness that they could not maintain self-respect or self-protection. The fact that people inherit unhappiness in the first alternative makes it totally unacceptable to Rawls. Rational individuals, he maintains, would not take a gamble where they could end up totally disadvantaged; they certainly would be unwilling to engage in a bet that might doom their children and grandchildren to such suffering.

From Rawls's perspective, the first principle of a well-ordered society is fairness, not happiness. Therefore, even if government must constantly intervene to prevent inequalities caused by luck, he asserts that fairness requires such interventions. He claims that reasonable and just programs could compensate the victims of bad luck and ensure that those who are born more fortunate do not take unfair advantage of this good fortune.

SUMMARY OF LIBERAL THEORY

Western liberalism begins and ends with the idea of individual rights and limited government. Clearly, it is a long way from the minimal government of John Locke and Robert Nozick to the interventionist government favored by John Stuart Mill and John Rawls. Nevertheless, all four writers agree on three important ideas:

1. Government must be limited.
2. The rights of the individual are prior to the rights of the state.
3. The proper role of government is to encourage liberty and happiness.

The next section addresses the question of how political institutions can accomplish the first of these important goals—limiting the power of government.

Constitutionalism

Although liberal theory provides the rationale for limited government, the development of constitutionalism gave real force to those limits. **Constitutionalism** is not an ideology, although its historical development corresponds closely to the emergence of democracy and liberalism. Neither is constitutionalism a theory produced by the systematic thinking of one or a few political philosophers. Instead, it is a set of political institutions that have the effect of guaranteeing individual rights and limiting government power.

The Constitution of the United States is often called "the world's first constitution." This position may suggest that the word *constitution* refers to a document. Long before the founders wrote the U.S. Constitution, however, the word had acquired a more general meaning. It refers to *a country's established governmental structure and process,* the way the government really works. Most written constitutions provide guidelines for the institutions of government and say something about their powers. Those provisions sometimes describe government characteristics. However, such a description is never complete and always is inaccurate in some respects.

The term *constitutional government* does not mean a government with a written constitution. Written documents underlie some constitutional governments but not others. Similarly, not all written constitutions call for constitutional governments. Some contemporary states have written constitutions that lay out tyrannical governments with virtually unlimited powers.

WRITTEN CONSTITUTIONS

The American Constitution, ratified in 1789, provided a powerful symbolic precedent for the French revolutionaries who wrote and adopted the French Constitutions of 1791 and 1793. Following both the American and French precedents, new revolutionary governments created throughout Europe during the 19th century also adopted written constitutions. Former colonies of European powers that gained independence after World Wars I and II did the same. The most recently enacted constitutions are those of the countries that became independent after the collapse of the Soviet Union.

Written constitutions display a common general format. An opening preamble states the authorizing power and purpose. The Preamble to the Constitution of the United States is a relatively brief example:

> We the people of the United States, in Order to form a more perfect Union, establish Justice, insure domestic Tranquillity, provide for the common Defence, promote the general Welfare, and secure the blessings of Liberty to ourselves and our Posterity, do ordain and establish this Constitution of the United States of America.

Constitutions typically name "the people" as authorizing powers. Most describe the basic organs of government (heads of state and of government; legislative, executive, administrative, and judicial bodies), and the methods for choosing officials. They also prescribe the powers of these organs. Most, but by no means all, contain provisions similar to the U.S. Bill of Rights. All provide for later amendments.

CONSTITUTIONALISM: BASIC PRINCIPLES AND HISTORICAL DEVELOPMENT

Constitutionalism's first principle, the rule of law, was clearly stated in modern times by the English political thinker, James Harrington (1611–1677). In his book *Oceana* (1656), Harrington described the ideal commonwealth as "an empire of laws, and not of men." This principle means that a government should govern by rules known to everyone, not by the whims or wishes of individuals. It assumes that a society can minimize conflict and benefit everyone by promoting social peace if people settle their disputes by general principles set down in laws.

Constitutionalism's second principle, limited government, simply requires limits on the powers of government. It assumes that the rule of law cannot prevail without such limitations. Citizens pay excessive costs if government abuses its powers, so they cannot leave government unrestrained. But a corollary provides that, even with limited power, government still must be able to operate effectively, especially in dealing with crises.

The third constitutional principle is the peaceful transfer of political power. One of the most common causes of severe political conflict is competition over the successor to a current ruler. Hereditary monarchy is one way to minimize such disputes. Democratic governments need other means.

Of these three principles, limited government has been the most difficult to maintain. This fact has led one noted modern analyst to define constitutional government as one that operates under "effective, regularized restraints."[23] In modern republican and democratic governments, periodic rotation of people in office serves that purpose.

PARTICIPATION TO LIMIT GOVERNMENT

Direct Democracy   The central practical problem for a constitutional government is to force rulers to abide by the limits in the constitution. One way to prevent the few from exploiting the many is to have the many rule. Early in the history of Athens, a hereditary nobility gradually supplanted a hereditary monarchy. The nobles ruled through an aristocratic Council, and members of ruling clans could take part in an Assembly.

Participation in the Assembly gradually extended to other segments of the population. By the middle of the 5th century B.C., the Assembly had become the central organ of Athenian government. All citizens (defined as free males) participated in its periodic meetings. The Council of 500 had the responsibility for the day-to-day business of governing. Athens chose these men by lot or by virtue of holding some office that entitled its occupant to a seat. Athenian government of this period was the model of Greek direct democracy, with all citizens participating. Through this system of direct democracy and the choice of Council members by lot, the majority of citizens in Athens could prevent a minority from imposing its will upon the majority.

The ability of the many to prevent rule by the few is one of the great benefits of direct democracy. However, direct democracy has two flaws within a system of constitutional government. First, all citizens in a large society cannot possibly assemble and engage in meaningful discussion, debate, and decision making. Therefore, as the nation-state became the dominant form of government, direct, national democracy became impossible. Second, as we shall discuss more fully in the next chapter, the majority can impose its will on the minority and infringe on their rights unless institutions specifically prevent it.

Representative Democracy   Representative democracy provides a remedy for the problem of direct democracy in a large nation-state. In the 13th century, the desperate need of English monarchs for money to finance their wars set in motion the development of representative government. Rulers made requests by calling the King's Council, composed of nobles summoned by the monarch. Over time, monarchs sought a wider tax base than the nobles alone could provide, but monarchs could not tax towns and counties without their consent. Rulers then began summoning people who had wealth other than land to meetings that coincided with King's Council meetings. Edward III summoned two knights from each county, two burgesses from each town, and also a number of the lesser clergy to a council meeting that became known as the "Model Parliament."

Membership in this ancestor of the English Parliament became regularized during the 14th century. At the same time, separation of this assembly's meetings from those of the King's Council left a Parliament made up of a House of Lords (nobles) and a House of Commons (knights and burgesses). Membership in the House of Lords was hereditary. Members of the House of Commons were at first selected by informal agreement among local notables of each group, but a system of voting for membership gradually evolved. A very small number of freemen and other local notables could vote for members of the House of Commons.

Over the next few hundred years, Parliament changed from a body that simply decided to accept or reject taxation into a legislative assembly. This characteristic developed by accident, not by design. First, representatives took advantage of the monarch's presence to submit petitions requesting a response to some violation of rights or some favor. If granted, the petition became law. Representatives agreed to consent to the monarch's taxes only if he granted their petitions. Petitions developed into bills when members began to frame their petitions in the language and form of the king's orders. These petitions or bills slowly came to form the basis of discussions in Parliament.

The final stage of parliamentary development in England culminated in the revolutions of the 17th century. These uprisings substantially deprived the monarch of law-making and tax-voting powers, and they imposed limits on the monarch's civil and military administration. Not long after that, Parliament compelled the monarch to choose his cabinet and major officers from the political party that had a majority in Parliament. Bills, when passed, became law without the king's assent. By the early 19th century, Parliament had become the paramount power in English government.

Over the next century, a generally peaceful, political revolution transformed the make-up of Parliament. For a long time, Parliament represented only a fraction of the English population—mainly nobles, wealthy landowners, and the wealthier members of the mercantile class. Beginning with the Reform Act of 1832 and continuing down to the mid-20th century, Parliament granted suffrage (the right to vote) to more and more groups and classes of citizens until suffrage was virtually universal among adults.

The pattern of development in England reoccurred in most contemporary democratic societies. Today, *representative government* means a mass electorate with universal adult suffrage to elect a representative body and sometimes the chief executive. Political philosophers did not design or generally foresee the development of this structure. It was the product of settlements reached in day-to-day political conflicts between groups and classes that held power and those that wanted to share it.

CHECKS ON MAJORITY RULE

Although representative government solves the problem of popular participation in large nation-states, it does not eliminate the possibility that the majority will act unconstitutionally and deprive the minority of their rights. In *The Federalist Papers,* three prominent Americans writing under the pseudonym Publius[††] attempted to show how the proposed American Constitution would reduce the problems of both majority and minority rule. Although the next chapter will discuss the political ideas expressed in *The Federalist Papers* in greater detail, many institutional mechanisms in the American Constitution reduce the opportunities for any group in society to carry out unconstitutional actions. Principal among these mechanisms are separation of powers, checks and balances, federalism, and judicial review.

Separation of Powers   The French historian and social theorist Montesquieu (1689–1755) first presented the idea of separation of powers in his book *The Spirit of the Laws* (1748).[24] James Madison cited him as "the oracle who is always consulted and cited on this subject," and restated his principle this way: "The accumulation of all powers, legislative, executive, and judiciary, in the same hands, whether of one, a few, or many, and whether hereditary, self-appointed, or elective, may justly be pronounced the very definition of tyranny."[25]

Checks and Balances   Madison went on to develop the case for constitutional checks and balances. Separation of powers, he wrote, "does not require that the legislative, executive, and judiciary departments should be wholly unconnected with each other. Rather, they should be so far connected and blended as to give to each a constitutional control over the others, . . . "[26] The American Constitution provides a practical application of this principle.

Thus, the U.S. Constitution, and those of countries that followed its model, divide legislative power between two legislative chambers. More importantly, this model gives some legislative authority to the executive branch. The president can check legislative power with a veto of its laws. The judiciary also shares legislative authority through its interpretation of laws and its ability in some countries to strike down unconstitutional laws.

Federalism   The authors of the U.S. Constitution relied on federalism to strengthen the national government, especially in a representative republic, and to safeguard the country against domestic insurrection.[27] If a leader of some faction should gain control in some region, federalism would help the country to isolate and defeat the renegade.

However, federalism also may help to prevent tyranny by dividing power between the national and subnational levels of government. By allotting certain powers to subnational units, a country divided by ethnic or religious strife may reduce the concerns of groups who are permanent minorities. This element of federalism could ensure that in certain regions the minorities could constitute majorities, so that they could control important areas of public policy.

[††] The name Publius referred to three persons, Alexander Hamilton, James Madison, and John Jay.

In the 200 years since adoption of the U.S. Constitution, the essentially American concept of federalism has spread throughout the world. The most recent extensive compilation of data reports that, of over 150 "sovereign" states in existence in 1991, 51 were "involved in formal arrangements utilizing federal principles in some way to accommodate demands for self-rule or shared rule within their boundaries or in partnership with other polities."[28]

Judicial Review   Judicial review gives courts the power to assess the compliance of government actions with the constitution and block those that fail the test. Most Americans consider this power the principal check on government. The U.S. Constitution does not, however, provide the courts with this power. Chief Justice John Marshall, in the case of *Marbury* v. *Madison* (1803), claimed this power for the court, and, in time, it became accepted practice. This particular form of judicial constitutional oversight is much more extensive in the United States than in most other countries.

Where a country's constitution provides for a review of the constitutionality of legislation, courts usually make this judgment, and they do so only after the passage of legislation. A few constitutions provide for prior scrutiny of proposed legislation. In Germany, for example, the president has the duty to make sure a bill conforms with the Constitution before signing it. In Finland, the president can refuse to sign an act that she considers unconstitutional, and she may ask the Supreme Court of Justice, the Supreme Administrative Court, or both for an opinion. If the president of Ireland thinks an act is unconstitutional, she may put it before the Supreme Court within 7 days of being notified of its passage. The court must then render its opinion within 60 days.

Many countries, even those with written constitutions, act on the belief that no rule of law should prevail over the will of the people and provide no control over the validity of legislation. In Belgium, Parliament decides a law's constitutional validity by passing it. In the Netherlands, parliamentarians' oath to abide by the Constitution guarantees a law's constitutionality. Among many other countries without formal control over constitutional validity are Indonesia, Israel, Laos, Spain, and Turkey.

A number of countries provide some means of nullifying the effectiveness of laws that violate constitutional limits. However, a recent report on practices in 41 countries around the world concluded that "no system of control over the constitutional validity of Acts of Parliament has ever been found entirely satisfactory."[29]

Summary

Liberalism and constitutionalism provide the theory and institutions to justify and implement limited government. Although the two concepts developed largely independently from each other, they have a strong common purpose. That purpose is to protect the rights of the individual by limiting the government's opportunities for tyranny.

Classical liberalism began as an attack on government power and a proposal for a minimal government. As industrialization showed the deficiencies and injustices that result from unrestricted individualism within a capitalist economy, reform liberalism argued for a broader role of government. Today, western liberalism dominates the worldwide debate concerning what should government do.

Just as liberalism dominates the discussion of appropriate government actions and limits of governmental intervention, constitutionalism dictates how to limit government and how to protect the unalienable rights that liberalism advocates. While democracy provides a remedy for minority tyranny by allowing the majority to rule or to select rulers, institutions developed through constitutionalism are necessary to protect the rights of both the majority and minorities. In the next chapter, we will examine in greater detail the development of democracy as the dominant form of liberal, constitutional government.

QUESTIONS AND EXERCISES

Questions for Reason

A. Government and Luck

Rawls's conclusion that the state should intervene on behalf of the least advantaged in society creates two problems. First, how should society decide who is advantaged and disadvantaged? Second, at what point does fairness require government intervention? Richard Epstein, a professor of law at the University of Chicago, argues that law and government are ill-equipped to deal with luck, including social or genetic advantages and disadvantages at birth and some later lucky or unlucky event.[‡‡] He recognizes the unfortunate plight of people who are born with disadvantages, but he also notes that the accidents of birth extend far beyond advantages and disadvantages caused by parents' income, education, and country of residence. Some people are born with severe physical handicaps and others are born physically strong; some are attractive, others ugly; some are born to kind parents, others to parents who neglect or mistreat them; some are smart, while others are stupid; some inherit genes that lead to long and healthy lives, while others have genes that lead to high blood pressure and heart disease. All of these characteristics greatly affect life chances and none is related to hard work and diligence.

Epstein suggests that citizens should ask themselves the question, "Should the state compensate people who happen to have been born poor by subsidizing their food, clothing, and medical care?" If you answered "yes," would you be equally willing to compensate people for hardships caused by being born ugly or with less-than-average intelligence? Must the government pay for plastic surgery for ugly people? Must it deny insurance companies the right to use actuarial tables to determine who is the best insurance risk? This restriction would ensure that people who are more likely to die young would pay no more for life insurance than those whose genes will likely let them live to ripe old age.

Epstein argues that once society compensates for one type of bad luck, it is not logical to exclude others. Luck certainly does not end with birth. Farmers who work equally hard earn different rewards because some get good weather while others receive bad. To illustrate the difficulties of compensating people who are lucky, Epstein examines the situation of a drunk driver who caused an accident that killed a pedestrian. Because the driver was unlucky and killed someone, she must pay compensation to the victim's family and go to jail. But not all drunk drivers that night were so unlucky. In fact, most drivers

---

[‡‡] Richard Epstein's article, "Luck," is a response to Rawls's answer to the question, "What can society do about inequalities of birth and natural endowment?

who were equally drunk that night had no accidents. If the government taxes lucky people to compensate people who are born with birth defects or into racial or ethnic groups against which society discriminates, should it not also find all the drunk drivers who did not have accidents and tax them to compensate the drunk driver who was unlucky enough to kill someone and go to jail as a result?

Epstein asserts that no clear philosophical principle separates types of bad luck for which government should compensate people from other types that should not cause government action; therefore, he believes, government should not attempt to compensate any unlucky people. Epstein contends that, "[I]n general the effort to use coercion to counter the adverse effects of luck tends only to make matters worse."[30] Certainly, the government incurs substantial costs to identify lucky and unlucky people. Would it find and administer a truth serum to all people who drove the previous night to discover who was drunk but lucky enough not to kill someone? How would it set the tax rate to compensate the unlucky drunk? Those who had more than five drinks might have to pay $1,000, while those who had only three might pay $500.

Although this example seems silly, try to provide a principle that justifies compensation for some types of bad luck and not for others. If you cannot, how should society decide when the bad luck is bad enough to require compensation and when the good luck is good enough to be taxed?

Choose either the position of John Rawls or that of Richard Epstein and write a single-page essay defending the position against the likely claims of the other writer. For example, if you choose Epstein's position, answer the criticism of Rawls that the differences in life chances caused by the luck of birth are simply too great to allow in a fair society. If you choose Rawls's position, explain how to determine when luck is sufficiently bad to receive compensation.

B. Mill's Empirical and Normative Arguments

Contemporary utilitarians accept Mill's position that utility is the ultimate standard for all ethical and policy questions and that this standard is grounded in the long-term interests of human beings. Therefore, while they acknowledge no natural rights, utilitarians still cite fundamental principles that government should follow to maximize benefits for the greatest number. These principles embody rights so important to the interests of society that short-term utilitarian considerations cannot justify violations. Mill believed that these principles include the right to free speech. Government must protect free speech, he argued, because only in the free marketplace of ideas can people test the worth of competing ideas and, thereby, improve the long-term well-being of society.

The exercises for Chapter 1 underscored the fact that most policy preferences include both empirical and normative components. This is true of Mill's position. The validity of his normative position depends upon the truth or falsity of his empirical claims. Mill rejected the intrusion of society and government into people's private lives, and he valued the free expression of ideas because he preferred a particular type of individual—one who leads a life of open exchange of views and intellectual debate. Mill's ideal individual is a critical, imaginative, and independent person. His *normative* belief held that a society with many such people would be better than a society composed largely of conformists. Mill based his rejection of government interference with citizens' private lives and freedom of speech on two *empirical* propositions: (1) The type of person he valued would more likely develop in a society that protected private life without censoring nonconformity, and (2) such a society will lead to greater long-term happiness than any alternative society.

While intuitively logical, the hypothesis that a free society will have more nonconformists and more original and creative ideas may be false. The emergence of imaginative and creative people from repressive societies such as the Puritans and totalitarian dictatorships suggests that Mill's empirical expectations could be wrong. Similarly, it may or may not be empirically correct that a society of nonconforming individualists leads to greater total happiness than a society in which clear social rules and norms lead to conforming behavior. If Mill's empirical propositions are false, then his defense of individual rights may fail because he bases his arguments on the beneficial impacts of these rights on the long-term maximization of pleasure.

Can you think of ways to test Mill's two empirical hypotheses? Write a single-page essay discussing how you might test the validity of Mill's two hypotheses.

Questions for Reflection

Using Individuals as Tools to Maximize the Greatest Good for the Greatest Number
Robert Nozick argues for a society that minimizes violations of individual rights and for prohibitions against a state (and its residents) violating one person's rights in the name of reducing greater violations of the rights of others. To see what Nozick means by this, imagine the following situation. Acting as an agent of the state, you're in Los Angeles in spring 1992 when a jury acquits four Los Angeles policemen of crimes after they were videotaped beating African American Rodney King. You are at the location where the initial riots are starting and you believe, quite correctly, that unless something is done quickly to stop the violence, many innocent people will die or suffer the effects of arson, looting, and other unlawful acts. Now, assume that you spot a single Los Angeles police officer in the area. You believe that if the discontent of the potential rioters can focus on that one person, the riots will not occur. As a result, however, the officer will be killed.

If you have a way to focus the rioters' attention on the officer, what will you do? If you place the person in the position that will cause his death, you will save many lives and millions of dollars in property. If you do not sacrifice the officer, then other innocent people will die.

Write a single-page essay to describe different actions suggested by the teachings of Bentham, Nozick, and Rawls. What would you do?

Question for Analysis

Using the technique for combining normative and empirical statements introduced in the Introduction, prepare three-statement arguments with empirical middle statements about what Locke, Bentham, Mill, and Rawls might prefer as the best possible society and the empirical justification for that choice. For example, Thomas Hobbes might write:

1. I prefer a society that minimizes the loss of life through violent means.
2. Societies ruled by monarchs with unlimited power will experience fewer violent deaths per capita.
3. Therefore, societies should give all power to a single ruler.

NOTES

[1] David Held, *Political Theory and the Modern State: Essays on State, Power, and Democracy* (Stanford, Calif.: Stanford University, 1989), p. 22.

[2] Kenneth R. Hoover, *Ideology and Political Life* (Monterey, Calif.: Brooks Cole, 1987), p. 16.

[3] Isaiah Berlin, "Two Concepts of Liberty," in *Liberalism and Its Critics,* ed. by Michael J. Sandel (New York: New York University Press, 1984), p. 21

[4] Thomas Hobbes, *Leviathan* (New York: Washington Square Press, 1964), p. 85.

[5] Francis P. Randall, "Editor's Introduction," in Thomas Hobbes, *Leviathan* (New York: Washington Square Press, 1964), p. xviii.

[6] Ibid., p. xix.

[7] Actually, the Hebrew name of the entity with whom God spoke translates as "The Adversary."

[8] John Locke, *Treatise on Civil Government and a Letter Concerning Toleration,* ed. by Charles L. Sherman (New York: Appleton-Century-Crofts, 1935), p. 56.

[9] Ibid., p.10.

[10] Ibid., pp. 82–83.

[11] Ibid., p. 83.

[12] Ibid., p. 58.

[13] Robert Heilbroner, *The Worldly Philosophers: The Lives, Times, and Ideas of the Great Economic Thinkers,* 5th ed. (New York: Simon & Schuster, 1961), p. 53.

[14] Ibid., p. 55.

[15] Quoted in Heilbroner, *The Worldly Philosophers,* pp. 66–67.

[16] Ibid., p. 63.

[17] Ibid., p. 124.

[18] Ibid., p. 126.

[19] John Stuart Mill, *On Liberty,* (New York: Henry Regnery, 1955), p. 20.

[20] Berlin, "Two Concepts," p. 20.

[21] Robert Nozick, *Anarchy, State, and Utopia* (New York: Basic Books, 1974).

[22] John Rawls, *A Theory of Justice* (Cambridge, Mass.: Harvard University Press, 1971).

[23] Carl J. Friedrich, *Constitutional Government and Democracy* (Boston: Ginn, 1946), pp. 20–23.

[24] Montesquieu's full name was Charles Louis de Secondat, baron de la Brede et de Montesquieu.

[25] Publius, *The Federalist Papers, No. 47,* ed. by Andrew Hacker (New York: Washington Square, 1964), p. 322.

[26] Ibid., p. 330.

[27] Publius, *The Federalist Papers, No. 48,* ed. by Andrew Hacker (New York: Washington Square, 1964).

[28] Daniel J. Elazar, comp. and ed., *Systems of the World: A Handbook of Federal, Confederal, and Autonomy Arrangements* (Harlow, Essex, England: Longman Group, 1991).

[29] Inter-parliamentary Union, *Parliaments: a Comparative Study on Structure and Functioning of Representative Institutions in Forty-one Countries* (New York: Praeger, 1961), p. 200.

[30] Richard Epstein, "Luck," *Social Philosophy & Policy* 6(1986): 17.

3

Democracy, Community, and Equality

Key Terms

Representative Democracy	Synthesis	Surplus Value
Direct Democracy	Historical (Dialectical)	Class Consciousness
General Will	Materialism	Bourgeoisie
Public Interest	Economic (Historical)	Proletariat
Political Equality	Determinism	Democratic Socialists
Popular Sovereignty	Forces of Production	Embeddedness
Communitarianism	Relations of Production	Association
Dialectic	Ideological	Hypothesis
Thesis	Superstructure	Variable
Antithesis	Class Conflict	Operationalize

The Development of Liberal and Constitutional Institutions

This chapter examines alternative theories of democracy, beginning with the development of representative democracy in a liberal, constitutional state. The chapter then turns to three alternative views of democracy: communitarianism, socialism, and Marxism.

Perhaps the greatest contributions of the United States to political theory and practice are the U.S. Constitution and the political principles that it embodies. The first written constitution, the U.S. Constitution, also was the first attempt to create a democratic government in a large nation-state. Perhaps the best explanation of the ideas embodied in the Constitution came from a set of essays written to persuade states to ratify it, *The Federalist Papers.* Written largely by Alexander Hamilton and James Madison, all the essays were published under the pen name "Publius."*

---

*John Jay also wrote three of the essays, all of which attempted to persuade New York to ratify the Constitution. The authors knew, however, that the essays would affect events in other states, as well.

Publius set out four goals for the essays: (1) to show the utility of the Constitution to political prosperity, (2) to demonstrate the need for a more powerful national government than then existed, (3) to confirm that the Constitution would become an instrument of true republican government, and (4) to prove that the Constitution would improve the young nation's security.[1] The previous chapter described the goal of constitutional government to limit the ability of rulers to tyrannize their subjects while simultaneously maintaining effective government. Democracy presents a way to prevent the few from tyrannizing the many, and Publius clearly supported the democratic principle. The words, *republic, democracy,* and *popular government* appear interchangeably throughout the essays. Despite a willingness to make the majority of the people the final authority, Publius argued that **representative democracy** provides better protection for liberty than **direct democracy** provides.

Publius described three problems in representative government:

1. The people may lose control of their representatives.

2. The majority may tyrannize the minority.

3. The majority may rule foolishly.[2]

The right of suffrage prevents the first problem by settling sovereignty firmly with the people. To prevent the second and third problems, the United States uses separation of powers, checks and balances, and federalism. Publius argues that the Constitution must divide power and pit ambition against ambition to prevent majority tyranny. The Constitution uses and extends Montesquieu's idea of separation of powers. The founders separated not only the executive, legislative, and judicial functions, but also legislative, executive, and judicial personnel.[3]

Publius expected that the legislature would be the institution most likely to practice majority tyranny. To prevent this, the Constitution gives the president and judges the means to defend themselves from the legislature. The president and judges will exercise this power to serve their personal interests and because they desire a good polity. Publius believed that representative government would reduce the likelihood that democratic action of the people would lead to foolish policy. He argued that representatives are more likely to have greater knowledge and virtue than the people who elect them. Publius did not count on this, however. Constitutional provisions for indirect elections for senators and the president and for the appointment of judges by the president with the approval of the Senate further remove some rulers from the direct oversight of the ruled.

In a particularly innovative insight, Publius argued that a large republic with representative government is more likely to avoid majority tyranny and foolish policy than a small republic. In small republics, the representatives are too much under the scrutiny and influence of the popular majority. For this reason, representatives cannot exercise independent judgment.[4] For the same reason, separation of powers does not work in small republics. However, in large republics, representation and separation of powers combine to ameliorate the excesses of the majority by giving the representatives greater discretion to use their own judgment.

For Publius, the central problem of popular government is the threat of many who have little property using the government to seize the wealth of a few who have a great deal of property. Publius argued that the size and economic complexity of the U.S. republic would prevent the majority of poor people from recognizing their common situation. In a small republic, the many poor can easily observe the vast difference between their situation and that of the wealthy few. A large republic with a federal structure also makes it more difficult for the many to organize and seize the property of the few.

A common thread that runs throughout *The Federalist Papers* is the Constitution's use of private interests to achieve public good. It pits faction against faction, ambition against ambition, and institution against institution. Any good constitution arranges institutions so that leaders acting for selfish motives will produce a safe, secure, limited, and democratic government.

The Federalist Papers show clearly how the U.S. Constitution is the prototypical liberal document. *Federalist No. 10* draws on almost every principle of classical liberalism. In it, Publius argues that if people have different talents and liberty, they will have different interests and levels of wealth. These differences inevitably lead to different factions, which inevitably want to use the government to improve their positions. Publius wrote, "Liberty is to faction what air is to fire."[5] Yet the protection of liberty is the first goal of government. As the government cannot eliminate factions and still maintain liberty, Publius asserted that a constitution should not structure government so that it can eliminate factions. Such a government would not be limited. Instead, Publius claimed that a constitution must structure government to reduce the worst effects of factions. Publius argued that the U.S. Constitution would achieve this through representative democracy, separation of powers, checks and balances, and the characteristics of a large, federal republic.

Although western liberalism and its emergence in constitutional, representative democracy have powerfully affected the development of democratic institutions, the critics of liberalism cite two major flaws. First, liberalism views individuals as isolated competitors. Second, it emphasizes protection for property rights rather than achievement of equality. The view of humans as isolated individuals ignores three seemingly obvious facts. First, most people are members of communities. Second, participation in these communities is a meaningful part of their lives and increases their happiness. Third, people have responsibilities to the community.

In addition, by emphasizing property rights, liberalism appears to accept extreme inequalities. Many democratic theorists argue, however, that people can convert economic resources into political power, so democracy becomes impossible under an extremely unequal distribution of wealth in society.

Jean-Jacques Rousseau and Communitarian Democracy

Jean-Jacques Rousseau attempted to cure both faults of liberal democracy by building both community and equality into a democracy. One of the most cataclysmic events in modern history was the French Revolution, which began in 1789. The successful revolution in America based on liberty and political equality contributed significantly to the

Jean-Jacques Rousseau

revolutionary movement in France and to the creation of the world's second republican government. The ideas cited to justify the French Revolution, however, were not those of John Locke, but those of the third great social contract theorist, Jean-Jacques Rousseau (1712–1778).

Although Rousseau wrote about familiar ideas of a social contract and a state of nature, he saw "nature" in more picturesque terms than either Hobbes or Locke. Rousseau presented an idyllic life in the state of nature. He assumed that people are naturally good: unselfish, pained by the suffering of others, caring, and kind. Above all, they are free. So long as they follow their instincts, they remain happy. They do not even have language.[†] Rousseau thought that humans in the state of nature are not rational in the sense that Locke and Hobbes believed. According to Rousseau, reason requires speech, and speech requires a society. Therefore, Hobbes and Locke were wrong about a natural law that all people know through their use of reason. Instinct, not reason, drives human action in the state of nature.

Rousseau contended that the forces of nature eventually became simply too strong for individuals acting alone to survive. In response, people organized themselves into civil societies. But these societies corrupted humans. People acquired vices, and their thoughts

---

[†] Rousseau described humans and their freedom in the state of nature in terms close to those in which he might have described other animals. The lion is not committing an immoral act when it kills its prey, nor is it moral when it protects its young, feeds and cares for other members of its pride, and shares its kills. In the same way, Rousseau's humans in the state of nature would follow their instincts. These instinctual acts might have negative or positive impacts on the welfare of other members of the group. The state of nature allows no crime or guilt. To speak of an action as either moral or immoral would be similar to speaking of the instinctual actions of lions as moral or immoral.

became depraved because the organization of societies discouraged virtue. Rousseau believed that humans learned vanity and vengeance when they began living in societies. They began comparing themselves to one another, and this led them to seek honor and wealth. Their vainglory became an endless source of quarrels.

Rousseau also believed that the individual who brought the greatest evil to humans was the first who said, "This property belongs to me."[6] Property creates inequalities and struggles, it promotes vanity, and, worst of all, it encourages bad laws. Rousseau argued that people with more property use the law to legitimize their wealth. The law becomes, therefore, an instrument of oppression of the poor maintained by public force.[7]

Rousseau's review of the development of society posed a problem in response to these observations: How do human beings regain their freedom? "Although humans were born free, they everywhere live in chains."[8] In the state of nature, humans acted on their own will and were, therefore, free. Rousseau argued that humans can regain their freedom only if they structure government so that all citizens can once more act on their own wills. Rousseau recognized the need for government to protect people and property, and he acknowledged that this need would require individuals to obey their government. Therefore, in an appropriately structured society, individuals must obey the state simultaneously as they obey their own wills.[9]

Rousseau solved the problem of simultaneous obedience by theorizing a social contract that required all members to surrender all of their rights to the community.[10] Such a contract creates a paradox, because when all citizens bind themselves completely, they regain their freedom. How can that be?

THE GENERAL WILL

This mention of individuals giving all their rights to government may seem reminiscent of Hobbes's Leviathan, but that is not what Rousseau envisioned. Hobbes thought a single ruler should have absolute power. Rousseau maintained that the people have absolute power; they determine what citizens must do and not do. The outcome of this determination is the **general will.**

Rousseau believed that people can develop a legitimate society if they share similar values, live in one place, have similar life experiences, and are bound together by a psychological bond. That society will be a harmonious one in which people live together peacefully and become virtuous. Such a society allows a true common or **public interest.** When little conflict arises between individual interests and the public interest, the factions that characterize liberalism do not occur. Only by keeping this ideal community in mind can you understand Rousseau's idea of the general will.

The general will is a strange concept for those who grew up in a society that values individualism and limited government. But Rousseau imagined a different form of government. The state, its government, and its citizens make an organic whole. The state becomes more than the sum of its parts. Its citizens could not be free and fully human outside of the community any more than a hand, heart, eye, and foot could exist unattached to the body. Just as it makes no sense to speak of a foot, hand, or brain having rights or a will of its own, Rousseau saw little sense in assigning rights or desires to individuals in a legitimate community except as these features help them to function as parts of the community.

Rousseau wrote that the community is a person whose life is in the union of its members. If a person's most important concern is self-preservation, then the same is true for the state. It must have the compelling force to use each part in the way that is most advantageous to the whole.[11] All citizens put all their power under the supreme direction of the general will, and all become indivisible parts of the moral person that is the community.[12]

All citizens participate in determining the will of the community, and all are bound by that will once it emerges. Citizens simultaneously determine the general will and act according to its dictates. The strongest statement of the absolute power of the general will is Rousseau's often-quoted statement that the general will may force people to be free: "[W]hoever shall refuse to obey the general will must be constrained by the whole body of his fellow citizens to do so: which is no more than to say that it may compel a man to be free . . ."[13]

Rousseau contended that an individual who opposes the general will does not understand her own interests. Therefore, to allow her to pursue those interests would harm both the individual and the society. Much as adults might prevent a child from behaving in ways that would prevent him from becoming an adult, the state must deny individuals the option of acting against the general will so that they will be free to do what is best for them.

On what matters may the general will act? It may take action on any matter that serves the public interest. Who decides whether or not a proposed action serves the public interest? The general will decides. Rousseau asserted that, if society is to decide the true general will, citizens must ask themselves whether a potential action truly promotes the public interest. If all citizens ask themselves this question and decide an issue under the principle of majority rule, then the result is the general will, and the general will cannot be wrong. What is more, the general will represents the true and free choice of each individual. Thus, by following the general will, the individual citizen experiences true freedom.

What prevents the general will from making a mistake? Imagine a community in which all members know their roles in society and society has socialized them to fulfill those roles. All are satisfied with their places in society because they know that all roles are essential. They are happy only when they are fulfilling the tasks appropriate to their roles and when attempting to make decisions that will benefit the entire community. Their socialization would make any other action as difficult for them as it would be for a lion to disregard its instincts.

Rousseau believed that when people in such a society meet and, through reason and discussion, make a decision, this decision must be correct. An individual or small group may misunderstand what is best for the community. The majority of the society, however, could not make a mistake because their discussion would present all perspectives. Because all want what is best for the community, this discussion leads to the correct decision.

Notice that Rousseau does not specify what choices can or cannot be part of the general will. He cannot predict this determination for a community because only its citizens can decide what is best for them. The decisions of the community are sovereign; no one can know in advance what issues will become important to a community or what they should decide.

Rousseau's conception of society and the method by which its citizens decide the general will have some extremely important consequences:[14]

- Inequality among citizens must be limited. Otherwise, vanity and envy lead people to ask, "What is in my interest?" rather than "What is in the public interest?"

- Sovereignty is an unalienable right. No individual or group within society has the right to make laws in place of the entire body of citizens.

- Representative government is impossible. Only direct democracy can allow all citizens to express their understanding of the best interests of the society.

- Majority rule is the only legitimate way to decide issues. In their votes, however, all ask what is good for the community rather than what is good for themselves.

- The society must forbid interest groups and political parties as representations of the particular wills of portions of the society.

- Separation of powers would imply an unacceptable principle that sovereignty is divisible.

- Nothing limits the scope of the law. Although individuals may decide what is not important to the society, it is impossible to know in advance what actions the society will have to take to preserve itself and improve its well-being.

Rousseau's society is neither liberal nor constitutional because government is not limited. Where Publius saw liberty as the freedom of individuals to follow their own interests, Rousseau saw freedom as voluntary obedience to the general will. Publius envisioned self-interested and competing citizens. Rousseau's vision of society rested on his belief that a community can encourage its citizens to lead the moral life and ask only what is good for the entire society.

Like Aristotle, Rousseau believed that individuals can become virtuous only in a community. Virtue requires that people interact with one another, and this requires that people leave the state of nature. The community then establishes a moral code and a set of institutions that allow people to become truly human by giving themselves over to the general will and following its dictates.

Rousseau's ideas of community have a powerful attraction. The ideal liberal citizen is an autonomous individual who is free because she stands alone, makes her own choices, and accepts responsibility for those choices. The liberal individual does not act to achieve the public interest, but her own interest. In contrast, Rousseau's ideal citizen gains freedom by participating in a community that depends upon her contribution to identify the public interest and by accepting the dictates of the general will as actions in accordance with her own will.

ROUSSEAU AND DEMOCRACY

Thanks to Rousseau, two primary principles guided development of democratic ideas in France: political equality and popular sovereignty. **Political equality** means that all citizens speak with equal voices in all matters of government; in every decision, each person's voice counts the same as every other's. **Popular sovereignty** means that the supreme power in the state resides in the people. The classic summary description of this conception of government by popular sovereignty is Abraham Lincoln's phrase "Government of the people, by the people, and for the people."

BOX 3.1

Modern Technology for Direct Democracy

Direct democracy, a process by which every citizen can vote on every major issue, is certainly possible in today's industrialized world. Current technology would allow government to hook up a box to every household television that would register an individual citizen's vote on every issue. Ross Perot, in his 1992 campaign, advocated such electronic town meetings. Experiments with nonambulatory, elderly populations in Pennsylvania have successfully allowed those individuals to express their opinions on public issues and vote on community decisions.*

The mechanism works through a two-way cable connection for each television. Partisans for each side debate an issue on television, and the audience can choose between two or more related policy alternatives. After the debate, citizens may call in questions. After a question-and-answer period, citizens enter their voter codes and cast their ballots. The votes are electronically tabulated almost instantaneously to allow an immediate run-off vote, if necessary.

Proponents of electronic democracy contend that through this mechanism, every person's vote can count equally and the society can realize the will of the majority. Equally important, direct participation will encourage political involvement and reduce the currently high levels of political alienation. By listening to both sides of the debate, the television audience would become informed voters and active citizens.

Opponents of electronic democracy argue that such a system violates the most important principle of democracy—reasoned and open debate among participants. In the course of this debate, people on both sides of an issue can come to understand the reasoning behind the opposite position, thus possibly promoting compromise and achieving better policy outcomes. Opponents contend that electronic democracy would encourage demagoguery, simplistic solutions, symbolic rather than substantive debate, and, ultimately, bad policy.

---

* James David Barber, *Strong Democracy* (New Haven, Conn.: Yale University Press, 1984); and R. Kenneth Godwin, *One Billion Dollars of Influence: The Direct Marketing of Politics* (Chatham, N.J.: Chatham House, 1988).

Most of today's "democracies" trace their origins to the American Revolution and Constitution (and thereby to Locke) or to the French Revolution (and thereby to Rousseau). Under the banners of political rights and popular sovereignty, from the American and French Revolutions until today, the right to participate in government has been steadily extended to more and more formerly excluded classes of citizens—indigent as well as propertied, women as well as men, and increasingly younger people as well as their elders. Universal suffrage is today more the norm than the exception, at least in nominally democratic societies. Popular participation has extended into policy making functions through new political institutions such as the initiative, referendum, and recall. All of these changes came about through political conflict, sometimes violent conflict. Although debate about the value of popular sovereignty and political equality continues, democratic theory today includes these two ideas that come directly from Rousseau.

Rousseau advocated the purest form of what people now call *direct* or *participatory democracy.* Popular government by the general will could occur only in communities like the city-states of classical Greece. The society must be sufficiently small, say 60,000 people or so, for each citizen to know virtually all other citizens. Some who share Rousseau's faith in the value of participatory democracy believe that modern communication techniques can achieve it in large nation-states, where every television could become a voting box. This would allow government to know the majority's will on all major policy issues. All citizens could participate in making government policy. Examine the ideas discussed in Box 3.1 and evaluate for yourself the modern-day idea of direct democracy.

ROUSSEAU AND TOTALITARIANISM

Despite Rousseau's contributions to democratic theory, several parts of his work foreshadow the excesses of 20th-century totalitarian regimes. His general will justifies absolute political power of the sovereign people. No individual has any right to disobey it or rebel against it, no matter what it commands.

Along with the absolute power of the general will, Rousseau linked participation, virtue, and patriotism. He was especially critical of the liberal position that the polity created by the social contract is the sum of individual interests. Rousseau believed that such a conception "implies neither public welfare nor a political community."[15] He derided liberalism for its premise of universal selfishness as the basis for society. To Rousseau, citizens are not just individuals who happen to join the same car pool or shop at the same supermarket. They are members linked with fellow citizens in their political community, an entity that has value in itself. Loyalty and patriotism bind members to the community and to each other.

Critics of Rousseau worry that this elevation of patriotism to the rank of a virtue above all others could help to create and justify totalitarian states. Rousseau wrote of patriotism that, "It is certain that the greatest miracles of virtue have been produced by patriotism; this fine and lively feeling, which gives to force of self-love all the beauty of virtue, lends it an energy which, without disfiguring it, makes it the most heroic of all passions."[16]

Without Rousseau's insistence on informed participation in governing, his community emphasizes patriotic passions where absolute authority fuels nationalistic fervor. Such a sentiment swept France like wildfire during and after the revolution, as that country became the first modern nation-state almost within a single generation.

The combination of patriotism, nationalism, and the absolute authority of the general will manifested itself in France's Reign of Terror immediately after the revolution. During this period, the state guillotined thousands in the name of protecting the revolutionary gains. Robespierre, the leader of the Reign of Terror, made this relationship clear when he claimed that, "Our will is the general will," and "The government of the Revolution is the despotism of liberty. . . ."[17] As French revolutionary armies, fired by patriotism, marched through Europe, they aroused similar nationalistic feelings elsewhere. The previously vague sense of common nationalities began to develop into the ideology of nationalism. That ideology was a critical element in many totalitarian regimes in the 20th century.

Rousseau never tied the totalitarian implications of the general will to the ideas of national patriotism or of the sovereign identity of the French people or that of any other nationality. But he would have approved of a modified version of John F. Kennedy's famous admonition: "Ask not what your city can do for you; ask what you can do for your city."

Modern Communitarians

In recent years, several theorists have attempted to apply many of Rousseau's ideas concerning the importance of community to provide a logically consistent political philosophy for modern societies. These theorists call their philosophy **communitarianism.**

Robert Bellah and his co-authors in *Habits of the Heart* define *community* as a group of socially interdependent people. These individuals participate together in discussions and decision making, share practices that define the community, and are nurtured by their community.[18] The Communitarian Platform, an explicit statement of this political perspective published in 1991 by 70 communitarian thinkers and community leaders, seeks to make government more participatory and to find ways to accord citizens more information and more authority, more often.[19] Communitarians argue that a responsive community is one whose moral standards reflect the basic human needs of all its members. If these needs compete with one another, the community's standards reflect the relative priority accorded by its members to some needs over others.

Communitarians would replace the principle of the individual choosing rationally to maximize self-interest with a new decision-making model based on collective decisions reached primarily through emotional reactions and value judgments.[20] Sounding much like Rousseau, communitarians argue that the only free individuals are those who live in communities that dictate those individuals' actions and obligations.[21]

Communitarians see people as situated in communities the moment they are born. Members are embedded in a history that locates each individual among others with whom the person shares norms, values, and goods.[22] The individual is defined, at least partially, by roles ascribed by the community. For communitarians, it is impossible for a person to speak of "I" without meaning "we."[23]

Modern communitarians do not expect that small cities will replace nation-states as the legitimate institutions of government. They do expect that neighborhoods, churches, schools, and families will provide each individual with community, meaning, and place. In addition, these institutions will act as buffers between the individual and the state.

An important aspect of communitarian theory harkens back to Rousseau. Communitarians believe that the goal of society is virtue, the realization of shared human good. This shared goal directs the lives of members and provides all in the community with a common purpose and common tasks.[24] Sociologist Amitai Etzioni argues that communitarians *assume* "that human beings pass moral judgment over their urges and that moral commitments are the *cause* for community."[25]

Policy Implications   What concrete policy proposals do the communitarian ideas support? At the level of the nation-state, communitarians argue that the state is an implied social contract among members of the community. This social contract "is an agreement to reach decisions together about what goods are necessary to our common life, and then to provide those goods for one another."[26] The social contract, writes Michael Walzer, "is a moral bond that connects the strong and the weak, the lucky and the unlucky, the rich and the poor, creating a union that transcends all differences of interest, drawing its strength from history, culture, language, and so on."[27]

Most communitarians support strong welfare state policies. For example, Walzer contends that a just society must allocate medical care by the individual's need for it rather than by ability to pay. He advocates putting medical care beyond the scope of the free market, thereby permitting the community to proclaim that the right to medical care is based on the need for it and on the duty of society to supply it.[28]

Communitarians do not allocate rights and needs based on arguments for natural rights (following Locke). Neither do they contend that rights and needs should be determined by some overriding principle such as maximizing social welfare (following Bentham and Mill) or improving the position of the least advantaged (following Rawls). In a communitarian society, consensus decides whether a woman has the right to choose an abortion and the right to have the state pay for that abortion or whether she has the duty to carry the fetus to term to protect its right to be born. *For communitarians, any right or need can have a priority that compels society to provide it without cost so long as the community has determined that the right or need has sufficient central cultural significance to create this moral requirement.*[29]

Communitarians want to replace the rights-based liberal society with a society that places equal emphasis on rights and responsibilities. For example, the society must balance the right to have children against the responsibility to care for those children in a family unit over the entire period of their childhood. Thus while the community may recognize the necessity of divorce in some cases, it takes the moral stand that the stable, two-parent family is the appropriate family unit. Communitarians oppose "no-fault" divorces because of the clear detrimental effects of divorce on children. The community should encourage parents to keep their marriage together for the sake of interests larger than their rights, convenience, and desires.

HIV policies are another area where a rights-based society might disagree with the emphasis on responsibility of communitarians. Do individuals infected with HIV have the right to keep their infections private, or are they obligated to inform anyone they may infect? If an HIV-positive individual does not notify sexual partners, what duties would that person's doctor have to people the individual might infect? What are the duties of public health officials? From the communitarian perspective, the duties of all individuals involved—the infected individual, the doctor, and the public health official—to notify those who are at risk outweigh any right to privacy of the HIV-infected individual.[30]

Critics of the communitarian approach ask how society should allocate priorities among rights. Presumably, a right has a higher priority if the community has reached a stronger consensus on its central cultural significance. A liberal such as John Stuart Mill, who greatly feared coercive social norms and mindless conformity, would find much to criticize in the communitarian vision of a good society if its emphasis on consensus were to lead to conformity. Locke, Mill, Nozick, and Rawls all would contend that individuals must have some rights, such as the right to one's life, independent of community consensus. Without such rights, the community might not prevent a consensus on a destructive value such as hatred for all Jews, African Americans, Caucasians, or members of any other group.

Another important criticism of modern communitarianism centers on its involuntary character. People are born into communities; they do not voluntarily choose them. Communitarians assume that a community requires a shared location, a common history, common activities, and *involuntary* obligations. An individual has no right to withdraw, because such a right would place the community continually at risk. Liberals see social meaning in *voluntary attachments* to groups, people, and institutions rather than coerced membership.

Marxian Socialism

The most fundamental and complete critique of liberalism comes from Marxism. Many people today identify Marxist theory mainly with totalitarian governments and their leaders like Joseph Stalin, Mao Tse-tung, and Fidel Castro. Marxism did not begin as a totalitarian theory, however, but as a comprehensive analysis of capitalist economics and liberal society. Its authors, Karl Marx and Friedrich Engels, believed in the essential goodness of all people, and they valued liberty. Chapter 4 will discuss how Marxism changed from democratic ideals to embrace totalitarian ideologies. In this chapter, we examine its relation to democracy.

KARL MARX AND FRIEDRICH ENGELS

Karl Marx (1818–1883) and Friedrich Engels (1820–1895) were political theorists, economic historians, and revolutionary organizers. Socialism became a political and social movement largely as a result of their efforts.

Marx grew up in Prussia. After receiving his Ph.D. in philosophy, he edited an opposition newspaper, *Rheinische Zeitung,* which the government suppressed to silence Marx's radical views. For virtually the rest of his life, Marx lived in exile in London, where he immersed himself in study and writing at the British Museum. He lived in poverty and was chronically ill. His sole earnings were occasional fees for serving as a correspondent for the *New York Tribune.* Marx and his family depended mainly on the financial support of Friedrich Engels.

Engels, the son of a wealthy German textile manufacturer, was successful in business. He met Marx in Paris in 1844, and they began the collaboration that continued until Marx's death in 1883. Engels and Marx worked together constantly in organizational activities and writing both individually and jointly authored works.[‡]

[‡] Although scholars usually refer to the body of Marx and Engels's work as *Marxism,* both writers contributed substantially to this body of literature. Engels wrote *The Condition of the Working Class in England, Socialism: Scientific and Utopian, Anti-Dühring,* and *The Origin of the Family.* Marx's major work, *Das Kapital,* was published in three volumes, the third completed after his death by Engels.

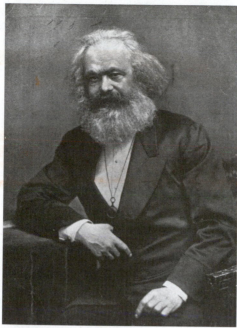

Karl Marx

PRINCIPAL SOURCES OF MARXIST THEORY

Undoubtedly the most significant influence on Marx's early intellectual development was the idealist philosophy of Georg Wilhelm Friedrich Hegel (1770–1831). Hegel saw his work as the instrument and guide for a total intellectual revolution. He deliberately broke with the fundamental premises and principles of Judaeo-Christian philosophy, Enlightenment doctrines of reason, and other philosophies of the time. To replace all existing world views, he offered the "logic of the dialectic."

Hegel believed that the historical dialectical process works continually to resolve contradictions among conflicting ideas. Each resolution brings people closer to the truth. Hegel's **dialectic** was not a logic to be applied by the reasoning of individuals. He considered it a historical process, a historical "necessity." He once described this evolutionary process of ideas as "the march of God on earth."

Hegel's dialectic starts with some particular proposition, such as the idea that profits should go to the capitalist because this person's investment of money in a project makes the profit possible and because this person assumes the risk. Call that proposition the **thesis.** That statement automatically implies its **antithesis**—any proposition about profits that contradict the thesis. In the example, the antithesis might assert that profits should go to workers because the true source of value is the labor required to produce it. The conflict between thesis and antithesis is the engine that drives historical necessity to produce the resolution of these contradictions. Hegel called this resolution their **synthesis.** For example,

Marx's synthesis might determine that neither the capitalist nor the worker owns the profits; rather profits should go to the entire society because the state protects both the capitalist and the worker. This synthesis becomes a new thesis, automatically generating a new antithesis and another conflict. This process continues until it reaches the ultimate synthesis, which Hegel saw as full realization of the Idea of Freedom.

ELEMENTS OF MARXIST THEORY

Marx rejected Hegel's belief that "ideas" are "real." He asserted that only material, physical, empirically sensible objects and phenomena have reality. But Marx accepted the idea that historical necessity drives the empirical world along a predestined historical course. He argued that the clashes of material theses and their antitheses results in a succession of societies. He anticipated a final synthesis not to produce Hegel's Idea of Freedom, but to produce the material freedom of communism. Marx claimed that he found Hegel standing on his head and just turned him right side up.

All his life, Marx was a voracious reader. In addition to his studies in philosophy, he researched the works of the classical economists, particularly Adam Smith and David Ricardo. He read the works of the early socialists and followed the output and activities of virtually all contemporary writers and radical activists. Marx and Engels merged diverse conceptions from all of these sources into their philosophy and their theory of society. The result remains the most comprehensive and systematic theory in all social science. Its key elements are captured in the summary labels by which it is often described—**historical materialism** or **dialectical materialism.**

As one element of this system, Marx and Engels developed the theory of **economic determinism.** Its major proposition holds that economic structures and processes determine all aspects of all people's lives, including all social and political relationships. Marx and Engels first distinguished between the forces of production and the relations of production. **Forces of production** are the physical elements (raw materials, human labor, capital equipment, tools, and land) that combine to make goods and services. **Relations of production** are the complex links among people that enable them to perform their various roles producing and distributing goods and services. Relations of production include laws and the institutions that make and enforce laws.

Ideas are important for Marx and Engels as tools to rationalize the behavior required to maintain society. In this way, ideas help to stabilize the existing social and economic system. Ideas themselves are not true or false, good or bad. They are part of the **ideological superstructure** of society and by-products of the workings of the economic system. Marx and Engels saw the entire ideological superstructure as a rationalization of the status quo. It is a defensive apparatus thrown up by the system of production to defend society's economic and political order.

Contradictions in Capitalist Society   The dialectical process is conflict. Hegel saw this conflict as a struggle between clashing ideas. Marx and Engels saw the conflict as a contest between the forces of production and the relations of production that drives history through cycles of economic and social revolutions. Marx and Engels outlined the historical parade of successive economic systems. With each revolution, property and political power change hands, and the very nature of property and property rights also changes. New ideas replace old ones in religion, philosophy, science, and politics.

Each successive economic system collapses because "contradictions" within each society inevitably destroy it. Marx and Engels argued that, at the very moment that capitalism gained supremacy, it began digging its own grave. The thesis of capitalism inexorably began generating the antithesis that would produce the synthesis that would bring about communism. Marx and Engels saw the **class conflict** that results from economic competition and technology as the fatal contradiction within capitalism.

Marx combined David Ricardo's labor theory of value with Malthus's ideas concerning the natural price of labor. From these, he created the theory of surplus value. Ricardo held that the true value, or "natural price," of any good or service is the cost of the labor that produces it. Malthus argued that the natural wage capitalists will pay laborers equals the cost of keeping the labor force alive and able to work. Thus the natural price of any object equals the number of hours necessary to produce a good multiplied by the natural wage. But manufactured products sell for more than the natural price. Marx called the difference between the natural price of an object and its selling price **surplus value**. The capitalists who own enterprises use their legal rights as owners to expropriate that surplus value from workers. This expropriation and capitalist competition are the roots of an ever-intensifying conflict between the forces and the relations of production.

That may sound too theoretical and complex to comprehend, but it is not. Adam Smith showed how competition among capitalists reduces profits. To get higher profits, each capitalist will look for technologies to lower the cost of production. Typically, technological advances reduce the amount of labor needed to produce a particular good. This gives the capitalist who first uses the new technology an advantage over competitors and increases that person's profits. The advantage, however, is only temporary. Competitors adopt the new technology, and again all capitalists producing the good earn small profits. They then search for even better technologies to reduce labor costs still further.

Notice the result of this process. Each new technology requires fewer workers to produce the same amount of the commodity. Because the natural price equals the cost of labor, the natural price of the commodity falls. But this does not increase profits, because competition forces down the selling price. Surplus value, the difference between the cost of labor and the selling price, decreases as the number of workers declines. In addition, because fewer factories can produce the same amount of goods, fewer people will own factories. Fewer factories mean fewer capitalists and more unemployed workers. The resulting reduction in profits intensifies the competition among the remaining capitalists and the entire process repeats itself.

The personal computer industry provides an example of this theoretical process. In 1985, numerous manufacturers produced personal computers in the United States, including IBM, Apple, Atari, Kaypro, Commodore, Radio Shack, Osborne, Texas Instruments, AT&T, and so forth. Today, far more computers are produced and bought, but most of these companies have either gone out of business or stopped making personal computers because they were losing money. The computer manufacturers that remain use far fewer workers. Marx correctly predicted that the number of producers, profits, and the labor force decline in all major industries as they mature.

To sum up Marx's argument, the inexorable historical dialectic working in capitalist society condemns workers to lives of poverty and capitalists to constant threats of failure and descent into the same conditions as workers. For both workers and capitalists, capitalism guarantees progressively worse lives for most people despite ever-increasing productivity.

Marx explained that capitalism cannot avoid the situation in which the economy produces vast commodities of goods but most people live in misery, because the structure of capitalism imprisons not only the workers but the capitalists, as well. All capitalists are caught in a prisoner's dilemma game. If they pay workers more than the minimum possible wage, other firms will undersell them and force them out of business. Workers are also caught in a similar game. They must work for the lowest possible wage because if they do not, other workers will. Thus, capitalists and workers who attempt to reform the system will be the first to fail and the first to starve.

Marx and Engels did not expect capitalism to change for another reason: It is captured in its own ideological superstructure. In liberal society, law, government, education, religion, and art socialize people to believe that private property is a natural right that government must protect. In Marx's time, Christian religions taught that hierarchy is natural, life in this world is temporary and unimportant, and workers will receive their rewards in the next world.[§] Art, music, and literature glorified capitalism. Newspapers did not attack the injustices of capitalism; they praised its productivity and condemned labor unions and other institutions that might encourage workers to demand a better system.

The steadily worsening condition of life for workers leads to steadily growing **class consciousness.** Workers become aware of their true class status and the character of the exploiting class. As the dialectic of history works itself out, the laws of economic behavior inevitably divide capitalist society into just two classes. Capitalists, the **bourgeoisie,** are not merely wealthy but also increasingly powerful in economic, social, and political spheres. Workers, the **proletariat,** are not merely impoverished but also exploited in those same spheres. Marx and Engels predicted that class conflict would ultimately erupt into a violent social revolution. This revolution would destroy capitalism and liberate the productive forces that capitalism created but could not put to work.

After the Revolution   The last step in Marxist theory is the synthesis that results from the contradictions within capitalism to produce a new socioeconomic system—communism. What does the new society look like? About all that Marx and Engels said about life after the revolution is that "the state withers away." The system that takes its place is not a government of people, but an "administration of things." In this final phase, people gain freedom from the economic power of the marketplace, the drudgery of the factory, and the patriarchal power of the family. Eliminating private property releases the forces of production and enables society to follow the rule, "From each according to her abilities; to each according to her needs." (See Box 3.2 for an example of how this works.)

Marx and Engels envisioned communist society as a peaceful, worldwide society, not a collection of nation-states. They saw more clearly than most economists of their time that the capitalist system was becoming an interlocking network of relations that

---

[§] One of Marx's best known aphorisms says that "religion is the opiate of the people."

BOX 3.2

Would You Want to Live in a Communist Society?

Marx wrote that in a communist society the rules for the production and distribution of goods and services would be "from each according to his ability, to each according to his need." Assume for a moment that such a society is possible and that you could live in it if you wished. If you were asked whether you would want to live in your current society or in the one in which Marx's rules are followed, what would you answer?

If you answered that you prefer your current society, why did you answer this way? Marx would argue that your answer is simply a product of your socialization by the capitalist superstructure. He would say that unless such indoctrination had taken place, every rational person would choose his society. We think that we can show you that perhaps Marx would be correct. Before we do, however, if you decided that you prefer your current society, make a list of reasons why this is so.

Marx's response to your list might go as follows. Think of a family with two children. One child is exceptionally bright, good-looking, and athletic; the other child is not bright, unattractive, and not athletic. How would you want the parents of the children to treat them? Say, for example, each had a math test on a particular day and the bright child did not study but made an A- anyway. The not-so-bright child studied very hard and earned a D. In addition, both children tried out for the basketball team and the athletic child made the team while the non-athletic child did not. The children come home and the parents must decide how to reward each child. If the family worked on the "merit system," then the bright and athletic child will receive the bulk of the praise. His performance, based on objective standards, was better than that of the other child. The parents can be proud of their bright, attractive, and athletic child and they can brag about his accomplishments to family and friends. However, the performances of the not-so-bright child are below average and merit no rewards. His D grade and his failure to make the team indicate that the parents should not reward him.

Now assume that you are the parent of these two children. How would you reward your children? Most of us believe that for parents to praise the gifted child and to fail to praise the challenged child would be unjust. In fact, because the gifted child did not study for his A-, perhaps he should receive less praise than his less-gifted sibling. How would you distribute rewards of love, affection, and praise to the two children to maximize the happiness and personal development of both? Now assume that you are a friend of the family with the two children. How would you evaluate the performance of parents who give more of their love, affection, and praise to the child who happened to be born with physical and mental gifts? Would you praise them for maximizing the future performance and happiness of their two children? Would you want to be a member of that family?

If most of you would treat your children, not according to some external measure such as the grade on a test or whether or not they made the basketball team, but wished to distribute rewards in a just manner, would not your expectations of your children be based on a rule quite similar to "from each according to his ability"? Would not your distribution be something extremely close to "each according to his needs"?

crossed national boundaries. They considered nationalism a confusing sentiment that blinds workers to capitalists' oppression. Patriotism misleads workers into supporting capitalist foreign adventures, and it inhibits the development of proletarian class consciousness. Marx and Engels confidently predicted that the revolution that ended capitalism would have a worldwide scope. The disappearance of the exploiting class would eliminate class conflict. Nation-states would disappear because international conflict would disappear with the private property that they attempted to protect.

In summary, the final stage of history, communism, would bring a society without government, that is, a state of peaceful anarchy. Marx and Engels predicted that the proletarian (workers') revolution that ended capitalism would also end the need for government. Government, merely "an executive committee of the ruling class," would not be needed as communist society would include no classes. The society of the future would be a worldwide, stateless, classless society. It would bring material plenty amid constant technological progress. It would embody almost perfect economic and social equality. Political equality would be unnecessary without any government or politics. With no government and no politics, people have no need for liberalism. People need protection neither from each other or from the state.

Democratic Socialism

Both John Stuart Mill and Jean-Jacques Rousseau argued that great inequalities undermine democratic government. Indeed, grinding poverty and inhumane working conditions led Malthus, Ricardo, Bentham, and Mill to repudiate the "natural laws of economics." These conditions led another group of writers to develop a set of political ideas and to propose a series of social and economic institutions that they believed would alleviate this suffering. These writers were the **democratic socialists.**

Rousseau's criticisms of liberal democracy addressed the first flaw of liberalism cited early in the chapter, its perceived disregard of community. Marx centered his critique on the second flaw, economic inequality. Democratic socialists also highlighted this second flaw, but their recommendations differed radically from those of Marx and Engels.

Economic power often translates into political power. Classical liberalism fails to recognize that political equality becomes impossible in the face of great economic inequality. Mill recognized this problem and advocated greater education and opportunities for the poor and more equal rights and opportunities for women. However, Mill's analysis stopped short of asking a critical question: At what point does economic inequality eliminate any real possibility of democracy? Democratic socialists answered this question by arguing that true democracy requires severe limits on individual economic power and wealth.

FABIAN SOCIALISM

Following many early socialists, such as Fourier, Saint-Simon, and Owen, Fabian Socialism is the best known body of democratic socialist writing and it had a substantial impact on politics. This fully developed theory addresses the practical problems and issues that face people and their governments.

The Fabian Society began in 1884. George Bernard Shaw, Beatrix Potter,[||] and Sidney Webb became its leading intellectuals. The Fabians issued a continual stream of pamphlets, tracts, and lectures expounding their views. They intended to spread socialist doctrine throughout the educated middle class and to persuade national and local governments in Britain to put those doctrines gradually into practice. The key word here is *gradually*. The Fabians rejected violent class struggle and the Marxist call to revolution. They expected socialism to develop by permeating existing social institutions. Shaw said that the Fabians had "agreed to give up the delightful ease of revolutionary heroics and to take to the hard work of practical policy reforms within the scope of existing political institutions."[31] The society's name symbolized its strategy and tactics. It was named after the famous Roman general, Fabius Maximus, who won his battles by following a "wait and win strategy." He dodged enemy attacks and avoided frontal attacks against opponents. Instead, he stalked them patiently, winning small battles one after another until victory came.

The Fabians analyzed proposed policies based on the criterion that the measures should promote a wide distribution of physical well-being and cultural opportunity. Specific objectives included nationalization of the land and state competition with private enterprise in every branch of production. The Fabians' justification for such policies rested on two principal lines of argument. First, they argued that unrestrained capitalism ended any hope of political equality. Wealth in a capitalist society becomes political power, and capitalism leads to such great differences that political equality is a bad joke. To preserve democracy, therefore, the state has only two choices. It can either dissolve large-scale industry (and lose the benefits of efficiency), or it can control concentrated units of economic power by government regulation or ownership.

The Fabians' second justification for their policies argued that the state creates value by protecting the workplace and the workers in the productive process. The state also provides the system of justice by which businesses and individuals settle their differences. Since the state creates value, society as a whole has the right to benefit from it. The objective of socialism is to get for the whole society the value that society creates. Therefore, the state rather than the workers or private investors should own the factories.

In 1900, at the urging of Beatrix Potter, the Fabians helped create the Unified Labour Representation Committee, which evolved into the British Labour Party. The Labour Party subsequently adopted the Fabians' tenets. The Fabians were important forces, and in many cases the principal causes, in most major practical reforms in England in this century. These include laws for a minimum wage, unemployment insurance, job security, health care, educational opportunities, taxation of inheritances and rents, and public ownership of utilities and transportation services. Today, all industrialized democracies have similar policies in those areas.

[||] Many readers will have seen Shaw's most famous play, *Pygmalion* (1913), which was later made into the musical *My Fair Lady*. The play represents clearly Shaw's belief that the distinctions between classes are based on social factors such as language rather than any innate differences in ability. Beatrix Potter's story, *Peter Rabbit,* also represents the Fabian perspective of capitalists (the farmer) and workers (Peter).

CONTEMPORARY SOCIALISM

Although the predictions of Marx and Engels never came true, socialist or social democratic parties have realized many goals of the Fabians when those parties have held power. What beliefs and principles did these parties have in common with the theorists examined so far in this chapter? What earns a person or a party the label *socialist?*

First, they all took for granted the liberal values of individualism—respect for the rights of life and liberty—and the liberal belief in popular consent as parts of the only legitimate basis of government. Socialist writers shared a deep, humanitarian concern about social evils that they saw as the wretched consequences of laissez-faire capitalism in actual life. All were sympathetic to the plight of the poor, the oppressed, and, above all, child-laborers and other wage slaves in 19th-century industrial enterprises. Popular answers to the questions posed in the Introduction of this book confirm that such humanitarian sentiments are by no means the sole property of the socialists. A wide variety of citizens, public and private, share these concerns.

All socialist and social democratic political parties contend that the social environment deeply influences and sometimes controls people's lives and fates. Every individual's fate depends above all on the social and economic status into which he is born. It also depends on the social structure and cultural patterns, customs, and habits that define society's social, economic, political, and legal institutions. Socialists recognize that these ingrained relationships constitute a social structure of which government and the economy are critically important parts. Indeed, socialism gets its name from the recognition of the powerful role of society as a structure of established relationships shaping and constraining people's lives, actions, and ideas.

Contemporary socialists and social democrats believe that, because humans create social evils, human action based on reason can relieve them. They believe that social legislation of the kind promoted by the Fabians will mitigate these evils. Most believe that substituting cooperation for competition would reduce injustice, but agreement becomes more elusive when they try to decide how to develop this cooperation. Some socialists believe that public ownership of some or all of the means of production would do that. None believe that violent class conflict or social revolution would help. All socialist and social democratic parties in industrialized democracies accept the basic ideals of political equality, popular sovereignty, and constitutional government.

Summary

Liberalism, communitarianism, Marxism, and socialism define a broad set of democratic values. Liberalism supplies the ideas of limited government, individual rights and civil liberties, equality before the law, constitutionalism, and representation. Rousseau and communitarians add the ideas of direct democracy, political equality, majority rule, the importance of community, popular sovereignty, and an emphasis on the public interest. Marxism emphasizes the possibility that great inequalities of wealth and power can create class conflict and revolution. Socialism shows that, because economic power can translate into political power, meaningful political equality requires limits on the economic power of individuals and private organizations.

Great conflicts also separate these sets of ideas. Liberals concern themselves with limited government, civil rights, and equality of opportunity through universal education; they acknowledge few goods that belong outside the marketplace. Liberals could never agree with Rousseau's idea of the general will, nor could Rousseau ever accept the liberals' ideas concerning the autonomy of individuals or representation. Whereas liberals tend to care most about equality of opportunity, socialists want equality of outcome. Where liberals and communitarians see state power as a major threat to freedom and liberty, socialists see private wealth as the major threat to liberty and democracy. The policies of and political debates within contemporary industrial democracies reflect these competing claims.

QUESTIONS AND EXERCISES

Questions for Reason

1. Why does the government advocated by Publius require a large republic, while that promoted by Rousseau requires a small one?

2. Today, television and movies show the vast differences in wealth in a country. Would a television-based program for direct democracy create the problems that Publius argued are inherent in small republics where the poor can see the great inequalities that exist?

3. How does the U.S. Constitution's use of the private interest to achieve public goals resemble Adam Smith's description of capitalism? In what ways do they differ?

4. How does the community enforce the obligations it prescribes? Presumably, for example, no one denies that the United States has a tremendous problem enforcing even a basic obligation that fathers provide financial support for their children. Would a more communitarian society help solve this problem? If so, how?

5. Marx argues that technology increases unemployment and decreases the number of capitalists. For the example of the computer chip, determine whether Marx's claim is true.

6. Does the demise of the Soviet Union and its eastern European allies mean that Marxism is dead? What important ideas remain?

Question for Reflection: The Feminist Critique of Liberalism and Communitarianism

Several feminist scholars have challenged the underlying ideas of liberalism and communitarianism. Political theorist Susan Hekman argues that neither the contractarian liberalism of John Rawls or the modern communitarianism of Michael Walzer can effectively eliminate the sexism inherent in their theories. Hekman contends that contractarian liberalism makes two mortal errors. First, it conceives of people as "disembodied" in the sense that liberalism denies the impact of social context on individuals' actions. This denial makes no logical or empirical sense. People's decisions reflect the identities they have developed through socialization by society, experiences within that society, and interpersonal relationships with members of that society. Hekman contends that any philosophy that denies this **embeddedness** of the individual is both empirically and morally wrong. Morality must be defined, at least in part, by social context.

Liberalism also errs in its recognition only of individuals who are socialized to separate their decision making and actions from the social contexts of those decisions. The people who are socialized in this way are males. In contrast, society socializes females to be emotionally involved and connected with people around them. Society discourages women from seeing themselves as separated, autonomous decision makers. Hekman contends that contractarian liberals have always divided the world into the public sphere of men (or women who enter this sphere as men) and the private world of women and the family.[32] Therefore, even if people could act as liberalism prescribes and separate their decisions from the effects of their past socialization, liberalism leaves women out of the public sphere. Only if a woman consciously rejects her involvement with the private sphere that both her biological and social roles as a female demand, can she enter the world described by contractarian liberals.

Feminist concerns may seem to fit well, however, with the communitarian orientation of writers such as Walzer. Alasdair MacIntyre, a leading proponent of the communitarian approach, writes that "We enter upon a stage which we did not design and we find ourselves part of an action that was not of our making."[33] Following Rousseau, MacIntyre contends that virtue is an acquired human quality that comes from people's understanding of their role in society. Hekman contends, however, that while communitarians resolve one of the critical problems with liberalism—its view of humans as disembodied decision makers—communitarianism also contains its own error. Hekman charges that communitarians accept patriarchal and sexist societies. The community envisioned by communitarians, "as it has been conceived in Western thought is hierarchical and ascriptive. This community ascribes a particular status to each category of individuals who comprise its members, and the status it has ascribed to women is clearly an inferior one."[34]

Hekman believes that only when political philosophy develops a view of humans as embodied in their community and interconnected with others, *and* when that embodiment recognizes differences among people without creating a hierarchy based on those differences, can people develop an empirically and morally appropriate political philosophy.

Using your knowledge of either liberalism or communitarianism, respond to Hekman's criticisms.

Question for Analysis: Operationalizing Hypotheses

The earlier chapters discussed the difference between normative and empirical statements. A normative statement makes a value judgment or indicates something that the speaker or writer believes ought to happen. Two examples would be, "All workers should realize that the capitalists are exploiting them," or "The only true democracies are direct democracies." Empirical statements refer to associations that occur in the real world. Empirical statements are either true or false. This exercise develops some of the skills necessary to do empirical analysis.

A. Noticing Associations
Many scientific advances began when a person noticed something.[35] For example, Alexander Flemming discovered penicillin when he noticed that a mold that had contaminated his culture in a petri dish prevented bacteria from growing. Flemming then

moved to the second step in empirical analysis. He experimented with many petri dishes and bacteria to test for a general association between the presence of the mold and stopping bacterial growth.

Once a scientist notices an **association** between two events, say high levels of new technology introduced into an industry and a decline in the number of firms that produce a product, the next task is to explain why the association occurs. Scientists typically use existing theories to develop reasons or rationales for the associations they observe.

Marx noticed the association between the age of an industry and the number of firms in the industry. Relying on economic theory developed by Adam Smith, Marx hypothesized that technological improvements allowed fewer firms to produce more goods. Because of competition among firms, the most efficient firms could produce enough of the industry's good to meet available demand at a low cost to consumers. These efficient firms forced less efficient competitors out of business.

B. Assumptions Required for Empirical Research

Although you may not have realized it, as you attempted to understand Marx's model, you were making two very important assumptions about how the world operates. First, as philosopher of science Ernest Gellner points out, you assumed the regularity of nature. You did not make this assumption because someone has proved that the world operates in an orderly fashion; that principle is impossible to prove. However, if cumulative knowledge is possible at all, then the principle of regularity of nature must apply.[36] Alan Zuckerman reports that political science, like any science, uses analytical techniques to posit and explore regularities in the world.[37] These writers essentially say that science is not possible unless observers assume that the world displays some order and that objects of observation exhibit some regularities.

The second essential assumption for science is that there are no hidden sources of truth and there are no people who are never wrong.[38] This means that scientists must be able, at least potentially, to evaluate all empirical claims that people make about the world. How do scientists evaluate empirical claims?

C. Theories and Hypotheses

All sciences try to make sense of the world by developing theories that relate abstract concepts to one another and to empirical observations. Observers evaluate theories by judging whether they are logically coherent and whether the events that they predict actually occur.

A scientific theory is a set of propositions that are deductively (logically) connected in a way that makes sense of empirically observed associations. For example, Marx's theory of capitalism argues that as technology increases in a society, so will the level of inequality. This overall conclusion is based on the following propositions:

1. Capitalists compete for markets for their manufactured goods.

2. Competition forces capitalists to sell their manufactured goods at the lowest possible prices.

3. Competition forces capitalists to search for and adopt new technologies that reduce production costs.

4. New technologies reduce the number of firms needed to manufacture higher levels of goods.

5. The reduction in the number of firms reduces the need for labor and increases unemployment.

6. A higher level of technology in society increases the inequality in that society.

7. As more and more workers become unemployed and wealth becomes more concentrated, class conflict will result.

These seven propositions are logically related and form a theory. Each is a hypothesis about empirical relationships. **Hypotheses** are statements that specify relationships among variables. **Variables** are the concepts that scientific observers study. In the seven hypotheses of Marxism, the variables included the type of property ownership (capitalist), competition, price, technology, unemployment, concentration of wealth, and class conflict.

A good theory provides a relatively simple model of how some portion of the empirical world operates. This model is made up of numerous, logically related hypotheses. For example, all of Marx's hypotheses relate logically to each other. They also explain an association that Marx thought he observed—as technology increased, so did the concentration of wealth in society.

Many readers may not clearly understand this material on scientific analysis. Some examples may help to clarify these very difficult concepts. Start with a simple hypothesis: "Tall people are more likely than short people to play in the National Basketball Association." This hypothesis relates two variables, height and probability of playing professional basketball in the NBA. To test the hypothesis, a scientist must **operationalize** the meaning of the word *tall* (define it in a way that allows measurement). A study might operationalize tall as being 6 feet 4 inches or more in height. This operationalization means that any person who is not at least 6 feet 4 inches in height is defined as "not tall."

The study must also specify the time period and the population to examine. Next, the scientist must decide how to make this test. The study might identify the time period for measuring the number of tall and not tall players as the 1997–1998 National Basketball Association regular season. If the percentage of males who played in the NBA during the 1997–1998 season who are at least 6 feet 4 inches tall is greater than the percentage of males who are at least 6 feet 4 inches in the general population, then the data support the hypothesis.

Try another example. You may hypothesize that money influences the decisions of politicians on important issues. Common Cause, a citizen action group in the United States, attempted to test this hypothesis. Common Cause operationalized the hypothesis by first operationalizing the word *money* as campaign contributions by political action committees (PACs) in the United States. Next, it operationalized the phrase *influences the decisions of politicians* as "increases the likelihood that members of the U.S. House of Representatives would vote favorably on bills related to the interests of the contributing organization." Common Cause then chose two PACs that contributed large amounts of money to political campaigns, the PAC of the American Medical Association and the PAC of the American Dental Association. Common Cause next selected a bill that these two groups strongly supported. The bill exempted doctors and dentists from regulation by the Federal Trade Commission.[39]

Common Cause obtained data on campaign contributions from reports to the Federal Election Commission of contributions of political action committees. Common Cause obtained records on votes from the *Congressional Record.* Members of Congress either voted for or against the measure or they did not vote.

Common Cause developed the following final, operationalized hypothesis:

> Members of Congress who voted for the bill to exempt doctors and dentists from regulation received significantly higher average contributions from the AMA and ADA than the average amount of money received by members of Congress who voted against the bill.

Common Cause found that members who voted for the position favored by doctors and dentists received an average of $10,875 in campaign contributions from these groups in the previous election cycle, while those who voted against that position received an average of $4,352.

Now look at a hypothesis derived from Marx's model that explains how capitalism leads to class conflict: "A higher level of technology in society corresponds to more inequality in that society." This hypothesis is difficult to operationalize because it states highly abstract variables: the level of technology and the level of inequality in society. Remember, to operationalize a variable, the study must define it in a way that indicates how to measure it. This process must move the study from the abstract concept to a specific, observable, and measurable event.

For purposes of this study, an observer might use the number of computers per capita as a measure of technology in a society. To operationalize the level of inequality in a society, the study might identify the ratio between the percentage of total income in a country received by the richest 5 percent of the population and the percentage of income received by the poorest 20 percent. For example, if the richest 5 percent receive 30 percent of the country's income and the bottom 20 percent receive only 5 percent of the country's income, the ratio would be 6 (30 percent divided by 5 percent).

After choosing a time period and a group of specific societies to study, the scientist can transform the abstract hypothesis, "A higher level of technology in society corresponds to more inequality in that society," into an operationalized hypothesis. Assume a time period of 1997 and take the list of societies to study from the list of countries for which the U.S. Department of State has data on both variables. The new hypothesis is, "In 1997, a higher number of computers per capita in a society will correspond to a higher ratio of the income of the richest 5 percent of a country's population to the income of the poorest 20 percent."

D. The Conflict between Generality and Specificity

Notice that operationalizing a hypothesis always sacrifices some of the generality in the original abstract concepts. When Common Cause operationalized the phrase *influence the decisions of politicians* it could not possibly include all types of politicians' decisions, so it used instead only one type, votes in Congress. Operationalized definitions must leave out many things. Using the number of computers per capita to measure technology measures only one aspect of technology. Other possible measures would include the number of engineers or energy consumption per capita. Similarly, operationalizing the concentration of wealth as the income ratio omits other important aspects of wealth, such as total stock ownership.

Whenever a scientist operationalizes a hypothesis, two things occur: (1) The scientist gains the ability to empirically test the hypothesis by defining the variables in observable and measurable ways, and (2) In return for this gain, the study loses some of the generality of the abstract concept. To make hypotheses as comprehensive as possible, scientists want them to be general. However, *whenever someone must choose between the generality of the hypothesis and the ability to test it, the choice must always favor testability.* Without the ability to empirically test a hypothesis, the scientist cannot determine whether the hypothesis is false.

E. Falsification

The most crucial aspect of a theory, model, or hypothesis is the potential to falsify it. *Unless a study can specify a situation that would falsify the theory or hypothesis under examination, the study does not form part of a scientific enterprise.* Look at the following statements and decide which ones are potentially falsifiable through empirical observation:

1. People with higher education are more likely to have higher incomes.
2. The important decisions in the United States are made by a small group of people who are so powerful that common citizens can never discover who they are.
3. Rush Limbaugh will become the president of the United States in 2005.
4. Rush Limbaugh will go to hell.
5. Students who are born into poor families deserve full scholarships to college.

Only Statements 1 and 3 are empirical. A scientist could specify situations that would falsify them. If someone other than Rush Limbaugh were to win the presidential election in 2004, then Statement 3 (Hypothesis 3) would prove false. On the other hand, it is impossible to disprove Statement 2. If someone identifies such an elite, then the proponents of the proposition could say, "You obviously have not found the real elite, because they can hide their existence." If a rigorous search does not find an elite, then the proponents would say, "See, we told you that they were too powerful to be discovered." Statement 4 is obviously not observable. Finally, Statement 5 is a normative statement. It depends upon the values and opinions of people for its truth or falsity. Whether you accept the statement as true does not depend upon empirical observations, but upon the values you hold concerning whether people who choose the wrong parents deserve special privileges from the society.

F. Examples and Explanations

We have now defined the characteristics of an empirically testable hypothesis:

1. It specifies a relationship between two or more variables.
2. Its variables are defined in a way that specifies how they are measured.
3. Its measures are observable.
4. It must be potentially falsifiable through the specified observations.

The material that follows provides additional examples of operationalizing abstract hypotheses.

Statement 1: People with conservative ideologies are more likely than those with liberal ideologies to believe that the United States should reduce spending on welfare programs.

What are the variables in this hypothesis? They are ideology and opinion on whether welfare programs in the United States should be reduced. Ideology is an abstract variable with two abstract values: conservative and liberal. Opinion on welfare also has two values: favor a reduction and do not favor a reduction. Finally, several terms need operational definitions: *conservatives, liberals, belief that welfare spending should be reduced.*

The definitions might be:

- *Conservatives:* People who responded to a question about their choice in the 1996 congressional elections that they voted for the Republican candidate
- *Liberals:* People who responded to a question about their choice in the 1996 congressional elections that they voted for the Democratic candidate
- *Believe welfare spending should be reduced:* People who answered "Yes" when asked, "Do you agree with the statement, 'The United States national government should spend less on the Aid to Families with Dependent Children program'?"

The operationalized hypothesis is: People who state that they voted for the Republican candidate in the 1996 congressional election are more likely than people who state that they voted for the Democrat to respond "Yes" to the question, "Do you agree with the statement, 'The United States national government should spend less on the Aid to Families with Dependent Children program?'"

Notice that the verb *believe* cannot appear in an operationalized hypothesis. *Beliefs, attitudes, and feelings are not observable behaviors; they are inferred states of mind.* For this reason, expressions of beliefs, attitudes, and feelings *never* appear in operationalized hypotheses. A study must substitute an observable phenomenon for these expressions. In this case, the observable phenomenon was the answer "Yes" or "No" to the question about reducing welfare expenditures.

One frequent mistake in attempts to operationalize a hypothesis is to substitute one abstract concept for another. For example, someone might replace *conservative* with *right-wing* or *traditional.* Neither of these words is any more useful than *conservative* because they do not indicate how to measure the concepts.

Statement 2: Rich nations are more likely than poor nations to spend more on education.

The variables are the wealth of the nation and the amount of money spent on education. The terms needing operational definitions are: *rich nations, poor nations, spend more on education.*

The definitions are:

- *Rich nations:* Countries with above-average per-capita incomes
- *Poor nations:* Countries with below-average per-capita incomes
- *Spend more on education:* Spent a higher percentage of the gross national product on schools for people 18 years of age and younger in the year 1997

The operationalized hypothesis is: In 1997, countries with above-average per-capita incomes spent higher percentages of their gross national products on public schools for persons 18 years of age and younger than countries with below-average per-capita incomes. The study can test this hypothesis by looking up the values for each variable in tables published by the World Bank or the United Nations.

Assignment: Determine whether the following statements are empirical or normative statements. Operationalize each empirical statement. For each operationalization write: (1) a list of the terms that need definitions, (2) your definitions of them, (3) the operationalized hypothesis, and (4) how you might obtain the information necessary to test the hypothesis:

1. Countries in which children have adequate diets will experience more rapid economic growth than countries in which children have inadequate diets.

2. Social justice is more important than economic efficiency.

3. All societies ought to reduce their levels of air pollution.

4. Most countries spend more on protecting the safety of their citizens than they spend on educating their children.

5. Rich people are more likely than poor people to participate in politics.

NOTES

[1] Martin Diamond, "The Federalist," in *History of Political Philosophy,* 3rd ed., ed. by Leo Strauss and Joseph Cropsey (Chicago: University of Chicago Press, 1963), pp. 573–593.

[2] Ibid., p. 669.

[3] Publius, *The Federalist Papers, No. 51,* ed. by Andrew Hacker (New York: Washington Square, 1964), pp. 122–123. All citations to *The Federalist Papers* refer to this edition.

[4] Diamond, "The Federalist," p. 674.

[5] *The Federalist Papers, No. 10,* p. 17.

[6] Allen Bloom, "Jean-Jacque Rousseau," in *History of Political Philosophy,* 3rd ed., ed. by Leo Strauss and Joseph Cropsey (Chicago: University of Chicago Press, 1963), p. 565.

[7] Ibid., p. 566.

[8] Hannah Pitkin, ed., *Representation* (New York: Atherton Press, 1969), p. 52. Unless otherwise noted, all quotations in this section from Rousseau's *Social Contract* are taken from Pitkin's abbreviated version of the Gerard Hopkins translation, edited by Sir Ernest Barker (London: Oxford University Press, 1960).

[9] Rousseau, *Social Contract,* p. 55.

[10] George H. Sabine and Thomas L. Thorson, *History of Political Theory,* 4th ed. (Hinsdale, Ill.: Dryden Press, 1973), p. 541.

[11] Rousseau, *Social Contract*, Book II.

[12] Ibid., Book I.

[13] Ibid., Book I, vii.

[14] Ibid., pp. 570–572.

[15] Ibid., p. 54.

[16] Cited in Sabine and Thorson, *History of Political Theory,* p. 538.

[17] Ibid., p. 543.

[18] Robert N. Bellah, Richard Madsen, William M. Sullivan, Ann Swidler, and Steven M. Lipton, *Habits of the Heart: Individualism and Commitment in American Life* (Berkeley: University of California Press, 1985), p. 11 and p. 333.

[19] "The Responsive Communitarian Platform: Rights and Responsibilities," in *Rights and the Common Good: The Communitarian Perspective,* ed. by Amitai Etzioni (New York: St. Martin's Press, 1995), pp. 11-23.

[20] Ibid., xi.

[21] Ibid.

[22] Michael Sandel, ed. *Liberalism and Its Critics* (New York: New York University Press, 1984), p. 9.

[23] Derek L. Phillips, *Looking Backward: A Critical Appraisal of Communitarian Thought* (Princeton, N.J.: Princeton University Press, 1993), p. 180.

[24] Alasdair MacIntyre, *After Virtue*, 2nd ed. (South Bend, Ind.: Notre Dame University Press, 1984).

[25] Amitai Etzioni, *The Moral Dimension Toward a New Economics* (New York: Free Press, 1988), p. x (emphasis in the original).

[26] Michael Walzer, "Welfare, Membership, and Need," in *Liberalism and Its Critics,* ed. by Sandel, p. 200.

[27] Ibid., p. 208.

[28] Ibid., p. 215.

[29] Ibid., p. 214.

[30] Ronald Bayer and Kathleen E. Toomey, "Preventing HIV: Rights, Duties, and Partner Notification," in *Rights and the Common Good: The Communitarian Perspective,* ed. by Amitai Etzioni (New York: St. Martin's Press, 1995).

[31] Quoted by Francis W. Coker, *Recent Political Thought* (New York: D. Appleton-Century, 1934).

[32] Susan Hekman, "The Embodiment of the Subject: Feminism and the Communitarian Critique of Liberalism," *Journal of Politics* 54 (1992), pp. 1,100; 1,107.

[33] Alasdair MacIntyre, *After Virtue,* 2nd ed. (South Bend, Ind.: Notre Dame University Press, 1984), p. 213; cited in Hekman, "The Embodiment of the Subject," p. 1,104.

[34] Hekman, "The Embodiment of the Subject," p. 1,107.

[35] W. H. Newton-Smith, *The Rationality of Science* (Boston: Routledge and Keegan Paul, 1981), p. 223.

[36] Ernest Gellner, *Relativism in the Social Sciences* (Cambridge: Cambridge University Press, 1985), pp. 88–89 (emphasis in the original).

[37] Alan Zuckerman, *Doing Political Science: An Introduction to Political Analysis* (Boulder, Colo.: Westview Press, 1990), p. 1.

[38] Gellner, *Relativism in the Social Sciences,* pp. 88–89.

[39] Common Cause, "$3.3 Million in PAC Money Pays Off in Key Legislative Victory for the AMA and ADA, Common Cause Study Shows," News Release, December 3, 1982.

4

Nonconstitutional Regimes

Key Terms

Fuehrer	**Unit of Analysis**	**Contingency Table**
Folk	**Case**	**Independent Variable**
Aryans	**Variable**	**Dependent Variable**
Charismatic Leader	**Value**	**Percentagize**
The Autumn of	**Probability**	
the People		

This chapter examines totalitarian and authoritarian governments. Students sometimes consider the terms *totalitarian* and *authoritarian* to mean the same thing as the two types of regimes display important similarities. Neither guarantees civil liberties or individual rights; both frequently use torture, murder, and terror to maintain power; neither recognizes constitutional limits on its power. As this chapter shall explain, however, important differences separate the two types of regimes.

Imagine two families, each ruled by a single person who keeps all family members under strict control. In the first family, the ruler gives no justification for his actions. He simply exercises the power to punish family members who do not act as he wishes. Other family members must either work for the ruler or surrender a large portion of their wages. In return, the ruler promises to protect them from harm by anyone other than himself. So long as the family members do not challenge the ruler, they are not in danger. In addition, if a family member does something that would draw punishment from the ruler but that remains undiscovered, then the person incurs no penalty.

In the second family, the ruler convinces other family members that God has chosen him to rule them and that he, and only he, knows The Truth. For this reason, the ruler has both the power to punish family members when they disobey him and the moral obligation to punish them, because by disobeying him they have sinned. Family members must report to the ruler any sins of other family members. If some family members disobey the ruler, all others think ill of them and assist in their punishment.

In some respects, the first family is analogous to an authoritarian state. The dictator's hold on authority depends on little other than the power to force his will on others. The second family is closer to a totalitarian regime. The ruler convinces citizens of the totalitarian state that they are part of a special community and that he is their legitimate ruler. The leader bases this claim on an ideology that the citizens accept as The Truth.

In both types of regimes, rulers maintain obedience by terror and force. The citizens of these regimes, however, perceive substantial differences. In the authoritarian state, the citizens know that their treatment is unjust. In the totalitarian regime, citizens believe that the subjects of the regime's discipline deserve their punishments. Citizens in totalitarian regimes believe that they are acting morally when they punish opponents of the ruler, even if the acts they commit would be considered crimes by anyone who did not accept the regime's ideology.

Totalitarianism

We start this chapter's analysis of nonconstitutional governments with totalitarian regimes because they developed as a reaction to the liberal democratic and constitutional principles studied in the previous chapters. Few totalitarian regimes existed prior to the 20th century because potential dictators lacked sufficient technological power to control most aspects of citizens' lives. Although pharaohs, kings, and queens might have claimed divine authority, they could not reach into the homes and control the minds of their subjects.

A modern totalitarian regime, however, can intervene extensively in the lives of its citizens. The ruler justifies this intervention with the argument that he knows The Truth.[1] In contrast, most authoritarian regimes repress their citizens only to the extent necessary to enjoy the benefits of a monopoly on power.[2]

This chapter illustrates totalitarian regimes with two cases, Nazi Germany (1932–1945) and Cambodia (1975–1978). Nazi Germany, one of the first totalitarian regimes in this century, had a rightist ideology, and the dictator came to power in an industrialized democracy. The totalitarian regime in Cambodia had a leftist ideology, and it developed in a rural society to replace a military dictatorship. Because of differences in ideologies, locations, economies, and preceding governments, a comparison of the two regimes should help students to identify characteristics that are common to all totalitarian governments.

Totalitarianism in Nazi Germany

Nazi Germany provides a classic model of the modern totalitarian state, but Mussolini's Italy (1922–1944) was the first. Hitler copied the Italian model for many of the trappings of Nazism, such as the Nazi Party's military-style uniforms and paramilitary auxiliary organization. Both regimes collapsed with their defeat in World War II (Italy in 1944, Germany in 1945).

Other regimes in modern Western history may have matched Nazi Germany in savagery and brutality, at least for short times, but only the Nazis gloried in their racism and barbarity. Nazi Germany advertised and justified virtually every policy and practice that the Nuremberg War Crimes Tribunal condemned.* Adolf Hitler's autobiography, *Mein Kampf,* offered the German people a holy faith, and many Germans professed a fanatical belief in its leader, its racism, and the divine destiny of the German *"Volk."*

ADOLF HITLER

Adolf Hitler (1889–1945) fought in World War I and won the Iron Cross for bravery. Intensely nationalistic, Hitler blamed Germany's defeat and the humiliating peace treaty on Marxists, Jews, and democracy. Upon his discharge from the army, Hitler joined the German Workers' Party, a group of nationalistic war veterans. In 1921, the party changed its name to *Nazionalistische Sozialistische Arbeiters Partei* (National Socialist Workers' Party), nicknamed "Nazis" from the party's name in German. Hitler transformed the party into a paramilitary organization with the SA (storm troopers) as its military arm. In 1923, Hitler and Nazi Party storm troopers failed in an attempt to overthrow the democratic German government. The government sentenced Hitler to 5 years in prison for high treason, but he served only 9 months of his sentence. He used his time in prison to write *Mein Kampf* (My Struggle), the book that became the bible of Nazi doctrine.[3]

Germany suffered more from the worldwide depression of the 1930s than most other countries because of the reparations imposed upon that country in the peace treaty that ended World War I. The economic catastrophe hit the middle class of salaried, white-collar workers and small shopkeepers particularly hard and generated mounting social discontent. With inflation running over 1,000 percent a month, a middle-class person's life savings or pension became worthless in less than a year. Shoppers had to take literally a wheelbarrow filled with paper money to buy bread. Only with this desperate situation in mind can outside observers begin to understand the willingness of many German people to accept Adolf Hitler and his vision of the Great Aryan Race and a Greater Germany.

In countless demonstrations and rallies around the country, Hitler's frenzied oratory condemned "Jew financiers," communist radicals, and trade unions. He promised to rid Germany of the evildoers and to establish control over the labor unions. At the same time, however, Hitler promised security to the workers. In 1932, Hitler lost a race for the presidency to the legendary war hero General Paul von Hindenburg, but the Nazi Party won more seats in the German legislature than any other party. Disorder and civil violence accompanied the elections, a good deal of it fomented by Nazi storm-trooper activity. After the elections, disorder increased and the government's ability to cope with it declined. When Chancellor Kurt Schleicher resigned on January 28, 1933, President Hindenburg invited Hitler to assume the post.

---

* The Nuremberg Trials were the first international tribunal ever to accuse, try, and convict individuals of war crimes.

Once in office, Hitler disregarded democratic procedures and institutions. Two months after he took office, a fire destroyed the Reichstag (Parliament Building). Hitler whipped up popular anger by blaming the communists. In the parliamentary elections of 1933, the Nazis won a bare majority. Nazi storm troopers then surrounded the Reichstag and barred communist members from the floor. In the absence of their opposition, Hitler obtained passage of the Enabling Act which gave him sweeping powers.[†] The Nazis claimed that this act constituted a legal and constitutional transfer of power. When Hindenburg died in 1934, the offices of president and chancellor were combined, with Hitler in both. Thereafter, the will of Adolf Hitler governed Germany. He became the supreme leader (**"Fuehrer"**) with authority over the party, the government, and the people.

NAZI PARTY DOCTRINE

German Nazis followed the policies that Hitler explicitly laid out in *Mein Kampf.* Nearly 1,000 pages long, this book provided a guide for action and an excuse to commit horrible crimes. The main themes in Hitler's thought show many of the underlying principles of totalitarianism. While Stalin, Mao, and others attempted to cover up their regimes' inhuman treatment and murder of their own citizens, Hitler glorified these acts. Therefore, his words reveal more than the statements of other totalitarian leaders about the lengths to which a totalitarian regime will go to impose its utopian dream.

Folk and State   Mussolini had earlier described the Italian nation as "an organism having ends, life, and means of acting superior to those of the separate individuals or groups of individuals which compose it."[4] For Mussolini, this living organism of the nation was an abstraction, signifying the insignificance of an individual compared with the imperial glory of the state. For Hitler, the German **Folk,** the relationship between the country's culture and its people, was more real than the chair on which you are sitting. Every aspect of German culture—art, literature, music, science, economic activity, and government—expressed the spirit of the Folk. For Hitler, individual Germans had value *only* as functioning parts (organs) of the living collective body.

Hitler believed that race distinguishes one folk from another. He described three different kinds of races: **Aryans** (those who created German culture), Jews ("parasites," who would destroy culture), and auxiliaries. He defined auxiliaries as races who gave labor and services to Aryans. Hitler considered them inferior to Aryans but superior to Jews. He identified the most important task of the state as preserving the purity of the blood of the Aryan race. To carry on its God-given mission, the Aryan race needed more land. A popular slogan made Hitler's purposes clear: "Today Germany belongs to us. Tomorrow, the whole world!"

[†] The act was officially entitled "An Act to Relieve the Distress of the People and of the Reich." It gave the cabinet unlimited legislative power, including the right to depart from provisions of the Constitution. It also provided that the powers of the president could not be curtailed. See Franz Neumann, *Behemoth* (New York: Octagon, 1983). After the passage of the Enabling Act, the German parliament wielded no power. Its infrequent meetings were attended by barely one-fourth of its members.

Leadership   Hitler believed that the mass public, including the German public, responds not to reason but to emotion:

> It is more difficult to undermine faith than knowledge, love succumbs to change less than to respect, hatred is more durable than aversion, and at all times the driving force of the most important changes in this world has been found less in a scientific knowledge . . . but rather in a fanaticism dominating them and in a hysteria which drove them forward.[5]

Hitler also believed that a natural elite constitutes the top layer of the mass of people. This elite is not identical with any existing social class. At the apex of this natural elite stands the leader *(der Fuehrer)*. He is "the unifying link that joins state, party, and people."[6] He leads not by virtue of his wisdom, his political skill, or any particular quality he possesses. Even less is he leader because the people choose him to lead. The leader emerges by natural selection because he is a leader.

Max Weber's description of the **charismatic leader**[7] fits Hitler perfectly. Followers of a charismatic leader do not accept his authority by tradition or because he holds a position of responsibility in some formal structure of power. They respond to the leader as a unique person, because they recognize what they consider to be qualities of leadership. They accept the leader's authority and offer loyalty and obedience because of what they think the leader is. The charismatic leader's relationship to the people has a mystical, rather than political or bureaucratic, basis. It is a matter of feeling, not reason.

THE POWER OF THE LEADER'S WORDS

Hitler demonstrated remarkable skill at manipulating the sentiments and feelings of people through virtuoso oratory and high-tech stagecraft. Hitler stressed the importance of dealing with humans in a mass. He advised that,

> The mass meeting is necessary if only for the reason that in it the individual, who in becoming an adherent of a new movement feels lonely and is easily seized with the fear of being alone, receives for the first time the picture of a great community, something that has a comforting and encouraging effect on most people.[8]

Hitler also stressed that the spoken word works better than written language:

> The pen has always been reserved to motivate . . . changes theoretically. But the power which set the greatest historical avalanches of political and religious nature sliding [is] . . . the magic force of the spoken word alone. The great masses of a nation will always and only succumb to the force of the spoken word.[9]

For the content of verbal propaganda, Hitler was the first to state that a leader can persuade people to a particular point of view more effectively by telling a big lie than a little one:

> . . . [S]ince the great masses of a people may be more corrupt in the bottom of their hearts than they will be consciously and intentionally bad, therefore with the primitive simplicity of their minds they will more easily fall victims to a great lie than to a small one, since they themselves perhaps also lie sometimes in little things, but would certainly still be too much ashamed of too great lies.[10]

THE NAZI REGIME

Guided, presumably, by Hitler's vision of the Folkish State and the policies that he considered necessary to implement its principles, the Nazis radically restructured German society. Absolute power of government was the Nazis' organizational principle; no area of life escaped that absolute control. The Nazis destroyed every institution of the short-lived German democracy that preceded them. Parliament virtually stopped meeting, since it was powerless to do anything if it did meet. Courts lost all independence. At the same time, new laws extended government jurisdiction into social, economic, and private life. Most people (except Jews, convicted criminals, and some other "inferior types") could still vote on some occasions. These votes were, however, plebiscites that allowed only one choice—to vote for approval of some government action.

Hitler understood clearly the value of political socialization. In education, he claimed that the government is "responsible for all factors influencing the mental life of the nation."[11] Government dictated not only the structure and procedures of education, but also every aspect of school administration—curriculum, textbooks, and teaching. "No boy or girl must leave school without having been led to the ultimate knowledge of the necessity and nature of the purity of the blood."[12] Of art, Hitler wrote, "The totalitarian state does not recognize the separate existence of art. . . . [I]t demands that artists take a positive position toward the state."[13]

In the government's ultimate intrusion into the lives of German men, women, and children, the government enforced rigid policies toward the perceived racial enemies of the Aryan race, the Jews. A series of laws enacted between 1935 and 1938 stripped them of their status as citizens and made them "state subjects." New laws prohibited marriages between Aryans and persons with one-quarter or more Jewish blood. The law also excluded Jews from all professions and many occupations, and it legally confined them to ghettoes.

In 1939, the government settled on the policy of extermination as the "final solution to the Jewish problem." Between then and the end of World War II in 1945, Germany murdered over 6 million Jews. It also murdered 6 million others who were political enemies of the Nazis and members of other "inferior races" (gypsies, Slavs, and other eastern Europeans). The state dispatched these victims wholesale by gas or gunshot in such camps as Belsen, Buchenwald, Dachau, Maidanek, and Treblinka. Before killing the victims, death camp personnel or slave laborers stripped them and deprived them of all possessions, especially jewelry, watches, or any other valuables. Before disposing of the victim's bodies (by wholesale cremation or mass burial), camp workers ripped teeth with silver or gold fillings from the mouths of the corpses.

The Nazi regime came to an end in spring 1945, $12\frac{1}{2}$ years after it was born, when Allied troops from the West met Russian troops at the Elbe River. An Occupation Government replaced the Nazi institutions with authority divided over four occupation zones (American, British, French, and Russian).

Communism and Totalitarianism

While *Mein Kampf* clearly foreshadowed the brutal acts of the Nazi regime, it may seem strange that the utopian and humanist vision outlined in Marx's writings could serve to justify totalitarianism. First in the Soviet Union and then in eastern Europe, North Korea, China, Cuba, and Cambodia, Marx's humanist dreams became totalitarian nightmares. Rather than retracing the development of the Soviet and Chinese regimes, the next section will examine a more recent example of communist totalitarianism from Cambodia.

Totalitarianism in Democratic Kampuchea (Cambodia)

In many respects, the Vietnam war harmed Cambodia more than it harmed either the United States or Vietnam. The rise and fall of the pro-American Lon Nol government in Cambodia and the rise to power of the communist Khmer Rouge army were related closely to the U.S. involvement in Vietnam.[14] The communist army, under the leadership of Pol Pot, defeated Lon Nol's army and took control of the capital city, Phnom Penh, on April 17, 1975. The new government renamed the country Democratic Kampuchea (DK) and initiated a war against its own people. In this war, the leaders sought to create a communist utopia by removing the causes of class conflict. According to Pol Pot's interpretation of Marxism, the principal causes of class conflict are private property, money, urban life, and corruption by foreign influences (especially those from Vietnam).

Shortly after taking control of Phnom Phen, Pol Pot ordered the evacuation of the 2½ million people living there.[15] The communist leadership insisted that this evacuation was necessary to escape the threat of American air strikes and the lack of food in the city. Certainly these reasons have some basis in reality, as the people could find little food in the city and additional supplies were unlikely to come from outside DK. The United States had been the major source of food for Phnom Phen for several years, but it was unlikely to assist the communist regime of Pol Pot.

Although the government may have cited good reasons to evacuate the city, its real reasons had more to do with the ideology of the ruling party than with physical necessity. The evacuation included both disabled and able-bodied people, and the former group quickly died. The evacuees found little food in the countryside, and the urban population sent there had neither the experience nor the necessary tools to grow food. During the next 3 years, one-third of the Cambodian population died of starvation, disease, or execution![16]

ELIMINATION OF *POTENTIAL* COUNTERREVOLUTIONARIES

The major goal for the evacuation was to "re-educate" the Cambodian people and eliminate those who would not become good citizens in the new utopia. In theory, the new government classified the population into three categories, called *Full Rights, Candidate,* and *Depositee*.[17] People with full rights included peasants and factory workers. Candidates were the upper middle-class peasants and the small shopkeepers. Depositees were capitalists and members of foreign minorities.

Once the evacuees reached the rural areas, the real class distinction was a dichotomy. One category, called the *new people,* were the evacuees from urban areas and those who lived in areas previously controlled by Vietnamese communists. The other category, the *old people,* included rural peasants who had lived in areas controlled by the Khmer Rouge before the end of the war.[18] The regime refused to allocate medicine or doctors to the new people. Large numbers of these people received the equivalent of death sentences when the regime sent them to carve new villages and fields out of forests but did not give them the tools to accomplish the task.

THE UTOPIAN VISION AND THE CORRUPTION OF THOUGHTS

Why did the communist regime choose to kill so many of its own citizens? This choice reflected the leaders' assumption that once a person had been corrupted, that individual was unlikely to understand and obey the true vision of communism. The class of corrupted people included anyone who wore glasses, had a high school education, had lived in a city, was associated with a past government, spoke a foreign language, owned land beyond the smallest family plot, or practiced a religion. A person was also corrupt if a family member had one of these characteristics. Once corrupted, an individual became a potential threat to the utopian vision of the Khmer Rouge leaders.

Between 1975 and 1978, out of an estimated population of 5.4 million, between 1.8 million and 2.5 million people died.[19] The leaders of Democratic Kampuchea used cadres of very young boys to discipline and execute the enemies of the state. These young people beat victims to death, force-fed prisoners their own excrement, and suffocated them with plastic bags (to save ammunition).[20] Pol Pot's forces were particularly hard on their past allies. They murdered Cambodian communists who had fled to Vietnam to avoid persecution by the pro-American regime when those people returned to help the Khmer Rouge. Pol Pot also ordered the massacre of citizens who aided Vietnamese troops fighting the Americans.[21]

Pol Pot's totalitarian state wanted to control the thoughts as well as the actions of its population. Recall from Chapter 3 that Marx and Engels argued that all art, culture, education, and religion are merely by-products of economic relations. This implies that a communist utopia will require new art, culture, and education appropriate to a classless, propertyless society. In the Soviet Union and China, Lenin, Stalin, and Mao had aggressively eliminated or re-educated "counterrevolutionary" elements of their own countries. The Khmer Rouge felt that the Soviet Union and China had failed in reaching the utopian vision of Marx and Engels. Therefore, leaders reasoned, their own war against counterrevolutionary elements would have to eclipse what Lenin, Stalin, and Mao had done.

To accomplish this goal, the government would have to transform people's thought, eliminate past economic structures, and eradicate past cultures. The Khmer Rouge government attempted to force changes in the ideological superstructure in order to safeguard the economic structures they desired. To achieve this, the leaders abolished education beyond the level necessary to work in a peasant-based, agricultural society.[22] The government attempted to destroy all family and religious ties. They were not satisfied with the state managing the economy; they felt that the state must radically restructure economic activity. The government eliminated markets, money, all independent exchange, private gardening, independent food gathering, and movement beyond one's state-assigned location. In short, the leaders of the Khmer Rouge government, particularly Pol Pot, did not wish to wait for changes in the economic structure to create the appropriate ideological superstructure; they decided to forcefully eliminate all vestiges of the past superstructure and the people who had been influenced by it.

Pol Pot's draconian policies led to dissension among the party leadership. Some wanted to reintroduce some market activity, gradually restore urban life, and relax discipline in the work camps. Pol Pot saw treason in any attempt to change his policies, and he successfully fought attempts to diverge from his chosen course. Periodic waves of arrests and executions of party members opposed to Pol Pot swept through the country in 1977 and 1978. In summer 1978, a civil war broke out between Pol Pot's faction and the party leaders in the eastern areas of the country closest to Vietnam. Pol Pot's forces won this civil war and then executed all the soldiers who fought against them.[23] During this period, Pol Pot's forces killed as many as 100,000 people, most of them peasants who lived in the area controlled by the dissidents. Pol Pot ordered that one-third of the remaining population be marched into western Cambodia. He announced that these people had "Khmer bodies with Vietnamese minds."[24]

Vietnam ultimately invaded Cambodia and established a puppet regime on January 8, 1979. The new government renamed the country the People's Republic of Kampuchea and ended the reign of terror by Pol Pot's forces.

What Is Totalitarianism?

This question has no easy answer. A description can begin with the characteristics shared by the two cases discussed so far in the chapter.

First, a totalitarian regime advocates an all-encompassing ideology with a single party and a single leader. The government promotes the belief in a single Truth that the leader knows. German Nazis accepted the mishmash of dogmatic assertions in *Mein Kampf* as The Truth of Nazism. The followers of Pol Pot believed that his interpretation of Marx and Engels identified The Truth. When people in a totalitarian state suggest that the leader's interpretation of The Truth is incorrect, this justifies their expulsion or death.[25]

The second critical characteristic of a totalitarian regime is a fully developed instrument of state terror to demonstrate the complete power of the state and to spread fear among the people. In Germany, Hitler used the Gestapo. Stalin used the KGB. Mao used the Red Army and the Red Guards. Pol Pot used both the military and gangs of teenagers to create terror among the citizens. All totalitarian states claim the right to murder citizens whose ideas *might be* detrimental to the state. This leads to a disregard for individual life. Perhaps the best example of the willingness to sacrifice lives occurred in Democratic Kampuchea. Although Germany, the Soviet Union, China, and Democratic Kampuchea all murdered millions of their own citizens, the particular terror of Democratic Kampuchea arose from the leaders' assumption about how easily people could become corrupted. If individuals had any contact with people who had different views of society, that contact was a sufficient reason for the state to kill them.

The final general characteristic of a totalitarian regime is the monopolistic control of communications, weapons, and all organizations.[26] The totalitarian state attempts to destroy the old social institutions and social norms and replace them with institutions designed by the new regime. The actual result of this process is a citizen who is alienated and alone without the support of ties to family, church, or other institutions. This fact highlights an ironic result of totalitarian rule: A regime that initially attracts citizens by appeals to patriotism and community ultimately makes citizens more isolated and fearful than they were before. In an attempt to escape from their frustration with liberal democracy, the German people embraced a society that left them not alone and autonomous in their choices, but alone, persecuted, and without choices.

Pol Pot and the other leaders of Democratic Kampuchea saw the creation of a sense of isolation as a necessary step to the creation of the new citizen. The regime destroyed religion, family ties, urban structures, art, and literature. It made education a crime. Finally, it placed the very young, who presumably were less corrupted by the past, in control of adults.

These totalitarian regimes teach some essential lessons for citizens in contemporary liberal democracies. First, when nationalism, militarism, and racism combine their enormously strong and irrational messages, everyone is in danger, even the supporters of the messages and the regime. Second, anyone in politics who claims to know The Truth presents a threat to democracy.

Authoritarianism

Authoritarianism is the most common form of government today, and it has been the dominant form of government throughout written human history. Chapter 1 explained that authoritarian government may have been the first type of regime in agrarian societies because it was logical for roving bandits to become stationary bandits. Such a change benefited both the bandits and the victims of their robbery. The analysis of a stationary bandit's situation applies to contemporary regimes, as well, demonstrating that most authoritarian regimes pursue straightforward goals. The rulers wish to eliminate political opposition, collect taxes, maintain order, enforce property rights, and supply collective goods that will increase their own wealth by increasing the wealth of the people they rule. In other words, the wise stationary bandit will maximize her own expected wealth over the length of time that she expects her rule and that of her heirs to survive.

This image of rulers as interested only in wealth maximization is, of course, a simplistic portrayal. Some rulers clearly act like stationary bandits and steal all they can from their subjects; other rulers put power, prestige, their place in history, and the well-being of their citizens ahead of personal wealth. These differences lead to an important question: Are some authoritarian institutional arrangements more likely than others to lead to better outcomes for citizens?

Thousands of authoritarian regimes have ruled in human history, and new ones emerge each year. Each regime partially reflects the history of the country and its current circumstances. However, some characteristics appear in almost all authoritarian regimes. First, the rulers do not depend on elections to remain in office. Second, they resort to repression if political opposition threatens their rule. They take this step regardless of any constitutional provisions that prohibit such repression. Third, they eliminate as many independent organizations and institutions as possible.

Until the end of the 19th century, one of the most common types of authoritarian rule was the monarchy. Monarchies are governments in which the succession from one ruler to the next is based on kinship to the previous ruler. Mancur Olson's analysis of stationary bandits indicates why both the ruler and the subjects may prefer monarchies to other types of authoritarian regimes. A monarch may desire the praise of future historians and continued wealth and prestige for his children and grandchildren; this encourages decision making with a long time frame. This priority will lead the monarch to pursue policies that improve the long-term wealth and happiness of subjects, since these policies also increase the wealth and stability of the monarchy.

Chapter 2 showed that monarchs often claim divine right to justify their rule. In other words, they claim that God chose them to rule. If the citizens accept this claim, then the rulers are likely to be seen as legitimate by their subjects. This improves the wealth of the society, because legitimate rulers do not need to invest as much of their resources to maintain their positions. If the citizens in a society did not see the ruler as legitimate, then the ruler would have to either buy loyalty or suppress rebellion. In either case, both the ruler and the subjects suffer a substantial net loss.

Although divine right monarchs seem preferable to alternative forms of stationary bandits, the view of monarchs as legitimate rulers has almost totally disappeared. The forces of rationalism, secularism, and democracy attacked the idea of divine right, and today only a few regimes in the Middle East have governments based on this principle.

Military dictators have replaced monarchs as the most typical form of rule by a single individual. Like monarchs, dictators can attempt to rule in the interests of all citizens, or they can attempt to maximize their own interests. Unfortunately, social science has been unable to predict authoritarians who will become enlightened leaders and who will become tyrants. More important, even when dictators attempt to rule in the best interests of their citizens, they have not developed a method for selecting successors who will continue their benevolent rule. Box 4.1 compares two 20th-century dictators, Anastasio Somoza and Gazi Mustafa Kemal (Atatürk), who chose different goals for their rule.

MILITARY RULE

Some scholars argue that authoritarian regimes are more likely to bring about rapid economic growth in less industrialized or rapidly industrializing countries. These observers contend that authoritarian regimes can prevent labor unrest and the overly rapid spread of political participation.[27] They argue that authoritarian regimes can constrain the demands of the urban labor force for higher wages and maintain the level of political stability necessary to attract foreign and domestic investment.

Those who accept any or all of these arguments often see rule by military officers as an attractive alternative to democracy. In the 1960s and early 1970s, many scholars argued that less industrialized countries would be better off ruled by soldiers rather than civilians. These scholars argued that military leaders possess organizational skills superior to those in the civilian sector. The nationalistic orientation of the military can help the country overcome religious, ethnic, and tribal divisions.[28] Also, the military

BOX 4.1

A Tale of Two Dictators

Nicaragua and Turkey provide two examples to illustrate the difference between a dictator who is a "stationary bandit" and one who attempts to rule in the interest of his country. A dictator ruled each country during the 1930s, and each dictatorship grew out of a violent history. Turkey was fortunate; its ruler was Gazi Mustafa Kemal. Later known as Atatürk (father of the Turks), Kemal created the nation of Turkey from the remains of the Ottoman Empire and transformed the country from a traditional society to a modern one. Nicaragua was less fortunate; its ruler was Anastasio Somoza García.

Atatürk and Somoza differed in how they came to power. Atatürk led a popular revolution against a monarchy that was a puppet of the imperialistic European powers. He defeated the Western-backed army of Greece in 1921 and forced the withdrawal of European forces from Turkey. Atatürk emerged from this struggle as the creator and legitimate ruler of the Turkish nation. Somoza was installed in power by the dominant imperialist nation of the Western Hemisphere, the United States. During the entire period in which Somoza and his two sons governed Nicaragua, U.S. power guaranteed their rule. Partially as a result of this dependence, Somoza never enjoyed the legitimacy in Nicaragua that Atatürk had in Turkey.

The two men also differed in their visions for their countries. Atatürk was the first of the modern dictators of a less industrialized country to devote his efforts to modernization. He wrote, "A person should not work for himself, but for those who come after him"[a]; he clearly attempted to follow his own advice. Atatürk's great popularity and strong charisma assured that he had little need to repress political opposition.[b] He could have used his immense popularity to establish himself as a stationary bandit. However, instead of devoting his efforts to generating wealth for himself, Atatürk worked to create a sovereign nation based on scientific values and peaceful coexistence. He renounced any imperialist ambitions for Turkey and ended the near-permanent state of war that had characterized the previous two decades of the Ottoman Empire.

Atatürk secularized public schools, separated church and state, simplified the Turkish alphabet and converted it from Arabic to Roman script, revised the legal code, and mandated legal equality for women. Dankart Rustow writes that, "Above all, Atatürk created a set of institutions that . . . responded effectively to the contingencies of the present, and equipped his people for the challenges of an uncertain future."[c]

Whereas Atatürk did not make himself wealthy, Somoza's major goals centered on personal wealth and power for himself rather than progress for the Nicaraguan people. Bernard Diederich writes that Somoza's assets reached staggering proportions; he seemed to own everything in sight. People who wanted to start businesses in Nicaragua had to bribe Somoza or include him as a partner. Businesses that attempted to compete with Somoza's enterprises soon closed their doors. Somoza stated of himself and his family, "Give us a finger and we take a hand. Give us a hand and we take an arm."[d] The corruption of the Somoza family wasted national resources, alienated and squeezed out local businesspeople, and skimmed off foreign aid and loans.[e] In his first 10 years in office, Somoza amassed a personal fortune of $120 million.[f]

To maintain himself in power, Somoza used his National Guard to torture and terrorize his political enemies. Ultimately, Somoza made himself such an inviting target that he became the first Nicaraguan president to die through assassination. Somoza's younger son, Anastasio Somoza, Jr., was deposed from power by Marxist guerillas, who took their name, the Sandanistas, from a leader murdered by the elder Somoza.

---

[a] Enver Ziya Karal, "The Principles of Kemalism," in *Atatürk: Founder of a Modern State,* ed. by Ali Kazancigil and Ergun Ozbuden (Hamden, Conn.: Archon, 1981), p. 14.

[b] Barry Rubin, *Modern Dictators: Third World Coup Makers, Strongmen, and Populist Tyrants* (New York: McGraw-Hill, 1987), p. 61.

[c] Dankart A. Rustow, "Atatürk as an Institution-Builder," in *Atatürk: Founder of a Modern State,* p. 57.

[d] Bernard Diederich, *Somoza, and the Legacy of U.S. Involvement in Central America* (New York: Dutton) p. 34.

[e] Rubin, *Modern Dictators,* p. 19.

[f] Ibid., p. 25.

---

requires new technology to remain effective, so it may more willingly accept the changes in society that technology requires. All of these factors would appear to make the military an ideal institution to help modernize a poor country.

In an influential study published in 1970, Eric Nordlinger found that military regimes in the least industrialized countries increased industrial growth, agricultural productivity, and levels of education.[29] However, other studies have failed to replicate Nordlinger's findings, and some have found the opposite relationship.[30] In addition, military regimes appear no more able than civilian governments to prevent abuses of civil liberties and political violence by one ethnic or tribal group against another. Finally, military governments are more likely than civilian regimes to violate the rights of their own citizens.

SINGLE-PARTY CIVILIAN REGIMES

In another common type of authoritarian regime, a single political party may impose its rule on a country. An earlier section of this chapter described how a totalitarian party can attempt to coordinate government actions and mobilize the population. A single ruling party in an authoritarian state can do the same things. Just as the army might integrate various tribes and ethnic groups into a nation, a single national party might undertake the same project.

A regime that allows only a single political party may seem to have trouble with legitimacy. People in other societies, however, may see political competition as an indication of weakness in the moral vision of the state. If the people see their society as a community with a common goal and a single public interest, then at least one of the competitors for power must support goals that are not in the public interest; such a threat to the state should be suppressed.

Military and revolutionary leaders have often attempted to rule by organizing government as a single political party and to use that party to mobilize mass support. For example, Atatürk governed Turkey unopposed from 1925 to 1945 through the Republican People's Party. The party in a single-party regime is a personal organization that a dictator puts together to support administration of the state and to help maintain power. Iraq, Syria, Indonesia, Libya, Ghana, and Tanzania are examples of such states.

Because of the almost universal legitimacy of democracy in the contemporary world, many single-party authoritarian regimes organize elections. These elections will not likely change who rules the country. Rather, elections provide opportunities for the authoritarian ruler to demonstrate her ability to mobilize popular support. In some countries, however, the dominant party is more open to criticism and to sharing power with people outside the party. This sharing of power may ultimately lead to political democracy.

KENYA AND MEXICO: EXAMPLES OF
SINGLE-PARTY AUTHORITARIAN REGIMES

Because of the universal appeal of democracy, single-party states often claim to be moving toward competitive democracies. Kenya and Mexico are two countries in which the ruling parties make this claim. In Kenya, Jomo Kenyatta ruled from 1963 to 1978. To assist him in modernizing the country, he founded a political party, the Kenyan African National Union (KANU). In reality, the party rarely did anything other than mobilize voters for the national elections. It allowed competition among members of KANU, but it did not allow other parties to develop. When Kenyatta died, his successor, Daniel Arap Moi, attempted to integrate the party and the government. He ordered all civil servants to join KANU and announced that only members of the party could hold government jobs.[31] To maintain the appearance of democracy, Kenya held multiparty elections in 1993, but it engaged in substantial fraud to ensure that its candidates won the presidency and controlled the legislature.

Mexico is an example of an authoritarian, single-party regime that allows competition from other political parties. The Institutionalized Party of the Revolution (PRI) came to power in 1929 and has kept power ever since. President Plutarco Elias Calles founded the PRI to serve as a mechanism to reduce violent conflict among contenders for power and to administer the government.[32] The PRI mobilizes the masses, administers and coordinates the government, and recruits future leaders. Through this work, it has made Mexico an anomaly in world politics by institutionalizing peaceful succession from one authoritarian ruler to another.

Every 6 years, a new president comes to power, and this ruler wields exceptional authority. Through the mechanisms of the PRI, the president controls all of the country's other political institutions.[33] Despite the current president's major role in selecting his successor, once a president leaves office, that successor holds and exercises the real power. Unfortunately, while the institutionalized succession process generally has allowed for peaceful transfers of power within the party, it also has led the president to act as a stationary bandit with a short time frame. Lopez Portillo, president of Mexico from 1976 to 1982, used his position to increase his wealth by $3 billion.[34]

In the 1988 elections, the PRI suffered major losses in the national legislature and in state and local government races. For the first time, the PRI's presidential candidate received less than a majority of the votes. Although the PRI's candidate, Carlos Salinas, still became president, he could count on only a bare majority of legislative seats won by the PRI. The 1988 elections made clear that fair balloting would remove the PRI's 60-year hold on power. In addition to the PRI's problems at the polls, a revolutionary movement in the south of the country has shown the weakness of Mexico's army and the questionable legitimacy of the PRI. In the 1994 elections, the PRI's chosen candidate was assassinated while campaigning and the party had to replace him with a less popular candidate. The PRI won the election amid widespread allegations of fraud.

At the same time that the PRI was losing its monopoly on political power, it voluntarily gave up control of a substantial portion of its economic power. The government privatized numerous state enterprises in the early 1990s. It also signed the North American Free Trade Agreement (NAFTA), which further integrated the Mexican economy with those of the United States and Canada. The PRI faces a critical challenge as it determines whether a decentralized, free-market economy must inevitably lead to institutions and organizations that will successfully challenge for political power.

Democratization

Although Kenya, Mexico, and other single-party, authoritarian states may be moving slowly toward democracy, other countries have shown much more rapid movement. The last 25 years have witnessed an astonishing increase in the number of democratic governments and a restructuring of much of the political world. The 1970s brought the end of western Europe's last three dictatorships in Spain, Portugal, and Greece. By the end of the 1980s, military regimes had abandoned power in South America. Central American countries such as El Salvador and Nicaragua ended their civil wars and held free elections. In Asia, South Korea and the Philippines had moved from dictatorships to more democratic regimes.

The most extraordinary political changes occurred in the Soviet Union and eastern Europe. The political and economic reforms begun in the Soviet Union in 1980 by Communist Party Secretary General Mikhail Gorbachev encouraged the fall of Communist Party dictatorships in Poland, Hungary, East Germany, Bulgaria, Czechoslovakia, and Romania. By 1991, many nations that previously had been parts of the Soviet Union were independent nation-states. Some of them had instituted democracies.

Eastern Europeans call the autumn of 1989 **The Autumn of the People.** During this brief season, numerous Communist Party dictatorships that had operated as puppet governments of the Soviet Union fell to prodemocracy forces. Perhaps the earliest indication that the Communist Party was going to lose control of eastern Europe occurred in Poland

in 1976. The event was the development of the Solidarity labor movement, an organization outside the control of the Communist Party. In 1981, political crises in Poland led to a coup d'etat that replaced the civilian communist regime with a communist military dictatorship led by General Wojciech Jarulzelski. Even direct military repression, however, could not prevent the prodemocracy forces from continuing to organize and protest. A general strike in the summer of 1988 led General Jarulzelski to compromise with Solidarity and share power with noncommunists. To the surprise of many, Gorbachev did not send Soviet troops to put down this move toward greater democracy.

The event that precipitated the rapid fall of the other communist regimes in eastern Europe was the decision by the communist government in Hungary to allow East Germans to refuse to return home and instead to proceed to West Germany. The communist government in Czechoslovakia followed suit and allowed the East Germans to board trains bound for West Germany. The East German government then made a fatal mistake. It agreed to let the trains containing the refugees pass through East Germany, while it organized demonstrations along the railway to denounce and humiliate the refugees. The demonstrators, however, cheered the trains. The government-organized demonstration turned into an antigovernment rally. Antigovernment demonstrations spread across East Germany and then throughout Poland, Hungary, Czechoslovakia, and Bulgaria.

In rapid succession, Communist Party regimes in these countries resigned from power. To the surprise of most who studied the Soviet Union, Gorbachev again declined to send Soviet troops into these countries to reestablish communist regimes. He also refused to act decisively to put down anti-Soviet demonstrations in Estonia, Latvia, and Lithuania, three countries that Stalin had forced into the Soviet Union in 1940.

In 1990, several high-ranking military and Communist Party leaders decided to overthrow Gorbachev and revoke his liberalization efforts. The coup leaders believed that unless they prevented him, Gorbachev would allow democracy to spread even in Russia, leading to the breakup of the Soviet Union. The overthrow failed when the Soviet army refused to back the coup leaders and instead backed the prodemocracy forces. This failed coup marked the end of the Soviet Union. In a short period of time, many nations that previously had been absorbed into the Soviet Union declared their independence and the Soviet Union ceased to exist. Russia, once again, became a nation-state.

Prodemocracy forces were not successful everywhere. In June 1989, students staged a mass prodemocracy demonstration in Tiananmen Square in Beijing. The Chinese Army crushed it. The image of the lone demonstrator blocking an armored column (see page 136 in Chapter 5) and the huge replica of the Statue of Liberty constructed by the students will remain in the memories of those who saw the events unfold on international television.

Authoritarian regimes continue to rule most African countries as well as the countries of Southeast Asia. By no stretch of the imagination could observers classify Honduras or Guatemala as democratic. Nevertheless, the last 25 years saw repressive authoritarian regimes succumb to democratic pressures in countries as diverse as Poland, Nicaragua, Chile, South Africa, and Russia.

WHY DID THE SOVIET EMPIRE FALL?

Political scientists would like to say that they accurately predicted the rapid demise of the Soviet Union and the sudden emergence of more than 20 new nations. However, as late as the spring of 1989, neither journalists, political scientists, or the intelligence agencies of Western governments predicted that the following autumn would change the world. Political scientists are still trying to understand what happened.

Perhaps Adam Przeworski best explained the rapid fall of the Soviet empire with an old Soviet joke:

> A man is distributing leaflets in Red Square. He is stopped by a policeman, who confiscates them only to discover that they are blank. "What are you spreading? They are blank. Nothing is written!" the surprised guardian of order exclaims. "Why write?" is the answer. "Everybody knows . . ."[35]

Przeworski goes on to argue that the Soviet empire fell for the same reasons that authoritarian regimes fell elsewhere: the people rejected the legitimacy of an authoritarian regime. In the Soviet Union, the people realized that the government had failed to protect the very people who needed protection according to the communist ideology, the working class. No one could present a legitimate reason to keep the state planners and party bureaucrats in power.

Of course, authoritarian regimes often survive without legitimacy. They survive as long as the military and police are willing to support the rulers and have sufficient force to repress rebellion. The authoritarian rulers in the Soviet Union and eastern Europe did not use their armies to put down the anticommunist rebellion for two reasons. First, by 1989, the bureaucrats no longer believed their own rhetoric. More important, the bureaucrats did not have the guns, and the armies refused to engage in repression.[36]

TABLE 4.1

CITIZEN SUPPORT FOR CIVIL AND POLITICAL RIGHTS IN EUROPEAN COUNTRIES AND MOSCOW

Right	France	Germany	Denmark	Britain	Moscow
Freedom of speech	75.9%	89.7%	74.9%	67.5%	77.0%
Freedom of association	59.7	61.9	63.8	67.2	50.0
Right to privacy	95.7	95.5	94.9	89.2	80.6
Right to property	79.2	86.2	75.5	81.5	90.7
Right to work	95.9	85.3	78.4	85.3	93.7
Right to education	95.6	92.1	87.3	95.9	95.0
Percentage who claim all rights	26.8	26.8	11.1	9.5	36.3

Source: "Democratic Values and the Transformation of the Soviet Union" by James L. Gibson, Raymond M. Duch, and Kent L. Tedin, *Journal of Politics* 54:2, pp. 329–343; by permission of the author and the University of Texas Press.

CAN THE NEW DEMOCRACIES SUCCEED?

What factors will decide whether the newly democratic nations built from the rubble of the Soviet system will remain democratic and whether the newly independent nations will become democracies? Many political scientists have argued that a nation needs a particular political culture to allow stable democracy to emerge. This culture must provide general support for democratic norms, tolerance for opposition groups, and a belief in civil liberties and political rights for everyone.[37]

Recent survey research shows little difference between democratic and nondemocratic countries in mass support for the basic ideas of democratic government.[38] Tables 4.1 and 4.2 reveal the prevalence of democratic values in most of the world. Table 4.1 shows the support for basic political and economic rights in western European democracies and

TABLE 4.2

SUPPORT FOR PARTICIPATION RIGHTS OF REGIME CRITICS AND ACTS OF CIVIL DISOBEDIENCE AMONG CITIZENS IN CENTRAL AMERICAN COUNTRIES

	Costa Rica	Nicaragua	El Salvador	Panama	Honduras	Guatemala	Average for Region
Support for Participation Rights[a]	5.79	5.69	5.21	7.10	6.99	4.60	5.92
Support for Civil Disobedience[b]	2.13	2.42	2.12	1.96	3.41	2.01	2.34

[a]Index of citizen support for participatory rights of regime critics (tolerance); range 0–10.

[b]Index of citizen support for acts of civil disobedience; range 0–10.

Source: John Booth and Patricia Bayer Richard, "Repression, Political Participation, and Support for Democratic Civil Liberties in Urban Central America" (Paper presented at the annual meeting of the Midwest Political Science Association, Chicago, April 1994).

in Moscow *prior* to the fall of the Soviet Union. Clearly, the people of Moscow supported most rights more vigorously than the citizens of Britain did. Similarly, Table 4.2 demonstrates rather uniform support for democratic norms among citizens of Central American countries. People's opinions do not differ despite Costa Rica's long history of stable democracy and similarly long histories of authoritarian rule in Honduras and Guatemala. If these surveys accurately measured support for democracy, then it had won the ideological battle in Russia prior to the fall of the Soviet Union. The surveys also show that democratic norms can enjoy high public support, even when a dictatorship controls a country.

RELIGIOUS, ETHNIC, AND NATIONALISTIC CONFLICTS

Although the legitimacy of democracy may be acknowledged worldwide, in certain conflicts, opposing sides have extreme difficulty accepting defeat at the polls or negotiating with each other. Earlier chapters explained that constitutional democracies often place some issues that divide citizens beyond majority rule. Three divisions that create great difficulties for democratic government are religion, ethnicity, and nationalism. These divisions present problems because people's psychological ties to particular religious, ethnic, or national groups help them to identify who they are. Paradoxically, because people typically do not choose their nationalities, ethnic backgrounds, or religions, these characteristics have tremendous meaning to them. These deep psychological attachments discourage compromises between the different groups and raise the stakes of political outcomes.

The critical components of the democratic culture may be tolerance of disliked groups and willingness to acknowledge that others must enjoy rights equal to one's own.[39] A review of internal national conflicts around the world demonstrates the critical roles of religion, ethnicity, and nationalism. Even when they do not spark civil wars, these issues generate severe problems for governments. In Germany, for example, the neo-Nazis justify their hate-filled speech and sadistic acts by appeals to racism. Race was a dominant and divisive issue in America before the origin of the United States, and it continues to be the single most dominant issue in American politics.[40] India, Turkey, Indonesia, Malaysia, Northern Ireland, and Israel illustrate the dangers that religious issues create for a state. Rwanda and Bosnia provide recent examples of the willingness of humans to kill thousands of other humans, including children, for no reason other than membership in the wrong religion, ethnic group, or nationality.

In some cases, ethnic or religious strife becomes so great that it overpowers efforts to maintain a democratic state. The violent breakup of Yugoslavia and the peaceful division of Czechoslovakia show that certain countries may not be able to remain unified when the underlying strife between groups is too great.

ELITE SUPPORT FOR DEMOCRACY

Wealth defines the fourth great division between citizens. Evidence shows widespread support for democratic norms throughout the world. Success of that ideal, however, depends not only on mass support for democratic norms but also on elite support. In most countries that have changed from military to democratic governments in Latin America, Asia, and Africa, economic inequality has prevailed. This means that if the poor organize sufficiently to defeat the wealthy in a democratic struggle, the elites may attempt to annul any electoral outcome.

A key factor in the democratization of eastern Europe and the Soviet Union was the refusal of the military to support the existing elites. In Latin America, Asia, and Africa, military leaders make the final decision whether democratization will occur and whether it will last. Traditionally, the military has intervened when economic and social elites feel threatened by the winners of elections.‡ Therefore, the democratization process faces a critical challenge to keep soldiers in their barracks. One way of achieving this goal has been to guarantee both the existing elites and the military that a potential leftist government will not undertake policies that severely threaten the wealth of the elites or the privileges of the military. Adam Przeworski contends that when political participation first extends to almost all in society, a country benefits if the conservatives win the next election. This encourages the existing economic elites to accept elections as the appropriate way to decide who rules, and it reduces the likelihood that the military will intervene.[41]

Ultimately, of course, democracy is a political system in which current rulers lose elections. At some point, traditional elites must lose in a truly democratic regime. Democracy becomes institutionalized only if elites choose not to exercise their initial power to overturn the outcome of an election. Democracy becomes stable when elites see it as "the only game in town,"[42] when all accept the outcomes of elections, even when their parties lose, because they expect that in the future they can win. As Chapter 9 will show, some democratic institutional arrangements encourage stable democracies while others make them more difficult.

Summary

A major theme of this chapter has been that nonconstitutional and nondemocratic regimes are likely to fail in a world where constitutional democracy enjoys overwhelming legitimacy. Totalitarian regimes are particularly dangerous to their own citizens because the dictator or ruling party claims knowledge of The Truth that will lead the society to a utopian world. This claim implies that the interests of the ruler (or ruling party) are synonymous with those of the state and all good citizens. In other words, the leaders cannot be wrong and, as with Rousseau's general will, they must force people to become utopian citizens. In such a situation, anyone who does not agree with the ruler or who seems unlikely to become a good citizen in the coming utopian society must be

---

‡ For Americans, perhaps the most familiar example of the military intervening to prevent economic reforms was the overthrow of President Salvadore Allende in Chile in 1973. Prior to 1973, Chile had been the most stable democracy in Latin America. However, when Allende became the first freely elected Marxist leader in the Western Hemisphere, he took actions that the economic elites saw as threatening their position and the Chilean economy. The military responded by overthrowing Allende and began almost two decades of military rule. The United States supported this coup and immediately recognized the new military government.

either reeducated or eliminated. As elimination seems much cheaper and easier, totalitarian regimes typically terrorize and murder large numbers of their own citizens.

An authoritarian regime also may murder and terrorize its own citizens, though generally on a much more limited scale. Pursuing the goals of a stationary bandit—to maximize personal wealth and to secure personal power—even a malevolent authoritarian ruler generally represses the population only to the extent necessary to achieve these limited goals. Despite their current disrepute, monarchies may be the best form of authoritarian rule for citizens. They simplify the problem of succession of power and thereby reduce the widespread violence that often accompanies leadership changes in other types of nonconstitutional rule. In addition, the time frame for wealth maximization of the monarchy can stretch beyond the lifetime of the current ruler. Such a lengthened time frame may encourage the monarch to invest in the long-term productivity of the subjects.

Ultimately, all totalitarian and authoritarian regimes suffer from at least three major flaws. First, they find it difficult to correct mistakes. In a democratic system, those who oppose the current government are only too happy to point out its mistakes and possible problems with existing policies. Even benevolent rulers such as Atatürk probably do not encourage the opposition to feel totally free to bring existing and potential errors to the attention of the public. A totalitarian leader would greet such free expression with swift and certain punishment.

The second critical problem with nondemocratic regimes is their need to spend valuable resources to protect the rulers from the ruled. The police state costs money that could otherwise purchase consumer goods or fund investments in economic growth. The diversion of these resources to protect the rulers from the people, therefore, impairs economic efficiency. The fall of the Soviet Union illustrates how nondemocratic regimes spread the seeds of their own destruction.

The final problem with nondemocratic regimes occurs when politically powerful elites identify correct policies as those that protect their own interests. As the interests of the ruling few often conflict with the interests of the many who are ruled and with the conditions for economic growth, policies of nondemocratic regimes often reduce the general welfare of a society's citizens. Judged by Jeremy Bentham's utilitarian standard that the best government maximizes the greatest good for the greatest number or by some other principle of good government and justice, most authoritarian regimes will fail the test. Nondemocratic regimes are essentially regimes of political and economic privilege. The ruling few very seldom structure taxing and spending to promote economic efficiency or social justice. For this reason, nondemocratic regimes not only lack political legitimacy, but they also suffer from economic inefficiency. In a world where democracy has become almost a secular religion, these problems almost certainly prove fatal for authoritarian regimes.

This analysis leaves two long-term questions concerning democratic and nondemocratic regimes. First, since liberal democracy requires tolerance of diversity and puts issues of religion, ethnicity, and nationalism outside of politics, can it meet public demands for community and identity? Second, can the huge inequalities of income encountered in most of the world coexist with liberal democracy?

QUESTIONS AND EXERCISES

Questions for Reason

1. Describe the basic differences between totalitarian and authoritarian governments.

2. In what ways are regimes based on religion similar to totalitarian regimes?

3. How did the totalitarian regimes in Germany and Cambodia differ?

4. How might you test the hypothesis that political tolerance is necessary for democracy?

Questions for Reflection

1. Why would Rousseau argue that Germany after World War I was an inappropriate site to attempt to build a community based on the general will?

2. Why would liberal theory represented by John Locke and John Stuart Mill have predicted the disasters created by 20th-century totalitarian regimes?

3. Can democracy function with only one political party? If you think it cannot, do states within the United States that are dominated by a single party practice democracy? If you think that democracy can work in a one-party system, then describe how it would hold rulers accountable to citizens?

4. Assume for the moment that you are the new leader in Rwanda, a country with a history of tribal warfare and genocide. Would you attempt to introduce democratic rule or would you attempt rule by establishing a single party? Justify your decision.

Questions for Analysis: Reading Tables

In this lab, you will learn to read tables. This skill is essential for many of the remaining exercises in the book. More important, learning to read and construct tables develops a helpful skill for getting through college and later employment. Start with a simple illustration. The letters and numbers in Table 4.3 represent the grade distribution from an introductory political science class.

This table supports a study of students. The objects of such a study are called the **unit of analysis,** and each individual unit is a **case.** In Table 4.3, the unit of analysis is *students.* The table presents data for 90 students (cases) (15 + 22 + 25 + 14 + 14 = 90). The table

TABLE 4.3

GRADES IN PSCI 101

Grade	Number of Students	Percentage
A	15	16.7%
B	22	24.4
C	25	27.8
D	14	15.6
F	14	15.6
	90	100.1%

includes only one **variable,** the grades that students received in the course. The **values** of the variable *grade* are A, B, C, D and F.

The third column in Table 4.3 shows the percentage of students who scored each value. What percentage of students scored the value *B* on the test? It is 24.4 (22 divided by 90 multiplied by 100). If you were to randomly choose a student from the class, what is the **probability** that the student you selected made a B in the course? It is 0.244 (22 divided by 90).

Assume that you are deciding whether taking PSCI 101 is likely to help or hurt your GPA. You want to know the probability that a student in the class will earn either an A or B. That probability is 0.411 [(15 + 22)/90]. In other words, 41.1 percent of the students made either an A or a B.

CONTINGENCY TABLES

A **contingency table** shows the relationship between two or more variables. Perhaps you want to check for a relationship between gender and grade in PSCI 101. To find out, you must categorize the students (place them into groups) by gender and determine how many males and females received each grade. If you did this, your table might look like Table 4.4

Table 4.4 includes two variables: gender and grade. Gender has two values, female and male. Grade has five values: A, B, C, D, and F. Table 4.4 gives data for 90 cases, 40 with the value *Female* for the variable *gender* and 50 with the value *Male* for that variable.

Before you can make comparisons using Table 4.4, you must do two things: (1) determine which variable is the **independent variable** and which is the **dependent variable,** and (2) **percentagize** the table according to the values of the *independent* variable. The independent variable is the one that you believe might affect the other variable; the dependent variable is the one affected. How do you tell which is which? *The variable you are trying to explain is the dependent variable.* Its values may depend upon the values of the independent variable. In Table 4.4, it is easy to pick the independent and dependent

---

TABLE 4.4

GRADES IN PSCI 101
BY STUDENT GENDER—RAW DATA

Grade	Gender	
	Female	Male
A	7	8
B	11	11
C	9	16
D	6	8
F	7	7
	40	50

TABLE 4.5		

GRADES IN PSCI 101
BY STUDENT GENDER—PERCENTAGES

	Gender	
Grade	Female	Male
A	17.5%	16.0%
B	27.5	22.0
C	22.5	32.0
D	15.0	16.0
F	17.5	14.0
	100.0%	100.0%

variables. Although you do not know whether gender affects the grades that students receive, you do know that students' grades cannot affect their gender. This means that gender cannot be the dependent variable.

What questions might you want to answer about the relationship between gender and grade? You might wish to know whether males or females are more likely to do well in PSCI 101. You could start with this hypothesis:

Females are more likely than males to do well in PSCI 101.

Before you can proceed, you must operationalize the phrase "do well." One possible operationalization would transform it to read "make either an A or a B in the course." The operationalized hypothesis becomes:

Females are more likely than males to make an A or a B in PSCI 101.

You must also percentagize the table. You do this by dividing the number of cases in each cell by the total number of cases with the same value of the independent variable. (A cell is the intersection of a row and a column; Table 4.4 has 10 cells.) To percentagize the first column of the table, divide the number of females who made an A (7) by the total number of females (40). The result (0.175) is the probability that a female will make an A. Multiplying that probability by 100 tells you that 17.5 percent of the females in the class made an A. If you percentagize all the cells, you get the results shown in Table 4.5.

You can now determine whether the data support your hypothesis. By adding the percentages of students who earned an A and a B, you find that 45 percent of females and 38 percent of males "did well" in PSCI 101. (A female had a 0.45 probability of doing well while a male had a 0.38 probability of doing well.) This result supports your expectation that females are more likely than males to do well.

To see why you must percentagize a table, try to simply look at the numbers in the table and determine whether they support the hypothesis. Table 4.4 shows that 19 males and only 18 females earned either an A or a B. This superficial view may lead to the mistaken conclusion that males were more likely than females to earn a high grade.

Deeper analysis reveals a huge difference between the two hypotheses, "More females than males made an A or a B," and , "Females are more likely than males to make an A or a B." The first statement is incorrectly formulated for the research because the study is interested in the probability that you, with your value on the variable *gender,* will make an A or a B. If you are female, that probability is 0.45. If you are male, that probability is only 0.38.

Before you proceed any further, notice two errors that people often make when they construct contingency tables. In the first error, they may compare probabilities of the dependent variable rather than probabilities of the independent variable. For example, if you hypothesized, "Students who earn an A are more likely to be male," you are badly confused about which variable is the cause and which is the effect. Presumably, the grade you make cannot change your gender. On the other hand, your gender may influence the probability that you will do well in class. You can avoid errors with contingency tables by making sure that the independent variable is at the top of your table and that your percentages for each *column* total to 100 percent. You can avoid errors in your hypothesis by making sure that you state the values of the independent variable before the values of the dependent variable in the sentence. For example:

Males are more likely than females to make a C.

The second mistake people often make is to write a hypothesis such as, "More females than males will do well in PSCI 101," rather than "Females are more likely than males to do well in PSCI 101." As Tables 4.4 and 4.5 demonstrate, these are quite different statements; generally, the second statement is theoretically more interesting.

Helpful Hints: A few suggestions will help you to read tables.

1. Before you do anything else, make sure that the independent variable is at the top of the table and that its values are at the tops of the columns. (In Table 4.4, gender is the independent variable and its values are male and female.) Usually, values of the independent variable are determined prior to the values of the dependent variable. For example, your gender was decided prior to your grade.

2. The total percentages of each column should add up to approximately 100 percent.

3. Hypotheses with two variables always begin with values of the independent variable and end with values of the dependent variable. ("Females are more likely than males to score an F in PSCI 101.")

PRACTICE EXERCISES

Examine Tables 4.6 through 4.8 and determine which one has the independent and dependent variables reversed. Table 4.7 is the incorrectly constructed table. Rather than the independent variable *Ethnicity* being at the top of the table, the dependent variable *Party Identification* is in that position. This error prevents you from confirming or rejecting hypotheses concerning how race may affect the political party a person chooses.

Using Tables 4.6 and 4.8, decide whether the following hypotheses are (A) correctly formulated and confirmed, (B) correctly formulated and rejected, or (C) incorrectly

TABLE 4.6

TYPE OF REGIME AND POPULAR SUPPORT AMONG CITIZENS IN LESS INDUSTRIALIZED COUNTRIES

Regime Support	Regime Type	
	Democratic	Authoritarian
Low	21%	38%
Medium	31	35
High	48	27
Total	100%	100%

formulated. Also, indicate the cases in those tables. (Hint: In Tables 4.3, 4.4, and 4.5, the cases are students.)

1. More people who live in democratic regimes than people who live in authoritarian regimes say they have high levels of support for their regimes.
   A. Correctly formulated and confirmed
   B. Correctly formulated and rejected
   C. Incorrectly formulated
   The cases in the table are _____ .

2. People living under authoritarian regimes are less likely than people under democratic regimes to say they have high levels of support for their regimes.
   A. Correctly formulated and confirmed
   B. Correctly formulated and rejected
   C. Incorrectly formulated

3. People who express high levels of support for their regimes are most likely to live in countries with authoritarian regimes.
   A. Correctly formulated and confirmed
   B. Correctly formulated and rejected
   C. Incorrectly formulated.

TABLE 4.7

ETHNICITIES AND PARTY IDENTIFICATIONS OF SURVEY RESPONDENTS

Ethnicity	Party Identification		
	Democrat	Republican	Independent
Anglo	67%	88%	76%
Minority	33	12	24
Total	100%	100%	100%

TABLE 4.8

EQUALITY OF EDUCATIONAL OPPORTUNITY AND
ECONOMIC GROWTH IN INDUSTRIALIZED COUNTRIES

Economic Growth	Equality of Opportunity		
	Low	**Medium**	**High**
Low	42%	31%	28%
Medium	39	35	30
High	19	34	42
Total	100%	100%	100%

4. Countries with high scores on equality of educational opportunity are more likely than countries with low and medium scores to have high scores on economic growth.
   A. Correctly formulated and confirmed
   B. Correctly formulated and rejected
   C. Incorrectly formulated
   The cases in the table are _____ .

5. More countries with high scores on educational opportunity have high scores on economic growth.
   A. Correctly formulated and confirmed
   B. Correctly formulated and rejected
   C. Incorrectly formulated.

6. Countries with high scores on economic growth are most likely to have high scores on equality of educational opportunities.
   A. Correctly formulated and confirmed
   B. Correctly formulated and rejected
   C. Incorrectly formulated

ANSWERS

The cases in Table 4.6 are the citizens interviewed in the less industrialized countries. The cases in Table 4.8 are industrialized countries.

1. This statement is incorrectly formulated because it uses "more" rather than "more likely."

2. This statement is correctly formulated and confirmed. To test the hypothesis, compare the percentage of persons in democratic regimes and authoritarian regimes with a value of *High* on the variable *Regime Support.* These percentages are 48 percent for democratic regimes and 27 percent for authoritarian regimes.

3. This hypothesis is incorrectly formulated, as it compares values of the dependent variable.

4. This hypothesis is correctly formulated and confirmed. Countries with high scores on equality of educational opportunity are most likely to have high scores on economic growth. In fact, 42 percent of countries with high equality of educational opportunity also have high economic growth. This percentage is greater than that for countries with either a medium level of equality of educational opportunity (34 percent) or a low level (19 percent).

5. This hypothesis is incorrectly formulated because it uses "more" rather than "more likely." Because you do not know the number of countries in each category of the independent variable, you cannot know whether the statement is confirmed or rejected.

6. This statement is incorrectly formulated as it compares values of the dependent variable.

EXERCISES

Using Table 4.1 (page 122), determine whether each hypothesis below is correctly formulated and, if so, whether it is confirmed or rejected. If it is incorrectly formulated, revise the hypothesis so that it is correctly formulated and confirmed. Residents of Moscow answered these questions in 1990, prior to the fall of the Soviet Union.

1. Citizens in France are more likely to support the right of privacy than citizens in Germany, Denmark, Britain, or Moscow.
   A. Correctly formulated and confirmed
   B. Correctly formulated and rejected
   C. Incorrectly formulated

2. Citizens in Moscow support the right to property more than citizens in France, Germany, Denmark, or Britain.
   A. Correctly formulated and confirmed
   B. Correctly formulated and rejected
   C. Incorrectly formulated

3. More citizens in Germany than citizens in France, Denmark, Britain, or Moscow support freedom of speech.
   A. Correctly formulated and confirmed
   B. Correctly formulated and rejected
   C. Incorrectly formulated

4. The country in which citizens are most likely to claim all the rights in Table 4.1 is Germany.
   A. Correctly formulated and confirmed
   B. Correctly formulated and rejected
   C. Incorrectly formulated.

5. Political scientists Gabriel Almond and Sidney Verba have hypothesized that "a civic culture"[43] is necessary for democracy. The civic culture includes democratic norms and support for civil rights. Using your knowledge about the countries in Table 4.1, do the data support the Almond and Verba hypothesis? Why or why not?

NOTES

[1] Ronald Wintrobe, "The Tinpot and the Totalitarian: An Economic Theory of Dictatorship," *American Political Science Review* 84 (1990), p. 849.

[2] Ibid., p. 849.

[3] Hitler dictated the work to Rudolf Hess, his closest party colleague throughout the party's early years. Hess remained Hitler's intimate associate until he defected by air to England during World War II. References to the work in this chapter cite a complete and unabridged edition produced under a distinguished editorial board: Adolf Hitler, *Mein Kampf* (New York: Reynal & Hitchcock, 1939).

[4] Italian Labor Charter, 1927, cited in George H. Sabine and Thomas L. Thorson, *History of Political Theory*, 4th ed. (Hinsdale, Ill.: Dryden Press, 1973), p. 821.

[5] Hitler, *Mein Kampf*, pp. 467–468.

[6] Franz Neumann, *Behemoth* (New York: Octagon, 1983), p. 83.

[7] H. H. Gerth and C. Wright Mills, eds. and trans., *From Max Weber: Essays in Sociology* (New York: Oxford University Press, 1958), pp. 295–296; also see Max Weber, *The Social Psychology of World Religions,* Vol. 1 (New York: Oxford University Press, 1922–1923), pp. 237–296.

[8] Hitler, *Mein Kampf*, pp. 714–715.

[9] Ibid., p. 715.

[10] Ibid., p. 313.

[11] Sabine and Thorson, *Modern Political Thought,* p. 840.

[12] Quoted in William McGovern, *From Luther to Hitler* (Boston: Houghton Mifflin, 1941), p. 655.

[13] Hitler, *Mein Kampf*, p. 636.

[14] Ben Kiernan, *How Pol Pot Came to Power* (London: Verso, 1984); and William Shawcross, *Sideshow* (London: Fontana Paperbacks, 1980). For a different view, see Michael Vickery, *Kampuchea: Politics, Economics, and Society* (London: Frances Pinter, 1986).

[15] Vickery, *Kampuchea*, pp. 28–31.

[16] Craig Etcheson, *The Rise and Demise of Democratic Kampuchea* (Boulder, Colo.: Westview Press, 1984), pp. 148–149.

[17] Vickery, *Kampuchea*, p. 29.

[18] Ibid., p. 30.

[19] Ruth Leger Sivard, *World Military and Social Expenditures* (Ann Arbor, MI: Inter-university Consortium for Political Science Research, 1991), p. 21; Etcheson, *Rise and Demise*, pp. 148–149.

[20] Sivard, *World Military and Social Expenditures,* pp. 150–151.

[21] Kiernan, *How Pol Pot*, pp. 386–389.

[22] Etcheson, *Rise and Demise,* pp. 157–158.

[23] Ibid., p. 35.

[24] Sivard, *World Military and Social Expenditures,* pp. 152–153.

[25] Arthur Koestler, *Darkness at Noon,* trans. by Daphne Hardy (New York: Macmillan, 1941). This book is a gripping account of the tribulations and behaviors of such confessors.

[26] Carl J. Friedrich, Michael Curtis, and Benjamin R. Barber, *Totalitarianism in Perspective: Three Views* (New York: Praeger, 1969), p. 126.

[27] Karl de Schweinitz, *Industrialization and Democracy* (New York: Free Press, 1964); and Samuel P. Huntington, *Political Order in Changing Societies* (New Haven, Conn.: Yale University Press, 1968).

[28] Manfred Halpern, *The Process of Social Change in the Middle East and North Africa* (Princeton, N.J.: Princeton University Press, 1963), p. 258.

[29] Eric A. Nordlinger, "Soldiers in Mufti: The Impact of Military Rule upon Economic and Social Change in the Non-Western States," *American Political Science Review* 64 (1970), pp. 1,131–1,148.

[30] See for example, Robert Jackman, "Politicians in Uniform: Military Governments and Social Change in the Third World," *American Political Science Review* 70 (1976), pp. 1,078–1,097; R. D. McKinlay and A. S. Cohan, "The Economic Performance of Military Regimes: A Cross-National Aggregate Study," *British Journal of Politics* 6 (1976), pp. 291–310; John Ravenhill, "Comparing Regime Performance in Africa: The Limitation of Cross-National Aggregate Analysis," *The Journal of Modern African Studies* 18 (1980), pp. 99–126; Gary Zuk and William Thompson, "The Post-Coup Military Spending Question: A Pooled Cross-Sectional Time Series Analysis," *American Political Science Review* 76 (1982), pp. 60–74; and Hamed Madani, "Socioeconomic Development and Military Policy Consequences of Third World Military and Civilian Regimes, 1965-1985" (Ph.D. dissertation, University of North Texas, 1992).

[31] Barry Rubin, *Modern Dictators: Third World Coup Makers, Strongmen, and Populist Tyrants* (New York: McGraw Hill, 1987), p. 296.

[32] Wayne Cornelius and Ann L. Craig, "Politics in Mexico," in *Comparative Politics Today: A World View*, 5th ed., ed. by Gabriel Almond and Bingham Powell, Jr. (New York: Harper Collins, 1992), p. 487.

[33] Ibid., p. 475.

[34] Mancur Olson, Jr., "Dictatorship, Democracy, and Development," *American Political Science Review* 87 (1993), p. 357.

[35] Adam Przeworski, *Democracy and the Market: Political and Economic Reforms in Eastern Europe and Latin America* (Cambridge: Cambridge University Press, 1991), p. 2.

[36] Ibid., p. 6.

[37] For a review of this literature and its application to the Soviet Union, see James L. Gibson, Raymond M. Duch, and Kent L. Tedin, "Democratic Values and the Transformation of the Soviet Union," *Journal of Politics* 54 (1992), pp. 329–371.

[38] Ibid. See also John A. Booth and Patricia Bayer Richard, "Repression, Political Participation, and Support for Democratic Liberties in Urban Central America" (paper presented at the annual meeting of the Midwest Political Science Association, Chicago, April, 1994).

[39] John L. Sullivan, Michal Shamir, Patrick Walsh, and Nigel S. Roberts, *Political Tolerance in Context: Support for Unpopular Minorities in Israel, New Zealand, and the United States* (Boulder, Colo.: Westview Press, 1985).

[40] Edward G. Carmines and James A. Stimson, *Issue Evolution: Race and the Transformation of American Politics* (Princeton, N.J.: Princeton University Press, 1989).

[41] Przeworski, *Democracy and the Market,* Chapter 2.

[42] Ibid., p. 26.

[43] Gabriel A. Almond and Sidney Verba, *The Civic Culture: Political Attitudes and Democracy in Five Nations* (Princeton, N.J.: Princeton University Press, 1963); Harry Eckstein, "A Culturalist Theory of Political change," *American Political Science Review* 82 (1988), pp. 511–529; Robert A. Dahl, *Polyarchy* (New Haven, Conn.: Yale University Press, 1971); and Lucian Pye and Sidney Verba, eds., *Political Culture and Political Development* (Princeton, N.J.: Princeton University Press, 1965).

PART 3

The Citizen
and the State

5

Political Participation

Introduction

Previous chapters outlined the two most important contemporary political ideologies, liberalism and Marxism-Leninism. That discussion explained that the governments envisioned by both ideologies require citizen participation to succeed. Chapter 4 reported that authoritarian regimes depend less on active input from citizens, and they may even discourage many forms of participation. Nevertheless, even authoritarian regimes require some level of citizen support, and totalitarian regimes also require substantial citizen activity. In this chapter, we answer several important questions: What is political participation? How do people participate in politics? Why do they do it? Who participates?

Before we begin to address these topics, please write your answers to the following questions about your own participation:

1. Are you registered to vote?
2. If you were old enough, did you vote in the last presidential election?
3. Did you vote in the primary elections?
4. In the last 12 months, have you participated in a community project such as collecting food for the poor or cleaning up a highway or park?
5. Have you ever attended a political rally?

6. Do you belong to a political organization (e.g., Young Republicans, Sierra Club, National Rifle Association)?

7. Have you participated in an illegal political activity?

It is important for your understanding of this chapter to actually write out your answers to these questions. Ask your friends and acquaintances why they did or did not participate in ways described in the list. Were their reasons similar to yours? How about your friends and acquaintances whose political behavior was different from your own? What reasons did they give for their action or inaction?

What Is Political Participation?

Until now, this book has dealt with political ideas and how those ideas relate to the structures of governments. In this chapter, we begin to look at the political process. We want to explore how governments operate and how citizens affect government and are affected by it. This chapter describes people who determine what becomes law and how their society implements law, and it reviews conditions that determine the success or failure of those efforts.

Above all, the political process involves conflict. People strive to make their own preferences about law and policy prevail over the preferences of other people. They often argue their cases with appeals to philosophical and normative views, but more often the true stakes are material. To repeat the words of political scientist Harold D. Lasswell, the political process determines "who [in society] gets what, when, and how."[1]

Adversaries in politics rarely gain total victory over their opponents. Rather, the political outcomes at any one point in time reflect the current distribution of power among contenders. Even wars and revolutions rarely culminate in total victory. In the absence of war or revolution, most disputants agree to an outcome because they believe that further effort would have higher costs than benefits. They may feel that prolonging a stalemate or escalating a conflict would endanger the institutions of decision making. For example, the Green Party in Germany certainly does not agree with many of the environmental decisions of the present government, but the Green Party currently does not have enough political power to force the government to change those decisions. The Greens must continue trying to convince voters to support them in order to gain sufficient seats in the Bundestag to change Germany's environmental policies.

Politics deals with both conflict and, paradoxically, conflict resolution. Each political decision *temporarily* resolves a particular conflict. The contestants tacitly agree, however grudgingly, to accept current decisions and their implementation. Nevertheless, the losers in the previous decision process will continue to work to change the outcome. They will continually try to gain sufficient power to prevail in the future. To prevent this, the winners must also continue their efforts. Political decision making is, therefore, an endless process. Important aspects of the political process concern the ways in which citizens affect the outcome of this process and how citizens react to government decisions.

Any study of participation by members of the mass public must deal with inputs into the political process. **Political participation** includes actions and "nonactions" through which persons attempt to influence, support, or reject governmental decisions and structures. It includes both conventional activities such as voting and writing letters to members of Congress and unconventional activities such as taking part in a protest demonstration to block the entrance to an abortion clinic. The definition embraces legal activities like giving money to political campaigns and illegal activities such as terrorist attacks. It encompasses the nonviolent actions like working for a political party or candidate and boycotting nonunion products; it also includes violent actions such as beating up minorities, vandalizing foreign cars, and shooting at workers who cross picket lines.

Political participation also encompasses actions that show support for or opposition to a regime or political structure. For example, in the United States, millions of citizens attend Independence Day parades, sing the national anthem, tie yellow ribbons to display support for troops at war, recite the Pledge of Allegiance, and fly the flag. All of these behaviors demonstrate support for the current political structures and institutions. In contrast, other citizens burn the flag, boycott elections, and engage in civil disobedience. In one such action, Rosa Parks, an African American woman, took a seat in the whites-only section of a bus in Alabama. Through this single act, she helped launch the civil rights demonstrations of the 1960s. Through nonsupportive actions, people show that they believe the current regime, structures, institutions, or laws are unfair and illegitimate.

WHY STUDY MASS POLITICAL PARTICIPATION?

Some may doubt the importance of understanding the political behavior of common citizens who are not in positions of leadership. Why, they may ask, should anyone care about the actions of people outside the elites. First and foremost, even totalitarian and authoritarian regimes depend upon the acquiescence of the vast majority of the public. The rapid downfall of the Soviet Union demonstrates that even totalitarian governments require some minimal popular support. Second, as democracy becomes more prevalent in a country, mass behavior has a greater impact on what the government does. Third, political participation affects the lives of those who participate. In totalitarian regimes such as Nazi Germany and in democratic regimes such as contemporary Germany, participation in politics can give meaning and importance to the lives of individual citizens.

CATEGORIES OF POLITICAL PARTICIPATION

Studies of political participation identify five distinct types of behavior through which people affect government policies: voting, campaign activity, communal activity, particularized contacting, and protest behavior. **Campaign activity** includes work to assist in electoral campaigns or attendance at campaign rallies. In **communal activities,** people may join neighbors in community projects or complain to public officials about a community problem. **Particularized contacting** occurs when a person contacts a public official about a problem that directly affects her or his family. **Protest participation** includes legal activities such as marching in a civil rights demonstration or standing outside an abortion clinic. It also includes illegal behavior ranging from civil disobedience like that of Rosa Parks and the Chinese student blocking the army's tanks to sabotaging fishing vessels that kill porpoises, shooting doctors who perform abortions, and burning down apartments that house migrant workers.

Why Do People Participate?

Perhaps the most interesting question concerning mass political participation is why any rational person would do any of these activities. Political economist Mancur Olson Jr.'s small book, *The Logic of Collective Action,* provides important insights into this question.[2] Olson demonstrates that if you are a rational actor, a person who attempts to maximize your own benefits and minimize your own costs, then normally you would not vote, attend a rally, give money to a candidate, engage in protest activity, or participate in a revolution. Rational people, he shows, will free ride and allow others to supply collective political goods.*

THE SIMPLE ACT OF VOTING

In the United States, less than 50 percent of the population is likely to turn out for a presidential election. For a local election, the figure is usually closer to 20 percent. In contrast, up to 90 percent of the population votes in countries such as Germany and Austria. These data raise two questions: Why would anyone vote? Why do voter turnout percentages differ so much among democracies?

Voting appears similar to the discussion in Chapter 1 of voluntary contributions to the national defense. Your vote is no more likely to determine the outcome of a national election than your taxes will decide whether your country's army will win a war. Chapter 1 discussed the idea that if paying taxes for national defense were voluntary, rational people would free ride. They would use the dollars they might have paid to the Department of Defense to purchase private goods such as cars, travel, and CDs. For exactly the same reasons, rational people should use the time and energy they would spend voting for other purposes. They might watch television, go to a movie, play ball, or put in 45 more minutes at work. They will enjoy the benefits of free elections whether or not they actually vote.

The odds that your vote will determine an electoral outcome in a national election are exceedingly small, much smaller than winning the grand prize in your state's lottery or the Publisher's Clearinghouse Sweepstakes. If only 10,000 people vote in an election and pre-election polls show the race to be a dead heat, your odds of casting the deciding vote are less than 0.019×10^{-251}. This number has 251 zeroes between the decimal and the 19.[3] In other words, the probability that *your* vote will decide an election is indistinguishable from zero. Yet the cost of gaining the information necessary to determine which candidate most closely reflects your political preferences, to register, and to vote is not zero.

It seems particularly irrational to take the trouble to become an informed voter. In the simplest case, consider an election for only one office, let's say for the U.S. Senate, with only two candidates running. To accurately determine which candidate best represents

---

*Refer to Chapter 1 for definitions and discussions of collective goods and free riders.

your preferences takes a tremendous amount of time and effort. A rational person would become an informed voter only if the following inequality were to hold:

$$PB > C_R + C_V + C_I \qquad (1)$$

The left side of the inequality represents the benefits (B) you expect to receive if the preferred candidate wins multiplied by the probability (P) that your vote will decide the outcome of the election. P is the probability that, if you failed to cast a ballot, the election would end in a tie or your preferred candidate would lose by one vote. On the right side of the inequality are the cost of voting. These include the time and effort required to register (C_R) and vote (C_V), plus the cost of finding out sufficient information about the candidates to choose one with the desired views (C_I).

The inequality really makes a simple statement. *It is simple because the probability that a particular vote will decide the election is so close to zero that the expected benefit of voting is zero!* No matter how great the expected benefits, any amount multiplied by a zero probability is still zero. What are the costs of voting? C_R and C_V, the actual costs of registering and voting, include at least the cost of the gas to get to the polling place and the time spent waiting in line to vote. In addition, this cost includes other considerations like the possibility of an auto accident going to the polls.

How about information costs? Now the voter faces some real expense. These costs include time spent in research on the past records of the two candidates and their stands on issues important to you. An informed voter would examine the voting record of the incumbent and compare the challenger's stands on those same issues. This means that, rather than watching a football game or sleeping late on Sunday, you must turn on the Sunday news programs. Rather than watching MTV, VH1, and *Oprah,* you must watch the evening news shows (even those on PBS). Instead of spending valuable time reading the sports pages, comics, and soap opera updates, you have to read the news and editorial pages. Rather than spending your money on subscriptions to magazines like *Sports Illustrated, Rolling Stone,* or *Vogue,* this money pays for *Time, Newsweek,* or *U.S. News and World Report.* Even worse, you must read them. By this time it should have become clear: *It is never in a citizen's rational self-interest to pay the costs of voting if the only benefits come from determining that a preferred candidate will win.*

Fortunately for democracies, citizens receive benefits from voting that do not depend on the probability that a single vote will decide the election. As indicated in Chapter 1, all regimes socialize their citizens to feel the duty to participate and to receive pleasure from fulfilling that duty. Television reports, newspaper editorials, and fellow-citizens all repeat the message, "If you do not vote, then you have no right to complain if elected officials do things you dislike." Friends may ask you if you voted, and they may think less of you if you did not. In addition, politics has entertainment value. On a typical day, you may choose to watch MTV or reruns of *Wings* rather than listen to the news. However, during national elections, most citizens have enough interest to watch the great electoral pageant. Voting affirms a person's citizenship and the importance of the electoral process. It allows us to participate in democracy's greatest ritual: elections.

The duty that people feel to vote and the entertainment value of participating in elections often provide social and psychological benefits greater than the costs of casting an *uninformed* vote. A person might decide whether or not to vote in an election based on an inequality like:

$$PB + D_V + E_V > C_R + C_V \qquad (2)$$

The *PB* term represents the sum of the benefits of each preferred candidate winning multiplied by the probability that your vote will decide the outcome of the election. D_V is the social and psychological benefit you receive from fulfilling a civic duty. E_V is the entertainment value of participating in the ceremony. As before, C_R is the cost of registering to vote, and C_V is the cost of actually voting. The right-hand side of the inequality no longer includes information costs, because you are not voting to influence the election, but to fulfill a duty and to enjoy the electoral process. Given that *PB* is indistinguishable from zero, Inequality 2 becomes:

$$D_V + E_V > C_R + C_V \qquad (3)$$

In this situation, if the benefits of fulfilling a duty plus the entertainment value of participating exceed the costs of registering and voting, then you probably will vote.

If Inequality 3 correctly describes voting behavior, it implies good news and bad news for democratic government. The good news is that it is now rational for many people to vote. The bad news is that, unless information is virtually free, most will cast uninformed votes. To participate in elections by voting and by watching the events that surround this important ceremony, voters need not actually inform themselves about the candidates. If most people vote out of duty and for the psychological benefits of participating in a ritual, then voting resembles singing "The Star Spangled Banner" more than substantive political behaviors that have an impact on public policy.[†]

TESTING ALTERNATIVE MODELS OF VOTING

Political scientists need to test whether people vote in the manner described by Inequality 1, or for the reasons described by Inequality 3. Inequality 1 expresses the **Informed Voter (IV) model,** the one you learned in high school civics and American government classes. This model predicts that people will vote if they perceive that their votes may affect the electoral outcome and they care who wins. In this model, voters inform themselves about candidates' positions on important issues and then cast their votes based on that information. The **Duty/Entertainment (DE) model,** Inequality 3, argues that the dominant variables that influence participation are citizen duty, the entertainment value of the election, and the costs of registering and voting. How might a researcher develop a test to determine which of these models best predicts voting behavior?

The expected benefit of voting in the Informed Voter model is the value of having preferred candidates win multiplied by the probability that one person's vote will decide the outcome. This model predicts, therefore, that voter turnout will increase along with the size of that probability. In other words, a greater probability that a single vote will decide

---

[†] As later chapters will show, free, fair, and competitive elections inspire wonder because, despite the individual irrationality of attempting to influence policy through the vote, elections do help make policy by making the elites more accountable to the masses.

the outcome increases the probability that a person will vote. In addition, anything that lowers information costs should have a strong positive impact on voting turnout. As Chapter 6 will show, political parties play key roles in reducing information costs to voters by promoting clearly distinct ideologies and inducing people to vote for parties rather than individual candidates. In such a situation, voters need to know only which party's view of the world is closest to their own. On the other hand, voters face high information costs if elections are nonpartisan, parties are ideologically similar, people vote for individual candidates rather than for political parties, and elected officials do not vote their parties' positions once they have gained office (or switch parties after they have been elected).

If the Duty/Entertainment model (Inequality 3) more accurately describes voting behavior, then factors that increase the social pressure to vote or the entertainment value of the election will increase voter participation. Because the DE model excludes information costs, the only costs of voting are the actual money and time spent registering and voting. Because the DE model predicts that voters do not care about the probability that a single vote will determine the election, neither the size of the voting population or the closeness of the election should affect voting rates. Finally, the DE model predicts that voters will not inform themselves about candidates or issues.

Exercises in earlier chapters explained that an empirical test of a model must operationalize hypotheses in order to test them. The researcher also must obtain data to test those hypotheses. If the Informed Voter model is correct, data will support the following hypotheses:

- H_1: A closer expected outcome of an election will be associated with a higher probability that a citizen will vote.
- H_2: A smaller voting population for an election will be associated with a higher probability that a citizen will vote.
- H_3: Countries with strong parties that express clear ideological differences will have higher voter turnouts than countries with weak parties that express similar ideologies.

If the Duty/Entertainment model of voting is correct, then data should lead the researcher to reject these hypotheses while supporting the following hypotheses:

- H_4: Voters will feel a much stronger sense of civic duty and find politics more entertaining than nonvoters.
- H_5: Voters will know little about the candidates or their positions on issues.

In one of the first tests of H_1, a closer outcome relates to a higher turnout, Harold Gosnell compared voter turnout in parliamentary districts in the 1924 British national election. Gosnell found that voter turnout was significantly higher in legislative districts where elections were close than in districts in which elections were not close. More recent tests generally confirm Gosnell's conclusions.[4] In another finding that supports H_1, as elections more frequently change the party in control of the national executive (president or prime minister), voter turnout in a country increases.[5] This suggests that if people perceive that an election can change who is in power, then they are more likely to perceive their individual votes as important.

Upon evaluating the second hypothesis, support for the IV model disappears.[‡] H_2 predicts that, because a voter presumably has a greater probability of casting the deciding vote in an election with a few hundred voters than in an election with 50 million voters, a higher percentage of citizens will vote when the number of probable voters is smaller. Studies relating the size of the voting population with voter turnout reject this hypothesis. In fact, the association between turnout and the number of voters often leans in the opposite direction. For example, in the United States, turnout is always lower for local elections than for national ones and for primary elections than for general elections.[§] Supporters of the Informed Voter model might argue that this is not a fair test because the benefits of a victory by a preferred candidate increase as the importance of an office increases. Thus, it makes sense that a higher percentage of the population votes in elections for president than in elections for mayor. The choice of the president or prime minister of a country generally matters a lot more to citizens than the choice of a mayor.

How might a researcher design a better test to determine whether to accept or reject this explanation of higher turnouts in elections with larger voting populations? One way would be to compare voter turnout in statewide elections for governor or U.S. senator to see whether the turnout percentages in less populous states exceed those in more populous states. Another way would be to compare turnout for elections for president and prime minister in large and small countries. These tests reveal that turnout percentages for statewide races do not vary significantly with state populations. Similarly, comparisons of voter turnout across nations find no relationship between the size of the voting population and the voter turnout. Switzerland, the smallest democracy among industrialized countries, has the lowest percentage of citizens who vote.[6] This suggests that the probability that a single vote will decide an election is relatively unimportant to the decision whether or not to vote.

[‡] Chapter 9 will show how organizations such as political parties and interest groups make it much easier for citizens to inform themselves. This reduces information costs and may allow political scientists to accept the Informed Voter model.

[§] A general election is the final election in the process; everyone who is registered can vote. In most primaries, only registered members of a party can vote in the race to determine that party's candidate. For this reason, the number of eligible voters in a primary is approximately half the number of eligible voters in the general election. Despite this limit, the turnout in the general election is almost always higher. Similarly, many local elections draw expected turnouts of only a few hundred or a few thousand voters. These limits should improve the probability that a single vote will be decisive. Nevertheless, these are precisely the elections with the lowest voter turnouts.

Because obtaining sufficient information to cast an informed vote is the most costly activity in voting, H_3 argues that information costs will strongly affect voter turnout. As strong, ideologically distinct political parties provide the simplest way of reducing information costs for all elections, H_3 predicts that countries where strong political parties give clear signals to voters are more likely to have higher turnout rates than countries where parties are weak and ideological differences are small.

Research has provided strong empirical support for this hypothesis. Among industrialized democracies, countries where strong parties promote easily identified ideologies have significantly higher voting rates than countries with weak parties and ideologies that are difficult to identify.[7] In addition, when political parties in a country identify closely with social or economic groups, they further reduce the costs of information. For example, if you are a farmer or a laborer and a party has the word *farm* or *labor* as part of its name, then you can more easily determine how to cast your vote. A Catholic who finds a party with the word *Catholic* in its name also gains some inexpensive and easily understood information. Political scientist Bingham Powell has found substantially higher voter turnout in countries where occupation and religion are closely linked to political parties.[8]

Studies that use data about individuals to predict who will vote also provide support for the importance of lowering information costs to increase voter turnout. In the United States and Switzerland, where party ideologies are relatively weak and neither occupation or religion closely overlaps with the positions of political parties, a person's level of education is the best predictor of voting. This connection is particularly strong among younger voters. As voters grow older, the difference in the voting rates of the most and least educated people declines. These findings suggest that both education and experience reduce information costs to voters, and this change increases their probability of voting.[9]

Although research provides strong support for the first and third hypotheses derived from the Informed Voter model, studies also offer substantial support for the Duty/Entertainment model. Numerous studies show that people are more likely to vote when they are interested in politics and when they support the political institutions of their country.[10] Notice how interest in politics changes the costs of gaining information. Someone who is really interested in politics finds entertainment in obtaining information about candidates, parties, and issues. This preference transforms a cost into a benefit. Someone might actually prefer reading *Time* to reading *Sports Illustrated*.

Research on individuals' attitudes and opinions also provides substantial support for Hypothesis 5. Voters know little about candidates, parties, and issues. In the United States, for example, opinion polls regularly show that less than 10 percent of voters in an election can state how the incumbent voted on a particular issue. Moreover, most Americans also hold highly contradictory opinions on political issues and show little understanding of the meanings of the labels *liberal* and *conservative*.[11]

Since the data provide partial support for both models of voting, you may wonder what to conclude about why some countries have higher voting turnouts than others and why anyone chooses to vote. First, the factor that best predicts differences in voter turnout is the cost of information. When parties promote clearly identified ideologies and when they conspicuously identify themselves with occupational or religious groupings, people are more likely to vote. Second, although people may realize that their individual votes are unlikely to affect the outcome of an election, close elections still increase voter turnout. In close elections, people seem to greatly overestimate the true probability that their votes might affect electoral outcomes. Third, citizens who feel strong obligations to vote and who enjoy obtaining information about politics are more likely to vote than those citizens who lack any strong sense of duty and who have little interest in politics. Finally, most voters know little about issues, ideologies, or candidates. In summary, the inequality that best describes voter turnout is Inequality 2:

$$PB + D_V + E_V > C_R + C_V$$

Participation Beyond Voting

Besides voting, people can participate in politics in other ways such as joining political parties or interest groups. Why do people participate in such activities? Do they think that they can affect political outcomes or do they participate for other reasons?

Prior to 1965, someone who asked a political scientist, "Why do people join political interest groups?" would have received the seemingly obvious answer, "To pursue shared political goals." This answer reflects a major assumption of **pluralist theory.** This theory assumes that when people wish to present their demands to government, they join existing groups or form new ones. These groups then represent the interests of members. For example, the pluralist theory postulates that a person joins the National Rifle Association so that the organization can present her views on gun ownership to political leaders. Similarly, doctors join the American Medical Association so that the group will represent their interests in Washington. Retired teachers join the National Retired Teachers Association to obtain better benefits and promote better education policies.

In pluralist theory, lobbyists for groups compete for collective goods. In this competition, more powerful and more persuasive groups obtain the policies they desire. Thus, to gain political representation for your interests, you must join interest groups and give them the necessary resources to participate in these struggles. Economist Mancur Olson's book *The Logic of Collective Action* challenges this view of why people join political groups. Olson argues that it is irrational for people to join groups for the purpose of helping to supply collective goods. As Chapter 1 showed, rational people would not voluntarily contribute to a $200 billion defense budget because their individual contributions would not affect the level of national defense, and they would enjoy defense whether or not they contributed. Olson argues that the political goals sought by interest groups are no different from national defense.

Assume that you strongly advocate wilderness preservation, and you believe that the most effective means of reaching your goal is to induce the government to enact legislation to preserve wilderness areas. Pluralist theory contends that this interest will lead you to join with others who share your ideas. You will donate money and other resources to the group so that it can persuade the government to provide the wilderness preservation you desire. Olson would say, "Nonsense!" Environmental interest groups in the United States spend annual budgets in excess of $100 million. The addition of your $35, $75, $100, or even $1,000 will not change the ability of the environmental groups to lobby government. Your individual contribution will not change the probability that government will act to preserve wilderness areas any more than your individual vote will decide the outcome of a national election or your individual taxes will change the level of national defense. Equally important, you will receive whatever wilderness preservation the government provides whether or not you contribute. It is, therefore, irrational for you to contribute to an interest group so that it can better represent your point of view.

But doesn't Olson make an obvious mistake? After all, millions of people join groups and pay membership dues. In fact, approximately 50 percent of the adults in the United States belong to at least one interest group. Even excluding union membership leaves approximately 40 percent of American adults as members of interest groups.[12] People join public interest groups such as Common Cause, the League of Women Voters, and the National Rifle Association. They also join economic trade associations such as the local Chamber of Commerce, the American Medical Association, the National Farm Bureau, the United Auto Workers union, and the American Political Science Association.

Olson responds to this criticism in two ways. First, he asserts that most people do not join most of the interest groups that work to achieve desired collective goods. Probably at least 25 million adults in the United States consider themselves "strongly environmentally oriented" and support the goals of groups such as the Wilderness Society. However, all environmental groups together receive contributions from fewer than 2.5 million citizens. Thus, Olson would argue that 90 percent of the population behave as he predicts; they free ride and enjoy the benefits provided by the minority who donate to environmental groups.

But why do those 2.5 million Americans contribute to environmental groups? Are they irrational or just stupid? Olson contends that most members join and contribute to groups not to achieve collective goods but to obtain **material goods** that only members receive. He calls these private goods **"selective incentives."** For example, members of the Sierra Club receive *Sierra*, a magazine filled with pictures of beautiful landscapes and animals. Club members get discounts on white-water raft trips through the Grand Canyon and guided trips through wilderness areas.[ii] Similarly, says Olson, doctors do not join the American Medical Association (AMA) to influence government policy on medical issues. Rather, they join to get referrals from other doctors, to receive the AMA's journals, and to practice at hospitals that require AMA membership. Olson argues that the *real reason* that people join groups is to get the benefits that only members receive. The achievement of collective goods—higher pensions for retired teachers, protection from restrictions on gun rights, preservation of wilderness areas, and higher doctors' fees—are only **"by-products"** of joining interest groups. If groups did not offer selective incentives worth the cost of membership dues, then no National Rifle Association, Sierra Club, or American Medical Association would exist.

Many sociologists and political scientists doubt Olson's argument that members join interest groups *only* for material incentives rather than for collective goods. Political

---

[ii] A comparison of the many environmental groups shows that membership size is closely correlated with the value of the private goods they provide and with the cost of membership. The largest group, the National Wildlife Federation, has the lowest membership dues, and it provides substantial selective incentives such as travel discounts and well-produced magazines. The smallest environmental groups provide the fewest selective incentives.

scientist James Q. Wilson suggests that people join groups to obtain selective material incentives, but they also join to receive what he calls **solidary benefits,** and to obtain the collective goods.[13] Solidary benefits reflect the pleasure that people receive from a sense of belonging to an important cause, meeting other people who share their values, and taking part in group activities.

Russell Hardin suggests that personal growth is an important reason that people participate in politics.[14] When you take part in great events, social movements, and elections, you have the opportunity to learn new ideas and refine old ones. Through participation, you meet new people, obtain information, learn new ideas, and develop your own personal capacities. Hardin suggests that many people participate for another reason: They vastly overestimate the probability that their own participation will have an impact.

Olson's arguments concerning the irrationality of joining an interest group apply to every form of political participation devoted to the goal of providing a collective good. Joining or contributing to a political party, campaigning for a particular candidate, writing to a legislator about a policy issue, and attending a protest rally are all alike. One person's action has an exceptionally small probability of changing a political outcome. At the same time, the activity costs time and money. Why, then, do citizens join interest groups, contribute to candidates, and attend political rallies?

What reasons did you cite for your past political participation when asked at the beginning of this chapter? Were selective incentives, solidary benefits, and opportunities for personal growth sufficient to make your participation rational? Did you participate because of duty, social pressures, or entertainment? Did you simply overestimate the probable impact of your participation?

Perhaps the most intriguing type of political behavior is protest activity, including both legal and illegal acts. Why are people willing to risk time in jail or even their lives for political causes? The probability that their individual participation would make a difference is close to zero. In addition, they often gain negligible direct benefits or none at all. For example, anti-abortion demonstrators risk fines and imprisonment even though they will not benefit materially from restrictions on abortion. The vast majority of people who demonstrate to preserve abortion rights do not expect to need abortions in the future. Even the demonstrators who risked their lives in the civil rights movement in the 1960s were unlikely to benefit significantly from any changes in the law. Most assuredly, the *material* benefits that these people expected from their political participation certainly were not worth the risking of their lives to face local police, fire hoses, attack dogs, and the Ku Klux Klan.

Throughout the world, young middle-class and upper-class university students participate in demonstrations for policies that, if adopted, would actually harm their own economic interests. Many young people participate in armed struggles against current regimes. Expectations based on rational self-interest cannot explain this participation.

TESTING OLSON'S MODEL OF COLLECTIVE ACTION

How might a researcher test Mancur Olson's hypothesis that people join interest groups primarily to obtain selective incentives? The simplest test would ask members why they joined. Did they join mainly because they wanted to help provide collective goods such as protection for wilderness or the right to own a machine gun? Did they join to obtain selective incentives such as a magazine, a trip down the Colorado river, or a good price on an Uzi?

A survey of members of environmental groups in the United States found four major reasons for joining:

1. To help supply collective goods for themselves and others
2. To obtain solidary benefits
3. To receive material goods (selective incentives)
4. To do their civic duty[15]

Members of environmental groups most frequently claimed that they joined to help provide collective goods. Fully 82 percent expressed the belief that their individual contributions would affect environmental policy outcomes.[16]

Members of most public interest groups would probably give similar reasons. For example, a woman might join the National Organization of Women (NOW) for several reasons. She may believe that her membership would help to improve life chances not only for herself, but also for her female friends and her daughters (collective goods benefits). She may enjoy the local NOW meetings and the friendships she makes there (solidary benefits). She may also enjoy the organization's bimonthly magazine and expect to improve her own career through the contacts she makes at NOW meetings (selective incentives). Also, she may believe that she must "do her part" in the struggle for women's rights (civic duty).

Do the reasons for joining economically oriented interest groups differ from reasons for joining to promote social causes? A survey discovered that 60 percent of economic trade association members believe that their individual contributions increase the success of the group's lobbying efforts.[17] This is true even of organizations with thousands of members.[18] Clearly, Hardin correctly anticipated that people who join groups vastly overestimate the impact of their individual participation on the provision of collective goods.

Despite their belief that their contributions affect supplies of collective goods, most members of economic groups listed selective incentives (private material benefits) as their main reason for joining the groups.[19] Asked whether they would remain in their associations only for selective incentives, most members in all of the groups indicated that they would remain. When asked if they would remain members if their groups stopped providing selective incentives but continued lobbying, most said that they would drop their memberships.

These studies suggest that people join public interest groups such as environmental organizations and pro-choice or pro-life groups primarily to help provide collective goods. Members believe that their contributions will increase the likelihood of environmental preservation, the woman's right to choose, the fetus's right to be born, or the right of citizens to carry automatic weapons. On the other hand, when a group's principal goals deal with economic concerns, individuals behave more as Olson would suggest. They join and remain members to obtain selective incentives rather than to provide collective goods.

UNLAWFUL PARTICIPATION

Political participation in illegal political actions normally has a much higher cost than participation in more traditional and socially accepted forms of political behavior.** For this reason, a researcher might expect an individual to cite different reasons for this participation than people who participate in legal ways.

In a series of studies, Edward Muller and his associates examined protest behavior and illegal political activity in several countries.[20] One of these studies involved citizens of Peru.[21] At the time of the study, that country suffered from a host of economic and political problems. Its inflation rate was over 100 percent per year, it had experienced seven consecutive years of recession, and the incomes of workers and members of the middle class had posted substantial declines. In addition, the government was fighting a Marxist guerilla army and terrorist group, the Shining Path. More than half of the country fell within "military emergency zones," and over 19,000 people had died in political violence during the previous 8 years.[22] If any country in the world was ripe for illegal political actions, it was Peru.

To examine the possible causes of illegal activity, Muller and his associates interviewed two sets of citizens. The first set included a national sample of adult citizens in all areas of the country except for the more remote rural areas. Students from two universities in the capital city of Lima comprised the second set. The government believed that the universities were strongholds of the revolutionary movement.

Muller and his associates tested the proposition that participation in unlawful rebellion is a rational decision. They hypothesized that whether or not a person took part in these illegal activities would depend on the benefits and costs to that individual of participating. However, the authors expanded their definition of *benefits* to include not only selective incentives, but also the rewards of conforming to group norms and acting in a manner consistent with personal ethical ideals. In other words, the authors included psychological and social rewards in their catalog of benefits.

The study also tested whether participation increases with people's estimations of (a) the likelihood that the rebellious activity will succeed and (b) the importance of the individual's contribution to the ultimate success of the revolution. Muller and his associates hypothesized that the expected costs of participation would powerfully affect a person's decision whether or not to take part in the illegal activities. To test this hypothesis, the interviewers asked respondents to estimate:

1. The probability that the government would catch them

2. The severity of the punishment they would suffer if caught

3. The financial gain or loss they would receive if the rebellion were to succeed

Analysis of these interviews shows that the desire to help create a better society is an important motivation for students and nonstudents. In both samples, the individuals'

** It is probably impossible to accurately measure the percentage of the population who participate in unlawful activities. Suppose that you have just participated in a terrorist attack. Someone comes to your door claiming to be a political scientist doing a survey and asks you if you have participated in a terrorist attack in the past 12 months. Would you give a truthful answer?

estimations of the likelihood that the revolt would succeed and whether their own participation would make a difference strongly influenced their probability of participation. In both samples, the encouragement of friends and their pressure to join in the protest activity increased the probability of participation. However, these social pressures were much stronger for the university sample than for the general population. An expressed desire to stand up for a belief in the illegitimacy of the current government increased participation in the nonstudent sample. The belief that rebellious behavior is morally wrong reduced participation for both samples, but the effect was stronger for nonstudents. Surprisingly, both sets of respondents said that possible negative sanctions did not reduce their participation.

IS PARTICIPATION RATIONAL?

If the test of rational participation in political activities requires that the material benefits of participation must exceed the costs of participation, then most political participation reflects irrational decisions. The expected material benefits of these actions almost never outweigh their actual costs. The probability that an individual's vote will decide a national election is much lower than the probability that the individual will be killed or seriously injured in an accident while traveling to the polling place. Only by including social and psychological benefits can a political scientist make sense of participation in politics.

Studies of different types of political participation have found several common factors that lead people to vote, join groups, and involve themselves in illegal activities. These factors are strong social norms, the expectations of friends and associates, personal beliefs about the morality of an action, the desire to take part in something important, and the belief that one's own actions make a difference.

Clearly, most people who participate in politics greatly overestimate the impact of their personal participation on political outcomes. We can say with complete confidence that no one reading this book has ever cast a ballot in a city, state, or national election that was decided by only one vote. Objectively, therefore, your vote does not matter because it never changes an election's outcome. Similarly, if you attended a rally for a presidential candidate during the 1996 elections, your attendance had no impact on the probability that your candidate would gain the party's nomination for president. It really does not matter whether 500 people or only 499 attend a rally or a protest demonstration. Neither does the political outcome of gun legislation or abortion policy depend on whether the National Rifle Association or the National Abortion Rights Action League has one more or one less member. Even a rebellion does not turn on the participation of one more or one less rebel.

Can political scientists conclude, therefore, that participation does not matter? They certainly cannot make this judgment. Harriet Beecher Stowe, Susan B. Anthony, Margaret Sanger, Rosa Parks, Malcolm X, and Lee Harvey Oswald all changed outcomes in American politics. In general, however, collective actions have more important effects than a single person's actions have. This is particularly true in democracies. A democracy can continue only when enough people participate in campaign-related actions to maintain the legitimacy of the electoral process.

Because elections are vital to maintaining democracy, society's educational system, the media, and people's family and friends help to socialize people to value the importance of civic duty. If no one comes to a candidate's political rallies, the candidate will not win a party's nomination. If too few persons had joined the civil rights movement in the 1960s, minorities in the United States would have far fewer rights in the 1990s. Similarly, a group can lobby for its goals only if enough people donate to the cause. Participation in politics is another example of a collective dilemma. If too many people free ride, no one will receive the collective good of a democratic society.

Who Participates?

Although a single individual's lawful participation rarely affects the outcome of the political process, political scientists care deeply about who participates. If people with one set of characteristics participate at higher rates than another set of people, then the activity of the members of the first set gives them a political advantage. For example, if people without school-aged children participate more than people with school-aged children, then society is likely to spend less on schools than it would spend if those proportions were reversed.

THE PARADOX OF PARTICIPATION

As mentioned earlier, the question of the irrationality of political participation leads to a remarkable conclusion about how much people routinely overestimate the impact of their own participation. If you believe that what you do or say can bring about a desired outcome, then a psychologist would say that you show a high level of *efficacy*. People who believe that they can personally influence political outcomes display what political scientists call **political efficacy.** High political efficacy does not mean that you can actually influence outcomes, only that you believe you can. Earlier discussions have revealed the unrealistic basis for this belief.

Notice, however, what happens if a set of people with common political values and goals also share the (mistaken) belief that their individual contributions toward the desired goal will make a difference. These people are far more likely to achieve their collective goal through their irrational action than if they had rationally declined to participate. To take politically effective action, a social class, ethnic group, or other set of individuals must convince its members that either (a) their individual participation will make a difference despite the fact that this belief is objectively incorrect, or (b) members have a duty to participate despite the fact that any one individual's participation will not make a difference.

If people with certain characteristics *feel* more efficacious, then they are more likely to overcome the free rider problems involved in political participation. This gives the people with those characteristics an advantage in politics because their demands are more likely to gain attention and responses from leaders. This is particularly true in democratic societies where citizens choose their leaders and, collectively, influence public policies.

DEMOGRAPHIC INFLUENCES ON PARTICIPATION

If groups can enjoy unusual political success through unusually active participation, do different sets of people in society show consistently different rates of political participation? They certainly do! In many countries, legal and social barriers based on race, ethnicity, or religion prevent citizens from participating in politics. South Africa denied black citizens the right to vote in national elections for most of its history. Voting restrictions in major portions of the United States discouraged minority ethnic groups from registering and voting. Not until the Voting Rights Act of 1965 did most of these ethnically biased practices begin to disappear in the United States. Turkey and Iraq still restrict participation by their Kurdish populations, and Israel limits the political participation of Palestinians. Germany and Japan deny rights to political participation to people born in their countries but who are not ethnic Germans or Japanese.

Obviously, if particular racial, ethnic, or religious groups encounter limits on their political participation, they are less likely to have their interests represented. The inferior schools that many African American and Hispanic children attend are part of the many consequences of their ancestors' past exclusion from the political process. Without opportunities to obtain the same quality of education as the majority population, most careers that led to upward social mobility were cut off for African Americans. The absence of blacks and other persons of color from good jobs in South Africa reflects their lack of full rights to participate in South African politics.

Age is another demographic characteristic that relates significantly to political participation. As people become older, they tend to participate more in politics. Two factors explain the differences in participation between younger and older adults. First, young people are not settled into their communities and are more concerned with establishing their careers and families than with active political roles.[23] As these individuals grow older, they become more attached to their communities. This helps them see the importance of politics to their lives and those of their children. This insight gives them a greater incentive to participate. For another reason, people participate more as they age because exposure to life's experiences provides the political skills and information that facilitate effective participation.

Because the elderly in democratic societies participate at higher rates than younger adults, older citizens receive government benefits far in excess of what one might predict based on their numbers. For example, people over 65 are much wealthier as a group than people under 35, but governments in western democracies still make substantial transfers of income from adults under 35 to adults over 65. The elderly wield this "gray power" because they participate more actively in all types of political life except for protest and revolutionary behavior.

Gender also significantly affects political participation. Like racial and ethnic minorities, women have suffered from de jure and de facto barriers to political participation. In most countries, women participate less than males with similar levels of education, income, and political interest.[24] Gender differences become even more pronounced in the change from mass to elite political behavior.

The Impact of Occupation, Income, and Education   The single demographic variable that best predicts rates of political participation in the United States is education. A study of legal participation in Austria, India, Japan, the Netherlands, the United States, Nigeria, and Yugoslavia has found that citizens with higher levels of education and income are significantly more likely to be active in all legal forms of political participation.[25] In their study of American voters, Raymond Wolfinger and Steven Rosenstone observe that, at least in the United States, education rather than income or occupation has the greatest impact on who votes.[26] They argue that education provides the information and skills that people need to understand political issues.

Although education is the most important influence on voting in the United States, its impact is not strong in most other democracies. In his study of a broad set of democracies, Bingham Powell has found that political institutions have a greater impact on voter turnout than characteristics of individuals. Powell analyzed voting turnout in 20 industrialized democracies for the years 1970 and 1980.[27] He included in his analysis seven characteristics of individuals—their levels of education, political efficacy, trust in political institutions, general level of political interest, strength of partisan identification, age, and occupation. Powell adds to these individual variables three political structure variables— the degree to which institutions make registration and voting more difficult, the competitiveness of political parties, and the extent of overlap between social groups and political parties.

Powell's research shows that if an electoral district is competitive (i.e., one where at least two parties have a good chance of winning) and if party and either occupation or religion overlap substantially, then individuals are much more likely to vote. Powell finds that a model that includes only three variables—the country's level of party competition, the overlap between social groups and political parties in a country, and an individual's age—explains 90 percent of the variation in who votes and who does not. Education is an important influence on voting turnout only in the United States and Switzerland.

Powell argued that education is so important in the United States and Switzerland because both countries make it difficult to register and to stay registered. For example, many areas of the United States drop citizens from registration lists if they fail to vote in consecutive statewide elections. Powell also noted that parties in these countries do not overlap highly with social groups based on criteria such as religion and occupation. Therefore, voters have less information about which party will best represent their interests. This puts a much larger burden on the individual citizen to obtain the information necessary to distinguish among parties and candidates. In the absence of such cues, most citizens in the United States act rationally and do not pay these information costs.

Summary

This chapter has tried to make sense of seemingly irrational activities involved in political participation. It began by asking you about your own participation and then moved on to explore the many ways in which people can choose to participate. The chapter examined in closer detail three kinds of participation—voting, joining an interest group, and participating in illegal activities. For each of these behaviors, the chapter asks, "Is it rational to participate in this activity?" Certainly if *rational* means that the individual expects material benefits from participating that exceed the personal costs of participation, then it is irrational to vote, to join an interest group, or to take part in a rebellion.

People participate in these ways because they receive benefits other than strictly material rewards. Neither the Informed Voter model or the Citizen/Duty model of political participation can explain entirely why voting turnout is greater in some countries than in others or why some people in a country vote while others do not. A complete explanation requires variables from both models. In countries such as the United States and Switzerland where ethnic, religious, and occupational allegiances do not overlap closely with partisan preferences, higher levels of education significantly increase political participation. As people grow older, the advantage of more educated people over their contemporaries declines as life experiences give people the skills and the sense of personal efficacy that encourage participation.

Mancur Olson Jr. correctly predicted that most people will not join interest groups unless they gain sufficient material incentives provided only to members. Even with these incentives, however, members of such groups probably would not join unless they also received solidary benefits such as new friends and the psychic benefits of "doing their part" to provide collective goods. Participation in interest groups becomes rational only when the definition of *benefits* includes these social and psychological rewards. Group pressure to do one's part motivates participants in unlawful protests and other rebellious activities. In all types of political behavior, those who participate vastly exaggerate the impact of their participation.

Finally, studies show that institutions critically affect who participates. Difficult registration procedures give an advantage to more educated members of society. Where party differences are clear, and where they overlap with other important characteristics such as occupation, religion, or social class, education becomes less important. These same factors increase voter turnout and reduce the advantage of more educated people.

How do the reasons discussed in this chapter correspond with your reasons for political participation or avoidance? Have you overestimated the probable impact of your vote or contribution to a political group? Did you vote to fulfill a duty or because you thought you might influence the outcome? If you were asked to explain why such a small percentage of the population votes in local elections, could you do it?

QUESTIONS AND EXERCISES

Questions for Reason

1. After reviewing the Informed Voter and Duty/Entertainment models of voting, which do you think better explains why people vote? Support your conclusion.

2. Would you expect the law that allows citizens to register to vote when they obtain their driver's licenses to increase voting? If so, which groups will it affect most?

3. Explain why the United States and Switzerland have the lowest voter turnout rates of industrialized democracies.

4. Among environmental interest groups, the National Wildlife Federation, the Audubon Society, and the Sierra Club have the largest memberships. If you had just finished

reading Mancur Olson Jr.'s book *The Logic of Collective Action* what variables might you examine to see why those three groups are much larger than others?

Questions for Reflection

1. Why do you think that voting rates are so low in the United States? Are any of your reasons different than those described in this chapter?

2. What difficulties might a researcher encounter in using a survey to study protest behavior in a country involved in a civil war? Why might subjects give untruthful answers?

3. If the United States were to adopt a multiparty system to replace its two-party system, how would this change affect voting turnout? Why?

4. Some countries make voting mandatory, and citizens who do not vote may be fined. What are the benefits and costs of such a scheme? Which party would benefit most from a mandatory voting law in the United States?

Questions for Analysis: Probability and Statistical Significance

Before attempting this exercise, you should have read either Appendix A or Appendix B and learned to use either the Micro-Crunch or SPSS software packages. Your instructor will tell you which statistical software is best for you.

This exercise explores two new tools for political science research: **probability** and **statistics.** At this point many students say, "Stop! I don't like math! I find it extremely difficult!" Don't worry. Although statistics uses numbers, the exercise requires almost no math. The computer will handle all the math, and you will supply the logic. Think of statistics as a collection of rules for describing data, testing hypotheses, and making decisions.[28] Don't panic—let Micro-Crunch or SPSS do all the difficult math.

Probability

Remember that science is about noticing associations, developing hypotheses, and then devising ways to test the hypotheses. Many of the advances in modern science came about because scientists tried hard to demonstrate the weaknesses of hypotheses derived from existing theories. In this tradition, one of the most important tasks in science is to determine whether to accept or reject a hypothesis. But how do scientists determine this?

To begin, suppose that you and a friend are going out to eat, but you disagree on where to go. You decide that whoever wins a coin flip will choose. Your friend hands you a coin and you flip it. She calls tails and it comes up tails. She chooses to eat pizza and it's time to choose the toppings. To see who gets to choose, you flip the same coin. Your friend calls tails and wins again. Later, you flip the same coin to see who pays. Your friend calls tails, and she wins once more. How many times must the coin come up tails before you begin doubting whether the coin is rigged?

The odds are 50–50 that an honest coin will come up tails on any given flip. That is, the probability on any flip of an unbiased coin is 0.5 that it will come up tails and 0.5 that it will come up heads. In two flips, the odds are 1 in 4 that an unbiased coin will come up tails twice. This means that the probability of two straight tails is 0.25 (0.5×0.5). The probability of three tails in a row is 0.125 (0.5 × 0.5 × 0.5). If you were to flip the coin a fourth time and it came up tails, you probably would begin to doubt that the coin was honest because the probability of four consecutive tails is only 0.0625 (1 in 16). Finally, if the coin were to come up tails five straight times, the odds of this occurring by chance would be only 0.03 (1 in 32). The laws of probability state how often a particular event such as a coin coming up five tails in a row occurs by chance; statistics is the study of those laws and how to calculate them.

In elementary physics or chemistry, the "laws" governing most physical properties seem *deterministic*. This means that a correctly run experiment will yield the same outcome every time. For instance, if a physicist throws a ball into the air, it should come down every time. In the social sciences, relationships are *probabilistic* rather than deterministic. Therefore, hypotheses include phrases such as "more likely to" or "have a higher probability of."

Knowing how often something could have occurred by chance is extremely important in life, and probability and statistics can contribute very useful insights to this question. Say, for example, that you need an expensive and painful operation. The surgery is not necessary to save your life, but if it succeeds, your life will improve. What will you do if the doctor tells you that, judging by the cases of everyone who has had the operation in the past, the odds are 0.75 that the operation will be successful? (This is the same as saying that 75 percent of the time the operation is successful or that the operation is successful three times out of four.) Will your decision be the same if the doctor says that the operation is successful only 5 percent of the time? (This is the same as saying that the operation has a 0.05 probability of success or that the operation succeeds in 1 in every 20 attempts.) Will you believe that the 0.75 probability of success is the true probability if the operation has been performed only four times? Might you think that the doctors chose to perform the operation only for patients with the most likely chances for success? How large a probability of success would you require to go ahead with the operation?

When people make decisions, they often want to know how frequently an association occurs by chance. For example, you might want to use statistics to help decide whether your friend's suspicious coin is rigged. After the fifth time the coin came up tails, you might hypothesize that your friend has tricked you. You cleverly keep the coin and decide to run an experiment with it when you get back to your room. You decide to flip the coin 100 times to see how frequently it comes up tails. The results will help you decide whether the coin and your friend are honest.

Logically, the experiment allows only two possibilities: (1) The coin is not rigged, and (2) the coin is rigged. Scientists call the first of these hypotheses the **null hypothesis.** The null hypothesis states that the observed association occurred by chance. In a test for a relationship between two variables, the null hypothesis states that any observed relationship occurred by chance, and the variables have no true relationship. The second hypothesis (the one the experiment actually tests) is called the **alternate hypothesis.** The alternate hypothesis for the coin flipping experiment states that the coin was weighted to come up tails more frequently than heads. The alternate hypothesis for a relationship between any two variables states that the observed association is a true one.

	TABLE 5.1	

VOTING BY STUDENTS AND NONSTUDENTS

	Student Status	
Vote	No	Yes
No	89	
	19.0%	22.5%
Yes	42	31
	81.0%	77.5%
Total	50	40
	$p = 0.37$	

You want to give your good friend the benefit of the doubt, so you decide to reject the null hypothesis only if the experiment yields overwhelming evidence that the alternate hypothesis is true. You flip the coin 100 times. It comes up tails 80 times and heads 20 times. Does this constitute overwhelming evidence of a biased coin?

It depends on what you mean by *overwhelming*. An unbiased coin flipped 100 times could possibly come up tails 80 percent of the time. Of course, you must determine the probability of this happening. Suppose that you would accept that the coin is unbiased if you were to find out that a fair coin could have had the result of 80 or more tails in 100 flips at least once in every 20 experiments. In other words, if the probability (p) is even 0.05 that the coin is not rigged toward tails, you will, for the sake of friendship, accept the null hypothesis. You will believe that the coin and your friend are honest. Unfortunately, the probability of 80 or more tails is less than 0.01. It would not occur even 1 time in 100 by chance. Oh, well. Perhaps your friend didn't know that the coin was biased.

Now try an example from political science using the data on political behavior in Peru discussed earlier in the chapter. This experiment will test the hypothesis, "Nonstudents are more likely to vote than students." Professor Edward Muller and his colleagues have kindly offered their data set from that study. From this data, the experimenter randomly chooses 50 nonstudents and 40 college students and checks to see if they voted in the last presidential election, giving the results shown in Table 5.1. The table shows that 81.0 percent of nonstudents voted while 77.5 percent of students voted.

The researcher now wants to answer this question: How likely is it that this result occurred by chance? In other words, how likely is it that the observed association between being a nonstudent and voting is not a true association? The null hypothesis is:

- H_0: Nonstudents and students are equally likely to have voted in the last presidential election.

  The alternate hypothesis is:

- H_a: Nonstudents are more likely than students to have voted in the last election.

TABLE 5.2		

EFFECTIVENESS OF NOAIDS DRUG

	Received Drug	
Developed AIDS	**No**	**Yes**
No	3	7
Yes	7	3
Total	10	10

$$p = 0.18$$

Because social sciences deal in probabilities, no matter which hypothesis the study concludes is correct, it can be wrong. A test of the null hypothesis really asks statistics to answer the question: How likely is it that the hypothesis of no relationship between two variables is correct? At some point, the chance is just too small to accept the null hypothesis, and the researcher rejects it. This leaves no option but to accept the alternate hypothesis.

Try another example. Assume that a tragedy occurs and you contract HIV. Your doctor tells you about a new drug called "Noaids." In a previous experiment using 20 subjects with HIV, 10 received a placebo and 10 received Noaids. The results of the experiment in Table 5.2 indicate that 70 percent of those who received the placebo developed AIDS while 70 percent of those who received Noaids did not. Unfortunately, Noaids has substantial side effects. Patients who take it feel sick for 2 days a month, and it slightly increases the chance that they will develop bone cancer. Your doctor offers you two options: Take Noaids, or wait and hope that another drug will come along soon. What should you do?

The null hypothesis in this decision states, "Patients who receive the placebo and those who receive Noaids are equally likely to develop AIDS." The alternative hypothesis states, "Patients who receive Noaids are less likely to develop AIDS than patients who receive the placebo." You want to know how likely is it that the null hypothesis is correct and how likely is it that the alternative hypothesis is correct. In this example, the probability that the null hypothesis is correct is $p = 0.18$. In other words, if Noaids had no actual relationship with preventing the disease, then the drug study would give a distribution at least as skewed as that shown in Table 5.2 18 percent of the time. The research reveals a probability of a relationship between receiving Noaids and not developing AIDS of 0.82. Although statistics and the laws of probability cannot tell you what to do, they can give you information you need to make an informed choice.

Now return to the much less serious example of who votes in Peru. In fact, the distribution of voting behavior by nonstudents and students in Table 5.1 could occur quite easily by chance. The null hypothesis—that nonstudents and students are equally likely to have voted in the past presidential election—has a probability of 0.37 of being correct. This means that the observed difference between voting and student status would occur 37

	TABLE 5.3	

CROSS TABULATION: VOTE BY STUDENT

	Student Status	
Vote	No	Yes
No	77	87
	15.6%	22.2%
Yes	416	305
	84.4%	77.8%
Total	493	392
	100%	100%
	$p = 0.02$	

percent of the time by chance if the two variables had no relationship. Suppose that a second survey samples 900 people. Because of missing data,[††] the research has only 885 cases to consider. Micro-Crunch and the file PERUCAT can indicate whether the difference observed in the small sample remains for the entire data set. The results in Table 5.3 confirm that the percentages do not change much from the small sample to the large sample.

Although the percentages in Tables 5.1 and 5.3 are similar, the likelihood that the null hypothesis is correct drops dramatically from Table 5.1 to Table 5.3. The probability that the distribution in Table 5.3 would occur by chance is 0.02. This leads the researcher to reject the null hypothesis and accept the alternative hypothesis that nonstudents are more likely to have voted than students.

Why did the probability that the null hypothesis is correct drop from 0.37 to 0.02 when the sample size increased? As the sample size increases, the confidence that an observed difference is a true difference also increases. Think of it this way. If you wanted to know whether a coin was biased, you might find that it comes up heads four times and tails only twice. You would probably not conclude that the coin was biased from such a small sample of data. If, however, it came up heads 40 times and tails only 20 times, then you probably would conclude that the coin was biased toward heads.

Similarly, say that you wanted to know whether men and women in Chicago held different attitudes toward affirmative action programs. Would you be willing to trust the results from a survey of just one man and one woman picked randomly from the city? How about five men and five women? What about 500 of each? People intuitively understand that, as the number of trials or respondents goes up, an observed association between two variables is more likely to be a true one, even if the strength of the

---

[††] As some of you are probably aware, respondents to surveys often refuse to answer certain questions. On other occasions the individual doing the survey may have entered an incorrect code. Both of these situations create missing observations in our data set. In this particular case we do not have answers on voting for seven nonstudents and eight students.

FIGURE 5.1

CROSS TABULATION: WILLLEGL BY EFFICACY

	1.000 Low	2.000 Moderate	3.000 High
1 Unlikely	80 38.8%	62 18.7%	82 25.2%
2 Possible	110 53.4%	179 53.9%	148 45.5%
3 Likely	16 7.8%	91 27.4%	95 29.2%
	206 100.0%	332 100.0%	325 100.0%

Valid Cases = 863   Missing Cases = 37

Chi-Square is 51.20 with 4 Degrees of Freedom. Min. Expected Cell: 48.2
Phi-Square: 0.057   Cramer's V: 0.169   Cnt. Coef.: 0.232
Gamma: 0.227   Lambda (A): 0.000   Tau-B: 0.146   Tau-C: 0.139

relationship stays constant. Statistics and the laws of probability confirm people's intuitive knowledge with more precision.

Calculating the Probability that the Null Hypothesis Is True
For each of the examples discussed so far, the text stated the probability that the null hypothesis was true. For example, in Table 5.3 that probability was 0.02. How did that figure come to be? The computer calculated the probability using the **chi-square statistic.** Chi-square is the statistic that political scientists often use to study contingency tables. To illustrate the use of chi-square with contingency tables, another example will examine a hypothesis about political behavior based on the data from Peru: The higher an individual's sense of political efficacy, the more likely that individual will participate in politics.

Using Micro-Crunch and the data set PERUCAT, the measure of political efficacy is the variable EFFICACY. This variable represents an index of responses to questions such as, How much do you think you can affect what the government does? The measure of participation in politics is the variable WILLLEGL. WILLLEGL is an index of individuals' responses to questions concerning how likely they are to participate in legal protest activities such as lawful demonstrations. Figure 5.1 shows the results of this analysis. The bottom row of the table shows that only 7.8 percent of people with low values for political efficacy answered that they would likely participate in legal protest activities, while 29.2 percent of respondents with high levels of efficacy said that they would likely participate in such activities.

FIGURE 5.2

CROSS TABULATION: WILLLEGL BY EFFICACY[a]

	1.000 Low	2.000 Moderate	3.000 High
1 Unlikely	54 26.0%	86 26.0%	85 16.0%
2 Possible	105 50.6%	168 50.6%	164 50.6%
3 Likely	47 23.4%	78 23.4%	76 23.4%
	206	332	325

Chi-Square = 0.00 with 4 Degrees of Freedom

[a]Expected distribution with no relationship between variables.

Look at the text below the figure. It reads "Chi-Square is 51.20 with 4 Degrees of Freedom." This material determines whether the researcher accepts or rejects the null hypothesis, which states: "People with low and high levels of political efficacy are equally likely to say that they probably will participate in legal protests."

How did those numbers appear in the figure? To understand this process, imagine what Figure 5.1 would look like if the study were to find absolutely no relationship between people's political efficacy and the likelihood that they would participate in legal protests. The figure should then look like Figure 5.2. *The critical characteristic of this figure is that each cell of the same row has exactly the same percentage of the total cases reported in the column.* In the top row, every cell shows 26 percent; in the middle row, every cell lists 50.6 percent; in the bottom row, every cell has 23.4 percent. If the figure were based on real data, it would indicate that knowing a person's level of political efficacy would not help you to predict the likelihood that she would participate in legal protests. In other words, the data would show no relationship between the independent variable and the dependent variable. In this situation, the researcher obviously would accept the null hypothesis that people with high and low levels of political efficacy are equally likely to participate in legal protests.

Notice, that absolutely no association between the variables in a table gives a chi-square value of zero. A figure with two strongly related variables will have higher chi-square values. Thus, a higher chi-square indicates a stronger relationship between variables.

The computer calculates the chi-square statistic by comparing the actual or observed frequencies in each cell in a table with the frequencies that would be expected with no relationship between the two variables. The formula for calculating the chi-square is shown below. Those who like math may feel free to calculate the chi-square in all the tables that this section will examine.

$$X^2 = \frac{\Sigma(O_i - E_i)^2}{E_i}$$

Where

X^2 is the symbol for chi-square

Σ is the symbol for a sum over all cells

O_i is the observed number of observations in a cell

E_i is the expected number of observations in a cell

To keep the promise that you will not have to do any difficult math, you need not memorize or use this equation. It is intended to help those who would like to know how to calculate the chi-square statistic.

Two factors determine the size of the chi-square. The first is the strength of the relationship between variables. A stronger relationship corresponds to a larger chi-square. The second factor that influences the size of a chi-square is the sample size. Larger samples generate higher chi-squares. This makes intuitive sense because, as discussed above, the confidence that a hypothesis states a true relationship increases as the number of observations increases.

Critical Values and Statistical Significance

Remember that scientists attempt to falsify hypotheses; they do not accept a hypothesis that establishes the truth of an observed association between two variables without strong evidence to support that association. Traditionally, social scientists have set one of three probability levels to guide the decision whether to reject the null hypothesis and accept the alternate hypothesis confirming the truth of an association. These probabilities are 0.10, 0.05, and 0.01. They call these probability levels **critical values.** In the test for bias in your friend's coin, you set a critical value of 0.05. This decision determined that even 1 chance in 20 that the coin was unbiased would lead you to accept the null hypothesis.

The scientist's choice of a critical value depends on how conservative she wants to make her test and the costs of rejecting a true hypothesis. A critical value of 0.10 implies that about 10 percent of the time, the researcher will accept as true an association between two variables that actually occurred by chance. The 0.05 level leaves only 1 chance in 20 of mistakenly accepting an association as true when it is not.

You might wonder why a researcher would not choose an even smaller critical value such as 0.001. This would create too much risk of accepting the null hypothesis when the alternate hypothesis is true. Remember the Noaids example. In real life, many people are quite willing to accept a 0.2 or even a 0.5 chance of incorrectly confirming a relationship between taking a drug and not dying of a disease such as cancer or AIDS.

Scientists also talk about a relationship's statistical significance. A **statistically significant** relationship is simply one in which the probability that the null hypothesis is true falls below the selected critical value. Social scientists and public opinion pollsters typically set the probability level at 0.05. Therefore, you can generally assume that when a television newscaster says that a research result is statistically significant, the statement really means that the study found less than 1 chance in 20 that the observed association between two variables occurred by chance.

TABLE 5.4

CRITICAL VALUES OF χ^2

Degrees of Freedom	Significance Level			
	0.10	0.05	0.01	0.001
1	2.71	3.84	6.63	10.83
2	4.61	5.99	9.21	13.81
3	6.25	7.81	11.34	16.27
4	7.78	9.49	13.28	18.47
5	9.24	11.07	15.09	20.51
6	10.64	12.59	16.81	22.46
7	12.02	14.07	18.48	24.32
8	13.36	15.51	20.09	26.12
9	14.68	16.92	21.67	27.88
10	15.99	18.31	23.21	29.59
12	18.55	21.03	26.22	32.91
14	21.06	23.68	29.14	36.12
16	23.54	26.30	32.00	39.25
18	25.99	28.87	34.81	42.31
20	28.41	31.41	37.57	45.31

Degrees of Freedom

In addition to the actual chi-square value, one other condition determines whether a particular chi-square test reaches statistical significance. This condition is the number of degrees of freedom in the contingency table, as in the notation "4 Degrees of Freedom" below Figures 5.1 and 5.2. The degrees of freedom in a table equal the number of rows minus 1 multiplied by the number of columns minus 1 $[(r-1) \times (c-1)]$. In a contingency table with two rows and two columns, the degrees of freedom equal 1 $[(2 - 1) \times (2 - 1)]$. For a three by four table, the number of degrees of freedom would equal 6 $[(3 - 1) \times (4 - 1)]$. For reasons that would take this discussion too far from its central subject, statistical significance requires higher chi-square values for tables with more degrees of freedom. Table 5.4 lists the chi square values necessary to reach statistical significance at the critical values of 0.10, 0.05, and 0.01. If you are using Micro-Crunch, you will need to check this table to judge the statistical significance of a relationship. If you are using SPSS, the table will provide the exact probability that the null hypothesis is correct.

SUMMARY

This list briefly summarizes all the material covered in the preceding discussion:

- Hypotheses in the social sciences deal with probabilistic relationships.
- To test these relationships, researchers gather data (or use data someone else has gathered) on the variables included in the hypotheses.

FIGURE 5.3

CROSS TABULATION: WILLNOLG BY EFFICACY

	1.000 Low	2.000 Moderate	3.000 High
1 Unlikely	94 46.5%	96 29.0%	115 35.8%
2 Possible	88 43.6%	143 43.2%	104 32.4%
3 Likely	20 9.9%	92 27.8%	102 31.8%
	202 100.0%	331 100.0%	321 100.0%

Valid Cases = 854   Missing Cases = 46

Chi-Square is 42.20 with 4 Degrees of Freedom. Min. Expected Cell: 50.6
Phi-Square: 0.047   Cramer's V: 0.153   Cnt. Coef.: 0.212
Gamma: 0.182   Lambda (A): 0.033   Tau-B: 0.120   Tau-C: 0.118

- The researcher formulates two possible hypotheses about any association that the data might reveal. The first, the null hypothesis, states that no true relationship exists between the variables; any observed association occurred by chance. The second, the alternate hypothesis, states that the observed association reflects a true relationship. Logically, one of these hypotheses must be false.

- To decide which hypothesis to accept, the researcher chooses a critical value. Generally this value is 0.10, 0.05, or 0.01.

- To determine whether an observed association reaches the critical value, the researcher refers to a computer-generated contingency table and its chi-square value. Together with the degrees of freedom in the table, this value determines whether the researcher accepts or rejects the null hypothesis. If the chi-square is smaller than the critical value of chi-square in Table 5.4, then the researcher cannot reject the null hypothesis. If the chi-square value is larger than that critical value, the study confirms the alternate hypothesis.

An Example

To demonstrate the simplicity of this task, consider another example from the Peru data set. Figure 5.1 reported the impact of political efficacy on participation in legal protests. This example will examine the effect of political efficacy on participation in illegal political activity. The measure of political efficacy is the same as above, the variable EFFICACY. The measure of illegal political activity, WILLNOLG, is a variable computed from respondents' answers to a set of questions concerning how likely they would be to

FIGURE 5.4

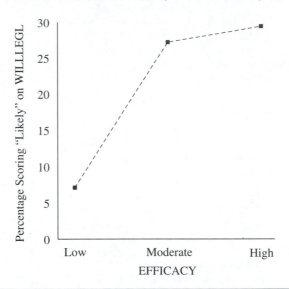

RELATIONSHIP BETWEEN POLITICAL EFFICACY AND
LEGAL PARTICIPATION (ACTUAL DATA)

participate in illegal political actions. WILLNOLG has three values: UNLIKELY, POS-
SIBLE, and LIKELY.

Set the critical value at 0.05. If the data give a chi-square that is below the value
necessary to reject the null hypothesis at the 0.05 level, then this will confirm the null
hypothesis. That will mean that the study finds no statistically significant relationship
between the measure of political efficacy and the measure of illegal political behavior.

Micro-Crunch (as described in Appendix A) gives the results shown in Figure 5.3.
The chi-square is 42.20 with 4 degrees of freedom. A quick check of Table 5.4 shows
that, at a critical value of 0.05, a chi-square of 9.49 or lower would lead to rejection of
the null hypothesis. Therefore, the research confirms the hypothesis that higher levels of
political efficacy are associated with higher probabilities of participating in illegal
political activity.

Graphing Relationships

Often researchers find it useful to graph relationships. They can relatively easily develop
graphs with only two variables. Figure 5.4 is the graph of the data in Figure 5.1. Notice
that the graph measures the independent variable, EFFICACY, along the X axis (at the
bottom of the graph) and it measures the dependent variable, WILLLEGL, along the Y
axis (up the side of the graph).

Observe how the information in Figure 5.1 translates into the graph. A graph normally represents the bottom row of data in a table. To develop the graph, for each value
of the independent variable, find the percentage of the cases that fall into each cell in the

FIGURE 5.5

CHART OF HYPOTHETICAL DATA SHOWING NO RELATIONSHIP BETWEEN EFFICACY AND WILLLEGL

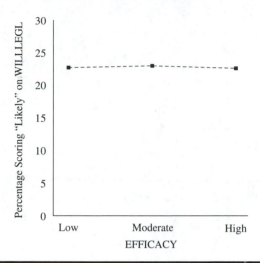

bottom row of the table. In Figure 5.1, these percentages are 7.8, 27.4, and 29.2. On graph paper, construct a set of axes with percentages along the side lower than the lowest value in the bottom row and higher than the highest value in that row. For instance, the percentages in Figure 5.4 go from zero to 30. Mark the points on the graph where the value of the independent variable intersects with the appropriate percentage, then connect the dots. If the line slopes upward, then the relationship between the two variables is positive. If the line slopes downward, then the relationship between the variables is negative. If the line is flat, it indicates no relationship between the variables. Figure 5.5 illustrates a flat line that indicates no relationship between the variables in Figure 5.2.

Recall the hypothesis that higher levels of efficacy will lead to higher levels of legal political participation. This led to an expectation of an upward-sloping graph for Figure 5.1; Figure 5.4 confirms this expectation. The steepest part of the slope in Figure 5.4 is between low and moderate levels of efficacy. After that, the relationship begins to become level. A graph of Figure 5.2 shows that the relationship between WILLNOLG and EFFICACY is almost exactly the same as that between WILLLEGL and EFFICACY. Again, the line slopes upward, indicating a positive relationship. Also, the steepest slope is between low and moderate levels of EFFICACY.

Analysis Exercise: Political Participation

This chapter examined various models of political participation. It found difficulties with the Rational Actor model because the costs of a political action appear to exceed the benefits for almost every behavior. Muller, and his colleagues tried to save the rational

---

FIGURE 5.6

RELATIONSHIP BETWEEN POLITICAL EFFICACY AND
ILLEGAL PARTICIPATION (ACTUAL DATA)

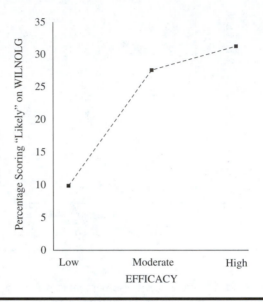

---

actor model by including in the benefits side of the equation the psychological value of acting in accordance with one's personal norms and the expectations of friends. In this exercise, you will test their hypotheses using a sample of the data they collected from Peru. Their model contains six abstract hypotheses:

1. Higher political efficacy makes a person more likely to participate.
2. People who consider politics more important are more likely to participate.
3. A person who perceives a greater likelihood that a collective action will be successful has a higher probability of participating in that action.
4. Stronger peer-group support for a political action increases the likelihood of participation in that action.
5. Individuals whose personal values more strongly support a political behavior are more likely to participate in the behavior.
6. Higher expected costs of a particular action to an individual reduce the probability that the person will participate in that action.

Muller and his associates believed that these benefits and costs would predict political participation such as voting, party activities, and taking part in unlawful protests. Their research addresses a critical question: Are the variables that influence legal political action the same as those that influence illegal political action? Figures 5.1 and 5.2

examined Hypothesis 1 for both legal and illegal participation. The data reveal the expected positive relationship (as shown in Figures 5.4 and 5.6) and the chi-square values were sufficiently high to reject the null hypothesis in both cases.

Constructing Contingency Tables[‡‡]

Micro-Crunch will easily construct contingency tables as directed by the user. To see how, consider a test of Muller's Hypothesis 2.

Start Micro-Crunch and select the data set PERUCAT. Micro-Crunch will display the screen shown on page 408 in Appendix A. Select the option "Tables." Next, select the option "Crosstab." Micro-Crunch will then ask for the *dependent* variable. To test Hypothesis 2, which relates legal activity to interest in politics, you might choose the dependent variable: **VOTE.** (Take a moment and think why VOTE is the dependent variable.)

Micro-Crunch will then ask for the *independent* variable. Enter **INTEREST.**

Micro-Crunch will now ask for a "filter variable." This is a request for a control variable. These exercises do not require a control variable, so simply press the Enter key.

Micro-Crunch will go about its crunching and then respond with a table that includes the chi-square and the number of degrees of freedom. Check Table 5.4 to see if the resulting chi-square is higher than the critical value. If it is, you can reject the null hypothesis.

For a measure of illegal political behavior, you might choose WILLNOLG. Use INTEREST as your independent variable. Generate the table and decide whether to accept or reject the null hypothesis.

You are now ready to test Hypotheses 3 through 6 in Muller's model. *Remember to operationalize two hypotheses for each abstract hypothesis: one for legal participation and one for illegal participation.* The codebook at the beginning of Appendix C (page 431) lists variables for these tests. The codebook lists the measures alphabetically. Think of a good reason for choosing each variable. You may keep the same dependent variable throughout the analysis, or you may choose to change them.

Choose measures of the following abstract variables:

1. Legal political actions
2. Illegal political actions
3. Expectation that legal collective action will be effective
4. Expectation that illegal collective action will be effective
5. Peer group and social norms for legal actions
6. Peer group and social norms for illegal actions
7. Individual's own values favoring or opposing legal actions
8. Individual's own values favoring or opposing illegal actions
9. Perceived cost of legal political behavior
10. Perceived cost of illegal political behavior

[††] If you are using SPSS for Windows, the Data Analysis section of Appendix B provides instructions for constructing contingency tables.

Next use your word processor to write eight operationalized hypotheses. Save this material to a file and give it a name such as LAB5.HYP. Now you are ready to enter Micro-Crunch and create the tables.

Follow these steps to accomplish this assignment:

1. Use the codebook for PERUCAT to choose measures.

2. Write out hypotheses relating legal behavior to Muller's Hypotheses 3 through 6.

3. Write out hypotheses relating illegal behavior to Muller's Hypotheses 3 through 6.

4. Save this work as the word-processing file LAB5.HYP.

5. Enter Micro-Crunch and select PERUCAT as the data file.

6. Select Tables from the menu.

7. Select Crosstabs from the menu.

8. Run your eight contingency tables and save them by choosing the Write to Disk option. Be sure to give this file a different name than you gave your word-processing file. For example, you might call it LAB5.TBL.

9. Exit Micro-Crunch and call up your word-processing file. Under each hypothesis, report whether Micro-Crunch confirmed or falsified it and report the percentages and the chi-square values.

10. Call your Micro-Crunch file into the word-processing file. Most word processors can treat the file from Micro-Crunch as a text file. You may have to choose a different font. (A proportionally spaced font will not work to print tables.) A safe choice is Courier 12 or New Courier 8.

11. Make sure that your name is on the first page and that the pages are numbered. The computer can number the pages for you.

12. Use the spell check feature of the word processor to catch spelling errors. Print the word-processing file.

13. Graph the results of each table on a separate piece of paper. You can choose to do this by pen and ink or you can use the computer.

NOTES

[1] Harold D. Lasswell, *Politics: Who Gets What, When, How* (New York: McGraw Hill, 1936).

[2] Mancur Olson, Jr., *The Logic of Collective Action* (Cambridge, Mass.: Harvard University Press, 1965), p. 51.

[3] Melvin J. Hinich and Michael C. Munger, *Ideology and the Theory of Political Choice* (Ann Arbor: University of Michigan Press, 1994), p. 42.

[4] Robert W. Jackman, "Political Institutions and Voter Turnout in the Industrial Democracies," *American Political Science Review* 81 (1987), pp. 405–423.

[5] G. Bingham Powell, "American Voter Turnout in Comparative Perspective," *American Political Science Review* 80 (1986), pp. 17–43.

[6] Jackman, "Political Institutions," p. 420.

[7] Powell, "American Voter Turnout" pp. 19–26.

[8] Ibid., p. 26.

[9] Alan S. Zuckerman, *Doing Political Science: An Introduction to Political Analysis* (Boulder, Colo.: Westview Press, 1991), pp. 18–33.

[10] Ibid., p. 27.

[11] Philip Converse, "The Nature of Belief Systems in Mass Publics," in *Ideology and Discontent,* ed. by David Apter (London: Free Press, 1964). For a more recent review of issue constraints, see Hinich and Munger, *Ideology and the Theory of Political Choice.*

[12] Kay Lehman Schlozman and John T. Tierney, *Organized Interests and American Democracy* (Cambridge: Harper and Row), p. 60.

[13] James Q. Wilson, *Political Organization* (New York: Basic Books, 1973).

[14] Russel Hardin, *Collective Action* (Baltimore, Md.: Johns Hopkins University Press, 1982).

[15] R. Kenneth Godwin and Robert Cameron Mitchell, "Rational Models, Collective Goods, and Nonelectoral Political Behavior," *Western Political Quarterly* 35 (1982), pp. 161–181.

[16] Ibid. Although some readers may wonder whether group members actually believe that their $35 could make a difference, compare this idea with the results of a survey done by a Tucson, Arizona, newspaper: Fully one-third of those who played the state's lottery expected eventually to win a prize worth more than $100,000.

[17] Terry M. Moe, *The Organization of Interests* (Chicago: University of Chicago Press, 1980). Trade associations are groups of firms that pursue the same economic activities. Moe studied a printing company association, a retail store federation, a hardware association, and two farm organizations. In return for paying dues, members of each association received individual services and benefits such as medical and casualty insurance and information on topics like the impact of new government regulations on their businesses and better ways to produce goods or collect bills. Members also received the collective benefit of the trade association's lobbying efforts for legislation and rules that would benefit the group's central economic activity.

[18] Ibid., p. 207.

[19] Ibid., p. 209.

[20] Muller and his associates studied protest behavior in the United States and Germany. See Edward N. Muller and Karl-Dieter Opp, "Rational Choice and Rebellious Collective Action," *American Political Science Review* 80 (1986), pp. 471–489. For a study of similar activity in Central America, see Edward N. Muller and Mitchell A. Seligson, "Inequality and Insurgency," *American Political Science Review* 81 (1986), pp. 425–452. See also Edward N. Muller, Henry A. Dietz, and Steven E. Finkel, "Discontent and the Expected Utility of Rebellion: The Case of Peru," *American Political Science Review* 85 (1991), pp. 1261–1282.

[21] Muller, Dietz, and Finkel, "Discontent and Expected Utility."

[22] Ibid., pp. 1262–1263.

[23] Sidney Verba, Norman H. Nie, and Jae-On Kim, *Participation and Political Equality: A Seven-Nation Comparison* (Cambridge: Cambridge University Press, 1978), p. 266.

[24] Ibid., pp. 255–257.

[25] Verba, Nie, and Kim, *Participation and Political Equality,* p. 266.

[26] Raymond E. Wolfinger and Steven J. Rosenstone, *Who Votes?* (New Haven: Yale University Press, 1980), pp. 17–28.

[27] Powell, "American Voter Turnout."

[28] W. Bruce Shepard, "Modern Political Analysis," Oregon State University, Corvallis, Ore., mimeographed (1990), p. 51.

6

Linking Citizens
to Government

Key Terms

Institution
Institutional Structure
Postmaterialist
  Ideology
Libertarian
Authoritarian

Voters' Paradox
Single-member
  Legislative District
Proportional
  Representation
Theory of Pluralism

Logrolling
Association
Time Priority
Rationale
Spurious Association

Chapter 5 examined the political behavior of citizens and discovered that almost all political behavior appears irrational if rational activities include only actions that provide higher material benefits than material costs. The expected costs outweigh the expected benefits for almost every possible political action. Yet, governments can function effectively only if citizens participate in politics. All political systems include both demands and supports from the public. Public inputs are particularly critical in democracies because those governments' decisions and policies should reflect the demands and desires of citizens. This chapter focuses on the institutions necessary to link citizen demands and desires to public policy.

Citizens demand particular policies and outcomes from policy makers, but how do public officials make sense of 50 million different sets of demands? Political science refers to the process of making sense of citizen demands as *demand aggregation*. In this process, leaders put your demands together with those of other citizens to form a meaningful and simplified whole. Only when this occurs can policy makers choose policies that respond to citizens' wants and desires. Obviously, policy makers cannot please everyone, and they cannot have a different set of policies for each of the 50 million sets of requests. How does the political system unify such a diverse set of demands? Four political institutions accomplish the critical task of linking citizen inputs and public policy decisions: ideologies, parties, interest groups, and elections.

Institutions

The political process continually expresses and resolves conflicts within an institutional framework. That is to say, the political process follows a *regularized (established) way of accomplishing public tasks*. Political conflicts and their resolutions conform to accepted patterns and norms. Sometimes the patterns are violent; other times they are nonviolent. These institutions affect any actions of legislators, executives, judges, bureaucrats, and all other political actors and how those people do their work. Institutions determine opportunities, costs, and benefits for political actors.

Institutions are patterns of behavior that persist over time. **Institutional structures** are the participants' conceptions of their own roles and their expectations about the roles of others within political institutions. These are extremely difficult concepts, and we expect many readers to wonder what the last few sentences mean. A few examples will help to clarify them. Most students read this passage because they are taking classes and their instructors assigned these pages. You expect when you take a class that the instructor will assign readings and will base your grade, at least in part, on how well you understand the material. The instructor expects that you will come to class, read the assignments, and participate in discussion. You expect the instructor to come to class, to help you learn and understand the subject matter, and to give fair grades on tests.

In short, the institution "college class" has a well-defined structure. This structure is the set of expectations concerning how you and your instructor will behave. These expectations shape your behavior and that of your instructor. If you or the instructor act in ways incompatible with these expected roles, the deviation may create tension.

Institutions are *not* buildings or laws; they are patterns of behavior. The institution "college class" does not depend on a particular classroom, college, building, teacher, or student. Even if your entire college burned down, the institution "college class" would continue. If you transfer to a different college, you will continue to observe similar patterns of behavior within the institution of the college class.

Institutions are immensely important in helping people get through their daily lives. They provide regularity of behavior to support efficient activity. Some simple but critical institutions include stopping at red lights, driving on the right side of the road, and yielding to pedestrians in a crosswalk. These particular institutions are written into law, but that is not true of most institutions.

Institutional structures are social norms concerning what people expect of one another. Suppose you go for a medical checkup, and the doctor's assistant tells you to go into a small room and to remove your outer clothing. This is a normal procedure, and you follow instructions without undue concern. But what would you do if you received the same instructions at the office of your dentist, minister, or professor? In these cases, the norms created by the institutional structure are not compatible with the suggested behavior.

INSTITUTIONS AND DEMOCRACY

Before the chapter can begin to examine the institutions that link citizens and policy outputs in democracies, it must first answer a fundamental question: Is democracy, including representative democracy, possible? Your response may be similar to that of the Southern Baptist when a sociologist asked, "Do you believe in baptism by immersion?" He responded, "Believe in it? Hell, I've seen it!" Most people not only believe that democracy is possible, but they believe that they live in one. But what does it mean to claim to live in a democracy?

Democracy, at least as most people use the term in ordinary language, means that citizens have a meaningful role in deciding government policy. The word comes from two Greek words, *demos* meaning ordinary people, and *kratia* meaning government. The notion of democracy has always implied popular participation in politics. But how does a society obtain this essential participation when it seems irrational and foolish for citizens to participate? One of the keys to this puzzle is the institution of ideology. Ideology increases the incentives to participate in politics, lowers the costs of information, and helps political parties, interest groups, and elections to function properly.

Ideology

What is an ideology? How does it assist democratic governance? In this book, we adapt the definition used by Melvin Hinich and Michael Munger in their book, *Ideology and the Theory of Political Choice:*

> An **ideology** is an internally consistent set of propositions that makes demands on human behavior. All ideologies have implications for (1) what constitutes ethically good and bad actions, (2) what are the rights and duties of citizens, (3) how resources should be distributed, and (4) where power appropriately resides.[1]

In other words, ideologies indicate what is good and bad, how people should behave to achieve good results, how to decide who gets what, and who should rule. Every ideology includes expectations concerning appropriate patterns of behavior.

Ideology helps citizens overcome the seeming irrationality of political participation in a democratic society, and it helps to communicate policy preferences to public officials. To see how, recall the Duty/Entertainment and Informed Voter models of participation discussed in Chapter 5. When that discussion confronted readers with the seeming irrationality of voting, many probably responded, "But what if everybody acted that way? Democracy couldn't exist!" Of course, they were absolutely correct. Democratic societies cannot afford nonparticipation by its rational citizens. For this reason, the ideologies underlying democracy identify voting and other supportive political behaviors as requirements for "good" citizens. In asking the question, "But what if everybody acted that way?" skeptical readers were repeating philosopher Immanuel Kant's categorical imperative.

The categorical imperative is the rule that requires a moral person to act as if the principle on which he bases his behavior were to become universal. Any ideology, whether a variation of contractarianism, utilitarianism, or communitarianism, includes the requirement that good citizens must participate in politics. In other words, every ideology strongly encourages participation because good citizens perform this duty. This means that social norms, peer group pressure, and personal desire to do what is right increase the psychological benefits of participating in politics. An ideology substantially increases the "duty" benefits in the Duty/Entertainment model of participation, thereby encouraging a participatory pattern of actions.

Ideology also drastically reduces the cost of information. It indicates how to distribute resources in society and the role of government in that distribution. Recall the discussions of the liberal philosophers Robert Nozick and John Rawls in Chapter 2. Each of these writers advocates a particular way of deciding how society should allocate resources and the appropriate role of government in this process. Nozick advocates what people in the United States recognize as a conservative position. He believes that so long as individuals obtain their property in a legal manner, government has no right to take those resources and give them to someone else. Needless to say, this position has strong implications for both the distribution of resources and what government can and cannot do. It says that government *cannot* tax the wealthy to help the poor, tax some to provide free public education and health care to others, or devise affirmative action plans that give children who chose their parents poorly opportunities to compete more equally with children who made better choices.

In sharp contrast, Rawls's ideology argues for greater equality in society. In his ideology, government *must* redistribute income from the wealthy to the poor, provide education and health care to those who cannot afford them, and act affirmatively to give greater opportunities to members of society who made unlucky choices of parents. In short, the ideologies of Nozick and Rawls tell a great deal about how they would distribute resources and what they see as the appropriate role of government in that distribution. From their ideologies, we have a good idea what health, education, welfare, and affirmative action policies they would choose.

Think for a moment about the benefits of all candidates for office and all voters developing clearly defined ideologies. Suddenly, it is almost rational to become an informed voter. If you have an ideology, then you can place political actions and choices in a coherent framework. The ideology helps you understand and decide your position on policy proposals that deal with similar situations. More importantly, the ideology helps you choose among competing candidates and parties. For example, if one voter's ideology places the highest value on equality of opportunity, then he supports the candidate whose ideological position most closely reflects that principle. If another voter's ideology gives the highest priority to maximum liberty, then she chooses the candidate whose ideology gives that principle the highest priority. By having an ideology and knowing the ideology of candidates, you no longer need to know every candidate's position on every important issue. In fact, you actually don't need to know a candidate's position on any issue! So long as a candidate's ideology guides political actions after the election, then by voting for the candidate whose ideology is most similar to your own, you have voted in an informed manner!

Of course, most people do not have ideologies as fully developed or as consistent as those of Robert Nozick and John Rawls. In fact, many people may not know that they have ideologies. Given that most people are not political philosophers, it becomes important to ask whether their political ideas and those of political candidates seem sufficiently cohesive to allow voters to act in an informed matter. Political scientists, sociologists, and psychologists have studied this question at great length. However, they continue to disagree about its answer.

Phillip Converse gives a compelling argument that most citizens do not have sufficiently coherent belief systems to call them ideologies.[2] Converse tries to determine whether the opinions of American adults on major policy issues are logically consistent and stable over time. To answer these questions, Converse interviewed the same American adults at three different times and asked them the same questions about their positions on political issues. He found that the opinions of most Americans on most political issues were only weakly correlated from one interview to the next. In addition, people held inconsistent positions among their preferences. The same person might support increasing federal aid to education in the first interview, oppose it in the second interview, and then support it again on the third interview. Similarly, an individual who told the interviewer that he supported federal aid to education might also have said that he strongly supported a reduction in the size and scope of the federal government.

Converse found that most people express consistent opinions only when they perceive clear cues about how an issue affects certain easily identifiable groups. For example, a citizen may hold a stable and logically consistent position on welfare and affirmative action programs. This occurs because the individual sees both policies as assisting ethnic minorities. Converse argues that only a small percentage of Americans have stable and logically consistent ideologies on most political issues. Any stability or logic comes not from an internally consistent set of propositions, but from strong likes and dislikes toward certain groups of people.

Many scholars reject Converse's conclusion that citizens are uninformed and lack sufficiently consistent positions on issues to constitute ideologies. For the purposes of this chapter, however, the importance of Converse's study is clear. If informed voters must have stable positions on *issues,* then the Informed Voter model cannot link citizens to policy outcomes. But you already knew that. You discovered in Chapter 5 that it is irrational to be informed about particular issues. The information costs are so great that a rational person will choose to remain ignorant about most of them.

Does Converse's study eliminate the role of ideology in linking citizen preferences to public policy? It does not. This linkage via ideology does not require that citizens have consistent positions on all issues. For ideology to help link citizen demands to public policy, citizens must have relatively stable and consistent views concerning how to distribute resources in society and the appropriate role of government in this distribution. Socialization by parents, life experiences, peer group pressure, and membership in certain ethnic, occupational, and income groups provide important cues to citizens that *may* allow them to develop reasonably consistent ideologies. If these socialization processes and cues help citizens develop ideologies, then voters need only find a method of identifying which candidates share their ideological preferences.

For example, suppose that your ideology stresses environmental preservation over economic development. You do not necessarily have to have an opinion on which toxic waste disposal policy is best or whether acid rain is really a problem. After all, you are not going to choose the actual policy. All you need to know is which candidate shares your basic belief that environmental preservation is an important social goal and which generally gives that goal a higher priority than economic development.

IDEOLOGICAL DIMENSIONS

Talk in the media and from politicians often refers to either liberal or conservative policies or politicians. Real world, issues rarely fall neatly along a single left–right or liberal–conservative dimension. Most people seem "liberal" on some issues and "conservative" on others. Political scientist Ronald Inglehart argues that the left–right ideological dimension based largely on economic issues no longer accurately characterizes the ideologies of citizens in advanced industrial societies. Instead, he says that a **postmaterialist ideology** focused on social issues is slowly replacing the old economic dimension. In particular, people who grew up in countries with high standards of living are less likely to focus on economic issues.[3] Inglehart writes:

> The postmaterialist outlook is linked with one's having spent one's formative years in conditions of economic and physical security. Hence it is more prevalent among the postwar generation than among older cohorts, and tends to be concentrated among the more prosperous strata of any given age group.[4]

Postmaterialists are more likely to favor equal rights for women, minorities, and gays along with strong environmental, consumer, and work safety regulations. Postmaterialists also stress the importance of popular participation in and influence on government. Inglehart believes that these are permanent changes. The new ideology is less concerned than previous ones with economic security and preserving traditional moral, religious, and nationalistic values. If Inglehart's analysis is correct, then people could take three basic positions: conservative on economic issues, liberal on economic issues, and postmaterialist.

Several scholars, using the same data as Inglehart, come to different conclusions. They argue that Inglehart's data indicate two distinct ideological dimensions, one economic and the other social.[5] The economic dimension tracks the traditional left–right split that deals with the level of government involvement in the economy and the distribution of income in the society. The other dimension deals with the social issues that concern Inglehart. However, a person can lean toward either a libertarian position on these issues or an authoritarian position. A **libertarian** will stress individual rights, tolerance for minorities, free speech, and environmental protection. An **authoritarian** might believe that government should prohibit homosexuality and abortion, promote law and order, implement nuclear power systems, support traditional religious values, and repeal endangered species legislation.

Although people's positions may reveal some correlation between leftist perspectives on economic issues and libertarian views of social issues, this is not a universal connection. In fact, studies suggest that these two ideological dimensions are clearly distinct.[6] You might conceptualize the two ideological dimensions as a grid similar to that shown in Figure 6.1.

Because potential voters fall into all four quadrants of Figure 6.1, candidates must deal with both the social and the economic dimensions of people's ideologies. For

FIGURE 6.1

PUSH TOWARD MODERATION
IN TWO-DIMENSIONAL IDEOLOGICAL SPACE

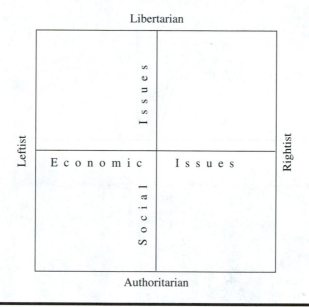

example, people in the upper-left quadrant of Figure 6.1 hold libertarian positions on social issues and liberal positions on economic issues. They want the government to stay out of what they consider private, personal decisions (abortion, sexual preference, styles of dress, and religion), but they want active government regulation of business to protect the environment and consumers. Their economic opinions also favor extensive redistribution of income by the government from the very rich to the very poor. These people generally support efforts to improve the positions of minorities.

The upper-right portion of the graph, represents libertarian positions on social issues combined with conservative economic positions. These people prefer that government stay out of personal affairs such as abortion and sexual preference, and they are open to new lifestyles and opinions. These individuals also support policies to protect the environment and promote consumer safety. On the economic dimension, people in this quadrant do not want the government to engage in extensive redistribution of income, they value a stable economy and comfortable lives, and they dislike inflation. They want government to tax and spend as little as possible.

At first glance, the individuals in this upper-right quadrant may seem to voice inconsistent priorities in wanting to limit government's role in people's economic welfare while simultaneously supporting an active government role in protecting the environment. Doesn't environmental protection require the government interference

and regulation that they criticize for other policies? Actually, this ideological position is consistent. Presumably, even Adam Smith would want producers and consumers to pay the full costs of their production and consumption. This means that producers must pay to clean up their pollution, and consumers must pay the social costs of their consumption. It makes sense, therefore, that a person in the upper-right quadrant will favor government policies that reduce substantial negative externalities.

The lower-right quadrant represents people who combine authoritarian priorities on social issues with conservative stands on economic issues. On the social issues dimension, they support prayer in the public schools, oppose abortion, wish to eliminate laws that protect gay rights, support the death penalty, and want to limit immigration. They value authority, discipline, and patriotism. Environmental concerns rank fairly low in this set of political priorities. On the economic dimension, they want to reduce government spending. They oppose affirmative action, redistribution of income, and welfare programs.

The lower-left part of the figure represents economic liberals who are also social authoritarians. These people want the government to intervene actively to protect their jobs and to provide medical care, unemployment insurance, and other social insurance programs. They also want government to reduce taxes on the middle and lower-middle classes. At the same time, they express authoritarian positions on issues such as abortion, prayer in the schools, gay rights, and environmental regulation.

Where would you put yourself in Figure 6.1? Most people know others who would fall into each quadrant. If you live in the Northeast or Midwest, you probably know a number of people who belong in the lower-left quadrant. Many such people belong to labor unions and support the economic liberalism that unions advocate. At the same time, they strongly oppose affirmative action plans, welfare programs, and the right of protesters to burn the American flag. On the other hand, if you live in suburban areas on the West Coast, then you are likely to know a number of people who fall in the upper-right quadrant. Many people in this region favor protection for abortion rights, the privacy of sexual preference, and the environment. At the same time, they hold conservative views on economic issues that involve redistribution of income.

Research on political ideologies in Western Europe and the United States has found two-dimensional ideologies for both individual citizens and political parties.[7] In all countries, the left-right dimension of economic policies constitutes one dimension. In some countries, the second dimension measures libertarianism versus authoritarianism. In other countries, a strong religious or ethnic division may replace social issues as the second dimension.

Multiple ideological dimensions complicate the linkage between public opinion and public policy. If your own ideological position is not compatible with that of a particular candidate on both dimensions, then you must decide whether the economic or the social dimension is more important to you. For example, in the 1996 presidential election, the Democratic Party's candidate, Bill Clinton, located himself close to the center on the economic dimension. Although he supported libertarian positions on many social issues, he attempted to appear as a moderate in this area, as well. In the ideological map from Figure 6.1, he probably would fall somewhere in the upper-left quadrant. (See Figure 6.2.) Robert Dole, Clinton's opponent from the Republican Party, portrayed himself as an economic conservative and an authoritarian on social issues. Voters probably saw Dole somewhere in the lower-right quadrant in Figure 6.2.

If your ideology places you in either the lower-left or the upper-right quadrant, then neither candidate's position was consistent with yours on both dimensions. To decide whom to support, you had to compare the importance of the economic dimension and the social dimension of your ideology. In the 1992 election, many voters judged President Bush's economic policies as failures, and Clinton successfully made the economy an important issue. Some voters in the lower-left quadrant, who had voted for Bush in 1988 to support his stand on social issues, decided to vote for Clinton in 1992. They may have done this because the economy had become the more important dimension to them.[8]

To attract voters in the upper-right quadrant, Clinton promised to reduce the deficit and to cut taxes for the middle class. These promises encouraged people in the upper-right quadrant to vote Democratic because Clinton assured them that his economic positions did not differ dramatically from their own. This allowed people in the upper-right quadrant to place more emphasis on social issues, the dimension on which they agreed with Clinton. This position proved particularly attractive for female prochoice voters who opposed the Republican Party's prolife position and for people who were angry that President Bush had broken his vow of "no new taxes."

What happened to Clinton's popularity? When he announced his policy to allow gays to serve openly in the military, Clinton alienated many of his previous supporters in the

FIGURE 6.2

CLINTON AND DOLE IN IDEOLOGICAL SPACE

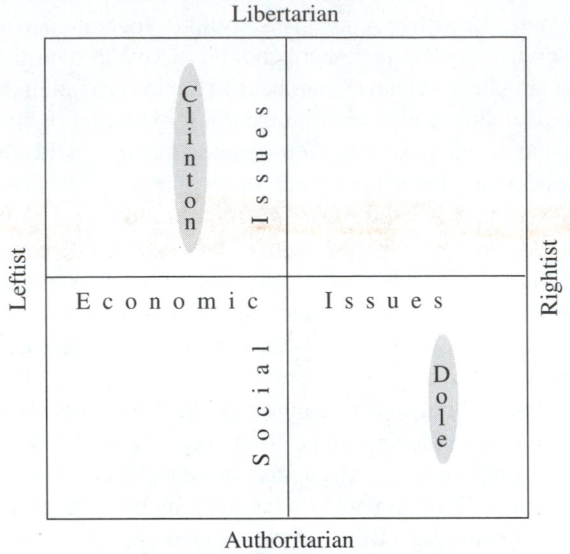

Libertarian

Clinton

Issues

Leftist

Rightist

Economic Issues

Social

Dole

Authoritarian

lower-left quadrant, who saw him as far too liberal on social issues. When the 1994 congressional elections came around and voters in the upper-right quadrant had not yet seen the middle-class tax cut and welfare reforms that Clinton had promised, they also became alienated. The votes of these two groups gave Republicans control of both the House of Representatives and the Senate. This relationship between the ideologies of candidates and their political parties emphasizes another linkage institution, political parties.

Political Parties

In 1950, the American Political Science Association published the report of its Committee on Political Parties. This document placed American political scientists on record as favoring one particular type of political system over all others. This system featured two strong parties, each choosing its positions on issues on the basis of a comprehensive ideology. Despite severe logical and empirical critiques of this stance,[9] most American political scientists probably continue to support the idea of a political system with two strong parties. They believe that the political party is the best institution to effectively link public preferences to public policy. Political scientists tend to believe stronger parties that establish more ideologically consistent platforms help citizens to make informed choices in elections and to hold elected leaders accountable for their actions in office. This, in turn, helps to ensure that the will of the majority actually does rule. Political scientists consider political parties to be the unsung heroes in making democracy work. Why do so many political scientists believe this?

Chapter 5 explained that rational people will not collect the information they need to make informed choices among several issues or candidates. Ideological political parties overcome this problem by drastically reducing the information necessary to vote in an informed way. If parties clearly state their ideologies and show how those ideologies relate to important issues, then people can easily become informed voters. In the United States, for example, the Democratic Party would take the more leftist or liberal position on each important issue, and the Republican Party would take the more rightist or conservative position. On abortion, Democratic candidates would favor prochoice policies and the Republican candidates, more prolife ones. Democrats would oppose the death penalty, while Republicans would favor it. Democrats would represent the interests of labor; the Republicans, those of business. Democrats would favor redistribution of wealth from the rich to the poor; Republicans would oppose such measures. Democrats would favor greater regulation of business to improve safety in the work place and to encourage environmental protection; Republicans would work to limit governmental regulation in these areas.

In this simple world, the citizen would have to answer only two questions to cast an informed vote: (1) Am I more liberal or more conservative? (2) Which party is conservative? Armed with the answers to these questions, the citizen would vote either for all Democratic candidates or for all Republican candidates. The voter could easily gather information on the parties. Each party has a strong incentive to alert the voters to its ideology and the beneficial effect of that position on policy outcomes. It has equally strong incentives to alert voters to the unpopular policy outcomes that result from the other party's ideology.

Supporters of strong parties believe that such a system would help to keep public officials accountable to citizens. In a strong party system, once the public elects a candidate, that official must vote as her party directs on every important issue. Officials who run as Republicans must vote the conservative position on each legislative proposal, and officials who run as Democrats must vote the liberal position. Each party enforces this rule by refusing to allow people who do not vote with the party's position to run as candidates in the next election. In such a system, voters would know which party to blame for policies that they did not like and which to credit for policies they did like.

Proponents of strong, ideological parties maintain that these organizations lead to a more active and involved citizenry. Currently, the average citizen has little incentive to vote because it is difficult to see the connection between a person's vote and eventual public policy. If parties have clear ideologies and connect these ideologies to policies that are important to citizens, then citizens will be more likely to understand how an election affects them.

CAN A STRONG, TWO-PARTY SYSTEM ACHIEVE MAJORITY RULE?

How can political scientists determine if this model with a strong party linkage would work as its proponents suggest? As with all other tests, they can do three things: (1) derive

FIGURE 6.3

VOTERS' PARADOX AND THE EVENING MEAL

	Jane	John	Lyn
First choice	Arab Delight	Burger Heaven	Cafe China
Second choice	Burger Heaven	Cafe China	Arab Delight
Third choice	Cafe China	Arab Delight	Burger Heaven

hypotheses based on the model, (2) examine the model and the hypotheses for logical inconsistencies, and (3) conduct empirical tests of the hypotheses. The model provides three critical hypotheses for the effects of a political system with strong, ideologically consistent parties:

1. The preferences of the majority will guide policies.
2. The parties will aggregate the demands of individual citizens in a way that makes elected leaders more responsive to citizens' demands.
3. Voter participation will increase.

On the basis of logic alone, the first two hypotheses have problems. In a large, heterogeneous society that faces multiple issues, the ideal of majority rule sometimes becomes impossible, because it is highly improbable that a majority of citizens will support one set of policies over all other alternatives. This problem arises for two reasons. First, on some issues no majority position emerges. Political scientists call this situation the **voters' paradox,** as discussed in the next section.*

The second reason that majority preferences are unlikely to determine policy results from the fact that there are two ideological dimensions. Once a political party places itself in the two-dimensional space shown in Figures 6.1 and 6.2, a majority of voters will disagree with it on at least one ideological dimension.

THE VOTERS' PARADOX

This potential problem of a two-party system deserves more attention as it illustrates why majority rule is unlikely in a large, heterogeneous nation. Assume a simple society with only three individuals—Jane, John, and Lyn. The society must resolve only one issue: At which restaurant will the three citizens eat for dinner? That issue has three possible policy options: Arab Delight, Burger Heaven, and Cafe China. Figure 6.3 shows each citizen's preferences.

---

*The French social scientist Condorcet first identified this paradox in the 19th century. Duncan Black and Kenneth Arrow made this paradox clear to social scientists in the 20th century.

Jane, John, and Lyn decide that the majority will rule, and they vote to see which policy option wins. In the first election, each restaurant receives one vote. Jane votes for Arab Delight, John for Burger Heaven, and Lyn for Cafe China. To resolve the three-way tie, the citizens decide to vote again, and they agree that the option that receives the most first and second place votes will win. The result is the same. Each restaurant receives one first place and one second place vote.

Lyn suddenly recognizes the problem as a situation described in her political science class, the *voters' paradox*. She knows that the group cannot reach a decision without completing two separate votes with each vote choosing between only two options. Lyn proposes that the group first vote between Arab Delight and Burger Heaven. They will then vote between the winner of the first vote and Cafe China. Arab Delight wins the first vote as both Jane and Lyn prefer it to Burger Heaven. Now the second vote must choose between Arab Delight and Cafe China. Cafe China wins as both John and Lyn prefer Cafe China to Arab Delight.

It appears that majority rule has led to the choice of Cafe China in free elections. After a moment's thought, however, John protests. He realizes that Lyn rigged the outcome by making sure that the vote on Arab Delight and Burger Heaven took place first. John argues for another round of voting between Burger Heaven and Cafe China. In this vote, John's position would win because both he and Jane prefer Burger Heaven to Cafe China. But if that vote were taken and Burger Heaven won, then Jane could protest that Arab Delight has already beaten Burger Heaven and therefore Arab Delight is the majority's choice. The hungry citizens soon realize that *no choice commands a majority; therefore, the majority cannot rule.* By structuring the order in which the society would vote on the alternatives, Lyn assured that Cafe China would win. This choice cannot represent the will of the majority, however, because there is no majority preference!

Does the voters' paradox ever happen in real life? It certainly does. The Vietnam War dominated the American political agenda and played an important part in deciding elections for an entire decade. From 1966 to 1973, surveys of the American population consistently listed Vietnam as the most important political problem facing the country. However, citizens favored no clear policy choice about the war. At least three options commanded some support: immediately pull out the troops; keep the military commitment at approximately the current level; and declare an all-out war that would, if necessary, include the use of nuclear weapons against North Vietnam. Substantial portions of the population supported each of these options. Figure 6.4 shows these groups and their preferences.

Doves, whose first priority was immediate withdrawal of all American troops, clearly preferred limited war to an all-out conflict. The Hawks argued that, if the country was not going to declare all-out war and do whatever necessary to win, then it should immediately withdraw the troops. The policy of committing only enough firepower to avoid defeat was their least favored alternative. Because no majority position emerged among these options, no candidate or party could obtain consistent support for the most important issue facing the nation. How often does the voters' paradox occur? No one knows. However, when it occurs, no political system can represent the majority.[10]

FIGURE 6.4

VOTERS' PARADOX AND VIETNAM

	Hawks	Doves	Moderates
First choice	All-out war	Withdraw immediately	Limited war
Second choice	Withdraw immediately	Limited war	All-out war
Third choice	Limited war	All-out war	Withdraw immediately

AGGREGATION OF CITIZEN DEMANDS

Will a strong, ideologically distinct, two-party system better represent public preferences than a system in which the parties do not promote highly ideological positions? Can a strong two-party system achieve majority rule in the absence of the voters' paradox? Obviously, if ideology defines two dimensions such as those shown in Figures 6.1 and 6.2, a system with only two ideological parties cannot represent individuals in all four quadrants.

Suppose, for example, that the Republican Party is both strongly conservative on economic issues and strongly authoritarian on social issues, while the Democratic Party is both strongly liberal on economic issues and strongly libertarian on social issues. Regardless of which party wins the election, the winning party does not represent the overall worldview of citizens in *three* of the four quadrants. The strong party model requires every elected official to follow the party's directive on every vote. If the Republicans win the election, on all social issues they will pass legislation in agreement with the authoritarian position. This will contradict the desires of all voters in the upper-left and upper-right quadrants. Similarly, the party will pass legislation that agrees with the conservative position on economic issues, over the objections of voters in the upper-left and lower-left quadrants. Only citizens in the lower-right quadrant receive the outcomes they prefer on both dimensions.

In summary, there is little reason to believe that an ideologically distinct, two-party system will aggregate citizen demands in a way that will lead to majority rule. To be sure, ideologically consistent parties provide clearer cues to voters, reduce the information necessary to cast informed votes, and increase the duty of citizens to vote. None of these attributes, however, assures that the position of a majority of citizens will prevail. Would a multiparty system do better?

MAJORITY RULE IN MULTIPARTY POLITICAL SYSTEMS

Recall the earlier statement that ideologies fall along only two dimensions in most countries. Why, then, do some countries have large numbers of parties while others have only two? Is it because a multiparty system can more effectively represent voters separated by more than one ideological dimension?

The number of political parties in a country reflects, in part, its electoral system. In countries with **single-member legislative districts,** two parties tend to dominate. Countries with **proportional representation** tend to favor multiparty systems. A multiparty system makes it easier for parties that represent ethnic, cultural, or religious minorities to win seats in the legislature.

In a system with single-member districts, only one candidate is elected from each area. Great Britain, Canada, and the United States elect officials using the single-member district system. In these countries, only the individual who receives the most votes in the district wins a seat in the legislature. This tends to prevent parties that appeal only to specific minority interests from winning an election. For example, three national parties have sometimes vied for power in Great Britain, and people have tried to start a fourth. In addition, nationalist parties from Scotland and Wales also run candidates in some districts. However, in a single-member district, only the candidate who receives the greatest number of votes is elected. As a result, two parties tend to dominate all others. Typically the Conservative Party and the Labour Party win the vast majority of seats in the House of Commons, Britain's major legislative institution. In the United States, whenever a third party has emerged, it has either been swallowed up by the Republican or Democratic Parties, or the third party has died quickly for lack of support at the polls.

In contrast to the single-member district system, Austria, Italy, Sweden, Norway, and Israel use a proportional representation system to elect representatives. This system allows several candidates from each district to win seats, allocating seats on the basis of the proportion of the total votes a party in the district receives. For example, if each district elects five legislators, then five different parties might win one seat each. If one party gets 49 percent of the vote, another party gets 28 percent, and a third party gets 23 percent, the first party wins three seats and each of the other two wins one seat. Any party that receives at least 15 percent of the votes in a district wins a legislative seat in that district under most versions of the proportional representation system.

An advantage of multiparty systems is the ability they give parties to provide extremely clear cues to voters concerning the relationship between party ideologies and those of voters. In Italy, for example, the Communist Party, the Socialist Party, the Social Democratic Party, the Green Party, the Christian Democratic Party, and the Liberal Party all compete for votes. Each of these names has a relatively clear ideological meaning to voters. In Sweden, the parties include the Left Party, the Social Democratic Party, the Christian Democratic Party, and the Centre Party. Once again, Swedish voters know pretty well the ideology associated with a party label. Similarly, the Labour Party in Great Britain clearly identifies itself with an occupational grouping. Environmentalists in several countries have started Green Parties. This name is a clear cue to voters that such a party espouses environmental concerns.

As Chapter 5 discussed, when political parties provide clear cues about their ideologies to citizens, political participation increases. Competition between more than two parties allows each party to give simple, straightforward cues to voters, and this increases voter participation. Most Americans know that the Democratic Party tends to support leftist positions and those that favor lower-income groups, as compared to the Republican Party's rightist orientation and emphasis on the concerns of higher-income groups. Because U.S. voters choose between only two major parties, both attempt to appeal to the large group of voters who consider themselves ideological moderates and members of the middle class. These individuals with moderate incomes may find it difficult to know whether the Democrats or the Republicans best represent their economic interests. In many elections, it may seem impossible to know which party would best represent a particular income group.

In countries with several parties, most voters know what the labels *Socialist, Social Democratic, Christian Democratic,* and *Conservative* mean; these terms imply specific ideologies, particularly as measured along the economic dimension. This means that party cues are clear, which increases voter participation.

For another advantage, proportional representation gives citizens a broader array of choices. For example, you might want to vote for a candidate from the Green Party because environmental issues are your primary concern. Another person might wish to vote for the Labour Party because a family member works as a union laborer in a factory.

The ability of the multiparty system to reflect more exactly the ideology of a smaller set of voters, as compared to a two-party system, is also its primary disadvantage. The price to a particular voter of a close match between personal and party ideology is the reduction in control over what the government will look like after the election. All democratic systems require majority rule at significant points in the decision process. If no party obtains a majority in the legislature, then it generally forms a ruling government by forming a coalition of enough parties to achieve a majority in the legislature. Unfortunately for the voters, they do not know what members will join the ruling coalition. The parties in the coalition may have close positions of political parties on ideological dimensions. However, parties often join together for reasons other than ideological proximity. In Israel, for example, the Labor and Likud Parties, despite their vast ideological distance, formed a coalition government in the 1980s.

OTHER FUNCTIONS OF POLITICAL PARTIES

Political scientists love political parties for reasons other than their ideologies. In most democratic countries, parties accomplish many tasks that are critical both to the linkage between people and policies and to the governing process. Parties recruit political leaders, and they select which potential leaders will run for office. In a parliamentary system, the party then decides which elected officials will hold the highest leadership positions. In other words, parties not only recruit leaders; they also attempt to screen those leaders to ensure that officeholders have the correct values and leadership qualities. Through the development of platforms and manifestos, parties also formulate policy alternatives for specific issues.

Chapter 7 will describe the critical role of parties in organizing the government, deciding which policy options will become law, and implementing those laws. In short, parties not only link citizens more effectively to their leaders, but they are also critical elements of effective government.

SUMMARY OF PARTY LINKAGE

Where does all this information on parties leave voters? Should they prefer strong parties or weak parties? Would ideological parties or nonideological ones better serve their interests? Is a two-party system better than a multiparty system, or do many parties do more for voters?

This discussion supports several important conclusions about political parties and linkage. First, linkage in a complex, heterogeneous society is impossible without parties. Second, each party promotes an ideology that provides cues to voters concerning what the party will do if it wins the election; these cues allow rational citizens to make informed choices. Third, no party system can actually represent the majority of voters on both primary ideological dimensions. Fourth, two-party and multiparty systems have strengths and weaknesses; neither is inherently preferable to the other. Finally, for reasons we will discuss below, strong parties support equality in representation better than weak parties. This last point can be understood only after consideration of the role of interest groups in democratic societies.

Interest Groups and Linkage

After ideologies and political parties, interest groups are the third institution that aggregates citizen demands into meaningful patterns. In general, the jobs of a political party are to win elections and then to govern. However, elections have two major difficulties as methods of communicating information about public preferences to policy makers. First, when people cast their votes, no one really knows why they voted as they did. Many people may vote for a Republican because they want to vote against the Democratic candidate. You may have voted against the Democratic candidate in the last election because you believed that he was too liberal on economic policies. Another person may have cast a vote against the Democratic candidate because she doubted the candidate's trustworthiness. Someone else may have voted against the Democrat because he disliked the candidate's wife. Still another person may have voted against the Democratic candidate believing that Democrats are prochoice, and the voter favors a prolife position. In short, voters may cast the same vote for a multitude of reasons. An equal number of voters may have wanted to vote *for* the Republican candidate for various reasons of their own. Because so many reasons lead citizens to cast votes for the same candidate, elections do not provide specific policy recommendations to public officials.

The second problem with an attempt to draw information from an election is that the vote count cannot indicate how strongly people feel about particular issues. For example, you may strongly favor affirmative action policies but care very little about abortion, free trade, or the environment. Similarly, you may strongly object to further environmental regulations, favor larger entitlements for the elderly, and care little one way or the other about foreign aid. When you cast a vote, the voting machine does not know how strongly you feel about any particular issue.

Interest groups help to solve both of these problems with elections by supplying policy-specific information. Like parties, many issue groups place themselves in ideological space. Figure 6.5 shows where some interest groups probably fall on the social and economic issue dimensions.

Some groups clearly fall into either the upper-left or lower-right quadrants. The National Organization for Women (NOW) and the National Association for the Advancement

FIGURE 6.5

INTEREST GROUPS IN IDEOLOGICAL SPACE

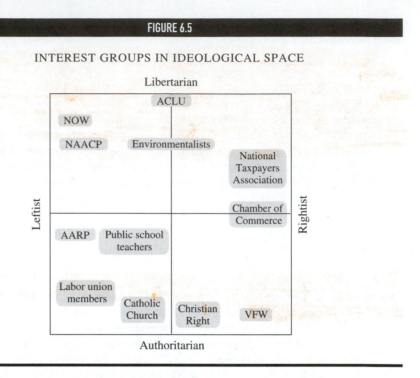

of Colored People (NAACP) share the upper-left section of the chart. They are liberal on the economic dimension and libertarian on the social issue dimension. On the other hand, the Veterans of Foreign Wars (VFW) and much of the so-called Christian Right fall into the lower-right quadrant. Both groups are conservative on economic issues (except pensions for veterans) and authoritarian on social issues. Presumably, members of NOW and the NAACP will vote consistently for the Democratic Party while members of the VFW and the Christian Right will vote consistently for the Republican Party.

However, some groups do not fall neatly into particular quadrants. Members of the American Civil Liberties Union (ACLU) and environmental groups are clearly libertarian on social issues, but they stake out no clearly defined locations on the economic dimension. Similarly, members of public school teacher organizations are liberal on economic issues, but it would be difficult to make a generalization about their position on social issues. The National Chamber of Commerce is conservative on the economic dimension, but it has no clear position on social issues.

Parties attempt to attract interest groups. They even allow some groups to assist in writing party platforms (called *party manifestos* in Europe). In this process, parties attempt to discern the strength of an interest group, the financial support the group will provide in the coming election, and how well the group can deliver the votes of its members on election day. In developing party platforms or manifestos, interest groups and parties can bargain over specific policy proposals and general ideological positions. Labor unions may press the Democratic Party to call for a higher minimum wage in its party platform, while the NAACP and NOW may push for strong affirmative action language. Notice, however, that party leaders must balance these various demands. The Democratic Party will attempt to appeal not only to the NAACP and NOW, but also to members of the American Association of Retired Persons (AARP), environmentalists, and public school teachers. If the party does not support affirmative action strongly enough to satisfy the NAACP or NOW, those groups may not go all out to help elect Democrats. Their members may stay home rather than vote. At the same time, if the Democratic Party focuses too much on affirmative action, it may lose the support of the AARP, the ACLU, and environmental organizations.

The Republican Party faces similar problems. If it stresses a prolife position too vigorously, it may lose the support of the National Taxpayers Association and the National Chamber of Commerce. These groups are conservative on economic issues, but they are not necessarily authoritarian on social issues. If the Republican Party stresses conservative economic policies too much, it may lose the votes of the working class and the elderly. This bargaining process among interest groups over political platforms can play an important role in moderating ideological extremism in a political party's platform and its candidates.

Interest groups help to link citizen desires to policy outcomes in several ways. They can ensure that parties and candidates keep their promises. Because most citizens do not seek out information on how their legislators voted on particular issues, they benefit when the interest groups to which they belong provide that information. Organizations often list the candidates they support and those they oppose. For example, the interest group Environmental Action keeps a list of "The Dirty Dozen," legislators that the group believes most consistently vote against environmental legislation. Many other groups also publish lists of candidates they want to see defeated. These activities by interest groups reduce information costs to potential voters. By officially endorsing or rejecting candidates, groups provide the public with information concerning the candidates' previous records and how the group expects them to act in the future. Thus, interest groups encourage linkage by reminding parties and candidates of their promises.

Interest groups also assist linkage by informing their members when policy makers are deciding specific issues. If the legislature is about to decide an issue critical to group members, the group can mobilize its members to write to legislators or the prime minister or president. This shows policy makers that those people place strong emphasis on particular issues. Policy makers know that people who take the time to write them letters are also likely to pay the costs of voting.

Finally, laws and rules work better if the citizens know about them. Interest groups assist this process. If you own a small business and join an interest group that represents small business interests, that group will provide information concerning the effects of new regulations and tax laws on your business.

In summary, interest groups can be key institutions in the linkage process. They transmit specific policy demands to political parties and candidates, bargain over various issues and ideological positions, and rally their members to campaign and vote for selected parties or candidates. Groups also keep track of officials' actions after the election and provide this information to members. This arms group members with the information they need to communicate their wishes to public officials between elections and to cast knowledgeable votes in the next election.

THE PROBLEMS OF SPECIAL INTERESTS

Although political scientists may have a high opinion of political parties, far fewer hold interest groups in such high esteem. Under the name *special interests, factions,* or *interest groups,* not many people see these organizations as good for politics or for society. Rousseau wanted to completely ban interest groups. James Madison, the author of the U.S. Constitution, designed it in a way that he hoped would reduce group influence.[11] Every president of the United States in the 20th century has castigated interest groups and their influence on Congress. Both Republican and Democratic presidents favor an item veto[†] to control the access of special interests to undeserved subsidies and tax loopholes. Perhaps the most frequently heard media complaint about the Congress is the easy access of special interests and members' dependence on the money these groups provide.

Criticism of interest groups is not confined to the United States. Every democracy in the world must deal with interest groups, and every democracy has great difficulty doing so. A recent article on Brazil's legislature concluded that it was almost totally dominated by special interests in a manner detrimental to national policy.[12] What do interest groups actually do that makes so many people dislike them so much? *The basic criticism of interest groups focuses on the nature of their task—to seek goods from the government for their members. Government generally provides these goods at the expense of someone else in the society.*

Recall from Chapter 2 that David Ricardo first explained how interest groups use government to provide themselves with unearned rents. Ricardo showed that the corn laws in England prevented merchants in that country from importing corn, wheat, and other grains from other countries. Because the population of England was increasing, the demand for food, particularly grain, also was rising. In a free market, consumers in England would have imported grain from other countries, and this would have limited domestic prices. This did not occur in England because landowners persuaded Parliament to put high tariffs on grain imports. These tariffs meant high food prices to English citizens and high profits for English landowners. In other words, the special interest (in this case the landowners) convinced the government to make them richer at the expense of other citizens. As Ricardo showed, this not only lowered the standard of living for consumers, but it also reduced the efficiency of the English economy.

Political interest groups seek unearned rents. For example, the U.S. sugar industry prevents significant imports of sugar from abroad and obtains huge subsidies for producing sugar cane and sugar beets. Winegrowers in France have convinced the French government to place high tariffs and low quotas on wine from other countries. Dairy farmers in Switzerland receive giant government subsidies that allow them to export large amounts of dairy products to other countries and make substantially higher profits than they would earn in the absence of such subsidies. Japanese rice growers have convinced their government that the country would suffer if inexpensive rice from the United States were allowed to enter the country. Each of these agricultural policies is the result of successful rent seeking. The beneficiaries are the producers of the agricultural products

---

[†] An item veto allows the chief executive officer to veto parts of a bill rather than having to approve or veto the entire bill.

BOX 6.1

The Great Federal Panty Raid

Last Friday, Bill Clinton nominated Laura Tyson—one of the nation's premier advocates of managed trade and industrial policy—to be chief of his Council of Economic Advisers. Coincidentally, the U.S. International Trade Commission on Monday will drop on President Bush's desk a textbook case of protectionist industrial policy. The government is on the verge of devastating dozens of manufacturers in a vain attempt to compensate two small companies for the fact that rubber trees do not grow in America.

Rubber thread is a key component of the waistbands of panties and other underwear, sock tops, and bungee cords. The ITC's three Democrats—David Rohr, Don Newquist, and Janet Nuzum—recently voted for an added tariff of as much as 25 percent on rubber thread imports. Imports from Malaysia, the main supplier, are already hit by various tariffs totaling 29 percent; the new levy will raise the tariff to 54 percent. The ITC's three Republicans—Anne Brunsdale (the Reagan-Bush administrations' unsung hero of free trade), Carol Crawford, and Peter Watson—voted against providing added protection.

After the two ITC factions forward recommendations to the White House, the president will have 60 days to decide whether to impose new barriers. If Mr. Bush passes the buck, Mr. Clinton will have to decide the case early on.

Rubber thread is composed primarily of latex, and Malaysia produces most of the world's latex from its rubber trees. Latex, which accounts for more than half the cost of producing rubber thread, is extremely expensive to transport, and Malaysian producers have many advantages from being next to the rubber plantations. The ITC concluded that, for 1990, the average cost of producing rubber thread was $1.79 a pound for U.S. companies but only 77 cents a pound for Malaysian companies. But, American trade policy makers refuse to be intimidated by mere facts of geography.

Though rubber thread imports are already heavily taxed, two Falls River, Mass., companies—Globe Manufacturing Co. and North American Rubber Thread Co.—want more. Globe and NART petitioned the ITC to impose more tariffs on Malaysian rubber thread imports to give themselves a chance to charge higher prices and modernize their equipment. The two petitioners have fewer than 150 workers employed making rubber thread, while total employment in U.S. companies using rubber thread is more than 3,000. Thus, additional protection could destroy 20 times as many jobs as it saves.

Globe and NART have been loudly damned by their American customers. Thomas Butler, president of Norbut Manufacturing Co. of Falls River, complained to the ITC that his company experienced "three weeks of constant rubber breaks in our [rubber] covering machines" after buying thread from NART. Michael Asheghian of Elastic West Industries of Los Angeles declared, "Because of late deliveries and sticky rubbers, the U.S. producers cannot meet customers' needs." Dave Casty, president of Elastic Corp. of America, the largest purchaser of rubber thread in the United States, denounced the petition at an ITC hearing: The rubber thread industry "abdicated that whole marketplace

(continued)

(continued)

years ago." (Even with high levels of protection, NART and Globe could not possibly supply American demand.)

The 29 percent tariff on Malaysian rubber thread imports is already pummeling rubber thread users. John Elliott, president of Rhode Island Textiles, which produces elastic, complained that his firm recently lost "a very large customer" in Los Angeles to a Hong Kong firm that can buy rubber thread at world prices (roughly 30 to 40 percent below current U.S. prices)—and must pay only an 8 percent U.S. tariff on its elastic exports. The high tariffs are also undercutting U.S. companies' efforts to export American-made elastic.

The ITC's Democrats even propose adding new tariffs on a specific type of rubber thread not produced in the United States. Food-grade rubber thread is used for mesh wrapping for hams and other meats, and strict production controls are necessary to avoid carcinogens. Timothy Carroll of C&K Manufacturing of Westlake, Ohio, railed: "I cannot fathom what the U.S. industry hopes to gain by requesting additional duties and quotas on this product when they don't produce them. . . ." Mr. Carroll also worried about the danger to U.S. companies of using tainted American-made thread: "All we have to do is have one product not meet the statute, and . . . we are sued and we are out of business."

Trade barriers divert capital from more productive to less productive uses. Globe is reaping large profits from producing Spandex—a frequent substitute for rubber thread. ITC Commissioner Nuzum asked Globe's Bob Bailey: "If you have essentially two different opportunities and one gives you a better return on your dollar, why isn't it that you would continue to devote more resources towards that more profitable line?" Mr. Bailey replied: "Because we still want to be a full service manufacturer. We don't only want to make Spandex." But corporate vanity should not drive U.S. trade policy.

According to U.S. trade law, before the president can impose these special higher duties, he must conclude that they would "provide greater economic and social benefits than costs." The U.S. government, by trying to forcibly enrich two small companies, could export a much larger industry. Several manufacturers warned the ITC that they may move their operations overseas if the ITC imposes new restrictions on rubber thread imports.

The rubber thread case vivifies the essence of protectionism—politicians intervening to allow floundering American companies to take successful American companies hostage. As Mr. Casty of Elastic Corp. warned, "If we lose that competitive entrepreneuring edge by actions like this, we just put America 50 leagues behind the rest of the world."

Source: *Wall Street Journal,* December 18, 1992. Reprinted with permission of The Wall Street Journal © 1982, Dow Jones & Company, Inc. All rights reserved.

protected by tariffs and subsidies. Consumers and taxpayers lose what the special interests gain. As Box 6.1 shows, such rents are certainly not restricted to agricultural products.

Politics is ultimately about winners and losers, who gets and who pays. If automobile manufacturers get the government to impose lower quotas and higher tariffs on Japanese cars, trucks, and minivans, consumers pay higher prices for all cars. If chemical companies get Congress to enact weak environmental legislation, others pay by involuntarily living with the pollutants the chemical companies produce. If students get higher subsidies for their studies, then the taxpayers must pay for these subsidies. If women and minority ethnic groups obtain jobs from employers according to defined quotas, then Anglo males pay by suffering a competitive disadvantage as compared to their prior position. If prolife forces get a government restriction on the availability of abortion, then women pay by losing the rights that the government eliminates.

PLURALISM: THE IDEAL WORLD FOR INTEREST GROUPS

Just as supporters of strong, ideologically distinct political parties imagine their ideal world, interest groups imagine a perfect world in which the political struggles among interest groups lead to informed policies that maximize the benefits and minimize the costs to all citizens. In this ideal world, people who share an economic interest or a particular value are either organized into an interest group, or they can organize if some event, law, or opposing interest group threatens them. Political scientists refer to this ideal interest-group world as the **theory of pluralism.** David Truman of Columbia University was perhaps the best-known proponent of pluralist politics. His book, *The Governmental Process,* attempted to show how this pluralist world works.[13]

Pluralism supposes three basic hypotheses:

1. The government is equally open to all interests.
2. All interests can organize with relative ease.
3. The political process will lead to the political outcomes that maximize everyone's preferences.

The last effect occurs because the interest group bargaining reflects both the importance of a policy to people as well as the number of people who favor or oppose that policy. By testing pluralism's hypotheses, a political scientist can examine its accuracy as a description of politics. These tests also show why so many political observers object to the activities of interest groups.

Pluralist Hypothesis 1: All Potential Groups Will Have Equal Access and Participation   If pluralism represents an empirically accurate model, then all potential groups must have an equal probability of becoming organized political interest groups. Political scientists can measure the accuracy of this proposition. In the United States, this hypothesis is false. Table 6.1 and Figure 6.6 show who belongs to interest groups in the United States and the percentage of groups that represent different interests in the population. Table 6.1 shows that in 1976 highly educated individuals were more than twice as likely to belong to interest groups as less educated people. People with high incomes were more than twice as likely as low-income individuals to be members of organized groups. Similarly, people in professional and technical occupations were almost twice as likely as people in sales and services to join political interest groups. People classified as laborers in the census were not quite as disadvantaged as sales or service

TABLE 6.1		
ORGANIZATIONAL MEMBERSHIP		
	Members of Organizations Other than Unions	**Members of Organizations or Unions or Both**
Total[a]	40%	52%
Education		
Grade school	10	35
Some high school	22	44
High school graduate	27	44
Some college	38	49
College graduate	56	60
Graduate school	73	80
Occupation		
Professional/Technical	63	70
Management/Administrative	48	51
Sales	34	39
Clerical	30	41
Crafts	35	64
Operative	23	48
Labor	13	56
Service	33	40
Income		
Under $6,000	24	29
$6,000–$10,999	27	42
$11,000–$15,999	35	52
$16,000 and over	55	65

[a] Metropolitan American workforce.

Source: Metropolitan Work Force Survey, 1976.

people because a significant percentage of laborers belonged to unions. That percentage has dropped significantly since 1976, however, and the figures for laborers today are probably close to those of sales and service workers.

An examination of the actual numbers of organizations that represent particular occupational groups reveals even more skewed figures. In fact, 71 percent of all organizations with lobbying offices in Washington, D.C., represent business interests! In sharp contrast, almost no consumer organizations have facilities in the capitol, and only 4 percent of these organizations represent workers. This does not mean that business is almost 20 times as powerful as labor. However, the figures suggest strongly that business interests can become organized more easily than either consumer or labor interests.

In other industrialized democracies, the advantages of political organization are not as powerfully skewed toward the upper classes and toward business as in the United States. Western European labor unions are stronger and more closely allied with leftist

FIGURE 6.6

THE PUBLIC AND THE PRESSURE COMMUNITY: ECONOMIC ROLES OF ADULTS AND ORGANIZATIONS

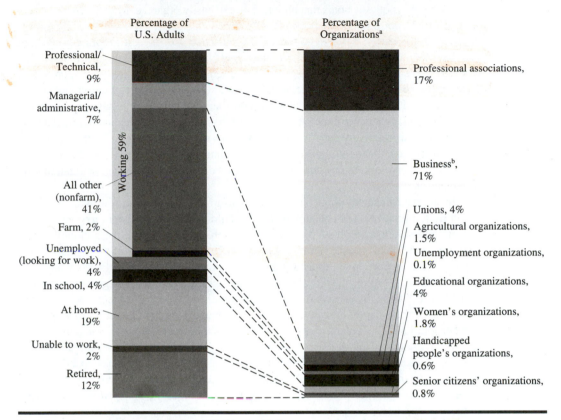

Percentage of U.S. Adults

Percentage of Organizations[a]

Professional/Technical, 9%

Managerial/administrative, 7%

Working 59%

All other (nonfarm), 41%

Farm, 2%

Unemployed (looking for work), 4%

In school, 4%

At home, 19%

Unable to work, 2%

Retired, 12%

Professional associations, 17%

Business[b], 71%

Unions, 4%

Agricultural organizations, 1.5%

Unemployment organizations, 0.1%

Educational organizations, 4%

Women's organizations, 1.8%

Handicapped people's organizations, 0.6%

Senior citizens' organizations, 0.8%

[a]Includes only organizations with offices in Washington, D.C.

[b]Corporations, trade associations, other business associations, and associations of business professionals.

Sources: Information about the public based on U.S. Bureau of the Census, *Statistical Abstract of the United States,* 102nd ed. (Washington, D.C.: U.S. Government Printing Office, 1981), pp. 379, 401–404. Information about organizations based on Arthur C. Close, ed., *Washington Representatives—1981,* 5th ed. (Washington, D.C.: Columbia Books, 1981), pp. 379, 401–404.

parties. Even in Western Europe, however, business organizations are certainly many times more numerous than all other categories of special interests. Similarly, individuals with higher education, more prestigious occupations, and higher incomes are more likely to be members of European interest groups.[14] *These data allow political scientists to reject the hypothesis of pluralism that all interests are equally likely to become organized. In all democracies, people of higher socioeconomic status are more likely to join interest groups, and business groups dominate the interest group community.* Political scientist E. E. Schattschneider summarized the empirical work on pluralism when he wrote in 1960 that Truman's first hypothesis was obviously false: "the flaw in the [pluralist] heaven is that the heavenly chorus sings with an upper-class accent."[15]

Hypothesis 2: All Interests Can Organize Easily in Response to Threats   Pluralism's second hypothesis holds that all interests can easily organize. Mancur Olson, Jr. attacked this hypothesis in his book, *The Logic of Collective Action.*[16] As Chapter 5 explained, it is almost never in an individual's rational self-interest to join a group that provides only collective goods. Olson argues persuasively that, although it is rarely rational to join a group for collective goods, some sets of individuals are much more likely to organize than others. If only a relatively small, homogeneous set of individuals share a concern, and they have substantial resources, then they are more likely to form an organized interest group. For example, any country has far fewer car manufacturers than car consumers. It is relatively easy for representatives of Nissan, Toyota, Honda, and Mitsubishi to get together and organize a trade association. The officers of these companies can use company funds to pay dues and to pay the costs of organizing and maintaining the organization.

In sharp contrast, any single automobile consumer faces an almost infinite cost of attempting to organize other consumers. How would such a person begin to contact consumers and solicit members? Who would trust this person to use their money in the specified way? Who would choose not to free ride? No single person's rational self-interest would support an attempt to organize all automobile consumers. As Chapter 5 showed, interest groups do represent consumers, environmentalists, gun owners, and other large, heterogeneous sets of people. However, only a small percentage of people who support these causes actually belong to the groups. Compared with business groups and corporations, consumer groups and other so-called *public interest groups* make up a small percentage of the interest group community. Certainly these organizations can draw on monetary resources nowhere near as large as those of producer groups. Public interest groups make up an even smaller percentage of the pressure group community in other democracies, where traditions of voluntary associations are much weaker than those in the United States.

In summary, *political scientists also reject the pluralist hypothesis that all groups can easily organize.* When numerous, heterogeneous people share an interest, and when they are spread across large regions and have few resources, their shared interest is unlikely to become focused to form an organized group. These people are certainly less likely to organize than small, homogeneous, business-related interests.

Hypothesis 3: The Political Process Will Maximize Preferences over the Entire Society   The final hypothesis of both normative and empirical pluralist theories holds that the interest group system will maximize total social benefits. Pluralists expect this result because groups provide decision makers with accurate estimates of (a) the importance of an issue to any set of people who share an interest and (b) the number of people who share that interest. Unfortunately, the truth of this hypothesis depends on the first two hypotheses. As those hypotheses are false, it follows that Hypothesis 3 is also false.

If the political system relies largely on interest groups to transmit demands to decision makers, then the pluralist system will maximize the preferences of those who are organized. In addition, it will give much higher weights to the preferences of those who belong to multiple organizations. These people generally have higher levels of education and income and more prestigious occupations. Thus, pluralism will not maximize the social welfare of all in the society; it will tend to emphasize benefits for those who already have many advantages. This trend exacerbates existing social, economic, and political inequalities.

WHY ORGANIZED MINORITIES DEFEAT UNORGANIZED MAJORITIES

In one of the most confusing aspects of democratic government, minorities rather than majorities appear to win many issues. Small, influential groups are most successful in achieving unearned rents when legislators engage in substantial **logrolling,** the practice among public officials of agreeing to support each other's special projects. In other words, they tell each other, "If you vote for my project, I will vote for yours." Consider an example of logrolling.

Morris Udall was a liberal Democrat and a representative in Congress from Arizona for more than two decades. On several occasions, Udall voted in favor of agricultural subsidies for tobacco farmers. Once on a television call-in show, a caller asked, "Why did you vote to subsidize cancer?" Representative Udall responded that the states of North Carolina, Kentucky, and Virginia accounted for a lot of congressional votes, and Arizona needed those votes to get Congress to approve building the Central Arizona Project (CAP). The CAP is a giant cement canal that brings Colorado River water to southern Arizona. Udall voted for tobacco subsidies in return for the tobacco legislators' votes for the CAP.

It is unlikely that either subsidizing tobacco or building the CAP promoted the national interest. The argument to "subsidize cancer" makes no more sense than a project to build a billion-dollar ditch to bring water to grow cotton in the desert. Why are legislators from Arizona, North Carolina, and other states willing to vote for projects that harm the nation as a whole? Because they are not elected by the nation as a whole; they are elected by voters from individual states and congressional districts. Representative Udall knew that few of his constituents knew about his vote on the tobacco bill. Udall also knew that if he could get federal funds to build the CAP, he would receive the enthusiastic support of cotton farmers, cement manufacturers, and construction firms in Arizona. Not only would they vote for him, but they would also contribute to his reelection campaign. Therefore, it was in Udall's political interest to support projects that did not promote the national interest.

Very few voters probably know how their legislators voted on any recent issue similar to the Central Arizona Project or tobacco subsidies. In fact, almost the only ones who know about legislators' votes on these issues are the few who receive direct benefits from those votes. The rational ignorance of voters concerning specific issues provides seemingly unlimited opportunities for politicians to bring substantial benefits to their constituents. Logrolling among legislators assures that most of them will vote for numerous bills that benefit certain minorities and harm the majority.

Proponents of strong parties contend that these political deals would not occur if legislators measured the value of policy proposals against ideological standards, and if parties punished legislators who voted against the accepted ideological positions. Republican legislators cannot argue that the tobacco subsidy and the CAP fit with an ideology that opposes government intervention in the economy. Democrats cannot claim that the bills fit with an ideology that values increasing equality of opportunity in society. After all, the primary beneficiaries of both projects were wealthy citizens. If parties adhere to their ideologies and force legislators to vote on the basis of those ideologies, then government would undertake few projects that would cost the nation more than they would benefit it.

A recent study attempted to evaluate the impact of weak, nonideological parties on logrolling and client politics in Brazil.[17] Brazilian elections center around candidates rather than party ideologies, and parties there are extremely weak. Running for the legislature is expensive and the largest donations come from major construction firms.[18] Not surprisingly, the legislature pays little attention to national issues such as health care and welfare. Instead, individual legislators support a president's proposals only if he directs government-funded construction projects to their districts. Barry Ames, the author of the study, writes: "The importance of [construction projects] to deputies speaks volumes about the absence of links, on issues of national scope, between voters and their representatives, and it goes far toward explaining the overall weakness of the legislature."[19]

SUMMARY OF INTEREST GROUP LINKAGE

This section's examination of interest groups indicates that, under the best circumstances, they can work with political parties to provide cues to voters and to hold elected officials to their promises. However, when organized interest groups replace political parties and ideologies as the major institution that aggregates citizen demands, then the political system will give greater weight to more easily organized sectors and interests in society. This will increase social inequality.

Elections

The final linkage institution discussed in this chapter is the one that people normally think of first, elections. Members of democratic societies have been socialized to believe that the free and fair election is the cornerstone of democracy. The authors of this book

Doonesbury

BY GARRY TRUDEAU

completely agree. Despite their importance, elections suffer from two major faults as links between voters and policy outcomes. First, they convey limited information from the voters to the policy makers. Second, voters often lack sufficient information to make meaningful choices.

William Riker, in his book *Liberalism against Populism*, contends that these faults should limit voters' expectations about their role in government. The possibility of majority governance diminishes further under the weight of the voters' paradox, the ability of elites to structure citizens' choices, and the fact that the governing party almost always represents a minority. Riker argues that realistic linkage between citizens and public policy preferences cannot occur.[20] He does not reject the value of elections or their importance to democracy, but he argues that elections and popular participation play extremely limited roles in government.

Riker argues that voters can generally decide only one issue: whether to retain the current elected officials or to replace them with another set. Examples of voters making this type of decision include the 1932 and 1980 U.S. presidential elections. In 1932, voters rejected President Herbert Hoover's program to deal with the Great Depression and gave candidate Franklin Roosevelt the chance to do a better job. In 1980, candidate Ronald Reagan asked voters, "Are you better off today than you were 4 years ago?" If voters thought they were, then Reagan said that they should vote for President Carter. If they felt worse off, as Reagan clearly thought they were, then he argued that they should vote to make him the next president.

Perhaps the most substantial rejection of any democratically elected government confronted the Progressive-Conservative Party in the 1993 Canadian elections. The party went from being the governing party with a majority of the 295 seats in the legislature to having just 2 seats! Clearly, the Canadian voters had formed a negative evaluation of the party's past performance.

Although we believe that Riker's model shows the importance of even a minimalist role for elections, we maintain that the institutions of ideology, party, interest groups, and elections provide the public with a powerful role in deciding public policy. Certainly where parties are strong and ideologies are clear, an election can provide a very direct message. However, even in America, with its notoriously weak parties, the loss of control of Congress by the Democratic Party in 1994 had a substantial policy impact. The Republican Party's Contract with America defined a clear stance on both ideological dimensions. In addition, the GOP identified aspects of the Democratic Party's government that members wished to reverse, and they had substantial policy success in the 1996 budget process.

Ethnicity, Religion, and Nationalism: The Dangerous Issues

Even the most cursory look at world events today shows that when issues of ethnicity, nationalism, tribalism, and religion come to dominate political debate, political conflict often makes humans commit inhumane acts. Consider Bosnia, Burundi, Guatemala, Israel, Lebanon, Northern Ireland, Rwanda, South Africa, the states formed from the republics of the former Soviet Union. These countries begin an almost unending list of sites where religious, ethnic, and cultural identity create huge strains on political systems and lead to violence and disaster.

Democracy has an extremely difficult time dealing with these issues. Although one might argue that conflict rages because such issues prevent compromise, we see a deeper problem. We have stressed in this chapter the importance of cues to help citizens understand politics. Some cues, however, lead not to principled ideologies, but to unthinking prejudices. Religious, ethnic, and tribal identities encourage people to think of themselves not as members of the same nation or civil society, but as members of different species. Just as war often encourages terrible stereotypes of citizens of the enemy nations, so too do identity issues. Once members of a society see other citizens as fundamentally different from themselves, they can begin to see them as somehow less deserving of the rights and privileges that members of society merit.

Edward Carmines and James Stimson wrote the award-winning book *Issue Evolution: Race and the Transformation of American Politics.* This book provides evidence that race is the dominant issue in American politics. Carmines and Stimson write:

> "Easy" issues have the attribute that they may be responded to, indeed even understood in a fundamental sense, at the "gut" level. They require almost no supporting context of factual knowledge, no impressive reasoning ability, no attention to the nuances of political life. Thus, they produce mass response undifferentiated with respect to knowledge, awareness, attentiveness, or interest in politics: none of these is a prerequisite of response.[‡]

Race affects positions along both the social and economic issue dimensions. Is affirmative action an economic issue, or is it a social issue? Given white stereotypes of African Americans and other minority populations, public responses to "welfare mothers," "illegitimate children," and "irresponsible fathers" become social issues with economic consequences. Membership in a minority ethnic group becomes associated with the "undeserving poor," drug abuse, and "threats to the American way of life." Questions about affirmative action move from a debate concerning legitimate ways to increase equality of opportunity for those who did not choose their parents well to the perception that the government wants to punish whites in order to give privileges to undeserving and irresponsible minorities.

The issues of nationalism, ethnicity, religion, and tribe create difficulties for any polity. As Chapter 12 of this book will explore further, these issues engender numerous opportunities for violent conflict. In Africa, Asia, Latin America, North America, and Europe, these issues often overwhelm ideologies and the standards of civil society. They are not healthy cues with which to link public opinion to public policy.

Summary

To understand the role of each institution in the linkage process, it is important to remember that the political system is dynamic. Although elections occur at discrete points

---

[‡] Edward Carmines and James Stimson, *Issue Evolution: Race and the Transformation of American Politics* (Princeton, N.J.: Princeton University Press, 1989), p. 11.

in time, individuals constantly reevaluate their ideologies based on life experiences. Candidates continually campaign. Parties always attempt to develop proposals and ideological cues that will attract voters. Interest groups ceaselessly pursue unearned rents.

Still, all four linkage institutions are instrumental in democratic government. Each has its influence despite the rational ignorance of voters, the voters' paradox, the inability of voters to predict coalition governments in multiparty systems, and the substantial advantages that the organized have over those who are not organized.

Because all linkage institutions can work simultaneously, they can link mass preferences to public policies with some degree of success in democratic societies.[21] The linkage institutions work best when they work in concert. The combination of ideology and political parties has an especially powerful effect. Chapter 7 looks at the various branches of government and how they work to transform citizen demands into public policies.

QUESTIONS AND EXERCISES

Questions for Reason

1. What is the relationship between political parties and ideologies? How do these institutions lower the costs of voting? Why do they lower those costs more effectively in some democracies than in others?

2. In which quadrant of Figure 6.1 do postmaterialists fit? Why is this? In what other part of Figure 6.1 would they feel most comfortable? Which party in the United States best represents postmaterialists? Why?

3. Explain why a majority of voters generally cannot agree on the major issues in an election.

4. Americans appear to dislike political parties as well as political interest groups. What prevents weak parties and weak interest groups from coexisting in a democratic country?

5. Explain why the proponents of a system with two strong, ideologically distinct parties are incorrect in their arguments about the likely democratic consequences of such a system.

Questions for Reflection

1. Is the move toward cultural diversity in the United States likely to change the nature of the American political party system? Why or why not?

2. Do the benefits for the political system created by public interest groups (such as Common Cause, Environmental Action, and the National Rifle Association) differ significantly from those created by private interest groups (like the Chamber of Commerce, the Farm Bureau, and the AFL-CIO)?

3. If you were writing a constitution for one of the newly independent countries of the former Soviet Union, would you choose single-member districts or proportional representation as the method for electing members of the legislature? Why?

4. Is the ability of citizens to throw out the current governing party both a necessary and a sufficient condition for democracy in a modern nation-state? If it is not, what additional characteristics does democracy require? What institutions might help achieve those conditions?

Questions for Analysis: Explanation and Spurious Association

Perhaps the single most important characteristic of science is its use of empirical tests to evaluate theories and models that explain and predict what happens in the world. Science assumes an orderly and regular world. Based on this assumption, science can develop models and theories that relate variables to each other in ways that help people to understand what they observe or experience. When something is properly explained, it "makes sense."

To see what we mean by "makes sense," assume that you look up suddenly and see a chair right in front of you that was not there when you started studying. Because of your understanding of how the world works, you probably would assume that somebody brought the chair into the room, but you were so engrossed in this book that you did not notice. (Another hypothesis might state that the book put you to sleep.) You do not assume that the chair simply materialized. What would you do if you did see a chair suddenly materialize? Unless a starship had beamed down the chair using known technology, you would doubt either your sanity, your entire view of how the physical world works, or both. A chair suddenly materializing does not "make sense."

In ordinary language, the word *cause* normally means that one event or set of events explains why another event or set of events occurred. For example, if your instructor says, "studying hard will cause your grade to improve," she is saying that the amount of time and effort spent studying helps to explain why one person earns better grades than another person earns. It "explains" the fact because it helps people to grasp the reasons or understand why something happened.[22] Most people want to understand why things happen, and all cultures include explanations of patterns of recurring events. For example, early cultures did not explain why the seasons of the year succeeded one another, why the moon changed shape or why people became ill in the same way that cultures explain those facts today. Despite their lack of scientific knowledge, most cultures developed explanations for these observed patterns.

The sciences normally require that any explanation meet four criteria for a good explanation: association, time priority, rationale, and nonspurious association.[23] Chapter 5 dealt with the first of these criteria, association. When scientists observe an **association**, they try to discover the probability that it could occur by chance. Based on that probability, they accept either the null hypothesis or the alternate hypothesis.

Time Priority

The second criterion for a good explanation (an accurate statement that variation in one variable leads to variation in another variable) requires that the change in the independent variable must occur before the change in the dependent variable. This standard requires **time priority.** For instance, suffering abuse as a child precedes becoming an abusive parent, smoking is antecedent to lung cancer, parents' income comes before children's income, and unsafe sex or sharing unclean needles precedes HIV infection.

Although the logic of the time priority criterion seems straightforward—something that happens later cannot cause something that happened earlier—researchers sometimes violate this requirement. For example, in the computer assignment for Exercise 6, some students may have used past participation in an illegal protest (DIDNOLG) as a dependent variable with an independent variable of either EFFICACY, INTEREST, or EFCYNOLG. Why did this violate the time priority criterion? Because the survey asked about *past* behavior and measured present levels of personal efficacy, interest in politics, and the perception that illegal acts are effective. Ignoring time priority may not have affected the results if an individual's scores on these three independent variables did not change from before the participation in the illegal action to the time of the survey. For some good reasons, however, one may suspect that these scores might have changed. It seems reasonable to expect that people's participation in a successful illegal behavior could increase the person's political efficacy, political interest, and estimation that illegal behavior works. On the other hand, participation in an unsuccessful activity might lower individuals' scores on these variables.

Rationale

Perhaps the most important test of a good explanation is its **rationale** (reason) for exactly how a change in one variable leads to a change in the other. In other words, a rationale lays out the steps by which X affects Y. For instance, a description of the methods by which people transmit disease through bodily fluids provides the rationale for the relationship between unsafe sex and the probability of contracting the HIV virus. Such exchanges can take place during sexual contact or while injecting drugs with a needle previously used by an infected person.

Unfortunately, it is all too easy to provide an incorrect explanation for a true association or to provide a likely sounding explanation for an observed association that actually happened by chance. One of the authors of this book runs an experiment every semester in which he describes the relationship between income and charitable donations. He tells one-third of the class that low-income people are significantly more likely to donate, one-third that middle-income people are more likely to donate, and one-third that high-income people are more likely to donate. Almost all students can develop perfectly reasonable rationales for what they believe is a true association, despite the fact that at least two of the described associations are false. Think how easily "experts" can always explain a drop in the stock market after the fact. Yet few of those same experts told their clients before the fall to sell their stocks and avoid the losses.

Because it is so much easier to explain why something happened after the fact than to predict it ahead of time, even if the association occurred by chance, science requires multiple studies to replicate observations and confirm that an association observed at one point in time also occurs the next time. For example, you may observe that during one spring it rained every day that you planned to have a picnic or the day after you washed your car. You might ascribe these associations to some cosmic law and believe that your planning a picnic or washing your car causes it to rain. To test this hypothesis, you might have picnics and wash your car during the following spring on days chosen at random and compare the percentage of times that it rains on those occasions with the percentage of times it rains on other days during the spring. If, over several springs, the probability of rain is higher when you plan a picnic or wash your car, then perhaps you should go into the

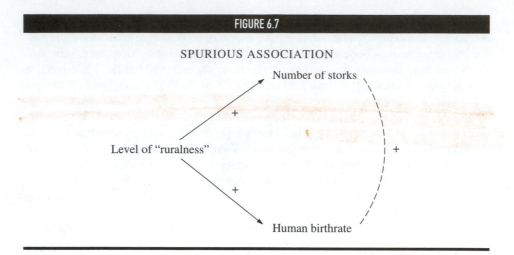

FIGURE 6.7

SPURIOUS ASSOCIATION

rain-making business. More than likely, however, you will find that you simply were unlucky during that one spring and the association was just a chance one.

Nonspurious Association

Scientists often observe associations between two variables for which they see no rationale. For example, someone in Germany once found an association between human birthrates and the number of storks in various locations in Europe.[24] Despite the greeting cards and diaper commercials that attest to this association, few people believe that storks influence human birthrates or that birthrates influence the number of storks. Something usually causes a repeatedly observed association between two variables (e.g., storks and high birthrates). In fact, a third variable, the rural character of an area, was positively associated with both high human birthrates and large stork populations. Storks like rural

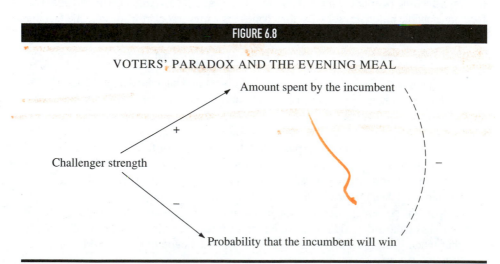

FIGURE 6.8

VOTERS' PARADOX AND THE EVENING MEAL

areas because they find more places to construct safe nests there than in urban areas. Birthrates are higher in rural areas because children born on farms cost less to raise and they contribute labor that increases family wealth. Figure 6.7 shows the arrows of influence among the three variables.

An observed association between two variables without any causal relationship between them is a **spurious association.** The number of storks and human birthrates were associated, but the association was caused by independent associations of each variable to a third variable (rural character). In scientific language, two dependent variables (stork populations) and (human birthrates) depend upon a single independent variable (rural character).

A political example of a spurious association is the negative association between how much an incumbent legislator spends on reelection campaigns and the likelihood of winning the elections. It does not make sense that incumbents who spend more are more likely to lose their race. If this were not a spurious relationship, then incumbents would simply spend less and win more. In reality, both the likelihood that incumbents will lose and the amount they spend on campaigns depends upon the strength of the candidates who challenge them. If a challenger is weak, the incumbent does not need to spend as much to win. If the challenger is strong, then the incumbent will spend more to increase the chance of reelection, but the candidate may still lose because the challenger is so strong. Figure 6.8 shows this relationship.

Form of the Hypothesis for a Spurious Association

A hypothesis that a relationship is spurious states, "Comparing only cases with similar values on the control variable reveals no relationship between the independent and dependent variables." For instance, looking only at rural areas, higher numbers of storks are not associated with higher birthrates. The same statement would be true for highly urban areas. Looking only at congressional races with strong challengers, higher rates of incumbent spending do not lead to higher percentages of incumbents losing. Similarly, looking only at congressional races with weak challengers, once again, no relationship becomes evident between how much an incumbent spends and the outcome of the election.

Scientists need a simple, yet precise way of formulating a hypothesis that the relationship between two variables is spurious. The best form of the hypothesis for spurious association is very similar to the good old null hypothesis from Chapter 5. For the link between storks and birthrates, the hypothesis of spurious association would look as follows: For regions of similar rural character, regions with many and few storks are equally likely to have high birthrates. A hypothesis for the spurious association between incumbent campaign spending and the probability of reelection would state: In congressional races with challengers of similar strength, incumbents who spend high amounts on their reelection bids and incumbents who spend low amounts on their reelection bids are equally likely to win reelection.

Notice that the spurious association hypothesis has an intuitively straightforward meaning. It says that for cases with the same or very similar values of the control variable, no relationship emerges between the independent and dependent variables. The form of the hypothesis for any spurious association dealing with contingency tables is this: For similar values of [the control variable], low and high values of [the independent variable] are equally likely to have high values on [the dependent variable].

Computer Exercise

Using Micro-Crunch or SPSS and the data set PERUCAT, test the hypotheses that married people are less likely than unmarried people to have participated in illegal activities (DIDNOLG)[§] and that unmarried people are more likely to say they will participate in illegal activities in the future (WILLNOLG). Then prepare hypotheses for the same relationships, using STUDENT as the control variable.

To run this test with Micro-Crunch, you follow the directions on using contingency tables in Appendix A, inserting the appropriate dependent and independent variables when requested. Then Micro-Crunch will ask you, "Filter Variable, If Any." You type:

STUDENT

Micro-Crunch will then ask you to set a value for the filter. You provide Micro-Crunch the first value of your control variable. In this case, you type,

1

[§] Notice this test assumes that people were married before they took part in the illegal activities. Unfortunately, the survey did not indicate how long the individuals had been married.

This is the value of the variable STUDENT that represents nonstudents. The screen will show the results between DIDNOLG and MARRIED only for nonstudents. Save the results to your disk. You then repeat the entire process of Crosstab, Tables, Dependent Variable, Independent Variable, naming STUDENT as the filter variable, and then typing the filter value, 2. The screen will now provide you with the results for students.

SPSS works much more quickly than Micro-Crunch in that you can supply all values of the control variable at the same time. Appendix B discusses how to do this in SPSS.

NOTES

[1] Melvin J. Hinich and Michael C. Munger, *Ideology and the Theory of Political Choice* (Ann Arbor: University of Michigan Press, 1994), p. 11.

[2] Phillip E. Converse, "The Nature of Belief Systems in Mass Publics," in *Ideology and Discontent,* ed. by David Apter (London: Free Press, 1964), pp. 219–241.

[3] Ronald Inglehart, *The Silent Revolution* (Princeton, N.J.: Princeton University Press, 1977); see also his "Value Change in Industrial Societies," *American Political Science Review* 81 (1987), pp. 1,289–1,303.

[4] Inglehart, "Value Change in Industrial Societies," p. 1,296.

[5] See, for example, Scott C. Flanagan, "Value Change in Industrial Societies," *American Political Science Review* 81 (1987), pp. 1,304–1,319; and Harold Clarke and Nittish Dutt, "Measuring Value Change in Western Industrialized Societies: The Impact of Unemployment," *American Political Science Review* 85 (1991), pp. 905–922.

[6] Flanagan, "Value Change in Industrial Societies," pp. 1,308–1,318.

[7] Norman Schofield, "A Theory of Coalition Government in a Spatial Model of Voting," working paper no. 162, Washington University Center in Political Economy, St. Louis, January 1992); and Hinich and Munger, *Ideology and the Theory,* Chap. 7.

[8] Robert D. Brown and Edward G. Carmines, "Materialists, Postmaterialists, and the Criteria for Political Choice in U.S. Presidential Elections," *Journal of Politics* 57 (1995), pp. 483–494. Brown and Carmines explore changes in the importance of social and economic issues from one election to the next.

[9] William H. Riker, *Liberalism against Populism: A Confrontation between the Theory of Democracy and the Theory of Social Choice* (San Francisco: W. H. Freeman, 1982).

[10] Not all political scientists agree that the voters' paradox happens frequently. Three writers who contest this point are Benjamin Barber, *Strong Democracy* (Berkeley: University of California Press, 1984); Carole Pateman, *Participation and Democratic Theory* (Cambridge: Cambridge University Press, 1970); and Elaine Spitz, "The Virtue of Numbers," *Ethics* 89 (1978), pp. 111–114.

[11] Publius, *The Federalist Papers, No. 10* (New York: Heritage, 1945), p. 106.

[12] Barry Ames, "Electoral Rules, Constituency Pressures, and Pork Barrel: Bases of Voting in the Brazilian Congress," *Journal of Politics* 57 (1995), pp. 324–343.

[13] David Truman, *The Governmental Process* (New York: Alfred A. Knopf, 1958).

[14] Sidney Verba, Norman H. Nie, and Jae-On Kim, *Participation and Political Equality: A Seven-Nation Comparison* (Cambridge: Cambridge University Press, 1978).

[15] E. E. Schattschneider, *The Semisovereign People* (New York: Holt, Rinehart and Winston, 1960).

[16] Mancur Olson, Jr., *The Logic of Collective Action* (Cambridge: Harvard University Press, 1965).

[17] Ames, "Brazilian Congress."

[18] Ibid., p. 331.

[19] Ibid., p. 342.

[20] Riker, *Liberalism against Populism.*

[21] For evidence of this success as well as the impacts of political parties, see Gerald C. Wright, Robert S. Erikson, and John P. McIver, "Measuring State Partisanship and Ideology with Survey Data," *Journal of Politics* 47 (1985), pp. 469–489; and Gary King and Robert X. Browning, "Democratic Representation and Partisan Bias in Congressional Elections," *American Political Science Review* 81 (1987), pp. 1251–1273.

[22] Abraham Kaplan, *The Conduct of Inquiry: Methodology for Behavioral Science* (San Francisco: Chandler, 1964), pp. 330–331.

[23] Alan S. Zuckerman, *Doing Political Science: An Introduction to Political Analysis* (Boulder, Colo.: Westview Press, 1991), p. 10.

[24] W. Bruce Shepard, "Modern Political Analysis" (Oregon State University, Corvallis, Ore., 1990, mimeographed), p. 65.

Institutional Arrangements

7

The Forms of Government: Parliamentary and Presidential Systems

Chapter 6 described how the institutions of ideologies, political parties, interest groups, and elections all have important roles in linking citizen demands to public policies. The exact process for forging these links depends on the structure of the institutions of government such as the legislature, executive branch, bureaucracy, and courts. Some formal body must enact a law, issue an executive order, or hand down a judicial decision.

This chapter and the two that follow it compare the structures of government institutions across nations. In this chapter, we distinguish between parliamentary and presidential forms of government and provide a step-by-step description of the arrangements through which the two forms prepare and pass legislation. We also focus on the duties of a legislature in a democratic political system.

Discussions of the appropriate structures of government are probably more relevant today than at any time in the last 40 years. New nations formed from the former Soviet Union as well as the countries of eastern Europe are still in the process of deciding what institutions they think will work best in their countries. In 1996 The Czech Republic continues to wrestle with its method for selecting members of its Senate and what duties senators will fulfill. Several countries are trying to define appropriate powers for their judicial branches. They must decide whether to follow Britain, which does not allow judicial review of laws, or India, where the highest court exercises extraordinary power.

Scholars studying Latin America have suggested that democracy would be more stable in that area with versions of a parliamentary system rather than the current presidential systems.[1] Many African nations decided they could not afford the political systems they inherited from the colonial powers (see Chapter 4); they are now attempting to build democratic structures appropriate to their cultures. Democratization has brought greater respect for human rights. This has lead to increased power for courts in many countries. All of these developments make the material you will be reading in the next few chapters particularly relevant to today's political world.

Parliamentary and Presidential Systems

Approximately 90 percent of the world's 200-plus countries make laws through national legislatures. These bodies range in size from the Costa Rican Legislative Assembly (56 members) to the 3,000-member Chinese National People's Congress. Most are called *National Assembly, Parliament,* or *Congress,* but some have more particular names, such as Israel's Knesset, Ireland's Dail, and Iran's Majlis. The goal of this chapter is to help you understand the legislative activities you watch or read about in print reports. Why does a legislature act as it does, and what results does it produce?

The chapter begins by pointing out the major institutional differences between the two basic types of legislative-executive relationships, **parliamentary systems** and **presidential systems.** Next, the chapter describes the general outlines of the **legislative process,** the activities of all legislatures, and the general routines for those activities in democratic political systems. It then explains how a legislature's institutional framework limits and affects what it does. After that, the chapter considers what part a legislature plays in a country's overall political system.

This discussion concentrates on the British Parliament and the American Congress. They are the standard models, respectively, of the parliamentary and presidential political systems. In addition, the British and American political systems define the far ends of the continuum of the concentration and fragmentation of political power in democratic polities. The British system concentrates political power, while the American system fragments and distributes it. Although the structures of most democracies reflect either presidential or parliamentary principles of organization, some nations have adopted mixed systems that combine elements of both.

Popular participation in government is critical to "keeping a bridle on the king." Previous chapters discussed how representative assemblies slowly emerged as the common form of popular participation in large nation-states. In the process, two major forms of representative government evolved: presidential systems and parliamentary systems.* A recent analysis of 136 governments shows that the vast majority reflect the presidential model. Most parliamentary systems are in Europe or former colonies of Great Britain such as Canada and Australia.[2] Presidential and parliamentary systems function quite differently from one another. For the most important difference, in parliamentary systems, the same people lead the executive and legislative branches of government. Presidential governments separate the powers and the leaders of the executive branch and the legislature. This separation is intended to limit government tyranny, but parliamentary systems are less fearful than presidential systems of tyranny and more concerned that government should be effective. For this reason, they place the executive and legislative branches under the same leaders.

Before the chapter can fruitfully examine differences between parliamentary and presidential systems, it must define a key term: **the Government.**[†] In a parliamentary system, people typically refer to the prime minister, other cabinet ministers, and the top advisors within the ruling party as "the Government." This name implies that these officials control the decisions of both the legislature and the executive branch. Although some authors refer to the president and cabinet in a presidential system as "the Government," we will not follow that practice; we believe that power is too dispersed in a presidential system to refer to a single group of people as "the Government."

HEADS OF STATE AND HEADS OF GOVERNMENT: CEREMONIES, SYMBOLS, AND POWER

Another difference between parliamentary and presidential systems is the division in a parliamentary system of the positions of the Head of State and Head of Government. Few ceremonies and rituals are more grandiose and elaborate than those that accompany and celebrate the coronation of a British monarch (most recently that of Elizabeth II in 1952). Compared even to the weakest of her royal predecessors, however, Queen Elizabeth II has virtually no political power. The coronation symbolized Queen Elizabeth's position as the Head of State of Great Britain and the nations of the British Commonwealth, yet the position brings little political authority. The symbolism surrounding her position dramatizes the differences between the functions of a **Head of State,** which the queen is, and a **Head of Government,** which she is not. The political responsibilities of a head of state are mostly ceremonial, while the powers and responsibilities of a head of government are greater than those of any other political official in a country.

The Head of Government is the chief political executive and the administrative leader of a country. In a parliamentary system, the prime minister is Head of Government. The most important, time-consuming, and attention-demanding task of this

---

*Names and labels alone are not reliable guides to a country's type of government. Some presidential governments label their legislatures *parliament,* and some parliamentary systems call them *congress.* Presidents, prime ministers, chancellors, and leaders with other titles can be found in both parliamentary and presidential systems.

[†] To avoid confusion, when the term *government* refers to the entire executive, legislative, judicial, and bureaucratic structure of the state, we will not capitalize it. In this book, "the Government," with the capital letter, refers to the prime minister, cabinet, and top party leaders.

position is to lead all other officials in making public policy. That job entails continual interaction with party leaders, legislative leaders, cabinet ministers, and countless other people. In almost all parliamentary systems, the Head of State and Head of Government are different persons. In a parliamentary system without a monarch, the Head of State typically holds the title of president, but this office does not correspond to the familiar one with the same name. The president in a parliamentary system generally has little political power.

In a presidential system, the president is both Head of State and Head of Government. A president fulfills ceremonial duties in the role of Head of State, such as receiving and entertaining ambassadors and foreign dignitaries and placing wreaths at war memorials. The president also accepts the power and responsibility that comes with the position of Head of Government.

HOW GOVERNMENTS ARE FORMED AND DISSOLVED

Presidential and parliamentary systems follow quite different practices to select political representatives and leaders. In a presidential system, voters elect the Head of Government, the president. In a parliamentary system, the voters do not directly select the Head of Government. Choosing a Head of Government in a parliamentary system involves three closely related practices that mystify many Americans:

1. Popular elections for members of the legislature do not occur by schedule or on any fixed date.

2. No popular elections for Head of Government (the prime minister) ever occur.

3. No practice or constitutional rule requires "single membership," as presidential systems demand.

The U.S. Constitution prohibits members of Congress from holding office in the executive branch or administrative agencies. British prime ministers and all principal cabinet ministers are also members of Parliament (MPs) elected from their districts. This double membership in the legislature and the executive branch is crucial to the Parliament's methods for conducting its business and to systems for keeping government responsible to citizens.[3] Figure 7.1 presents a schematic overview of the presidential and parliamentary forms of government.

Notice how the fusion of legislative and executive powers in the same group of leaders radically changes the relationship of the Head of Government to the legislature. Presidential systems allow situations in which the Head of Government, the president, does not control a majority of votes in the legislature. Executive and legislative leaders often compete with each other for power, and both can have substantial impacts on legislation. This competition for power does not occur in parliamentary systems because the same people lead both branches. Normally, a prime minister controls a majority of members of parliament and can instruct those members how to vote. Therefore, parliament typically passes any legislation the Government introduces and rejects legislation that the Government opposes. In presidential systems, even if the president's party controls a majority of the seats in both chambers of the legislature, this does not guarantee that the

---

FIGURE 7.1

PRESIDENTIAL AND PARLIAMENTARY FORMS OF GOVERNMENT

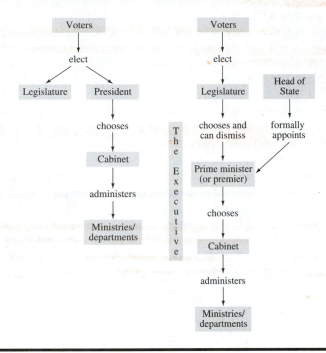

---

president controls the legislature or that the legislature will not pass measures the president opposes.

In either a parliamentary system or a presidential system, the voters elect members of the lower house of the legislature. Unlike a presidential system, however, voters in a parliamentary system do not directly decide who becomes the prime minister (Head of Government). The members of the newly elected legislature decide this. Typically, the Head of State asks the leader of the party that won the most seats in the legislature to "form a Government." The party leader submits to the Head of State a list of cabinet appointments agreed upon within the party; of course, the party leader heads the list as prime minister. The Head of State then formally appoints the cabinet ministers. For example, in Great Britain, either the Conservative Party or the Labour Party typically controls a majority of seats in the House of Commons after an election. The queen requests that the leader of that party form a Government.

COALITION AND MINORITY GOVERNMENTS

If a single party wins a majority of seats in the lower house of the legislature, then it forms the Government through a straightforward process. The leader of the majority party, in consultation with other party leaders, chooses the members of the Government.‡ What happens, however, when voters divide their loyalty among a number of political parties and no party wins a majority of seats in the legislature? The lower house of the legislature must then form a **coalition Government.** The leaders of two or more parties that together hold a majority of seats in the legislature reach an agreement to form a Government. The agreement specifies which cabinet posts each party will control, the priorities of legislative measures in the new Government, and the proposals that the Government will block. The person designated to become prime minister takes the proposal to the Head of State, who makes the appointments that install the new Government.

When such an agreement breaks down after a coalition Government takes office, a cabinet crisis results. Unless the coalition partners can negotiate a new agreement, the Government usually holds new elections. Italy, with legislative seats split among many parties, has had 54 Governments in the 50 years since World War II. In Germany as well as Italy, neither of the larger parties typically can form a majority Government without one or more of the smaller parties; this need often gives small parties critical power in coalition Governments.

As another solution to the problem of forming a Government when no party has a majority in parliament, one of the larger parties may take responsibility by forming a **minority government.** The proposed minority Government undertakes the task of ruling the country, even though it typically cannot enact any proposal that is unacceptable to the other major party.

CABINET RESPONSIBILITY AND THE DISSOLUTION OF PARLIAMENT

A parliamentary system does not schedule elections at set intervals. Typically either the constitution or custom dictates that an election must occur within some time period, generally 5 years from the previous election. As elections theoretically can occur any time within this 5-year span, the power to decide when to hold votes gains enormous importance. In this *political* decision, the Government tries to choose the best possible time to hold an election to maximize its own position. When the electoral climate seems favorable, the prime minister asks the Head of State to dissolve the sitting parliament and order new elections. Elections occur soon after the request to dissolve.

Votes of Confidence The decision to dissolve parliament and hold new elections does not always reside in the Government's hands, though. The Government faces a **vote of confidence** when a member of parliament proposes a resolution expressing a loss of confidence in the Government's ability to govern. Such a motion may result from a particular aspect of the Government's policy, or the overall Government performance may dissatisfy members of parliament.

---

‡ Typically a party conference chooses the party leader prior to the election. Party conferences are gatherings that resemble American national party conventions, but parties hold them annually instead of every 4 years.

A confidence vote has priority over all other legislative business. Ordinarily, the Government controls the parliament's agenda and the terms of debate, but on confidence motions it must yield control to the opposition. Should the Government lose the vote, its officials must resign. Typically rigid discipline in parliamentary parties ensures that a Government almost never loses a confidence vote. Only when a number of its own members desert or when a party abandons a coalition Government can the Government lose. Of course, the media pay close attention to confidence votes and the debate that precedes them.

The idea of votes of confidence stems from the parliamentary principle of **cabinet responsibility** to the legislature. This responsibility imposes both individual and collective liability. Each minister is individually responsible for actions by administrators and employees in the ministry. The prime minister and the cabinet are collectively responsible for the overall performance of the Government and also for egregious malfeasance by individuals in any ministry or administrative agency.

Cabinet responsibility and votes of confidence are characteristic of parliamentary governments, but not all countries implement procedures and customs that follow exactly the British pattern. A noteworthy variation is the **constructive vote of confidence** in the German Bundestag. This motion requires that any confidence vote to oust a Government include the name of the chancellor (prime minister) who will replace the current chancellor.

Question Hour Another check on the power of the ruling party in the British system is the **question hour.** Members of opposition parties can question the Government's policies during this regularly scheduled time, and cabinet ministers and other Government officials must answer these questions. Questions must be written and given to the Government ministers before they appear in Parliament to answer them. Opposition and Government speakers in Britain are all seasoned parliamentarians with sharp debate skills. This assures that the media provide extensive coverage of question hours.

The Institutional Framework

Every legislature works within an institutional framework made up of constitutional rules, established practices, and accepted ethical norms. This framework channels and constrains the actions of legislators. The precise nature of these constraints and their effects on legislative actions vary, of course, from country to country. Even so, the similarities among established procedures are more striking than the differences.

LEGISLATIVE COMPETENCE

Constitutional prescriptions provide the most visible institutional constraints on **legislative competence** within a government. These provisions list actions that lie within the theoretical scope of the legislature's authority, and they define how the legislators will carry out their duties. For example, Article I of the U.S. Constitution prescribes the organization and powers of Congress. It lists:

1. The necessary qualifications for becoming a member of Congress and how qualified candidates become legislators

2. The organization scheme for Congress's business (one session per year, choosing officers, punishing and expelling members, and time of adjournment)

3. Legislative procedures

4. Above all, the specifically enumerated powers of Congress, that is, the subjects upon which Congress may act

Article I also prescribes the role of Congress in amending the Constitution.

Since the British government operates without a written constitution, Parliament has theoretically unlimited discretion to take or withhold any action. However, a number of unwritten rules accomplish in Britain much of what Article I of the Constitution does in the United States. For example, legislation that would change the customary limits on Parliament (perhaps limit the Bill of Rights or abolish the House of Lords) must pass the House of Commons in two succeeding sessions in order to become law. Still, Parliament recognizes few subjects on which it is not competent to act if it chooses to do so. The limitations on the scope of Parliament's authority have political, not legal, origins.

NUMBER OF CHAMBERS

The U.S. Congress, the British Parliament, and most other national legislatures are legislatures composed of two chambers. *Unicameral* legislatures do make law in a few countries, however, including the National People's Congress of China and the legislature of New Zealand. Several successor states to the former Soviet Union, as well as of some communist states elsewhere in the world, have also adopted the unicameral model.

For primarily historical reasons, the so-called "upper chamber" is the smaller of the two houses in most bicameral legislatures.[§] In almost all countries other than Italy and the United States, the upper chamber wields much less power and authority than the lower chamber. In some countries, the current memberships and modes of selecting members of the upper houses reflect surviving practices from the countries' constitutional histories, as in Great Britain and France. In others, these characteristics reflect the countries' regional or federal structures. That is the case in the United States, Germany, Switzerland, the Netherlands, Italy, and Spain.

Members of almost all lower houses are elected by individual voters in geographically defined districts. Universal suffrage is the general rule in most countries today, but this practice has not been long established. Women won the vote only about two generations ago in the United States, and only in 1971 in Switzerland. Voters must meet property qualifications in legislative elections in a few places. In other countries, ethnic and religious identities may prohibit individuals from voting. In Croatian elections in 1995, for example, only people of ethnic Croatian descent could vote.

[§] The terminology reflects the nomenclature of the earliest legislatures, when the terms described the class status of the members—nobility and clergy on top, commoners on the bottom.

As one consequence, a legislature with two chambers instead of one must carry proposals through essentially the same process twice: if the two houses pass different versions of a proposal, the versions must go through some special procedure to generate a single set of provisions that both chambers will accept. Complex problems arise when the two chambers represent different combinations and patterns of interest. For instance, in the United States, the Democrats sometimes control one chamber of Congress and the Republicans control the other.

RULES OF PROCEDURE

Each legislative chamber adopts its own rules of parliamentary procedure to govern its proceedings. These resemble *Robert's Rules of Order*, but they lay out far more extensive and detailed requirements. Chapter 6 explained the tremendous political advantage of the individual who controls the order in which members vote on alternatives. (See the discussion of voters' paradox and Figure 6.3.) Knowledge of the rules and when to apply them is, therefore, a potent legislative resource. This is a particularly valuable tool for those who control the agenda of either the entire legislature or its committees.

Unwritten **rules of the game** also govern legislative behavior. Old hands in the legislature know these rules and expect new legislators to learn and follow them. For example, such rules in state legislatures in the United States include supporting another member's bill if it does not hurt one's own interests, notifying political allies well in advance of any intention not to support them, keeping one's temper, accepting defeat graciously, and not trying to win a vote by trickery.[4] It is important to learn and follow these rules because failure to do so will lead other legislators to apply informal sanctions.

Both formal and informal rules of procedure and unwritten rules of the game help to determine the fates of legislative proposals. These rules determine when and how legislators can introduce bills, when and how they can bring legislation to the floor for deliberation, if and how they can propose amendments to bills, when and for how long they will debate a bill, and much more. All rules of procedure serve essentially the same purpose as rules in any group. Where people have to act together, chaos results unless almost everyone follows the same rules. Formal rules of procedure act as traffic regulations, preventing verbal traffic jams and chaos on the floor of the legislature. Informal rules encourage civility in legislators' behavior. They minimize interpersonal conflicts among the members, so that they can accomplish their tasks.

On the whole, the formal and informal rules of procedure succeed remarkably well in helping legislatures get their business done in an orderly fashion and in preventing abusive language and violent conflict. Almost every legislature has suffered at least a few violent disruptions to its proceedings. Several times in recent years, mass fistfights have broken out on the floor of the Japanese Diet. Until fairly recently, legislators' riotous behavior often disrupted Italy's Chamber of Deputies. These incidents highlight the surprising truth that, even in times of crisis and acute political conflict, reasonable peace and quiet prevails in most legislatures, legislators are civil to one another, and legislative business stays on track. These facts underscore the remarkable effectiveness of well-established political institutions.

AUTHORITY AND LEADERSHIP STRUCTURE

A legislature needs leadership and authority to keep its business moving expeditiously and according to the rules. The nominal head of virtually every legislative chamber is a **speaker** (usually addressed by that name). The speaker usually presides over sessions of the chamber and manages the proceedings. The vice president of the United States is presiding officer of the U.S. Senate, but other members usually perform these duties. The speaker of the U.S. House of Representatives, who is also the leader of the majority party in that chamber, is the most powerful authority there. The speaker of the British House of Commons, on the other hand, is a scrupulously nonpartisan presiding officer elected by the members; this official usually retains the position as long as she wishes. When elected, she abandons any prior partisan attachments.

Political parties are important components of each chamber's authority structure. Chapter 6 explained the essential contribution of parties to the process of aggregating citizen demands and linking those demands to legislation. Each party must decide its priorities and devise its legislative strategy. This means that leaders must be aware of business that will come before the legislature and when each issue will arise. In a parliamentary system, party leaders tell the legislators how to vote. Even in a presidential system with relatively weak parties, like that in the United States, party affiliation is the best predictor of a legislator's votes on bills.

The most visible party leadership in every legislature is that which manages day-to-day business. Each party has a **floor leader,** usually called the *majority leader* and *minority leader* in a political system in which two parties dominate the legislature. The

speaker of the House in the U.S. Congress is the actual majority leader there, but the party also selects a floor leader to assist the speaker along with party **whips.** The whips keep members advised of party positions on upcoming measures and round them up for imminent roll calls. They also keep tabs on members' votes and advise leaders of deviations from party positions. When a member of Parliament votes against the prime minister of the same party, the party may not allow the member to run for office in the future. When a member of the U.S. Congress deviates from the directions of party leaders, however, the voters back home often reward this display of independence. For this reason, the job of the floor leader or whip is not usually very difficult in a parliamentary system. In a presidential system, however, these officials often struggle to maintain party discipline.

COMMITTEE SYSTEMS

Most legislatures cope with the high volume of work they must process by parceling it out to committees. The number of committees and the division of labor among them varies widely from country to country and between chambers in bicameral systems. Both houses of the U.S. Congress evaluate legislative proposals through a number of permanent committees, each dealing with a particular subject matter such as agriculture, banking, small business, taxes, and so forth. The German and Italian legislatures each maintain large networks of committees usually numbering in the 30s. The British House of Commons and the French Chamber of Deputies, however, have far fewer committees, and the work of these groups of legislators is not specialized by subject matter.

The committees examine the purpose and intent of a piece of proposed legislation, its adequacy for achieving that purpose, its compatibility or conflict with other policies, and its expected social, economic, and political effects. Most committees examine bills in considerable detail, usually line by line, and they often suggest changes. They then formulate judgments about the proposed legislation and send their recommendations to the full chambers.

Membership on a committee is roughly proportional to each party's representation in the chamber. Some legislatures distribute committee chairs in a similar proportional fashion. In the legislature of a bipartisan system, members of the majority party chair all committees. In the American Congress, seniority is a governing factor both in individual members' committee assignments and in choosing committee chairs. The chair is almost always the ranking (senior) member among the committee members of the majority party. Seniority also preserves legislators' seats on committees, unless they choose to change assignments.

The personal skills, ambitions, and parliamentary stature of a committee chair enhance the power and influence of the committee. In the United States, particularly in the Senate, committee chairs frequently block action on measures by simply refusing to permit discussions or reports on them. In 1995, Senator Jesse Helms, chairman of the Foreign Relations Committee, held up for months bills authorizing actions to implement State Department and U.S. Army activities in eastern Europe that had already been approved by Congress. He also prevented any committee action on nominations of ambassadors to a number of countries.

A unique instance of committee power and influence occurs in Italy, however. Each of the many specialized committees in the Chamber of Deputies has constitutional authority to enact *leggini* ("little laws") on subjects within its competence. No further action by the full house is required to enact these laws. While Italian committees cannot pass measures dealing with taxes, defense, and such major subjects, they can and do pass legislation of vital concern to various interest groups in the country.

SUMMARY FOR LEGISLATIVE INSTITUTIONS

A biologist might say that modern legislatures all display the same genotype. What they have in common affects the way each goes about its work, so they do many things in quite similar ways. As with people, however, the individual makeup and character of each particular legislature (*phenotype* in the biologist's terms) constitutes the framework within which it carries out legislative action. Seemingly small variations in structure and organization sometimes make for large differences in typical activities. To understand fully the activities in any particular legislature requires both general knowledge of legislative procedures and some familiarity with particular characteristics. The next section reviews some of the differences in the legislative process that result from these institutional differences.

The Legislative Process

The main business of every legislative body is to do something about proposals of law. Different bodies adopt varying methods for determining what proposals come before them, how those proposals reach legislators, and how those legislators deal with the proposals. Despite these differences, all take essentially the same final action on a proposal: Members of each legislative chamber vote either to pass or to reject it. The diagrams in Figure 7.2 outline the main steps in the legislative processes of both U.S. and British systems. As you follow the process, notice an important difference in the two systems. In a parliamentary system, the outcome of a Government-sponsored bill is almost a foregone conclusion. In a presidential system, a bill faces a much more problematic fate.

INITIATION

The legislative process formally begins when a legislator (or a group of them) presents a bill and requests that the clerk of the chamber register it for consideration and action. Where a proposal originates is more important than who initiates it, however. In most instances, sponsors and cosponsors submit proposals drafted outside the legislature. In a parliamentary system, most proposals come from the Government. Each minister introduces bills that most directly affect his particular ministry, but only after the Government has agreed on each bill's contents. Since 1945, the Government has introduced 82 percent of all bills in the British House of Commons, and 95 percent of the bills the Government has introduced have become law. In the French Fifth Republic, 95 percent

FIGURE 7.2

THE LEGISLATIVE PROCESS IN THE U.S. CONGRESS AND THE BRITISH PARLIAMENT

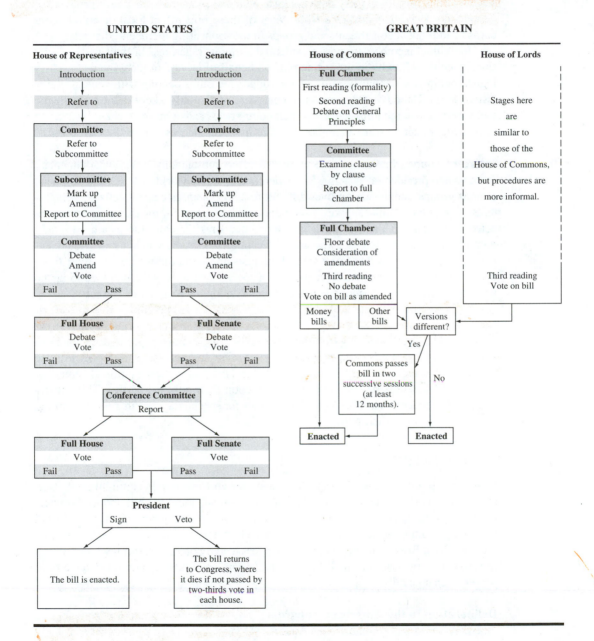

of all bills originate as Government bills.[5] In a typical presidential regime, many measures originate in the president's office.

In a major difference between parliamentary and presidential systems, individual members in most presidential countries can introduce legislation on their own proposals. In the British House of Commons, all MPs who are not officials in the Government or leaders of the opposition party must compete with one another for the scarce privilege of introducing **Private Member's Bills.** Most of these bills affect local or private concerns of individual constituents and groups in the sponsoring members' districts.

Individual members in most presidential systems, regardless of their party affiliations, face no difficulty in proposing bills on behalf of private or local interests. Many legislators in presidential systems also introduce measures dealing with general policy issues. In the United States, committee chairs are particularly likely to introduce legislation pertinent to the jurisdictions of their committees, and committee chairs as a group have a higher success rate than the president in obtaining passage of their proposals.[6]

Interest Groups   Interest group activity also differs substantially between parliamentary systems and presidential systems. Every democracy in the world must deal with special interest groups, and this task proves difficult for all of them. In a presidential system, interest groups try to enlist support from individual legislators for measures they want enacted. For example, a recent article concluded that Brazil's legislature is almost totally dominated by special interests who use its decentralized structure to have individual legislators introduce bills that favor special interests and harm the nation.[7] Chapter 6 described how interest groups achieve passage of special interest bills through logrolling, the process of trading votes among legislators representing local or private interests.

The centralized structure of a parliamentary system generally allows it to restrict interest group influence more effectively than a presidential system can. Aware of the Government's near monopoly over introduction of bills, an interest group does not try to get individual legislators to sponsor desired legislation. Instead, the group works with the leaders of the major political parties. In a parliamentary system, the political careers of individual legislators depend almost entirely upon their political parties. This critical feature discourages legislators from doing favors for special interests that would hurt the national interests of their parties.

DELIBERATION

Legislative proposals usually receive the most time and attention in committees. A committee gathers information, both technical and political, about the bill and its likely effects. Committee hearings are an important means of doing this in many political systems, including those of the United States, Germany, and Italy. Other systems, like those of Great Britain and France, rely much less heavily on these hearings. Committees in some countries can drastically alter bills. In some countries, committees have little power to change bills.

Deliberation in the American Congress   The deliberation process is probably as time-consuming and complex in the American Congress as in any legislative body in the world. As Figure 7.2 shows, all bills are first assigned to committees (and delegated further to subcommittees), mainly on the basis of their subject matter. In a presidential system, committee chairs can exert considerable influence at this stage. If they wish, they often can kill a legislative proposal in its early stages. For a bill to succeed, the chair of the committee must assign it to a subcommittee for hearings where proponents and opponents testify on particular points of the proposal. Following the hearings, the subcommittee works through the bill clause by clause and submits recommendations to the parent committee, which further examines it. The bill then finds a place on the House or Senate agenda.

At this stage, the majority party leadership can expedite the bill, delay it, or block further action. Most measures reported out of committee eventually come to the floor. Some bills have amendments added to them there. If a bill passes, it goes through a similar process in the other house. If the two houses pass different versions, both go to a conference committee made up of members from each chamber. This committee brings the two versions into agreement and reports the single, consolidated measure back to each house, where it is put to a vote without amendment. If passed, it goes to the president who decides whether to sign the bill or veto it.

Deliberation in the British Parliament   Deliberation in the British legislature bears little resemblance to the American process. For one difference, the House of Lords does not play a decisive role in deliberations. After the conclusion of the major deliberations on a bill in the House of Commons, the House of Lords can neither block nor delay passage of a bill that appropriates or raises money.

Committees also play a fundamentally different role in Britain than in America. Before the Government refers a bill to a committee, the House of Commons gives it a "first reading" and conducts extensive debate on its general principles. The Government and opposition parties select their speakers and the order in which they will speak. After this debate, the bill goes to a committee in the House of Commons. Committees go through bills line by line, refining their language and form. Committees conduct few if any hearings, and they take no lengthy testimony from interested parties. Committees may make minor amendments, but they may not change the character of proposals. If a committee has made changes, the full house may debate the changes but not the whole measure. A vote to pass, as indicated in Figure 7.2, sends a money bill to the queen for her signature. Other bills go to the House of Lords, which may refuse to pass the bill as passed in Commons. But if the House of Commons passes the bill twice by simple majority within two sessions (1 year) it becomes law without the Lords' approval.

ENACTMENT

The final vote on a legislative proposal is the simplest action in the legislative process. When the outcome of an important bill remains uncertain, the final vote may be a dramatic occasion. More often, however, the outcome appears so predictable that it may be difficult to find the quorum necessary to take a vote. In most legislatures, the speakers record members' votes in final decisions to pass or reject important bills. The American

Senate holds roll calls for individually recorded votes. Members of the House of Representatives vote through an electronic system.

Notice the differences between the deliberative processes in parliamentary and presidential systems. In a parliamentary system, few proposals not sponsored by the Government reach the legislature. Debate on a bill creates an opportunity for the Government to explain the rationale for the bill to the public. The opposition also has its chance to explain why the bill should not pass. Committee action in a parliamentary system clarifies a bill and catches errors in its drafting; it does not give opponents an opportunity to gain substantive changes in the bill. The upper house cannot prevent bills from becoming law. As long as party discipline holds and no party abandons a coalition Government, a bill's final passage is a formality. Thus, a parliamentary system provides no way to prevent the passage of a Government bill, unless the Government decides to withdraw it. This reflects the power of the prime minister and the priority in a parliamentary system of the ability of a Government selected by a majority of the population to effectively implement its programs.

Presidential systems are quite different. The separation of powers, along with political arrangements that further fragment power, gives opponents of a bill numerous opportunities either to kill it or to gain substantial changes. Subcommittees and committees in both chambers can kill or radically alter bills. Weaker party discipline in a presidential system allows floor amendments in each house that can alter a bill; floor votes can even kill it. Finally, the president can veto the bill. The deliberative process in a presidential system reflects the goal of those who first developed the procedural rules to restrain government tyranny, even if it represents the will of the majority.

Legislative Performance

Most citizens think of legislatures primarily in terms of their law-making activities. Recall from Chapter 3, however, that the law-making functions of legislatures developed after the establishment of their representative function. Legislatures in democracies also oversee and restrain the executive.

REPRESENTATION

Representation is a difficult concept, not only to operationalize for empirical tests, but also to clarify for basic understanding. Dictionary definitions offer little help. Most political thinkers would agree that *representation* means generally acting on behalf of the person or persons represented. A firmer definition might seem to require no more than answers to two questions: (1) Who or what is represented? (2) How does a representative make decisions? Do representatives attempt to do what is best for the people who elected them or for the whole country? Equally important, do representatives use their own judgment about what is best, or are they expected to do what their constituency instructs?

The first national assemblies performed important functions of representing the interests of at least some social classes against those of the monarch. As democratic theory and institutions developed, liberal democracy settled on the basic tenet that government must be responsible and responsive to the people. This seems to give an easy answer to the first question about representation: "The people are represented." This answer, however, is inadequate.

If "the people" select their representatives by district or region, should the representatives speak on behalf of the entire country or only on behalf of the people in their own districts? Perhaps, they should speak only on behalf of those who voted for them, leaving supporters of their opponents without representation. As Chapter 6 pointed out, however, even if "the people" refers only to those who voted for the representative, many disagreements still emerge. Every conception of "the people" to be represented combines individuals with all kinds of interests and opinions. Representatives face a basic difficulty because these interests and opinions conflict with varying intensity in countless ways.

Many people believe that a representative's first obligation is to protect the interests of the home district and to base actions on the opinions of constituents. But even if a legislator's constituency agreed widely on economic matters, their opinions would differ on social issues. Liberal theorists such as Publius have argued that such conflict comes from the nature of humankind, and Chapter 6 confirmed that no representative can pretend to speak for the majority of constituents on all interests. This underlying problem led Rousseau to reject the very idea of representation.

Chapter 6 also showed that neither a two-party nor a multiparty system can resolve the problem of inability to represent a majority of voters. Even if legislators could represent the wishes of the majority of their own constituents, a basic problem would remain. The representative must ask, "Am I sitting in this chamber to act on behalf of all the people in the country or just those in my own district?" At one time, many legislators believed that legislatures should function as assemblies of wise persons rather than politicians or spokespersons for districts or special interests. Representatives were supposed to apply their wisdom and judgment and do what they thought best for the common interest of all citizens. Edmund Burke gave the classic statement of this view:

> Parliament . . . is not a *congress* of ambassadors from different and hostile interests; which interests each must maintain, as an agent and advocate, against all other agents and advocates; but Parliament is a *deliberative* assembly of *one* nation, with *one* interest, that of the whole; where, not local purposes, not local prejudices ought to guide but the general good, resulting from the general reason of the whole.[8]

Burke told his constituents explicitly that he could not be bound by instructions or orders from them; he would be guided by "his unbiased opinion, his mature judgment, his enlightened conscience."[9]

The rising tide of democracy over the next century, with its emphasis on "the voice of the people," overwhelmed Burke's conception of the representative as **trustee** of the national interest. Instead, democracy moved toward the idea that the representative should be a **delegate,** taking orders from the people and doing nothing they do not want and everything they do want. For the modern representative, political parties further complicate the picture. Legislators now have to reconcile the demands of their own conceptions of the public interest, conflicting demands from various competing interests in their own constituencies, and forceful demands of the leaders of their political parties.

Whose public interest comes first, the nation's or the district's? How far should representatives work to execute instructions from voters, and when must they use their own best judgment? Should representatives function as delegates who take orders or as trustees with special expertise and corresponding obligations to use their judgment to further the interests of citizens? How can political scientists evaluate how well legislators represent or serve the people?

Political scientists Heinz Eulau and William Riker argue that the answer to this question in a liberal democracy is concerned less with what decisions to make or whom to represent than with whether the decision process follows the formal and informal rules decided by the country's constitution and by the legislature itself. Decisions that follow the rules are legitimate for that reason. So long as the people can elect a different set of representatives at the next election, then the representative process has met the requirements of a liberal democracy.[10] Studies of attempts at democratization in eastern Europe, Haiti, Nicaragua, and Korea confirm that the ability of the people to vote a different set of leaders into office is probably the single best indicator of how well democracy is developing.[11]

EVALUATING LEGISLATION AND PUBLIC POLICY

Producing legislation is the chief activity of a legislature. How can citizens evaluate the content of that legislation or determine how well the policies are working for the affected people? Every year, a legislature enacts hundreds of laws, changes hundreds of others, and fails to enact thousands that specific groups of citizens think it should have passed. One simple criterion for judging that output is its coherence, that is, the absence of laws that contradict or conflict with other laws. One simple example is conflicts in policies concerning tobacco; one set of government actions actively discourages its use through regulation and taxation, and another actively encourages the production of tobacco by paying subsidies to growers.

Another simple criterion might be the number of self-contradictory or nonsensical laws passed. Classic examples of such laws were passed in Indiana and Oregon. The first decreed that, when an auto and a train arrived at a railroad crossing simultaneously, neither should proceed until the other had passed. Second, in an attempt to prevent lewd behavior in and near public parks, a town council passed an ordinance banning sexual intercourse in all public and private places.

Meaningful evaluation of public policy calls for an examination of the effects of laws. This effort encounters essentially the same problem, however, as an attempt to objectively define "the public interest." All laws that legislatures pass inevitably have unequal effects on different people. Many analyses of public policy focus on which interests in society most powerfully influenced the process of making particular policies and which interests benefited or lost as a result. Clearly, if a democratic polity excludes citizens from representation, whether by law or by process, then the legislature fails an important democratic test. Thus, if the procedures of a presidential system favor organized minorities, or if those of a parliamentary system fail to protect minority rights, then the policies of those legislatures are likely to lead to outcomes that liberal theory would reject. This raises more of the normative issues with which this book began, and it highlights the importance of integrating normative and empirical issues.

OVERSIGHT AND CONTROL OVER THE EXECUTIVE

Representative government evolved historically as the most effective known device for limiting tyranny of the minority. The third important function of a democratic legislature is to keep the bridle on the king, that is, to limit abuse of power by the executive. In a parliamentary government, the principle of collective cabinet responsibility to parliament theoretically maintains ultimate legislative control over the Government. Party dominance of parliament, however, makes the vote of confidence an uncertain instrument for maintaining that control, since the opposition rarely has enough votes to defeat the Government. Legislatures in both parliamentary and presidential governments have some power to keep tabs on the executive branch and its agencies. In many parliamentary systems, the question period is effective in bringing abuses of power to light. Many legislatures in presidential systems have authority to impeach the chief executive and high-ranking officials, as well as high-court justices. Legislative committees may focus on inappropriate administrative actions and policies. American congressional committees in recent years have investigated and criticized awards of contracts by the Defense Department and harassment of taxpayers by the IRS. More prominent congressional investigations have explored the Iran-Contra affair, scandals at the Department of Housing and Urban Development, and Whitewater loans.

As Chapter 8 will detail, the executive and administrative activities in most countries are much too extensive for any of the instruments of legislative oversight to encompass more than a very small fraction of government activity. Legislatures, even strong ones in presidential systems, cannot match the information and technical expertise available to the executive. The legislature may force the removal from office of guilty officials and require the executive to take corrective action to prevent further abuses. If abuses become too numerous or too scandalous, public exposure through legislative investigations may ultimately lead to voters' taking punitive action at the polls against the party in power.

OTHER FUNCTIONS

One legislative function with which individual legislators in many systems become all too familiar is **constituency service.** Many legislators dislike this "errand running." The errands may actually be run by members of a legislator's staff at the capitol, but they usually involve phone calls or correspondence with individual constituents. In performing constituency service, the legislators represent constituents in dealings with government agencies by helping them cope with problems. For example, your grandmother might be having difficulty obtaining her Social Security check, or your parents' business may be having difficulty with unfair enforcement by a particular inspector in the Occupational Health and Safety Administration. Almost any agency that comes into direct contact with people is likely to create some difficulties for a legislator's constituents, and the constituents may call the legislator for assistance.[‖] Many constituents, of course, seek legislators' help in lobbying for passage of bills that interest them and in lobbying bureaucrats for establishment of favorable procedures or rules.

Legislatures also perform a less obvious function: **recruitment of political elites.** In this way, legislators help to expand the reservoir of people who are interested in and knowledgeable about government and willing to seek office. Service in a regional or provincial legislature socializes political elites to the necessity of recognizing diverse interests and viewpoints, all claiming validity, on every matter with which they deal. They learn the importance of coping with conflict, and they learn by observation and experience how to do it in such bodies. Many members of national legislative bodies have profited by serving first in state and regional legislatures. Similarly, service in the national legislature helps to prepare public officials who later become governors, cabinet members, or chief executives. In local positions, these officials refine their ideas of executive-legislative relationships and the appropriate functions of the two branches of government.

Finally, legislatures have very important symbolic functions. Some legislative activity involves ceremonies and rituals that focus attention on the community as whole and not on conflict among members of the community. For example, when legislators take the oath of office, they promise to uphold the constitution and to preserve the welfare of the entire country. In taking this oath, they demonstrate the value of government itself and not just the regime currently in power. Legislative rituals such as the final vote on a bill symbolize democracy in action, the rule of law, and the presumed agreement of all parties on these fundamental values in spite of political conflicts.

Summary

Most citizens agree with John Stuart Mill that direct democracy is impractical and that the ideal form of government for a nation-state is representative democracy. Although they may see representative government as an ideal, many citizens living in democracies are dissatisfied with their legislatures' conformance to the ideals of representation. The media report stories about corruption, sordid party politics, and public disinterest in legislative activity. These complaints occur not only in the United States but in all democracies with a free press.[12]

European and American scholars have argued, however, that legislatures do their jobs no more poorly today than they ever have; in many respects, in fact, they do better. French scholar Yves Meny has argued that legislatures never have expressed the democratic will of the people, exerted effective control over the executive, or dominated the legislative process.[13] American political scientists Gerhard Loewenberg and Samuel C. Patterson have emphasized an absolutely critical role for legislatures in democratic politics:

[‖] One of the authors sought and received help from his Senator in securing immediate discharge from the Army of his son, who was kept enlisted (without pay, but still with bed and board) beyond an agreed 3-year enlistment. (The Army unit lost all of the soldier's papers and claimed to have no record of him.) In fact, the Army post in question was already under investigation by the Senate Armed Services Committee, which happened to be chaired by the senior senator from the author's home state.

In the management of political conflict, legislatures translate the fundamental conflicts existing in all societies into forms amenable to political action. . . . The manner in which legislatures cope with conflict affects the level of conflict in society, raising or lowering it, redirecting it, and ultimately generating allegiance or hostility to the men and women in political office, to the institutions of government, and to the political community itself.[14]

Such collective representation is the ultimate link between citizens and their government. How well a legislature performs that complex collective assignment depends on the adequacy of the legislative institutions examined in this chapter.

The quality of a legislature depends on the character, talents, political skills, and motivations of the individual legislators. Although not all legislators behave as statesmen instead of irresponsible political manipulators, many do. In addition, citizens must remember that the quality of representation they receive depends equally on what they demand of their representatives. An unknown cynical observer once said that people get the kind of representation they deserve.

QUESTIONS AND EXERCISES

Questions for Reason

1. Explain briefly the roles of Head of State and Head of Government. What are the benefits of separating the two offices? What are the benefits of fusing them?

2. What are rules of the game in legislatures? Why are they so important? What might cause a breakdown in these important standards of behavior?

3. Describe and explain the differences in the roles of the legislatures in the deliberation process in the U.S. and British systems? How do their committee structures reflect these differences?

Questions for Reflection

1. Which chamber of the legislature is more powerful in most bicameral legislatures? Why is this? How does it fit with democratic theory?

2. Edmund Burke saw the role of the legislator as one of a trustee of the national interest. Do you want your legislator to act as a trustee or as your delegate? Does your opinion on this question differ for varying issues?

3. Why does a legislature need committees, even in a parliamentary system?

4. By what standards should citizens evaluate a legislature? Do your standards indicate why Americans typically dislike Congress but love their own representatives and Senators?

Questions for Analysis: Control Variables

The previous chapter introduced the idea of spurious association. (Remember the problem with storks and birthrates.) To determine whether an association between two variables is spurious, a political scientist generally needs two things: a third variable that influences both of the original variables and an explanation of why that third variable really causes the observed association. Recall that the negative relationship between the level of incumbent spending and the probability of winning the election made no sense without the third variable, challenger strength. Challenger strength influenced both the likelihood that the incumbent would spend a lot of money trying to retain a seat and the likelihood that the challenger would win. (See Figure 6.7, page 206.)

Notice that a scientist can never truly "know" that any association is spurious, even the strange one between storks and birthrates. The decision that the association is spurious rests on the judgment that an alternative explanation "fits better" with the accepted understanding of how the world works. Similarly, no one can prove that an incumbent does not raise the chances of electoral defeat by spending more money; the alternative theory is simply more logical, and it fits better with other knowledge about why candidates win elections.

Look at one final example of the importance of spurious association for public policy about important political issues. If you were to examine the salaries of male and female professors at your university, you probably would find that male faculty members earn higher average salaries than their female colleagues. Does this mean that your university is discriminating against women? Actually, it could mean just the opposite.

In recent years, graduate schools have actively recruited and graduated more female Ph.D. students than they did in the past. To improve the percentage of female faculty members, schools are actively competing to hire these women. Because colleges have only recently begun graduating and hiring females with Ph.D. degrees, females have a much higher probability than males of being relatively new faculty members. As in other professions, people with more experience in their jobs earn more money. On average, a faculty member who has served longer will receive a higher salary. As a group, females have been faculty members for shorter periods, so they receive less pay than males. Thus, the observed negative relationship between female faculty members and low salaries may indicate that a university is trying hard to act affirmatively to diversify its faculty rather than that it is discriminating against females.

To discover if your college or university currently practices gender discrimination, you must first "hold constant" the length of time that individuals have been faculty members. You could do this by comparing the salaries of male and female professors with comparable teaching experience, for example, by grouping faculty members by the number of years they have been working since they received their Ph.D. degrees. Perhaps you would define three groups: little experience, moderate experience, and high experience. Now you might compare the average salaries of males and females in each group to check for bias against female faculty members.

Interaction

The examples cited so far "control for" the effects of a third variable to check for a spurious association. Scientists call this third variable a **control variable,** because they control for its effects when examining the association between the two original variables. A control variable may help in many ways to explain relationships. One is to identify spurious associations. A second reason is to measure **interaction.**

Suppose that a sociologist hypothesizes that society practices height discrimination; tall people are more likely than short people to be promoted in their jobs. The sociologist collects data and finds that taller people are more likely to be promoted than

FIGURE 7.3

THE RELATIONSHIP BETWEEN HEIGHT AND JOB PROMOTION,
CONTROLLING FOR GENDER

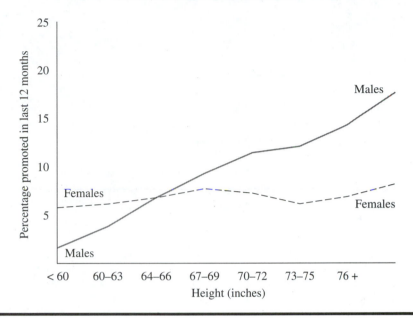

shorter people, but the relationship is weak. A colleague suggests that the relationship is not stronger because being tall helps males, but it does not help females.

To test this hypothesis, the sociologist divides her data into two groups, males in one and females in the other. She then repeats the chi-square analysis and finds a very large chi-square for the male group and an insignificant chi-square for the female group. A graph of the results might look similar to Figure 7.3.

In the real world, a relationship between the independent and dependent variables often holds for one value of the control variable but not for another value. An infamous such case is the relationship between the ages of male college students and car insurance. Insurance companies keep very extensive data on auto accidents, and they run many statistical analyses to see if different groups in the population are more likely to have accidents. Because of the past performance of all young males, insurance companies typically charge males between the ages of 16 and 25 much higher insurance rates than they charge females. Once males reach age 25, their rates drop, and rates drop still further when they reach the age of 30. For females, insurance rates show little variation with age, and the rates of young females are much lower than those of young males. Thus, controlling for gender, males experience a negative relationship between age and insurance rates, and females see no relationship between age and insurance rates. A graph of that interaction would look like Figure 7.4.

FIGURE 7.4

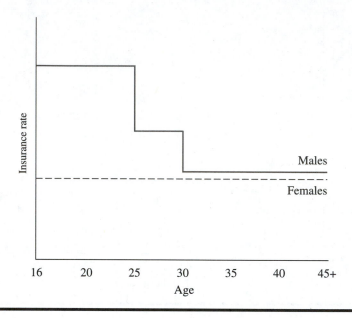

INTERACTION: THE RELATIONSHIP BETWEEN AGE AND
INSURANCE RATES, CONTROLLING FOR GENDER

The two examples with height discrimination and auto insurance rates use gender as the control variable. In the first case, the variable height had a different effect on job promotion for men than for women. The same was true of the effect of the variable age on car insurance rates. In each of these cases, interaction has occurred. *Interaction occurs when the control variable and the independent variable combine to produce different relationships between the independent and dependent variables for different values of the control variable.*

Formulating Hypotheses for Interaction
To test for interaction between the control variable and the independent variable, a researcher must develop more than one hypothesis. This adjustment reflects the expectation that the relationship between the independent and dependent variables will change with changes in the value of the control variable. Two hypotheses would describe the relationships shown in Figure 7.3:

- For females, short and tall people are equally likely to have been promoted during the last 12 months.
- For males, tall people are more likely than short people to have been promoted during the last 12 months.

Notice that hypotheses for interaction have the following form:

- For [first category of the control variable], [standard hypothesis predicting the expected relationship between the independent and dependent variables].
- For [another category of the control variable], [standard hypothesis predicting the expected relationship between the independent and dependent variables].

A particular test requires as many hypotheses as different hypothesized relationships. If you were to use ethnicity as the control variable when studying the relationship between education and affirmative action, you might need several hypotheses like these:

- For Anglos, people with higher social status will have higher support for affirmative action programs.
- For African Americans and Hispanics, people with higher social status will have lower support for affirmative action programs.
- For Asian-Americans, people of high and low social status are equally likely to have high support for affirmative action programs.

Accepting or Rejecting the Null Hypothesis
The decision whether to accept or reject the null hypothesis is more complex for a study with interaction than for one with spurious association. The researcher must confirm or disprove a number of hypotheses equal to the number of expected different relationships between the independent and dependent variable. The researcher must test each hypothesis separately and decide whether to reject or accept it. He also must test whether the relationships between the independent and dependent variable are, in fact, different for at least some values of the control variable.

EXERCISES

To keep the analyses as simple as possible, continue to use the data set PERUCAT and repeat the computer procedures you learned in the exercises in Chapter 6. Use any independent variables you think are appropriate—either WILLLEGL or WILLNOLG as your dependent variable and either STUDENT or MARRIED as your control variable. Using your word processor, prepare statements of two hypotheses that predict spurious association and three hypotheses that predict interaction. Explain why you expect either spurious association or interaction for each hypothesis or set of hypotheses. Each explanation will require two or three well-thought-out sentences.

Following the procedures you learned in the previous chapter, use either Micro-Crunch or SPSS to test your hypotheses. Explain whether you accept or reject each hypothesis. *Your results need not actually show either spurious association or interaction. You need only to prepare the appropriate hypotheses and have a rationale for each.*

Carry out these steps to complete this exercise:

1. Using your word processor, prepare the necessary statements of hypotheses and rationales for each.
2. Save the file for later use.

3. Using Micro-Crunch or SPSS, test your hypotheses. Save the material by writing it to disk. Give the file a different name than your word-processing file.

4. Combine your word-processing and data-output files and decide whether to accept the null or alternate hypothesis in each case.

5. If data falsify your hypothesis, explain results that they actually support.

6. Save the combined file and print it. Make sure that your name is on your output.

7. (Optional) Draw the graphs for each set of tables. Be sure to include the significance level.

NOTES

[1] Adam Przeworski, *Democracy and the Market: Political and Economic Reforms in Eastern Europe and Latin America* (Cambridge: Cambridge University Press, 1991).

[2] Jan-Erik Lane and Svante Ersson, *Comparative Politics: An Introduction and New Approach* (Cambridge, Mass.: Polity Press, 1994), Table 7.1, p. 158.

[3] In the Netherlands, Norway, and Sweden, parliamentary regimes operate on the single-membership principle. In Tanzania and Kenya, presidential systems allow double membership. See Jan-Erik Lane and Svante Ersson, *Comparative Politics: An Introduction and New Approach* (Cambridge, Mass.: Polity Press, 1994), p. 20.

[4] John Wahlke, Heinz Eulau, William Buchanan, and Leroy Ferguson, *The Legislative System* (New York: John Wiley & Sons, 1962), pp. 146–147.

[5] Yves Meny, *Government and Politics in Western Europe,* trans. by Janet Lloyd (New York: Oxford University, 1993).

[6] Jean Reith Schroedel, *Congress, the President, and Policymaking* (Armonk, N.Y.: M. E. Sharpe, 1994), p. 132.

[7] Barry Ames, "Electoral Rules, Constituency Pressures, and Pork Barrel: Bases of Voting in the Brazilian Congress," *Journal of Politics* 57 (1995), pp. 324–343.

[8] Edmund Burke, "Speech to the Electors of Bristol," *The Works of the Right Honorable Edmund Burke,* vol. 2, 5th ed. (Boston: Little Brown, 1877), p. 12.

[9] Ibid., p. 12.

[10] Riker, *Liberalism Against Populism/Lesiglative System,* and Heinz Eulau, in Wahlke, et al., *A Confrontation between the Theory of Democracy and the Theory of Social Choice* (San Francisco: W. H. Freeman, 1982), p. 271.

[11] Prezworski, *Democracy and the Market*, pp. 51–99.

[12] Gerhard Loewenberg and Samuel C. Patterson, *Comparing Legislatures* (Boston: Aldine, 1979), pp. 264–265.

[13] Yves Meny, *Government and Politics in Western Europe,* pp. 226–228.

[14] Loewenberg and Patterson, *Comparing Legislatures,* p. 303.

8

Choosing, Making, and Implementing Policy: The Process of Government

---

Imagine how a government might make new laws regulating the environment, providing housing for low-income families, changing the tax structure, or developing a new land use plan for a large city. Where would policy makers get the information they needed to make suitable decisions? Who would prepare alternatives for discussion? Who would write the actual language of the legislation? Once the legislation became law, who would decide how to apply it in different situations?

This chapter examines how governments make and implement policy. This focus directs the inquiry toward two institutions of government, the executive and the bureaucracy. High school students learn that legislatures create laws, chief executives sign them, and bureaucracies, under the supervision of chief executives, implement them. That picture of government overestimates the importance of legislatures, and it vastly underestimates the roles of chief executives and bureaucracies.

The executive and the bureaucracy dominate all aspects of the policy-making process in almost every country. Executive dominance becomes obvious in an authoritarian regime, as legislators typically serve at the pleasure of the ruler. Even though the legislature in a democracy typically must pass a law for it to become policy, the executive remains the dominant policy-making institution.

Throughout this chapter, *the executive* refers to Heads of Government and their cabinets, immediate advisors, and support staff. In a parliamentary system, this term refers to the Government (defined on page 217 in Chapter 7). In a presidential system, the executive includes the president, the cabinet, immediate advisors, and the staff that reports to the president and those advisors.

The bureaucracy refers to the various departments, ministries, and agencies that the executive oversees. For example, in the United States, the bureaucracy includes cabinet departments such as Education, Health and Human Services, and Defense. It also includes agencies such as the Environmental Protection Agency and the Federal Trade Commission. In most countries, most elements of the bureaucracies fall under the authority of various ministries such as a Ministry of Trade, Ministry of Education, and Ministry of Defense.

The Policy-Making Process

To understand why the executive dominates the policy-making process, students need a basic understanding of that process. Figure 8.1 shows the various stages in the procedure of policy making: (1) agenda setting, (2) formulation, (3) legitimation, (4) implementation, and (5) evaluation and feedback.

FIGURE 8.1

STAGES OF POLICY MAKING

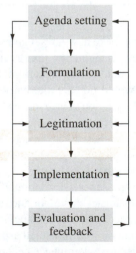

Agenda setting is the name that political scientists give to the process of choosing the issues that the government will address. A study of agenda setting seeks answers to the question, "How does a government decide which social problems it will attempt to solve and which problems it will ignore?" At any one time, hundreds of issues compete for the attention of policy makers. Most items on a government's agenda have inspired debate for a long time. These include taxes, public safety, education, national defense, regulation of various commercial activities such as the production of medicines, and entitlement programs (payments to individuals including Social Security and unemployment benefits).

Although these programs continue from one year to the next, each requires resources every year. One of the better methods by which political scientists can identify a government's real priorities is to study changes in the budgets of these programs. For example, a prime minister may campaign on the promise that his government will give education a higher priority than any other goal. If the prime minister's budget decreases the allocation to education while substantially increasing the amount given to farm subsidies, however, observers have good reason to believe that he assigns a higher priority to farmers than to students.

For a new issue to reach the political agenda, someone must successfully argue that the problem merits an attempt by the government to solve it. Chapter 6 showed that political parties and elections play crucial roles in bringing government's attention to new problems. For example, a party may pledge to balance the budget, improve health care, or provide employment. If it subsequently wins the elections, then its campaign promises become part of the government's agenda, and citizens expect the government to put forth legislation that will accomplish the promised goals.

After agenda setting, the next stage of the policy-making process is **policy formulation.** Once an issue gains a place on the political agenda, the government must decide what to do about that issue. During this stage, decision makers collect information on the causes of social problems that the government wants solved. Policy makers review alternative methods to reduce those problems and design various options. Say, for example, that the party that won the last election promised during the campaign to improve air quality. The government could try to achieve this goal in many ways. It could place strict regulations on car and truck emissions, require smokestack industries to reduce emissions (perhaps by burning natural gas rather than coal), or increase the use of nuclear power. Each policy alternative or combination of alternatives achieves the same level of air quality at a different cost. In other words, some methods of reducing pollution are more efficient than others. How do elected officials identify the most efficient method? Typically, they obtain information from the government's bureaucracy. In the United States, the Departments of Energy and Transportation as well as the Environmental Protection Agency would probably provide information about the effectiveness and efficiency of each potential approach.

While each policy alternative may have different total benefits and costs to the entire country, it also imposes costs and provides benefits to specific sets of people. For example, switching from coal to natural gas would harm coal miners and coal producers, and it would benefit the producers and distributors of natural gas. Reducing car and truck emissions would raise the prices of those vehicles to consumers; reducing the emissions of smokestack industries would raise the prices of their products. Elected officials typically ask the bureaucracy to provide estimates of who would benefit and who would lose from each alternative. For example, the most efficient policy choice might reduce the use of coal and increase the use of nuclear power. However, an official whose political constituencies include coal miners and antinuclear activists might not choose this alternative. Ultimately, public officials settle on a policy that considers both social and political costs and benefits.

The next stage of the policy-making process is **legitimation.** In a country with a legislature, its members pass the laws necessary to achieve the policy goals at this point in the process. In a democratic political system, this action requires the support of at least a majority of legislators. The important condition of legitimation, as its name implies, is to ensure that any action of officials at this stage must follow rules and procedures that the population perceives as standards for legitimate conduct. If citizens perceive a new law as legitimate, they are more likely to obey it. Citizens who perceive a new law as illegitimate are more likely to disregard it. They may also be less likely to support the existing government.

In the fourth stage of the policy-making process, **implementation,** the government obtains sufficient resources to carry out the law. For example, if the government chooses to regulate factory emissions, it must take steps to monitor those emissions and penalize factories that do not comply with the new regulations. These activities require personnel and equipment. If the government allocates too little money for implementation, then the law will fail to achieve the desired effect. Typically, the government's bureaucracy plays the major role in the implementation process. As later sections of this chapter will show, policy implementation often involves considerable policy-making activities.

The final stage of the policy-making process is **evaluation and feedback.** Policy actions lead to results. One part of the evaluation process looks at whether a policy has actually achieved its stated goals. If it has not, then demands for additional or different policies may emerge. Policies also have political results. Were the economic costs to the losers so great that they created political costs to public officials? Does political pressure from the losers require policy makers to propose changes? Did the law encourage the opposition party to advocate a different policy? If so, did the opposition party win the next election? Whatever results or outcomes a policy has, policy makers and those affected by the policy will decide whether to try to make changes. This evaluation will result in new demands on policy makers.

Agenda Setting, Formulation, and Legitimation in Different Types of Regimes

NONDEMOCRATIC GOVERNMENTS

The chief executive in a nondemocratic regime clearly dominates the entire policy-making process. This leader sets the agenda, determines priorities among goals, and then selects from alternative policies those that might reach the chosen goals. The chief executive may receive information concerning the efficiency and political costs of various alternatives from the country's bureaucracy or from other advisors. A chief executive who acts as a stationary bandit (see Chapter 1) will choose among alternatives on the basis of their impact on her own wealth and ability to remain in office. For reasons explained in Chapter 4, the chief executive will not choose policies that alienate the military.

In most nondemocratic governments, legislatures approve and thereby legitimize the policy alternatives chosen by the chief executives. Members of the national legislature in a nondemocratic system know that they must demonstrate continuing loyalty to the chief executive. Legislators who attempt to act independently from the executive do not retain their offices. The chief executive may well dissolve or suspend a national assembly that fails to pass desired legislation or that attempts to pass undesirable legislation. Authoritarian executives suspended legislatures in Chile, Pakistan, and the Philippines in the 1970s and in India, Nigeria, and Turkey in the 1980s. More recently, the military rulers of Algeria canceled elections because a fundamentalist Muslim party seemed likely to win a majority of legislative seats. This result would have been unacceptable to the military and the country's secular elites.

An authoritarian ruler is not necessarily obliged to legitimize policies in the eyes of the public. Decisions may focus solely on the preoccupation of holding onto power at all costs. Under these circumstances, the executive automatically interprets opposition as a threat and an intolerable act of betrayal. A legislature could provide a potential center of resistance around which political opponents could cluster and organize. This possibility makes an authoritarian ruler extremely wary of legislative activity.

An authoritarian chief executive can respond in two ways to the threat a legislature presents to her own power. The first response destroys a potential center of opposition by eliminating the legislature. This is a common response in the aftermath of a military seizure of power through a coup d'état. The second response allows the legislature to exist, but the ruler co-opts it by restricting its permissible activities and its membership. In the Islamic state of Iran, for example, a legislature meets, but it excludes non-Muslims from membership.

An authoritarian leader may choose not to call on a legislature to legitimize policies without surrendering completely to self-interest and a hunger for power. Some may well attempt to impose policies that improve the welfare of their citizens. Several African countries provide examples of this situation. Nationalist leaders won freedom from European colonial powers for their countries by creating broadly based independence movements. After independence, the leaders believed that they needed to keep these movements together to achieve national goals, particularly for economic development. These leaders faced serious problems, however, since their independence movements often encompassed class, ethnic, linguistic, and religious groups with long histories of mutual distrust and hostility. Disputes can result, such as the unending conflict between the Hutu and Tutsi tribes in Rwanda and Burundi.

Since democracy actively encourages competition between groups, it may risk extremely dangerous contention in circumstances such as those in Rwanda and Burundi. An independent legislature offers a forum where animosities between groups can surface, inflaming violence and distracting groups from national goals. It may not seem surprising, then, that many African nationalist leaders opted for strong executive authority and abandoned the parliamentary institutions left to them by departing colonial powers. In one of the first examples of this pattern, Kwame Nkrumah abandoned Ghana's parliamentary constitution in 1966 and assumed the title president for life. Nkrumah assumed a wide range of legislative, executive, and judicial powers, clearly demonstrating that the only legitimate policies were those he approved. Whether an authoritarian chief executive's underlying rationale is self-interest or collective interest, policy outcomes generally have been the same: The legislatures in authoritarian regimes have become rubber stamps for executive actions, or they have been disbanded.

Totalitarian regimes often express greater concern for policy legitimacy than authoritarian governments. Totalitarian leaders justify their rule as an attempt to transform the society to realize a utopian vision. To succeed in this quest, the government must convince the population to accept change and to participate in the transformation. A totalitarian regime, particularly a communist one, typically attempts to achieve legitimacy for new policies by showing how those measures will move the society toward its utopian goals. By allowing an elected legislature to follow constitutional procedures when passing new laws, the regime encourages citizens to feel like participants in its activities and to believe that it is working for them. For this reason, communist regimes rarely disband their legislatures.

Despite the legitimizing function of the legislature, policy making in a communist regime remains totally within the preserve of the Communist Party, especially its national leaders gathered together in the Politburo. (The Politburo is the name for the executive in most communist countries.) Communist constitutions, however, deny this concentration of power. The constitutions state that directly elected legislative assemblies make all policies. Article 108 of the 1977 Soviet constitution makes the sweeping assertion that "the Supreme Soviet [the national legislature of the former Soviet Union] . . . is empowered to deal with all matters within the jurisdiction of the Union of Soviet Socialist Republics." The 1936 predecessor of this document provided still more explicitly that "the legislative power of the USSR is exercised exclusively by the Supreme Soviet of the USSR." The reality, though, was quite different.

The Politburo dominated the Supreme Soviet, and the secretary general of the Communist Party often dominated the Politburo. While Soviet voters cast ballots in direct, universal, equal, and "secret" elections to the Supreme Soviet, they could choose only a single candidate for each seat, and the Communist Party nominated all candidates. Once members were elected, infrequent sessions of the Supreme Soviet lasted only about 10 days. Debate was not free, dissent was unknown, and members rubber-stamped the party's nominees for the prime minister and other ministers. In short, the legislature played no part in agenda setting or policy formulation. Its sole role was legitimation.

The denial of policy influence to a communist legislature is the inevitable consequence of totalitarian, one-party rule. Under Mao, the Chinese National People's Congress (NPC) experienced the same subjugated status as the Supreme Soviet. After Mao's death in 1976, party leaders introduced some modest reforms to enliven the legislature. Voters saw limited choices among candidates, even including some nonparty candidates. The Chinese Politburo eased restrictions on debate and permitted the formal questioning of ministers.

Two restrictions greatly limited the impact of these reforms. First, electoral procedures guaranteed the continuing dominance of the Communist Party. Second, the leaders demanded that deputies "act responsibly" when taking advantage of the reforms. In a nutshell, the reforms allowed legislative debate in exchange for consent to one-party rule and active support for party policy.[1]

DEMOCRATIC REGIMES

Democratic regimes must resolve more complex executive-legislative relations than nondemocratic regimes in the agenda setting, formulation, and legitimation stages of the policy-making process. While a nondemocratic regime exerts all-but-complete executive control, in a democratic regime, the influence of the legislature varies. The degree of dominance by the executive depends largely on two factors: (1) the confidence of the executive in the support of its followers in the legislature and (2) whether the executive commands a majority of legislative seats. Members of some legislatures faithfully follow the leadership-defined party line. Other legislatures treat the wishes of the party as only one of several cues to which legislators respond when making laws.

Chapter 7 described differences between parliamentary and presidential systems that determine whether the executive can always expect to control a majority of seats in the legislature and whether parties will enforce strict discipline. In a parliamentary system, officials in the executive (the Government) are the leaders of either the majority party or the coalition of parties that control a majority of seats in the parliament. In a presidential system, however, the president's party frequently does not control a majority of seats in one or both chambers of the national legislature. If the executive in a parliamentary system cannot control a majority of votes in parliament, then a vote of no confidence is likely to force new elections and/or reorganization to define a new executive that does control a majority of seats. Presidential systems do not hold confidence votes because both the president and members of the legislature are elected for fixed terms.

Nelson Polsby has argued that presidential legislatures, typified by the U.S. Congress, are **transformative legislatures.** Transformative legislatures possess and frequently exercise the independent capacity to transform proposals from any source into laws.[2] In other words, such a legislature can have a major impact on policy outcomes. At the other extreme are **arena legislatures.** These legislative bodies, typified by the British House of Commons, rarely affect the substance of policy. Conflict and disagreement occur in arena legislatures, but Chapter 7 showed that the conflict is staged for public show. Floor debate does not change policy because the executive makes all important policy decisions before it introduces bills into the legislature. The purpose of a debate on the floor of the legislature is to inform the public of the reasons for the Government's policy and the opposition's objections.

Agenda Setting   Democratic political systems complete a great deal of their agenda setting when political parties write their platforms or manifestos. Chapter 6 showed how competing political parties present alternative worldviews or ideologies to voters. The policies that a party advocates during an election demonstrate this worldview to the electorate. In a parliamentary system, the leader of the party that wins a majority of legislative seats becomes the prime minister. The Government's agenda is, therefore, composed of the policy goals of the majority party. In a presidential system, parties and candidates, including candidates for the legislature, introduce all sorts of issues in campaigns. If the goals of the president differ from those of the majority in the legislature, then many more issues reach the political agenda, and debate raises more options for solving the problems on the agenda. This complicates the process of policy formulation and increases the uncertainty of the outcome.

Formulation and Legitimation The executive in a parliamentary system, with the help of the bureaucracy, dominates policy formulation. For example, if the majority party's platform promises to improve air quality, then the minister of environment will work with the bureaucracy in that ministry to formulate policy alternatives. The minister might then present these alternatives to the ministers of transportation, energy, and the treasury to obtain comments from experts in those ministries. The minister of environment might then submit several policy proposals for the prime minister and the cabinet to consider. These officials will discuss the alternatives and choose one. The minister of environment will then prepare a bill that reflects the Government's decision and introduce it to the legislature.

The executive also dominates a presidential system, but the legislature plays a greater role in the policy process. As in a parliamentary system, the minister of environment (in the United States, the director of the Environmental Protection Agency) would prepare policy alternatives for reducing air pollution. The various alternatives would go to the Executive Office of the President. The president and advisors (or the cabinet) would discuss the merits of the alternatives and the president would choose one. Either the appropriate bureaucratic agency or the president's staff would then prepare a bill for submission to the legislature.

At this point, the presidential and parliamentary policy-making processes begin to display drastic differences. Remember that the minister of environment in a parliamentary system is also a member of Parliament. Therefore, this official can personally introduce the executive's air pollution bill to the legislature. In a presidential system, a member of the cabinet or other executive agency cannot simultaneously hold a position in the legislature. Therefore, the president must ask a friendly member of the legislature to submit the bill.

Three aspects of presidential systems combine to reduce the dominance of the executive in policy making. First, the president and members of the legislature are directly elected. More importantly, they run as candidates first and as party representatives second. For this reason, the president often does not control the votes of a majority of members of the legislature. Often when the president's party holds a minority position in the legislature, and sometimes when it is the majority party, the executive and the legislature become locked in a stalemate.*

Second, the president and the legislators are elected for fixed terms. This means that disagreements between the executive and a majority of members of the legislature cannot

---

*In a classic example of the president's inability to control a majority of his own party, President Clinton was unable to pass a welfare reform bill in the 1993–1994 session of Congress when Democrats controlled both houses. A stalemate caused the government to shut down in late 1995 and early 1996 when President Clinton and the Republican Congress could not agree on a new budget.

result in a vote of confidence and either replacement of the executive or new elections. Voters cannot resolve policy disagreements until the next scheduled election, perhaps leaving conflicts to persist for years.

Finally, presidential systems rarely feature strong party discipline. Instead, members of the legislature often vote for the special interests of their districts rather than in support of the ideologies of their parties. Without party discipline, even if the president's party controls a majority of seats in the legislature, the president cannot always count on the votes of fellow party members.

All of these factors increase the power of the legislature in the policy-making process. To compete effectively with the president for preeminence in policy making, however, the legislature needs its own information and expertise. For this reason, the U.S. Congress has, among other things, its own library and budget office. Members of Congress also have large personal staffs. Most importantly, Congress carries out the large majority of its business in small, specialized, and experienced committees with permanent mandates to meet frequently to scrutinize, criticize, and often amend policy initiatives. A committee may choose to kill a bill or radically alter it. In addition, legislators, especially committee chairs, often introduce their own bills that propose solutions to social problems entirely different from those proposed by the president. The critical characteristic of a transforming legislature is the possibility that a final bill may or may not embody the wishes and preferences of the president.

Judging by the American example, the separation of powers in a presidential system of government seems to guarantee a substantial role for the legislature in shaping public policy. The executive cannot impose its will on the legislature, nor must it take orders from legislators. Policies result from bargaining and compromise between the two branches of government.

Unfortunately, this conclusion does not hold for all presidential democracies. In presidential systems outside the United States, disagreements between the executive and the legislature commonly result in a stalemated and unstable government. In other words, when an elected executive cannot govern, no one governs. This situation encourages the eventual overthrow of the democratic government. A president faced with hostile and uncompromising legislators may declare a state of emergency and try to rule by decree. In such a situation, the legislature can no longer legitimate policy and the president attempts to govern without the legitimacy of constitutional rule.

A recent book examining presidential governments found that since World War II, only 13 of 39 parliamentary democracies (33 percent) have been replaced by nondemocratic regimes. In contrast, nondemocratic regimes replaced presidential democracies in 10 of 13 (77 percent) countries.[3] This high rate of breakdown suggests that stalemate is the normal pattern of executive-legislative relations in presidential democracies outside the United States.

What makes the United States different from other presidential democracies? What allows the U.S. Constitution to work and affords Congress an effective and constructive role in shaping public policy? The distinctive feature of government in the United States is the consensual *and* pragmatic political culture that shapes the expectations and behavior of both elites and the mass of citizens. Americans overwhelmingly accept the social, economic, and political principles underpinning their system of government. This makes political radicalism a vice and moderation a virtue to Americans. Almost everyone shares a consensus on the rules of the game of politics. Pragmatism reigns. Neither the public nor elected officials value obstructionism; both generally see bargaining, compromise, and concession as necessary elements of effective policy making in government.[†] This philosophy is well summed up in the popular American adage: "You have to go along to get along."

In many Latin American presidential democracies, however, the nature of the party system works against such mutual accommodation. Often political parties interact with extreme hostility, and no single party can win a majority of seats in the national legislatures. Two results follow. First, presidents rarely command majority support in their countries' legislatures. Unlike presidential relations with the two-party U.S. Congress, Latin American presidents must win the support of numerous parties to pass their legislative proposals. Second, parties not in control of the presidency often resist cooperating with the president because they are so ideologically opposed to him and his policy stands. The result is an immobilizing executive-legislative deadlock. In the short term, the conflict leaves a policy-making vacuum and instability. In the longer term, regimes often break down and the military steps in to restore a semblance of government.

The overall conclusion is that the presidential system of government helps to give the legislature a substantial influence in the formulation of public policy, but it does not guarantee that result. Institutions provide incentives for elites to engage in certain types of behavior, but the elites have to want to make the institutions work. They have to willingly play according to a shared set of rules and values. They must accept compromises and respect alternative viewpoints.

SUMMARY FOR AGENDA SETTING, POLICY FORMULATION, AND LEGITIMATION

In every political system, the executive plays the leading role in placing issues on the political agenda and in formulating policy options. In nondemocratic regimes, this dominance is almost complete. If the legislature is unwilling to legitimate the executive's proposals, then legislators often find themselves entirely excluded. In democratic systems, elections play a significant role in the agenda-setting process. Parties and candidates promise to deal with various issues in particular ways, and the results of elections help to decide which issues will reach the nation's policy agenda and which specific policies the government will formulate. Although the executive dominates policy formulation in all democratic systems, this domination is greater in parliamentary systems than in presidential ones. In both parliamentary and presidential systems, legislatures make key contributions by legitimating policies proposed by the executive. In both systems, legislatures openly debate policies, and they must pass resulting legislative proposals to allow them to become law. In a parliamentary system, the legislature does not significantly alter policy

---

[†] It may be that American politics are changing with respect to compromise. The inability of President Clinton and the Republican Congress to compromise during 1995 and 1996 led to numerous stalemates and government shutdowns. However, public opinion polls showed clearly that the citizenry expected the two sides to compromise and each side attempted to make the public believe that it was trying to do so.

proposals. In a presidential system, the legislature exerts more independence from the executive and often makes substantial changes in policy proposals. The price for legislative independence, however, is often policy stalemate and an unstable political system.

The Bureaucracy and Policy Implementation

The fourth stage of the policy-making process is implementation. The normal image of the bureaucracy emphasizes implementation (or administration) of the laws that other officials have formulated and legitimated. Still, policy implementation involves a substantial amount of policy making. This is true in both nondemocratic and democratic systems.

The earlier section described the critical role of bureaucracies in formulating legislation. An elected official who wants to solve a problem begins by finding out what the government currently is doing about the problem and how well the existing policy is working. The public servant turns to the bureaucracy for help in this mission. Bureaucrats are often the first to know when a law, rule, or regulation is not working. In addition, bureaucrats bring expertise about specific policy areas to the political process. For this reason, elected officials often request help designing new laws from bureaucrats in the agency that implements the old laws.

Chief executives, cabinet members, and legislators rarely have sufficient expertise to judge the safety, efficiency, or likely effectiveness of nuclear plants, air pollution regulations, or alternative health care plans. Therefore, members of the executive and the legislature must rely on other government personnel who have the appropriate expertise. Most government bureaucrats are not elected or even appointed by elected officials. Hiring standards partially shield them from political pressures. Bureaucratic norms encourage a climate that generally reduces the effect of partisan influences on their opinions and decisions. Because they are not working to maximize the profits of a business or consumer group, decision makers expect bureaucrats to speak objectively and to work for the public interest.

Although the bureaucracy plays a critical role in policy formulation, its major job is to implement the laws enacted by the legislature or executive. In this process, bureaucrats make a great deal of additional law. Historical developments like the Great Depression, World War II, rapid population growth, and technological, industrial, and social change have created new responsibilities for governments. One result of this growth in government responsibility has been a corresponding growth in bureaucracies. The sections below discuss the expanding role of bureaucracies in contemporary societies, why bureaucrats make law as well as administer it, and why bureaucracy is the core of modern governments.

MAKING AND IMPLEMENTING LAWS
THROUGH BUREAUCRACIES

When a legislature passes laws to ensure clean air, equal credit opportunity, or worker safety, explicitly stated provisions often consist only of general guidelines. Bureaucratic agencies then write the specific rules that elaborate those guidelines and stipulate how people must behave. For example, if a law states, "the work place will be as safe as possible," a bureaucratic agency must specify the meaning of "as safe as possible" for each type of business and each industry. If air pollution legislation mandates that a factory use the "best practicable technology," a bureaucratic agency must set standards for that technology for each industry. Administrative agencies often encounter obstacles in deciding what a particular law means. The targets of regulations often resent the additional costs that result. They may see bureaucrats as overzealous interlopers whose regulations exceed the intentions of the original law. Those who sought protection through government regulations often believe that the bureaucrats do not go far enough.

One of the easiest examples of the role of the bureaucracy in making law is in the area of tax collection. In most countries, bureaucrats interpret the tax laws that the legislatures have passed. Typically, the ministry or agency that collects revenues publishes a multivolume tax code that states its interpretation of the tax laws enacted by the legislature. In order to clarify the tax legislation, the bureaucrats may write 20 pages of tax law for every page of the legislative act. The likelihood of changing the law increases with each additional page of the code.

KEY PRINCIPLES OF BUREAUCRATIC ORGANIZATION AND DECISION MAKING

The earliest major civilian apparatus of government was not an executive, legislative, or judicial organization. It was an administrative agency. Bureaucracy, often called the "core of modern government,"[4] was well developed in virtually all major civilizations of the ancient world. One scholar describes the bureaucracies of early China and Egypt as

---

FIGURE 8.2

ORGANIZATION CHART FOR A BUREAUCRACY

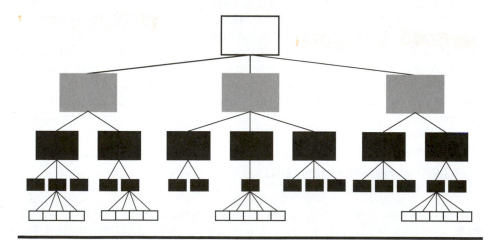

"the two outstanding institutions of this type in all history."[5] Sociologist Max Weber, one of the first to analyze bureaucracies systematically, lists four essential characteristics of large-scale administration:

1. *Hierarchical organization.* Organizational authority forms the structure of a pyramid, where decisions run from one or a few individuals at the top to many workers at the bottom. Each person is responsible to only one supervisor, and each supervisor is responsible to one higher-level supervisor. (See Figure 8.2.)

2. *Specialization of functions.* An administrative organization's overall job, or mission, is logically divided up into the different steps or distinct operations needed to complete it.

3. *Division of labor.* Individuals receive job assignments according to their individual skills, talents, and competence, and they do well-defined tasks. In law enforcement, one group of bureaucrats may concentrate on homicide, another on burglary, another on vice, and another on bookkeeping.

4. *Merit.* Meritorious performances rather than favoritism, social class, or ethnicity determine who gets jobs and who receives promotions or raises in salary.

POLICY IMPLEMENTATION IN DEMOCRATIC REGIMES

Bureaucratic decision making follows some basic rules: treat everyone fairly, show no favoritism, and act according to approved procedures. These rules also lead to the biggest problems with bureaucracies: Their actions and decisions appear rigid, show little innovation, and often fail to adapt to the characteristics of a particular situation. (See Box 8.1.) The most important norm of bureaucratic behavior is to apply rules equally to everyone. This rule leads bureaucracies to develop **standard operating procedures (SOPs)** that guide bureaucrats' behavior in situations that they commonly encounter. This preoccupation with evenhanded treatment can drive citizens crazy because the SOPs may require bureaucrats to treat people the same despite differences in their situations. Even though obvious and excellent reasons may support suspending an SOP in a particular situation, bureaucrats are much safer if they do not vary from the prescribed procedure.

SOPs often lead to bureaucratic rigidity. For example, perhaps you are waiting at an airport check-in counter in a line so long that some customers may miss their flights. In this situation, airline personnel typically do not insist on helping the next person in line. Rather they give priority to passengers whose flights are about to leave. Bureaucrats rarely have the discretion to make similar decisions. When lines are long, employees at the Department of Motor Vehicles do not first serve people who will be late for appointments. Other customers probably would object if bureaucrats were to act in these ways.

Even when rules appear totally nonsensical, bureaucrats are rarely free to change them. If a scientist invents a new drug that might save the lives of people dying with lung cancer, the ministry or agency charged with guaranteeing drug safety may prohibit its use until it passes through tests using all of the SOPs for the introduction of new drugs. People who are dying of lung cancer may assail bureaucrats for this totally unreasonable decision. As part of the long-term search for cancer cures, however, society wants researchers to follow all required scientific procedures in testing the drug to confirm expectations about its impact on cancer and its side effects.

BOX 8.1

What's Wrong with Bureaucracy?

It often seems that government bureaucracies are less efficient than private sector organizations. In his book *Bureaucracy: What Government Agencies Do and Why They Do It* James Q. Wilson argues that this opinion reflects an oversimplification. Wilson gives an example from the City of New York where, after 6 years and nearly $13 million in costs, the ice-skating rink in Central Park still had not been rebuilt. Donald Trump, the New York and Atlantic City real estate developer, contacted Mayor Ed Koch and offered to finish the job in 6 months. The city appropriated $3 million, and Trump promised to pay any cost overruns out of his own pocket. The work was completed in 5 months and $750,000 under budget.

Some critics would see a clear case of an inefficient public bureaucracy as compared to private industry. Wilson argues that Trump was able to complete the job so much more easily because he did not have to work under the constraints that limited government bureaucrats. Trump could hire a familiar general contractor or a contractor who had a superior record of rebuilding ice rinks. He did not have to treat all potential contractors the same. Trump could allow the general contractor to hire any subcontractors he chose for different components of the job such as plumbing and electrical wiring. For example, the general contractor could give the plumbing contract to her brother-in-law knowing that he would do good work and complete the job on time. If the general contractor or any subcontractor were to complete the job for less money than they bid, they could keep the difference. Finally, Trump had to worry about only one objective, finishing the rink in 6 months at a cost of $3 million or below.

The city enjoyed none of these benefits. New York City hired workers through an open-bid process, and laws required the city to take the lowest bid regardless of experience with the contractor's past work. In addition, the city had to specify exactly how the rink would be built prior to letting the contract, and every subcontract had to be let in the same way. The general contractor could not choose the subcontractors. These rules ensured that all bids were open to all competitors and that the subcontractors would work to the exact specifications the city desired. Certainly, the general contractor could not choose a relative for the job.

An official would be fired for favoritism after any attempt to ensure that the city hired a particular contractor or subcontractor, even if the official knew that the person would do good work on time. Because the city had to pay for the fuel to cool the ice and operate the rink, its bureaucrats had to first determine the most energy-efficient solution and then build the rink around that solution. Donald Trump did not have to pay for future fuel costs, and he did not worry about them.

Which of the constraints on the City of New York, or any other public bureaucracy, would you be willing to eliminate? Would you be willing to let a bureaucrat choose a contractor because the official liked and trusted the person, or would you force the official to accept the lowest bid? Would you be willing to allow the general contractor to subcontract to his brother-in-law? Would you be willing to pay the public official a $750,000 bonus for completing the project on time or under budget? Would you allow a public official to disregard future fuel costs?

Most of the constraints on public bureaucrats serve good purposes. Policy makers want to prevent unfairness to potential contractors, nepotism, kickbacks, and public officials lining their own pockets. Also, public officials must normally work toward multiple goals. As Wilson summarized the New York skating rink situation: "A government that is slow to build rinks but is honest and accountable in its actions and properly responsive to worthy constituencies may be a very efficient government *if* we measure efficiency in the large by taking into account *all* the valued outputs."

Source: James Q. Wilson, *Bureaucracy: What Government Agencies Do and Why They Do It* (New York: Basic Books, 1989), p. 318. Reprinted with permission of HarperCollins Publishers, Inc.

MANAGING THE BUREAUCRACY

On paper, officials manage the bureaucracy in today's complex government through a straightforward process. Each ministry or agency displays the top-to-bottom structure shown in Figure 8.2. The ministers who head the various ministries are nominally responsible for the actions of everyone in their departments. The Head of Government is generally responsible for all national bureaucracies. Figure 8.3 shows (in much simplified form) the structure of the U.S. national bureaucracy. The president, from a position at the apex of the pyramid, exercises responsibility and authority over all cabinet departments. Figure 8.3 also lists many independent agencies that do not fit into the hierarchical pattern of authority. The picture is much the same in most modern democratic governments.

Responsibility for overseeing administrative agencies falls primarily on the top levels of administrative staff within each ministry. The effectiveness of that supervision varies enormously from one ministry to another. It depends not only on the competence and integrity of individual workers and supervisors, but also on different customs and office cultures that grow up and persist in different office environments. Reformers encounter extraordinary difficulty in trying to change organizational structure, SOPs, or personnel in an established bureaucracy. The sheer size and complexity of the administrative apparatus in any large nation-state makes effective control an almost impossible task. Every ministry, department, or agency has its supportive clientele. These citizens resist any changes in the agency that serves them. In most countries, for example, ministries of agriculture enjoy strong support from farmers and farm lobbies. Ministries of education have the support of professional educators, and ministries of trade rely on the loyalties of various business interests.

The problem of ensuring responsible actions by a bureaucracy is not simply a matter of proper management. Administrative agencies often exercise much more authority

FIGURE 8.3

ADMINISTRATIVE STRUCTURE OF THE U.S. GOVERNMENT

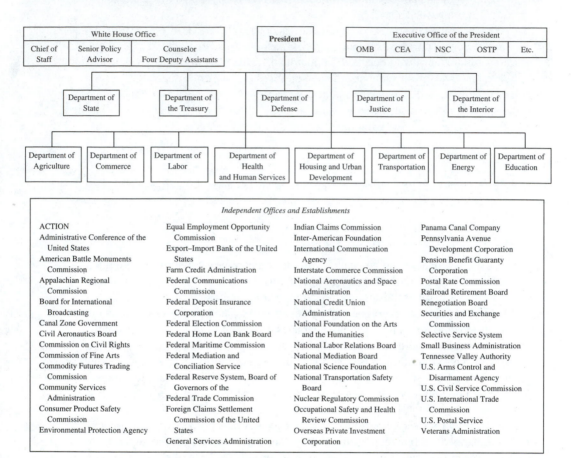

Independent Offices and Establishments

ACTION
Administrative Conference of the United States
American Battle Monuments Commission
Appalachian Regional Commission
Board for International Broadcasting
Canal Zone Government
Civil Aeronautics Board
Commission on Civil Rights
Commission of Fine Arts
Commodity Futures Trading Commission
Community Services Administration
Consumer Product Safety Commission
Environmental Protection Agency

Equal Employment Opportunity Commission
Export–Import Bank of the United States
Farm Credit Administration
Federal Communications Commission
Federal Deposit Insurance Corporation
Federal Election Commission
Federal Home Loan Bank Board
Federal Maritime Commission
Federal Mediation and Conciliation Service
Federal Reserve System, Board of Governors of the
Federal Trade Commission
Foreign Claims Settlement Commission of the United States
General Services Administration

Indian Claims Commission
Inter-American Foundation
International Communication Agency
Interstate Commerce Commission
National Aeronautics and Space Administration
National Credit Union Administration
National Foundation on the Arts and the Humanities
National Labor Relations Board
National Mediation Board
National Science Foundation
National Transportation Safety Board
Nuclear Regulatory Commission
Occupational Safety and Health Review Commission
Overseas Private Investment Corporation

Panama Canal Company
Pennsylvania Avenue Development Corporation
Pension Benefit Guaranty Corporation
Postal Rate Commission
Railroad Retirement Board
Renegotiation Board
Securities and Exchange Commission
Selective Service System
Small Business Administration
Tennessee Valley Authority
U.S. Arms Control and Disarmament Agency
U.S. Civil Service Commission
U.S. International Trade Commission
U.S. Postal Service
Veterans Administration

than the term *administrative* might suggest. The statutes that establish government policies often create agencies to administer those policies and delegate necessary power to
issue and implement binding regulations and rules. For example, legislation may require that factories use the best available technology to reduce air pollution, but it gives
the ministry of environment the power to specify that technology for each industry.
Even when the chief executive retains legal authority, the technical and professional
training of bureaucrats may encourage elected officials to defer to their judgment. Either
the chief executive or members of the legislature may not be able to exercise effective
bureaucratic control over an issue that requires a Ph.D. in nuclear engineering or organic chemistry to make an informed decision.

SUMMARY FOR POLICY IMPLEMENTATION

The increased scope of government in the 20th century simultaneously increased the sizes of government bureaucracies. Because the solutions to so many modern problems require technical expertise, bureaucrats formulate, make, and evaluate policy as well as implement it. For better or for worse, as the world becomes an increasingly complex and interdependent place, the need for bureaucrats expands. As long as students want loans, farmers desire price supports, the elderly demand entitlements, businesses crave protection from international trade, citizens require police protection, government needs taxes, and the legislature and executive pass laws that require interpretation, bureaucracy will continue to flourish.

Policy Evaluation

A totalitarian regime evaluates policies based primarily on their contribution to stronger government control over society and to the society's movement toward the utopian vision dictated by the ruling party's ideology. For example, Stalin chose to combine much of Soviet agriculture into large, state-owned farms despite the policy's negative impact on agricultural production. To justify this policy, he argued that privately owned land is unacceptable in a communist society because it leads to social classes. Similarly, the totalitarian regime of Pol Pot in Cambodia did away with money, even though this change complicated commerce and state planning. The regime evaluated the policy not on its economic efficiency, but on the basis of how its projected outcomes fit with the leaders' utopian image of society.

Policy evaluation and feedback is straightforward in most authoritarian societies. Two questions guide this judgment: Did the policy increase or decrease the wealth of the ruler? Did the policy tighten or loosen the ruler's grip on power? To the degree that authoritarian rulers are concerned with the collective welfare of their citizens, the effects of a policy on social welfare and its efficiency are also considerations.

Policy evaluation encounters a difficulty in all nondemocratic regimes when those who do not rule hesitate to inform the rulers that a policy is not working. If a ruler holds power through personal charisma (see, for example, the discussion of Hitler in Chapter 3), then the regime's legitimacy relies in part on the assumption that he cannot make a wrong decision. If the rulers govern on the basis of communist principles, they can never admit flaws in those principles (though they may accept adaptations to particular circumstances). These situations permit only strictly limited discussion of policy options. More important, because the ruler and the ideology cannot be mistaken, any policy failure is attributed either to inadequate effort by those who implement the policy or to treason. This threat gives bureaucrats a strong incentive to make sure that a policy works. It also encourages them to provide positive evaluations of bad policies and to coerce responses from people whose behavior must change to make a policy succeed.

In a democratic regime, policy evaluation means many things. Public policy analysis has been recognized as a field of scholarly interest since the 1970s. Such efforts have compared the benefits and costs of each alternative for achieving relatively specific goals. For example, in evaluating an air pollution policy, the analyst would ask whether the level of sulfur dioxide fell as desired and whether the policy achieved this reduction at the lowest possible cost.

This type of policy evaluation is, however, only one half of the task. Observers must evaluate political institutions in a broader framework. Political conflict and compromise focus not primarily on means and methods, but on more basic goals and values. Such decisions are not limited to the best way to pave a highway, police the streets, immunize children, or teach reading. More important decisions determine how much to allocate to highways, how much to police, how much to health care, and how much to education. While there may be no Democratic or Republican way to pave a street, the two parties often promote different choices about whose streets get paved.

Chapter 7 advocated evaluating legislatures based on whom they represent and how well they promote those people's interest. Is a country's legislature effectively preventing abuses of power by either the executive or the bureaucracy? Is the legislature preventing abuses of minority rights? Any evaluation of the executive and the bureaucracy in a democratic society must answer similar questions. Whose interests does the executive represent? Does the bureaucracy make fair decisions? Is it accountable to elected officials? Finally, and perhaps most importantly, does the entire executive-legislative-bureaucratic system function democratically to promote both effective and stable government?

Summary

This chapter and Chapter 7 have explored the important roles of institutions in the policy-making process. Democratic and nondemocratic governments reach different decisions in different ways. While democracy may have worldwide legitimacy as the best form of government, some conditions such as violent ethnic hatred may leave a democratic country at risk of death and violence.

Within democracies, it is important to recognize a government's parliamentary or presidential characteristics, or some combination of the two. Government institutional arrangements affect the policy process, policy outcomes, and, perhaps, whether democracy even survives in a country. This chapter's brief examination of executive authority suggests that a country's political structures must fit its political culture. While a presidential system may work well in the United States, it may not be appropriate for a society with extreme divisions and where the culture does not value compromise and pragmatism.

In future courses in comparative politics, you will have opportunities to study various institutional relationships in much greater detail. That study will show probable mismatches between a highly centralized and majoritarian system such as that of Great Britain and societies such as Belgium or Switzerland. One of the great lessons of a comparative study of political institutions is the importance of societies' efforts to develop institutions appropriate to their characteristic cultures and conflicts.

QUESTIONS AND EXERCISES

Questions for Reason

1. What stages of the policy process are most likely to be dominated by the executive? The legislature? The bureaucracy? Explain the reasons for your answers.

TABLE 8.1

SYSTEM FAILURE FOR PRESIDENTIAL AND
PARLIAMENTARY DEMOCRACIES

COUP	Experienced Coup	SYSTEM		
		Presidential 1	Parliamentary 2	Row Total
	No	3	27	30
		23.1%	67.5%	56.6%
	Yes	10	13	23
		76.9%	32.5%	43.4%
COLUMN TOTAL		13	40	53
Marginal Percent		24.5%	75.5%	

Corrected Chi-Square = 6.18, 1 *df*, $p = 0.01$

2. Explain why the executive in a parliamentary system is so much more dominant than the executive in a presidential system during policy formulation.

3. Why do many scholars believe that presidential systems are ill-suited to most less in-dustrialized countries? How might a political scientist test this hypothesis?

4. Why are policy evaluation and feedback much easier in democratic systems than in nondemocratic ones?

Questions for Reflection

1. If you were designing the constitution for a new nation such as Bosnia, would you choose a system that is closer to a presidential model or a parliamentary one?

2. If you chose a parliamentary model, what constitutional powers and other resources would you give the legislature to encourage an active role for it in agenda setting and policy formulation?

3. Why is the bureaucracy the core of a modern government? Looking back at Box 8.1 (page 254) what changes would you make to improve the efficiency of the New York City bureaucracy? What potential problems do you foresee for these reforms?

4. Socialist regimes collapsed in the Soviet Union and eastern Europe for many reasons. What factors discussed in this chapter might have contributed to this widespread loss of political power by those regimes?

5. Why do you think so many elections in eastern Europe and Russia have led to the reemergence of communists and socialists as major political parties?

6. Table 8.1 shows a contingency table that details the association between the type of gov-ernment and the likelihood that democracy will fail and give way to a military gov-ernment or other undemocratic regime. Why might you argue that this is a spurious association? How might you test this hypothesis?

Questions for Analysis: Correlation Analysis[‡]

You are now ready to make an important step in using statistics to examine relationships. Thus far you have worked with probabilities, percentages, contingency tables, control variables, spurious associations, and interaction. The only major research topics left to introduce are how to measure the strength of relationships, how to predict the values of one variable using the values of another, and how to analyze more than three variables. This exercise teaches one statistic that measures the strength of an association between two variables: **correlation.**

One of the really powerful benefits of contingency tables comes from their ability to present all types of data. They can help researchers to compare relationships between gender and voting, hair color and car color, or age and income. They can make these comparisons whether they call the values for gender "male" and "female" or "1" and "2." Similarly, the computer could compute a chi-square for a contingency table on age that combines everyone between the ages of 1 day and 18 years into a category called "young," everyone from 19 to 29 into a category called "middle aged," and everyone over 30 as "very old," or it could deal with the same groups labeled "1," "3," and "-2." Contingency table analysis does not change for different labels for the value of the variable under study. It would give the same chi-square value no matter what names the researcher gives to the groups.

For other types of statistics, this situation changes. Researchers must give up some of the flexibility of contingency tables in order to gain additional statistical power.

If the age-based study were to state people's ages in years rather than dividing them into three groups, the researcher could use more powerful statistics to measure the strength of a relationship between one variable and another. As researchers use statistics to learn as much as possible about their data, they often want to use more powerful statistics than the chi-square. Those statistics typically require, however, that the numbers assigned to values of variables accurately represent the order of the values for variables. What does this statement mean?

The numbers assigned to male and female in a study of gender have no meaning. The label 1 does not indicate lower status than 2; it is only a label that classifies people according to their genders. When a researcher classifies objects of data such as people or countries into groups and then gives each group a name or label, this action creates a **nominal measure.** The word *nominal* indicates that the variable simply names categories. The statistical calculations do not change whether the researcher assigns each group a name composed of numbers or a name composed of letters. Examples of nominal variables are region of the world, eye color, ethnicity, and party identification.

The next level of measurement, an **ordinal measure,** indicates values with a definite order. Say you went out on a date last night. This morning a friend asks, "How was your date?" All of the following answers convey meaning: "Super," "OK," "Lousy," and "The best part of the evening was when I ate spoiled food and threw up." These answers could form an ordinal measure of the variable labeled "quality of date." An example of a familiar ordinal rating measure is that used by movie critics. These people often rank

---

[‡] This exercise was written in collaboration with W. Bruce Shepard.

FIGURE 8.4

ORDINAL SCALE FOR MOVIE RATINGS

Q		R	S		T	U

0 stars	1 star	2 stars	3 stars	4 stars

---

movies from zero to four stars depending on their perceptions of the films' quality. Presumably, if a critic is consistent, then a two-star movie is better than a zero-star or one-star movie, but not as good as a three-star or four-star movie.

It is important to remember that the distances between pairs of numbers or labels in an ordinal measure may not be the same. For example, the movie critic might rate films along a scale that looks like Figure 8.4. Few movies deserve no stars and few deserve four. Imagine that this critic reviews and ranks five movies—Q, R, S, T, and U—and publishes only the number of stars assigned to each movie in the local newspaper. Movie T has a higher rating than Movie S and a lower rating than Movie U. The distance between each set of movies is not, however, the same. Figure 8.4 shows that the difference between Movies R and S is quite small, while a large space separates S and T. Remember that an ordinal measurement does not indicate the *magnitude* of the differences between each value in the scale. Sometimes, correctly phrased survey questions can change a nominal measure (Republican or Democrat?) into an ordinal measure (Strong Democrat, Weak Democrat, Independent, Weak Republican, or Strong Republican?).

The third level of measurement is the **interval scale.** As the name suggests, each value along the scale marks off the same interval or distance from the previous value. For example, the distance between 65 inches and 66 inches tall is the same as the distance between 72 and 73 inches tall. Political scientists often use interval scales like the number of years of school an individual has completed, a legislator's scores on issues from various lobbying groups such as the Conservative Coalition, and the amount of money a candidate spends to get elected.

Correlation analysis, the statistical technique for this lab, requires either interval data or very good ordinal data.[§] Once again, the computer will do all of the actual calculations required to compute the measure of correlation, the correlation coefficient. To see how correlation works, look at Figure 8.5. It shows a **scatterplot**[ǁ] of scores of Supreme Court justices since 1946 on two variables: ideological liberalism before joining the court and the percentage of liberal votes in civil liberties cases after joining the court.[6] The chart measures scores on ideological liberalism along the *x* axis ranging

---

[§] Computer simulations allow researchers to test the amount of likely error due to treating ordinal data as interval data. For discussions of these problems, see Hubert M. Blalock, Jr., ed. *Measurement in the Social Sciences: Theories and Strategies* (Chicago: Aldine, 1974).

[ǁ] A scatterplot is a figure that plots the location of individual cases on both the *x* and *y* axes.

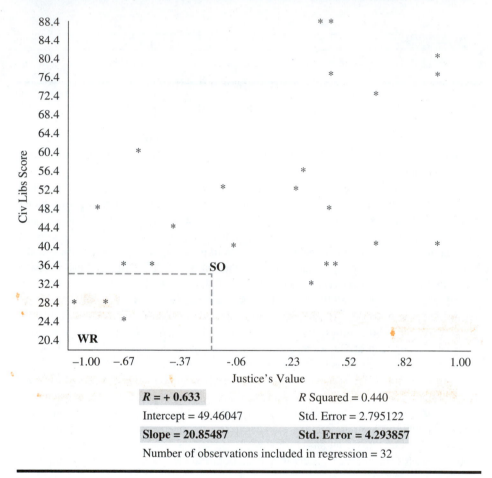

FIGURE 8.5

SCATTERPLOT OF PRIOR IDEOLOGY SCORES AND CIVIL LIBERTIES VOTE[a]

R = + 0.633 R Squared = 0.440

Intercept = 49.46047   Std. Error = 2.795122

Slope = 20.85487   **Std. Error = 4.293857**

Number of observations included in regression = 32

[a] Developed using Micro-Crunch and its Quik-Plot command

from −1.00 for the most conservative to +1.00 for the most liberal. The chart measures civil liberties votes along the *y* axis with scores in a theoretical range of 0 percent to 100 percent.

Each asterisk represents a justice. The figure labels two justices, Sandra Day O'Connor (SO) and William Rehnquist (WR) to show how to read the figure. Look vertically downward from SO to the *x* axis to determine Justice O'Connor's score on ideological liberalism: −0.17. Look horizontally to the left to see the percentage of times she has voted with the liberal side on civil liberties cases, 34.1 percent. The same steps for

FIGURE 8.6

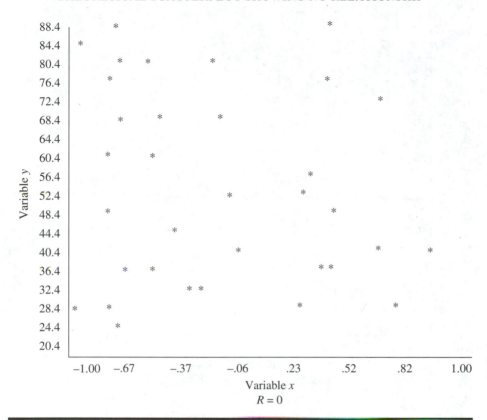

THEORETICAL SCATTERPLOT SHOWING NO RELATIONSHIP

Chief Justice Rehnquist reveal a score of −0.91 on the ideological liberalism scale and a score of 20.4 percent on the civil liberties scale.

Think of a scatterplot simply as a contingency table for interval data. Both of these devices draw pictures of research data. The scatterplot in Figure 8.5 shows that, as judges' scores on ideological liberalism increase, the percentage of their votes for liberal resolutions of civil liberties cases also tends to increase. In other words, as the values of variable x increase, the values of the variable y also tend to increase. This is an example of a *positive relationship*. If the data revealed no relationship between the value for liberal ideology and votes on civil liberties cases, the asterisks would be scattered randomly throughout the scatterplot. Figure 8.6 shows what a scatterplot between two unrelated variables might look like.

To show a negative relationship, recall the data on participation in Peru. The chart from Quik-Plot in Figure 8.7 shows the relationship between the variables WILLNOLG

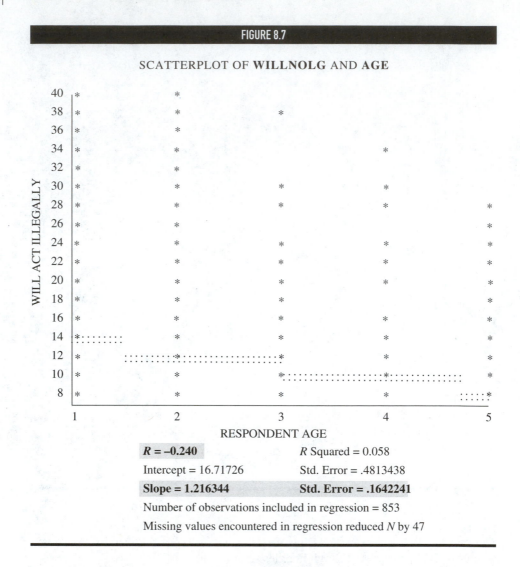

FIGURE 8.7

SCATTERPLOT OF **WILLNOLG** AND **AGE**

$R = -0.240$ R Squared = 0.058

Intercept = 16.71726   Std. Error = .4813438

Slope = 1.216344   **Std. Error = .1642241**

Number of observations included in regression = 853

Missing values encountered in regression reduced N by 47

and AGE. Because the interviewers asked respondents to place themselves in age groupings rather than to state their actual ages, the study gave ordinal data. This causes all of the cases to fall in columns immediately above the value given to the age group. For example, Group 1 is made up of people under 21, while Group 5 includes people over 60.

Correlation Coefficient

Most of the time in the social sciences we want to know not only whether there is an association between variables, but also the strength of the association. The **correlation coefficient** (denoted by the letter R), allows us to determine both the direction and the strength of an association. For a positive relationship like that in Figure 8.5, R has a value greater than zero; for a negative relationship, as in Figure 8.7, it has a value less than zero. If data confirm no relationship between x and y, as in Figure 8.6, then $R = 0$.

FIGURE 8.8

SCATTERPLOT SHOWING PERFECT POSITIVE CORRELATION

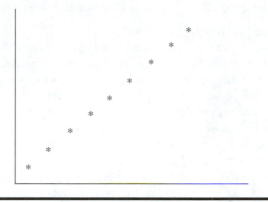

The second powerful benefit of the correlation coefficient is its indication of the strength of an association. A perfect positive association has an R of +1.0. This means that for any two cases, if the score on the x variable moves up a particular amount (e.g., 3), then the score on the y variable will also move up a specific amount (e.g., 2). In other words, at any spot on the x axis, if the value of x increases by 3 intervals, the score on the y variable will move up 2 intervals. Figure 8.8 shows an example of a perfect correlation where an increase of 1 unit in x corresponds to the same increase in y for every interval of x. Every case falls along a straight line on the scatterplot.

A perfect negative relationship would yield a correlation coefficient of −1.0. In this case, an increase of a specific amount in x would correspond to a reduction in y by a precise amount. For example, if the value of x moved up by 2 units, the value of y would drop 1 unit. The R for Figure 8.5, which measures ideological values and civil liberties votes of Supreme Court justices, is 0.663. Figure 8.7 shows that the R for age and expected participation in illegal activities is −0.240.

A third characteristic of the correlation coefficient makes it easy to use. It can help a researcher to study relationships between variables with quite different measures. It can evaluate associations like those between the percentage of women in a country who have attended secondary school and national birthrate or between age and responses to an attitude survey.

Correlation and Probability

As for a chi-square statistic, a researcher can calculate the probability that a particular correlation coefficient will occur. Also, as for the chi square, this probability is a function of both the size of the correlation coefficient and the number of cases. For example, an R of 0.15 is not statistically significant for 20 cases, but it is significant for 1,000 cases.

Sometimes students confuse the measure for the statistical significance of R and the actual value of R because both are similar-looking decimal fractions. For example, the relationship between variables x and y might have an R of 0.85 and a probability of 0.001. These numbers mean that x and y have a strong positive association ($R = 0.85$), one that could have occurred only 1 time in 1,000 by chance ($p = 0.001$).

One-Tail and Two-Tail Tests of Significance

When using correlation analysis researchers may not know whether they expect a positive or negative relationship between two variables. For example, say an observer is testing to see if there is a relationship between level of religious commitment and the level of tolerance for opposing political opinions. One hypothesis might be that the more religious a person, the more tolerant that person will be. The researcher might reason that most religions teach us to respect and value the opinions of others. Therefore, the more religious a person, the more that person will respect the right to hold opinions that differ from one's own. An alternative hypothesis is that more religious people are less tolerant of opposing political opinions. The researcher might reason that people who believe they know The Truth are less likely to respect the opinions of people who do not believe in that Truth. In situations where researchers do not know whether two variables will be positively or negatively correlated, they use a two-tail test of statistical significance.**

If, on the other hand, the researcher expects that an association between two variables has a specific direction, then a one-tail test of significance is appropriate. For example, a researcher might hypothesize that persons for whom the cost of illegal participation are great are less likely to participate in illegal political activity. Because the researcher specifies the direction ahead of time, a one-tail test of statistical significance is appropriate.

This and other exercises assume that the reader has expectations concerning the positive or negative directions of associations. For this reason, the reader will use one-tail tests of significance.

Student's t (t-score)

The statistic that determines the significance of a correlation coefficient is the **student's t.** The student's t statistic, like the chi-square statistic, indicates the likelihood that the observed distribution between x and y could have occurred by chance. The degrees of freedom for the student's t equal the number of cases minus 1 ($n - 1$). For example, Figure 8.5 charts data for 32 justices, and each justice is a case. Therefore, the degrees of freedom equal 31 (32 cases minus 1).

This exercise requires simple division to compute the student's t. Divide the **slope** of the dotted line by its **standard error.** Statistical software packages print these numbers beneath a scatterplot on the last line of numbers (the shaded sections of the charts in Figures 8.5 and 8.7). To calculate the t-score, divide the slope (20.85487 in Figure 8.5) by its standard error (4.2939), giving a t-score of 4.86.

The researcher then checks the student's t statistic in much the same way as the chi-square. Data for Figure 8.5 included 31 degrees of freedom (32 justices minus 1). Using the distribution of student's t in Table 8.2, check the size of the t-score necessary to reach statistical significance for 30 degrees of freedom. Because the calculated t-score of 4.86 is

---

** A one-tailed test is stronger than a two-tailed test because the chances of finding any relation at all, whether positive or negative, are much greater than the chances of finding either one you specify.

	TABLE 8.2			

STUDENT'S t DISTRIBUTION

Level of Significance (one-tail test)

df	0.10	0.05	0.025	0.01
10	1.372	1.812	2.228	2.764
20	1.325	1.725	2.086	2.528
25	1.316	1.708	2.060	2.485
30	1.310	1.697	2.042	2.457
40	1.303	1.684	2.021	2.423
60	1.296	1.671	2.000	2.390
120	1.289	1.658	1.980	2.358
∞	1.282	1.645	1.960	2.326

greater than the table value of 2.457, the correlation coefficient is statistically significant at the level of $p < 0.01$. The researcher can reject the null hypothesis that the data reveal no relationship between the prior ideological ratings of Supreme Court justices and their votes on civil rights cases. In short, Quik-Plot confirms that the two variables have a positive and statistically significant relationship.

Using Micro-Crunch to Find the Correlation Coefficient
Micro-Crunch can calculate the correlation coefficient, and the researcher calculates the associated t-score. This example will use the two variables from the PERU data set that produced Figure 8.7.

One way that Micro-Crunch discovers the correlation coefficient between two variables is with the Quik-Plot command, one of the options in the Linear Tables menu. Quik-Plot displays the scatterplot for the x and y variables and computes several statistics, including the correlation coefficient. The following steps show how to do this for the variables WILLNOLG and AGE:

1. Enter Micro-Crunch.
2. Select the data set PERU.
3. Choose the option Linear Models.
4. Choose Quik-Plot.

At this point, Micro-Crunch will display the instruction:

Enter y axis variable:

Enter **WILLNOLG,** and press the Enter key. Next, Micro-Crunch will display the instruction:

Enter the x axis variable:

Enter **AGE,** and press the Enter key. Micro-Crunch then asks:

Compute and Plot the regression line? (Y/N)

Press **Y.** Micro-Crunch then provides the display in Figure 8.7 (without the shading).

How do you interpret all of this information? First, the asterisks (*) indicate locations on the scatterplot where at least one case is located. The dots (::::::) indicate the direction of the relationship. The line of dots slopes downward in Figure 8.7, indicating a negative relationship between WILLNOLG and AGE.

To determine whether a relationship is statistically significant, divide the slope of the line by its standard error to find the student's t-score of 7.41 with 852 degrees of freedom. Checking the row along the infinity sign (∞) in Table 8.2 confirms that you can again reject the null hypothesis. The data confirm that, in Peru, age and the willingness to participate in illegal demonstrations are negatively associated. The R value of -0.240 indicates, however, that the relationship is not nearly as strong as that between ideology scores and votes in Supreme Court civil rights cases.

SUMMARY

Many readers probably got a little lost somewhere in the discussion so far. A summary might help to clarify what a researcher needs to know to use the correlation coefficient.

1. Correlation coefficients measure the strength of associations. A perfect positive relationship will have a correlation coefficient of $+1.0$; a perfect negative relationship will have a correlation coefficient of -1.0.

2. A stronger association produces a correlation coefficient further from zero. For example, the coefficients of -0.40 and $+0.40$ indicate equally strong associations; a coefficient of -0.75 indicates a stronger association than a coefficient of $+0.65$.

3. The probability (p) that a correlation coefficient (R) is statistically significant is determined both by the size of R and the number of cases. Although both R and p are expressed as decimal fractions, they have opposite meanings. Larger absolute values of R indicate stronger associations between variables. A smaller value of p indicates greater statistical significance for the association.

4. Quik-Plot provides the correlation coefficient (R) for a relationship. To find the value of p, calculate the t-score by dividing the slope by its standard error. Quik-Plot provides these numbers, but you must do the division. Remember that the number of degrees of freedom equals the number of cases minus 1. (If you are using SPSS, the program calculates the t-score and the level of statistical significance for you.)

EXERCISE

Test five of the hypotheses that you generated in Chapter 5 to examine the relationship between political behavior and various independent variables. Generate a scatterplot for each hypothesis. Compare the results of your chi-square analysis with those of the correlation analysis. For this exercise use the file PERU rather than the file PERUCAT.

NOTES

[1] Kevin J. O'Brien, *Reform without Liberalization: China's National People's Congress and the Politics of Institutional Change* (New York: Cambridge University Press, 1990), p. 177.

[2] Nelson Polsby, "Legislatures," in *Handbook of Political Science, V,* ed. by Fred I. Greenstein and Nelson W. Polsby (Reading, Mass.: Addison-Wesley, 1975).

[3] Juan J. Linz and Arturo Valenzuela, eds., *The Failure of Presidential Democracy* (Baltimore, Md.: Johns Hopkins University Press, 1994), p. 74.

[4] Carl J. Friedrich, *Constitutional Government and Democracy* (Boston: Ginn, 1946), p. 36.

[5] E. N. Gladden, *History of Public Administration,* Vol. 1 (London: Frank Cass, 1972), p. 53. Gladden also suggested, more than half seriously, that the job of public official, not that (as legend has it) of prostitute, is the oldest profession in the world.

[6] Jeffrey A. Segal and Albert D. Cover, "Ideological Values and the Votes of U.S. Supreme Court Justices," *American Political Science Review* 83 (1989), pp. 557–566.

9

Courts and Judicial
Policy Making

Key Terms

Mechanical Conception of
   the Judicial Process
Triadic Conflict Resolution
Go-between
Mediator
Arbitrator
Judge
Administrative Tribunal
Appeal

Legal Realist
Stare Decisis
Scope
Depth
Judicial Review
Constitutional Courts
Concrete Judicial
   Review
Abstract Judicial
   Review

Administrative
   Judicial Review
Trial Court
Regression Analysis
Regression Equation
Intercept
Slope

Of all the institutions of government, courts and judges seem most fascinating to people. Outside observers are engrossed by what they assume to be the day-to-day work of courts and judges—holding trials. This activity is fodder for a vast array of popular entertainments, from important and powerful movies like *Judgment at Nuremberg* and *Twelve Angry Men* through such diversionary fare as *L.A. Law* and *Law and Order*. By contrast, images of daily activities of officials in the executive, legislature, and bureaucracy seem to engage the imaginations of many fewer people (except for the activities of those special bureaucrats, the police, the military, and the spies). Examples of government themes in entertainment (like *The Last Hurrah,* a true-to-life story of a Boston political boss elected mayor) are scarce when compared to courtroom dramas. The ratings for Court TV coverage of the O. J. Simpson trial far outshone those of even the most-watched C-SPAN coverage of the U.S. Congress.

Certainly, the authors enjoy a good courtroom drama as much as anyone. Political scientists worry, however, about the depictions in popular culture of what courts and judges usually do. Most careful students of the courts would agree that trials, especially strongly contested courtroom encounters, constitute only a relatively small part of the activities of most courts and judges. To explore this fascinating segment of the political system, this chapter must begin by correcting the popular stereotype through an accurate look at what courts are and what they actually do.

Courts and Judges: What They Are and What They Do

The traditional definition of the role of the courts comes from the civics-book understanding of the separation of powers: If the legislature makes laws and the executive implements them, then judges apply them to particular situations to resolve disputes. Taken broadly, this understanding of the judicial function is not inaccurate, but it gives too narrow an image. This narrow focus seriously misinterprets the process by which judges should and do make decisions. We call this misinterpretation the **mechanical conception of the judicial process.** In addition, narrowly limiting the role of judges to dispute resolution distracts attention from other important functions that courts perform.

TRIADIC CONFLICT RESOLUTION

One influential analyst of the functions of courts and judges sees their origins in **triadic conflict resolution.** * Courts and judges become a third party to a dispute to assist its resolution. In any society, even the simplest, individuals and groups come into conflict over things they mutually value. To avoid violent consequences of these conflicts, societies devise ways of using third parties to help resolve them. The least intrusive of these third parties is the **go-between,** who ferries arguments and bargaining positions back and forth between opposing sides. Skillful go-betweens defuse tensions that arise in face-to-face arguments between conflicting parties. With the trust of both parties, a go-between can make significant contributions to resolving a dispute.

A **mediator** plays a more active role, not only shuttling information back and forth between the conflicting parties, but also suggesting possible solutions that neither of the parties might have contemplated. Imaginative suggestions of mediators may make major contributions to resolving disputes. However, mediators have no power to enforce their suggestions; both parties must agree to these actions for them to go into effect. More active and authoritative than a mediator, an **arbitrator** has all the duties of the mediator plus the authority to impose solutions that the conflicting parties must accept. An arbitrator has this authority because the disputing parties agree in advance to accept a proposal put forward by this intermediary.

Why might conflicting parties agree to bind themselves to accept the arbitrator's solution? They probably make a rational choice to do so because both parties expect to continue dealing with each other, so they willingly accept the risk of a present loss rather

---

*This discussion follows the analysis of Martin Shapiro, *Courts: A Comparative Analysis* (Chicago: University of Chicago Press, 1981, Chapter 1).

than tolerate persistent and continuing losses that result from an unresolved conflict. Given this expectation, arbitration makes a lot of sense if the conflicting parties can find a third party whose fairness and expertise they trust. Once both sides agree to arbitration, resulting solutions to their dispute become binding choices.

Go-betweens, mediators, and arbitrators represent increasingly authoritative and formal means of triadic conflict resolution. Still, none can deal with a conflict when the disputing parties cannot agree on a third party to turn their bilateral disagreement into a triadic search for a solution. What happens when such agreements cannot be achieved? Society's answer is to replace the go-between, mediator, or arbitrator with an authoritative third party, the **judge.** The judge undertakes triadic conflict resolution in institutions called *courts*.

The key difference between judges and the less formal third parties is the authority of judges to impose solutions without the agreement of the parties to accept those solutions. Government gives this authority to judges, and government can use its coercive powers to force disputing parties to accept judges' solutions.

The independence of a judge from the consent of both parties to participate in or accept a conflict resolution has extremely important effects. On the surface, the absence of consent would seem to guarantee that at least one of the parties would regard the solution as an improper and illegitimate burden. The loser might complain that two parties are ganging up against one. If one of the parties denies the legitimacy of the judge's dispute resolution, this disappointment leaves little incentive to abide by the resolution. The government would seem to have no alternative but to threaten or coerce losing parties to ensure that they accept judges' decisions. This would require undesirable and expensive intervention to force compliance to a dispute settlement. In addition, enforcing a judge's decision by coercion increases the chance of violence, thus negating the reason for resorting to triadic conflict resolution in the first place.

To avoid this undesirable outcome, governments have developed norms, or perhaps myths, intended to increase the chances that all parties in a dispute settled by a judge will accept the result without being coerced. These norms specify that, while the parties to a dispute may not consent to having their conflict resolved by a judge, they can have confidence that the judge will arrive at a proper resolution worthy of acceptance. It is proper, the norms assert, because the judge is:

- *Independent* of the control of others who might have an interest in the dispute
- Fair or *impartial* with respect to the interests of the parties to the dispute
- *Expert* in applying the rules that everyone, or at least most people, agree should be applied to resolve such disputes[†]

The traditional view of judges presents their decisions as worthy of acceptance because they represent the *inevitable* results of impartial experts applying relevant rules fairly to specific disputes. Judges decisions do not represent their personal preferences. This view of the role of judges is part of the mechanical conception of the judicial process. Other scholars prefer the phrase "traditional conception of the judicial process." The chapter shall return to it later.

[†] For a useful discussion of these norms, see Theodore L. Becker, *Comparative Judicial Behavior-The Political Function of Courts* (Chicago: Rand McNally, 1970).

The preceding description does not imply that all contemporary or historical governments have asserted these norms as appropriate for judges. Some governments (the Nazis and communist China, for example) have claimed exactly the opposite. They believe that the ideology and personal objectives of the current ruler should guide judges' decisions. In such a regime, the only relevant judicial expertise is knowledge of and devotion to the dominant ideology and objectives.

Finally, governments and judges may argue for the independence, impartiality, and expertise of the judiciary without really believing their own assertions. Governments often act to hinder judicial independence, impartiality, and expertise. Judges are, after all, part of the government. Expecting them to act independently or impartially when government interests are at stake may ask too much of their abilities. Furthermore, the self-interests of other government officials might lead them to encourage judges to ignore the official norms of independence, impartiality, and expertise. The preceding discussion mentioned societal *norms* and *myths* for this very reason. To protect the image of legitimacy for judges' decisions, a government will maintain that fairness and neutrality prevail over considerations of self-interest.

SOCIAL CONTROL

In addition to conflict resolution, courts perform the function of social control. (Recall the discussion of this topic under the headings "Protection and Order" and "Political Socialization" in Chapter 1.) To promote social control, judges regulate the behavior of individuals to ensure their conformity to the rules or laws established by the government. The courts are far from the only institutional guardians of social order. Indeed, they are not even at the front lines of social control. Police and other bureaucrats have the primary duty of compelling individuals to conform to the laws and applying sanctions to those whose behavior does not conform.

Courts and judges retain nominal involvement in social control because they are the official third parties in disputes between the government and those accused of breaking its rules or laws. These legal disputes differ from conflict resolution situations, however. Courts do not work to resolve direct disagreements between law breakers and their victims. In part, this reflects the fact that violations of many regulations or laws—so-called victimless crimes—do not produce any real harm to any specific individual. But even when specific victims do suffer the effects of violations of the law, most governments do not allow them to take action against the law breakers. Instead, government takes the place of the victims. This establishes the convention that a dispute of violation of laws becomes a conflict between the people (the government) and those who have broken the people's (the government's) laws.

Government substitutes itself for the victims of crime to provide protection and effective representation for the weak and to prevent citizens from resorting to vigilante justice. Vigilante justice may cause even more law breaking and violence than it deters. Attempts at "quick justice" run a serious risk of punishing people who have not been proved guilty of breaking any law.

In disputes between the government and criminals, judges serve as the third parties who officially choose appropriate resolutions. In this work, they are supposed to observe the same norms of independence, fairness, expertise, and avoidance of arbitrary (personal) discretion that regulate their resolutions of other conflicts. A judge acts most obviously as a third party in a criminal trial. The prosecuting attorney is paid by the people to represent them. The defense attorney represents the accused. Although the judge serves the people, she is, nevertheless, expected to make neutral decisions rather than to act as another representative of the people. Many, perhaps most, judges do their best to live up to these norms when they decide the government's claims against accused criminals. They try to see to it that defendants get fair trials and receive just penalties, if found guilty.

In practice, the role of the judge in a dispute between the government and a citizen appears to amount to bureaucratic processing. The judge ratifies the application of a regulation in a common administrative circumstance rather than personally resolving the conflict. In the United States, this activity is especially evident because the parties conclude so many criminal cases through "plea bargaining." In plea bargaining, the government and an accused criminal or the lawyer for such a defendant seeks out a solution to the dispute. This reduces the time and trouble that the government must expend to apply some relevant sanction to a law breaker. A plea bargain weakens the sanction that the law breaker must suffer in return for agreement to plead guilty to a violation and avoid the need for a trial. Even where plea bargaining is not common, the activities of judges in criminal cases appear to be more like bureaucrats involved in social control than independent, impartial third parties involved in resolving genuine conflicts.

JUDGING AND ADMINISTRATION

The actions of judges performing their social control function resemble those of bureaucrats involved in the day-to-day administration of government programs with fixed guidelines. This resemblance shows some overlap in the activities of judges and bureaucrats in the administration of justice.

The overlap between judging and administration becomes obvious in the activities of a special class of bureaucratic organizations, **administrative tribunals.** Many nations set up administrative tribunals outside of their regular legal systems to deal with certain kinds of conflicts that arise in modern societies and economies. Labor tribunals deal with disputes between workers, their unions, and management. Employee compensation commissions hear and rule on disagreements over compensation for workers injured on the job. Agrarian reform commissions consider problems arising from agricultural landlord-tenant relations; this activity becomes especially common as part of efforts to redistribute land ownership.

These administrative tribunals may resolve disputes with specialized content, but their decision processes are not very different from those of regular courts. Yet it is often difficult or impossible to appeal the decisions of administrative tribunals to the regular courts. Why is this the case? Indeed, why do governments set up administrative tribunals outside their regular judicial hierarchies in the first place? The answer lies in the history of the development of social policy in industrial nations.

In many countries, representatives of leftist parties became very suspicious of courts. This mistrust grew when those parties gained control of governments and enacted progressive social and economic legislation to redress social harms created by industrialization. This kind of legislation expanded significantly the scope of government, and dominant economic and social elites often viewed the new laws as dangerous or subversive violations of accepted standards. Frequently, these elites found allies in the courts, which often overturned the new legislation or frustrated its intentions.

Because judges need extensive education and training, they come overwhelmingly from the most privileged classes in society. Whether for this reason or because their legal training, orientations, and beliefs made them conservative, judges often appeared hostile to progressive reforms or ignorant of the socioeconomic conditions the reforms addressed. As a result, as part of their efforts to promote socioeconomic reform, governments set up tribunals within their bureaucracies to administer specific reforms and to resolve related disputes. Where possible, the governments excluded the regular courts from handling such disputes to bypass possible judicial bias in favor of economic elites.

LAWMAKING

Traditional notions of separation of powers define lawmaking as the principal function of the legislature. But Chapters 7 and 8 have already described the executive dominance in lawmaking over legislatures. If the legislative and executive branches come into conflict over a particular lawmaking issue, a third party must decide the dispute. Thus, no one should be surprised to find judges involved in lawmaking, since they sometimes resolve these intergovernmental conflicts.

Still, well-informed and knowledgeable people, including many attorneys and judges, argue vigorously that judges do not—or at least *should* not—make laws. They argue that the legitimacy of judges' decisions in triadic conflict resolution depends upon their ability to render unbiased verdicts. It is very difficult to maintain such neutrality if the judges make laws and then provide expert interpretations of those laws. Societies developed the mechanical conception of the judicial process to enhance the acceptability of judges' decisions in triadic conflict resolution. Because conflict resolution produces winners and losers, judges need both winners and losers to believe that their decisions reflect societies' rules, not their personal wishes.

THE MECHANICAL CONCEPTION OF THE JUDICIAL PROCESS

The mechanical conception of the judicial process stresses that the decision of a judge, or at least a proper judge, to resolve a conflict depends upon only two things: the circumstances of the dispute (the facts) and the rules established by society to apply to those circumstances (the law). A proper judicial decision is determined entirely by the facts of the situation and the law that society orders the judge to apply when those facts appear. In essence, judges' decisions should resemble machine outputs: They should depend only on the inputs received by the machine and the mechanical rules established by the makers of the machine to guide its production of outputs. A judge's decision, like the machine's output, should have nothing to do with the judge's personal or political values or biases, or the values or biases of anyone else, no matter how powerful those people may be.

In lawmaking, by contrast, decision makers directly apply their political and personal values and ideas about desirable outcomes. Lawmakers instill their values in the rules they create to deal with political problems. Such laws might be established by dictatorial or monarchical decrees, by majority votes of a legislature, or by majority votes in two legislatures accompanied by a formal executive assent. People do not expect these outcomes to resemble automatic results of a mechanical process free from the influence of political values or political influence.

The mechanical view of judicial decision making ignores an important obstacle: Judges cannot always easily identify the facts in disputes before them or decide how the law applies to those facts. If these determinations were obvious, the parties to a dispute might not need to submit their case to the decision of a judge. They could simply read the rule that governs the facts of their dispute and, perhaps with the aid of a go-between or mediator, quickly settle the dispute.‡ The mechanical view of the judicial process deals with this obstacle by stressing that the proper judge is not only independent and impartial, but also *expert* in applying rules to facts.

The expertise of a proper judge comes from thorough knowledge of the law developed through extended study and legal experience. These legal sages can apply their expertise correctly and faithfully because their personalities, training, and experience have given them the proper judicial temperament. This temperament allows them to concentrate solely on the facts and the law to determine the inevitable outcome in the case, totally ignoring their personal views about an appropriate solution for the dispute.

This traditional conception of the judicial process, that is, how proper judges decide disputes, clearly bolsters the authoritative image of the judge in conflict resolution, and it defines clear inconsistencies with the idea that judges may be lawmakers. Proper judges never apply their values to make laws; instead, they apply their training and experience to find the laws that apply to the particular facts of the disputes they settle. How, then, can anyone assert, as an earlier section of this chapter did, that one of the basic functions performed by judges necessarily involves lawmaking?

LAWMAKING AND "WRONG" JUDICIAL DECISIONS

The mechanical conception of the judicial process can allow only one plausible answer: While proper judges do not engage in lawmaking, not all judges meet proper standards. Some judges may have inadequate knowledge, training, or experience. Others, despite thorough training and experience, may give way to their own values or to the desires of others. These judges may, improperly, end up making law.

This is the explanation stated by proponents of the mechanical conception of the judicial process when they disagree with the decision of a judge or a court in a given case. They label a decision "wrong" because the judge or court misread or misunderstood the facts or the law or allowed other factors to influence the decision about how to apply the law to the case. Practical planners anticipate such improper decisions. For this reason, societies normally provide for **appeals** to higher, and presumably more expert, courts so that such errors can be corrected.

---

‡ The same logic does not necessarily apply in social control situations.

But even the highest courts can reach poor decisions, according to most proponents of the mechanical conception of the judicial process. In fact, since multijudge courts typically hand down decisions in appeals, individual members of these panels may disagree on what the law requires in a given case. When judges on a court disagree, those in the minority often, and usually politely, criticize perceived defects in the decision of the majority.

Challenge to the Mechanical Conception The frequency of appeals and dissent in multijudge courts suggests that the judicial process may not operate in the mechanical fashion of the traditional model. Wrong decisions by ordinary judges are common enough to require appeal systems and provisions for disagreements among the presumably expert judges of multijudge courts. These circumstances cast doubt on the plausibility of the argument that the judges make wrong decisions only when they lack sufficient skills or training or when they display improper judicial temperament. In this century, many legal scholars (called **legal realists**) and most political scientists have rejected this conclusion. They have argued instead that the facts and the law in a court case are rarely so clear and compelling that they require a judge to reach only a single, correct decision.

Judges face choices among two or even more outcomes that are equally appropriate for a case, even if everyone agrees about the facts. Since the parties to a case often dispute the facts, appropriate outcomes can multiply. The number of choices expands greatly at times because judges must decide what evidence (facts) represent admissible and relevant information.

THE RULE OF PRECEDENT

How can a judge choose appropriately between more than one outcome justified by the relevant facts and the law of a case? The mechanical conception of the judicial process provides an answer accepted in many legal systems: The judge should avoid relying on personal views or values by following the rule of precedent (**stare decisis**). The judge should do what other judges have done in similar cases. Stare decisis, tradition asserts, will provide maximum stability and predictability for the law; and it will minimize the personal influence of judges on case outcomes.

Lawyers and judges in legal systems based on the rule of precedent receive rigorous training in identifying precedents that should govern the decisions of their cases. Furthermore, substantial research evidence confirms that precedents influence judges.

The Multiplicity of Precedents Does reliance on precedent restore the mechanical conception of the judicial process by removing the opportunity for judges to exercise their discretion? Legal realists and most political scientists would answer "no." Even well-understood and widely acknowledged precedents can be found to set improper standards, leading courts to overturn them. Most Americans, for example, are familiar with the Supreme Court decision *Brown* v. *Board of Education* which declared in 1954 that racially segregated schools constitute inherently unequal and therefore unconstitutional treatment. To reach this conclusion, the Supreme Court had to overturn a precedent established by an earlier court in the 1890s (*Plessy* v. *Ferguson*) that upheld the constitutional basis for racially segregated public facilities so long as they were "separate but equal."

In addition, lawyers on both sides of a dispute follow their training to find precedents that support their desired decisions. This means that, at least in important and controversial cases, judges must weigh precedents that support several different case outcomes. As a result of the lawyers' arguments and their own legal knowledge, therefore, judges in such cases must select from at least two decisions. According to the mechanical conception, the judge's decision would coincide with the conclusions of well-trained legal specialists who display proper judicial temperaments about the law's requirements. Thus, criticism of such a decision usually reflects personal desire for a different decision rather than a sound basis for a different conclusion.

CODE LAW DECISION MAKING

The rule of precedent cannot remove all discretion from judicial decision making. For one reason, not all legal systems formally emphasize the rule of precedent. Legal systems like those of France or Germany, for example, have voluminous legal codes governing civil, criminal, and administrative matters; judges are supposed to refer to these detailed standards when they determine applicable law in a given case.[§] Since only the code is supposed to matter, the actions of other judges in similar circumstances should not govern later decisions. If the code does not provide a rule for a particular case, the judge cannot simply create one. Instead, the judge is supposed to alert the legislature about the absence of a rule and wait for it to take appropriate action. In principle, then, proper judges under code law never substitute their judgment for that of the legislature.

Even the most rigorous and traditional defenders of this code law (or civil law) basis for judicial decision making recognize that judges must exercise their discretion in some circumstances and choose among apparently equally appropriate alternatives. Societies that use code law have developed additional rules to guide judges in this exercise of discretion. In this century, stare decisis has taken its place among those interpretive rules.

JUDICIAL DISCRETION AND LAWMAKING

To choose among alternative decisions, then, judges must exercise discretion. When they make a binding rule in a dispute on this basis, they engage, to a greater or lesser extent, in lawmaking. Since judicial discretion seems an inevitable feature of the legal process, so is judicial lawmaking.

Judicial lawmaking through decisions in individual cases may not seem to have sweeping effects. However, some scholars emphasize a large cumulative effect of small-scale lawmaking that governs individual disputes in local courts. The effect is large because these courts create law that influences the distribution of resources for large segments of the population.[1] Beyond such cumulative effects, however, the normal image of judicial lawmaking centers on the most important and controversial cases in the judicial system.

[§] This discussion draws loosely on Lafon, "France," in *The Global Expansion of Judicial Power,* ed. by C. Neal Tate and Torbjorn Vallinder (New York: New York University Press, 1994), pp. 289–306.

SCOPE AND DEPTH OF DECISION MAKING

The potential of a particular court to engage in lawmaking depends most clearly on the scope and depth of its decision-making authority.[2] **Scope** refers to the variety of types of legal disputes that a court must resolve. A court that makes decisions over a broader scope has greater lawmaking potential. Legally, the scope of a court's decision making is determined by its jurisdiction. In practice, courts may have the opportunity to decide a full range of important questions included within their jurisdictions; they may even decide what falls within their jurisdictions. For example, the Supreme Court of the Philippines must have the broadest scope of decision-making authority of any court in the world. The view prevails in Philippine society that no dispute, no matter how big or small, is definitely settled unless the Supreme Court has finally ruled on it. The Supreme Court justices, recognizing this view, accept their legal and social responsibility to decide hundreds of disputes of no earth-shaking significance, even though this active role limits the time they can spend resolving truly great controversies. By contrast, the courts of Great Britain have been known historically for deciding only very restrictive ranges of issues.

Depth of decision-making authority refers to the ability of a court to question and even to invalidate laws. A court with deeper decision-making power has greater law-making potential. Courts with great decision-making depth can even overrule laws made or planned by other institutions by citing unconstitutional provisions or other faults. A court that has the power to declare a law unconstitutional has the power of **judicial review.**

JUDICIAL REVIEW

American courts are well known for actively exercising their power of judicial review. They regularly find violations of the Constitution in acts of state legislatures, governors, Congress, and the president. This activity is somewhat ironic, since the U.S. Constitution did not specifically grant judicial review powers to the courts. The Supreme Court gave courts this power in the landmark case of *Marbury* v. *Madison.* Ironic or not, however, the power to review the constitutionality of the acts of other government agencies and officials is now a firmly established part of the power exercised in the United States by *all* courts and judges. Even the lowest court can declare some action unconstitutional and the decision becomes legally binding without the approval of any higher authority.

Many other nations have adopted some form of judicial review since *Marbury* v. *Madison,* but not all have followed exactly the American practice.[3] For example, an increasingly popular version of the practice restricts it to specially established **constitutional courts.** Perhaps the leading example of such an institution is the German Constitutional Court. Established in the post–World War II German constitution, this court has come to play a dramatic role in German law making.[4] It is being widely replicated in the constitutions of the newly democratic states of eastern Europe and the former Soviet Union.

Judicial review does not end with the power of American courts to decide the constitutionality of duly enacted or officially issued acts of other government institutions. Instead of this form of **concrete judicial review,** courts in some countries have the power to engage only in **abstract judicial review,** judicial review before the fact. For example, the French Constitutional Council can declare, upon request, whether a proposed act of parliament is constitutional, but only *before* the act is officially promulgated as law. Some courts, including the German Constitutional Court, can exercise both abstract and concrete judicial review. Still others, such as those of Great Britain, have no official power at all to declare government acts unconstitutional.

The identification of judicial review with the United States and its dramatic exercise by the U.S. Supreme Court sometimes obscures the worldwide importance of the practice. Canada's leading constitutional scholar has concluded that constitutional changes in the 1980s made judicial review as important in Canada, if not more important, than it is in the United States.[5] A prominent student of European courts has noted that "in practice" these bodies have recently been "noticeably more aggressive" in exercising judicial review than their American counterparts.[6] A final example is the Supreme Court of India. A court could scarcely conceive a more dramatic application of judicial review than the ruling by this one striking down legally adopted amendments to the Indian constitution as unconstitutional because they violated not specific provisions but the "basic structure" of the Indian constitution.[7]

Administrative judicial review completes the range of powers of courts over actions of other government institutions. While no judge in Great Britain can declare a law of Parliament unconstitutional, courts there and in many other countries exercise judicial review over the actions of administrators. Administrative, as opposed to constitutional, judicial review "occurs when the courts consider whether the actions of government agencies (other than the courts) are legally proper or whether they represent an abuse of discretion beyond what the law allows."[8] Courts in many countries have exercised this type of review for more than 200 years.

Most observers of legal systems and courts probably see constitutional judicial review as the most important type of lawmaking by judges. The effect of this activity on national politics justifies that conclusion. The effect on ordinary citizens, however, may make administrative judicial review a more important practice. This ability of courts to review the abuse of discretion by government agents may represent citizens' only protection against unfair taxes or inadequate public services and benefits. Perhaps nowhere else can a citizen find redress for a complaint.

Court Hierarchies

The structures of court organizations reflect differences in (1) the scope and sometimes the depth of their decision-making authority and (2) the principal activities in which they engage. Like most complex organizations, courts are structured in hierarchies, with broader decision-making scope at the top than at the lower levels. In addition, the day-to-day duties of courts tend to change from the bottom to the top of the hierarchy. A simplified example of a court hierarchy is given in Figure 9.1.

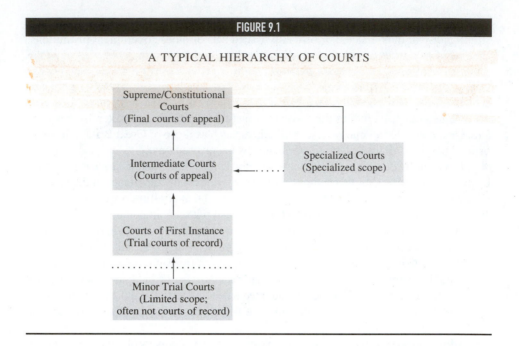

FIGURE 9.1

A TYPICAL HIERARCHY OF COURTS

TRIAL COURTS/COURTS OF FIRST INSTANCE

The courts at the first level of the hierarchy above minor trial courts (above the dotted line) are general **trial courts** or courts of first instance. As these names suggest, the courts at this level hear the first formal trials of disputes between parties or accusations that defendants have violated laws. In the U.S. national government, these courts are called *district courts.* The principal trial courts in the governments of most American states carry the same name, as do those in Australia, Sweden, and Japan.[||] In Canada, the principal trial courts, the *provincial superior courts,* have various specific names. In England, the *crown courts, county courts,* or *High Court of Justice* preside depending upon whether a trial is criminal or civil in nature and how serious it is. In Italy, these courts are *tribunals;* in the Philippines, they are *regional trial courts.*

Large judicial hierarchies may send simple cases to minor courts below the general trial courts or courts of first instance; these bodies make decisions within limited scope and simple procedures. Courts below the dotted line in Figure 9.1 are intended to deal routinely, cheaply, and quickly with small or less serious disputes. The issues involve only minor harms, small amounts of money, or violations of law that are not considered very serious—minor traffic violations, petty theft, and public drunkenness. The U.S. national judicial hierarchy includes no such courts, but they resolve minor matters in every American

---

[||] Australia and Japan also have family courts at this level; Sweden and many other code law countries also have administrative courts at the trial court level. For hierarchy diagrams and names for a selection of national courts, see Jerold L. Waltman and Kenneth M. Holland, *The Political Role of Law Courts in Modern Democracies* (London: Macmillan, 1988).

state.** These include justice of the peace courts, traffic courts, some county courts, some juvenile and family relations courts, and small-claims courts. In Canada, so-called *section 92* provincial courts do this work. In Japan, they are *summary courts.*

While these minor courts stay within a narrow scope of decision making and follow informal procedures, they play a critical role for society and government. They interact with the greatest number of citizens of all types of courts. If the courts of limited jurisdiction are slow, poorly run, or corrupt, their reputation can have a substantial negative impact on the legitimacy of a regime or even of the state.

Though these minor courts are the first courts encountered by people involved in such limited disputes, they are usually not courts of record. They do not follow the practice of courts of first instance of keeping full, written records of all proceedings that occur before them. Instead, a court of limited jurisdiction typically records the names of the parties, the nature of the dispute, the outcome decided upon by the judge, and little else. If one of the parties to a case wants to exercise a right to appeal the outcome, the dispute is heard all over again (*de novo* in legalese) in a court of first instance, where a full record of any trial proceedings will be kept.

A trial, of course, is a ritual in which the contending parties to a dispute—or the government and the accused in a criminal case—present the facts and the law that they hope will persuade the court to make a decision that favors their interests. In some societies (the United States, Canada, and Great Britain among them), juries participate in judicial decision making. The courts summon these groups of citizens specifically to hear the arguments in civil or criminal trials and to make judgments about which side should be favored in the trials' outcomes. In other countries, such as Germany, panels composed of professional and nonprofessional (*lay*) judges perform the same function. In Japan and the Philippines, among other countries, one or more judges hear each trial and make the court's decision.

It is important to remember that many disputes that people bring to courts of first instance do not actually result in trials. Through procedures described earlier, the judicial system frequently resolves cases through out-of-court settlements and plea bargaining to avoid the trouble, expense, and risky outcomes of actual trials. But whether an outcome in a court of first instance results from a settlement, a plea bargain, or a verdict rendered in an actual trial, it represents the official result of a case. A party to the case who disagrees with the verdict may register an appeal with a higher court in the hierarchy, a court of appeal.[††]

APPEALS AND COURTS OF APPEAL

The parties involved in a court case (the *litigants*) are allowed to appeal the decision of a trial court under conditions that vary widely across societies and legal systems. Most

---

** The American judicial system is by far the most complicated in the world. It consists of 51 judicial hierarchies, one for the United States national government and one each for the governments of the 50 states. Nevertheless, this simplified diagram is a fair summary of the national hierarchy and most of those in individual states.

[††] Because both parties agree to accept plea bargains and settlements, they can appeal these outcomes only under very limited circumstances.

legal systems allow most litigants at least one appeal. This principle seems to reflect a presumption that legal errors occur more frequently in courts of first instance than in appeals courts, and that every litigant should have a chance to have such errors corrected. This does not imply, however, that a litigant can challenge any aspect of the first hearing of the case.

An appeal almost never involves another trial, so the appeals court has no opportunity to review the entire proceeding. In addition, appeals must usually cite errors in the procedures and legal rulings from the case's first hearing; courts call these issues "questions of law." Suppose, for example, that a jury concluded, based on their judgment of the facts, that you committed a breach of contract and the court ordered you to pay a $1 million penalty to your opponent in the case. You can appeal this decision only to ask a higher court to correct an error in a question of law. You cannot get the higher court to hear an appeal in which you simply argue that the jury assessed the facts incorrectly and urge the appeals court to reverse that assessment of the facts. In principle, the appeals court must deny your appeal because you have not raised a substantial question of law.

We say "in principle" because in actual practice, distinctions between questions of fact and questions of law may be very difficult to make. In addition, a skillful attorney can often find an error of law that opens up questions of fact, perhaps allowing the litigant to argue that the trial court erred in its judgment about a breach of contract or crime. Perhaps the jury or the judge considered a crucial piece of evidence that should not have been admitted, or the court did not consider a similarly crucial piece of evidence that was incorrectly excluded. In fact, an appeals court may well discuss the facts of a case just as seriously as it discusses whether the trial court committed errors of law. While most legal systems promise every litigant at least one appeal from the decision of a trial court, relatively few litigants actually take advantage of the opportunity to appeal. No doubt most of them (or their attorneys) conclude that a loss at trial probably implies a loss on appeal. Appeals, after all, are not free; they cost time, trouble, and money, and most litigants have little enough time and money and far too much trouble already. This decision illustrates, however, that the legal system includes a bias in favor of those who have money.

SUPREME COURTS: FINAL ARBITERS

At the top of a country's judicial hierarchy, the highest court is intended to be the final arbiter. This institution has the last word on disputes within the whole legal system or within specific segments. In the United States, Canada, India, Japan, the Philippines, and many other countries, a single Supreme Court occupies this position. In other countries, a similar single court is known by a different name: High Court (Australia) or Lords of Appeal in Ordinary (Great Britain), for example.

France, Germany, Italy, and Russia, among other nations, have multiple top courts. One top court acts as a constitutional court, considering only questions involving the interpretation and application of the national constitution. Another supreme court (or sometimes more than one) serves as the final arbiter for legal questions involving civil, criminal, or administrative law.[‡‡]

Its role as a final arbiter involves a supreme court in several kinds of activities. A national constitution may assign it to give the first and only decision on certain very special kinds of disputes such as those involving foreign diplomats or those between regional governments. A national supreme court may also serve as the first court of appeal for the actions of other government agencies (e.g., the president, the legislature, or administrative decision-making bodies within the bureaucracy). But most decisions by supreme courts give final resolutions of cases that have already been passed through other courts, often more than once.

For a litigant, the supreme court provides a last-chance appeal of unsatisfactory previous decisions, including the decisions of lower appellate courts. Litigants are rarely automatically entitled to an appeal to a supreme court. To merit the attention of this body, they must usually persuade its judges that their cases are really special for one of three reasons: First, they can claim that the court that most recently heard the case committed an extraordinarily egregious error of law. Second, they can point out that different lower

---

[‡‡] Usually, these jurisdictions subdivide the trial and appellate courts below them into similar divisions that hear only civil, criminal, or administrative cases. In many countries, these represent important organizational subdivisions within the judicial hierarchies. Americans find them a little strange because in the United States, and in most states, the courts of first instance are trial courts of general jurisdiction; that is, they are authorized to hear any kind of case.

courts have made different decisions in their cases and similar ones. Third, they can convince the judges that the issue raised in their appeal is so unusual or important that it deserves a decision by the highest court in the land.

Supreme courts exercise decision-making authority over a very broad scope when compared to those of lower courts. Because a supreme court has the authority to define the meaning of a country's constitution, it regularly becomes involved in some of the most politically important disputes. This political role persists even if, like the Lords of Appeal in Ordinary in Great Britain, the court lacks the power to declare laws unconstitutional and invalidate them. In Great Britain, a constitutional interpretation stands until Parliament overrules it by an appropriate action. In nations where courts have great depth of decision making, an effort to overrule the courts must normally enact a constitutional amendment. Recall the case from India, where the Supreme Court ruled that its interpretations of the constitution superseded even a constitutional amendment if the amendment would violate the "basic structure" of the constitution. Of course, the Supreme Court gets to decide what is the basic structure of the Indian constitution!

Important as this role is, we do not want to overemphasize the constitutional decision-making activities of supreme courts. Constitutional courts and some general-jurisdiction supreme courts, like that of the United States, spend significant portions of their time on broad, constitutional issues. Other countries' supreme courts, however, may spend relatively little time and effort on such issues. Instead, their decisions may resolve the same kinds of legal issues that occupy the time of the trial courts: economic suits, criminal cases, administrative regulations, and private disputes. The important characteristic of a supreme court is its authority as the final arbiter of these disputes. Its decisions establish a range of policies that govern broad areas of political, social, and personal life. Some courts make laws vigorously, with a flourish. Some do so quietly, almost with reticence. Because of their positions atop their countries' judicial hierarchies, however, all have the power to make laws.

The Importance of Legal Policy Making

The powerful actions of a supreme court raise the question, "How important is the policy making of courts?" A hackneyed traditional answer holds that the courts are the weakest branch of government because they have "neither the purse nor the sword." This position implies that, because judges lack the power to raise and spend government revenues or to command police or military forces, they can affect policy less powerfully than legislatures and executives. Like most clichés, however, this one oversimplifies.

It is true that judges do not directly command police or military forces. If implementation of a court's order requires police or military force, the judge must depend upon the willingness of the executives or bureaucrats who command these forces to order them into action. A quote from U.S. President Andrew Jackson suggests that such commands may not inspire the intended actions. When the Supreme Court decided a case contrary to Jackson's desires, he said: "The Supreme Court has made its decision; now let it enforce it."

But the comment from the 19th century and President Jackson may obscure more relevant or telling actions of the 20th century by Presidents Eisenhower and Kennedy.

Despite some personal misgivings, both sent troops and federal marshals to enforce court-ordered school desegregation in Arkansas, Mississippi, and Alabama after the Supreme Court's *Brown* v. *Board of Education* decision. When the Supreme Court gave the order, President Richard Nixon meekly turned over to other authorities the tapes that he knew would bring a swift end to his presidency. Outside the United States, the French and German governments conform to requirements that they *anticipate* their constitutional courts will lay down.[9] When the Philippine Supreme Court ruled illegal the high-tech national lottery, the president and executive branch promised to concentrate on launching it without violating any laws.

In none of these cases, nor in a thousand others, did the executive or legislative leaders say what Andrew Jackson said. In every case, they complied with court orders. No doubt they did so on any number of occasions with some irritation and against their better judgment. But they complied. Why?

Each of these constitutional governments valued the rule of law. Their executives and legislatures complied with the orders of their supreme courts because they felt that the law required them to do so. Thus, the characterization of courts as weak policy-making institutions because they lack the purse and the sword simply does not hold water in a state with a constitutional government.[§§] In such a state, if the Supreme Court needs support from the executive's sword or money from the legislature's purse to have its orders enforced, it is likely to get what it needs.

Courts are regarded as weak policy makers also because they are generally passive and negative rather than active and positive policy makers. Suppose, for example, that a nation needed a new immigration policy. To establish such a policy, the chief executive or a member of the bureaucracy would draft a proposed bill embodying the provisions of this new policy. If the legislature passed the bill, then the framework for a new immigration policy would be in place. On the other hand, suppose that the members of the supreme court wanted a new immigration policy. The court would lack the authority to draft or implement such a policy, however desirable or however well the judges could do this job. In order to have any effect on the current policy, the court would have to wait until someone appealed a case involving immigration policy. Even then, the court could only outlaw the old policy as illegal or unconstitutional and suggest to the legislature and the executive what kind of immigration policy could pass legal muster.

But the court's passivity may not, in fact, pose such a serious problem. Though they cannot actually solicit cases, skillful courts know how to communicate to attentive members of the public the judges' interest in receiving cases in certain policy areas. In many societies, a wide variety of interest groups will happily bring test cases that will help the courts make the policies the interest groups desire. In such circumstances, the courts will not lack opportunities to make policy.

[§§] To see how little logic underlies the argument "neither the purse nor the sword" to explain the purported weakness of the courts, think about the dependence of those who supposedly do control the purse and the sword on the actions of others. Suppose the president, having lawfully issued an executive order that military leaders do not like, orders the generals to deploy the army in support of this order. What can the president do if the generals refuse? The question does not imply that the president would really be helpless in such a situation. It simply stresses the fact that all branches of government depend upon the willingness of other officials to enforce their orders, if only because they are lawful orders.

The greatest limitation on the policy-making power of the courts is its negative character. No string of policy-making opportunities allows a court to initiate a positive policy change. But even in their narrow position, think about how the courts compare to other policy-making institutions. In a parliamentary system, members of parliament who are not part of the Government have quite limited and passive roles. Both the executive and the legislature in a presidential system may face difficulties initiating policies. Recall from Chapter 8 that the executive and legislature often find themselves in a stalemate. Neither can act without the cooperation of the other.

With a few exceptions, however, judges do not seek the kind of positive role that the executive and legislative branches fulfill. They, and others whose opinions matter, believe that courts simply should not set policy. Keep in mind the logic of the triad of conflict resolution, which leads society to insist on independent, impartial, and expert courts. If judges were to actively pursue policy leadership roles, they surely would risk losing at least the perception of independence and impartiality. The belief that judges should not actively make policy may be the most important reason for the policy weakness of the judiciary relative to the other branches of government. The courts have been relatively restrained (timid?) policy makers in such nations as Great Britain, Canada (before about 1980), the Scandinavian countries (until recently), and Japan. They have played dramatic and sometimes controversial roles in policy making in the United States, India, and Germany. Critics of policy making by the Philippine Supreme Court have accused its judges of establishing a judicial tyranny that overpowers the other government institutions. Within the beliefs of judges about their appropriate role, courts clearly can find room for a great deal of variation in actual policy making.

Global Expansion of Judicial Power?

Incidents around the world provide considerable evidence that the actual policy-making importance of courts and judges is on the rise. Judges appear to be making public policy in areas that previously were dominated by legislative and executive officials. Why is this happening? What is contributing to this apparent expansion of judicial power?

Several factors support this development. The most stunning of these has been the breakdown of totalitarian communism in eastern Europe and the disappearance of the Soviet Union. These changes left the United States, the birthplace of the expansion of judicial power, as the world's only superpower. In a closely connected trend, democratization has spread in Latin America, Asia, and Africa. The circumstances from which many new democracies have emerged have encouraged them to include strong judiciaries in their constitutions to protect democratic political rights.

Institutions of the developing European Union, especially the European Convention on Human Rights and the European Court, have enhanced judicial power. The rulings of this court and the debates about rights that will accompany the new European system have led some countries to strengthen their domestic courts to protect human rights.

What conditions increase the likelihood of an expansion of judicial power? Based on examples from around the world, at least six factors appear to lead to greater judicial power: democracy, separation of powers, respect for human rights, strong interest groups, ineffective majoritarian institutions, and willful delegation by other institutions.

Dictators probably resist allowing even nominally independent judges to increase their participation in the formulation of major public policies. Democratic government thus appears to be a necessary condition, though certainly not a sufficient one, for the expansion of judicial power. Separation of powers may increase judicial power because a constitutionally separate and equal judicial branch can assert itself in policy making when the executive and legislature disagree and policy bogs down in a stalemate.

Whether or not a country has enacted a formal bill of rights for courts to apply, leaders may accept the principle that individuals or minorities have rights that can be enforced against the will of majorities. This possibility increases the policy significance of courts and judges. Observers have dubbed such an acceptance a "politics of rights" and noted its development in many modern nations.[10]

Readers should not, however, form the misleading impression that the expansion of the policy-making authority of courts develops in isolation from the central social and economic interests that structure a country's politics. To the contrary, interest groups discover that courts can help them achieve their objectives in ways that other political means cannot match. This trend has led to an overall expansion of the power of courts in several countries. When the executive cannot govern because political parties are weak and undisciplined or it cannot win the support of an effective legislative majority, the courts can provide policy leadership. Sometimes the public and the leaders of interest groups and major economic and social institutions see self-serving or corrupt motives for the actions of the executive and legislature. Under such circumstances, it is hardly surprising that citizens come to prefer policies made by judiciary officials, with their reputations for expertise and rectitude, over those of the executive and legislature, the majoritarian institutions.

Sometimes, the policy-making power of courts expands when majoritarian institutions delegate to courts certain issues that they do not wish to decide. Outsiders often interpret this delegation as willful avoidance of responsibility. Why do other decision makers delegate authority? This action seems most likely when the political costs of dealing seriously with an issue are too great. If the issue leaves no winning position for elected decision makers, they are happy to leave it to the judges. Perhaps the best example of such an issue in the United States is abortion. In Canada, a comparable issue may be language rights.

Judicial Power and the Attitudes of Judicial Policy Makers

Even when general political conditions favor an expansion of judicial policy-making power, the actual expansion requires more. Judges must have the appropriate personal attitudes and policy preferences. An expansion of judicial power develops only when judges decide that they *should* participate in policy making and wish to substitute their own policy solutions for those of other institutions.

ACTIVISM/RESTRAINT AND VALUES

What attitudes must underlie the development of any significant, active expansion of judicial power? The literature of judicial politics suggests two: judicial activism/restraint and judicial public policy preferences or values. Judicial activists believe that judges should rely on their own public policy preferences or values to decide disputes rather than deferring to the values of other policy makers. The opposite belief, judicial restraint, asserts that judges should not substitute their own policy values for those of other policy makers.

The policy preferences or values of judges reflect their beliefs about the nature of appropriate kinds of government policies on the issues that come before their courts. Like other people's preferences, the values of judges usually fall somewhere in two-dimensional ideological space (see Chapter 6, page 179). In the United States, where judicial policy values have been most extensively studied, judges—especially Supreme Court justices—are most often described as liberals or conservatives based on their opinions about civil rights and liberties and about economic principles.

CIVIL RIGHTS AND LIBERTIES ISSUES

In the United States, these issues refer to a set of citizen rights and liberties guaranteed in or implied by the Bill of Rights: freedom of speech, press, and religion; due process of law and other rights of criminal defendants; and privacy rights. For example, people often dispute whether the government should limit or punish the publication and dissemination of disloyal or libelous materials; whether a local government should allow anyone to place a religious symbol such as a cross or menorah on public property; what authorities must do to preserve the right of criminal defendants to be represented by attorneys; or to what extent government regulations about abortion violate a woman's right to privacy. Liberals on civil rights and liberties issues usually vote in favor of the these kinds of claims put forward by plaintiffs in such disputes; conservatives usually vote against such claims.

Disputes over civil rights and liberties issues have been very prominent in American politics, especially in Supreme Court decision making, since the late 1930s. While other nations may not have equivalents of the U.S. Bill of Rights, most disputes about civil rights and liberties issues become important in most of their policy-making arenas.[IIII] The controversy over abortion and the right to privacy, for example, has been just as prominent in Canadian and German politics as it has in the United States.

ECONOMIC ISSUES

Economic disputes in the courts cover a wide range of policy issues. In most industrialized democracies, as in the United States, the disputes have involved government regulation and control of business activity to protect the interests of the public, the interests of less privileged people, and the interests of labor unions against those of management.

[IIII] Unfortunately, political scientists lack sufficient information about the decision-making routines of the judiciaries in most countries to be able to make confident generalizations about the importance of civil rights and liberties and other kinds of issues in their policy making.

Economic liberals usually support the claims of governments, underdogs, and unions in such cases; economic conservatives argue for the opposite groups.

Economic issues have always been important in politics, but they become especially contentious and prominent during and after a country's period of industrialization. In the United States, economic issues featured prominently in Supreme Court decision making during the late 19th and early 20th centuries. They remain important today, but they have taken a back seat to civil rights and liberties issues since World War II. In Great Britain, similar issues were important at about the same time. As described earlier, the perceived economic conservatism of British courts and those of other European countries led to the creation by leftist-controlled parliaments of administrative tribunals designed to remove many economic issues from the scope of judicial decision making. In many countries, economic issues are probably far more important than civil rights and liberties in judicial policy making. It seems especially likely the courts in the nations of eastern Europe and the former Soviet Union will have to address these issues. These countries are undergoing democratization and conversions to market economics—conditions that encourage disputes between the courts and other government institutions.

ACTIVISM, VALUES, AND DECISION MAKING

A judge's activism or restraint is largely independent of her liberal or conservative position on policy issues. Research on the U.S. Supreme Courts suggests that justices behave like activists if it will serve their policy preferences. Only infrequently, it seems, will a justice's belief in judicial restraint motivate a rejection of a chance to make a decision that would advance personal policy preferences.

Outside the United States, traditional legal standards have held the values of judges as irrelevant to explanations of their decision making; but little research has tried to determine whether this expectation is more fact than myth. If judicial power continues to expand in other nations, it may become harder to sustain the traditional view of politically irrelevant judges against evidence of their entry into the policy arenas previously dominated by majoritarian institutions.

Summary

This chapter should take the reader's understanding of the judicial process far beyond the limited portrayals in popular media. Much of the information in the chapter seems prosaic when compared to the intrigues of the O. J. Simpson trial, but the issues it raises point to fundamental concerns of politics that transcend the glitter of Hollywood.

Modern observers assume that judicial decisions provide the primary avenue for legitimate resolutions of disputes between citizens and even between governments. This assumption reflects the perception in most parts of the world that judges are neutral third parties that hand down unbiased (legal) decisions. While this principle sounds simple enough, the research of judicial behaviorists reveals that judges probably cannot reliably base decisions on mechanical decision rules. This change in perception has very striking results, considering the vast array of public issues that fall within the scope of judiciary control. Judicial review may represent the greatest power of courts. In some cases, courts even decide the most serious national questions, namely the meaning of a nation's constitution. If judges interpret the very basis of law itself, it is critical to know what drives these decisions.

The courts in most industrialized countries have had to deliberate on economic issues and more recently on individual civil rights. Earlier chapters have explained that questions about individual liberty and private property lie at the very core of modern liberalism. As developing countries in eastern Europe and elsewhere move toward democracy, these same legal questions have come inevitably to the forefront. While trials presented in the national media seem more interesting, more mundane court decisions resolve high-stakes questions concerning the day-to-day business of modern political life. These actions of the judiciary have especially powerful effects for those who do not take democratic institutions for granted.

QUESTIONS AND EXERCISES

Questions for Reason

1. Explain briefly the importance of triadic conflict resolution. Why should the two parties in a conflict choose this alternative rather than attempting to resolve the issue between themselves?

2. How do judges make decisions, according to the mechanical conception of the judicial process? What do legal realists say about this theory?

3. What is the principle of stare decisis? How does it differ from code law?

4. What characteristics must judges display to avoid making decisions based on personal prejudice?

Questions for Reflection

1. Why does the court take the place of the injured party in a criminal case? If a citizen is the victim of a crime, should that person determine the fate of the criminal? Why or why not?

2. If judges base decisions on personal ideology rather than the mechanical rule of law, what dangers do they impose on society? Keep in mind that strict legal codes helped political opponents block many social reforms in the early part of this century. If special administrative tribunals and activist judges had not intervened, people would live in a very different world today. Why is this question still important today, especially in countries that are attempting to move toward democracy?

3. Why is judicial review such an important role of courts? Wouldn't it be more democratic if a majority of the electorate decides such issues?

4. Describe the role of administrative courts compared to civil and criminal courts. How is this difference reflected in the hierarchies of most judicial systems? Which type of court is most important for (a) governments, (b) citizens, and (c) social control?

Questions for Analysis: Regression***

Through empirical analysis, scholars found that the decisions made by U.S. Supreme Court justices strongly reflect their policy preferences or values. The pioneering work of Glendon Schubert established that the most consistent and parsimonious way to account for the patterns of voting exhibited by the post–World War II justices was to compare their attitudes toward the "C-scale" (civil rights and liberties) and "E-scale" (Economics) issues that dominated the court's important cases.[11]

You can document for yourself the sharply different degrees of liberalism in the votes of Supreme Court justices on civil liberties and economic decisions by examining the data set that accompany this text. The data set, COURT, allows you to apply sophisticated techniques to study the justices and their decisions. This exercise will present the final statistical technique to be covered in the book, regression analysis.

The data set covers the 32 justices serving on the Supreme Court since its 1946 term. The data detail the personal, educational, career, appointment, and decision-making characteristics of the justices. Appendix C of this book contains the full codebook for COURT.

The exercise introduces only one new idea, using scores on the independent variable to explain scores on the dependent variable. The statistical tool for this explanation is **regression analysis.** The computer commands duplicate those from the previous chapter's discussion of the scatterplot. Both Micro-Crunch and SPSS then provide additional commands to obtain regression statistics, as this exercise will detail.

Imagine you stop at a carnival's weight-guessing booth. Rather than guessing your weight, the attendant offers to pay you $1,000 if you can guess, within 5 pounds, the weight of the next person to walk by the booth. Assume that the game is honest and random chance determines who will come by next. To play the game you must pay the booth attendant $100, for which you will learn one piece of information about the person whose weight you will guess. What piece of information might you want to know?

Perhaps you would choose to know the person's height. Are you ready to make the guess based on that information? The booth attendant now offers one additional piece of information about your subject for an additional $100. Perhaps this time you would like to know the person's sex.

You might decide to play if you had an electronic encyclopedia that would accept input about the height of the person and then return the average weight of all the people of that height at the carnival that night. If you could also input the sex of the subject after paying another $100, your encyclopedia could also calculate the average weight of everyone at the carnival who meets the height and sex criteria. If you could add age information, your encyclopedia would refine its average for everyone with the chosen height, sex, and age. Each additional piece of information would increase the accuracy of your prediction. Before you decide to play, you want to know how closely you might guess and how much closer your guess would come if you were to pay an additional $100 for another piece of information.

Regression analysis works like the electronic encyclopedia. Because this method provides so much useful information, it is the statistical technique that appears most often

***This exercise was co-authored by W. Bruce Shepard.

in social science journals. Once you understand how to use regression analysis, you will be able to read journal articles in sociology, anthropology, public administration, psychology, and political science. In addition, regression will become a powerful tool for your own research. Should you go into business, regression will provide you with a powerful tool for making business decisions.

Prediction

Regression analysis focuses on predicting the value of the dependent variable given the values of various independent variables. To understand how it does this, recall your eighth grade math class, where you probably saw an equation like this one:

$$Y = 5 + 3X$$

This is an equation for a straight line. Knowing the value of X allows you to predict Y. For example, if $X = 5$, then:

$$Y = 5 + 3(5)$$
$$= 5 + 15$$
$$= 20$$

If $X = 1$, then $Y = 5 + 3(1) = 8$. If $X = 100$, then $Y = 305$.

Table 9.1 shows a selection of the values of X and Y for this equation. A scatterplot for Table 9.1 would show all values in a straight line. Recall from Chapter 8 that such a graph implies a correlation of either 1.0 or −1.0.

Now make the equation more general:

$$Y = a + bX$$

This is the standard form of a **regression equation.** The a and b stand for any numbers. Plug in any two numbers for a and b, and then assume a series of numbers for X. *Whatever values you choose, the resulting equation will be the equation for a straight line.* If you choose different values for a and b, then the equation will represent a different straight line. For *any* equation, you can plot the data points and draw the corresponding line on a scatterplot. More importantly for researchers, they can reverse this process. For any line on the scatterplot, they can compute the equation that describes it.

TABLE 9.1

VALUES FOR THE EQUATION $Y = 5 + 3X$

X	Y
10	35
5	20
7	26
15	50
2	11
20	65

Karl Pearson, who invented the correlation coefficient, developed regression analysis based on the knowledge that a researcher can represent points on a scatterplot with a graph. Pearson wondered how well the heights of fathers would predict the heights of their sons. More generally, he wanted to know the best way to use the values of any variable *X* to predict the values of any related variable *Y*. Furthermore, Pearson wanted a measure of how accurately *X* predicted *Y*.

Given that a father's height does not perfectly predict his son's height, how could Pearson make the best prediction possible based on knowledge of the father's height. First, he plotted data points for a sample of fathers and sons on a scatterplot. He then drew the straight line that would minimize the divergence of all data points.

To see how Pearson did this, return to the example of Supreme Court justices' votes on economic cases and their ideological values before joining the court. (The exercise in Chapter 8 did this with civil liberties votes and ideological values.) Figure 9.2 shows a moderately strong, positive association between liberal ideological values and liberal votes on economic cases. The upward sloping stepped row of dots is the straight line that reduces the total error in the predictions of votes based on prior values scores. This dotted line is the **regression line;** it shows the economic vote score that a researcher would predict given a justice's score on prior ideological values.

To interpret the figure, choose a score on the values scale ranging from −1 (most conservative) to +1 (most liberal). For example, take a justice whose values score falls exactly halfway between the most conservative and most liberal justices. This is Justice White with a score of 0. To find the best prediction of Justice White's economic votes, move upward from the 0 point on the values scale until the vertical line at that point intersects with the regression line. Then move left along the horizontal line at that point until it intersects with the vertical axis and note the score. Using only the information on Justice White's ideological values before he joined the court, a researcher would predict that he would vote liberal on economic cases 54.0 percent of the time. This prediction turns out to be slightly low. Justice White actually voted liberal on 59.2 percent of the cases.

How would the regression equation, $Y = a + bX$, predict a justice's economic votes from a score on prior ideological values? In Figure 9.2, *Y* represents the predicted percentage of cases on which a justice will vote for the liberal position. *X* represents the justice's score on the values scale. The letter *a* gives the **intercept,** that is, the value of *Y* when *X* equals 0. In Figure 9.2, *a* is 54.05176. The letter *b* designates the **slope** of the regression line, that is, how many units *Y* moves up when *X* increases by 1 full unit. In Figure 9.2, *b* is 11.47757. A researcher could easily predict the percentage of time that Justice White would vote for the liberal position. Because his *X* score is 0, his predicted *Y* score is the intercept, 54.05176.

Now predict the scores of Justices Scalia and Marshall, respectively the most conservative and most liberal justices in the data set. Justice Scalia has a score of −1.0 on the values scale. The same regression equation of $Y = a + bX$, predicts his votes in economic cases:

$$\text{Scalia votes} = 54.05176 + (11.47757 \times -1)$$
$$= a + b \times X$$

FIGURE 9.2

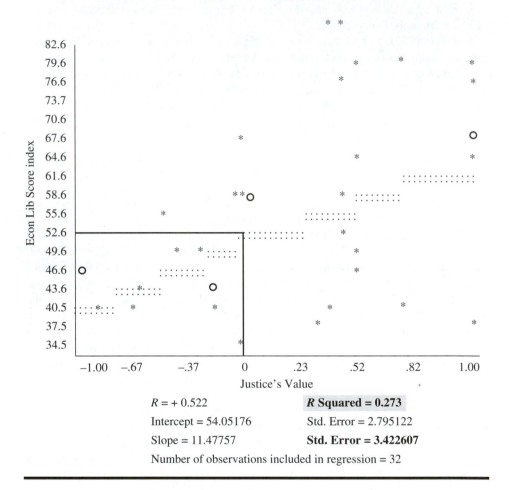

SCATTERPLOT FOR REGRESSION
ECONOMIC VOTES AND IDEOLOGICAL VALUES

$R = + 0.522$ **R Squared = 0.273**

Intercept = 54.05176   Std. Error = 2.795122

Slope = 11.47757   **Std. Error = 3.422607**

Number of observations included in regression = 32

The equation predicts that Justice Scalia will vote for the liberal side in economic cases 42.57 percent of the time. Similarly, Justice Marshall has a score of +1.0 on the values scale, giving a prediction of votes in economic cases of:

$$Y = 54.05176 + (11.47757 \times +1) = 65.53$$

Now try to predict the percentage of economic cases on which Justice O'Connor will vote for the liberal position given her ideological values score: –0.17. The positions of all four justices mentioned so far are circled in Figure 9.2. The regression equation gave slightly low predictions for Justices Scalia, White, and Marshall and a slightly high prediction for Justice O'Connor.

How do you find the right regression equation to apply to the data set? In Micro-Crunch or SPSS, simply choose the regression procedure. Indicate to the computer which variable is dependent and which is independent, and it magically spits out the equation that minimizes the errors in predictions of the dependent variable based on values of the independent variable. Figure out the *t*-score using the slope and the standard error of the slope, then check the Student's *t* table to determine if your results reflect a statistically significant relationship.

How Well Does Regression Predict Reality?

Finally, consider how much variation the regression analysis explained. Notice the shaded material in Figure 9.2: *R Squared = 0.273*. The exercises at the end of Chapter 10 will deal with this concept more completely, but notice now that if an independent variable could perfectly predict a dependent variable, then *R* squared would equal 1.00. The values of the independent variable would then perfectly predict the values of the dependent variable for every case. Needless to say, this does not happen in real life. However, a higher value for R^2 indicates a better prediction. Just as its name implies, R^2 is the square of the correlation coefficient.

Exercise

For dependent variables, choose the percentage of liberal votes in civil rights cases (CLVOTE) and in economic cases (ECONVOTE). Produce hypotheses for the relationships between those variables and the following independent variables:

BEGNYEAR   The year a justice first began to serve on the court
TENURE   The number of years a justice served on the court
JUDEXFED   The number of years a justice served as a judge in the federal courts prior to joining the Supreme Court
PTYIDRID   The justice's political party

Choose a critical value (e.g. $p < 0.05$) and use either Micro-Crunch or SPSS to produce scatterplots. You will have a total of eight hypotheses and eight scatterplots. To determine whether to accept your hypotheses, compute the *t*-scores and check the Student's *t* table in Chapter 8, page 267). Assemble your results in a report using a word processor.

Based on your results, how strongly do you think the individual backgrounds of justices influence their judicial decisions?

NOTES

[1] Herbert Jacob, *Justice in America,* 4th ed. (Boston: Little, Brown, 1984). See also Lynn Mather, "Policy Making in State Trial Courts," in *The American Courts: A Critical Assessment,* ed. by John B. Gates and Charles A. Johnson (Washington, D.C.: CQ Press, 1989), pp. 119–157.

[2] Jean Blondel, *An Introduction to American Government* (New York: Praeger, 1969); C. Neal Tate, "Judicial Institutions in Cross-National Perspective: Toward Integrating Courts into the Comparative Study of Politics," in *Comparative Judicial Systems,* ed. by John R. Schmidhauser (London: Butterworths, 1987), pp. 7–33.

[3] For a more complete discussion of the varieties and importance of judicial review, see C. Neal Tate, "Comparative Judicial Review and Public Policy: Concepts and Overview," in *Comparative Judicial Review and Public Policy,* ed. by Donald W. Jackson and C. Neal Tate (Westport, Conn.: Greenwood Press, 1992), pp. 1–13.

[4] Christine Landfried, "Germany," in *The Global Expansion of Judicial Power,* ed. by C. Neal Tate and Torbjorn Vallinder (New York: New York University Press, 1994), pp. 307–324; Alec Stone, "Complex Coordinate Construction in France and Germany," in *The Global Expansion of Judicial Power,* ed. by C. Neal Tate and Torbjorn Vallinder (New York: New York University Press, 1994), pp. 205–229.

[5] Peter H. Russell, "The Growth of Canadian Judicial Review and the Commonwealth and American Experiences," in *Comparative Judicial Review and Public Policy,* ed. by Donald W. Jackson and C. Neal Tate (Westport, Conn.: Greenwood Press, 1992), pp. 29–40.

[6] Mary L. Volcansek, "Judicial Review and Public Policy in Italy: American Roots and the Italian Hybrid," in *Comparative Judicial Review and Public Policy,* ed. by Donald W. Jackson and C. Neal Tate (Westport, Conn.: Greenwood Press, 1992), pp. 89–106.

[7] G. C. Mirchandani, *Subverting the Constitution in India* (Columbia, Mo.: South Asia Books, 1977).

[8] C. Neal Tate, "Concepts and Overview," in *Comparative Judicial Review and Public Policy,* ed. by Donald W. Jackson and C. Neal Tate (Westport, Conn.: Greenwood Press, 1992), pp. 1–13.

[9] Landfried, "Germany."

[10] See Mary Ann Glendon, *Rights Talk: The Impoverishment of Political Discourse* (New York: The Free Press, 1993).

[11] Glendon Schubert, *The Judicial Mind* (Evanston, Ill.: Northwestern University Press, 1964).

Contemporary Problems and Issues

10

Issues Facing Less Industrialized Countries

Imagine that you have just been elected president of Ecuador. In your campaign, you promised greater equality in the distribution of income, more jobs for the urban poor, and increased economic development. When you take office, you find a multitude of problems. The most pressing one requires you to refinance Ecuador's huge foreign debt; the International Monetary Fund (IMF) is the only source of such funds.* The IMF tells you, however, that it will refinance the debt only if your government first institutes major economic reforms. Specifically, you must reduce tariffs on imports, cut government subsidies to the agricultural and manufacturing sectors of the economy, end price ceilings on food, and slash government expenditures by one-third.

Although you may feel tempted to follow your first impulse and tell the IMF to stuff these requirements someplace, you know that this is not a realistic option.[1] If you decline to follow the IMF's advice, then Ecuador cannot get foreign loans. Without those loans, the country will face bankruptcy, leading to the loss of almost all foreign aid and all trade with other countries except for imports for which Ecuador can pay in a foreign currency such as dollars. As your country has few dollars, it can buy few imports.

---

*The International Monetary Fund is a consortium of central banks from the more industrialized countries. Through its affiliation with the United Nations, the IMF promotes worldwide monetary cooperation, currency stabilization, and expansion of trade.

Without food imports, segments of the population will go hungry. Without imported replacement parts for equipment, industry will face a dramatic decline in its manufacturing output. In short, without the IMF loans, Ecuador's entire economy will descend into chaos.

If you do what the IMF requires, however, Ecuador will suffer other hardships. First, the price of food for the urban population will increase by at least 100 percent. The urban poor in your country, the people primarily responsible for your election, will live even more impoverished lives than they knew before you took office. Second, importing low-cost food from other countries may destroy much of Ecuador's agricultural sector. This will throw many peasants out of work and into starvation. Third, cutting government spending by 33 percent will require you to fire large numbers of government workers and, perhaps, to reduce military expenditures. Government bureaucrats will fight this change by every means possible, knowing that they will not find enough jobs in the private sector. If you cut military spending, the military may even overthrow your government. In short, you are between a proverbial rock and a hard place. What would you do?

Almost every new leader in the less industrialized countries (LICs) faces this kind of trouble. Both elected and nonelected leaders come to power with the intent of industrializing their countries, reducing dependence on foreign aid, and improving economic performance. When they take office, however, they face seemingly impossible situations where any policy choice will have negative consequences.

The Current Situation in Most Third-World Countries

People in almost every LIC live under grim economic conditions. First, and most importantly, the people are poor. In 1990, more than 3 billion people in 43 countries had per-capita incomes below $610 per year. Compare that amount to what you spend each *month* for food, clothing, and shelter. Imagine what it would be like to live on $610 for an entire year. In addition to this terrible poverty, in a typical LIC, the labor force is unskilled, the financial system provides insufficient capital for investment, the economy depends on only one or two export products, limited social infrastructure provides weak support for daily life, and agricultural production employs inefficient methods. In addition, LICs typically labor under huge and inefficient government bureaucracies, entrenched policies that lead to inefficient allocation of resources, and immense inequalities between the wealthiest and poorest sectors of their societies. Finally, high birthrates create enormous demands upon scarce health and educational services so that the country must spend increasingly large sums of money just to provide the same services that it provided the previous year. Table 10.1 compares data on several key indicators of quality of life for low-income, middle-income, and high-income countries.

Why have so few countries developed economically while so many have not? Explanations of underdevelopment fall into three broad categories: (1) economic, (2) cultural, and (3) political. None of these explanations is adequate by itself to explain the successes and failures in economic development. Each interpretation identifies different variables as critical to the development process, and each proposes distinct policies that

TABLE 10.1

BASIC INDICATORS OF ECONOMIC DEVELOPMENT

	GNP		Inflation Rate	Life Expectancy	Adult Illiteracy (percent)	
	Per capita 1991	Growth 1980–1991	(percent) 1980–1991	(years) 1991	Female 1990	Total 1990
Low-income economies	$350US	3.9%	12.6	62	52	40
Upper-middle economies	$3,530US	0.6%	95.4	69	17	14
High-income economies	$21,530US	2.3%	4.3	77	5	4

Source: World Bank, *World Development Report 1993: Investing in Heath* (New York: Oxford University Press, 1993), pp. 238–239. Copyright © 1993 by The International Bank for Reconstruction and Development/The World Bank. Reprinted by permission of Oxford University Press, Inc.

governments should pursue in order to encourage development. Together, all three explanations promote understanding of both the breadth of problems that face the LICs and the uncertainty of economists, sociologists, anthropologists, political scientists, and policy makers about actions to foster economic progress.

Economic Explanations

Two sets of economic arguments attempt to explain the failure of LICs to develop. One theory, the neoliberal theory, is based largely on Adam Smith's belief in the superiority of the unrestrained marketplace in guiding economic activities. The theory contends that LICs can develop most effectively if governments intervene as little as possible in their economies. This theory contends that every country has a *comparative advantage* in production of some set of goods. If government stays out of the economy, then the market will provide the necessary price and profit signals to guide investment by local entrepreneurs to the sectors that represent the country's comparative economic advantage. The free-market orientation of the government will attract international capital and advanced technology into the country. The combination of local investment, international capital and technology, competition, and the profit incentive will maximize the country's economic efficiency. This entire process will lead to long-term economic growth, as Box 10.1 explains.

In this view, the movement of capital and the diffusion of technology from more industrialized countries (MICs) to less developed ones leads to modernization and industrialization. Progress will occur as savings and investment increase in response to the economic opportunities that the free market produces. Economic progress and free enterprise will lead to political democracy as a pluralistic economy encourages a pluralistic

BOX 10.1

The Law of Comparative Advantage

David Ricardo (see Chapter 2) developed the law of comparative advantage to explain why nations (or individuals) benefit from specializing in production of certain goods and then trading them without restriction. For example, assume that your parents assign you and your brother the tasks of mowing the grass, washing the car, and cleaning the house every weekend.

At first, you divide all of this work by weeks. One week you do all the chores; the next week your brother does them. Suppose that it takes you a total of 2 hours to mow the grass, $1/2$ hour to wash the car, and 3 hours to clean the house ($5^1/_2$ hours of labor). It takes your less efficient sibling $3^1/_2$ hours to mow the grass, 1 hour to wash the car, and 4 hours to clean the house ($8^1/_2$ hours of labor). In fact, however, you and your sibling could work fewer total hours if you were to mow the yard and wash the car every week while your sibling cleaned the house. You would end up working $2^1/_2$ hours each weekend (instead of $5^1/_2$ hours every other weekend) and your brother would work 4 hours per week (instead of $8^1/_2$ hours every 2 weeks).

In the absence of cooperation, you would average 2 hours and 45 minutes of work per weekend, and your brother would average 4 hours and 15 minutes. Through specialization you each gain 15 minutes of leisure each week.

David Ricardo explained the law of comparative advantage with an international example:

| **Labour Hours to Produce** | | |
	1 Gallon wine	**1 Yard cloth**
Portugal	80	90
England	120	100

Workers in Portugal produce both wine and cloth with less labor than workers in England. Nevertheless, each country will be better off if Portugal specializes in wine and England specializes in cloth. Without trade, people in Portugal pay more than the cost of 1 gallon of wine to buy 1 yard of cloth. (To produce 1 yard of cloth, Portugal must give up the production of $1^1/_8$ gallons of wine; as it takes workers 90 hours to produce either quantity of goods.) In England, however, 1 yard of cloth costs less than 1 gallon of wine, as workers there take more labor to produce a gallon of wine than to produce a yard of cloth.

Both countries benefit if England produces only cloth and Portugal produces only wine. Portugal can then trade 1 gallon of wine to England for 1 yard of cloth. For each gallon of wine traded, Portugal gains a surplus of 10 hours of labor to devote to the production of other goods, to the increased production of wine, or to leisure. (Workers there must spend 10 fewer hours to produce wine and trade it for cloth than they would spend to make the cloth itself.) Similarly, in the same exchange, England gains 20 hours of labor for each gallon of wine that it obtains from Portugal by trading cloth. (It gains the wine by spending only 100 hours to make cloth and then trading.)

polity.[2] The hypothetical IMF recommendations to Ecuador correspond closely to the policy proposals of neoliberal theory; the IMF strongly supports the free-market approach to economic development, and it attempts to force the leaders of LICs to accept the policies prescribed by this approach.

A second set of economic advancement principles stress the development of human capital. Studies of families in industrialized countries have demonstrated that families with fewer children invest more time and money in each one than do families with many children.[3] Also, investments in prenatal care, infant feeding, and pediatric public health pay rich dividends in developing countries.[4] Similarly, countries that target resources to education for comparatively high percentages of their populations generate the skills necessary to compete with more industrialized countries. Studies have found that expenditures for educating females are particularly critical for expanding economic growth.[5] A country gains a double advantage from such an emphasis on human capital. It simultaneously improves the lives of citizens and increases economic growth. In addition, this method gives a country control over many of the steps necessary to improve economic productivity.

DEPENDENCY THEORY

A third economic explanation for variations in industrialization comes from **dependency theory.** Dependency theory contends that free enterprise and the international market cannot solve problems with poverty in the LICs; they are the causes of this poverty. This theory explains that less industrialized countries remain underdeveloped because of the structure of the world economy.[6] Foreign capital does not help LICs develop. Rather, foreign corporations (usually referred to as *multinational corporations*) maintain their profits by holding down wages in the LICs. The multinationals do not reinvest their profits in the LICs; they send them back to the stockholders in the more industrialized countries. In addition, the multinationals form cartels to avoid competition, and these combinations prevent achievement of economic efficiency.[7]

In some versions of dependency theory, the first-world countries maintain their dominance because the multinational corporations form alliances with elites within the LICs and buy their loyalty. These elites then adopt policies that maintain both their own wealth and that of the multinational corporations. In return, the local elites receive the necessary income and foreign military support to maintain themselves in power.

The policy recommendations of dependency theory vary. Early dependency theorists saw the root of the problem in the fact that the LICs export raw materials and food while the more industrialized countries export manufactured goods such as machinery, automobiles, and computers. This trade pattern harms the LICs because the prices of raw materials fluctuate widely and do not rise as rapidly over time as those of manufactured goods. Also, increases in productivity due to new technologies do not affect production of raw materials as much as production of manufactured products. Because of this difference in the impact of technology, LICs will fall further behind the MICs; in the process, they will always experience wide price fluctuations in their export goods which will lead to economic crises.

For these reasons, according to dependency theory, the "comparative advantage" of the LICs in production of raw materials such as copper and agricultural products such as sugar and coffee becomes a comparative disadvantage. Ricardo argued that Adam Smith's invisible hand could become an invisible foot that would step on the aspirations of some people and lead to class conflict and unearned rents. In the same way, dependency theory argues that the economic laws of comparative advantage are a cruel hoax perpetrated by wealthy countries on poor ones.

To overcome this problem, economists who support dependency theory recommend that LIC governments follow policies of **import substitution.** This policy, developed by Argentine economist Raul Prebisch, requires that a government place high tariffs on imported manufactured goods and invest in the industrialization of its own country. The high tariffs protect industries in the country while the infusion of capital from the government develops these industries sufficiently to compete on the international market. Until that time, however, only goods produced in the country are available to domestic consumers.[8]

Import substitution policies have not generated long-term success for LICs for several reasons. The most important reason is that the protected status of the LIC industries reduces their incentive to improve efficiency. In addition, technological advances in the rest of the world leave the LIC industries with two equally bad options: They can depend upon foreign corporations for technology or develop their own. If the country chooses the first alternative, then it once again becomes dependent, and a large portion of its profits will leave the country. If the country attempts to develop its own technology, it will fall further behind the more industrialized countries. The existing advantages of technologically advanced industries fuel accelerating increases in productivity, allowing them to outpace the less technologically advanced industries of the third world.

A more radical version of dependency theory, sometimes referred to as **world systems theory,** contends that the international economic system represents a class struggle between the dependent LICs and the dominant capitalist class located in the MICs. This capitalist class has conspired, according to the theory, to keep the LICs in poverty. In this view, the world is divided into the states of the **core** (also referred to as the **North**) and those of the **periphery** (also referred to as the **South**).[†] The more industrialized

---

[†] The terms *North* and *South* stem from the locations of most of the core nations in the northern hemisphere, while the vast majority of the periphery nations are in the southern hemisphere.

countries form the core; the less industrialized countries constitute the periphery. Multinational corporations from the core invade the periphery, quieting resistance by promising capital, technology, and growth. Rather than keeping their promises, however, the multinationals exploit the periphery. Using the puppet governments of domestic elites, the core countries maintain economic and political dominance.

The proponents of world systems theory argue that the solution requires a **new international economic order.** This new order would redistribute wealth from the core to the periphery, radically restructuring the world's economic system and improving equity among nations.[9] The core nations have a moral obligation, the theory asserts, to provide debt relief and increase economic development assistance to the nations of the periphery. The new international economic order would revise the international trading system by providing needed goods to the nations of the periphery on more favorable terms.[10]

Decision makers in LICs encounter difficulties with both the free-market and world systems theories of development. The free-market theory conveniently neglects the substantial disadvantages to third-world countries of policies set in first-world countries. While governments in the United States, Europe, and Japan preach free trade, they subsidize their own agricultural and industrial sectors. The U.S. government provides billions of dollars in subsidies to the producers of agricultural products from sugar and honey to tobacco and peanuts. Along with these subsidies, it also places quotas on imports of sugar, beef, tobacco, and numerous other goods. Similarly, France, Switzerland, Japan, and most other first-world countries protect their farmers with both subsidies and tariffs. Japan subsidizes research and development in many industries, and it places substantial barriers in the way of foreign interests that want to sell their products in Japan. The British and French heavily subsidize their aviation industries, while the United States provides indirect subsidies to aircraft manufacturers through defense development contracts. In short, while the IMF prescribes free markets for the nations of the South, it allows the nations of the North to engage in practices and policies that substantially undermine the promised worldwide free market.

Under the class-based world systems theory the LICs cannot escape their place in the international economic system through their own efforts. The policy prescription of this theory requires the core nations to admit their past and present wrongdoings and make restitution to the countries in the periphery by giving them money and technology. The industrialized countries that agreed, however would harm the interests of their own citizens. Can you imagine a presidential candidate in the United States or a party leader in Japan campaigning to reduce domestic economic well-being in order to improve the lives of people in other countries? Would the U.S. growers of sugarcane and beets voluntarily give up their subsidies and go out of business so that the Dominican Republic and Cuba could have an increased share of the sugar market? Would IBM and Digital Computer provide their technology to third-world countries free of charge?

A more import problem arises because world systems theory cannot explain why the newly industrialized countries (NICs) of South Korea, Taiwan, and Singapore have achieved such rapid development. World systems theory predicts that no LIC will ever overcome the international economic system that exploits it.

Cultural Explanations

Elites and intellectuals in the LICs typically blame the international economic system for weak economic development in their countries. Elites in the more industrialized countries often blame the cultures and policies of the LICs. Beginning in the 1960s, a popular explanation for the failure of development in the LICs faulted their "traditional" rather than "modern" cultural values and attitudes.[11]

Every society has a culture—a set of norms, institutions, attitudes, values, behaviors, and customs. Monte Palmer writes that each culture accomplishes three social tasks:

1. It explains and sanctifies established social, economic, and political relationships.

2. It prescribes desirable values and behaviors and identifies right and wrong.

3. It prescribes how to handle such events and institutions as marriage, child rearing, death, and interpersonal conflict.[12]

According to cultural explanations of underdevelopment, "modern" values stress saving, investment, risk taking, achievement, acceptance of change, reverence for science, belief in democracy,* and personal identification with the nation and its progress. Cultural explanations may also cite the treatment of women in society; the inferior position of women in many LICs, these theories note, encourages high birthrates and low per-capita investment in children. In contrast to modern cultures, traditional cultures rely on superstition and fatalism. Instead of encouraging saving and investing, traditional cultures favor spending on feasts and celebrations. Traditional people make hiring decisions based on family, tribe, or friendship ties rather than merit. A market economy requires that people interact with others outside their immediate circles of acquaintances; traditional people do not trust strangers enough to do this. Instead of viewing work positively, traditional cultures often have negative attitudes toward work, especially manual labor. Rather than studying science, engineering, or business, university students in less industrialized countries study subjects that contribute less to social development like social science, law, and philosophy.[13] Graduates of higher education do not go into business and use their education to increase the productivity of the country. Instead, they expect to take jobs in government bureaucracies.

The prevailing cultures in LICs represent adaptations to poverty and the impossible lives of poor people in these countries, according to cultural explanations. Why should people save when they have barely enough to survive? Why invest if they have too little wealth to expect any dividends? Why take risks when they live so close to starvation that a failure may mean death? Why welcome change when people like them have suffered the same fate for 100 years? Since traditional attitudes represent rational adaptations to unchanging prospects for harsh lives that cannot get better, they do not nurture the changes necessary for people to break with traditions, take risks, and believe that their actions can improve their lives and the lives of those around them.

Proponents of cultural theories of modernization also contend that the political culture affects the type of regime in a country. Ronald Inglehart has argued that, "[C]ertain

---

* A belief that life chances should not be determined by birth.

societies are characterized relatively strongly by a durable set of orientations that roughly respond to the 'civic culture' . . . and this cultural pattern shows a strong empirical link-age with stable democracy even when I control for related aspects of social structure and economic development."[14] Several scholars agree, contending, for example, that Latin America has not developed stable democracies because it inherited an antidemocratic culture from Spain. This culture is Catholic, corporate, stratified, authoritarian, hierar-chical, patrimonialist, and semifeudal to its core.[15]

Recent writings concerning the role of culture in economic development suggest that the Confucian culture has promoted the development of the NICs of South Korea, Taiwan, Singapore, and Hong Kong.[16] Confucianism teaches that all members of a well-ordered society should work to make the society a better place to live for all its members. Individuals who work harder for their community gain higher status. In addition, the Confucian ethic stresses respect for authority and social harmony.[17] Political scientist Harmon Zeigler argues that the Confucian emphasis on achievement and merit encourages economic progress, while the values of the good of the community and respect for au-thority reduce corruption and create the stability and trust necessary for investment.

The theories that stress culture, attitudes, and values as independent variables in ex-planations of economic development lead to sweeping policy recommendations. The governments in LICs must socialize their populations to accept more modern values. Progressive elites must force value changes to create attitudes favorable toward merit, trust, and risk taking. Schools, military training, and government programs must spread the right values. Palmer refers to this process of breaking down traditional values and replacing them with more modern ones as "disintegration and reintegration."[18]

Like the economic explanations of underdevelopment, cultural theories have signif-icant practical, theoretical, and empirical problems. If culture is the one critical indepen-dent variable in the process of economic and political development, then an LIC that lacks the right cultural values faces a hopeless situation. Changing an entire culture is an almost impossible task. How could a leader convince elites to encourage policies that would eliminate their own privileges by changing the attitudes, values, and norms that supported their elite status? If behavioral patterns and attitudes reflect the culture, and cul-ture dominates all aspects of life and society, where could the change process begin? Even if elites do want to change the culture of their society, an LIC government rarely has the organization necessary to do this. Even when the regime is willing to apply the full co-ercive power of the state to make the cultural change, the effort generally fails. Mao at-tempted to erase Confucianism from China during the Cultural Revolution (1966–1976), and the Khmer Rouge tried to remake the culture of the people of Kampuchea (formerly known as Cambodia); both ended in disaster and death. Ultimately, the Cultural Revo-lution failed, and, when Mao died, the leaders of this program were arrested.[19] Simi-larly, the new society of the Khmer Rouge led to wholesale murder, economic disaster, and the collapse of the government.

An attempt to treat culture, values, and attitudes as the critical *independent* variables in the process of development faces another, more theoretical problem: These variables may be the *dependent* variables. In other words, changes in the social environment may create changes in the culture more rapidly than changes in the culture alter the environ-ment. Research concerning modern attitudes has found that the best predictors of these

BOX 10.2

Why the Israelites Worshipped Bael and Why Athletes Wear Dirty Socks

Discussions of the cultural differences between less industrialized countries and more developed ones often draw a false dichotomy between the two sets of cultures. In reality, all cultures exhibit both traditional and modern traits. So-called "modern" people still appeal to god or fate to intervene in their lives, just as "traditional" people do.

Many know only as much about traditional societies as they have read in biblical stories about the Hebrews. From these stories, the authors have always wondered why the Hebrews kept returning to worship the god Bael despite witnessing all the miracles that Yahweh performed.

The answer may lie in the fact that prior to their arrival in the Promised Land, the Hebrews were nomadic herders. They had to make the transition to an agricultural society. Imagine yourself in the position of a nomad trying to learn how to farm. You observe your neighbors, the Moabites or the Philistines, planting their crops. You plant yours. Theirs grow; yours do not. In explanation, your neighbors explain that they worship Bael, the god who takes care of crops, while you worship Yahweh, a god who prefers those who raise sheep and goats.* As an afterthought, they also show you how deep to plant your seeds and how frequently to water and weed the crops. Sure enough, you worship Bael, and your crops grow.

In any society that asks a god to bless the land, to bring the rains, and to prevent plagues, people assume without question that divine actions cause one set of crops to grow and another to fail. If events, whether good or bad, simply represent god's will, then people develop fatalistic attitudes. Their most important actions center not on trying new agricultural techniques, but on placating the appropriate gods with worship and sacrifices.

How different are modern people? Farmers who know more about horticulture still pray for rain or sun, depending on their needs. A basketball player wears the same set of socks she was wearing during her best game in the hopes that the socks will bring more magic. Fans at sporting events frequently pray for miracle finishes, and baseball teams wear "rally caps" to encourage fate to intervene on their behalf. Sick people continue to ask a god to heal them when medicine fails or at least to give medicine a helping hand. One of the authors vividly remembers clutching the radio and asking Oral Roberts to intercede with his god to relieve the pain of the author's first hangover.

Obviously, superstitious and fatalistic behaviors occur in all societies. As people better understand and control the factors that influence outcomes, such as crop yields, they depend less upon fate. Given the lack of scientific knowledge in most traditional societies, particularly in agricultural methods, requests for divine intervention and acceptance of bad luck are simply rational responses to an environment over which the farmer has little control.

---

*See Gen. 4: 2–5 for a discussion of Yahweh's preference for keepers of sheep over tillers of soil.

attitudes are the amount of time an individual has lived in an urban area and whether or not he has worked in a factory or other modern setting.[20] This finding suggests that living and working in a setting that requires modern behavior leads to changes in attitudes, values, and, ultimately, culture.

Imagine for a moment that you are no longer the president of Ecuador; now you are a peasant who has been thrown off of your land. You are forced to leave the countryside and move to the city to find work. You arrive with traditional attitudes toward time and interactions with strangers. You are fortunate and land a job in a factory, but you lose that job because you keep coming to work late. In your next job, however, you arrive on time because experience has taught you that city people do not measure time by the sun or by seasons; they measure it by minutes and hours. To keep your job, you too must measure time in this way. Ultimately, you will come to realize that a factory's assembly line requires that workers start and end work at the same time. This understanding, combined with your forced change in behavior, is likely to change your traditional attitude toward time. In the same way, your new situation may also alter your attitudes toward interacting with strangers. Because you can call on no family members, only strangers can provide assistance, advice, or companionship. If these interactions succeed, then you have a much higher probability of learning to trust people who are not family members.

Changing an individual's environment is likely to alter her values and behaviors, even in the central areas of religion and superstition. The strength of religious conviction depends, to some degree, on the region of the country in which a person lives. In the United States, people raised in the South or Midwest are, on average, more religious than those raised in the Northeast and the West. If you were raised as a fundamentalist Christian, the likelihood that you will continue with that set of beliefs will depend upon your life experiences. The probability that you will change your beliefs about dancing, card playing, cursing, and premarital sex depends upon whether you attend a bible college or a large state university. Similarly, if a member of your family were to die in a car accident after the seat belt failed, you might attribute the death to God's will or to mechanical failure depending upon your religious beliefs. However, a lawyer might call and tell you that you can sue the automobile manufacturer for $1 million; this event could encourage you to blame God less and the automaker more. (See Box 10.2.)

In reality, causal relationships are reciprocal. Culture influences the social environment, and the social environment changes culture. The environment affects behavior, and behavior affects the environment. Values and beliefs influence how people perceive their environment, and changes in the environment alter values and beliefs. In short, culture is constantly changing. For this reason, although broad cultural values such as Confucianism, Hinduism, or Catholicism may well assist or inhibit development, the absence of modern values does not constitute an insuperable barrier to economic progress.

Political Explanations

Political variables inspire the third set of explanations for uneven economic development in the LICs. These interpretations of the causes of economic progress contend that countries develop more rapidly when political leaders, institutions, and policies promote economic growth. Scholars who emphasize the influence of political factors generally identify three specific variables: the level of government control over the economy, the level of corruption, and the stability of the government.

GOVERNMENT CONTROL OVER THE ECONOMY

U.S. citizens may have difficulty imagining how actively the state influences the economic system of a less industrialized country. In the United States, tens of thousands of different investors and entrepreneurs simultaneously decide where to invest, how much to produce, and what price to charge; in most LICs, however, government representatives dominate these decisions. In more industrialized countries, capital markets such as the Tokyo Stock Exchange allow capital to move relatively easily from one firm to another. If you expect your Mitsubishi stock to decline in value, you can call your broker and move your capital out of Mitsubishi and into another stock. In most LICs, state decisions dominate the capital markets. An LIC government borrows money from international lenders such as the IMF. It then decides which enterprises will receive investment capital, which will receive subsidies or tariff protection, and whether to allow foreign interests to own firms in a particular industry. LIC governments often implement centralized plans that dictate what goods their countries produce, what prices consumers pay for goods, and how much their countries save for investment. Why are LIC governments so intimately involved in their economies?

Most nations in Asia and Africa became independent in the 1960s and 1970s. Prior to independence, the colonial government of such a country allowed the bureaucracy to determine what goods the country would produce for export, what goods it would import, what crops farmers would grow, and what goods and resources local people could buy and sell. When these countries gained their independence, the new leaders inherited this model of government control over the economy. The new leaders also inherited the perception that economic decisions are too important to be left to vagaries of the market or the whims of individual producers and consumers.

Political elites in the LICs see economic development as their major responsibility, and they doubt that giving up control will promote this goal. In addition, political elites believe that central planning will lead more rapidly than free-market chaos to desired development. Worldwide, 50 LICs did not obtain independence from colonial rulers until 1960 or later. After their countries gained independence, numerous leaders wanted to match the rapid industrialization, economic growth, and rise in international stature of the Soviet Union after the 1917 revolution. They tried to copy Stalin's single-party dictatorship in which economic planners allocated scarce resources, considering it the best strategy to achieve rapid industrialization. Rather than allowing citizens to squander money on consumer goods such as imported automobiles, leaders wanted to invest as many national resources as possible in building their industrial bases.

To achieve industrialization, a country must generate an economic surplus and invest that surplus in economic activities that support industrial production. The Soviet Union changed from a nonindustrialized nation to a world industrial leader in a relatively short period by using the government's coercive force to extract a surplus from its own population, particularly the agricultural sector, and then investing that surplus under the guidance of government economic planners. Stalin did not depend on IMF loans, so he did not have to follow IMF instructions. In addition, during the 1960s and 1970s, centrally planned economic systems reported economic growth rates as high as or higher than those of free-market systems.

The model of a centrally planned economy run by a single political party makes sense to LIC elites because their countries often suffer from shortages of trained personnel. In many places, colonial rulers actively repressed educational aspirations of indigenous populations. For example, when the Republic of Chad gained its independence from France in 1960, eight members of the indigenous population had attended college. While other countries were not in such difficult situations, they also could call on only scant technical and entrepreneurial talent after independence. LIC elites argued that political and economic competition would waste scarce human resources. They preferred to unite the efforts of educated and talented citizens, and they asserted that the state must plan effective use of available human resources, just as it planned use of other resources. LIC elites also tend to prefer a centrally planned economy because they doubt the value of any kind of competition to a good society. As Chapters 3 and 4 demonstrated, many cultures, ideologies, and religions expect more benefits from cooperation among elites than from competition.

The problems of centrally planned economies are much more obvious today than they were in earlier decades, as the economic and political systems of the Soviet Union and eastern European countries have failed. Even prior to the fall of the Soviet Union, however, economists who specialized in economic development were arguing that the LICs face one of their greatest difficulties in the inability of central governments to coordinate programs and ensure timely delivery of materials and services. Development economist Dennis Rondinelli studied more than 200 African development projects and identified the single, biggest obstacle to their success: the inability of central governments to organize and run them.[21] Demand for education, expertise, communication, and all the other requirements for effective central planning far exceeded the supply of those resources. Michael Todaro writes that perhaps the most binding constraint on economic progress in the LICs is administrative and managerial capability. This is perhaps the single scarcest resource in the developing world.[22]

To understand the monumental tasks facing bureaucrats in a centrally planned economy, consider the responsibilities of the Soviet Union's government planners prior to the dissolution of that state. The planners had to set the prices of between 20,000 and 30,000 goods.[23] Firms relied on correct prices to carry out their own efficient production of goods and services. For example, if the planners set the price of steel too low, then the steel mills had insufficient income to purchase the raw materials they needed to produce the steel; at the same time, demand for steel soared, far outpacing supply. If they set the price of steel too high, however, then the factories that needed steel to produce their products could not buy enough of it. Prices and profits in a planned economy do not tell planners about the efficiency of a particular firm or factory, because they cannot compare it against competitors. If a steel mill in the Soviet Union produced goods worth 1 million more rubles than it spent to make the goods, what does this mean? Did the mill do its job well, or did planners set an excessively high price for steel?

Some observers may doubt the importance of correct prices. In fact, however, economic development requires that the costs of goods and services in a society must

accurately reflect their value in a free market. The World Bank found a correlation of −0.48 between the level of distortion of prices in a society (measured as deviations from the prices that would occur in a free market) and the level of economic growth.‡ The correlation between the rate of savings and the rate of economic growth is only 0.24! No one denies that a society must save to accumulate resources that it can invest, yet the association of that variable with economic growth is only half as strong as the correlation between price distortion and growth.[24]

GOVERNMENT CORRUPTION

Corruption by public officials constitutes a serious problem in every country. This problem is particularly serious, however, in most LICs. Corruption is so pervasive in some LICs that the languages include special terms for bribes demanded by public officials. These include *la mordida* (the bite), *baksheesh* (something given), and *chai* (tea). Anyone doing business with bureaucrats, judicial officers, or the police in such a country must provide these bribes to get needed services. For example, a citizen may have to bribe a bureaucrat to get the necessary papers for a car license, registration records to enroll a child in school, or a permit to open a new business.

Harmon Zeigler attempts to distinguish between relatively petty graft and "destructive graft" that makes economic and political development almost impossible to achieve.[25] Graft becomes destructive, Zeigler contends, when elites use their political power primarily to enhance their personal wealth. Recall the discussion in Chapter 6 of the Somoza family in Nicaragua. In Mexico, President Lopez Portillo (1976–1982) appears to have used his position to become $3 billion wealthier during his 6-year term.[26] The relatives of the Shah of Iran stole $3.4 billion in 1978, an amount equal to 25 percent of

---

‡ Remember that a negative correlation, such as −0.48, means that a higher level of price distortion is associated with a lower rate of economic growth. See the discussion of correlation in Chapter 8.

Iran's oil revenue. The head of the national oil company stole an additional $60 million, and a cabinet minister took $40 million more.[27] President Ferdinand Marcos stole $10 billion from the Philippines! In countries such as Nigeria, Colombia, Uganda, Bangladesh, Zaire, and El Salvador, political office represents the path to economic success, because political elites use their power to steal economic wealth from their countries and stash it in Swiss or American banks.

Bribery and graft pervade the Mexican political system. This bribery is not limited to petty theft by a police officer, who might take the license plate from a car because of a parking or traffic violation and return it only after the violator pays the "fine" directly to the officer. The graft that debilitates the Mexican economy, according to Alan Riding, is a combination of bribery, drugs, and the use of the police to break rather than enforce the laws.§ This combination has led to political institutions that destroy rather than build the Mexican economy.[28]

GOVERNMENT INSTABILITY

Because the state plays such an important economic role, many political scientists and economists believe that political stability is essential to economic development. At any given time, however, approximately one-third of the governments of the world's LICs are fighting rebellions within their borders, and other countries are subject to frequent coups d'état.‖[29] This kind of political instability reduces the willingness of foreign investors to finance new industry, and it leads the citizens of the LICs to place their savings in more industrialized countries with stable political institutions. Various estimates of this movement of capital out of the LICs indicate that if their own citizens kept their savings within their own countries, then the average country's foreign debt would be less than 30 percent of the current amount.[30]

One of the major reasons for political instability in less industrialized countries is the extreme and violent character of the divisions between political opponents as compared to those in industrial democracies. If an opposition party takes control of the government when divisions are intense, the losers suffer substantial harm. If a leftist government gains power, the landed elites may fear the **expropriation** of their land for redistribution among peasants. Foreign interests may also fear governmental expropriation of their property. At the same time, military leaders may believe that a leftist government will create and arm a people's militia to counterbalance the army's coercive force. On the other hand, if a rightist government wins the election, labor unions may worry that its actions

---

§ Before condemning Mexican officials, we should remember that bribery pervades the U.S. government, as well. During a trip to Mexico, one of the authors twice had to pay local *policia* to get his U.S. license plate returned. On the same trip, during a stop in Albuquerque, N.M., the same author's out-of-state license plate attracted the attention of a traffic officer, and he had to bargain directly with the officer and the justice of the peace over the size of a fine. In neither case did the author receive a citation. While this helped his insurance rates, it is highly doubtful that the fine ever reached the treasury of the beautiful state of New Mexico. More seriously, police in numerous cities throughout the United States have been prosecuted for extorting money from drug dealers.

‖ In a coup d'état, one elite takes power by force from another elite. Usually this seizure of power involves the armed forces.

BOX 10.3

The Ultimate Kleptocrat: Mobuto Sese Seko

Although Ferdinand Marcos of the Philippines probably stole more money from his country than any other kleptocrat, the president of Zaire, Mobutu Sese Seko, appears to have achieved the most efficient pillage of his country's wealth. Harmon Zeigler reports that Zaire "loses" about 60 percent of all government revenue. Of this amount, President Mobutu controls about one-fourth for his personal use, and another 30 percent goes through the office of the presidency without any budgetary control. The president of a country with a per-capita GNP of less than $200 per year, Mobutu is reported to have a personal fortune of $10 billion. He controls and distributes all government offices, revenue, and promotions. His personal holding company employs 25,000 people.

No one can accurately measure the economic effects of Mobutu's theft, as many factors contribute to a country's economic performance. From 1968 to 1986, however, Zaire's average GNP growth was −2.2 percent, the second-worst performance in the world.

Source: Harmon Zeigler, *The Political Community: A Comparative Introduction to Political Systems and Society* (New York: Longman, 1990), p. 209.

will outlaw unions and deal violently with striking workers. Peasants may fear that the new government will oust them from their lands and return them to the old elites. The opposition may expect to be arrested and tortured. Certainly, most LIC opposition leaders doubt that they will soon be able to compete in a fair and free election.

Those who see political factors as critical elements in the process of economic development recommend varying policies, depending upon their opinion of the most serious impediment to economic progress. Those who see too much government intervention in the economy or too much centralization of authority recommend that the government loosen its grip on the economy. In this respect, their proposals match those of the advocates of neoliberal theories about economic development. In addition, politically oriented critics recommend decentralizing development programs. Instead of relying on the central bureaucracy in the capital city to plan, coordinate, and implement programs such as education, health care, and agricultural projects, development economists advocate launching decentralized projects that depend upon local leadership, local funding, and local control.[31] Often these same people also call for increased use of price information to assist planners in measuring demand and to help pay for the project or service.[32]

Corruption is much more difficult to control than government interference. While corruption plagues all countries and all governments, prevailing social and cultural norms in most industrialized countries restrain it. Few mothers in industrialized countries talk proudly of "My son the thief." In many LICs, however, social norms encourage rather than inhibit acceptance of bribes. Robert Price contends that families of public officials in Ghana view those offices as valuable possessions to be used to benefit their families. He writes:

> Giving aid and showing generosity to one's relatives and others to whom one has a personal tie is a primary social virtue. . . . From the vantage point of the civil servant, not only does his position within the extended family depend upon his full exploitation of the resources of his office, but how well he does for his family will also greatly affect his standing in the larger community.[33]

In this situation, the son who takes bribes and gives out favors is not a despised thief, but a noble defender of the family. The discussion later in this chapter of political institutions will explain the beliefs of some observers that ideological political parties or military rule would reduce corruption.

Efforts to achieve government stability may prove even more difficult than measures to prevent corruption. No regime desires its own demise, particularly through violent means. Presumably, every government tries to preserve the stability of the state. Yet, later discussion will confirm that few LICs have been able to retain stable governments for long periods of time. Communist regimes have the best record for maintaining themselves in power, but they have accomplished this feat only through totalitarian coercion and control.

Regime Types and Development

Students of life in less industrialized countries often wonder what form of government most effectively promotes economic development—totalitarian, authoritarian, or democratic? Different scholars argue for each. Totalitarian governments may effectively mobilize their populations and coerce them to produce the surplus that becomes savings, which in turn fuel investment. Authoritarian governments may assure political stability and willingly make the hard political choices necessary to achieve long-term growth. Finally, democratic governments may discover their mistakes quickly as opposition parties and competing candidates identify them. In addition, a democratic polity may encourage the decentralized economic system favored by economists.

Whatever the form of government, three institutions—political parties, the military, and the bureaucracy—play major roles in determining how effectively the political system functions in a less industrialized country. Political parties can provide a foundation for mass support of government decisions, assist in national integration, mobilize resources, and restrain corruption and erratic behavior by political leaders.[34] The military ultimately decides whether the existing regime will remain in power. Its leaders can also engage in nation-building activities such as educating recruits; integrating various regional, tribal, and ethnic groups into a single, national organization; and assisting in development projects such as supplying potable water. Finally, the bureaucracy is the largest employer of educated people in a typical LIC. In every country, the skill, corruption, commitment to the political system, and orientation toward economic development of the bureaucracy affect capabilities for both political and economic development. The bureaucracy must ultimately implement and maintain the development goals that LIC leaders choose; also, as discussed earlier, the bureaucracy plays a central role in choosing economic priorities and investing capital.

TOTALITARIAN GOVERNMENTS AND ECONOMIC GROWTH

Totalitarian governments are rare in less industrialized countries because these regimes lack sufficient technological capacity and bureaucratic efficiency to spread government control to all aspects of the society. Recall how the rapid industrialization of the Soviet Union attracted many LIC elites to the Soviet model. Like all totalitarian regimes, Soviet leaders used a single political party to control and direct the military and the bureaucracy. Ultimately, of course, the Soviet political and economic system disintegrated for reasons that scholars do not yet understand. Was the economic collapse inevitable because central planning could not manage a modern economy, or did political reasons cause the fall?

Currently, the only states that come close to the totalitarian model are China, North Korea, Albania, and Cuba. Using the organization of the Communist Party, each country's government attempts to control almost every aspect of life and to penetrate every institution from the military to the family. Unfortunately, observers cannot judge their economic performance because people outside the political elites have no access to accurate data. The statistics that these governments provide concerning changes in GNP, literacy, infant mortality, and life expectancy may bear no relationship to the truth. Scholars can confidently state, however, that China's Great Leap Forward (1958–1960) and Cultural Revolution (1966–1976) did not achieve either their economic or political goals. On the other hand, China is certainly a world military power, and it is becoming a world power in science.

Clearly, the levels of adult literacy and life expectancy in China and Cuba are much higher than those in other countries with comparable GNPs. However, observers may gain insight by comparing Albania to the noncommunist countries around it, Cuba to countries in Latin America at similar stages of development when Castro took control, and North Korea to South Korea. These exercises suggest that totalitarian governments are not the most effective agents of economic modernization.

AUTHORITARIAN GOVERNMENTS AND DEVELOPMENT

Authoritarian governments rule in most LICs. A large number of these governments are those of stationary bandits with short time horizons. The likelihood of either economic or political development in these countries is small, as the political elites use their positions to extract wealth from their countries rather than to make their countries wealthier. (See Box 10.3 for an egregious example of a stationary bandit.)

Although stationary bandits frequently rule authoritarian governments in LICs, some authoritarian governments do devote their energies to achieving economic development. This section will briefly examine three types of authoritarian regimes: charismatic leadership, military rule, and single-party domination. In reality, these three types frequently overlap. Many charismatic leaders come to power through military coups or successful revolutions and then establish single-party regimes with themselves in control of the parties. Similarly, a military coup may lead to a nominally civilian government in which the leader of the coup establishes a political party to institutionalize power and mobilize resources.

CHARISMATIC LEADERSHIP

Perhaps the most interesting figures in politics, charismatic leaders are particularly likely to rise to power in LICs. To complete a swift modernization program, a society must undergo fundamental changes in its social, economic, and political structures. These radical alterations in the lives of citizens lead them to look for hope and guidance, for someone with whom they can identify and in whom they can trust. In such situations, individuals who can satisfy these needs often assert their personalities to become national leaders.[35] This development creates a **charismatic leader.** In the first attempt to explain charismatic leadership, sociologist Max Weber wrote that the authority of such a leader rests on the people's "devotion to the specific and exceptional sanctity, heroism, or exemplary character of an individual person. . . ."[36]

Often the charismatic leader comes to power as a leader in an independence movement. Gandhi of India, Nkrumah of Ghana, Nasser of Egypt, and Mao of China were all charismatic leaders who played key roles in helping their countries achieve independence from colonial rule. Still, charismatic leaders need not be among the founders of a nation. Fidel Castro in Cuba and Kemel Atatürk in Turkey took control of long-established nations.

Every charismatic leader, however, demonstrates strength to the masses. Nasser evicted the British from Egypt, nationalized the Suez Canal, and thwarted an invasion of Egypt by Britain, France, and Israel. Castro began with only a few soldiers and defeated the American-trained Cuban army. He then defied the United States and nationalized numerous properties belonging to U.S. citizens. Mao led legendary armed struggles against the Japanese and Nationalist Chinese armies. Although charismatic leaders demonstrate strength most commonly through military exploits and images, some have found other ways. Gandhi demonstrated his strength through civil disobedience and moral courage. The Ayatollah Khomeini used his strength as a religious leader to gain control over Iran.

As an agent of economic development, charismatic leadership has advantages and disadvantages. Because the people identify with the charismatic leader, she can use her personal status to help create a nation where one did not exist. This is particularly likely in a country where national boundaries reflect a colonial ruler's administrative decisions rather than the natural limits of a common language or culture. At the time of its independence, India encompassed hundreds of dialects and multiple ethnic and religious groups. Gandhi's demonstration of strength of character and the people's belief in his integrity allowed him to begin building a nation from these diverse elements. Kwame Nkrumah became the president of Ghana and then assumed chiefly titles to all the major tribes within the new nation.[37]

The charismatic leader is in a good position to advocate the adoption of modern values and behaviors. As Palmer has written:

> Political leaders must "sell" development to the masses, persuading their subjects to strive and sacrifice for the sake of development and to set aside traditional values that stand in opposition to economic modernization. They must persuade their subjects to walk away from centuries of debilitating ethnic and religious conflict and to be tolerant and patient.[38]

A charismatic leader is in an ideal position to sell modernization because the public believes that she knows what to do in difficult and stress-filled times. The charismatic leader can also serve as a role model for citizens. Through personal behavior, this leader can show the masses what a citizen of the nation should be.

A charismatic leader generally creates a political party to support continuing rule. Gandhi created the Congress Party of India, Mao developed the Communist Party of China, and Nkrumah established the Convention Peoples' Party of Ghana. The charismatic leader uses the party to mobilize mass support for government programs and to control the bureaucracy and the military. Because so many charismatic leaders in the third world come from the ranks of military leaders, they often draw initial support from their countries' armed forces. As long as military leaders continue to accept the charismatic leader as the legitimate ruler of the state, they are unlikely to challenge the regime's authority. In addition, a charismatic leader who is the first leader of the country or who achieves power through a revolution can build a bureaucracy with personal loyalty to her. In summary, the charismatic leader often has the opportunity to form and control all three major modernizing institutions.

The advantages of charismatic leadership rest on the strength of the leader's personality and identification with the nation. Similarly, the disadvantages of charismatic leadership stem from the highly individual nature of the leader's authority. Unfulfilled promises, government errors, and economic downturns seriously threaten charismatic leadership. Such events make the leader appear more like a normal human than a national savior. To complete the perilous task of economic development, the leader must make difficult choices that will dissatisfy some citizens; also, even a successful program will suffer economic setbacks. Over the long term, events invariably will undermine the leader's charismatic authority.

The extreme dependence of national authority on a single person creates difficulties in the development process. Even a hero can work only 24 hours in the day. If the leader's decisions alone are considered legitimate, then the task of governing will exceed one person's capabilities. The leader must extend the people's loyalty to political institutions so that the party, regime, and state can make legitimate decisions.

Other common disadvantages of charismatic leadership include unwillingness of the leader to give up power peacefully and obstacles to any peaceful transition from one head of state to another. Charismatic leaders such as Kwame Nkrumah, Idi Amin, Muammar al Qaddafi, Fidel Castro, Adolf Hitler, and Juan Peron employed huge security forces to prevent organized opposition, and they used murder, torture, and exile to eliminate actual and potential opponents. Whether the leader dies of natural causes or flees to escape a coup, charismatic leadership presents a severe transition problem. If the leader did not transfer legitimacy to the country's political institutions while in power, then citizens probably will not accept the legitimacy of new leaders. If political opponents forcefully deposed the leader with her charisma intact, then members of the public who continue to identify with her will refuse allegiance to the "illegitimate" new regime.

Charismatic leaders have compiled a mixed overall record in economic development. Many charismatic leaders in LICs have established extensive health and education programs for their citizens. On the other hand, none of the newly industrialized countries achieved its rapid development through charismatic leadership. LICs headed by charismatic leaders have posted lower rates of growth in gross national product than LICs without such leaders. This simple test is not a fair one, however. Charismatic leaders have often taken over countries just as they achieved independence or just after revolutions, situations that always limit economic growth. In other countries, such as China and Cuba, governments have consciously assigned lower priorities to rates of economic growth than to measures of economic equality.

MILITARY REGIMES

For most of the time since 1946, military governments have ruled most LICs.[39] In any given year, military leaders in many LICs attempt to overthrow their countries' existing governments, and a number of these coups always succeed. Despite the universal acceptance of democracy as the most legitimate form of government, either direct military rule or a nominal civilian ruler established by the armed forces is the most common type of government in the LICs.

Probably the major reason for frequent military intervention is its simplicity. Military coups occur regularly in third-world countries because generals expect little opposition from weak political leaders and institutions that lack legitimacy. A country's armed forces can easily control finance, industry, and communication concentrated in only one or two cities; and the military also enjoys an overwhelming advantage over any potential rivals in both organization and coercive power. In addition, civilian governments frequently call on military power to deal with internal threats rather than external ones, so military leaders become accustomed to political battles. Finally, existing regimes often fail to achieve economic growth and control the rampant corruption of the bureaucracy, so military leaders come to believe that they could more effectively foster economic development.

Theoretically, military officers may be in a better position than civilian regimes to assist economic development. Morris Janowitz provides three justifications for this belief. First, the military practices more modern values; military personnel are more nationalistic, more disciplined, and more likely to reward performance than kinship or tribal connections. Second, because military regimes do not have to worry about winning elections, they may be able to make the difficult decisions necessary for long-term economic progress. Finally, military leaders possess the coercive ability to enforce their decisions.[40] Unfortunately, only the ability to apply coercive force has moved from theoretical possibility to empirical reality. Empirical analyses show that military regimes do no better and no worse than civilian regimes in bringing about economic progress.[41]

The development records of military governments resemble those of civilian governments because they face the same problems. While one might expect less corruption in the military, no evidence supports this hypothesis. Large, hierarchical, centralized bureaucracies face structurally similar problems whether the bureaucrats are civilians or soldiers. The many scandals in defense procurement in the United States and the extremely bureaucratic structure of the Department of Defense confirm that military officers may be more likely rather than less likely to tolerate corruption and senseless red tape.

Several political scientists have more favorable views of potential and actual contributions of the military to the modernization process. These scholars contend that if military leaders participate in a revolutionary movement, then a country will gain the expected advantages of military rule.[42] They hypothesize that revolutionary soldiers are more likely to commit themselves to the cause of development and to sacrifice for it. Unfortunately, this hypothesis is impossible to test. Only in totalitarian countries have armies participated in revolutions and then remained in power. It is impossible to evaluate the prospects for the expected benefits of rule by a revolutionary military devoted to modernization, because observers cannot empirically separate the consequences of rule by a revolutionary military from those of totalitarian rule. However, as totalitarian regimes have not outperformed noncommunist regimes in their economic growth, many doubt the expected benefits of military rule, even revolutionary military rule.

SINGLE-PARTY, NONCOMMUNIST REGIMES

In the most common form of civilian regime in the LICs, a single party rules according to its own principles. Some countries, such as Kenya and Mexico, hold elections in which opposition parties win legislative seats. Such an opposition party, however, never wins either the presidency or a majority of seats in the national legislature. In other countries, such as Taiwan, dominant parties do not allow significant opposition. In both situations, however, only the party that controls the government at the time of the election has any realistic chance of ruling the country after it.

Once again, leaders in many LICs view the absence of effective opposition as a positive sign. A dominant single party indicates harmony among the political elites. This is particularly true if the party unites representatives from most major economic and political groups. For example, the Institutionalized Revolutionary Party (PRI) in Mexico includes all major economic groups other than employer associations. The PRI nominates candidates in legislative or mayoral elections according to the wishes of the strongest sector in that particular constituency. For example, in a largely agricultural constituency, party leaders from the agriculture sector choose the candidate. If the constituency contains mainly urban workers, then the labor sector chooses the party's nominee. The PRI decides policy issues through a process of bargaining among representatives from its various sectors.

Parties have most successfully maintained power and popularity over a long period by blending nationalism, socialist ideologies, and traditional beliefs. This combination allows a regime to build a nation while maintaining the support of workers, traditional elites, and the military. Socialist ideologies effectively manipulate egalitarian rhetoric and prevent appeals from left-wing opposition groups. Traditional structures and beliefs encourage the support of both agricultural workers and traditional political elites. The nationalist focus encourages the support of the military.

A single-party, authoritarian state has four potential advantages. First, a single party suppresses the potentially disruptive effects of party competition. Political losers in the less industrialized countries lose a lot. The party that wins an election or seizes power through a coup will use its power to harass and destroy its opponents. By keeping competition outside the electoral arena and allowing most major sectors in the society to participate in their internal political processes, single parties reduce this harassment and destruction. Second, a stable, single-party system encourages all citizens to become involved in the party's organizations, as the party becomes the only realistic source of political benefits. This process can enhance national identity by the mass public and institutionalize the process of peaceful bargaining. Third, a single party can examine its long-term goals and develop policies to implement them while assuring those who must sacrifice today that they will gain in the future. Finally, the party can legitimate the peaceful transfer of power from one leader to another. All of these functions of a single party encourage the political stability that assists economic growth.

Although some countries have enjoyed the four advantages just discussed, most single-party, authoritarian regimes have suffered from the same problems that besiege other LICs. In particular, single-party regimes must confront three serious problems. First, they often cannot include all major national interests within their party structures. Regardless of its official structure, a party cannot maintain the loyalty of all important interests in society. The political process allocates scarce resources to one group rather than to another. Because LIC governments create such large bureaucracies and because public office offers exceptional opportunities for economic advancement, the allocation of these positions becomes an extremely important political question. Groups that are disappointed with their shares of benefits may choose to leave the party and form opposition organizations.

Personal authority provides a second source of problems for a single-party government. Typically, a military officer or a charismatic leader such as Gandhi, Nasser, or Nkrumah forms the party. When the leader rewards personal followers more generously than other party members, dissension surges and unity weakens. If leaders rather than institutions form the basis for loyalty within the party, then unity dissolves into personality struggles.[43] Finally, when the leader's importance overshadows that of the party, a single-party state suffers from the same legitimacy and transition problems as a regime headed by a charismatic leader.

Bureaucratic institutionalization is a third problem of a single-party state. As the party retains power longer, party functionaries often become more secure in their positions and less responsive to the mass public. In addition, the party may lose the revolutionary zeal that originally propelled it to power. Rather than welcoming political reform and economic progress, the party leaders begin to resist change, particularly when it threatens their positions. This transformation from the party of change to the defender of the status quo may reduce economic innovation and erode political support among the mass public. Disaffection with such a party becomes particularly strong among the country's young people.

DEMOCRATIC REGIMES

The 1980s and the first part of the 1990s brought a large number of new democracies in the LICs. In Latin America, Argentina, Bolivia, Brazil, Chile, Nicaragua, Peru, and Uruguay replaced repressive military governments with democratically elected regimes. In Asia, South Korea and the Philippines moved from one-party, authoritarian regimes to establish democracies, and both Taiwan and Singapore relaxed political repression. In the Middle East, Turkey changed from an authoritarian, military government to a democratically elected regime. In Africa, the ruling parties in Kenya and Ghana suffered substantial election losses even though the presidents of both countries held onto power. Even South Africa made substantial strides toward a more democratic government. What accounts for this surge of democracy and liberalization among some of the world's more repressive single-party, authoritarian regimes?

Perhaps the most important force behind the emergence of new democratic regimes is the universal legitimacy of democracy. Rarely will even the most repressive leader willingly acknowledge a lack of democracy or admit that the government is not striving to achieve democracy in the future. For this reason, the failure of an existing regime leads people to call for the preferred alternative of most members of society—some form of democratic rule.

Poor economic performance provides the second major reason for the resurgence of democratic government. The 1970s brought difficult economic times for the entire world. The rapid increase in oil prices caused by the OPEC cartel drastically reduced standards of living and created economic crises in countries at all stages of development. Just as American voters blamed Jimmy Carter for inflation in the United States, citizens in the LICs blamed hard times on their leaders. Military leaders who took power expecting to solve their countries' economic problems found that they could not. Many returned willingly to their barracks. When Brazil experienced a severe economic depression in the early 1980s, the military decided that it was time to restore civilian rule.

Another reason for the emergence or restoration of democracies is the commitments of elites to democratic rule. In one such example from Nicaragua, the Sandinista government chose to hold free and fair elections and then abided by the results of those elections even though the people voted the communist regime out of power.

But will those democratic governments achieve economic progress? Adam Przeworski contends democracy may fail to promote economic growth, because all basic economic reforms necessary to create growth will cause short-term dislocations, unemployment, inflation, and volatile changes in relative incomes. A democratic regime, Przeworski contends, will either resist policies that have these effects or lose power in the next election.[44]

Recent studies, however, show no significant difference between the economic performance of democratic and nondemocratic regimes. Still, some authors attribute the failure of rapid development in democratic countries to their governments' willingness to accommodate demands of individual groups and their reluctance to take the drastic steps necessary to reform their economies.[45] This conclusion ignores similar failures of nondemocratic regimes, which feel little obligation to accommodate and have undertaken quite radical economic steps. Certainly, the totalitarian regimes of China, North Korea, Albania, and Cuba have not had to compromise, and yet they have achieved standards of economic performance generally below those of more democratic regimes in similar circumstances. Similarly, comparisons of democratic regimes with one-party, authoritarian governments reveal no consistent evidence of economic superiority of authoritarian regimes.

Democratic governments do encounter special problems in the development process, though. Most importantly, if the government's economic policies do not improve the lives of the majority of voters, then a new set of leaders may well replace the current set at the next election. In addition, to obtain popular support, candidates often make promises that they cannot keep. For example, presidential candidates Carlos Menem in Argentina, Victor Paz Estenssoro in Bolivia, and Henrique Cardosos in Brazil all campaigned on promises not to repay their countries' huge foreign debts because those payments would impose excessive hardships on the poor in their countries. Each decided later that he had to make these payments.[46] Such broken promises may not only reduce the reelection chances of these leaders, but they also may reduce the legitimacy of democratic government and increase the appeal of rule by authoritarian regimes.

Summary

Successive sections of this chapter appear to have rejected totalitarian, authoritarian, and democratic regimes as appropriate political systems for economic development. Does any type of regime succeed in this important work? In reality, no type of regime or set of political structures can guarantee economic development. Scholars can look for guidance, however, from countries that appear to have beaten the odds. The three most obvious recent examples of sustained economic growth come from Singapore, Taiwan, and South Korea.** Between 1965 and 1990, these three countries grew at an average annual rate of approximately 8 percent. In addition, people suffer much less economic inequality in all three countries than in almost any other part of the third world.[47] What makes these countries special? What characteristics do they share?

Harmon Zeigler points out that the cultures of all three, like that of Japan, stress Confucian principles of achievement and social order. These single-party, corporatist regimes include input from most important political actors to make critical economic decisions. Finally, the government of each country has provided capital and sponsored research to assist export-driven enterprises. Each government selected export enterprises for subsidies to maximize its country's comparative advantages on the world market.

Does this mean economic development absolutely requires all or any one of these policies? If a country must adopt a Confucian world view to develop, then is the rest of the third world doomed? If a country must adopt a single-party, authoritarian, corporatist structure, then is democracy inappropriate for rapid economic development? Can a country achieve economic success only by identifying and subsidizing industries in which it has a comparative advantage on the world market? The answer to all three questions is, "Probably not."

Non-Confucian countries have developed and continue to do so. Spain is the most obvious current example of a country that has rapidly caught up to its neighbors after falling far behind. In addition, Spain achieved its growth after it moved from an authoritarian government to a democratic one. Obviously, non-Confucian countries, including the more industrialized countries of western Europe and North America, industrialized before any others in the world, and relatively democratic governments ruled most of them. In short, neither Confucianism nor authoritarian, single-party government is a necessary condition for development.

How about the choice of economic strategies? Must all LICs subsidize industries in which they expect to have comparative advantages? Hesitate, at least briefly, before jumping to the conclusion that all LICs should follow this strategy. If this book had been written in 1975 rather than in 1995, the economic systems that depended upon centralized planning and import substitution would have appeared the best choices. If this book had

---

** Hong Kong would fall into this group if it were a sovereign country rather than a colony temporarily run by the British.

been written in 1965, the economic strategy of the Soviet Union would have seemed most attractive with its emphasis on exploitation of the agricultural sector in order to invest in the industrial sector. In other words, although the common economic strategy of South Korea, Taiwan, and Singapore *may* offer the best hope for other LICs, past experience suggests that no single economic approach works for all countries, and no approach remains the best for very long.

QUESTIONS AND EXERCISES

Questions for Reason

1. How might you test the ability of the neoliberal and dependency models to explain current levels of development and growth rates among less industrialized and newly industrialized countries?

2. Why are core nations referred to as the *North* and periphery nations as the *South* in the dependency and world systems theories?

3. Explain the difference between the dependency and world systems theories.

4. Which economic development theory does the North American Free Trade Agreement (NAFTA) represent?

5. Why is corruption such an obstacle to economic development?

6. What advantages and disadvantages does military rule bring to a country? Single-party rule?

Questions for Reflection

1. What similarities do you see in the Confucian ethic that dominates newly industrialized countries and the Protestant ethic that was dominant during the economic development of many countries in North America and western Europe? What key differences might separate these two worldviews?

2. If neoliberal theory is correct, what policies should the more industrialized nations pursue to encourage economic development in less industrialized nations? What if dependency theory is correct?

3. What policies might a government pursue to reduce the problem of corruption?

4. What forces have driven the democratization of so many LICs? What conditions are likely to help these new governments establish democratic institutions?

Questions for Analysis: Multiple Regression

Many less industrialized countries face serious problems with high birthrates, which place tremendous demands on government education and health services, keep women out of the labor force, and reduce the resources that parents can invest in each child. In countries such as China, India, and Haiti where populations are already too large for arable land, any increase in population is likely to lead to environmental degradation. In response to this problem, almost all less industrialized counties have adopted population-control policies. This exercise evaluates alternative methods to identify those that most successfully reduce birthrates.

To do this, the exercise will extend the discussion of regression started in the previous chapter. One of the reasons Karl Pearson developed regression was to evaluate the accuracy of predictions. Pearson wanted to answer this important question: How much of the variation in a dependent variable can the regression equation "explain"? To understand this idea, return to the example from the previous chapter of the weight guessing game. Remember, you have to guess the weight of the next person who passes by the booth. In the absence of any knowledge about the individual who is about to pass by, your best guess is the average weight of all the people attending the carnival that night. Statisticians call this average score the **mean.**

The discussion requires one other statistical term: **variance.** If everyone at the carnival weighed the same, the variable WEIGHT would show no variation. Of course, people's weights do differ, and statistical analysis of the guessing problem must determine how much they differ. Variance is the statistic that indicates this. As shown in the formula below, to find the variance in (V in the formula) the weights of everyone at the carnival, you would begin by subtracting the mean (average) weight $(\overline{Y}) / (Y_i) / (Y_i - \overline{Y})^2$ from each individual's actual weight and squaring the result. (One reason you square the difference is to avoid potential problems with negative numbers.) You would then add up all the results (Σ means " take (N) the sum of all the $[Y_i - Y]^2$) and divide the sum of the results by the number of people at the carnival. The formula for computing the total variance is:

$$V = \frac{(Y_i - \overline{Y})^2}{N}$$

If the variable HEIGHT explained 100 percent of the variation in WEIGHT, then simply knowing an individual's height would predict perfectly that person's weight.

Figure 10.1 is a scatterplot of imaginary people at the carnival who played the guessing game. (Fortunately, the small number of participants simplifies life.) The horizontal axis measures each person's common sense. The vertical axis measures the number of times the game master was able to convince each person to play the guessing game. The thick, flat line in the figure shows the average (mean) number of times people played the game. The dotted line from the upper left to the lower right is the regression line that predicts how many times each participant will play based on that individual's score on the measure of common sense. (Notice that the relationship is negative.)

The distance of each dark bar from the flat line shows the number of times above or below the average that each participant played the game. Squaring each of these distances and adding up the results gives the **total variation**[††] in the dependent variable, the number of games played. The length of each light bar represents the error in predicting how many games each person would play based on the measure of the participant's common sense. For example, the figure indicates that the measure of common sense correctly predicts how many games A, D, and G would play; it vastly underestimated how many times E would play; and it overestimated the number of times C would play. Squaring the difference between the predicted and actual number of games each individual played and summing all the results gives the total variation that the regression *did not* correctly predict. Not surprisingly, this amount is called the **unexplained variation** in *Y*.

[††] Statisticians usually refer to the total variation as the total sum of squares.

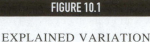

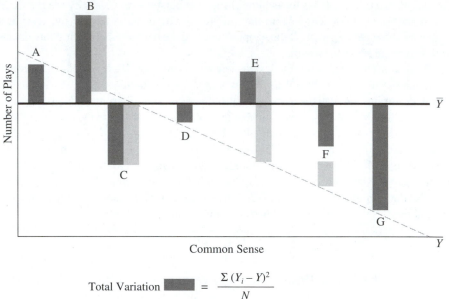

EXPLAINED VARIATION

$$\text{Total Variation} \quad \blacksquare \quad = \quad \frac{\Sigma\,(Y_i - \overline{Y})^2}{N}$$

$$\text{Unexplained variation} \quad \blacksquare \quad = \quad -\frac{\Sigma\,(Y_i - \hat{Y})^2}{N}$$

$$\text{Explained variation} = \text{Total Variation} - \text{Unexplained Variation}$$

$$\text{Percent of variation explained} = \frac{\text{Explained variation}}{\text{Total variation}}$$

Figure 10.1 shows that subtracting the unexplained variation from the total variation gives the **explained variation.** Dividing the explained variation by the total variation gives the percentage of the variation in the dependent variable that the regression equation explains. This number represents the ability of the independent variable to accurately predict values of the dependent variable. Micro-Crunch gives this number as the R squared from the Quik-Plot or Scatterplot command. The previous chapter showed that it is also the square of the correlation coefficient. The amount of variation that an independent variable explains can range from 0 percent to 100 percent.

Of course, numbers do not really "explain" any variation in Y. Explanation deals with causality; the theory provides the rationale for why variation in the independent variable causes variation in the dependent variable.[48]

Combining Several Independent Variables

In real life, most events have more than a single cause. Therefore, an accurate prediction of the values of a dependent variable often requires more than one explanatory variable. For instance, the model of political participation tested in exercises from earlier chapters included six explanatory variables: (1) the benefits that the individual would receive if the collective action were successful, (2) the perceived probability that the individual's participation would make a difference, (3) the perceived probability that collective action would be successful, (4) the social norms surrounding participation, (5) the individual's own values concerning political behaviors, and (6) the expected costs of participation. Contingency tables support only two simultaneous explanatory variables. Multiple regression can include all of the variables in a model simultaneously, and it can weight the relative importance of each in predicting the outcomes.

To see how multiple regression works, consider the problem of high birthrates in less industrialized countries. Assume once more that you are the president of Ecuador, and that you wish to lower the birthrate in your country. How would you choose which policies to implement? For the moment, assume that you have hired the authors of this book as consultants to come to Ecuador and help you choose policies. First, you ask us to determine what variables are associated with low birthrates in less industrialized countries. Given that you are probably an authoritarian ruler, we quickly comply with your request.

To find out what variables are associated with low birthrates, we review the existing literature on the topic. Unfortunately, experts disagree. Some say that strong statements from political leaders have important effects. Others argue that just making contraceptives available will reduce birthrates. Still others contend that education and job opportunities for women are most closely associated with low birthrates. Finally, one specialist contends that vigorous economic growth has the most important influence.

We decide to test these hypotheses using multiple regression. We gather data from numerous sources on the previously identified variables, and the total fertility rate in a country serves as the dependent variable. Computer programs for regression analysis can determine which variables are statistically significant predictors of low birthrates and the relative impact of each variable.

Introducing more than a single independent variable, however, makes visual representation of a regression equation impossible. However, the computer can use several independent variables to find the equation that will minimize the errors in predicting the values of the dependent variable. The statistical procedure that combines more than one independent variable to make predictions is called **multiple regression.**

An equation that includes statements of political leaders, the availability of contraceptives, female education, and gross domestic product to predict birthrates would look like this:

$$Y = a + b_1 X_1 + b_2 X_2 + b_3 X_3 + b_4 X_4$$

where

Y = the predicted birthrate of a country
b_1 = the partial slope for female education
X_1 = the measure of female education

FIGURE 10.2

MULTIPLE REGRESSION: PREDICTING TOTAL FERTILITY RATES

$N = 80$

Sums of Squares

Total	Unexplained	Explained
210.995	63.342	147.654

R Squared	Adjusted R Squared
0.700	0.684

Regression: TFR90 Is Dependent

Variable	B	Std. Error	t	Beta
Constant	8.8604	0.7997	11.0796	0.0000
FMLITB89	– 0.0222	0.0050	– 4.4699	– 0.3790
POLI89	– 0.0217	0.0228	– 0.9508	– 0.0902
AVAIL89	– 0.1023	0.0233	– 4.3866	– 0.4600
LGDP87	– 0.1994	0.1140	– 1.7494	– 0.1388

b_2 = the partial slope for the strength of statements by leaders
X_2 = the measure of the strength of statements by leaders
b_3 = the partial slope for availability of contraception
X_3 = the measure of availability of contraception
b_4 = the partial slope for the gross domestic product (in logarithmic form)
X_4 = the measure of the gross domestic product (in logarithmic form)

Notice that b no longer refers to the slope of the regression line. It is now called the **partial slope.** The partial slope indicates how much the dependent variable will change if an independent variable changes 1 unit *and all the other independent variables in the equation remain the same.*

A scatterplot can no longer depict the data because it cannot represent five-dimensional space. Instead, the computer evaluates all the cases in the sample of less industrialized countries to generate the equation for the straight line that minimizes the error in the prediction of birthrates in LICs. The computer responds with the information in Figure 10.2.

How can you, the president, read Figure 10.2? At the upper left, $N = 80$ tells you that the regression equation included information on 80 countries. The lines below that report the total variation to explain (210.995). Of this total variation, 63.342 is unexplained and 147.654 is explained by the chosen independent variables. Dividing the explained variation by the total variation indicates that the regression equation explains 70 percent of the variation. Of course, you need not do that because the material in the shaded box tells you that the R squared is 0.700. Next, another R squared figure appears, the adjusted R squared. Statistical software programs make all sorts of adjustments to the R squared for reasons that will become clear in statistics courses. For the moment, simply recognize that the actual explained variation is 68.4 percent, not 70.0 percent.

The next line in the table restates the dependent variable: the total fertility rate of a country in 1990. Now comes the interesting material. The leftmost column below the dotted line gives the variable names: the female literacy rate in 1989 (FMLITB89), the policy statements on birth control and family size by political leaders in 1989 (POLI89), the contraceptive availability in 1989 (AVAIL89), and the log of the country's gross domestic product in 1987 (LGDP87).

The second column gives the intercept (constant) and the partial slope of each variable. *Always check here to see if the variables have the predicted signs.* In this table, they do. The minus signs suggest that female literacy, statements by leaders, contraceptive availability, and high gross domestic products all reduce the birthrate.

Are the variables statistically significant? You must turn to your trusty student's *t* table (Chapter 8, page 267) to find the answer. (If you are using SPSS, you already know.) Assume 0.05 as the critical value and check the row for 60 degrees of freedom. (The problem actually allows 79.) Apparently, all independent variables except for the statements of leaders (POLI89) have statistically significant associations with the dependent variable. The final, shaded column headed "Beta" indicates the importance of each variable in predicting the outcome. The beta value for POLI89, the statements of leaders, is very small (−0.09). As the variable was statistically insignificant, this should not cause any surprise. Two variables have large beta values: female literacy and the availability of contraceptives. Although we will not show the table here, those two variables alone have an adjusted R^2 of 68 percent. The variables gross domestic product and leaders' statements add little to our explanation.

We are quite pleased with our results. Social scientists rarely explain more than two-thirds of the variation in anything. However, a friend who is a demographer (someone who studies population variables like birth, death, and migration) warns us that we have omitted a very important variable. This variable is whether or not a country is in sub-Saharan Africa. Because of the property rights to children and the attitude toward nursing infants among the upper class there, women in sub-Saharan Africa have higher rates of fertility than women in other parts of the world. The demographer suggests that we should include a dummy variable for sub-Saharan Africa.

Dummy Variables

Social scientists often study relationships between nominal and interval variables. For example, in the study of birthrates we would like to use a nominal variable to indicate the region sub-Saharan Africa in a regression equation. Regression, however, requires interval level data. Fortunately, regression analysis can use what appears to be a nominal level variable if the variable has only two values. For an ordinal or nominal variable with only two categories, the researcher can assign values of 0 to one category and 1 to the other category. For example, the birthrate regression might include a variable AFRICA for which all countries in sub-Saharan Africa have a value of 1 and countries in all other regions have a value of 0. We call nominal level variables with only the values 0 and 1, **dummy variables.**

FIGURE 10.3

REGRESSION WITH DUMMY VARIABLE

$N = 80$
Sums of Squares

Total	Unexplained	Explained
210.995	58.760	152.236

R Squared	Adjusted R Squared
0.722	0.703

Regression: TFR90 Is Dependent

Variable	B	Std. Error	t	Beta
Constant	8.3686	0.8020	10.4346	0.0000
POLI89	− 0.0371	0.0230	− 1.6138	− 0.1546
AVAIL89	− 0.0805	0.0244	− 3.3030	− 0.3620
FMLITB89	− 0.0206	0.0049	− 4.2351	− 0.3516
LGDP87	− 0.1770	0.1109	− 1.5960	− 0.1232
AFRICA	0.5867	0.2442	2.4022	0.1797

The demographer hypothesizes that a regression equation that includes the dummy variable AFRICA will explain more variation, making it a more accurate model of actual events. (In statistical jargon, the model will be "better specified.") We decide to run our regression equation again, adding the dummy variable AFRICA. Figure 10.3 shows the results.

The outcome confirms the demographer's hypothesis concerning birthrates in sub-Saharan Africa. The adjusted R squared for the equation moved from 68.4 percent to 70.3 percent. This change doesn't really give us anything to write home about, but it represents an improvement.

The new method has more interesting effects on the t-score for the statements of political leaders and the measure of gross domestic product. The t-score for the statement of leaders now approaches statistical significance, and the measure of gross domestic product drops slightly below the critical value. The betas for female literacy and the availability of contraceptives continue to dominate the equation.

These effects force a researcher to decide what to do about variables in the equation without statistical significance. This question gives social scientists problems. If an equation includes a variable that has no relationship to the dependent variable, then it is a **misspecified equation.** This flaw increases the error in the estimate. On the other hand, an independent variable might really affect the dependent variable, but the measure of it in the equation may not very effectively capture the relationship or the association may have only a weak effect. To leave such a variable out of the equation would also lead to a misspecified equation.

Some social scientists deal with this problem by dropping independent variables for which their regression equations show no statistically significant relationships with the dependent variable. The researchers revise their models to exclude those variables and repeat their regression calculations including only statistically significant variables, or those that came close, in the earlier equation. Other social scientists object to this process. They argue that it would invalidate the first set of results to alter a theoretical model after testing it and then test the altered model on the same data. These critics would prefer to revise the theory and then collect new data on which to test the revised theory.

The following exercise assumes that once a researcher has developed a model and tested it using a particular data file, the researcher should not then revise the model and test it again with the same data set. Thus, the results you get are the ones you keep.

EXERCISE

As the president of Ecuador, you review our research results. You are unimpressed and complain that we have studied the wrong dependent variable. Although you said you wanted to know the causes of current fertility rates, you really wanted to know how to bring about rapid drops in fertility rates. Some forces may take a long time to work, others may produce quicker results. By studying only the level of fertility in a single year, we may not have identified the causes of such a rapid drop. You want to know which combination of variables would have a large impact over a short period of time.

Unfortunately, our time as consultants in your country has come to an end. If you want the answer to this question, you will have to get it for yourself, although we leave you our data set. It includes two variables that you might use as your dependent variable: TFRT85 and TFRT95. The first measures the drop in the total fertility rate from 1980 to 1985, and the other measures the drop in the fertility rate from 1990 to 1995. Another dependent variable you might wish to evaluate is the rate of contraceptive prevalence, PREVL89. After all, people who use contraceptives may well have small families.

To complete this important analysis, choose one or more of these variables and develop a regression model that you think will best explain either fertility decline or contraceptive prevalence. Your model should include at least four independent variables and no more than six. Begin with a hypothesis for each independent variable indicating the direction of its relationship with the dependent variable. As with all other exercises, use your word processor to prepare a statement of your hypotheses and a discussion of your results. In your discussion, be sure to discuss the beta values of the different variables.

Appendix C provides a full list of the variables available in the data set POPULATN.

NOTES

[1] Adam Przeworski contends that, "While all kinds of considerations may be insufficient to propel [political leaders] onto the path of reforms, one is irresistible. If the government is bankrupt—if it runs a deficit and cannot borrow money—all politicians, regardless of their ideological orientations, electoral programs, and social bases, will be willing to do what it takes to restore creditworthiness." Adam Przeworski, *Democracy and the Market: Political and Economic Reforms in Eastern Europe and Latin America* (Cambridge: Cambridge University Press, 1993), p. 166.

[2] Ronald H. Chilcote, "The Search for a Class Theory of the State and Democracy: Capitalist and Socialist Perspectives," in *Comparative Political Dynamics: Global Research Perspectives,* ed. by Dankwart A. Rustow and Kenneth Paul Erikson (New York: Harper Collins, 1991), pp. 75–97.

[3] Gary Becker, *A Treatise on the Family* (Chicago: University of Chicago Press, 1981).

[4] Michael P. Todaro, *Economic Development,* 5th ed. (New York: Longman, 1994), pp. 80–90.

[5] Ibid., Chapter 11.

[6] Monte Palmer, *Dilemmas of Political Development: An Introduction to the Politics of Developing Areas,* 4th ed. (Itasca, Ill.: Peacock Press, 1989), p. 293.

[7] For examples of dependency theory, see Fernando Henrique Cardoso, "Associated-Dependent Development: Theoretical and Practical Implications," in *Authoritarian Brazil,* ed. by Alfred Stepan (New Haven, Conn.: Yale University Press, 1973), pp. 142–178; and Guillermo O'Donnell, *Modernization and Bureaucratic Authoritarianism* (Berkeley: University of California, Institute for International Studies, 1973).

[8] Raul Prebisch, *The Economic Development of Latin America and Its Principal Problems* (Lake Success, N.Y.: United Nations Economic Commission for Latin America, 1950).

[9] Palmer, *Dilemmas of Political Development,* p. 335.

[10] Ibid., p. 343.

[11] The best known of the cultural explanations for industrialization and modernization is Max Weber's classic, *The Protestant Ethic and the Spirit of Capitalism: The Relationships between Religion and Economic and Social Life in Modern Culture,* trans. by Talcott Parsons (New York: Charles Scribner's Sons, 1958).

[12] Palmer, *Dilemmas of Political Development,* pp. 63–64.

[13] Many studies have investigated the relationship of modern attitudes and values to economic development, including David C. McClelland, *The Achieving Society* (Princeton, N.J.: D. Van Nostrand, 1961); Lucian Pye, *Politics, Personality, and Nation Building* (New Haven, Conn.: Yale University Press, 1962); Gabriel A. Almond and Sidney Verba, *The Civic Culture* (Boston: Little, Brown, 1965); Edward Banfield, *The Moral Basis of a Backward Society* (New York: Free Press, 1967); Joseph A. Kahl, *The Measurement of Modernism* (Austin: University of Texas Press, 1970); and Kenneth S. Sherrill, "The Attitudes of Modernity," *Comparative Politics* 1 (1969), pp. 184–210.

[14] Ronald Inglehart, "Value Change in Industrial Societies," *American Political Science Review* 81 (1987), p. 1,221.

[15] Howard Wiarda, *Politics and Social Change in Latin America: The Distinct Tradition* (Amherst: University of Massachusetts Press, 1974), p. 269; cited in Mitchell A. Seligson and John A. Booth, *Elections and Democracy in Central America: Revisited* (Chapel Hill: University of North Carolina Press, 1995), p. 9.

[16] Harmon Zeigler, *The Political Community: A Comparative Introduction to Political Systems and Society* (New York: Longman, 1990).

[17] Palmer, *Dilemmas of Political Development,* p. 333.

[18] Ibid., p. 45.

[19] Zeigler, *The Political Community,* p. 245.

[20] Kahl, *The Measurement of Modernism;* Albert O. Hirschman, "Obstacles to Development: A Classification and Quasi-Vanishing Act," *Economic Development and Cultural Change* 13 (1965), pp. 385–393; John H. Kunkel, "Values and Behavior in Economic Development," *Economic Development and Cultural Change* 13 (1965), pp. 257–277; Kenneth Godwin, "Two Thorny Theoretical Tangles: The Relationships between Personality Variables and Modernization," *Journal of Developing Areas* 8 (1974), pp. 181–198; and Mitchell A. Seligson and John A. Booth, "Political Culture and Regime Type: Evidence from Nicaragua and Costa Rica," *Journal of Politics* 55 (1993), pp. 777–792.

[21] Dennis A. Rondinelli, *Development Projects as Policy Experiments: An Adaptive Approach to Development Administration* (London: Metheun, 1983).

[22] Michael P. Todaro, *Economic Development in the Third World* (White Plains, N.Y.: Longman, 1981), p. 483.

[23] Nikolai Petrakov and Evgeni Yassine, "Economic Methods of Planned Centralized Management," in *Sovietskaia ekonomitcheskaia reforma: Poiski i reshenia* (Moscow: Nauka, 1988), pp. 54–86; cited in Przeworski, *Democracy and the Market.*

[24] Zeigler, *The Political Community,* pp. 365–366.

[25] Ibid., pp. 354–355.

[26] Ibid., p. 357.

[27] United Press International, November 28, 1978.

[28] Alan Riding, *Distant Neighbors* (New York: Vintage, 1986), p. 193.

[29] Palmer, *Dilemmas of Political Development,* p. 298.

[30] Donald R. Lessard and John Williamson, *Capital Flight: The Problem and Policy Responses* (Washington, D.C.: Institute for International Economics, 1987).

[31] See John C. Akin, Nancy Birdsall, and D. de Ferranti, *Financing Health Services in Developing Countries* (Washington, D.C.: World Bank, 1987); Paul Gertler and P. Glewee, *The Willingness to Pay for Education in Developing Countries: Evidence from Rural Peru* (Washington, D.C.: World Bank, 1989); and Rondinelli, *Development Projects as Policy Experiments.*

[32] Akin, Birdsall, and de Ferranti, *Financing Health Services;* Richard Rose, "Charges as Contested Signals," *Journal of Public Policy* 9 (1989), pp. 261–286; and R. Kenneth Godwin, "Charges for Merit Goods: Third World Family Planning," *Journal of Public Policy* 11 (1992), pp. 415–429.

[33] Robert M. Price, *Society and Bureaucracy in Contemporary Ghana* (Berkeley: University of California Press, 1975), pp. 148–199; cited in Zeigler, *The Political Community,* p. 355.

[34] Palmer, *Dilemmas of Political Development,* p. 200.

[35] Ibid., pp. 157–158.

[36] Max Weber, *The Theory of Social and Economic Organization,* ed. and trans. by A. M. Henderson and Talcott Parsons (New York: Free Press, 1947), p. 328.

[37] Henry L. Bretton, *The Rise and Fall of Kwame Nkrumah* (New York: Praeger, 1966), p. 88.

[38] Palmer, *Dilemmas of Political Development,* p. 155.

[39] Talikder Maniruzzaman, *Military Withdrawal from Politics: A Comparative Study* (Cambridge, Mass.: Ballinger, 1987).

[40] Morris Janowitz, *Military Institutions and Coercion in the Developing Nations* (Chicago: University of Chicago Press, 1977).

[41] Kareen Dep Singh, "Comparative Regime Performance in Economic Development: A Time Series Analysis," (Ph.D. diss., University of North Texas, 1992).

[42] Amos Perlmutter, *The Military and Politics in Modern Times* (New Haven, Conn.: Yale University Press, 1977).

[43] Palmer, *Dilemmas of Political Development,* p. 213.

[44] Przeworski, *Democracy and the Market,* p. 161.

[45] Palmer, *Dilemmas of Political Development,* pp. 230–231.

[46] Przeworski, *Democracy and the Market,* pp. 166–167.

[47] Michael Don Ward, *The Political Economy of Distribution* (Beverly Hills, Calif.: Elsevier, 1977), p. 181.

[48] Alan S. Zuckerman, *Doing Political Science: An Introduction to Political Analysis* (Boulder, Colo.: Westview Press, 1991), p. 10.

11

Politics in More Industrialized Countries

At the beginning of Chapter 10, you became president of Ecuador. You had to deal with the country's international debt, inflation, and urban slums, along with the requirements of the International Monetary Fund. As president of Ecuador, you would have to take actions that no sane politician would choose, yet a responsible leader would have to act to improve the country's economic situation.

Now imagine that you are the new president of France. You have just come to power as the leader of the dominant party in a coalition government with one other political party. What economic, social, and political problems do you face? What policies will you pursue?

Your first task is to get France out of its current economic slowdown. France's economic growth rate, adjusted for inflation, has averaged less than 1.5 percent annually during the past 15 years. Your predecessor's government ran huge budget deficits in an attempt to increase economic growth, and France's national debt grew to levels unknown prior to 1980. Current unemployment stands at a much higher rate than was common during the 1960s and 1970s, and previous governments have tried and failed to reduce it. Finally, France is integrating its economy with the remainder of Europe. Economic integration will require the government to reduce subsidies to many industries, including agriculture. This action will create higher unemployment in the short term as some farmers and firms go bankrupt. These are your *short-term* problems.

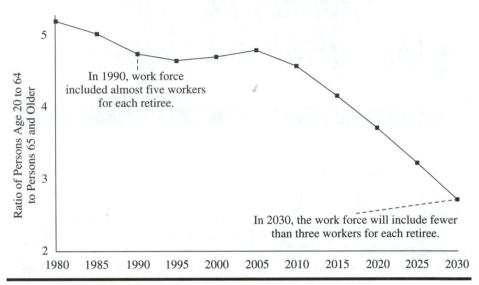

FIGURE 11.1

AN AGING POPULATION: FEWER WORKERS TO SUPPORT
EACH RETIREE'S BENEFITS

Bipartisan Commission on Entitlement and Tax Reform (Washington, D.C.: GPO, 1994).

Even these severe short-term economic problems pale beside your long-term problem: French industry is losing competitive strength in the world market. At the same time, the country's aging population will impose tremendous demands upon state pension and health-care programs. France must create far more rapid economic growth, and it must change its welfare structure so that the aging population will not bankrupt the state.

Previous governments passed politically popular legislation that increased old-age pensions and expanded income-maintenance programs. These two programs grew from 16 percent of the country's gross national product in the early 1960s to nearly 25 percent by 1996. Because the number of older people in France is growing much more rapidly than the work force, the number of workers available to support each retired person will drop from more than 3.0 in the 1950s to approximately 1.6 by 2010, and it may fall as low as 1.2 by 2030.[1] This change in the ratio of workers to retirees will require either a huge increase in taxes to support pensions for the elderly or a drastic cut in their benefits. However, increasing taxes may reduce economic growth. Figure 11.1 shows this pattern for the United States; almost every industrialized country faces similar prospects.

Also, the aging population corresponds to a growing cost of health care. Due to increases in life expectancy, the number of French citizens over age 85 will double between 1990 and 2010. (See Figure 11.2.) As the health-care expenses of a person over 85 are five times greater than the expenses of a person under 65, the change will impose

---

FIGURE 11.2

DOUBLING OF THE NUMBER OF AMERICANS OVER AGE 70

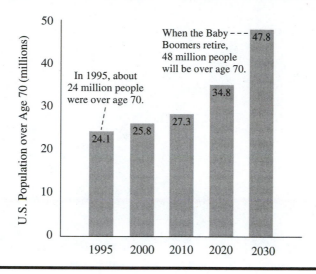

gargantuan requirements for financing the public health-care system. (Figure 11.3 indicates a similar situation in the United States).[2] In summary, unless your government causes substantial reductions in either the after-tax incomes of working people or the pension and health-care benefits of the elderly, the entire social welfare system will fail. If your government does take these actions, however, you may be out of a job. Attempts to reduce pensions for the elderly resulted in massive labor strikes and student unrest in both 1994 and 1995.

Will you choose to raise taxes or cut benefits? If you choose either, can your party win reelection? Will your coalition partner agree to either a tax increase or a decrease in benefits, or will it leave the government and blame you for raising taxes and reducing pensions and health-care benefits? Can you imagine the headlines that your coalition partner could make if its leader were to publicly withdraw from the Government amid statements about refusing to go back on the promises France has made to the elderly, who have worked all their lives to have a decent retirement, and refusing to raise taxes on already overburdened French workers? Certainly, the political parties who helped create the huge deficit by increasing social programs will remind citizens that *they* voted for policies that benefited rather than harmed French citizens. Of course, if your coalition partner withdraws, then you no longer command a majority vote in the national assembly. You will either have to find a new coalition partner or hold new elections. Can you win such an election after proposing politically unpopular policies?

In addition to these economic issues, your Government faces important social issues. Chapter 6 discussed at least two major ideological dimensions in more industrialized countries. One deals with economic issues, while the other deals with social issues such

FIGURE 11.3

GROWTH OF THE SHARE OF THE POPULATION OVER 65

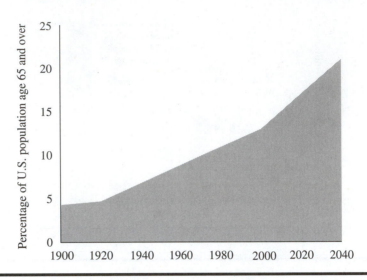

Source: Bipartisan Commission on Entitlement and Tax Reform (Washington, D.C.: GPO, 1994), p. 7.

as environmental protection, women's rights, tolerance for minorities, and preservation of traditional morals and social norms. You must be careful not to alienate voters who supported your stand on economic issues in the last election but whose support would evaporate if you were to take the wrong positions on social issues. Similarly, your economic policies must not alienate voters who supported your stands on social issues. Like any governing party, yours can rely on support from only a minority of the voters for your positions on both social and economic issues.*

You may have recognized these problems of the president of France as similar to those of the president of the United States and the prime ministers of England and Canada. In fact, similar problems confront the leaders of every more industrialized country (MIC). When the Organization of Petroleum Exporting Countries (OPEC) more than tripled the price of oil in the 1970s, four things happened: a massive redistribution of wealth from the oil importing nations to the oil exporting nations, double-digit inflation in almost every oil importing country, a substantial slowdown in economic growth, and significantly higher unemployment. While American voters blamed Presidents Nixon and Carter for these problems, all oil-importing countries experienced the same inflation and economic slowdowns as the United States. Similarly, many industrialized countries attempted to spur economic growth in the 1980s through tax cuts, spending increases, and huge government budget deficits. Although the U.S. government ran larger budget deficits than those of

---

*For a discussion of this fact, see Chapter 6 on linkage.

other MICs, all of these countries significantly increased their debt. How can the president of France, or the leader of any MIC, overcome these difficulties?

In this chapter, we first examine the category of more industrialized countries and consider which countries belong. We then examine the development of the current policies of these countries and the economic, distributional, and social issues that they currently face. Next, we discuss the institutional similarities and differences among the MICs and evaluate the performance records of alternative institutions in meeting shared economic, distribution, and social challenges. Finally, we consider why the MICs may have difficulty in dealing with the challenges of the 21st century.

Criteria for More Industrialized Countries

After considering the problems of the less industrialized countries and the difficulty of their struggle for economic development, we now turn to the high standards of living and generally democratic methods of settling political conflicts common in the more industrialized countries. On every economic indicator, the MICs are clearly better off than the LICs. The MICs have high per-capita incomes, excellent medical facilities available to most of their populations, long life expectancies, low infant mortality rates, high levels

TABLE 11.1

BASIC INDICATORS—MICS AND LICS

Country	GNP per Capita	Average Growth Rate 1980–1991	Life Expectancy (years)
Ireland	$11,120	3.30%	75
Israel	11,950	1.70	76
New Zealand	12,350	0.70	76
Spain	12,450	2.80	77
United Kingdom	16,550	2.60	75
Australia	17,050	1.60	77
Italy	18,520	2.20	77
Netherlands	18,780	1.60	77
Belgium	18,950	2.00	76
Austria	20,140	2.10	76
France	20,380	1.80	77
Canada	20,440	2.00	77
United States	22,240	1.70	76
Germany	23,650	2.20	76
Denmark	23,700	2.20	75
Finland	23,980	2.50	76
Norway	24,220	2.30	77
Sweden	25,110	1.70	78
Japan	26,930	3.60	79
Switzerland	33,610	1.60	78
Average MICs	20,106	2.11	77
Average LICs			
Lowest 42	350	1.10	56
Middle 41	1,590	−0.10	67
Highest 21	3,530	0.60	69

Source: World Bank, *World Development Report, 1993* (New York: Oxford University Press, 1993), Table 1, p. 2.

of education, adequate diets, and good housing. All of the MICs are **welfare states.** This term refers to countries have market-oriented economies that depend on the institutions of private property, and have broad public-assistance programs for the unemployed, the needy, and the elderly. Finally, all of the MICs are constitutional democracies with excellent records for protecting individual freedom and liberty over the past 40 years. What countries belong in this lucky group?

Every MIC, with the exception of Japan, has a predominantly Caucasian population; most were colonial powers. All except New Zealand and Australia are in the northern hemisphere. Table 11.1 lists these fortunate countries and their scores on various socioeconomic indicators, along with the average scores of the LICs for the same variables. Clearly, the living conditions of the more industrialized nations differ dramatically from those of less developed ones. If you lived in an LIC, you might wonder how citizens of MICs could think that they have problems. Nevertheless, the citizens of the MICs see numerous problems with the economic, social, and political conditions in their homelands, and those citizens are correct to worry.

The Development of the Welfare State

To understand the difficulties that currently face the more industrialized countries, one must understand how characteristic social programs developed in these countries. Hugh Heclo, a scholar of comparative public policy, writes that the welfare state began to emerge in the late 19th century. From the 1870s to the 1920s, most countries of western Europe began to experiment with unemployment compensation, dispensations for the poor, and pensions for the elderly.[3] During this period, these programs passed through many false starts as new arrangements were enacted and then canceled. Some governments developed social programs aimed only at the "deserving poor" and the most vulnerable members of society; others offered comprehensive protection for all destitute people. Some governments justified programs on the basis of charity, others on the basis of social obligation.

Heclo maintains that three key values competed during this period. Conservatives stressed order, liberals emphasized liberty, and socialists emphasized equality. Conservatives, liberals, and socialists alike shared a belief that proved vital to social policies: They agreed that appropriate public policies *could* reconcile these three fundamental values. **Social insurance programs** appeared to achieve this goal. Shocked by labor uprisings and abortive attempts at revolutions, conservatives called for programs that would enhance order. Unemployment insurance and mandatory pension programs provided security for workers who would otherwise listen to the appeals of political agitators. Conservatives believed not only that social insurance would facilitate social order during downturns in the business cycle, but that they would also encourage poor people to help themselves through contributions to state insurance premiums.

Liberals, following John Stuart Mill and other reformers, confronted the effects of the material deprivations in which most working-class families lived. Scarce resources rendered individual liberty meaningless if the individual was at liberty only to starve. Liberals held that social insurance programs minimized interference with individual rights while simultaneously allowing people to escape from the conditions of severe physical deprivation that deprived liberty of its meaning. Socialists, particularly those who favored evolutionary rather than revolutionary socialism, supported policies that moved society toward egalitarian goals. They saw insurance programs as mechanisms through which the state would force more fortunate members of society to contribute to programs that would benefit the poor and working classes.

Four catastrophes and a single economic theory helped to consolidate elements of the welfare state and to expand both social insurance programs and other state efforts to reduce the economic insecurity that capitalism created. The two world wars fostered feelings of nationalism, community, and common purpose among citizens. These feelings encouraged concern for less advantaged citizens. If a nation asked these unfortunates to fight and die for their country, then it should respond more readily to the needs of those citizens.

The other two catastrophes were the great flu epidemic that immediately followed World War I and the Great Depression of the 1930s. These two events showed that almost everyone was vulnerable to economic disaster. People who had worked hard all of their lives suddenly saw how rapidly a family could fall into poverty if the breadwinner died suddenly, lost a job because of a severe downturn in the economy, or lost savings because of a bank failure. In short, these catastrophes made everyone look to government for greater economic security than laissez-faire capitalism could provide.

Sometimes critical events coincide with the development of new theories, and this combination allows the formation of new solutions to old problems. The welfare state developed in the wake of the catastrophes described earlier with the support of a new idea: Keynesian economics. John Maynard Keynes, an English economist, showed that economic downturns did not necessarily correct themselves as classical economics had previously taught. If more and more people were losing their jobs as consumer demand declined, their loss of income reduced their ability to buy goods and services. This, in turn, led to more unemployment. More unemployment further reduced demand, and the vicious circle continued.

Keynes argued that the government could use its taxing and spending policies to reduce the severity of these recessions and to curb inflation in better economic times. Through deficit spending during recessions, government could increase the demand for goods and services and prevent further unemployment. Its social insurance programs could provide purchasing power for people suffering temporary unemployment. By building roads, dams, housing projects, schools, and weapons, government could put people back to work and boost the economy enough to prevent a recession from becoming a depression. Similarly, during times when full employment created inflationary pressures, government could cut back its expenditures and increase its taxes. This would take money out of circulation and reduce the demand for goods and services. Following these techniques, government economic policies could keep the national economy on a path of steady growth.

Those who accepted Keynesian economics argued that spending for social purposes also would achieve economic goals. Thus, the economic and social spheres became integrally related. The Great Depression eliminated blind faith in capitalism and private-sector solutions to social and economic problems. Almost all parts of the electorate and almost all political parties came to accept the need for government intervention in the economy and social insurance programs. Heclo writes:

> The prevailing assumption [after World War II], created by hard experience, was now that collective social policy arrangements were required for everyone's good and not merely for the working class or some special group of deserving poor. In country after country, World War II carried in its wake a commitment to social services and income maintenance programs that would have been unthinkable to the turn of the century reformers.[4]

This grand consensus encountered a major difficulty. While the new social policies emphasized basic economic security and equality, they did not set priorities among these values. The welfare state became a composite of diverse ideas that included social betterment, human progress, secular individualism, and conservatism. Because the welfare state encompassed so many seemingly competing goals, it allowed paternalistic institutions to emerge in predominantly liberal states.[5] It also encouraged a faith in the benign power of government to undertake collective responsibilities and to generate solutions to collective problems. Because support for the welfare state was not based on a coherent set of ideas, when societies faced the need to make hard choices among competing goals, they could refer to no standard to evaluate the priorities of those goals.

Fortunately for elected officials during the 1950s and 1960s, unparalleled economic growth in the MICs allowed governments to avoid hard choices. Still, while the economies of the more industrialized countries grew rapidly, the growth of government social programs and taxes set an even faster pace.[6] The demands of less advantaged groups in society resulted in government expenditures, and more advantaged groups also demanded and received government transfers. Most people in the MICs took sustained economic growth for granted.[7] Neither the general public nor their elected officials worried that government transfer payments were growing much more rapidly than the GNP. Politicians did not concern themselves that population growth had slowed dramatically and that the number of elderly was posting exponential growth. This demographic combination was silently creating a huge problem in which a relatively large percentage of the population would reach retirement age early in the 21st century when a relatively small percentage of the population would be working to support the government transfers and medical-care programs that these retirees would expect.

Heclo and others have argued that the sustained economic growth of the middle decades of the 20th century undermined political leadership in the MICs.[8] Economic growth, with its accompanying increases in tax revenues, allowed officials to expand social policies with almost no political cost. Groups asked and they received. Governments provided higher benefits, more services, wider coverage, and greater subsidies. Any increase in a social program prior to 1950 required an elected official to build a strong political coalition and to justify the new benefits; later, however, governments in the 1950s and 1960s avoided "confronting, debating, and resolving political problems." They did not ask, "Who is losing and gaining? What are the implications for personal liberty? What rights and duties are owed by whom? Is it worth it?"[9] They no longer justified actions through appeals to shared risks, vulnerability, or social order. Instead, if any group felt it was not getting its share of government benefits, it did not hesitate to demand more.

Thus the late 1960s witnessed a . . . paradox of affluence . . . with everybody joining in as claimants for justice and improved public policies. Students were oppressed. Poverty persisted. Women were suppressed. Capital wasn't getting a fair return. Jobs weren't meaningful. Workers weren't getting their fair share of the expanding product. The disabled were discriminated against. In short inequality was rediscovered. Economic growth was not enough. The welfare state would have to do more.[10]

Of course, no linear trend forever continues its familiar course. Economic growth in the MICs slowed dramatically beginning with the 1973 recession. Governments in the 1970s found their citizens accustomed to ever-larger government benefits without having to cut back on private consumption. Beginning in 1973, economic growth no longer allowed this. While almost everyone agreed that something had to be done to resolve the problems of the welfare state, no one stepped forward and said, "Cut my benefits, I can afford it." In the words of the country-and-western song, "Everybody wanted to go to heaven, but nobody wanted to die."

MIC governments briefly forestalled this problem through massive deficit spending during the 1980s. By the end of that decade, however, this solution was requiring burdensome interest payments, and governments could no longer continue their rapid increases in borrowing. Many leaders and citizens agreed that the accumulating debt was placing an unfair burden on future generations.

Reasons for the Slowdown in Growth among the MICs

What has caused the decline in economic growth rates among the MICs? At least three factors have combined to produce this effect. First, technological advances pioneered in the MICs have created opportunities for other countries. The less technologically advanced countries could catch up to the more advanced ones by copying others' innovations rather than inventing new technologies of their own. Economists call this situation "opportunities of backwardness."[11] As developing countries can imitate existing technologies more quickly and more cheaply than they can complete research and development for entirely new technologies, countries such as Brazil, South Korea, and Taiwan can produce products of comparable technological quality to those produced in Japan, France, and Germany while paying lower labor costs and lower taxes.[12] This places the MICs at a competitive disadvantage and slows their economic growth. Although empirical research shows that opportunities for backwardness have allowed less technologically advanced countries to reduce the competitive advantage of the MICs somewhat, these opportunities actually have a relatively small overall impact on the growth rates of the more industrialized countries.[13]

The increasing cost of maintaining the welfare state has also contributed to the slowdown in growth in the MICs. Political economist Mattie Dogan contends that growing entitlement programs, increasing costs of health care, rapidly rising interest payments on these countries' national debts, and dysfunctional bureaucratic regulations are leading the MICs to economic failure. Government spending on entitlement programs, health care, and interest payments leave insufficient funds for investment in production, while the economic costs of regulations encourage industries to make investments in countries with fewer obstacles.[14] Dogan contends that the growth of the service sector in a country's economy is not a positive development, but an indication that the country is "deindustrializing" and devouring rather than investing its capital.[15]

Public education, pensions, unemployment compensation, and assistance to the needy take up one-third or more of the GNP in every MIC. In France, these payments equal almost 45 percent of the GNP.[16] Because the less industrialized countries and newly industrialized countries need not pay for this huge social overhead, and because they impose less restrictive safety and environmental regulations, the more industrialized countries are becoming less competitive despite their technological superiority. In separate studies, political scientist Erich Weede and economist Hakan Nordström found that social programs are negatively associated with economic growth in the MICs.[17]

Mancur Olson, Jr. provides a third explanation for the decline in growth rates among the MICs. Olson believes that economic growth depends on the flexibility and efficiency of resource allocation. As the discussion in Chapter 2 of Adam Smith pointed out, efficiency in a market-based economy requires that investors shift resources to the enterprises that can produce the greatest profits.[18] Although this process promotes economic efficiency and growth, the reallocation of resources harms some investors and reduces employment in less competitive businesses. Olson contends that in a democracy, interest groups force government to protect profits, jobs, and wages from the harsh realities of capitalism. This protection creates economic inefficiencies as investors no longer move capital to the most efficient industries. Members of the society gain temporary security at the cost of economic growth.

To see how interest groups seeking protection can reduce economic growth, imagine that you are an investor deciding whether to invest in Company A or in Company B. Company A produces steel, generating an expected rate of return before taxes of 10 percent. Company B produces computer software and generates an expected pretax rate of return of 15 percent. The expected rates of return reflect the efficiency of the corporations and their potential for growth. In the absence of government intervention, you certainly would invest in Company B.

But the steel industry and its labor union have powerful lobbies. They argue that if people quit investing in steel manufacturing, then the industry will collapse and leave the country vulnerable in times of war. The industry's collapse will create severe unemployment and damage the economy. The government responds to this argument by providing tax credits to steel companies to invest in new equipment, setting quotas and tariffs on foreign steel to raise its price, and reducing the corporate tax rate on steel producers. These government actions increase Company A's expected rate of return to 18 percent, and you prudently divert your money away from efficient Company B into inefficient Company A.

Olson would argue that such government actions not only lead people to invest in inefficient companies, but they also increase the price of steel to everyone. This price increase drives up the cost of production for all goods that use steel and makes the country's products less competitive on the international market. Company B, and other companies that do not receive special government protection, encounter more difficulty attracting capital to expand. This further harms the economy as workers remain in the inefficient steel industry rather than retraining to work in the more efficient software industry. Ultimately, these inefficiencies generate the very problem that the politicians attempted to prevent—large-scale unemployment and national economic vulnerability.

Olson contends that democratic rule, with its protection of the rights to assemble and to petition the government, encourages the formation of groups that lobby government to distort prices in favor of their members. A country with a longer history of democracy thus generates slower economic growth. Olson believes that all of the MICs have reached an advanced stage in this process of government-generated inefficiency. This gives the less democratic or more recently democratic of the newly industrialized countries (NICs) a competitive advantage over older democracies of the MICs.

ECONOMIC INEQUALITY

The economies of the more industrialized countries face other problems in addition to slow growth. Underlying redistribution issues between more wealthy and less wealthy members of society also cause strains. High rates of unemployment coupled with slow economic growth have encouraged intolerance of minorities as well as ethnic strife. In Germany, neo-Nazis have killed immigrant workers and their families by burning down their apartment buildings. Battered by the effects of slowing economic growth in the last 10 years, many Germans blame the imported workers for their own economic problems. Perhaps for this reason, many tend to accept the neo-Nazi ideology more readily than they would in other economic circumstances.

Leftist critics of more industrialized countries point out that their governments give the largest subsidies to the most affluent people while giving little relief to truly poor citizens. As one example of this policy, all MICs give subsidies to relatively affluent students to support their college educations. In Great Britain, less than one person in five enters higher education, and the vast majority of these individuals come from the wealthiest one-third of the population. Despite their wealthy backgrounds, Great Britain provides grants to students that cover almost the entire cost of university education. Because pursuit of college education strongly correlates with social class in all countries, almost all public subsidies to university students redistribute wealth and opportunity from poor families to rich families.

In the United States, wealthier people receive higher Social Security payments than poorer people, despite the fact that the investments and private pensions of the wealthy make these checks less important to their retirement incomes. In most MICs, the largest farm subsidies go to the wealthiest farmers. The MICs report that they maintain systems of **progressive taxes.** In a progressive tax system, a person with a higher income must pay a larger percentage of that income in taxes. In reality, however, after tax deductions that benefit special interests such as mortgage payments on second homes, business expenses, and home offices, the income tax in an MIC is not as progressive as it is supposed to be. At the same time, sales and payroll taxes are clearly **regressive taxes.** Working-class and middle-class families often pay higher percentages of their incomes in taxes than wealthy families pay.

Problems with income distributions across age groups also plague MICs. In a study of eight more industrialized countries, Timothy Smeeding, Barbara Torrey, and Martin Rein found that all of their governments provide sufficient incomes to allow most elderly families to escape poverty. Only Sweden and Norway, however, provide sufficient incomes to families with children to keep them out of poverty. The six other countries do not come close to meeting this standard. In the United States, for example, single-parent families in 1985 received only 58 percent of the income necessary to escape poverty.[19] With cuts in welfare, Medicaid, and other programs for the less advantaged that occurred in 1996, this figure has dropped still lower.

Social concerns as well as economic concerns divide citizens in the MICs. Many noneconomic issues partition the electorates in the MICs, including the rights of minorities, women, and gays; environmental protection; abortion; and religion. In Germany, the Green Party built its political platform around environmental issues, and the party has won representation in both the Bundestag and state legislatures. In other countries, special interest groups and political parties pursue social issues. In the United States, advances in direct marketing techniques, particularly direct mail, have generated a financial base for advocates for women's rights, children's rights, gay rights, consumer rights, abortion rights, fetus rights, rodent rights, tree rights, and gun owners' rights.

Three social problems currently create problems for almost all MICs: drug addiction, family dissolution, and crime. The sales volume of illegal drugs in the United States has been estimated at $100 billion to $150 billion, making this illicit commerce larger than the automobile industry. Sweden has almost as many drug addicts per capita as the United States; Germany has the highest addict death rate among MICs.[20] A longitudinal study of crime by Gurr, Grabosky, and Hula found that violent and nonviolent crimes have increased substantially for 60 years in every western democracy.[21] The rates of white-collar crime in London and Stockholm rose by nearly 700 percent between 1945 and 1970.[22] Britain, France, Sweden, the United States, and Germany all more than doubled their divorce rates between 1955 and 1985. The increases in both single-parent households headed by females and illegitimacy rates have sharply increased the number of children living in poverty. In the United States, the percentage of children born to unmarried mothers grew from 10.7 percent in 1970 to 28.0 percent in 1990.

In summary, although a citizen in a more industrialized country clearly enjoys a higher quality of life than one in a less industrialized country, the MICs still deal with many unsolved economic and social problems. As their populations age, their public expenditures change from investment in the young to consumption by the old. High rates of unemployment and slowing economies suggest that the MICs will have difficulty fighting off the economic challenges of the newly industrialized countries of Asia. While they try to cope with slowing economic growth, the demands for government services to assist the elderly, fight poverty, improve education, and cope with drug addiction place tremendous strains on the public treasuries and the social fabrics of these countries. Can their political institutions resolve these issues while maintaining the individual liberty that has been the greatest accomplishment of these societies?

Institutions and Ideologies in MICs

INSTITUTIONAL SIMILARITIES

The more industrialized countries exhibit striking similarities in their institutions despite their very different histories. Every MIC has a written or implied constitution that limits government, protects the rights of citizens, and prescribes the processes by which citizens will choose rulers and governments will make decisions. More importantly, the governments of the MICs generally abide by their constitutions. The constitutional protection of liberty and the development of the welfare state have led to societies that realize, to an exceptionally high degree, the basic ideals of liberalism described in Chapter 2.

Political competition also characterizes the MICs. In every country, more than one political party has a real chance to become part of the ruling government. In some countries, such as the United States, Canada, and Australia, only two such parties compete. In others, such as Germany, Austria, and France, voters can choose among several. All citizens of MICs consider their countries' legislatures to be critical parts of the legitimate decision-making structures.[23] Also, in both presidential and parliamentary systems, popular elections of legislators contribute an integral component of government legitimacy.

Recall from Chapter 8 that, despite the importance of the legislature, the chief executive is the most powerful political leader in every MIC except Switzerland. The president or prime minister develops a budget, sets policy priorities, and tries to convince the legislature to pass her programs. Although some countries give their legislators substantial autonomous power to formulate their own programs and budgets, legislatures still play clearly secondary roles. In Germany, for example, when the prime minister sends her budget to the Bundestag (Germany's main legislative body), the legislators may only pass or reject the entire budget. The Bundestag cannot change the budget without the approval of the finance minister, an individual appointed by the prime minister.

All MICs have built extensive national bureaucracies that not only implement laws passed by the legislatures, but also make laws by interpreting legislative acts and deciding issues in administrative courts. These bureaucracies develop policy proposals and represent specific social interest groups. For example, agriculture ministries not only implement the farming laws that emerge from the legislatures, but they also recommend levels of subsidies and tariffs, draft proposed legislation, and provide numerous services to farmers. Although graft and corruption affect policies in all countries and in almost all bureaucracies, public or private, MICs generally do not experience the debilitating corruption found in LIC bureaucracies.

In every more industrialized country, the left-right distinction in economic policy is a defining characteristic of politics. Parties identify themselves with either more leftist (*liberal* in American terminology) or more rightist (*conservative*) economic orientations. Even in the United States, the MIC with the smallest ideological difference between the major parties, the Democratic Party promotes policies significantly to the left of those of the Republican Party.

Parties on the left advocate greater economic equality among citizens, and they pursue this goal through policies that redistribute wealth from more advantaged members of society to less advantaged members. Leftist parties support active government economic planning and intervention. They recognize and encourage the rights of labor and encourage the growth of social welfare policies. The major leftist parties in the MICs are the **social democrats,** the socialists, and the communists. Although social democratic parties pursue programs designed to increase economic and social equality, they differ from socialists and communists in that they accept the important economic role of private property and advocate evolutionary rather than revolutionary means for achieving greater equality.

Parties on the right advocate planning in the private marketplace rather than government bureaucracies to direct economic outcomes. Rightist parties contend that the classical economic forces of supply and demand are far more likely than government planning to encourage economic growth. Although the rightist parties in almost every country accept social welfare programs, they prefer to limit the sizes and scopes of these programs. When it must intervene in the economy, a rightist government tends to take actions that assist the business community.

Students in the United States and Canada often have trouble understanding the goals of parties in other countries with the word *liberal* in their names. This label does not necessarily indicate a leftist party. In Japan and Italy, *liberal* indicates a rightist party, while in England it refers to a centrist party. In most countries, parties that call themselves *socialist* and *social democratic* represent leftist views.

In all MICs, interest groups play significant roles in aggregating public preferences and communicating these priorities to policy makers. As the next section of this chapter will discuss, the relationships between interest groups and government institutions, and between interest groups and political parties, create different patterns of government in the MICs.

INSTITUTIONAL DIFFERENCES

In an important analysis of culture and institutions, Arend Lijphart divides regimes into two major categories: **majoritarian states** and **consensual states.**[24] According to Lijphart's argument, culturally unified countries that lack major religious, ethnic, and racial divisions are likely to develop majoritarian structures. By *majoritarian,* Lijphart means that the institutions in these countries allow majorities of voters to decide issues, and they prevent minorities from blocking majority decisions. Majoritarian societies concentrate power in the political executive, and their political parties assume positions along a simple left-right economic dimension. Interest groups attach themselves to parties according to this same left-right economic dimension. Examples of such countries include Australia, Great Britain, New Zealand, Norway, and Sweden.

A consensual state structures decision making so that the government must achieve a consensus or supermajority to make a major policy decision. To accomplish this objective, the constitution in a consensual society often divides power through federalism, separation of powers, and multiple legislative chambers.[25] The Constitution of the United States is an example of an attempt to disperse political power in order to protect minority rights. Belgium, Canada, Switzerland, the Netherlands, and the United States have consensual government structures.

Lijphart claims that majoritarian institutions may function in a country when the losers in an election do not fear that the winners will take away their rights or seriously infringe on their deeply held values. Because no ethnic or religious differences encourage groups of citizens to see themselves as inherently different from others, most important political issues tend to focus on economic questions rather than race, ethnicity, and religion. In a society such as Japan, where almost the entire population belongs to a single ethnic group, citizens see each other as members of the same community who share similar cultural values and norms.

Policies in consensual countries, such as Switzerland, cross several major nationalistic, ethnic, or religious divisions. Often, economic well-being strongly overlaps with these divisions. Major cleavages in society lead people to see political decisions as potential threats to their basic values and interests. Lijphart maintains that the constitution of a country with major religious, ethnic, or racial divisions will structure political decision making so that majorities cannot destroy minority values or liberties.

Pluralism or Corporatism?   Another distinction between pluralism and corporatism in industrial democracies focuses on the extent of coordination between interest groups, parties, and the government in the development of public policy. In **pluralist states,** numerous groups organize around relatively narrow interests and lobby all branches and levels of government. For example, several national and many regional organizations may claim to represent farmers. Rather than a single major labor union for industrial workers, separate unions may organize workers in various industries.

The idealized pluralist system is a descendent of the liberal theories discussed in Chapter 2, particularly the liberal ideals that emphasize individualism and rational self-interest. Pluralism postulates that individuals will pursue their self-interest by joining groups because they rationally expect benefits from those associations.[†] Because an individual acting alone cannot easily influence political outcomes, people see that they must join groups if they wish to participate effectively in the political process.[26] As Gabriel Almond and Sidney Verba wrote in their classic work, *The Civic Culture,* "Voluntary associations are the prime means by which the function of mediating between the state and the individual is performed. Through them the individual is able to relate . . . effectively and meaningfully to the political system."[27]

A political interest group can organize around any common concern from a tariff on imported rice to a regulation protecting spotted owls. Groups represent savings and loan associations, copper smelting plants, hardware store owners, auto workers, school teachers, medical doctors, and government employees. Groups lobby for subsidies to sugar growers, beef producers, and steel manufacturers and for tax breaks to automobile producers and parents who send their children to private schools. *Pluralist politics do not assume that everyone works together to promote an underlying public welfare.* Rather, in a pluralist political system, almost every interest has a legitimate claim to government preference. Each interest pursues the policies it desires and the values it prefers. Tobacco

---

[†] As Chapters 1 and 8 explained, rational individuals will not necessarily join interest groups. Because of the potential benefits of free riding, a rational individual will allow others to join groups and pay membership dues to provide a desired collective good.

producers, nonsmokers, smokers, and those who must pay the medical costs of smoking all plead their cases, if they can organize and gather sufficient resources, and public officials accept an obligation to provide each group the opportunity to be heard. Robert McCormick and Robert Tollison summarize the basic idea of pluralism: The "public interest" is an outcome of people's pursuit of personal interests within a given institutional framework. People do not vote for options that they expect to promote the public interest, and they do not pursue some "private interest" when they buy groceries; they seek "self-interest" in both cases.[28] Among the MICs generally classified as pluralist states are the United States, Canada, Great Britain, New Zealand, Australia, and France.

Corporatist states follow a radically different pattern of interest group involvement. Corporatism does not grow out of liberal theory or share its emphasis on individuals. Instead, the ideal corporatist state reflects communitarian ideologies. *Corporatism assumes that some identifiable "public welfare" should guide social actions and some "good" policies will achieve "just" solutions and the "best" outcomes for the community.* Although the corporatist institutions follow communitarian rather than liberal standards for government and society, the corporatist MICs nevertheless protect individual liberties identified in classical liberal theories.

A corporatist political system replaces the many, narrow interest groups of pluralism with a few, broad interest organizations called **peak associations.** The state recognizes these peak associations as the official representatives of legitimate interests in the society; it acknowledges only one peak association as the representative for each major economic interest. For example, one association represents all industry employers and one association represents all industry employees.

Rather than pluralist clamor with hundreds of groups attempting to affect policy at numerous locations, the corporatist system invites state-sanctioned peak associations to meet with government bureaucracies. Elected government officials then develop policies to maximize overall social welfare. Most political studies classify Norway, Sweden, Austria, and the Netherlands as corporatist systems. Germany, Denmark, and Japan exhibit both corporatist and pluralist tendencies, and most empirical research classifies them as mixed systems.[29]

The Success Records of Alternative Political Systems in MICs

For almost two decades, political economists have searched for ways to evaluate political institutions. They have studied whether leftist or rightist parties spend more on social welfare, reduce poverty more effectively, and encourage more equal distributions of income. They have also examined whether majoritarian or consensual systems foster more rapid economic growth and different distributions of income. Similar studies have compared corporatist and pluralist institutions.

WELFARE EXPENDITURES, POVERTY, AND INEQUALITY

People often assume that leftist regimes spend more than rightist governments on programs to help disadvantaged citizens. After all, a major goal of leftist governments is greater income equality. In fact, however, research results do not support this seemingly obvious conclusion! The regimes that actually spend the largest amounts on social welfare programs are coalition governments made up of centrist and rightist parties that face strong opposition from the left.[30] This finding suggests that when no party can achieve a majority in the legislature, a coalition made up of the center and right attempts to purchase support by expanding government spending on welfare programs.

In possibly the most important conclusion about the impact of political ideologies and political institutions on governments' spending patterns, researchers have found that no political variable explains a large percentage of the variation. In a study of more industrialized nations, Harold Wilensky found that a country's per-capita GDP, the age structure of its population, and the length of time since the country introduced social welfare programs predict which countries spend a lot or a little on programs to help the less advantaged.[31]

The finding that demographic and economic variables predict social welfare spending better than political variables may surprise some. Surely the ruling party's expressions of support for or opposition to increases in welfare spending should have a major impact on such spending. Remember, however, that all more industrialized countries are democracies; presumably, a democratic government should try hard to accurately translate the preferences of the population into public policy. An individual's age and wealth strongly influence her preferences for goods and services. If the government accurately translates voters' preferences into public policy, then the economic and demographic characteristics of the country will strongly influence how much the government spends and what it buys.

Examine briefly how your income and age influence how much you spend and what you buy. Whatever your age, you must spend some money for food, housing, and transportation. People with higher incomes spend more on all of these commodities. Similarly, wealthier nations can spend more on all programs than other nations. How do you allocate money between expenses such as education and health care? A 20-year-old college student probably directs a large portion of expenditures to education-related goods and services. A 75-year-old grandparent spends a larger portion of personal income on health care. Similarly, a nation with a large percentage of its population aged under 25 will spend more on education, while a nation with a large percentage of its population over 65 will spend more on health care and retirement pensions.

In the same way, it makes sense that countries with long-established welfare programs spend more on them than countries that set up these programs in recent times. Government programs tend to grow over time. During periods of economic growth, politicians may choose to expand benefits because the nation can afford to do so and because voters often reelect politicians who provide such benefits. During recessions, however, politicians do not cut spending on these programs because it is unpopular to reduce benefits, particularly when the population is already suffering. Because elected officials expand programs during good times but do not cut them during bad times, social welfare programs tend to grow more rapidly than the economy in general. Officials seem especially willing to expand programs and unwilling to cut them in governments where no single party can command a legislative majority.

Although political variables do not accurately predict government expenditure patterns, Arend Lijphart and Markus Crepaz found that consensual parliamentary democracies outperformed other institutional arrangements with respect to some goals. They achieved higher voter participation and reduced political deaths, political riots, inflation, unemployment, and economic inequality as compared to majoritarian systems.[32] Consensual and majoritarian democracies did not differ in their ability to encourage economic growth.

A number of authors argued in the early 1990s that political variables do influence expenditure patterns.[33] Using more sophisticated statistical techniques than were available to earlier studies, these writers have attempted to show that corporatist, highly centralized governments did spend more than others on social welfare programs. More recent research using corrected statistical procedures has found results quite similar to those of earlier research, though. The most important predictors of welfare spending are the age of a country's population and the age of its welfare program. The research confirmed the earlier finding that competition from a strong, leftist *opposition* party has a stronger impact than any other political variable on social welfare spending.[34]

UNEMPLOYMENT, INFLATION, AND ECONOMIC GROWTH

Can some forms of government achieve economic goals better than others? All MIC governments attempt to achieve three macroeconomic goals: high rates of real economic growth, high employment, and low inflation. Unfortunately, when economic growth rates are high and unemployment is low, inflation is likely to increase. Inflation is a problem for three reasons: it discourages savings, harms those who live on fixed incomes, such as many retirees, and it makes imports from other countries more expensive. This raises the cost of living for everyone. The economic objective of MIC governments is to achieve the highest possible rates of sustained economic growth and employment without creating high rates of inflation. Both of these effects reduce consumption. Could some arrangement of political institutions prevent this?

The United States relies on the Federal Reserve Board to implement fiscal policy to speed up or slow down the economy. When unemployment drops to a level that drives up the cost of labor, the Federal Reserve Board raises interest rates and reduces the supply of money. The board intends in this way to slow investment and prevent inflation. But, countries want investment to create new jobs and fuel economic growth. Similarly, employed people produce more than unemployed people. Does one institutional arrangement maximize investment without driving up prices? Can a country keep inflation low without creating unemployment?

Adam Przeworski and Michael Wallerstein formulated a logical model to show that corporatist agreements among business, labor, and government could achieve these economic goals.[35] Przeworski and Wallerstein assert that workers and capitalists are caught in a situation similar to the prisoner's dilemma game discussed in Chapter 1. Workers want high wages and low unemployment, while capitalists want high profits and low inflation. It seems as though one side can win only if the other loses. In fact, all of society loses because no country seems able to combine full employment and corresponding high productivity with stable prices; instead, those forces cause inflation.

Przeworski and Wallerstein contend, however, that countries can escape the dilemma through an agreement between capital and labor that the government enforces. They contend that some countries have found this solution: a corporatist government led by a leftist political party.

The argument for this particular form of government goes as follows. Both workers and capitalists would benefit if workers would agree to accept lower wages in the short term to achieve full employment. Workers will do this, however, only if capitalists agree to reinvest the profits they make through low labor costs. If capitalists increase their investment, growing production will increase the demand for labor. If investment increases sufficiently, the economy reaches full employment. The national economy will grow faster and productivity will increase as a result of high investment and full employment. Because of this growth in productivity, labor can receive higher wages without creating inflation. Labor will agree to the required wage restraints, however, only if they control the government so they can force the capitalists to keep their side of the agreement.

The **Przeworski-Wallerstein model** of economic growth includes five institutional requirements. First, labor organizations must be able to bind individual workers to the wage agreements reached with the capitalists. Second, capitalist organizations must be able bind their members to the agreements reached with workers. Third, capitalists must reinvest the profits they gain from paying lower wages. Fourth, government must be willing and able to enforce agreements between worker and capitalist organizations. Fifth, the government must ensure that the coalition that forms the compromises can win popular support in elections. This implies that the government must consider the interests of those who do not take part in the bargaining process.[36] The Przeworski-Wallerstein model clearly requires the institutional arrangements found in corporatist societies. They argue that examples include Norway, Sweden, and Austria, all countries that have grown rapidly and consistently since World War II.

Several scholars have attempted to operationalize and test the hypotheses of the Przeworski-Wallerstein model. They have found evidence to support it,[37] but the model appears to work for some time periods and not for others.[38] The model seems unlikely to describe future rates of growth because it requires a relatively closed economic system. The system that Przeworski and Wallerstein propose does not allow either labor or capital to move freely across national boundaries. Businesses cannot invest profits abroad, and foreign goods cannot undersell domestic goods. As the next chapter will show, none of these conditions holds completely today, and they are even less likely to persist in the future. The economies of the MICs are highly integrated into the world economy. The economic integration of western Europe as well as the North American Free Trade Agreement will continue to increase the international character of MIC economies.

One additional flaw disrupts the Przeworski-Wallerstein model. Remember that it supposes workers will accept lower wages because government will force businesses to reinvest profits. MIC governments do not, however, control investment decisions of firms. Only in a planned economy such as China can government guarantee investment.

While a government may be willing to pursue policies that encourage investment, the critical variable that guides this decision is the individual firm's expectation that such investments will generate higher returns than alternative uses of capital. Empirical research shows that government tax policies have relatively little impact on this variable.[39] Further, the failure of the planned economies suggests that when governments control investment, their economies grow at lower rates than economies in which firms can invest where they expect to find the highest returns.

One set of political institutions does clearly appear to improve economic performance, however. That institution is the protection of private-property rights. Distinguished economic historians such as Douglass North have made this argument for many years.[40] Recently, David Leblang reported a study of 50 countries from 1960 to 1990 showing that protection of property rights has a strong, positive impact on economic growth.[41] As indicated in Chapter 1, effective private property rights allow people to buy, sell, consume, and invest. In short, they improve security for economic transactions and clarify incentives. Leblang found strong evidence that clear and well-protected property rights encourage economic growth. His study also made the important discovery that democracies encourage clear and effective property rights and protect those rights significantly more effectively than do authoritarian regimes.

Summary

This chapter examined those fortunate countries that enjoy relatively secure political liberty and economic wealth. Despite this happy condition, even the wealthiest nations face difficult economic and social problems. The ideological orientation of a government has little impact on that country's welfare expenditures, and the economic interdependence of all more industrialized countries with the world economy complicates attempts to solve economic problems through single-nation economic policies. One institutional variable that clearly appears to influence economic growth across all societies is explicitly defined and well-protected property rights.

QUESTIONS AND EXERCISES

Questions for Reason

1. Explain Mancur Olson's argument that interest groups in democracies create economic inefficiencies. Why are older democracies more likely to have greater inefficiencies?

2. Explain why the tax structure of the United States would become regressive if the national government adopted a flat-rate income tax and the states continued to rely on property taxes and sales taxes to generate income.

3. How do majoritarian states differ from consensual states? Why do these states develop different institutions? Does the choice of consensual institutions reduce economic efficiency in a country?

4. Explain the difference between pluralist and corporatist regimes. In which of these categories would you place each of the world's industrialized democracies?

Questions for Reflection

1. Why did Lijphart not classify the United States as a consensual democracy? What effects would the classification decision have on his reported relationship between consensual governments and lower levels of political deaths, political riots, inflation, unemployment, and economic inequality?

2. Why, according to pluralist theory, did the U.S. Congress in 1995 make larger percentage cuts in the programs for poor children than from programs for wealthy elderly people?

3. Economic analyses of income inequality and rates of economic growth in industrialized countries consistently show that higher rates of inequality lead to lower rates of economic growth.[42] Why have these findings not led to a greater emphasis on policies intended to change income distributions in countries with the highest rates of inequality?

4. This chapter began with a description of the coming crisis in entitlement payments in MICs caused by aging populations and declining economic growth rates. Research indicates that different institutional arrangements within industrialized democracies have only slight impacts on economic growth. Is it likely, however, that some institutional arrangements will deal better than others with the expected shortfall of funds both to pay for entitlements of the growing number of elderly recipients and to fund the investment necessary for economic growth?

    To illustrate the responses of pluralist and corporatist systems to the forthcoming crisis, imagine two hypothetical MICs, one pluralist and one corporatist. Assume that each country elected a new government in 1997. The government in each country joins two parties in a coalition. Further assume that the prime ministers of these governments believe that when the baby boomers are old enough to retire (between 2005 and 2015), both government health-care programs and Social Security pension programs will face crises.

    The prime minister in each country meets with economic advisors and determines that a responsible leader must initiate policies that will reduce the severity of that crisis. Both prime ministers come up with the following policy proposals: (1) small increases in payroll and sales taxes, (2) reductions in the cost-of-living raises built into the government-funded pension plans, (3) reductions in government coverage of medical procedures that do not significantly prolong life, and (4) a new tax on the pensions and health-care benefits of the wealthiest one-third of elderly people. The prime ministers believe that these policies will substantially reduce the problems that their countries will face a decade from now. How might political parties and interest groups in pluralist and corporatist countries respond to these proposals? How successful would you predict the prime minister will be in each system?

Questions for Analysis: The Impact of Political Culture on Economic Growth

In a recent effort to determine whether cultural values affect economic development, Jim Granato, Ronald Inglehart, and David Leblang compared models of economic growth based on cultural variables with models based on economic variables. The

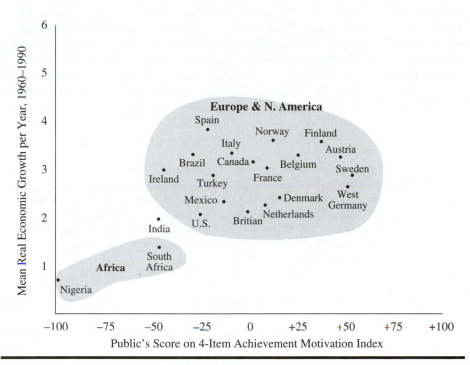

FIGURE 11.4

ECONOMIC GROWTH RATE BY ACHIEVEMENT MOTIVATION SCORES

Note: The Achievement Motivation index is based on the percentage in each society who emphasized "Thrift" and "Determination" as important things for a child to learn, *minus* the percentage emphasizing "Obedience" and "Religious Faith."

Source: Adapted from James Granato, Ronald Inglehart, and David Leblang, "The Effect of Cultural Values on Economic Development: Theory, Hypotheses, and Some Empirical Tests," *American Journal of Political Science* Volume 40, Number 3 (August 1996): 612. Reprinted by permission of the University of Wisconsin Press.

authors studied both LICs and MICs in a combined sample over the period 1960 to 1989. They hypothesized that cultures that taught achievement values would experience higher economic growth than those that did not emphasize those values in countries that stressed postmaterial values (see Chapter 6), the study expected lower economic growth.[43] Figure 11.4 shows the scatterplot of the distribution of growth rates and the achievement motivation scores of the countries included in the study.

The economic model for the study was based on investment. It included variables for the initial level of development in a country, physical capital investment rates as a percentage of GDP, and human capital investment measured by the percentage of children in the appropriate age groups enrolled in elementary and secondary education. In their original models, the authors found statistically significant associations for all variables. The economic model based on investment indicators explained 55 percent of the variation in economic growth. The cultural model explained 59 percent.

Your task is to use multiple regression to combine these two models to determine whether cultural or economic variables are more significant and which cultural and economic variables have the strongest associations. First, run a scatterplot regressing economic growth on each of the dependent variables. Then use multiple regression to see which variables continue to show statistical significance. Include all independent variables in your model, including the level of economic development in 1960. Your dependent variable is the average rate of growth over the 30 years between 1960 and 1989. The codebook in Appendix C contains the names of all variables, an explanation of how they were measured, and the countries included in the sample.

NOTES

[1] Denis Kessler, "Les retraites en peril?" *Revue Francaise Des Affaires Sociales* (June 1984), pp. 69–83.

[2] George Schieber, *Financing and Delivering Health Care: A Comparative Analysis of OECD Countries* (Paris: Organization for Economic Cooperation and Development, 1987).

[3] Hugh Heclo, "Toward a New Welfare State," in *The Development of Welfare States in Europe and America,* ed. by Peter Flora and Arnold J. Heidenheimer (New Brunswick, N.J.: Transaction Books, 1981), pp. 383–406.

[4] Ibid., p. 392.

[5] Ibid., p. 393.

[6] Jürgen Kohl, "Trends and Problems in Postwar Public Expenditure Development in Western Europe and North America," in *The Development of Welfare States,* pp. 309–311.

[7] Richard Rose, "Ordinary People in Extraordinary Circumstances," *Studies in Public Policy* 11 (1986).

[8] Heclo, "Toward a New Welfare State," passim.

[9] Ibid., p. 397.

[10] Ibid., p. 398.

[11] A. Maddison, *Phases of Capitalist Development* (Oxford: Oxford University Press, 1982).

[12] Erich Weede, "Sectoral Reallocation, Distributional Coalitions, and the Welfare State as Determinants of Economic Growth Rates in Industrialized Democracies," *European Journal of Political Research* 14 (1986), pp. 501–519.

[13] See Robert J. Barro, "Economic Growth in a Cross Section of Countries," *American Economic Review* 106 (1991), pp. 407–443; Gregory N. Mankiw, David Romer, and David Weil, "A Contribution to the Empirics of Economic Growth," *Quarterly Journal of Economics* 107 (1992), pp. 407–437; and Torste Persson and Guido Tabellini, "Is Inequality Harmful for Growth?" *American Economic Review* 84 (1994), pp. 600–621.

[14] Mattie Dogan, "Crisis of the Welfare State," in *Comparing Pluralist Democracies,* ed. by Mattie Dogan (Boulder, Colo.: Westview Press, 1988), pp. 214–215.

[15] Ibid., pp. 213–214. Ross Perot attempted to make this argument in his 1992 independent campaign for president of the United States.

[16] Theodore Stanger and Marcus Mabry, "Liberté, Egalité, Médiocrité: France: The glory is gone," *Newsweek,* June 20, 1994, p. 50.

[17] Weede, "Sectoral Reallocation,"pp. 501–502. Hakan Nordström, *Studies in Trade Policy and Economic Growth,* Monograph No. 20 (Stockholm: Institute for International Economic Studies, 1992).

[18] Ibid., p. 503. For the original argument, see Mancur Olson, Jr., *The Rise and Decline of Nations* (New Haven, Conn.: Yale University Press, 1982).

[19] Timothy Smeeding, Barbara Torrey, and Martin Rein, "Patterns of Income and Poverty: The Economic Status of Children and the Elderly in Eight Countries," in *The Vulnerable,* ed. by John Palmer, Timothy Smeeding, and Barbara Torrey (Washington, D.C.: Urban Institute, 1988), p. 111.

[20] John Nagel, *Introduction to Comparative Politics: Political System Performance in Three Worlds,* 3rd ed. (Chicago: Nelson Hall, 1992), p. 138.

[21] Ted Gurr, Peter Grabosky, and Richard Hula, *Politics of Crime and Conflict* (Beverly Hills, Calif.: Sage, 1977).

[22] Ibid., 635–636.

[23] Gabriel A. Almond and Bingham Powell, "Government and Policymaking," in *Comparative Politics: A World View,* 5th ed., ed. by Gabriel A. Almond and Bingham Powell (New York: Harper Collins, 1992), p. 97.

[24] Arend Lijphart, *Democracies: Patterns of Majoritarian and Consensus Government in Twenty-One Countries* (New Haven, Conn.: Yale University Press, 1984).

[25] Almond and Powell, "Government Policy Making," p. 96.

[26] Harmon Zeigler, *Pluralism, Corporatism, and Confucianism: Political Association and Conflict Regulation in the United States, Europe, and Taiwan* (Philadelphia: Temple University Press, 1988), pp. 4–5.

[27] Gabriel A. Almond and Sidney Verba, *The Civic Culture: Political Attitudes and Democracy in Five Nations* (Boston: Little, Brown, 1965), p. 245.

[28] Robert E. McCormick and Robert D. Tollison, *Politicians, Legislation, and the Economy: An Inquiry into the Interest-Group Theory of Government* (Boston: Martinus Nijhoff, 1981), pp. 5–6.

[29] For rankings of MICs on both the consensual-majoritarian and pluralist-corporatist dimensions, see Arend Lijphart and Markus Crepaz, "Corporatism and Consensus Democracy in Eighteen Countries: Conceptual and Empirical Linkages," *British Journal of Political Science* 21 (1992), pp. 235–256.

[30] Kohl, "Trends and Problems," p. 324.

[31] Harold Wilensky, *The Welfare State and Equality: Structural and Ideological Roots of Public Expenditures* (Berkeley: University of California Press, 1975). More recent studies include Douglas Hibbs, Jr., *The Political Economy of Industrial Democracies* (Cambridge, Mass.: Harvard University Press, 1987); and Alexander M. Hicks and Duane H. Swank, "Politics, Institutions, and Welfare Spending in Industrial Democracies," *American Political Science Review* 86 (1992), pp. 658–674. Another excellent study shows that the method of measuring corporatism and labor union strength as well as the time period chosen for the study determines whether relationships will occur: Marco Wilke, *Corporatism and the Stability of Capitalist Democracies* (Frankfurt: Peter Lang, 1991).

[32] Lijphart and Crepaz, "Corporatism and Consensus Democracies"; and Arend Lijphart, "Democracies: Forms, Performance, and Constitutional Engineering," *European Journal of Political Research* 25 (1994), pp. 1–17.

[33] For an example of this literature and a review of earlier work, see Alexander Hicks and Duane Swank, "Politics, Institutions, and Welfare Spending in Industrialized Democracies, 1960–1982," *American Political Science Review* 86 (1992), pp. 658–674.

[34] Nathanial Beck and Jonathan N. Katz, "What to Do (and Not to Do) with Time-Series-Cross-Section Data in Comparative Politics," *American Political Science Review* 89 (1995), pp. 634–647.

[35] Adam Przeworski and Michael Wallerstein, "The Structure of Class Conflict in Democratic Capitalist Societies," *American Political Science Review* 76 (1982), pp. 215–238.

[36] Ibid., p. 236.

[37] See, for example, Peter Lange, "Unions, Workers, and Wage Regulation: The Rational Bases of Consent," in *Order and Conflict in Contemporary Capitalism,* ed. by John H. Goldthorpe (Oxford: Clarendon Press, 1984), pp. 98–103; Peter Lange and Geoffrey Garrett, "The Politics of Growth: Strategic Interaction and Economic Performance in the Advanced Industrial Democracies, 1974–1980," *The Journal of Politics* 47 (1985), pp. 792–827; R. Michael Alvarez, Geoffrey Garrett, and Peter Lange, "Government Partnership, Labor Organization, and Macroeconomic Performance," *American Political Science Review* 85 (1991), pp. 539–556; and Nathanial Beck et al., "Government Partisanship, Labor Organization, and Macroeconomic Performance: A Corrigendum," *American Political Science Review* 87 (1993), pp. 945–949.

[38] Ibid.; and Beck and Katz, "What to Do," pp. 634–642.

[39] For a formal model refuting the Lange et al. theory as well as empirical evidence, see Wilke, *Corporatism and Stability,* pp. 132–133.

[40] Douglass North, *Institutions, Institutional Change and Economic Growth* (Cambridge: Cambridge University Press, 1990).

[41] David A. Leblang, "Property Rights, Democracy, and Economic Growth," *Political Research Quarterly* 49 (1996), pp. 5–21.

[42] See Torste Persson and Guido Taballini, "Is Inequality Harmful for Growth?" *American Economic Review* 84 (1994), pp. 600–621.

[43] James Granato, Ronald Inglehart, and David Leblang, "The Effect of Cultural Values on Economic Development: Theory, Hypotheses, and Some Empirical Tests," *American Journal of Political Science* 40 (1996), pp. 607–631.

12

Global Politics in a Changing World

Key Terms

Isolationism	International	Genocide
Foreign Policy	Nongovernmental	Human Rights
Political Realism	Organization (INGO)	Economic and Social Rights
National Interest	Multinational Corporation	Personal-Integrity Rights
Neorealism	(MNC)	International
Idealism	Pragmatism	Governmental
	Interstate War	Organization (IGO)
	Imperialism	

Events remind us fairly frequently of the fact that we are citizens of a particular nation-state. We celebrate the efforts of our Olympic heroes, we see our chief executive board a helicopter on the evening news, or stand for our national anthem. Only rarely, however, do persons identify themselves as members of the human race or the world system. Although we rarely think about the connection, all of us participate in the global system and its many interrelated and overlapping political subsystems, as Figure 12.1 demonstrates.

Most of us rarely think about how much global affairs touch our lives. (See Box 12.1.) That we do not take the time to reflect on these matters is understandable. We are too busy with the hustle and bustle of our everyday lives to sit around and ponder our relationships with the rest of the world. One of our goals in this chapter is to help you to reflect on global politics and their importance to your life. We also hope to teach you some of the major theories of international relations and to introduce you to some of the problems that dominate the thinking of social scientists who specialize in world politics.

In this chapter we first discuss technological developments that have changed world political relationships in the last hundred years. We then summarize the predominant

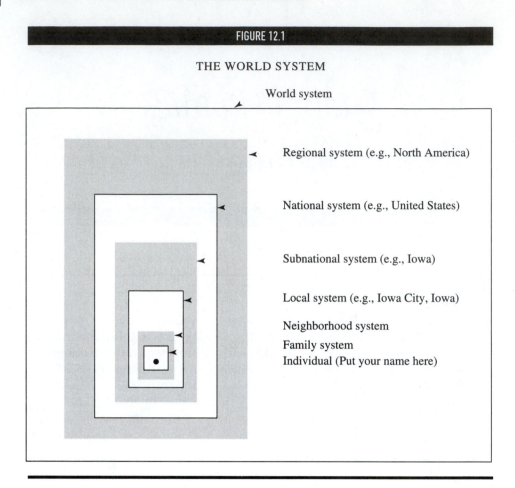

FIGURE 12.1

THE WORLD SYSTEM

Source: Adapted from Bruce Russett and Harvey Starr, *World Politics: The Menu for Choice,* 4th ed. (New York: W. H. Freeman & Co., 1992), p. 493. Copyright © 1992 by W.H. Freeman and Company. Used with permission.

theory that has guided the study of world politics during the past two millennia and outline some of the arguments of its critics. Next we look at some of the major problems that face the world system today, along with a few recent achievements. Finally we assess the chances of the human race successfully meeting its current challenges.

Improved Technology, Increasing Interactions

People today often observe that "The world is becoming a much smaller place." The essence of this statement is true, because technological developments have vastly expanded human abilities to travel, transport goods, and communicate. Alvin Toffler, in his book *Future Shock,* showed the effects of technology on the ability of people to transport themselves and their goods over long distances.[1] He pointed out that in 6,000 B.C.,

BOX 12.1

The World Politics Game

Let's play a game. Imagine what your life would be like if the United States were to follow a strict isolationist foreign policy, maintaining no political or economic relations with any other country in the world. Check where your belongings were manufactured. Chances are that some of your favorite possessions—a car, TV set, stereo system, or perhaps all three—will vanish into thin air.

As an experiment, I set some time aside to play the game. A cold draft provided me with the first clue that something was terribly wrong. I had lost my Costa Rican pants and my shirt, manufactured in Thailand. I reached up to scratch my head in bewilderment and found my beloved Chicago Cubs hat was also missing. (It had been made in China. So much for the national pastime.)

In fact, I couldn't finish writing this paragraph because my computer quit working due to missing parts. To meet the publisher's pressing deadline, I immediately had to get to a store where I could find a replacement computer. I dressed in my best "made in the U.S.A." clothing, and hurried to my good old, American-made Ford Escort, which waited loyally in the driveway. Unfortunately when I tried to start it I found it wouldn't run because some of those things under the hood (whose purposes have always been a complete mystery to me) had vanished because they had come from foreign sources. My Fuji bike was gone. So were my favorite Nike running shoes.

I grumbled bitterly about my losses as I walked to the store, my American-made dress shoes giving me blisters with every step. At the store, I loudly object to the high prices. Due probably to the sudden disappearance of the advantages gained through U.S. participation in the global marketplace, my new computer doesn't cost a lot more and work nearly as quickly as the one I had before.

Okay, you get the point. My game is officially over. This story illustrates some of my connections outside the United States. Give it a try yourself to find out how other countries touch your life. You would probably face similar hardships without your international relationships. Many of you, and members of your family, would lose jobs and as a result would face an uncertain future fraught with financial hardships.

Don't get the impression that all of the outcomes would be bad, though. Some of you would be pleasantly surprised to have brothers, sisters, uncles, or grandfathers who had died in foreign wars come knocking at your doors. Also, if we were to accept some international-relations theories and their implications, conditions in less industrialized countries might actually improve. Certainly, life would be much different, because world politics have come to affect people's lives all over the world each and every day in innumerable ways we rarely, if ever, bother to consider.

the fastest method of transportation over long distances was the camel caravan, which averaged around 8 miles per hour. In 1825, the swiftest mode of transportation, the first steam locomotive, could move at 13 mph. Thus in some 8,000 years of human history, there was only a very slight improvement in the speed at which people could move. In the last two centuries, however, and particularly in the last generation, the speed of travel has increased phenomenally. Another steam engine broke the 100 mph barrier in the 1880s. In the 1960s, jets traveled at around 4,000 mph, and during the *Apollo 15* mission that carried humans to the moon, astronauts reached speeds of 24,000 mph.[2]

A similar trend has transformed communications. Through a global network of telephone lines and interconnected computers, people can carry on conversations with others and send documents instantaneously to the other side of the world. During the Gulf War, Saddam Hussein was probably watching the same news source as many Americans and their government officials—the Cable News Network (CNN)—thanks to satellite TV. Leaders of foreign governments are not the only ones watching. Satellites carry classic American TV shows like *Gilligan's Island, Leave It to Beaver,* and *Dallas* that, for better or worse, carry images of American culture abroad.

As a result of these technological advances, international events transform the lives of people around the world. Improved technology is clearly a large part of the reason that world politics affects people's lives so much today. Studies in all social sciences show clearly that families, marriages, friendships, work, leisure, agriculture, housing, travel, electoral politics, and every other aspect of life have recently undergone changes of great magnitude.[3] As Box 12.1 shows, a political or economic upheaval in one society can adversely affect the lives of customers in other countries who depend on the goods that those societies produce.

Technological developments also affect the way governments act and react toward one another. During much of its history, the United States government adhered to an isolationist foreign policy. It chose to stay out of the political affairs of other countries, focusing its efforts mainly on what was happening at home. In today's "smaller world," such an isolationist policy would be nearly impossible for the United States or any other major country. The shrinking-world phenomenon, coupled with the United States' position of world leadership, entangles the U.S. government in situations around the world. Even Bill Clinton, a president elected after expressing much more concern with problems at home than with those abroad, has found himself bogged down in crises in Somalia, Haiti, the Balkans, and North Korea.

Realism in World Politics

Most of this book has dealt with domestic politics within national political systems. Though some might say that world politics as a field was founded over 2,000 years ago, relatively few scholars have chosen to study them. This lack of attention has caused developments in the subdiscipline of world politics to lag behind those in political science and economics, which focus on domestic issues. This is unfortunate, since only global political efforts can deal with many of the serious challenges now facing the human race such as environmental decay, war, and weapons proliferation.

To better understand how world politics work we must know the different kinds of social units that act in the world system. Most scholars of world politics agree that the most important actor in world politics over about the last three centuries has been the nation-state (e.g., the United States, Ghana, Argentina). The objectives, goals, and political strategies adopted by governments of these units toward other nation-states make up those nations' **foreign policies.**

Because of the importance of the state, world politics scholars have thought a good deal about foreign policies. The Greek historian Thucydides pioneered the field of international relations some 2,000 years ago. Scholars also refer to him as the father of **political realism** because of a book (or more accurately, a scroll) he wrote on the Peloponnesian War. For most of the two millennia since Thucydides world politics has been dominated by scholars and practitioners who have expanded on his theory and assumptions. Among the thinkers associated with political realism is Henry Kissinger, secretary of state under President Richard Nixon.

Like all theories, the theory of political realism makes some basic assumptions about human nature and how the world works.[4] Let's look at those assumptions and their strengths and limitations.

First, most realists share a pessimistic view of human nature. Many realists agree with Thomas Hobbes that humans are naturally greedy and nasty, and that they probably cannot improve their basic nature. Because of natural human greed and the improbability of improvement, realists believe there will always be conflict in world politics. They believe that permanent harmony between human beings, and their nation-states, is possible only in the minds of dreamers.

Realists simplify world politics by making a second assumption that nation-states are the key actors on the world scene. They admit that subnational actors such as multinational corporations and local governments may have important effects. Still, realists contend that they can explain most important phenomena in world politics by looking only at nation-states.

In their third assumption (an extremely important one), realists posit that the highest priorities of nation-states are power and security. In fact, one realist argued that power is the "currency of the political system in the way that money is the currency of the economy."[5] Much as economists assume that firms seek to maximize profits, realists accept that a nation-state most effectively promotes its interests by accumulating all the power necessary to protect its borders. Realists deduce from this assumption, and their assertion of the primary importance of the nation-state, that world politics is, and will be, full of conflict between states with competing interests. They often argue that international relations resemble the state of nature as it was described by Hobbes.

Fourth and finally, realists believe that nation-states normally act in a rational manner. That is, governments routinely calculate the costs and benefits of alternative actions to reach their goals and then choose the actions that they judge best *for their nation-states.*

Armed with these four assumptions, a realist can provide an explanation for almost any course of action that a nation-state would take. If these assumptions are correct, then the realist does not need to know much about decision makers in a particular country, what those decision makers think, or what they know. This simplification is particularly convenient in the study of world politics because governments almost always make foreign-policy decisions behind closed doors.

BOX 12.2

Do the Ends Justify the Means?

A rather difficult question one can ask of a realist is, "Does what is right and wrong matter to you, or is power all-important?" Few realists would admit to taking a position of amorality, where morals are believed to be completely unimportant to world politics. One well-known position on this question was offered by Hans J. Morgenthau, the 20th century's most prominent realist scholar.

Morgenthau distinguished between abstract notions of morality and something he called *political morality,* which referred to the application of moral principles to judge the outcomes of foreign-policy actions. According to Morgenthau:

> There can be no political morality without prudence—the weighing of the consequences of alternative political actions—to be the supreme virtue in politics. . . . Ethics in the abstract judges action by its conformity with the moral law; political ethics judges action by its political consequences.*

To justify his position, Morgenthau quoted the greatest of American presidents, Abe Lincoln, who made a similar distinction, but expressed it in much simpler terms:

> I do the very best I know how, the very best I can, and I mean to keep doing so until the end. If the end brings me out all right, what is said against me won't amount to anything. If the end brings me out wrong, ten angels swearing I was right would make no difference.†

Thus, in answer to our questions, Morgenthau, and many other realists, would argue that in foreign affairs achieving "good" ends justifies actions that many would consider unethical. From the realist perspective an American president who directly promotes morality instead of his country's power interests would be like the spectacle of Emmit Smith, the great halfback for the Dallas Cowboys football team, performing a ballet dance after receiving the ball on a handoff. The football coach would say, "Ballet is an honorable pursuit, Emmit, but please, not in a professional football game!" (Admittedly the coach's language might be "less polite".) Similarly, the realist would say "morality and ethics are admirable, but please Mr. President, not in the game of world politics!"

---

*Hans J. Morgenthau, *Politics among Nations (*New York: Alfred A. Knopf., 1967), p. 10.

† Ibid.

One goal of realist theory is to *explain* why things happen in world politics. Clearly, however, many realists also seek to help government decision makers by *prescribing ways they should act.* Realists believe that it is the statesman's duty to act in the **national interest,** that is, officials in charge of their country's foreign policy should seek to increase the country's power base. The exact meaning of *power,* the central concept in realist thought, is sometimes not carefully defined, though.[6] Realist scholars differ in their definitions of this key term.

CRITICS OF REALISM

Although political realism has been the dominant way of thinking about world politics for quite some time, it currently is losing ground to its critics. In recent years the strongest group of critics has come to be known as the **neorealists.** Neorealists accept some realist assumptions, but they often reject one or more of them. They argue that if realists would relax certain assumptions, realism would better explain world political events. In short, neorealists seek to build on political realism, but try to improve on what they perceive to be its weaknesses.

Some neorealists contend that realists make a huge error when they assume that foreign policies reflect rational decisions. Neorealists argue that governments often take irrational actions. Government decisions often emerge from long, arduous political processes in which substantial bargaining and negotiation determine the outcomes. These outcomes, therefore, are not rational, in the sense that they are the best means to achieving particular goals. Rather, they are composite positions pasted together to gain the support of enough key people to become policy. The North American Free Trade Agreement and the General Agreement on Tariffs and Trade were products of such negotiation.

Of course, ignorance or mistaken perceptions on the part of government decision makers can lead to apparently irrational decisions. For example, Napoleon believed that if he captured Moscow, Russia would surrender or sign a peace treaty with terms very favorable to France. Clearly, he did not understand how the czar made his decisions. Similarly, when Germany clearly was going to lose World War II, Hitler seems to have preferred that the nation-state be completely destroyed rather than surrender. In 1962, Soviet leaders attempted to put missiles in Cuba. They undoubtedly misperceived the probability that the United States would detect their actions in time to stop them. In addition, Soviet leader Kruschev did not believe that President Kennedy would risk nuclear war in order to keep the missiles out of Cuba. Kruschev was clearly wrong, and his mistake proved costly to Soviet foreign policy, and to his own political career. Similarly, when General MacArthur invaded North Korea and moved his troops close to the border with China, he mistakenly believed that the Chinese would not dare attack U.S. forces. Thousands of American soldiers paid for that error with their lives. Citing the many cases where a nation-state's actions reflect mistakes and misperceptions, many neorealist scholars have relaxed the rationality assumption and examined how decision makers' ignorance and misperceptions affect their actions.[7]

Another common neorealist criticism assails the lack of scientific rigor in the realists' position. Neorealists claim that realists should more carefully define and operationalize important terms such as *power* and *system.* More careful operationalizations might lead to a testable, scientific theory of world politics. Because many of you have struggled with operationalizing important concepts, you know just how difficult it is to operationalize a concept as broad and vague as "power." You also know that if you cannot operationalize a concept, then you cannot possibly falsify a hypothesis or theory. This means that those realists who do not operationalize their concepts cannot possibly "explain" anything—at least not in a way which would satisfy a scientist. You also know that different operationalizations of key concepts can lead to quite different conclusions concerning the validity of a theory.

A much smaller group of critics called the **idealists** provide an even more critical view of realist theory. Like neorealists, idealists criticize some of the basic assumptions of political realism. They differ from the neorealist school, however, in their belief that the difficulties with realism are much more serious. Many of the important differences between idealists and realists can be explained by the contrast in their assumptions about basic human nature. Idealists are much more optimistic about the basic nature of humans, and, for this reason, they see greater possibilities for a peaceful world.

Idealists contend that even if humans are currently greedy and violent, they can be changed for the better. No one is born evil, they claim, and successive generations can escape their greedy past. Instead, idealists believe that imperfections of character result mainly from the influence of human institutions. They say that imperfect socialization and counterproductive incentive systems create human flaws. If humans were to create better institutions, they would become less greedy and more peace-loving beings. Many, but not all, idealists see creation of a world government as one means toward this end.

Some idealists argue that the realists' assumption of the innate persistence of human greed is one of the causes of that failing. They assert that leaders act greedily in large part because realist thought conditions them to believe that every other leader will do the same. They must, therefore, act in a similar fashion in order to protect the security of their nation-states. Educating and socializing society and its leaders to believe that governments must strive for power in a world full of violent conflict will only, in the words of Captain Jean-Luc Picard, "Make it so."

Idealist thought was most prevalent after World War I. Though the onset of World War II crippled the idealist movement of that era, descendents of this line of thought are still around today. One of the most frequently cited examples of an idealist is President Woodrow Wilson, who sought to build world peace through his vision of world government, the League of Nations. Through his efforts, the league was created. Ironically, it was doomed to fail, because the U.S. Senate would not ratify the treaty, meaning that the United States, which was fast emerging as the world's most dominant country, would not take part.

REALIST FAILURE: POLITICAL ACTORS OTHER THAN NATION-STATES

Neorealists and idealists agree on what may be the most persuasive criticism of realist assumptions. Robert Keohane, a prominent neorealist, argues that it is unrealistic to assume that the nation-state is the *only* important actor in the world system. This argument has become even more persuasive as the world has grown smaller due to better transportation and communications, and closer economic ties. These developments have increased the importance of other types of world political actors.[8] Among these are **international nongovernmental organizations (INGOs)**.

The **multinational corporation (MNC),** such as Coca-Cola or Honda, is a type of INGO that often wields more economic power than many nation-states. For example, in 1989, the total sales of General Motors exceeded the gross national products of such countries as Austria, Italy, and Venezuela. In that same year, 38 multinational corporations had total sales greater than the GNP of Libya.[9] For more personal evidence of the importance of MNCs, think about how many important personal possessions (television, compact-disk player, car, or clothes) you would lose if MNCs had not supplied them. Some other examples of INGOs are the International Olympic Committee, the Salvation Army, Amnesty International, and a long list of churches and church-related organizations.

Idealists and neorealists also argue that individual human beings can be important actors in world politics. Roy Prieswork, a modern-day idealist, asked, "Could we study international relations as if people mattered?"[10] One reason idealists sometimes pose this question is their belief that most of the abstract theory produced by social scientists is pretty irrelevant to the plights of ordinary persons in need of help. Another reason is that they believe that individuals' actions can make a difference in world politics, and that the importance of individuals has been ignored by political realists. The bumper sticker message "Think globally, act locally" sums up the idealists' hope that, taken together, the sum of the actions of many individuals can bring about positive global changes. Individuals can form coalitions and try to affect their countries' foreign policies and, therefore, world politics. An example arose during the national debate over the North American Free Trade Agreement when various labor and business groups lobbied Congress, taking their case directly to the American people through advertisements.

Individuals can matter in many other ways. Individual terrorist actions can start wars and create substantial tension among nations. The assassination of Prime Minister Yitzhak Rabin of Israel is a recent example of how a criminal action perpetrated by a single individual can affect relations between countries in important ways, and in the process, significantly alter the lives of millions of people. Individuals can also draw attention to external events and apply pressure to their own governments. When Muhammad Ali refused induction into the armed services because of religious convictions, he brought substantial attention to the Vietnam War and helped to focus the opposition of African Americans against that conflict. Certain individuals conduct relations directly with foreign governments or societies; this routinely happens with foreign-exchange programs.[11] Famous people have used their prestige to reduce conflict among nations. Ex-president Jimmy Carter attempted to avert war and increase the chances for peace through his efforts in Korea, Haiti, and Bosnia. The Nobel Peace Prize recognizes individuals who act, often privately, to bring about peace.

Are you a realist, a neorealist, or an idealist? To answer this question you must first ask yourself, "What is my view of human nature?" If you believe that human nature can be improved considerably and maybe even perfected through socialization, then you fit best with the idealist camp. If you are more pessimistic about the likelihood for improvement in the human character, you are probably either a realist or a neorealist. You can determine which position you favor by considering the four key assumptions of political realism. If you disagree with one or more of them, or if you think the scientific method should be used to help us understand foreign policy, then you probably fit better with the neorealists than the realists.

Some of you might deny that you fit into any of these three groups. You might think like a realist one day when reading about one international issue and like an idealist the next day when evaluating another. If this description fits you, then you are probably a **pragmatist.** Pragmatists do not wholly accept any of the theories discussed so far; they believe that each theory has its strengths and weaknesses. Pragmatists try to apply the theory that seems to best fit with their evaluation of international issues as they arise. Pragmatists may sometimes seem wishy-washy, but the pragmatic position has a fine and honorable history. Some of the finest U.S. presidents and the world's greatest political leaders have been pragmatists.[12]

However, a pragmatist should recognize the danger of emphasizing no position in particular. If pragmatists fail to devote enough time and energy to carefully consider the facts pertaining to an issue, they may tend to be blown too much by the changing winds of public opinion, or to have their reactions colored too much by their own moods. The ill-fated U.S. relief mission to Somalia in 1993 might be cited as an example of presidents falling prey to this tendency. One might argue that two rather pragmatic U.S. presidents, George Bush and Bill Clinton, inadvisably allowed themselves to be carried away by public passions aroused by images of starving Somalian children appearing nightly on the country's television screens. Both Bush and Clinton have attracted criticism for having aimless foreign policies that simply reacted to world events as they happened instead of actively pursuing American interests.

A Brief Survey of World Problems

Scholars of world politics view similar world events, issues, and questions through different theories. Since Thucydides, they have paid more attention to questions related to war and peace than to any other problems. Today, however, a whole host of difficult problems vie for our attention. Table 12.1 lists 11 such problems and their likely impacts. Most of these concerns have been around for awhile, but a few such as AIDS and environmental decay, are relatively new. Widespread international concern about repression of basic human rights is also relatively new, though, arguably, the problem has troubled people throughout human history. Ethnic and religious violence provoke greater concern today, among both academics and the public at large, probably because of the highly visible case in the Balkans.[13] In 1987, ethnic and religious violence occurred in 25 locations around the world.[14] Such conflicts, however, have been going on in many places around the world for thousands of years.

A brief inspection of the impacts listed in the table will lead you to the inescapable conclusion that many of the world's most serious problems are interrelated. For example, lack of education is associated with the population explosion, since female literacy is one of the strongest determinants of contraception use. The population explosion, in turn, exacerbates poverty. Poverty itself is associated with another set of problems, including an increased probability of political instability and political repression. To be honest, we often cannot tell which problems cause which other ones. Sometimes, causation runs in both directions. For example, if a less industrialized country has to reduce its per-capita spending on female education, it can expect an increase in the birthrate as one consequence. This increase will further reduce per-capita spending on education, creating a vicious circle. Social scientists are desperately trying to understand the complex pattern of interrelationships among these kinds of variables in an effort to build theories to explain why these problems happen and what can be done to resolve them. We are always on the lookout for talented, creative individuals to join us.

TABLE 12.1

A SUMMARY OF ELEVEN WORLD PROBLEMS, AND THEIR LIKELY IMPACTS

Problem	Impacts
1. War	Worst Case: In the case of all-out nuclear war, extinction of the human race. Known Impact: Death on a large scale; large number of injured place strain on society; poverty, disease, damage to the environment, increased repression in participating countries. Likely Impact: Further arms proliferation.
2. Repression of Basic Human Rights (imprisonment, torture, disappearance, political execution)	Likely Impacts: Death on a large scale; large number of injured potentially places strain on society; political instability leads to inability to deal effectively with poverty, education, health care.
3. Conventional-Arms Proliferation	Worst Case: Weapons used in war (see impacts of war above). Likely Impacts: increased likelihood of war due to increased tension; less money spent on social issues such as poverty, education, health care, which means those problems are exacerbated. Absence of sufficient money to improve economic infrastructures.
4 Nuclear-Arms Proliferation	Worst Case: Weapons used in nuclear war that spreads, leading to all-out unlimited nuclear war and extinction of the human race. Likely Results: Increased tension leads to conventional arms proliferation, and increased probability for war (see impacts listed above).
5. Population Growth	Probable Impacts: Increased poverty; lack of sufficient resources to deal with poverty, education, health care; damaged environment, and increased probability of repression due to strain on the the political system.
6. Poverty	Known Impacts: Death on a large scale; absence of resources to deal with health care, education; absence of adequate sanitation leads to environmental damage; political instability leads to repression of basic human rights.
7. Lack of Education	Known Impacts: Population growth, since the educated are more likely to use contraception (see effects of population growth above). Likely Impact: Inability to achieve large-scale economic growth.
8. Absence of Sufficient Health Care	Known Impacts: Large-scale death; health problems proliferate, exacerbating poverty.
9. Environmental Damage	Known Impacts: Disease and death on a large scale as a result of cancer caused by depletion of the ozone layer, or diseases associated with excessive pollution; poverty and starvation as a result of the loss of arable lands. Likely Impact: Scientists theorize that a phenomenon called the greenhouse effect might change the climate of the planet Earth, raising temperatures and bringing drought and starvation.
10. Auto-Immune Deficiency Syndrome	Known Impact: Disease and death on a large scale. Probable Impact: Strain placed on health care systems. Likely Impact: Exacerbates poverty.
11. Ethnic and Religious Violence	Probable Impacts: Small- to large-scale death, increased repression of basic human rights, environmental damage, conventional-arms proliferation. Probable Impacts: Increased poverty and disease, strain placed on health care systems.

Table 12.1 provides only a rough representation of the relations between 11 of the world's serious problems. Because we do not fully understand all of these linkages, some of the impacts that are listed must be considered likely or probable results instead of certain outcomes. The table almost certainly overlooks other effects. This creates a difficult task for the politician or political activist who wants to improve people's living conditions. Imagine for a moment that you are an independently wealthy social activist who wants to make the world a better place. Lacking a valid scientific theory to tell you what causes what, you do not know how to attack a particular problem. In the absence of this vital knowledge, you probably will act based on common sense mixed with a healthy dose of your own ideological biases. You are in a position similar to that of doctors prior to the development of modern medicine and medical research. They administered common-sense and folk medicine as well as some remedies based on superstition and misunderstandings about how the human body works.

To complicate the undertaking still further, you may want to fight one problem and end up confronting the whole intimidating mess of them because of their many interrelationships. The entire undertaking is pretty intimidating whether you are a political scientist seeking to explain the problems or a political leader interested in solving them. Of course, it is impossible to give a full treatment of each of the problems listed in Table 12.1 within a single chapter. We can begin an overview, however, by examining the issue that has fascinated scholars of world politics since Thucydides—war.

War

THE COSTS

War has received more attention from scholars than any other issue in world politics. One reason for this is that the costs of war are horrific. The most obvious and frequently cited cost of war is the number of human lives that are lost. One analyst has estimated that over 23 million people, roughly the population of Canada, have died in wars since 1945.[15] Not counted in such figures are the refugees who have been forced to flee their homes. The United Nations cared for over 18.9 million of the "international homeless" in 1992.[16]

War also has important opportunity costs: resources used to prepare for and fight wars or those damaged during wars might otherwise have been used to achieve other, more productive ends. It is difficult, if not impossible to assess the potential achievements of the human race if people had not prepared for and taken part in wars. After all, what value would this calculation place on each human life that was lost? Who can tell how many Einsteins, Curies, Picassos, and Edisons perished among the 23 million who died in wars during the last 50 years? Though it is still quite difficult, we can think about the opportunity costs of preparation for war by imagining what might have been achieved if the money spent on the military had been used for other purposes. Ruth Leger Sivard estimates that the United States alone spent $5.54 trillion on the military from 1946 to 1993.[17] She estimates world military expenditures from 1960 to 1990 to be roughly $21 trillion.[18] The world expenditure is roughly equivalent to the value of all goods and services produced by the people of the planet Earth in the year 1990.[19] In her frequent publications on military and social expenditures, Sivard asks readers to imagine the schools, hospitals, and roads that could be built and the diseases that could be wiped out if we could all work on those problems for one full year, instead of working to pay for military costs. Along these lines, she points out that the price of one ballistic-missile submarine (about $1.4 billion) would double the education budgets of 18 less industrialized countries with over 129 million children to educate.

Even after the end of the Cold War, the U.S. government keeps spending extraordinary amounts of money on high-tech weapons systems: The B-2 (Stealth) bomber is expected to cost about $2.3 billion, roughly equivalent to three times its weight in gold.[20] Thus, if Thomas Jefferson was correct in stating "The care of human life and happiness, and not their destruction, is the first and only legitimate means of government,"[21] then war surely represents governments' greatest failure.

TRENDS IN WARFARE

The two most important goals of political science are to explain why political phenomena happen and to predict when they will happen. Although most political scientists today are concerned more with explanation than prediction, some observers do seek to forecast the wars of the future based on historical evidence and trends evident today.

Political scientist John Mueller has generated some controversy in the last few years, by arguing that major war has disappeared and will not occur in the future.[22] He contends that the idea of war was born in the minds of men and that it can end there. War is not a necessity of human existence, but something that mankind brings upon itself. Gradually, people have become aware of the great costs of war.

> Over the centuries war opponents have been trying to bring about . . . [the end of war] by discrediting war as an idea. In part their message . . . stresses two kinds of costs: (1) psychic ones—war, they argue, is repulsive, immoral, and uncivilized, and (2) physical ones—war is bloody, destructive, and expensive.[23]

Although it has taken quite a long time, the efforts of generations of war's opponents have paid off, according to Mueller. A revulsion toward war has gradually evolved in the more industrialized countries, and the practice of warfare will become extinct among them much like other revolting human practices such as slavery, dueling, and human sacrifice have disappeared.[24]

This all looks good in theory. However, the obvious question is whether the disappearance of war is found in the data. To answer this question, a political scientist must first define *war*. This is no easy task. After many years of arguing, scholars have not reached a consensus on the definition. However, in order to get started on the process of testing theories, political scientists must formulate operational definitions to guide their data collection. Today, the most prevalent operationalization of the term *war* is one used in a large data set identifying wars that took place between 1816 and 1980. This project defined **interstate war** as, "a hostility between two or more nation-states culminating in at least 1,000 battle deaths."[25]

Using this operational definition, political scientists Charles Kegley and Eugene Wittkopf count 181 wars between 1816 and 1988. They examine the distribution of interstate wars and conclude that their frequency has not changed much over time.[26] However, if we take into account the larger number of countries in the international system in more recent years, we find that the number of interstate wars *per country* has declined over time.[27] Thus, it would seem that Mueller's thesis may have some validity.

A seemingly slight difference in the operational definition of *war* leads to a more pessimistic conclusion. Ruth Leger Sivard defines *war* as "any armed conflict involving one or more governments and causing the deaths of 1,000 or more people per year." This statement expands the operationalization to include not only wars between nation-states but also civil wars and some ethnic, religious, and tribal conflicts.[28] Using this operationalization, Sivard calculates the number of ongoing wars and the number of war-related deaths from 1945 to 1993. She concludes that there is an obvious upward trend in both.

Unfortunately we have yet to find persuasive evidence that war is disappearing on a global basis. There are good reasons to be skeptical of reports that war, an institution that has plagued humanity for pretty much its entire history, is disappearing. To be fair to Mueller, though, we should note that Sivard includes less industrialized countries in her assessment of trends. Mueller meant his argument to apply only to the more industrialized and former communist countries.

WHY WAR?

Political scientists have expended a great deal of time puzzling over the question of why humans go to war. This contemplation has produced nearly as many theories about why war takes place as there are theorists. One way to make more sense of the volumes of research on this question is to distinguish theories according to their units of analysis. As political scientist Kenneth Waltz explained, theorists seeking to explain war have generally focused on one of three "images" or levels of analysis to explain war: characteristics of individuals, characteristics of nation-states, or characteristics of the international system.[29]

Several theories of war cite causes related to innate properties of human beings. Perhaps the most famous writer who saw war as the result of innate human properties was Sigmund Freud. Early in his career, Freud argued that human aggression, of which warfare is one expression, results from the frustration of sexual urges. After World War I, he posited the existence of a death instinct that attracts people to take part in war. This death instinct leads humans to aspire to death, Freud said, which provides a solution to all urges. Most people choose to live on, however, and prefer not to go to war because of a counterbalancing instinct to live. Though still widely read, most of Freud's theories have been rejected by the majority of psychologists today.[30]

Konrad Lorenz offers another theory that is relevant to an explanation of man's preoccupation with violence. Drawing on studies of animals, Lorenz argues that human beings, like other animals, have aggressive instincts toward other members of their species. In the state of nature, these instincts assist species' efforts to survive. According to Lorenz, aggression prevents members of the same species from living too close together. Instead, it forces members of the same species to spread out across the habitat, thus increasing their chances of survival.[31] When viewed in the context of this theory, the substantial increase in the world's population during the last century does not bode well for humans, who would be expected to fight more when forced to live in close proximity to each other. Lorenz does leave some room for hope, however. He mentions that some animals have developed "aggression-inhibiting mechanisms or appeasement gestures." For example, the wolf, though armed with great natural weaponry, has developed means to stop conflicts by "baring its neck to the fangs of a victorious foe."[32] Lorenz hopes that humans will be able to follow in the footsteps of these "lower" animals and develop sufficient customs to resolve or settle conflict and survive as a species.

Though attractive because of their simplicity, theories of war based on innate characteristics are problematic. While these theories might provide some insight into the characteristics of humans that lead us to be aggressive, they do not help much in our efforts to understand why nation-states (and human beings) act aggressively in some instances and not in others. Stated differently, an aggressive instinct might be a necessary condition for wars to occur, for without this instinct humans might have no desire to fight. But just because humans have an instinct to fight, it does not mean that they will go to war. The vast majority of people (and nation-states) go through each day without fighting (or making war). Therefore, political scientists need a different kind of theory to help us to identify the conditions under which wars are apt to occur.

Substantial research has sought to explain war based on the characteristics of nation-states. One issue that has inspired considerable argument over the years is the effect of a country's economic system on its propensity to go to war. The liberal economist J. A. Hobson and the communist revolutionary V. I. Lenin both linked the capitalist economic system to **imperialism,** which can be defined as taking over geographic areas by force for the purpose of economic exploitation. Hobson argued that the unequal distribution of wealth and the large populations of poor persons in the capitalist systems of his time left the rich without sufficient markets for their goods in their home countries. This forced capitalists to invest their capital and look for markets abroad, which led to competition and conflict with the capitalists of other countries, who had been forced to go abroad for similar reasons.[33]

For Hobson, however, imperialism was not a necessary result of a capitalist system. Hobson believed that conflict was simply a product of the unequal wealth distribution of capitalist systems during his time. Following the teachings of liberal economist John Stuart Mill (discussed in Chapter 2), Hobson believed that the distribution of wealth could be changed through economic policies. Lenin agreed with most of Hobson's argument, but he disagreed with the idea that capitalist countries could successfully redistribute wealth. Thus, he concluded that the very nature of capitalist countries predisposes them toward aggression.[34]

On the other side of the argument, some theorists including the Marxist thinker Karl Kautsky believed that capitalism might lead to peace, because international cartels would come to dominate the world and enforce their will.[35] Also, some liberal, pacifist thinkers have argued that free trade, which characterizes the capitalist system, is a means to reach peace. War, they argue, is an "unprofitable anachronism" whose costs clearly outweigh its benefits for most capitalists.[36] Therefore most capitalists do not want to take part in war, because they stand to lose more than they gain.

Each of these two seemingly opposite theories finds support in reasonable explanations. As political scientists we must at this point ask, what do the data say? One piece of important anecdotal evidence is that the stock market commonly falls when an international crisis raises the probability of war. This would seem to indicate that capitalists are more concerned about the costs of war than they are excited about the alleged economic opportunities that wars might bring. Bruce Russett and Harvey Starr consider studies evaluating the hypothesized imperialist origins of World War I. They conclude that, while individual capitalists might want peace, their drive to expand markets to other regions may well produce political pressures that lead to crises, which, in some cases, lead to war.[37]

Another theory of nation-state behavior is currently a hot topic in international-relations research. This theory deals with the relationship between democracy and war. Many scholars have followed in the footsteps of philosopher Immanuel Kant, who argued that there is an important relationship between democracy and peaceful foreign relations. Political scientists who have examined the evidence on this relationship have concluded that democracies tend to go to war at about the same rate as nondemocracies, but *never* (at least not yet) with one another. The best explanation offered for this intriguing phenomenon is the theory of bounded competition. This theory argues that leaders of democracies are socialized to believe that certain rules limit how far leaders should go in their pursuit of power within their own national systems. One of those rules states that violence should not be used to dispose of political rivals. Thus, when tense situations arise between democratic nations, each leader's tendency is to recognize the other party's socialization is similar and to trust that the two countries can eventually settle the conflict without resorting to violence.[38]

Finally, certain explanations of war refer to characteristics of the international system. Many of the theorists who focus on this level of analysis observe that nation-states are the most important international actors and there is no world government to enforce international laws, agreements, and property rights. Therefore, they contend, the countries of the world clash in a state of anarchy similar to a Hobbesian state of nature. (This is consistent with realist claims.) In such a system, the distribution of power has an important impact on the way countries act.

To illustrate the point that an actor's behavior is affected by the location of power in a system, consider how you would act in two scenarios. In the first scenario, you decide to go out with four friends. You have $200 in your pocket, but your friends have no money. In the second situation, each person in the group has $40. Assume that you disagree with each other about how to spend the evening. In the first situation, although you might talk about what everyone wants to do, if you decide to express a preference, your friends probably will go along. After all, you have all the money. The second situation will probably lead to a much more equal negotiation process. Your friends might not listen as carefully to your preferences. If they did listen, they would be less apt to agree with you than if you intended to pay for everyone. The distribution of money affects the way you and your friends act and the kinds of discussions you will have; in the same way, international-systems theorists argue that the distribution of power in the international system affects the probability that wars will occur and the sizes of the wars that do happen.

Systems theory evokes tremendous interest among specialists in world politics, because the world system appears to be evolving from a bipolar one with two major powers, into a multipolar world with several major actors. For half a century the bipolar system characterized the international system. Now that has changed, due to the disintegration of the Soviet Union. An obvious question is whether this change is a positive one that will lead to a more stable and peaceful world, or a negative one which will increase the probability of wars.

Interestingly, though systems theorists agree that the structure of the world system is important, they disagree about whether current changes will yield more peaceful international relations. One set of analysts emphasizes that the bipolar power structure leads to a rivalry between the major powers, which in a nuclear world raises the danger of the destruction of human society. They argue that the move toward multipolarity significantly reduces the probability of nuclear war because the conflictual relationship between two major powers will disappear. They also argue that the move to multipolarity will reduce the frequency and destructiveness of conventional wars. This argument is based on the idea that in a bipolar world, most nation-states tend to group themselves into two major alliances around the most powerful actors. In such a world two countries in separate blocs tend to interact infrequently. In a multipolar world, though, larger numbers of nation-states interact with more frequency. The larger number of interactions with a larger number of countries, proponents of the multipolar system argue, will lead to greater stability and less violent conflict.[39]

On the other side of this argument, theorist John Mearsheimer explains "why we will soon miss the Cold War."[40] He and other scholars argue that a bipolar international system tends to be more stable and peaceful than a multipolar one. In a bipolar system the two major powers will try to maintain a balance of power in order to keep stability in the world. The bipolar system has the advantage of power inequality *within* the two blocs of countries. This allows the two superpowers to impose their will on other alliance members without using violence, much like you could when you had all the money and your friends had none. Mearsheimer and others have argued that during the Cold War, this kind of relationship kept some latent ethnic and religious conflicts from becoming civil wars. Now that the Cold War is over and there is no Soviet Union to keep discipline in eastern Europe, age-old ethnic conflicts have flared up again with calamitous results.

Proponents of the bipolar system argue that it offers a further benefit by limiting most wars to rather small skirmishes fought by proxies. Most of these skirmishes will result from one superpower's efforts to take a nation-state from the alliance of the other superpower (e.g., Korea, Vietnam). The bipolar system may promote stability in another way, as each of the two powers knows who its major rival is and can maintain a careful watch. This makes it difficult to mount a successful surprise attack.

Unfortunately, though each of the explanations of war based on the international system seems to make sense on paper, when we look at the actual data we see that "the findings are mixed," meaning that neither of the theories is either convincingly supported or falsified by the data. Perhaps one of the reasons for this ambivalence is that the research designs used thus far have been looking for relationships.[41]

International Wars and Human-Rights Violations
VIOLENCE AGAINST FELLOW CITIZENS

Although war causes horrible trouble in the world, another problem is worse as measured by the number of human lives lost. In the 20th century, more than 95 million people have died in political violence. This number becomes truly frightening when deeper analysis reveals that more than 75 percent of those deaths were caused not by international wars, but by internal violence.[42] In other words, people in the 20th century have had more to fear from fellow citizens and their own governments than from foreign governments and their armies.

Why would the citizens and government of a country murder other residents of their own country? The willingness of humans to torture, rape, and murder other human beings clearly increases with the eagerness to view the victims as, in some sense, different from and inferior to the aggressors. Politically caused deaths in the 20th century clearly demonstrate this fact. Because of ethnic, religious, ideological, and national differences, those who murder and torture people in their own country see their victims as unworthy of human rights.

Hitler convinced the German people that the Jews and other non-Aryans were inferior beings and not part of the nation-state of Germany. By blaming ethnic groups, particularly the Jews, for Germany's economic problems, Hitler made killing them seem like a legitimate action. In the Balkans, Bosnian Serbs, Muslims, and Croatians have committed thousands of criminal acts against women and children of the other ethnic groups. In Rwanda and Burundi, members of the Hutu tribe have killed hundreds of thousands of members of the Tutsi tribe, and Tutsis have killed hundreds of thousands of Hutus. These events illustrate this terrible willingness of humans to commit **genocide,** murders of many members of one ethnic group by members of another. The awful Serbian term *ethnic cleansing* clarifies the distinction that each ethnic group sees between itself and other groups. Whites in the United States have demonstrated a similar willingness to almost exterminate Native Americans, to enslave African Americans, to intern Japanese Americans in concentration camps, and to commit war crimes against the Vietnamese population; these acts show that U.S. citizens also have been willing to justify similar crimes by appeals to ethnicity.

Appeals to religion have also traditionally justified violations of one group's human rights by another. The current struggles in the Middle East between Jews and Muslims and between different Muslim sects, as well as the conflict in Northern Ireland, illustrate this willingness of believers in one religion to violate the rights of those who do not share the same faith. The suicide bomber who straps explosives to his body and then sets the explosive off in a crowded bus or shopping center illustrates the depth of this hatred and the difficulty of attempting to stop such terrorism by rational deterrence.

Political ideology is a third variable that may also encourage extensive murders of fellow citizens. Communist regimes have caused the deaths of as many as 60 million of their own citizens. Stalin and Mao committed many of these atrocities in their various purges. Regardless of the actual reasons for these deaths, the standard official reason branded these individuals as "enemies of the state." They were killed for attempting to hold back the communist regime from reaching its utopian vision. The movie *The Killing Fields* shows the horror of such mass killings in Kampuchea (Cambodia) by the Khmer Rouge Party led by dictator Pol Pot. The government murdered people or starved them to death because they had lived too long in cities or had lived in areas that had been under the control of the Vietnamese. Therefore, according to official rationale, they had been improperly socialized and would make poor citizens of the new communist society that the Khmer Rouge wished to build.[43]

A critical aspect of all three factors that we have named—ethnicity, ideology, and religion—is the nonrational basis for people's attachments to them. The nonrational character of basic attachments should give liberals pause when they expect that reason will ultimately lead people to reject war and internal political violence. When nonrational motivations drive political actions, the results often resemble the state of nature feared by Hobbes more than the one envisioned by Locke.

THE GROWING CONCERN FOR HUMAN RIGHTS

After wrestling with the problems of international war and internal conflict, you may feel like throwing in the towel. As tempting as it may be to conclude that our problems are insurmountable, there are some reasons to be guardedly optimistic about the prospects for the human race. One such reason is that since World War II there has evolved an unprecedented international concern with respect for **human rights.** International organizations and individual countries have put new tools into place to improve respect for human rights. If the current interest in human rights can be maintained, there is every reason to believe that governments might well respect these rights more in the future than they have in the past.

POLITICAL SCIENCE AND THE STUDY OF HUMAN RIGHTS

A necessary first step in discussing human rights is to define the term. When scholars talk about human rights, they usually adopt one of two common views of what that term means. The first image resembles the Lockean view of the relationship between citizens and the state. Humans must sign away some of their rights to the state so that it has the power to protect others. But some rights are so basic to human life that no rational individual would give them to government, and government should not choose to interfere with these natural rights.

Central among these rights are those pertaining to the right to life, which are sometimes called **personal-integrity rights.** These rights include freedom from torture and from politically motivated or arbitrary abduction, imprisonment, or execution. Other rights suggested by this Lockean view are the rights to a fair public trial, freedom of thought, freedom of conscience and religion, freedom of speech, freedom of the press, and freedom to participate in government. This class of rights is sometimes called "negative rights," because, following Locke, government ensures these individual liberties by *not doing things* (e.g., not torturing, not arresting people for joining opposition political parties). That said, the role of the government is to guarantee that others do not infringe upon each individual's rights. The government does this through its police power and a

BOX 12.3

Is International Law Really Law?

Many of the ideas and theories about domestic politics discussed in this book also apply to politics at the international level. There are some important differences, however, in the nature of law in these two distinct realms. In international politics, unlike domestic politics in the United States and most other countries there is no legislature that passes laws which apply to the world's inhabitants. The closest thing to such a legislature is the General Assembly of the United Nations, which can only pass recommendations and declarations about what it believes should be done. None of these declarations or recommendations impose binding requirements on national governments.

Instead of coming from a legislature, international laws usually emerge from two sources. Many are the product of customs agreed upon by national governments for their mutual convenience, usually over the course of many years. Second, international treaties and conventions signed by government representatives are also considered to be international law.

Another big difference between domestic and international law is that there is no police force to bring violators to justice. In fact, some would argue that international law is not really law at all, because laws must be backed up by effective enforcement. These critics would argue that powerful countries can choose to ignore international law if they wish, as the United States did when the World Court found it guilty of illegally mining Nicaraguan harbors in the 1980s. There was no enforcement mechanism that could have forced the United States to make restitution, and therefore, critics claim, no law existed.

In rebutting this argument, proponents of international law would acknowledge that enforcement of international law is imperfect, but they would assert that enforcement of domestic law often fails, as well. For proof, take a drive on any interstate highway in the United States and set your cruise control at the speed limit. Keep track of how often other cars pass you and how often those drivers are stopped for speeding. Over a long drive, my suspicion is that the percentage of speeders who were actually stopped by police will be about zero.* If effective enforcement is a necessary condition for there to be law, then there is now no law in the United States or in most other countries of the world either.

Of course, this example intentionally highlights one of the most frequently violated of all laws to make a point, just as critics often focus on frequently violated international laws in order to make their arguments persuasive. In fact, most laws, both domestic and international ones, are followed most of the time, because people and nation-states recognize that lawful behavior usually serves their best interests. Although countries would behave with more respect for international law if there were a more effective enforcement mechanism, most scholars of world politics today accept its validity.

---

*For a similar argument see Frederic S. Pearson and J. Martin Rochester, *International Relations: The Global Condition in the Late Twentieth Century* (New York: McGraw-Hill, 1992), pp. 320–321.

court system that openly and fairly prosecutes alleged violations of one person's rights by another person.[44]

The second meaning of *human rights* stems from historical developments in reform liberalism and socialism that advocated government action to ensure that all individuals have certain important opportunities. This conception emphasizes **economic and social rights,** including rights to a job, rest, and leisure; a standard of living that provides for a family's physical needs; and universal education, participation in cultural life, and protection of intellectual property.[45]

Ironically, as human-rights expert David Forsythe points out, international progress toward greater respect for human rights began as a result of war.[46] In 1864, a group of mostly Western nations negotiated, wrote, and signed the first Geneva Convention, an international treaty that protected medical personnel giving aid to injured soldiers. This treaty recognized the principle that "the individual soldier was entitled to at least a minimum respect for his essence as a person, to a minimum degree of humanitarianism—even in war, the greatest denial of humanitarianism."[47] Between 1919 and 1939, the League of Nations reached more comprehensive agreements that dealt not only with practices in war but also with issues like labor rights and the rights of minorities.[48]

The greatest steps toward protection for human rights have been taken in the last 50 years. After World War II, in response to the horrific images of human-rights violations in German concentration camps, a push for an international bill of human rights began.[49] This effort led to the United Nations Declaration of Human Rights of 1948. This declaration by the world's best-known **international governmental organization (IGO)** asserted the validity of both images or definitions of the human rights discussed in this section. Later treaties formalized many of the principles declared in that first document, giving them the force of international law. (Box 12.3 discusses international law.) These treaties and declarations included assurances of women's rights and the rights of racial and tribal groups.

At the same time that the U.N. efforts occurred, countries in several regions of the world took additional steps to protect human rights. In 1953, the countries of Europe agreed to set up an institutional apparatus to investigate and rule on allegations of human-rights abuses. Similar institutions have been established in the Americas and Africa.

The realist would correctly point out that these international institutions can promote human rights only as effectively as the national governments allow. Experts have commented on the tendency of these regional institutions to carefully avoid challenging state interests in their rulings, even when clear evidence documents that human-rights abuses have occurred. Still, some successes, such as the sanctions imposed on the white government of South Africa, raise hopes, and existing institutions are constantly being revised and refined to improve their effectiveness.[50]

POLITICAL SCIENTISTS' STUDIES OF HUMAN RIGHTS

As interest in and concern for human rights have increased in the political arena, political scientists have begun to investigate the topic, too. One question they have recently sought to answer is, "why do human-rights abuses occur?" Most of the work on this question so far has focused on personal-integrity rights. Analysts have gathered data on

FIGURE 12.2

A GLOBAL MAP OF HUMAN-RIGHTS ABUSES, 1990–1993

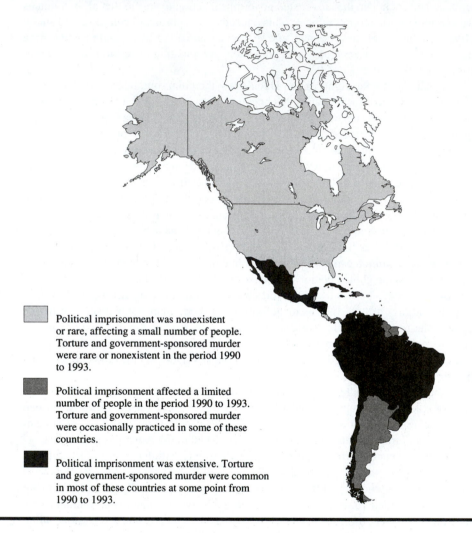

Political imprisonment was nonexistent
or rare, affecting a small number of people.
Torture and government-sponsored murder
were rare or nonexistent in the period 1990
to 1993.

Political imprisonment affected a limited
number of people in the period 1990 to 1993.
Torture and government-sponsored murder
were occasionally practiced in some of these
countries.

Political imprisonment was extensive. Torture
and government-sponsored murder were common
in most of these countries at some point from
1990 to 1993.

abuses of these rights from around the world and then sought to develop and test theories
that explain country-to-country variations.

The world human rights map presented in Figure 12.1 shows considerable worldwide
variation in respect for human rights. Some human-rights abuses, including political imprisonment, torture, and arbitrary execution, occur in most regions of the world. Recent
history in Europe reveals widespread respect for human rights which has led to establishment of regional institutions to adjudicate related complaints. Still, even in that region
some countries have abused human rights.

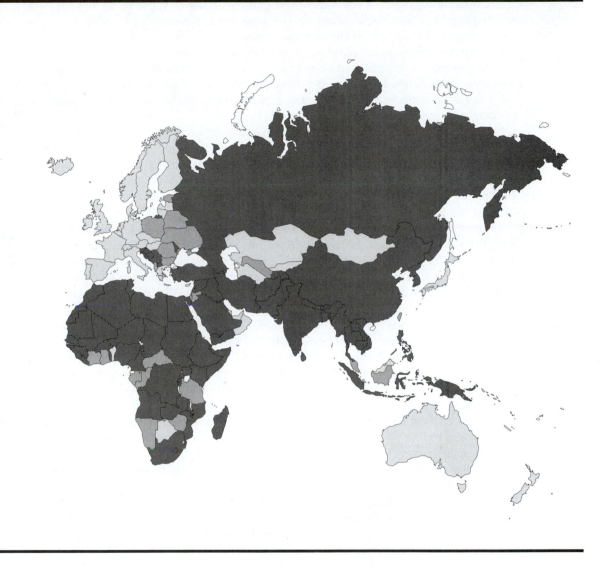

On the positive side, though most of the countries in some regions such as Africa and Latin America have a greater tendency to commit human-rights violations, there are countries with good human-rights records in most regions of the world, separated by large differences in culture and heritage. Thus, it is reasonable to conclude that decent respect for human rights could conceivably be achieved almost anywhere.

Why do regimes choose to imprison, torture, and even kill innocent citizens? One way researchers try to develop theories to explain why decision makers make choices is to try to put ourselves in their shoes (an approach that works well on a variety of questions of interest to world politics). As distressing as it might be for us to imagine ourselves in the position of someone who considers these horrible crimes as viable policy options, we do it because it helps us to understand why these crimes are committed. Political scientists who are working on explaining human-rights abuses hope that someday, as a result of our work, some of these crimes can be predicted and prevented.

As you begin to imagine yourself as a national leader, try to think like the realists for a moment. Assume that keeping power is more important to you than anything else. Now ask yourself what kinds of things are going to make it more likely that a person in your position will commit human-rights violations?

Perhaps the type of government system over which you preside would influence your decision-making environment and ultimately your decisions. First, consider yourself the leader of a democratic country like the United States. Next, imagine yourself as the authoritarian leader of an otherwise similar country that lacks any democratic institutions. In which of these conditions would someone be more likely to commit human-rights violations and why?

You may expect the democracy to commit fewer human-rights violations because that country would socialize citizens to favor negotiation, bargaining, and compromise to solve political disputes instead of violence. A leader would hesitate to break with this tradition, which would violate socialization and invite retribution in the next election. In contrast, a country with a tradition of autocratic rule does not socialize its leaders to value less coercive solutions. Also, the autocrat need not worry about losing the votes of the victims of abuse. While the nondemocratic leader might offend the will of the people enough to be overthrown, the autocrat's control of the military typically keeps people under a tight lid. Thus the democratic country's incentive system encourages leaders to promote respect for human rights. No such force protects people's rights in nondemocratic countries, leading researchers to expect a negative relationship between democracy and human-rights abuses.

In this case our thinking (or theory) is supported by the data. Studies focusing on human-rights violations in the 1980s have found that democratic countries abused human rights less than others, other factors being equal.[51] Some democratic governments do commit human-rights abuses, however. Clearly there are additional factors that enter into leaders' decisions to imprison, torture, and murder.

Getting back into the leader's shoes, what kinds of situations might lead someone to begin to commit human-rights abuses? Certainly, if things were running smoothly there would be no reason to risk these crimes, but what if your leadership position were threatened? Leaders might be more apt to initiate repressive policies if they perceive some threat to their continued rule. When would a leader perceive such a threat? Two likely causes are acute international or civil conflicts. Once again, the implied hypotheses are supported by the findings of political-science studies. Governments are more likely to commit human-rights abuses when they are engaged in international or civil wars.[52]

Two other factors found to increase the probability of human-rights abuses are large populations and lack of economic development. Every government must respond to demands made by citizens. Both large populations and resource shortages make it more difficult for governments to respond positively to these demands. When such demands are not met the probability of violent opposition increases. In turn, this creates conditions where some leaders might choose to use repression in order to maintain control.

Besides studying why human-rights abuses occur, world politics scholars also wonder how human rights fit into foreign policy and relations between nations. Studies in this vein have examined the impact of human rights on countries' foreign policies, often as a way of testing the realism of the realist theory, discussed earlier. Remember that realists believe that power and the pursuit of a nation-state's self-interest are the dominant motives of foreign policy. From this view, ethical considerations such as human rights would influence foreign policy only when power interests are not at stake.

In order to gauge the impact of human rights on U.S. foreign policy, analysts have examined how foreign aid is allocated. These studies have found that a recipient's human-rights record is probably one of many factors considered when the government allocates aid dollars, but that respect for human-rights conditions does not have a very great impact. Further, if leaders perceive that serious strategic or political interests are at stake in a country, they tend to overlook human-rights abuses.

U.S. aid to El Salvador during the early to middle 1980s illustrates this point. The Salvadoran government and its supporters committed serious and well-documented human-rights abuses, including political imprisonment, torture, and murder of political enemies, yet that country was one of the largest recipients of U.S. foreign aid. The reason? Key congressmen and executive branch officials believed that communism threatened the Central American region, and the government of El Salvador was perceived to offer a pro-American, anticommunist ally. This benefit outweighed that country's frightfully bad human-rights record in the minds of U.S. decision makers. This is a piece of evidence that clearly is consistent with realist thinking on world politics.

HUMAN RIGHTS AND NATIONAL SOVEREIGNTY

Before we conclude this discussion of human rights and world politics, it is important to consider the ramifications of the human-rights movement for the realists' idea that the nation-state is the primary actor in the world political system. In fact, the primary role of the nation-state has been institutionalized, until very recently, as one of the most steadfast principles of international law. Tom J. Farer points out that until World War II:

> [M]ost legal scholars and governments affirmed the general proposition, albeit not in so many words, that international law did not impede the natural right of each equal sovereign to be monstrous to his or her subjects. Summary execution, torture, arbitrary arrest, and detention: these were legally significant events beyond national frontiers only if the victims of such official eccentricities were citizens of another state.[53]

International laws aimed at improving respect for human rights directly confront this principle by asserting that there are limits to what a nation's government can legally do to its people. As such, these laws also directly challenge the strength of the nation-state and the theory of political realism.

One does not have to be a realist to question whether international laws passed to govern human rights are effective in the real world. Thus far, human-rights treaties and conventions are international laws in the sense that, by signing them, governments have agreed that the rights specified therein are worthwhile goals. In reality, however, no government, including that of the United States, follows the letter of the law. Clearly some countries sign treaties and conventions with no intention of ever trying to comply with them; this fact is consistent with the observation that "hypocrisy is the homage which vice pays to virtue."[54]

Like other international laws, enforcement of human-rights laws can be difficult. Nation-states that are confronted by U.N. criticism for their human-rights abuses frequently cite the Charter of the United Nations, Article 2(7), which states that the United Nations cannot intercede "in matters which are essentially within the domestic jurisdiction of any state."[55]

With these caveats in mind, it can still be argued that these international laws have been somewhat effective, and promise to become more effective if current trends continue. In some countries (e.g., South Africa), international efforts have apparently been successful in pressuring countries to change for the better. International laws on human rights, though they serve mainly to set goals, are providing a new and improved standard on which the legitimacy of governments is increasingly being judged. These principles are gradually replacing the "old standards of divine right, revolutionary heritage, national destiny, or charismatic authority."[56]

Positive Development in World Politics: A Few Rays of Hope

A few years ago, I began all my world politics classes by discussing several of the problems listed in Table 12.1 and their potentially calamitous effects. In my first lecture of each semester, I argued vehemently that students simply *had* to interest themselves in world politics because the survival of the human race depended on their generation's learning to conduct world politics in a way that would avoid nuclear war, and catastrophic damage to the ecosphere. I tried to interest students in world politics by scaring them. Many of my students were, understandably, discouraged.

The problems that face the human race are, by and large, about as pressing today, but now my first lecture sets a different tone. I now outline some reasons to be cautiously optimistic about the fate of the earth. Indeed, there have been some recent positive accomplishments in world politics that give us cause to hold out hope for the future of the human race. One of them, an increased awareness of human-rights issues, has already been discussed in some detail. Other positive developments include some impressive accomplishments:[57]

- The dissolution of the Soviet Union signaled the end of the Cold War, a period of tension between the United States and the Soviet Union. The number of nuclear weapons in the world is now decreasing for the first time in 50 years. Nuclear tests are rarer, too. These changes probably decrease the likelihood of all-out nuclear war.[58]

- A 1993 treaty would require the destruction of all chemical weapons within the next 15 years.

- Major powers have cut the amounts they spend on weapons in general. In each year between 1988 and 1992 (the last date for which data are available) worldwide expenditures on weapons declined. This makes more money available for social expenditures and economic research and development. (Note, however, that the worldwide decline is a result of less spending by developed countries. Spending on weapons has remained almost constant in the LICs.)

- The United Nations is attempting to take a more active role in settling and resolving international disputes and, for the first time, violent domestic conflicts. Though some current efforts to stop violent conflicts have failed so far (e.g., Somalia), a look at history tells us that many U.N. missions have been very successful. Reforms that would increase the effectiveness of peace-keeping are currently being considered.

- Over the last 30 years, infant mortality rates have been cut in half. Part of the reason is a World Health Organization program that immunizes children in LICs. A decade ago, only about 15 percent of the children in LICs were immunized. Today, over 80 percent are immunized against six major childhood diseases, thanks in large part to this program.

- The average human life span has increased substantially in that same time frame. Even in the less industrialized countries, the average life span has increased by "12 years or more."[59]

- World spending on education has increased in recent years, as have educational opportunities for women. As a result, literacy is up, particularly for women, in each of the less developed regions of the world. Positive trends associated with increased literacy include decreased fertility rates and declining infant mortality rates.

The eleven problems outlined in Table 12.1 are serious, continuing problems, to be sure, and people will suffer their horrible effects for years to come. Though the positive trends just summarized may seem rather insignificant in comparison to these problems, those trends do illustrate an important point—the human race *is* capable of changing its course for the better. Though impossible to prove conclusively, it would benefit us to assume that our fate, and that of the world in which we live, is ultimately up to us.

Summary

This chapter discussed the theory of political realism that has dominated human thinking about world politics for 2,000 years, as well as the arguments of neorealists and idealists who have taken issue with that theory for a variety of reasons. How we interpret world politics, our positions on key issues, and to a degree, our assessment of the prospects for the world's future are dependent on which theoretical perspective we choose.

In this chapter we briefly discussed 11 major world problems. We emphasized that these complex and interrelated problems require careful analysis by political scientists seeking to understand them.

Having surveyed world problems, we next considered one in detail—war, which world politics scholars have studied more than any other. Sigmund Freud and Konrad Lorenz offered theories explaining the occurrence of war by focusing on individuals and their instincts. We also discussed theories based on the attributes of nation-states, which seek to explain the effects of economic systems and political systems on nation-states' proneness to participate in war. Finally, we discussed theories focusing on the linkage between the power structure of the international system and the occurrence of war.

A second international problem we discussed was government repression of basic human rights. We discussed two human-rights traditions, one that dealt with political and personal-integrity rights and another that defined human rights in terms of social and economic factors. We discussed the evolution of human-rights law since World War II and summarized the findings of political-science literature dealing with human rights.

Finally, we listed a few positive political accomplishments from recent history and discussed the prospects for the world's future. Hopefully as a result of this chapter you will have a clearer idea of the serious challenges facing the human race. At the same time, we hope that you will retain some hope that a more peaceful and just world can be achieved.

QUESTIONS AND EXERCISES

Questions for Reason

1. Explain briefly the major differences between the idealist and realist positions.

2. How do neorealists differ from pragmatists?

3. Explain why multinational corporations present such a problem for national foreign policy.

Questions for Reflection

1. Would you prefer that the next president of the United States be a realist, a neorealist, or an idealist?

2. If you were the president of France, how might you encourage the expansion of human rights in Europe?

3. If you were the president of Ecuador, how might you encourage the expansion of human rights in Ecuador, Columbia, and Peru?

4. What factors are most likely to initiate internal conflicts in countries? What factors are most likely to encourage interstate wars?

Questions for Analysis: Global Human Rights

This exercise will test hypotheses on the important question of why governments abuse their citizens' personal-integrity rights, defined and discussed in this chapter. Put another way, we will do research on the question of why some countries' regimes choose to imprison, torture and execute their political opponents, while others do not. This research will refer to a data set we call HRIGHTS gathered by Poe and Tate for a study published in 1994. These data cover a nearly global sample of countries for the years 1980 through 1987.*

---

* Steven C. Poe and C. Neal Tate, "Repression of Human Rights to Personal Integrity in the 1980s: A Global Analysis," *American Political Science Review* 88 (December 1994), pp. 853–872. The variables in this and the other data sets used in exercises are listed and described in Appendix B.

Earlier exercises have analyzed cross-sectional data sets, or data sets gathered for large numbers of units (usually people or countries) at one point in time. In a pooled cross-sectional data set like HRIGHTS, each cross-sectional unit (in this case, a country) appears several times (in this case, in data for each of 8 years, from 1980 to 1987). Researchers measure the independent and dependent variables for each country for each year included in the data set. Thus the unit of analysis in this data set is the country-year. If a pooled cross-sectional data set covers enough years, it allows us to see dynamics, or changes as they evolve throughout time. Even when data are available for only a few years, as is the case here, the time dimension still gives us a greater number of cases to analyze. This, in turn, increases our confidence in statistical results. The exercise relies on regression analysis, as discussed in the exercises of previous chapters, to investigate the causes of repression.[†]

Measuring Violations of Human Rights
Scholars have proposed a number of hypotheses to explain why some regimes violate human rights, while others accord these rights great respect. The chapter text discussed some of these hypotheses. The pooled cross-sectional data set HRIGHTS gives data on several different factors that have been linked by theorists to repression of these rights. Before proceeding further, the research must address a very basic problem: how, if at all, one can measure human rights.

We confront several difficulties in measuring human rights. Defining the term is not an easy task because conceptions of human rights inevitably differ from person to person and culture to culture. In this chapter we have already dealt with that problem as best as we can, by carefully defining the *personal-integrity rights* on which HRIGHTS rests.

Another problem arises because many of the regimes that most seriously violate human rights are closed societies where the media are more or less closely controlled by the government, thus giving the government a means to keep its activities quiet. (The list includes China, Iraq, and North Korea.) Though abuses probably happen frequently in these countries and others, researchers can rarely find exact information on what happens and when. In some cases, an absence of reports of human-rights abuses is good news; in other cases, fewer reports might actually reflect a crackdown on the media in order to hide serious abuses. Thus analysts need to use their own careful judgement in their attempts to measure human rights.

Finally, debate and discussion of human rights is almost always charged with emotion, and personal positions on this topic are often affected by political biases. Any researcher should realize these biases and try not to let them affect measurement attempts.

Researchers have, however, found a couple of sources of human-rights information from which they have derived measures of the seriousness of violations of personal

[†] Data sets like HRIGHTS create some complex methodological difficulties. (See James A. Stimson, "Regression in Space and Time: A Statistical Essay," *American Journal of Political Science* 29 (1985), pp. 914–947.) However, this exercise will not address any of those problems. Familiar regression analysis will usually yield results very similar to those of more sophisticated and complex techniques designed to deal with these difficulties.

integrity rights. Reports published by Amnesty International and the U.S. State Department summarize human-rights conditions in countries around the world.[‡] While these sources provide no summary data, researchers can analyze their contents and classify countries on an ordinal scale. This scale ranges from 1 to 5, where a 1 represents the most respect for human rights and a 5 represents the most complete disregard for these rights. The five categories are as follows:

1. "Countries . . . under a secure rule of law, people are not imprisoned for their views, and torture is rare or exceptional. . . . Political murders are extremely rare. . . ."

2. "There is a limited amount of imprisonment for nonviolent political activity. However, few persons are affected, torture and beating are exceptional. . . . political murder is rare. . . ."

3. "There is extensive political imprisonment, or a recent history of such imprisonment. Execution or other political murders and brutality may be common. Unlimited detention, with or without trial, for political views is accepted. . . ."

4. "The practices of [Level 3] are expanded to larger numbers. Murders, disappearances are a common part of life. . . . In spite of its generality, on this level terror affects primarily those who interest themselves in politics or ideas."

5. "The terrors of [Level 4] have been expanded to the whole population. . . . The leaders of these societies place no limits on the means or thoroughness with which they pursue personal or ideological goals."[§]

Based on these criteria, researchers analyzed the contents of both the Amnesty International and State Department reports in order to create two separate measures of personal-integrity rights abuse. The SDNEW variable in the data set came mainly from the researchers' analysis of the contents of the State Department reports, while AINEW mainly reflects the information published by Amnesty International.[‖] Although neither scale is perfect, they give two measures, gathered from information from two separate organizations, with different sets of biases.

Having established a basic understanding of the dependent variables we can proceed with an assignment. You will be asked to conduct two sets of analyses. You will conduct one analysis with SDNEW, and one with AINEW, employing identical sets of

---

[‡] See Amnesty International, *Amnesty International Report* (London: Amnesty International Publications, annual); and U.S. State Department, *Country Reports on Human Rights Practices* (Washington, D.C.: U.S. Government Printing Office, annual.) Michael Stohl, Mark Gibney, and others at Purdue University, as well as Poe and his coauthors, have gathered the data in HRIGHTS. Note, however, that Amnesty International attempts to discourage researchers from using its information for the purpose of measurement.

[§] Raymond Gastil, *Freedom in the World: Political Rights and Civil Liberties, 1980*. (New Brunswick, N.J.: Transaction Books, 1980), p. 37; quoted in Michael Stohl and David Carleton, "The Foreign Policy of Human Rights: Rhetoric and Reality from Jimmy Carter to Ronald Reagan," *Human Rights Quarterly* 7 (1985), pp. 212–213.

[‖] A few cases were originally missing from both the Amnesty and U.S. State Department measures, because one of the sources did not cover a country in a particular year. If one of the measures was available while the other was missing, HRIGHTS substitutes the present data for the missing value. The high correlation among the variables from the two sources ensures against corruption of data.

TABLE 12.2

INDEPENDENT VARIABLES IN THE DATA SET HRIGHTS

Variable Name	Description
LEFT	Dummy variable; 1 indicates countries with socialist governments and no nonso-cialist opposition, while 0 indicates all other countries.
PCGNP	Per-capita GNP, a standard measure of economic development, in thousands of U.S. dollars
DEMOCRA	Created from the Freedom House Political Rights scale, a 7-category ordinal scale where 1 is least democratic and 7 is most democratic
IWAR	Dummy variable; 1 indicates countries that participated in international wars, while 0 indicates countries that did not participate in international wars.
CWAR	Dummy variable; 1 indicates countries that were embroiled in civil wars during the year in question, while 0 indicates countries without civil wars.
LPOP	Populations logged so that outlying cases, such as China and India, do not exercise inordinate effects on the results
MILCTR2	Dummy variable; 1 indicates countries with regimes controlled by the military, while 0 indicates countries with civilian governments.
BRITINFL	Dummy variable; 1 indicates countries with histories of British colonial rule, while 0 indicates others.

independent variables to explain variations in each of these human-rights measures. Table 12.2 outlines several independent variables that you can use to test hypotheses.

Steps to Complete the Assignment

1. From your study of political theory in the first part of the text and your knowledge of socialism from sources outside this class, formulate a hypothesis linking the dummy variable LEFT to repression. Indicate whether you expect this variable to have a positive or negative effect on repression, and carefully offer the reasons for your expectation.

2. Do the same for the democracy variable, DEMOCRA.

3. Now repeat this process for at least three other hypotheses that you might want to test based on the variables that are summarized in Table 12.2. (Of course, you can do more if you want.)

4. Test the hypotheses by running simple bivariate correlations between the independent variables and SDNEW.

5. Repeat Step 4 substituting AINEW for SDNEW.

6. Run a multiple regression testing the four hypotheses that you posed, first with SDNEW and then with AINEW.

7. In a short essay, discuss your results. Address the following points:
   a. The similarities between the results yielded with AINEW and those with SDNEW
   b. Any important differences in results from these two human-rights measures

c. Explanations for any substantial differences, conclusions about the biases of your two human-rights measures. State conclusions, if any, about the hypotheses where the results differed.**

8. Come to class ready to discuss your interpretation of the results. Hand in your printouts with the essay.

NOTES

[1] Alvin Toffler, *Future Shock* (New York: Random House, 1970), p. 26.

[2] Frederic S. Pearson and J. Martin Rochester, *International Relations: The Global Condition in the Late Twentieth Century* (New York: McGraw-Hill, 1992), p. 19.

[3] James N. Rosenau, *Turbulence in World Politics* (Princeton, N.J.: Princeton University Press, 1990), p. 17.

[4] The first assumption regarding human nature mentioned here is discussed in James E. Dougherty and Robert L. Pfaltzgraff, *Contending Theories of International Relations* (New York: Harper & Row, 1990), pp. 82, 102; for discussions of the last three, see Robert O. Keohane, "Realism, Neorealism, and the Study of World Politics," in *Neorealism and Its Critics*, ed. by Robert O. Keohane (New York: Columbia University Press, 1986), pp. 1–27.

[5] Robert J. Lieber, *Theory and World Politics* (Cambridge, Mass.: Winthrop, 1972), p. 93.

[6] See the discussion of Morgenthau in Keohane, "Realism, Neorealism," p. 10. Other analysts define *power,* but their definitions differ considerably from one to another. For a good discussion of these differences, see Dougherty and Pfaltzgraff, *Contending Theories,* pp. 84–90.

[7] See for example, Glenn H. Snyder and Paul Diesing, *Conflict among Nations: Bargaining, Decision Making, and System Structure in International Crisis* (Princeton, N.J.: Princeton University Press, 1977).

[8] Dougherty and Pfaltzgraff, *Contending Theories,* pp. 276–277.

[9] Pearson and Rochester, *International Relations,* pp. 470–471.

[10] Roy Prieswork, "Could We Study International Relations as if People Mattered?" in *Peace and World Order Studies: A Curriculum Guide,* 3rd ed., ed. by Gordon Feller, Sherle R. Schwenninger, and Diane Singerman (New York: Institute for World Order, 1981), pp. 2–24.

[11] J. David Singer, "The Global System and Its Subsystems: A Developmental View," in *Linkage Politics: Essays on the Convergence of National and International Systems*, ed. by James N. Rosenau (New York: Free Press, 1969).

[12] John G. Stoessinger, *Crusaders and Pragmatists* (New York: W. W. Norton, 1979).

[13] Another contributing factor is the break up of the bipolar power system at the end of the Cold War, which the chapter will discuss in a later section. These recent changes in international interactions have led the press and scholars to shift some of their attention away from traditional Cold War questions and toward issues such as ethnic and religious violence that have previously been neglected.

[14] *Washington Post,* June 8, 1987; cited in Bruce Russett and Harvey Starr, *World Politics: The Menu for Choice,* 4th ed. (New York: W. H. Freeman, 1992), p. 51. These conflicts occurred in Corsica, Cyprus, Northern Ireland, Spain, Yugoslavia, Angola, Chad, Ethiopia, Nigeria, South Africa, Sudan, Uganda, Zimbabwe, Burma, India, Iran, Iraq, Israel, Lebanon, New Caledonia, Pakistan, Philippines, Sri Lanka, Syria, and Turkey.

** See Poe and Tate, "Repression of Human Rights," p. 866, to discover how the original researchers interpreted similar results. If you think you have a better interpretation than the one they give, e-mail Poe and tell him about it! His e-mail address is: SPOE@WOOTEN.UNT.EDU.

[15] Ruth Leger Sivard, *World Military and Social Expenditures, 1993,* 15th ed. (Washington, D.C.: World Priorities, 1993), p. 21.

[16] Ibid., p. 22.

[17] Ibid., p. 11.

[18] Ruth Leger Sivard, *World Military and Social Expenditures, 1991,* 14th ed. (Washington, D.C.: World Priorities, 1991), p. 11.

[19] Ibid.

[20] Sivard, *World Expenditures, 1993,* p. 56.

[21] Quoted in Sivard, *World Expenditures, 1993,* p. 1.

[22] John Mueller, "The Obsolescence of Major War," in *Conflict after the Cold War: Arguments on Causes of War and Peace,* ed. by Richard K. Betts (New York: Macmillan, 1994).

[23] Ibid., p. 22.

[24] Ibid., pp. 25–28.

[25] Melvin Small and J. David Singer, *Resort to Arms: International and Civil Wars, 1816–1980* (Beverly Hills, Calif.: Sage Publications, 1982).

[26] Charles W. Kegley, Jr. and Eugene R. Wittkopf, *World Politics: Trend and Transformation,* 4th ed. (New York: St. Martin's Press, 1993).

[27] J. David Singer, "Peace in the Global System: Displacement, Interregnum, or Transformation?" in *The Long Postwar Peace,* ed. by Charles W. Kegley, Jr. (New York: Harper Collins, 1991), pp. 56–84; *World Politics.*

[28] Sivard, *World Expenditures 1993,* p. 20.

[29] Kenneth Waltz, *Man and the State* (New York: Columbia University Press, 1965).

[30] Dougherty and Pfaltzgraff, *Contending Theories,* pp. 276–277.

[31] Konrad Lorenz, *On Aggression,* trans. by Marjorie Kerr Wilson (New York: Bantam, 1967), pp. 28–32; cited in Dougherty and Pfaltzgraff, *Contending Theories,* pp. 278–282.

[32] Lorenz, *On Aggression,* p. 127; as paraphrased in Dougherty and Pfaltzgraff, *Contending Theories,* p. 180.

[33] J. A. Hobson, *Imperialism: A Study* (London: Allen & Unwin, 1902); summarized in Bruce Russett and Harvey Starr, *World Politics,* pp. 193–194.

[34] Russett and Starr, *World Politics,* pp. 193–194.

[35] Ibid., p. 195.

[36] Norman Angell, *The Great Illusion: A Study of the Relation of Military Power to National Advantage* (New York: G. P. Putnam, 1910); cited in Dougherty and Pfaltzgraff, *Contending Theories,* p. 200.

[37] Russett and Starr, *World Politics,* p. 197.

[38] William Dixon, "Democracy and the Peaceful Settlement of International Conflict," *American Political Science Review* 1 (March 1988), pp. 14–32.

[39] Karl W. Deutsch and J. David Singer, "Multipolar Power Systems and International Stability," *World Politics* 16 (1964), pp. 390–407.

[40] John J. Mearsheimer, "Why We Will Soon Miss the Cold War," *The Atlantic Monthly,* August 1990, pp. 35–50.

[41] In case you are interested, most of the studies of this relationship have used statistical tools like O.L.S. regression that assume a linear relationship between independent and dependent variables. But such studies may yield unclear results because the relationship between international system structure and the frequency of war may not be linear. The international system structure may be important because it determines the opportunity structure for countries that are considering aggression. As such, the structure of the international system may set boundaries within which the frequency of war is likely to vary, without determining exactly how many wars there are at any given time. This is apt to produce a nonlinear relationship between international

system structure and war, which might not appear to be important when methods like O.L.S. regression are used. For an argument that runs in this direction see Benjamin A. Most and Harvey Starr, *Inquiry, Logic and International Politics* (Columbia, S.C.: University of South Carolina Press, 1989).

[42] Bruno Leone, *Nationalism: Opposing Viewpoints,* 2nd edition (St. Paul, Minn.: Greenhaven Press, 1986), p. 112.

[43] Chapter 4 discussed the Khmer Rouge in detail.

[44] Burns H. Weston, "Human Rights," in *Human Rights in the World Community: Issues and Action,* 2nd ed., ed. by Richard Pierre Claude and Burns H. Weston (Philadelphia: University of Pennsylvania Press, 1992), p. 19.

[45] Ibid., p. 7.

[46] David P. Forsythe, *Human Rights and World Politics* (Lincoln, Neb.: University of Nebraska Press, 1981), p. 7.

[47] Ibid., p. 5.

[48] Ibid., pp. 5–6.

[49] Claude and Weston, *Human Rights in the World Community,* p. 8.

[50] Burns H. Weston, et al., "Regional Human Rights Regimes: A Comparison and Appraisal," in ibid., p. 254.

[51] Steven C. Poe and C. Neal Tate, "Repression of Human Rights to Personal Integrity in the 1980s: A Global Analysis," *American Political Science Review* 88 (1994), pp. 853–872.

[52] Lo and behold, each of our theories was supported by the data! If only political scientists were so lucky in real life, your professor would smile a lot more and perhaps let class out early!

[53] Tom J. Farer, "The United Nations and Human Rights: More than a Whimper, Less than a Roar," in *Human Rights in the World Community,* p. 227.

[54] La Rochefoucauld, quoted in *Human Rights in the World Community,* p. 11.

[55] U.N. Charter (1945), Art. 3(7), quoted in Claude and Weston, *Human Rights in the World Community,* p. 3.

[56] Ibid., p. 11.

[57] Sivard, *World Military and Social Expenditures 1993,* p. 9.

[58] Some would argue, however, that the probability of smaller nuclear attacks may actually have increased because of arms proliferation coupled with the breakdown of the bipolar international system that emerged from the end of World War II.

[59] Ibid., p. 9.

Conclusion: The Functions of Government Revisited

Chapter 1 explained that a society would preserve order, develop mechanisms to supply collective goods, reduce negative externalities, and assign rights and duties even under the rule of a stationary bandit concerned only with her own welfare and that of her children. Recall also a basic difference between a government of bandits and a good government: Responsible leaders display their concern with justice, while bandits concern themselves with power and personal well-being. As Saint Augustine put it almost 1,600 years ago, Set justice aside, then, and what are kingdoms but great robberies?[1] Once the development of justice through law became an appropriate function of government, rulers gained legitimate authority to expand their roles in other areas in order to create a more just society.

The writings of Plato and Aristotle clearly articulate some critical questions in politics as early as the 5th century B.C.:

- What is a just government?
- How can government create good and just citizens?

The state's response to the second question allowed it to vastly increase its sphere of legitimate action. It began to apply law not only to settle disputes, but also to change society.

The scope and depth of politics took another great leap with the development of the nation-state and the challenge to the divine right of monarchs. Just as the process of industrialization would do in later years, the development of the nation-state greatly enlarged the scope of government. As soon as developments permitted people to question and reject the divine right of monarchs, they took the short step to some related questions:

- What should the state do about accidents of birth?
- What is the source of legitimate political authority?

Although the first of these questions remains perhaps the major battle in politics, contemporary societies have settled on an answer to the second. Political authority comes from the people. Hobbes, Locke, and Rousseau, though they advocated quite different forms of government, all identified the same source for government authority—it resides in the hands of the people whom rulers govern. The worldwide support for the ideology of democracy clearly demonstrates that most people in the world see sovereignty as a property of the people. As the fall of the Soviet Union and the communist regimes of eastern Europe showed, governments that deviate from this norm, with the possible exception of those that claim authority based on religious dogma, have substantial problems with legitimacy.

Followers of Publius, Rousseau, and Marx continue a great battle about what democracy should look like, and this struggle continues to define a critical issue in political regimes. For Publius, democracy had to maintain liberty and promote equality before the law; it also had to observe limits to its own authority. The modern pluralist states exemplify many of the individualistic ideas of Publius and the forms of government he advocated. The communitarian ideas of Rousseau and Marx remain evident in the contemporary corporatist democracies dominated by social democratic parties and others on the left. Regardless of the pluralist or corporatist orientation of a democratic regime, democracy requires that citizens play a meaningful role in choosing their leaders. Also, these states rely heavily on institutions that effectively link citizen preferences to policy outcomes.

Chapter 3 showed how the distribution of property is perhaps the critical question in matters of social justice. The great political philosophers all addressed the problems of inequalities in property and opportunity among members of society. Given the large role of inheritance in matters of property, talents, and disposition, societies must choose how they will deal with the good or bad fortune that individuals receive at birth. Almost all writers in democratic theory recognize that great inequalities leave small chances for effective democracy. More recent work in economics has shown that great inequalities also slow economic growth, at least among the more industrialized countries of the world. (See Chapter 11.) In one of their key roles, the social sciences can explain how inequalities affect societies and their ability to realize their conceptions of the good life.

Some enduring questions continue to influence both normative political theory and empirical political science:

- What role does citizen participation play in the policy process?
- What role *should* it play?

Political science should also answer:

- To what degree and how are citizen preferences linked to public policy?
- How do the people exercise effective control over current leaders?

Chapters 5 and 6 showed that political participation varies from country to country, and institutional arrangements strongly affect who will participate. Political parties make critical contributions, not only in democratic regimes, but in totalitarian and authoritarian regimes as well. Those chapters also observed that majority rule, defined as a system in which the preferences of a majority decide particular policy issues, is not really possible; still, elections give democratic societies effective majority control over the actions of elites.

Chapters 7, 8, and 9 traced the labyrinth of political institutions and how these institutions go about translating demands for government action into public policies. These activities differ for democratic and authoritarian governments and for democratic governments with largely parliamentary and largely presidential structures.

Parliamentary systems have much to recommend them, particularly in societies with deep divisions among groups of citizens. A parliamentary system with proportional representation provides an effective way for minority opinions to be heard. It also reduces the likelihood of stalemate and democratic failure as compared to other types of democratic systems. Presidential systems have worked well in societies that value compromise and where ideological divisions remain limited; in countries with deep divisions that favor confrontation over compromise, however, presidential systems have a higher probability of degenerating into nondemocratic regimes.

Chapters 8 and 9 showed the substantial policy-making activities of the nonelected branches of government, the bureaucracy, and the courts. These two institutions are common to both democratic and nondemocratic states. As technology increases and society grows more complex, the bureaucracy expands its policy-making role. Similarly, as respect for human rights increases around the world, so too does the role of courts.

The last section addressed the multitude of problems that face contemporary regimes. Less industrialized countries, particularly the poorest among them, face perhaps insurmountable economic development problems. The international economy is not structured in their favor, and the great gap between the resources of the wealthy few and those of the impoverished many may cripple any form of democratic government. History, culture, politics, and economics all seem to conspire to keep the poorest of the less industrialized countries in poverty.

Although their people live in less dismal conditions, the middle-income countries of the world such as Mexico, Brazil, Turkey, and Iran also face tremendous economic and political obstacles. In some countries, yawning gaps between rich and poor make economic development difficult and politics more so. An abundance of natural resources does not provide a sufficient condition for development. Nigeria, Brazil, and Mexico are only three of the many countries that have been unable to achieve sustained economic growth despite enormous stocks of natural resources.

In other countries, cultures of bribery and corruption in politics ranging from police officers to the prime ministers inhibit effective growth and altogether prevent legitimate politics. Countries that have achieved rapid economic development illustrate the powerful influence of culture. The achievement motivation in the Confucian cultures of South Korea, Taiwan, and China appear to have helped these countries overcome obstacles that have disrupted progress in countries with cultures less oriented toward economic achievement.

Although the people of the more industrialized countries enjoy many comparative blessings, their political systems also confront substantial problems. Foremost among these are crime, drugs, environmental damage, and the strains that rapidly aging populations place on social welfare systems. Between 1994 and 1996, Italy, France, and the United States all faced political crises when elected officials attempted to prepare for growth in those countries' elderly populations, which will increasingly focus attention on consumption rather than production. Whether the economies of the MICs can grow rapidly enough to pay for their welfare systems is a serious question. Certainly these countries must increase their rates of investment and economic growth to avoid significant declines in real per-capita wealth.

Finally, Chapter 12 looked at the issues facing the international political system. Is the nation-state an outmoded political unit when several multinational corporations make allocation decisions that control larger budgets than half of the nations of the world? How can a state protect its citizens when an external entity owns the country's information network and energy resources? How can the state survive when its external debt exceeds its government budget? Can a state retain its sovereignty in such a situation? Who dictates public policy, the International Monetary Fund or the current regime?

Chapter 12 also sounded alerts about the issues of human rights and the huge problems of violence between ethnic, tribal, and religious groups. Although the scope of human-rights protection continues to grow in international law, mass murders due to membership in particular religions, ethnic groups, or tribes continue. The conflict rages in world politics, as international law demands that governments protect human rights and individual countries grossly violate those laws. This presents a critical problem for foreign policy. Under what conditions should the United Nations, the United States, France, or any other external actor intervene in countries like Bosnia, Haiti, and Rwanda? What should the international community or any individual state do when another state breaks down, as happened in Somalia? Does the international system still languish in the horror Hobbes described 600 years ago, a brutish state of nature without real law and effective rights? Should states follow realist or idealist approaches to their international relations? If external forces intervene, under what circumstances can they expect to succeed? What obligations do the states of the core (the rich states) have to the states of the periphery (the poor countries)? If the states of the core want to assist those of the periphery, what policies would work best to achieve their goals?

This book has attempted to introduce the great normative questions of politics and to show how those questions relate to important empirical concerns. As promised at the beginning of the book, it focused more than other texts on political economy as a subject area and public choice as an approach. When any political scientist chooses an approach to the study of politics, that choice inevitably narrows the questions that the observer asks; in this way, it influences the answers that the observer finds. This book is no exception to that rule. In concentrating on political economy, it omits important philosophical questions. In stressing public choice, it primarily explores the self-interested side of human nature rather than the altruistic side.

While the authors believe that political conditions justify this emphasis of subject matter and approach, we want to point out three issues that did not receive as much attention as we would have liked. First, as Chapter 1 indicated, the first task of government is to establish and maintain order. Chapters 11 and 12 indicated that crime and violence in both the national and international arenas are continuing and growing problems. As Hobbes so clearly showed, most people in most societies will choose order over liberty when they encounter life-threatening disorder.

Second, the book has not examined the environmental issues facing individual nations and the entire planet. Environmental degradation, if it continues at its present pace, will force a redefinition of property rights, and it may even encourage nondemocratic government.

Third, the book has not assessed the full impact of the feminist revolution and the resulting restructuring of society and ideology. The authors agree with Nancy Hirschmann[2] that liberal principles stressing equality of opportunity define a sufficiently encompassing political philosophy to respond to the rights claims of women and minorities. History has not yet worked out satisfactory arrangements, though. As Marx made clear, any time society restructures, political philosophy and ideology will follow.

Despite these omissions, we believe that the book has developed skills in critical thinking and provided substantive information to substantially improve students' skills in decision making and in evaluating the truth of claims of politicians, journalists, and social scientists. We also hope that the book's introduction of some of the world's great political philosophers will encourage students to reflect more clearly on their own ideas and to seek out the wisdom of those who write on the enduring questions of political science.

NOTES

[1] Augustine, *Concerning the City of God* (trans. by John Healy), bk. iv, ch. 4; quoted in Leslie Lipson, *The Great Issues of Politics: An Introduction to Political Science,* 9th ed. (Englewood Cliffs, N.J.: Prentice-Hall, 1993), p. 55.

[2] Nancy J. Hirschmann, "Rights, Gender, and Multiplicity: Toward a Feminist Liberalism" (paper presented at the annual meeting of the American Political Science Association, Chicago, September, 1995).

Using Micro-Crunch

We recommend using the data from the computer disk that accompanies this book to complete the end-of-chapter exercises. In this way, the course can help students to develop two of the basic skills necessary to survive in a modern society—understanding and preparing simple data presentations and using personal computers. At the user's command, the computer will construct tables and graphs and carry out almost instantaneous statistical analyses. You will not have to compute statistics, draw tables, or use your calculator. The computer will also print out the results of your work without difficulty.*

Learning to Love Your PC

Many political science students find no aspect of their studies more frustrating than learning to use the computer. If it is any consolation, the same is true for many political science professors. Before you get started with the computer, it may be helpful to remember some vital facts:

---

*This appendix assumes that you will be using a personal computer (PC) to complete the exercises. If you have a terminal with a modem and access to a computer center, personnel there can tell you how to connect. We cannot describe the routines for accessing (logging in), using, and logging out of any specific mainframe computer system. Those procedures differ from one computer center to another. Consult your instructor or computer center personnel about working through a particular system and about installing SPSS if it is not already installed there.

1. The computer is stupid. It cannot think for you or figure out what you want to tell it. Say, for example, that you are attempting to type the number 10, and you accidentally type the letter *O* rather than a zero. If the computer had any common sense, it would recognize that you meant to add zero rather than *O* to change 1 into 10. However, the computer has no common sense. It records exactly what you enter.

2. It is extremely difficult to hurt a computer. You can hit all the wrong keys, turn the power on or off at the wrong time, and do all sorts of other things that the computer's programming does not expect. Nevertheless, you will not hurt the computer. The only problem created when you battle the computer is the additional time that it will take to do the work you need to accomplish.

To do the analyses for exercises in this course, you will use one of two statistical software packages: Micro-Crunch for MS-DOS or SPSS for Windows. This appendix tells you how to install Micro-Crunch and carry out the statistical procedures necessary for the analysis exercises in the text. Micro-Crunch requires an IBM-compatible PC running the MS-DOS operating system. The instructions assume some minimal familiarity with such a machine. The first thing you have to do is install Micro-Crunch on the hard disk of your PC from the $3^1/_2$-inch diskette that came with this book.

Installing Micro-Crunch

If you are using a computer in a college computer lab, you do not need to install Micro-Crunch. Your instructor will have made arrangements to offer Micro-Crunch through the local area network (LAN) or mainframe computer; you need only get instructions about how to get to Micro-Crunch.

If, however, you are installing Micro-Crunch on your own computer or that of a friend, follow these instructions:

1. Turn on the machine's power. You should see a prompt that looks like **C:>**

2. Insert the Micro-Crunch Install diskette into the $3^1/_2$-inch drive.

3. If you put the diskette in the A drive, type **A:** If you put it in the B drive, type **B:**[†]

4. Type **Install** and the screen in Figure A.1 appears.

When you press a key other than Esc, the computer will display the following questions:

1. "On which disk drive do you wish to install Micro-Crunch?" The words *Drive C* will be flashing. If you want to place the program files on drive C, press the Enter key. If you want to store them on another drive, use the arrow keys to highlight the appropriate drive (to make its designation flash), and then press the Enter key. For most users, C is the appropriate drive.

[†] Throughout this and other appendices, you should type the material that is in capital letters and bold type. This includes the punctuation marks.

FIGURE A.1

MICRO-CRUNCH INSTALLATION SCREEN

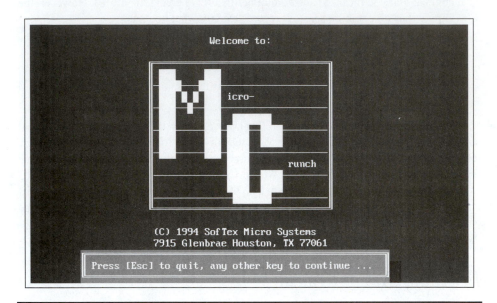

Welcome to:

(C) 1994 SofTex Micro Systems
7915 Glenbrae Houston, TX 77061

Press [Esc] to quit, any other key to continue ...

2. The screen will instruct you to specify the "disk destination subdirectory." Unless you already have a subdirectory called "Crunch," simply press the Enter key. If you want to use a different name, type it and press the Enter key. Micro-Crunch will begin installing on the designated drive and subdirectory, and you should see lots of stuff rapidly passing across your screen.

3. The screen will ask whether the program can create or modify your AUTOEXEC.BAT file, if necessary. If you are on your own PC, type **Y** in response. Micro-Crunch will then add the path C:\CRUNCH to your AUTOEXEC.BAT file.

4. The screen will ask whether the program can create/modify your CONFIG.SYS file. Type **Y** in response. In all probability, the screen will state that no changes need be made. Only if you are using an older PC will this file be changed. At this step, Micro-Crunch is making sure that it has enough files available to store working files. Micro-Crunch is a small program and does not need much space.

5. The screen will then ask whether you can see colors on your screen. Answer **Y** if you can or **N** if you cannot. If you have a color monitor, Micro-Crunch will ask if you like the colors you are viewing or if you wish to modify the screen. Answer **N** unless you want to change the screen.

Micro-Crunch will then indicate that the installation is complete. You now need to install the data sets. Remove the Micro-Crunch Install diskette from drive A and insert the Data diskette. Your computer should show

C:\CRUNCH>

Type:

COPY A:\MCDATA*.* C:\CRUNCH

This will copy all of the data sets into the subdirectory \CRUNCH on the C drive to make them available to you. If you wish, you can also store a copy of the codebooks for the individual data sets on your computer. You can do this by typing the following command:

COPY A:\CODEBOOK*.* C:\CRUNCH

The files were created and stored using Microsoft Word 6.0.

Although the creators of Micro-Crunch designed it so that students will find it easy to use, do not be fooled by this claim. At first, you may not agree with their claim. Nevertheless, you will find it possible to use the program to do the analyses. Although you may never come to love your PC or Micro-Crunch, you need not fear them.

Making Micro-Crunch Work for You: A Trial Run

The exercises in this text require you to do at least four types of analyses: contingency tables, correlations, scatterplots, and multiple regressions. The next few sections take you through the steps necessary to do each one. You can begin by practicing each type of analysis by following all of these steps. When you must execute each type of analysis for the exercises, you will find it helpful to refer to these sections.

CONTINGENCY TABLE ANALYSIS

This type of analysis produces tables of data and computes chi-squares and other statistics appropriate to contingency table analysis. We will use the data set PERUCAT for this trial analysis. Follow the numbered steps below to determine whether married or single people in Peru are more likely to agree with the statement that it is sometimes necessary to break the law to have an impact on government.

1. Turn on your computer. At the DOS prompt (C:>) type **CD \CRUNCH** and then press the Enter key. Then type **CRUNCH** and press the Enter key. You will see a screen similar to that in Figure A.2.

2. Use the arrow keys to choose the data set PERUCAT and press the Enter key. A new screen gives the "variable map" for the file C:\PERUCAT. This should look similar to Figure A.3.

3. Press the Enter key once more to see the rest of the variables in the data set PERUCAT.

   The variable map indicates that the data set includes 900 cases (900 respondents to survey questions) and 31 variables. You specify variable names to tell Micro-Crunch what to do. You must give correct spellings for these names. Each variable also has a

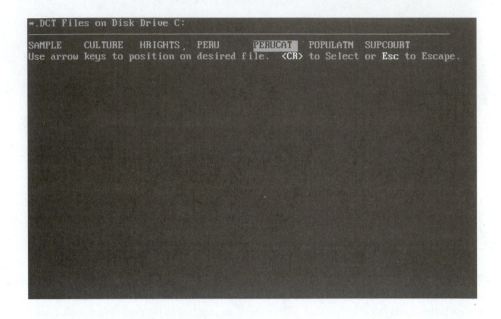

FIGURE A.2

MICRO-CRUNCH DATA SET SELECTION SCREEN

variable label that describes it in a bit more detail. All variables have identification numbers; the computer will use them more than you will. The submenu at the bottom of the screen lists three options: Print-to-Printer, Write-to-Disk, and Neither. If you are working on your own computer, use the arrow keys to highlight *Print-to-Printer*. This will give you a printout of the variables in the file PERUCAT.

4. Now you should see a screen with two rows. The word *Tables* should be highlighted. As you want Micro-Crunch to create tables at this point, press the Enter key.

5. Use the arrow keys to move over to *Crosstab*. Press the Enter key.

6. Micro-Crunch now asks for the dependent variable. When you are actually doing your analysis, you will choose which variable you want. For this analysis, type **BREAK-LAW** and press the Enter key.

7. Micro-Crunch now asks for the independent variable. Type **MARRIED** and press the Enter key.

8. Micro-Crunch now asks if you have a filter variable. You do not have a filter key, so press the Enter key.

9. Micro-Crunch produces your results.

MICRO-CRUNCH VARIABLE MAP SCREEN

```
         Variable Map for File: C:PERUCAT                 Cases:  900
Variable          Variable Label                   Format Missing Values

1    LOCCASE   CASE# FOR EACH FILE                  F4.0
2    INTEREST  HOW INTERESTED IN POLITICS           F8.2  -9
3    PROBLEMS  EQUALITY ISSUES PROBLEMS             F8.2  -9
4    IDEOLOGY  HOW CONSERVATIVE THE RESPONDENT      F8.2  -9
5    EDUCATN   LEVEL OF EDUCATION                   F8.2  -9
6    EFCYLEGL  HOW EFFECTIVE LEGAL ACTIONS          F8.2  -9
7    EFCYNOLG  HOW EFFECTIVE ILLEGAL ACTIONS        F8.2  -9
8    EFFICACY  LEVEL OF PERSONAL EFFICACY           F8.2  -9
9    BREAKLAW  SOMETIMES NECESSARY TO BREAK LAW     F8.2  -9
10   IMADEDIF  HOW MUCH OF A DIFFERENCE RESPONDENT MADE F8.2  -9
11   SUCCESS   HOW SUCCESSFUL LAST COLLECTIVE ACTION F8.2  -9
12   NORMLEGL  FRIENDS WILL THINK WELL OF LEGAL ACT F8.2  -9
13   RESPECT   RESPECT PEOPLE WHO ENDANGER SELVES   F8.2  -9
14   ALCONTRB  EACH MUST CONTRIBUTE TO GROUP ACTS   F8.2  -9
15   GUILT     WOULD FEEL GUILTY IF BROKE THE LAW   F8.2  -9
16   DORIGHT   FEEL GOOD FOR LEGAL POLIT ACTS       F8.2  -9
17   RELIGOUS  LEVEL OF RELIGIOUS AFFILIATION       F8.2  -9
18   LOSSLEGL  EXPECTED LOSS FROM LEGAL ACTS        F8.2  -9
19   LOSSNOLG  EXPECTED LOSS FROM ILLEGAL ACTS      F8.2  -9
20   LOSSTIME  TOO MUCH LOSS OF TIME TO ACT         F8.2  -9
<CR> to continue ...
                         Esc to interrupt              Time: 15:19:15
```

These results include a contingency table and statistics similar to those in Figure A.4. At the top of each column the table gives values for the independent variable MARRIED: 1 NO and 2 YES. Along the side are the values for the dependent variable BREAKLAW: 1 STRNGDIS, 2 DISAGREE, and 3 AGREE. The table states that 28.6 percent of single people agree that it is sometimes necessary to break the law to have an impact on government, while only 18.1 percent of the married people agree with this statement.

At the bottom of the screen, Micro-Crunch asks what you want to do with the results, Print-to-Printer, Write-to-Disk, or Neither. This time use the arrow keys and move the highlight to *Write-to-Disk* and press the Enter key.

10. Micro-Crunch asks what file name you want to give your results. It offers the default name of PERUCAT.OUT. Rather than accepting that choice, type the file name **C:\CRUNCH\PRACTICE.OUT** and press the Enter key.

File names can contain only 11 total characters. You can use between one and eight characters before the period and from zero to three after the period.

You have now created the file, PRACTICE.OUT in the subdirectory C:\CRUNCH. That file contains your table and statistics.

FIGURE A.4

CROSS TABULATION OF BREAKLAW VERSUS MARRIED

BREAKLAW by MARRIED

	0.000 NO	1.000 YES	
1 STRNGDIS	131 21.0%	90 36.1%	
2 DISAGREE	315 50.4%	114 45.8%	
3 AGREE	179 28.6%	45 18.1%	
	625 100.0%	249 100.0%	

Valid Cases = 874 Missing Cases = 26

Chi-Square is 24.77 with 2 Degrees of Freedom. Min. Expected Cell: 63
Phi-Square: 0.028 Cramer's V: 0.166 Cnt. Coef.: 0.164
Gamma:-0.299 Lambda (A): 0.000   Tau-B:-0.154   Tau-C: -0.156

If you are working in a computer lab, you will probably save your PRACTICE.OUT file on a drive other than the C drive. In this case, ask your lab assistant or instructor which drive should store your personal files; type that letter, a colon, and the name PRACTICE.OUT. For example, you might type **H:PRACTICE.OUT** to store the file on drive H.

Other computer labs require you to bring your own diskette to save files. If that is the case, type **A:PRACTICE.OUT** after inserting a diskette.

USING YOUR WORD PROCESSOR TO PRINT RESULTS

Readers will use many different word processors and printers, and we cannot hope to explain how to use all of them. Many readers will be working in college computer labs through local area networks. The instructor or lab assistant can tell you how to bring your file into the word processor, format it nicely, and print it. The general directions that follow should help you with any word processor and printer. However, if you are new to the computer, you will probably need the assistance of either the instructor, a computer lab assistant, or a friend in the class who knows a little bit about word processing on computers.

1. Call up the word-processing package that you intend to use. For example, you might be using Word or WordPerfect. The file you saved is a text file (sometimes called an

ASCII file or a *DOS Text file.* Use the open command and request the file **C:\CRUNCH\PRACTICE.OUT.**

For users of Windows 3.1 or Windows 95, the word-processing package will display a dialog button for opening files. Both WordPerfect 6.0 and Word 4.0 (and higher versions of these programs) can easily recognize a text file and properly import it. Other packages may ask what kind of file you want to import. Try any of these options: **txt, text, ASCII,** or **Dos Text** (without the commas). One or more of these should work.

2. At this point, you may have to change the font to properly display the table. You should NOT choose a proportionally spaced font. A good choice for a font is Courier New; a font size of 8.5 points or 16.67 points will work. In Word and WordPerfect, you can use the Edit option to Select All and the Format and Font options to choose the appropriate font. Once you have done this, your table should line up in neat columns.

3. Go to the top of the page and insert your name.

4. Print the document.

CORRELATION ANALYSIS

The exercises for Chapter 8 explain how correlation analysis measures the relationship between two variables. The strength of the relationship goes from 0 to 1 for positive relationships and from 0 to −1 for negative relationships. A correlation coefficient of +0.75 indicates the same degree of association as a correlation coefficient of −0.75.

To do correlation analysis, follow the steps from the section on contingency tables to bring in Micro-Crunch. For this example, choose the data set SUPCOURT.

As usual, Micro-Crunch will display a list of variables that you can print out or save to a disk. Remember, if you need to check variable names, you can press F2 to get a list. This example will examine the relationships between the justices' personal values and their voting records on civil-rights issues and economic issues. The variable for justices' votes on civil rights cases is CLVOTE. The variable for their votes on economic cases is ECONVOTE. The variable for personal values is VALUES. All three variables follow scales described in the Supreme Court codebook in Appendix C. Lower scores on the variables indicate more conservative votes or conservative values; higher scores indicate more liberal votes or values.

To instruct Micro-Crunch to perform correlation analysis, follow these steps:

1. After starting your computer, entering Micro-Crunch, and choosing the data set SUP-COURT, use your arrow keys to highlight the option *Linear-Models.*

2. Use arrow keys to highlight *Correlation* and press the Enter key.

3. When the screen reads, "Listwise or Pairwise missing value deletion" with a flashing *L,* press the Enter key.

4. When the screen reads, "Write matrix to disk" with a flashing *N,* press the Enter key.

5. The screen will now tell you to "Enter variables following prompts. <CR> To terminate list." This simply means to enter each variable you wish to examine. After you type each

---
FIGURE A.5

CORRELATION ANALYSIS OUTPUT

Correlation

Number of Valid Cases = 32

Variable	Mean	Std. Dev.
CLVOTE	52.700	19.871
ECONVOTE	55.834	13.895
VALUES	0.155	0.632

Listwise Correlation Matrix, N = 32

	CLVOTE	ECONVOTE	VALUES
CLVOTE			
ECONVOTE	0.786		
VALUES	0.663	0.522	

---

variable, press the Enter key. When you have included all the variables, press the Enter key once more. In this example, you will type the following:

CLVOTE and press the Enter key.

ECONVOTE and press the Enter key.

VALUES and press the Enter key twice.

That's it! Micro-Crunch will now do the correlations. It will give you a table that looks like the one in Figure A.5. This figure indicates that all three variables are positively associated. CLVOTE and ECONVOTE have a correlation coefficient of 0.786; CLVOTE and VALUES have a correlation coefficient of 0.663; finally, ECONVOTE and VALUES have a correlation coefficient of 0.522.

SCATTERPLOTS

One of the exercises in Chapter 8 asks you to use a scatterplot to examine the relationship between two variables. A scatterplot is a figure that places individual cases on a graph by their values of the dependent and independent variables. The graph locates values of the dependent variable along the y axis and the values of the independent variable along the x axis.

Micro-Crunch can easily convert data into a scatterplot. Simply follow the steps outlined in this section. The example will use the data set SUPCOURT, which reports the voting patterns of the justices on the U.S. Supreme Court from 1946 to 1995. CLVOTE is the dependent variable, and VALUES is the independent variable. (See the Supreme Court Codebook in Appendix C for definitions of these variables.)

1. Following the same directions as for correlation analysis, bring up Micro-Crunch and choose the data set SUPCOURT.

2. Use the arrow keys to choose *Linear-Models*.

3. Use the arrow keys to choose *Quik-Plot*.

4. When the screen reads "Enter Y axis variable," type **ECONVOTE** and press the Enter key.

5. When the screen reads "Enter X axis variable," type **VALUES** and press the Enter key.

6. When the screen reads "Compute and plot regression line? (Y/N)," press **Y.**

After showing the bivariate regression analysis (just press the Enter key to continue), Micro-Crunch will show the scatterplot and ask you if you want to Print-to-Printer, Write-to-Disk, or Neither. The scatterplot looks similar to the one in Figure A.6. Each asterisk (*) represents the scores of a Supreme Court justice on both ECONVOTE and VALUES. The shaded dots indicate the regression line. It slopes upward, indicating a positive relationship. The correlation coefficient, *R,* is equal to +0.522. The line "R Squared = 0.273" indicates that knowing justices' scores on the variable VALUE explains 27.3 percent of their scores on ECONVOTE.

MULTIPLE REGRESSION

The last statistical technique in this appendix is multiple regression. By now, Micro-Crunch is an old friend, so you will easily finish all of these instructions. Once again, get into Micro-Crunch and choose the data set SUPCOURT. As the exercises for Chapter 9 describe, multiple regression allows researchers to use several independent variables to predict scores of a dependent variable.

This example will use a single justice's votes on economic cases (ECONVOTE) as the dependent variable. It hypothesizes that the following variables all have negative impacts on ECONVOTE: (1) if a justice lived in a southern or border state (SOUT-LIFE), (2) if the justice attended a high-status law school such as Yale or Stanford (HI-LAWSCH), and (3) if the justice attends an Episcopal or other high-Protestant church (HIPROT).

1. As with correlation analysis and Quik-Plot, use the arrow keys to choose *Linear-Models*.

2. Now choose *Regression*.

3. The screen will ask for the dependent variable. Type **ECONVOTE** and press the Enter key.

4. The screen will now ask for the independent variables. Type:

   SOUTLIFE and press the Enter key

FIGURE A.6

SCATTERPLOT OF ECONVOTE VERSUS VALUES

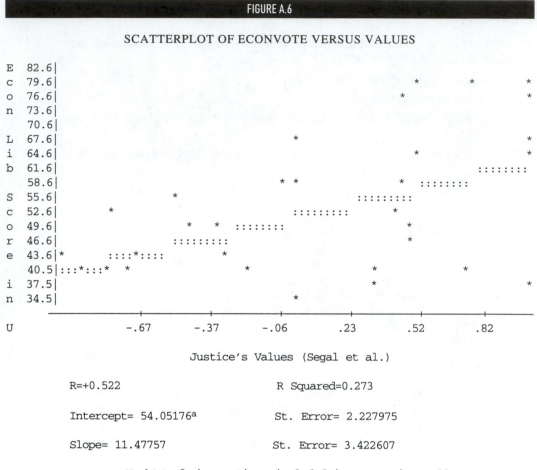

```
E  82.6|
c  79.6|                                               *        *        *
o  76.6|                                          *                       *
n  73.6|
   70.6|
L  67.6|                        *                                         *
i  64.6|                                          *                       *
b  61.6|                                                         :::::::::
   58.6|                             *  *              *         :::::::::
S  55.6|              *                            :::::::::
c  52.6|        *                         :::::::::            *
o  49.6|             *    *    :::::::::                   *
r  46.6|                 :::::::::::                        *
e  43.6|*      ::::*::::              *
   40.5|:::*:::*   *              *                *            *
i  37.5|                                          *                       *
n  34.5|                             *
```
```
U            -.67      -.37      -.06      .23      .52      .82
```

Justice's Values (Segal et al.)

R=+0.522   R Squared=0.273

Intercept= 54.05176[a]   St. Error= 2.227975

Slope= 11.47757   St. Error= 3.422607

Number of observations included in regression = 32

[a]The computer's plot of the line describing the relationship is only a rough estimate. Notice that it appears here to intercept the y-axis at about 40.5. But the computed intercept shown in the figure is 54.05176. You should rely on the computed value.

HILAWSCH and press the Enter key

HIPROT and press the Enter key twice

5. That's it! You are done. Micro-Crunch will respond with two screens that together provide the information in Figure A.7. Write the material to disk and give the file an appropriate name such as C:\CRUNCH\REGRES.TRY. Now bring the material into your word processor and fix the fonts and page breaks so that the output looks similar to Figure A.7.

FIGURE A.7

MICRO-CRUNCH VARIABLE MAP SCREEN

Regression

N = 32

Variable	Mean	Std. Dev.
ECONVOTE	55.834	13.895
SOUTLIFE	0.188	0.390
HILAWSCH	0.750	0.433
HIPROT	0.344	0.475

Sums of Squares

Total	Unexplained	Explained
6178.664	5824.425	354.239

R-Square	Adjusted R-Square
0.057	-0.044

Regression: ECONVOTE Is Dependent

Variable	B	Std. Error	t	Beta
Constant	61.4386	5.9329	10.3556	0.0000
SOUTLIFE	0.9248	6.8806	0.1344	0.0260
HILAWSCH	-5.3991	6.1286	-0.8810	-0.1682
HIPROT	-5.0279	5.4365	-0.9248	-0.1719

Using SPSS 6.1 for Windows

We recommend using the data from the computer disk that accompanies this book to complete the end-of-chapter exercises. In this way, the course can help students to develop two of the basic skills necessary to survive in a modern society—understanding and preparing simple data presentations and using personal computers. At the user's command, the computer will construct tables and graphs and carry out almost instantaneous statistical analyses. You will not have to compute statistics, draw tables, or use your calculator. The computer will also print out the results of your work without difficulty.*

Learning to Love Your PC

Many political science students find no aspect of their studies more frustrating than learning to use the computer. If it is any consolation, the same is true for many political science

---

*This appendix assumes that you will be using a personal computer (PC) to complete the exercises. If you have a terminal with a modem and access to a computer center, personnel there can tell you how to connect. We cannot describe the routines for accessing (logging in), using, and logging out of any specific mainframe computer system. Those procedures differ from one computer center to another. Consult your instructor or computer center personnel about working through a particular system and about installing SPSS if it is not already installed there.

professors. Before you get started with the computer, it may be helpful to remember some vital facts:

1. The computer is stupid. It cannot think for you or figure out what you want to tell it. Say, for example, that you are attempting to type the number 10, and you accidentally type the letter *O* rather than a zero. If the computer had any common sense, it would recognize that you meant to add zero rather than *O* to change 1 into 10. However, the computer has no common sense. It records exactly what you enter.

2. It is extremely difficult to hurt a computer. You can hit all the wrong keys, turn the power on or off at the wrong time, and do all sorts of other things that the computer's programming does not expect. Nevertheless, you will not hurt the computer. The only problem created when you battle the computer is the additional time that it will take to do the work you need to accomplish.

To do the analyses for exercises in this course you will use one of two statistical software packages: Micro-Crunch for MS-DOS or SPSS for Windows. This appendix tells you how to copy the data sets for SPSS from the disk that came with this book to your own computer and how to do the statistical analyses required in the exercises.

Loading Data from the Data Diskette into Your Personal Computer

Most users of SPSS for Windows (or SPSSPC+) will find that their instructors have loaded the data sets on the appropriate computers. If, however, you have your own version of SPSS and want to copy the data sets to your computer, follow the instructions in this section.

When we instruct you to type material into the computer, the material you type will be in bold type and in capital letters.

First, place the data diskette in the A drive of your computer. Second, move to the subdirectory where SPSS is located. For example, if you have stored SPSS in C:\Windows\SPSSWIN, then type:

CD\WINDOWS\SPSSWIN

Your computer will respond with the prompt:

C:\WINDOWS\SPSSWIN>

Now type:

COPY A:\SPSSDATA*.* C:

If you want to put the codebooks for the data sets on your C drive, you can do this by typing:

COPY A:\CODEBOOK*.* C:

Loading Data from the C Drive into SPSS for Windows

The first step in data analysis is to load a data set into SPSS 6.1 for Windows. This exercise uses the data set PERUCAT.SYS as an example. It also assumes that the data sets are stored in the C:\SPSSWIN directory. To load the data set PERUCAT.SYS into SPSS follow these steps:

1. Click on the command _File_. A menu window will appear.
2. Click on the command _Open_. A menu window will appear to the right.
3. Click on the command _Data_. The Data menu window will appear.
4. Note that the file PERUCAT has a .sys extension. To access it, move the cursor to the _File Type_ window and click once. A number of options will be available, but this example will focus on accessing .sys files. Click once on the line _SPSS/PC+ (*.sys)_ and several files should appear in the _File Name_ window. Move the cursor to the file PERUCAT.SYS and click twice.
5. Congratulations! You have just loaded the file PERUCAT.SYS.
6. To exit SPSS, click on _File_ and then on _Exit_. SPSS will ask, "Save contents of data window Newdata?" Click on _No_.

Loading Data from the M Drive of a Network into SPSS 6.1[†]

This exercise will use the data set PERUCAT.SYS as an example. To load the file PERUCAT.SYS into SPSS from the M drive follow these steps:

1. Click on the command _File_. A menu window will appear.
2. Click on the command _Open_. A menu window will appear to the right.
3. Click on the command _Data_. The Data menu window will appear.
4. Move the cursor to the small window in the center of the screen titled _Drives_ and click once.
5. Move the cursor to the line _M:_ and click once.
6. The file PERUCAT has a .sys extension. To access it, move the cursor to the _File Type_ window and click once. A number of options will be available, but this exercise will access only .sys files. Click once on the line _SPSS/PC+ (*.sys)_ and several files should appear in the _File Name_ window. Move the cursor to the file PERUCAT.SYS and click twice.
7. Congratulations! You have just loaded the file PERUCAT.SYS.

[†] We will assume the M drive is a drive on your network system. Your drive, most likely, will be different.

8. To exit SPSS, click on *File* and then on *Exit*. SPSS will ask, "Save contents of data window Newdata?" Click on *No*.

Data Analysis Using SPSS 6.1

CHI SQUARE ANALYSIS

Part 1: Chi Square without a Control Variable   This sample exercise will use a chisquare test to examine the relationship between two variables in the PERUCAT.SYS data set. (To load the correct file, refer to the earlier instructions.)

The directions in this section assume that you have opened a file in a word processor that uses Windows. For example, you might have a Microsoft Word file open in which you have written the hypothesis, "Individuals with higher political efficacy scores are more likely to say that they are willing to participate in legal political activities." You will use the measures EFFICACY and WILLLEGL to test this hypothesis.

Using the minimize arrow in the upper-left corner of the screen, minimize the word-processing application and enter SPSS for Windows. To obtain a chi-square statistic:

1. Click on the command *Statistics*. A menu will appear.

2. Click on the command *Summarize*. A menu will appear (normally on the right side of the screen).

3. Click on the command *Crosstabs*. A Crosstabs menu will appear. Move the cursor to the down-arrow box in the variable list and click a couple of times to scroll through the variable list.

4. When the variable WILLLEGL appears, move the cursor to it and click once. You will notice that it is highlighted. Move the cursor to the right arrow beside the box titled *Row(s):* and click once. You have added the variable WILLLEGL to the list of variables to be analyzed.

5. To add EFFICACY to the *Column* list, move the cursor to the variable EFFICACY and click once. It will be highlighted. Move the cursor to the right arrow beside the box titled *Column(s):* and click once. You have just defined the row variable and the column variable.

6. In order to calculate a chi-square test statistic, you must perform a couple more steps. Move the cursor down to the gray box titled *Statistics* and click once. A Crosstabs: Statistics menu will appear. Move the cursor to the *Chi-Square* box and click once. An *X* will appear to the left of the word *Chi-Square*.

7. Click on the command *Continue* and you will return to the Crosstabs menu.

8. Next, instruct SPSS to calculate column percentages. To do this, click on the command *Cells* and a Crosstabs. Cell Display window will appear. Click on the command *Column* and an *X* will appear in the box to its left. Click on the command *Continue* and you will return to the Crosstabs window.

9. To run the chi-square test, click on the command *OK*. Your output will appear in the Output window looking similar to Figure B.1. The shaded area in the figure indicates the statistical outputs of interest in this exercise.

CHI-SQUARE TABLE WITHOUT A CONTROL VARIABLE

WILLLEGL   WILL ACT LEGALLY IN FUTURE   by   EFFICACY   LEVEL OF PERSONAL EFFICACY

```
                    EFFICACY              Page 1 of 1
            Count |
            Col Pct |LOW      MODERATE   HIGH
                    |                                      Row
                    | 1.00   |  2.00   |  3.00  |  Total
WILLLEGL            ----------------------------------
            1.00    |   80   |   62    |   82   |   224
   UNLIKELY         |  38.8  |  18.7   |  25.2  |  26.0
                    ----------------------------------
            2.00    |  110   |  179    |  148   |   437
   POSSIBLE         |  53.4  |  53.9   |  45.5  |  50.6
                    ----------------------------------
            3.00    |   16   |   91    |   95   |   202
   LIKELY           |  7.8   |  27.4   |  29.2  |  23.4
                    ----------------------------------
            Column     206      332       325      863
            Total      23.9     38.5      37.7    100.0
```

Chi-Square	Value	DF	Significance
Pearson[a]	51.20421	4	.00000
Likelihood Ratio	57.36699	4	.00000
Mantel-Haenszel test for linear association	25.22042	1	.00000

Minimum Expected Frequency -   48.218

Number of Missing Observations: 37

[a]NOTE: "Pearson" is Pearson Chi square

To move your results from SPSS into your word processor, continue with the following steps:

10. Use your mouse to block the chi-square output material shown in Figure B.1.

11. Click on *Edit* and then on *Copy*.

    If you plan to return to SPSS to do more analysis, minimize the SPSS screen and restore the word processor screen, then follow the directions in Steps 14 and 15. If you are finished with the SPSS analysis, exit by following Steps 12 and 13.

12. Click on *File* then click on *Exit*.

13. SPSS will ask two questions, "Save contents of data window Newdata?" and "Save contents of SPSS output windows !Output1?" Click on *No* for both questions and then continue with Step 14.

14. Move the cursor to the location where you wish to place your output, then complete one of two actions:

a. Click on the icon for paste (a small bottle of glue in WordPerfect, a small clipboard with a note pasted on it in Word).

b. Click on the command *Edit* then click on the command *Paste.*

15. Block the material you have pasted and use a font such as Courier New in the size 8.5 or Courier in the size 16 characters per inch to ensure that your material fits. You may also need to adjust the margins.

Part 2: Chi-Square with a Control Variable

1. Using the same steps as in the previous section and the file PERUCAT.SYS, click on the commands *Statistics* then *Summarize* and then *Crosstabs.* This example will use DIDNOLG as the dependent (row) variable, MARRIED as the independent (column) variable, and STUDENT as the control (level) variable.

2. Scrolling down through the variables, choose DIDNOLG and place it in the box for the row variable.

3. Scroll up to the variable MARRIED, and move it into the box titled *Column(s).*

4. To add STUDENT as the control variable, move through the list of variables until you get to STUDENT, then click on it. Next, click the arrow below the line:

Previous   **Layer 1 of 1**   **Next**

5. Follow Steps 6 through 10 in the previous section to calculate a chi-square for each value of the control variables.

6. Your output will appear in the Output window looking similar to Figure B.2.

7. To place this material in your word-processing file, follow Steps 10 through 15 in the previous section.

CORRELATION ANALYSIS

Correlation analysis measures the strength of relationships among variables. This exercise will analyze the strength of associations (i.e., correlations) among three variables in the SUPCOURT.SYS data set. Specifically, it examines the relationships between the personal values of Supreme Court justices and their votes on cases involving civil liberties and government economic regulation. The first variable, CLVOTE, gives the percentage of time a Supreme Court justice votes on the more liberal side of a civil liberties case. The second variable, ECONVOTE, reflects the percentage of time a Supreme Court justice votes on the more liberal side of an economic regulation case. The third variable, VALUES, measures a justices' ideological liberalism before becoming a member of the Supreme Court.

To begin the exercise, go into SPSS and bring in the file SUPCOURT.SYS.

1. Move the cursor to the command *Statistics* and click once. A statistics menu will appear.

==
FIGURE B.2
==

CHI-SQUARE TABLES WITH A CONTROL VARIABLE

DIDNOLG   HAS ACTED IN ILLEGAL DEMONSTRATION by MARRIED   RESPONDENT MARRIED
Controlling for..
STUDENT   RESPONDENT A STUDENT   Value = 1.00   NO

```
                       MARRIED        Page 1 of 1
              Count |
              Col Pct |NO        YES
                    |                     Row
                    | 1.00   | 2.00   |Total
DIDNOLG       --------+--------+--------+
              1.00 |  184   |  161   |  345
    NEVER          | 80.3   | 78.2   | 79.3
                   +--------+--------+
              2.00 |   25   |   30   |   55
    SOMETIME       | 10.9   | 14.6   | 12.6
                   +--------+--------+
              3.00 |   20   |   15   |   35
    FREQUENT       |  8.7   |  7.3   |  8.0
                   +--------+--------+
              Column   229      206     435
              Total   52.6     47.4   100.0
```

Chi-Square	Value	DF	Significance
Pearson	1.49024	2	.47468
Likelihood Ratio	1.48972	2	.47480
Mantel-Haenszel test for linear association	.01629	1	.89845

Minimum Expected Frequency -   16.575

DIDNOLG   HAS ACTED IN ILLEGAL DEMONSTRATION by MARRIED   RESPONDENT MARRIED
Controlling for..
STUDENT   RESPONDENT A STUDENT   Value = 2.00   YES

```
                       MARRIED        Page 1 of 1
              Count |
              Col Pct |NO        YES
                    |                     Row
                    | 1.00   | 2.00   |Total
DIDNOLG       --------+--------+--------+
              1.00 |  167   |   10   |  177
    NEVER          | 47.7   | 47.6   | 47.7
                   +--------+--------+
              2.00 |   88   |    4   |   92
    SOMETIME       | 25.1   | 19.0   | 24.8
                   +--------+--------+
              3.00 |   95   |    7   |  102
    FREQUENT       | 27.1   | 33.3   | 27.5
                   +--------+--------+
              Column   350       21     371
              Total   94.3      5.7   100.0
```

Chi-Square	Value	DF	Significance
Pearson	.57299	2	.75089
Likelihood Ratio	.58084	2	.74795
Mantel-Haenszel test for linear association	.10977	1	.74041

Minimum Expected Frequency - 5.208

Number of Missing Observations: 94

FIGURE B.3

BIVARIATE CORRELATION

```
- -   Correlation Coefficients    - -

            CLVOTE        ECONVOTE      VALUES

CLVOTE      1.0000         .7863         .6635
            (    32)      (    32)      (    32)
            P= .          P= .000       P= .000

ECONVOTE     .7863        1.0000         .5222
            (    32)      (    32)      (    32)
            P= .000       P= .          P= .001

VALUES       .6635         .5222        1.0000
            (    32)      (    32)      (    32)
            P= .000       P= .001       P= .


(Coefficient / (Cases) / 1-tailed Significance)        " . "
is printed if a coefficient cannot be computed
```

---

2. Now move the cursor to the command _Correlate_ and click once. A submenu will appear to the right.

3. Move the cursor to the command _Bivariate_ and click once. A Bivariate Correlation menu will appear. The box on the left lists all of the variables in the SUPCOURT.SYS data set.

4. Move the cursor to the variable CLVOTE and click once. You will notice that it is highlighted. Move the cursor to the right arrow beside the variable box and click once. You have just added the variable CLVOTE to the list of variables to be analyzed.

5. Follow Steps 3 and 4 to add the variables ECONVOTE and VALUES. When you have finished, three variable names should appear in the window titled _Variables_.

6. In the box titled _"Correlation Coefficients"_ make sure that the box beside Pearson has an _X_ in it.

7. In the box titled _"Test of Significance,"_ click on _One-tailed Test_.

8. Make sure that the box next to the statement "Display actual significance level" has an _X_ in it.

9. Now click on the _Options_ command. Click on the statement "Exclude cases pairwise" in the Missing Values box. Now click on _Continue_.

10. Move the cursor to the OK box and click once. SPSS will perform the calculations and display the results in the Output window. They should look similar to Figure B.3.

11. Check your results. Are the correlations among the variables positive, as the hypothesis expects? Do the results indicate strong or weak relationships?

12. To copy your results from SPSS into your word processing file, follow the steps in the section on chi-square analysis.

SCATTERPLOT ANALYSIS

This sample exercise explains how to use a convenient tool called the *scatterplot*. A scatterplot indicates relationships and patterns among variables by plotting their values against each other. The exercise will use two files, SUPCOURT.SYS and PERU.SYS. From the data set SUPCOURT, it will analyze the variables VALUES and CLVOTE. VALUES is a measure of the ideological values of U.S. Supreme Court justices; higher scores indicate more liberal personal values and lower scores indicate more conservative personal values. CLVOTE is the percentage of cases in which a justice voted in favor of the more liberal position on a civil liberties case. To demonstrate a scatterplot with ordinal variables, the exercise will analyze the relationships and patterns between the two variables WILLNOLG and AGE from the data set PERU.SYS.

Scatterplot with Interval Data   Bring the data set SUPCOURT.SYS into SPSS using the procedures described in the first exercise. To obtain a scatterplot, complete the following steps:

1. Move the cursor to the command *Graphs* and click once. A menu will appear.

2. Move the cursor to the command *Scatter...* and click once. A Scatterplot menu will appear.

3. Move the cursor to the command *Define* and click once. A Simple Scatterplot menu will appear.

4. Move the cursor to the down arrow and click until the variable CLVOTE is highlighted. Click once on the variable name, then move the cursor to the right arrow next to the box titled *Y Axis* and click once. You have just instructed SPSS to use CLVOTE as the *y*-axis variable.

5. Move the cursor to the variable name *VALUES* and click once. The variable name will be highlighted. Then move the cursor to the right arrow next to the box titled *X Axis* and click once. You have just instructed SPSS to use VALUES as the *x*-axis variable.

6. Move the cursor to the command *OK* and click once. SPSS will open a Chart Carousel window and display the scatterplot of the two variables CLVOTE and VALUES. Have SPSS fit a regression line to the scatterplot to provide a useful way of interpreting it. To do this, follow these steps:

7. From the Chart Carousel window, move the cursor to the command *Edit* (directly under the title bar Chart Carousel) and click once.

8. Move the cursor to the command *Chart* along the top of the SPSS screen and click once.

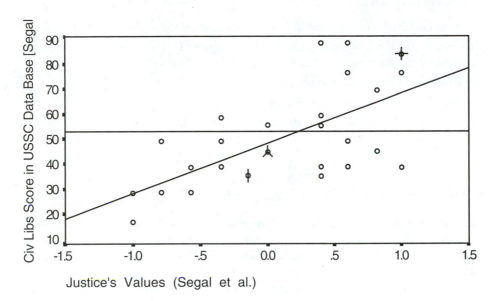

FIGURE B.4

SPSS SCATTERPLOT OF CLVOTE AND VALUES

A mark of 'o' indicates a single case. This is the center of the sunflower. Petals added to the sunflower indicate that more than one case has the same scores for CLVOTE and VALUES. Thus the mark 'A' indicates that three judges have the same scores on the two variables.

9. Move the cursor to the command *Options* and click once. A Scatterplot Options window will appear.

10. Move the cursor to the command *Total* located in the Fit Line box and click once. (An *X* should appear in the box.)

11. Move the cursor to the command *Total* located in the Mean of Y Reference Line window and click once. (An *X* should appear in the box.) You have just instructed SPSS to estimate a line and to estimate the mean of *Y*.

12. Move the cursor to the command, "Sho<u>w</u> Sunflowers" in the Sandflowers box and click once.

13. Click on the box ▭ SUNFLOWER OPTIONS

14. Click on the bar ▭ CONTINUE

15. Move the cursor to the command *OK* and click once. Your scatterplot will appear in the Chart window looking similar to the one in Figure B.4.

Moving a Chart to the Word Processing File   To print this chart, you must copy it into a word processor. This example will give instructions for the word processors Microsoft Word and WordPerfect for Windows. The procedure within SPSS is the same for other word processors.

1. From the Chart Window in SPSS, click on the command *Edit*. A menu will appear.
2. Click on the command *Copy Chart*. The scatterplot is now saved in the temporary memory of your computer.
3. Minimize SPSS 6.1 for Windows.
4. Open Microsoft Word or WordPerfect for Windows.
5. Move the cursor to the point in the document where you wish to insert the scatterplot, then take one of two actions:
   a. Click on the icon for paste (a clipboard with a note attached to it in Word, a small bottle of glue in WordPerfect).
   b. Click on the WordPerfect command *Edit* then click on the command *Paste*.

Scatterplots with Categorical Data   Political scientists usually do not use scatterplots to represent categorical data. However, from time to time this tool will contribute to an understanding of the nature of a particular relationship. This example will use the data set PERU.SYS, so follow the commands in the earlier sections to bring that file into SPSS.

The example will work with the variables DIDLEGL and INTEREST. DIDLEGL, the dependent variable, is measured on an interval scale. It indicates the number of legal political demonstrations the respondent reports attending in the previous 12 months. INTEREST is measured on an ordinal scale that records a respondent's expressed interest in politics ranging from "Not at all interested" to "Very interested."

The commands to obtain the scatterplot are the same as Steps 1 through 10 in the procedure for a scatterplot with interval data except that you specify the variable DIDLEGL for the *y* axis and INTEREST for the *x* axis. In Step 11, however, rather than having SPSS draw a horizontal line at the mean, tell it to show each point on the graph where a case lies as the center of a sunflower. SPSS will add a petal to the sunflower for each case at that point on the graph.

After you have completed Step 10, move your cursor down to the lower left of the screen and click on the box beside *Sunflower* in the Sunflowers box. Move the cursor to the command *OK* and click once. Your scatterplot will appear in the Chart window looking similar to the one in Figure B.5.

BIVARIATE REGRESSION

This exercise introduces bivariate linear regression and multivariate linear regression. These are some rather large, abstract-sounding words, but with SPSS and the following instructions, even abstract ideas can become manageable tools. Just remember, the primary objective of a linear regression is to study the dependence of one variable on one or more explanatory variables. The example will use the data set SUPCOURT to attempt to explain the dependence of the variable VALUES on CLVOTE.

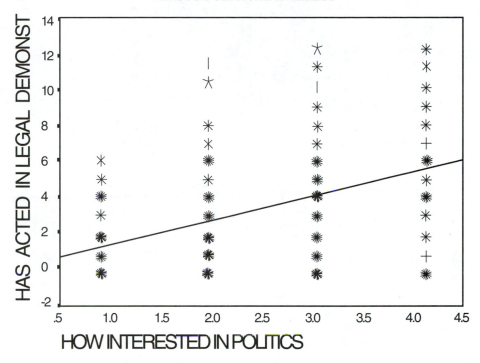

FIGURE B.5

SCATTERPLOT OF LEGAL POLITICAL ACTIVITIES
VERSUS POLITICAL INTEREST

To obtain a bivariate regression output, complete these steps:

1. Move the cursor to the command *Statistics* and click once.

2. Move the cursor to the command *Regression* and click once. A menu will appear to the right.

3. Move the cursor to the command *Linear* and click once. A Linear Regression menu will appear. The box on the left-hand side lists all of the variables in the SUPCOURT.SYS data set.

4. Move the cursor to the down arrow until the variable CLVOTE is highlighted. Click once on the variable, then move the cursor to the right arrow next to the box titled *Dependent:* and click once. You have just instructed SPSS to use CLVOTE as the dependent variable.

5. Move the cursor to the variable name VALUES and click once. The variable name will be highlighted.

6. Move the cursor to the right arrow next to the box titled *Independent(s)* and click. You have instructed SPSS to use VALUES as the independent variable.

FIGURE B.6

BIVARIATE REGRESSION

* * * *   M U L T I P L E[a]   R E G R E S S I O N   * * * *

Listwise Deletion of Missing Data

Equation Number 1   Dependent Variable..   CLVOTE   Civ Libs Score in USSC Data

Block Number 1. Method: Enter   VALUES

Variable(s) Entered on Step Number 1..   VALUES   Justice's Values (Segal et al.)

Multiple R[a]	.66347	.66347Analysis of Variance		
R Square	.44019		DF	Sum of Squares	Mean Square
Adjusted R Square	.42153	Regression 1	5561.82478	5561.82478
Standard Error	15.35496	Residual 30	7073.24732	235.77491

F =   23.58955   Signif F = .0000

———————————— Variables in the Equation ————————————

Variable	B	SE B	Beta	T	Sig T
VALUES	20.854865	4.293857	.663468	4.857	.0000
(Constant)	49.460666	2.795122		17.695	.0000

[a]This a bivariate regression, but SPSS labels all regressions "multiple," leaving reader to notice there is only one independent variable here.

---

7. To perform the regression, simply click the *OK* box and wait. Your regression output will appear in the Output window looking similar to Figure B.6.

8. Check and interpret your results.

MULTIVARIATE REGRESSION

To perform a multivariate regression output, follow these steps:

1. Perform Steps 1 through 4 of the bivariate regression procedure described in the previous section.

2. Move the cursor to the other variable names you would like to include in the multivariate regression model. Note, you may specify multiple independent variables, but only one dependent variable.

MULTIPLE REGRESSION

```
* * * *   M U L T I P L E   R E G R E S S I O N   * * * *


Listwise Deletion of Missing Data

Equation Number 1    Dependent Variable..   CLVOTE   Civ Libs Score in USSC Data

Block Number  1.  Method: Enter      VALUES   FAMSTAT  JUDPARTY


Variable(s) Entered on Step Number  1..   JUDPARTY   Judge Political Party
                                    2..   FAMSTAT    Family Status
                                    3..   VALUES     Justice's Values (Segal et al.)



Multiple R          .71158        Analysis of Variance
R Square            .50635                      DF    Sum of Squares    Mean Square
Adjusted R Square   .45346        Regression     3       6397.76615     2132.58872
Standard Error    14.92518        Residual      28       6237.30594      222.76093

                                  F =      9.57344      Signif F =  .0002


———————————————— Variables in the Equation ————————————————

Variable          B         SE B       Beta        T       Sig T

VALUES      16.423103    5.587322    .522478     2.939     .0065
FAMSTAT    -10.886191    5.743239   -.265227    -1.895     .0684
JUDPARTY     1.961630    3.460983    .096723      .567     .5754
(Constant)  54.807311    5.500539                9.964     .0000


End Block Number   1   All requested variables entered.
```

3. When you have finished, click OK and your multivariate regression output will appear in the Output window. Figure B.7 shows a sample of one multivariate regression with CLVOTE as the dependent variable and JUDPARTY, FAMSTAT, and VALUES as the independent variables.

4. Check and interpret your results.

Saving Your SPSS Output File to a Floppy Disk

When you have completed data analysis using SPSS, you may want to save the output file rather than copying the material directly into a word-processing file. To save an SPSS output file that is not a chart, follow these steps:

1. Click on the command *File*.

2. Click on the *Drives:* window, and move the cursor to the line labeled *B:*. If you are working on your own personal computer, you may want to save on the C drive in the subdirectory where you keep your political science files.

3. Click on the line *File Name:* and delete the characters **.LST*. Then type the name of the file (for example, **C:\POLYSCI\ASSIGN5.LST**). Remember, the file should have the extension .LST.

4. Click on the command *OK*.

5. Some word processors (including WordPerfect and Word) can read SPSS output files. To take advantage of this capability, go into your word processor. If you are using Microsoft Word, click on *File* and then on *Open*. Type in the name **C:\POLYSCI\ASSIGN5.LST** and Word will ask what type of file you want to open. Indicate that it is a text-only file. For WordPerfect for Windows, type in the name and, when WordPerfect responds by indicating that it plans to convert the file as an ASCII (DOS) text file, click *OK*. For both Word and WordPerfect, you will have to block the entire file and assign a monospaced (nonproportionally spaced) font in a size that will allow the material to fit horizontally within applicable margins.

Codebooks for Data Sets*

Codebook for File PERUCAT

AGE   RESPONDENT AGE
Explanation: The respondent's age divided into four categories

    1.00 <22   2.00 23–25

    3.00 25–29   4.00 30>

ALCONTRB   EACH MUST CONTRIBUTE TO GROUP ACTS
Explanation: An index of the respondent's perception that all members of a group must contribute to allow an action to succeed. The index has been divided into three categories.

    1.00 DISAGREE   2.00 DONTKNOW

    3.00 AGREE

BREAKLAW   SOMETIMES NECESSARY TO BREAK LAW
Explanation: An index of the respondent's answers to questions concerning whether or not a group must sometimes break the law to succeed in politics. The index has been divided into four categories.

    1.00 STRNGDIS   2.00 DISAGREE

    3.00 AGREE   4.00 STRNGAGR

DIDLEGL   HAS ACTED IN LEGAL DEMONSTRATION

---

* Additional data sets and codebooks are available at the Internet address, www.psci.unt.EDU.

Explanation: The extent of the respondent's previous participation in legal political demonstrations.

1.00 NEVER   2.00 SOMETIME

3.00 FREQUENT

DIDNOLG   HAS ACTED IN ILLEGAL DEMONSTRATION

Explanation: The extent of the respondent's previous participation in illegal political demonstrations.

1.00 NEVER   2.00 SOMETIME

3.00 FREQUENT

DORIGHT   FEEL GOOD FOR LEGAL POLIT ACTS

Explanation: The extent of the respondent's agreement with the statement, "When I participate in legal political actions, I feel good about it."

1.00 ALITTLE   2.00 SOMEWHAT

3.00 ALOT

EDUCATN   LEVEL OF EDUCATION

Explanation: The respondent's number of years of formal education divided into four categories.

1.00 NONE   2.00 PRIMARY

3.00 SECONDRY   4.00 COLLEGE

EFCYLEGL   HOW EFFECTIVE LEGAL ACTIONS

Explanation: The extent of the respondent's agreement with the statement, "Legal political actions are likely to succeed."

1.00 ALITTLE   2.00 SOMEWHAT

3.00 ALOT

EFCYNOLG   HOW EFFECTIVE ILLEGAL ACTIONS

Explanation: The extent of the respondent's agreement with the statement, "Illegal political actions are likely to succeed."

1.00 ALITTLE   2.00 SOMEWHAT

3.00 ALOT

EFFICACY   LEVEL OF PERSONAL EFFICACY

Explanation: An index of the respondent's answers to questions concerning perceived personal political efficacy. The index has been divided into three categories.

1.00 LOW   2.00 MODERATE

3.00 HIGH

GOVPERFM   GOVT PERFORMANCE ON EQUALITY ISSUES
Explanation: An index of the respondent's ratings of the government's performance on issues dealing with political equality. The index has been divided into four categories.

    1.00 POOR   2.00 OK

    3.00 GOOD   4.00 EXCELNT

GUILT   WOULD FEEL GUILTY IF BROKE THE LAW
Explanation: The extent of the respondent's agreement with the statement, "I would feel guilty if I were to participate in a political activity that broke the law."

    1.00 ALITTLE   2.00 SOMEWHAT

    3.00 ALOT

IDEOLOGY   HOW CONSERVATIVE THE RESPONDENT
Explanation: An index of the respondent's perception of personal conservatism on various issues, divided into three categories.

    1.00 LEFT   2.00 CENTER

    3.00 RIGHT

IMADEDIF   HOW MUCH OF A DIFFERENCE RESPONDENT MADE
Explanation: Respondent's estimation of the difference made by past personal political participation.

    1.00 LITTLE   2.00 SOME

    3.00 ALOT

INTEREST   HOW INTERESTED IN POLITICS
Explanation: Respondent's self report of interest in politics.

    1.00 NONE   2.00 ALITTLE

    3.00 SOMEWHAT   4.00 VERY

LOSSLEGL   EXPECTED LOSS FROM LEGAL ACTS
Explanation: An index of the respondent's estimation of the personal cost of participation in legal political demonstrations. The index has been divided into three categories.

    1.00 ALITTLE   2.00 SOMEWHAT

    3.00 ALOT

LOSSNOLG   EXPECTED LOSS FROM ILLEGAL ACTS
Explanation: An index of the respondent's estimation of the personal cost of participation in illegal political demonstrations. The index has been divided into three categories.

    1.00 ALITTLE   2.00 SOMEWHAT

    3.00 ALOT

LOSSTIME   TOO MUCH LOSS OF TIME TO ACT
Explanation: An index of the respondent's estimation of the time lost to participate in various political activities. The index has been divided into three categories.

    1.00 ALITTLE   2.00 SOME
    3.00 ALOT

MARRIED   RESPONDENT MARRIED

    0 NO   1 YES

NORMLEGL   FRIENDS WILL THINK WELL OF LEGAL ACT
Explanation: The extent of the respondent's agreement with the statement, "If I participate in legal political actions, my friends will think well of me."

    1.00 DISAGREE   2.00 NOTSURE
    3.00 AGREE

PROBLEMS   EQUALITY ISSUES PROBLEMS
Explanation: An index of the respondent's answers to questions that indicate that inequality is a problem. Higher scores indicate that respondents see inequality as a larger problem.

    1.00 ALITTLE   2.00 SOMEWHAT
    3.00 ALOT

RELIGOUS   LEVEL OF RELIGIOUS AFFILIATION
Explanation: The respondent's self-report of the personal importance of religion.

    1.00 NOT   2.00 ALITTLE
    3.00 VERY

RESPECT   RESPECT PEOPLE WHO ENDANGER SELVES
Explanation: The extent of the respondent's agreement with the statement, "I respect people who endanger themselves by participating in illegal political actions."

    1.00 ALITTLE   2.00 SOMEWHAT
    3.00 ALOT

STUDENT   RESPONDENT A STUDENT
Explanation: Respondent is currently enrolled in a university.

    0 NO   1 YES

SUCCESS   HOW SUCCESSFUL LAST COLLECTIVE ACTION
Explanation: The respondent's estimation of the success of his or her group in its most recent collective political activity.

    1.00 LITTLE   2.00 SOME
    3.00 ALOT

VOTE   VOTED IN LAST PRES ELECTION
Explanation: The respondent's self-report of voting in the most recent presidential election.

   0 NO   1 YES

WILLLEGL   WILL ACT LEGALLY IN FUTURE
Explanation: An index of the respondent's answers to questions concerning the likelihood of future participation in legal political activities. The index has been divided into three categories.

   1.00 UNLIKELY   2.00 POSSIBLE
   3.00 LIKELY

WILLNOLG   WILL ACT ILLEGALLY IN FUTURE
Explanation: An index of the respondent's answers to questions concerning the likelihood of future participation in illegal political activities. The index has been divided into three categories.

   1.00 UNLIKELY   2.00 POSSIBLE
   3.00 LIKELY

Codebook for File PERU

AGE   RESPONDENT AGE
Explanation: Respondent's age divided into four categories

   1.00 <23–25
   3.00 25–29
   4.00 30–39
   5.00 40+

ALCONTRB   EACH MUST CONTRIBUTE TO GROUP ACTS
Explanation: An index of the respondent's perception that all members of a group must contribute to make a political action succeed. Higher scores indicate stronger agreement with the idea that all must contribute.

BREAKLAW   SOMETIMES NECESSARY TO BREAK LAW
Explanation: An index of the respondent's answers to questions concerning whether or not a group must sometimes break the law to succeed in politics. Higher scores indicate stronger agreement that it is sometimes necessary to break the law. Range 3–15.

DIDLEGL   HAS ACTED IN LEGAL DEMONSTRATION
Explanation: The number of times the respondent has participated in legal political demonstrations. Range 0–12.

DIDNOLG   HAS ACTED IN ILLEGAL DEMONSTRATION
Explanation: The number of times the respondent has participated in illegal political demonstrations. Missing data indicate no past participation; set to 0. Range 0–14.

DORIGHT   FEEL GOOD FOR LEGAL POLIT ACTS
Explanation: The extent of the respondent's agreement with the statement, "When I participate in legal political actions, I feel good about it."

    1.00 NOTATALL   2.00 ALITTLE
    3.00 SOMEWHAT   4.00 ALOT

EDUCATN   LEVEL OF EDUCATION
Explanation: The respondent's number of years of formal education, divided into four categories.

    1.00 NONE   2.00 PRIMARY
    3.00 SECONDRY   4.00 COLLEGE

EFCYLEGL   HOW EFFECTIVE LEGAL ACTIONS
Explanation: The extent of the respondent's agreement with the statement, "Legal political actions are likely to succeed."

    1.00 NOT   2.00 LITTLE
    3.00 SOME   4.00 VERY

EFCYNOLG   HOW EFFECTIVE ILLEGAL ACTIONS
Explanation: The extent of the respondent's agreement with the statement, "Illegal political actions are likely to succeed."

    1.00 NOT   2.00 LITTLE
    3.00 SOME   4.00 VERY

EFFICACY   LEVEL OF PERSONAL EFFICACY
Explanation: An index of the respondent's answers to questions concerning personal political efficacy. Higher scores indicate higher levels of political efficacy. Range 1–6

GOVPERFM   GOVT PERFORMANCE ON EQUALITY ISSUES
Explanation: An index of the respondent's ratings of the government's performance on issues dealing with economic inequality. Range 0–20

GUILT   WOULD FEEL GUILTY IF BROKE THE LAW
Explanation: The extent of the respondent's agreement with the statement, "I would feel guilty if I were to participate in political activity that broke the law."

    1.00 NONE   2.00 ALITTLE
    3.00 SOMEWHAT   4.00 ALOT

IDEOLOGY   HOW CONSERVATIVE THE RESPONDENT

Explanation: An index of the respondent's perception of personal conservatism on various issues. High scores indicate a conservative respondent. Low scores indicate an individual with a leftist political orientation. Range 1–10.

IMADEDIF   HOW MUCH OF A DIFFERENCE RESPONDENT MADE
*Explanation:*The respondent's estimation of the difference made by past personal political participation.

1.00 NONE	2.00 LITTLE
3.00 SOME	4.00 ALOT
5.00 GRATDEAL	

INTEREST   HOW INTERESTED IN POLITICS
Explanation: The respondent's self-report of personal interest in politics.

1.00 NONE	2.00 ALITTLE
3.00 SOMEWHAT	4.00 VERY

LOSSLEGL   EXPECTED LOSS FROM LEGAL ACTS
Explanation: An index of the respondent's estimation of the personal cost of participation in various legal political activities. Higher numbers indicate greater losses. Range 0–12.

LOSSNOLG   EXPECTED LOSS FROM ILLEGAL ACTS
Explanation: An index of the respondent's estimation of the personal cost of participation in various illegal political activities. Higher numbers indicate greater losses. Range 3–12.

LOSSTIME   TOO MUCH LOSS OF TIME TO ACT
Explanation: An index of the respondent's estimation of time lost to participate in various political activities. Higher scores indicate loss of more time.

MARRIED   RESPONDENT MARRIED
0 NO   1 YES

NORMLEGL   FRIENDS WILL THINK WELL OF LEGAL ACT
Explanation: The extent of the respondent's agreement with the statement, "If I participate in legal political actions, my friends will think well of me."

1.00 NOTATALL	2.00 ALITTLE
3.00 SOME	4.00 ALOT
5.00 GRATDEAL	

PROBLEMS   INEQUALITY A PROBLEM IN PERUVIAN SOCIETY
Explanation: An index of the respondent's answers to questions that indicate that inequality is a problem. Higher scores indicate that respondents see inequality as a larger problem. Range 5–25.

RELIGOUS   LEVEL OF RELIGIOUS AFFILIATION
Explanation: Respondent's self-report of the personal importance of religion.

    1.00 NOT   2.00 ALITTLE
    3.00 VERY

RESPECT   RESPECT PEOPLE WHO ENDANGER SELVES
Explanation: The extent of the respondent's agreement with the statement, "I respect people who endanger themselves by participating in illegal political actions."

    1.00 NOTATALL   2.00 ALITTLE
    3.00 SOME   4.00 ALOT
    5.00 GRATDEAL

STUDENT   RESPONDENT A STUDENT
Explanation: Respondent is currently enrolled in a university.

    0 NO   1 YES

SUCCESS   HOW SUCCESSFUL LAST COLLECTIVE ACTION
Explanation: The respondent's estimation of the success of the most recent collective political activity of his or her group.

    1.00 NOTATALL   2.00 ALITTLE
    3.00 SOME   4.00 ALOT
    5.00 GRATDEAL

VOTE   VOTED IN LAST PRES ELECTION
Explanation: The respondent's self-report of voting in the most recent presidential election.

    0 NO   1 YES

WILLLEGL   WILL ACT LEGALLY IN FUTURE
Explanation: An index of the respondent's answers to questions concerning the likelihood of future participation in legal political activities. Higher scores indicate more expected participation. Range 5–25.

WILLNOLG   WILL ACT ILLEGALLY IN FUTURE
Explanation: An index of the respondent's answers to questions concerning the likelihood of future participation in illegal political activities. Higher scores indicate more expected participation. Range 8–40.

Codebook for File SUPCOURT.SYS

JUDGEID
Explanation: Identification numbers reflect the appointment sequence.

Value	Name
76	BLACK
77	REED
78	FRANKFURTER
79	DOUGLAS
80	MURPHY
81	BYRNES(NOT included)
82	JACKSON
83	RUTLEDGE
84	BURTON
85	VINSON
86	CLARK
87	MINTON
88	WARREN
89	HARLAN
90	BRENNAN
91	WHITTAKER
92	STEWART
93	WHITE
94	GOLDBERG
95	FORTAS
96	MARSHALL
97	BURGER
98	BLACKMUN
99	POWELL
100	REHNQUIST
101	STEVENS
102	O'CONNOR
103	SCALIA
104	KENNEDY
105	SOUTER
106	THOMAS
107	GINSBURG
108	BREYER

CLVOTE   CIVIL LIBERTIES SCORE IN USSC DATABASE[1]

Explanation: An index of a justice's overall liberalism in civil liberties cases contained in the U.S. Supreme Court database through December 1995. Each score indicates the percentage of such cases in which the justice cast a liberal vote—(one in favor of a claimed civil right or liberty).

ECONVOTE   ECON LIB SCORE IN USSC DATABASE[2]

Explanation: An index of a justice's overall liberalism in economics cases contained in the U.S. Supreme Court database through December 1995. Each score indicates the percentage of such cases in which the justice cast a liberal vote—one in favor of government regulation of economic activity or in favor of economic underdogs.

VALUES   JUSTICE'S VALUES[3]
Explanation: An index of a justice's political values derived from preconfirmation editorials about justices published in major newspapers. Values range from −1.00 to +1.00, with higher scores indicating greater liberalism.

NORTEAST   APPOINTED FROM NORTHEAST
Explanation: Was a justice appointed from a northeastern state?

   0 No   1 Yes

SOUTBORD   APPOINTED FROM SOUTHERN/BORDER STATE
Explanation: Was a justice appointed from a southern or border state?

   0 No   1 Yes

SOUTLIFE   CHOSE SOUTH/BORDER STATE
Explanation: Did a justice choose to live most of her or his adult life in a southern or border state?

   0 Nonsouthern life   1 Souther/border Life

SIZTOWN   BIRTHPLACE TOWN SIZE
Explanation: In what size or type of place was a justice born?

   1 Rural   2 Urban

   3 Metropolitan

FAMSTAT   FAMILY STATUS
Explanation: Was a justice born into a family of relatively low or high social status?

   0 Low   1 High

HIPROT   HIGH STATUS PROTESTANT
Explanation: Was a justice a member of a high-status Protestant religious denomination?

   0 No   1 Yes

NONPROT   NONPROTESTANT
Explanation: Was a justice a member of a non-Protestant religious denomination (e.g., Catholic or Jewish)?

   0 No   1 Yes

FATHGOVT   FATHER A GOVT OFFICER[4]
Explanation: Did a justice's father hold any elective or appointed government office?

   0 No   1 Yes

FATHFARM   Father a Farmer
Explanation: Was a justice's father a farmer or agricultural land owner?

0 No   1 Yes

HIPRELAW   High Status Prelaw Education
*Explanation:*Did a justice receive prelaw education in a high-prestige institution?

0 No   1 Yes

HILAWSCH   Attend High Status Law School
Explanation: Did a justice receive legal education in a high-prestige institution?

0 No   1 Yes

BEGNYEAR   BEGIN SERVICE YEAR
Explanation: The last three digits of the year a justice began service on Supreme Court (e.g., 925 = 1925).

ENDYEAR   END SERVICE YEAR
Explanation: The last three digits of the year a justice ended service on Supreme Court (e.g., 925 = 1925).

APPTAGE   AGE AT APPOINTMENT
Explanation: A justice's age in years at appointment.

TENURE   TENURE IN YEARS
Explanation: The number of years a justice served on the Supreme Court as of December 31, 1995.

LASTOFFC   LAST OFFICE BEFORE APPOINTMENT
Explanation: The type of public office held by a justice immediately prior to appointment to Supreme Court.

   1 NOT A PUBLIC OFFICIAL

   2 PUBLIC OFFICIAL BUT NOT A JUDGE

   3 JUDGE

   4 APPEALS COURT JUSTICE

TYPLWYR   TYPE OF LAWYER (PREAPPOINTMENT)
Explanation: The principal type of legal career pursued by a justice prior to appointment.

   0 NOT LAWYER AT ALL (not represented in the data)

   1 POLITICIAN-LAWYER (lawyers who were primarily politicians)

   2 GENERAL PRACTICE (lawyers primarily in general private practice)

   3 CORPORATE/BUSINESS (lawyers primarily in corporate/business practice)

   4 ACADEMICIAN (lawyers who were primarily law professors)

5 JUD ADMINIS (lawyers who were primarily court administrators)

7 NONE, OTHER

JUDEXPER   FEDERAL JUD EXPERIENCE-YEARS
Explanation: The actual number of years of *federal* judicial experience a justice had prior to appointment to the Supreme Court.

XPROCJUD   PROSEC/JUDIC EXP INDEX (AJPS)[5]
Explanation: A justice's record of prosecutorial and judicial experience

0 JUDGE NOT PROSEC (The justice was a judge, but never a prosecutor.)

1 PROSEC-JUDGE (The justice was a prosecutor and also a judge.)

2 PROSEC NOT JUDGE (The justice was a prosecutor but never a judge.)

PRESLIB   PRESIDENTIAL LIBERALISM[6]
Explanation: An index of the general political liberalism of appointing presidents devised by Jeffrey Segal; values for George Bush and Bill Clinton are estimated by the authors. Range +14.2 to +77.7.

PRESNTNT   PRESIDENTIAL INTENTIONS INDEX
Explanation: Apparent intentions of the appointing president in making Supreme Court appointments. See the value explanations below.

−1 CONSCIOUS CONSERV PRES (The president consciously intended to appoint ideological conservatives.)

0 NOT CONSCIOUS PRES (The president did not consciously intend to represent any ideology in appointments *or* the president consciously intended to appoint ideological moderates.)

1 CONSCIOUS LIB PRES (The president consciously intended to appoint ideological liberals.)

PRSPARTY   APPOINTING PRESIDENT'S POLITICAL PARTY
Explanation: The political party of the president who appointed a justice.

1 Republican   2 Democrat

JUDPARTY   JUDGE'S POLITICAL PARTY IDENTIFICATION
Explanation: A justice's party identification.

0 Republican   1 Independent

2 Democrat

RACE   JUSTICE'S RACE

0 White   1 African-American

GENDER   JUSTICE'S GENDER

0 Male   1 Female

REAGBUSH   APPOINTED BY REAGAN OR BUSH

0 No   1 Yes

Codebook for File POPULATN

CNUM   Standard Country Code assigned to each country by many studies.

ABORTION   LEGAL AVAILABILITY OF ABORTION IN 1985
Explanation: An index of the ease of obtaining a legal abortion in the country in 1985.

   1 none   3 moderate
   2 low   4 high

AVAIL82   AVAILABILITY OF CONTRACEPTIVES IN 1982
Explanation: An index of the overall availability of contraceptives in both the public and private sectors of a country in 1982. Range 0–24.

AVAIL89   AVAILABILITY OF CONTRACEPTIVES IN 1989
Explanation: An index of the overall availability of contraceptives in both the public and private sectors of a country in 1989. Range 0–24.

POLICY82   STATED POPULATION POLICY OF THE GOVERNMENT IN 1982
Explanation: An index of the strength of the country's stated population policy as provided by the current political leaders in the country in 1982. Range 0–31.0.

POLICY89   STATED POPULATION POLICY OF THE GOVERNMENT IN 1989
Explanation: An index of the strength of the country's stated population policy as provided by the current political leaders in the country in 1989. Range 0–30.3.

PRIVAT82   LEVEL OF PRIVATE SECTOR INVOLVEMENT IN FAMILY PLANNING 1982
Explanation: An index of contraceptive availability in the country from private sector delivery in 1982. This includes both not-for-profit organizations such as Planned Parenthood and for-profit organizations such as local pharmacies. Range 0–40.6.

PRIVAT89   LEVEL OF PRIVATE SECTOR INVOLVEMENT IN FAMILY PLANNING 1989
Explanation: An index of contraceptive availability in the country from private sector delivery in 1989. This includes both not-for-profit organizations such as Planned Parenthood and for-profit organizations such as local pharmacies. Range 0–43.50.

RECORD82   LEVEL OF RECORD KEEPING AND EVALUATION 1982
Explanation: An index measuring the quality of record keeping and program evaluation in public and private family planning systems in the country in 1982. Range 0–11.50.

RECORD89   LEVEL OF RECORD KEEPING AND EVALUATION 1989
Explanation: An index measuring the quality of record keeping and program evaluation in public and private family planning systems in the country in 1989.Range 0–11.5.

AFRICA   COUNTRY IS IN SUBSAHARAN AFRICA
Explanation: A dummy variable to indicate whether the country is located in the sub-Saharan portion of Africa.

0 No   1 Yes

REGION   REGION OF THE WORLD WHERE THE COUNTRY IS LOCATED

1 LATNAMER   3 MIDEAST
2 SUBSAHR   4 ASIA

CATH   CATHOLICISM IS THE DOMINANT RELIGION
Explanation: A dummy variable to indicate whether Catholicism is the dominant religion in the country.

0 No   1 Yes

CHRISTN   CHRISTIANITY THE DOMINANT RELIGION
Explanation: A dummy variable to indicate whether Christianity (Protestantism or Catholicism) is the dominant religion in the country.

0 No   1 Yes

ISLAM   ISLAM DOMINANT RELIGION
Explanation: A dummy variable to indicate whether Islam is the dominant religion in the country.

0 No   1 Yes

ISLAND   ISLAND OR SEMI-ISLAND STATUS
Explanation: A dummy variable to indicate whether the country is an island or a small peninsula.

0 No   1 Yes

FEMLIT83   FEMALE LITERACY RATE 1983
Explanation: The percentage of females in the population with at least 3 years of formal schooling in 1983.

FEMLIT89   FEMALE LITERACY RATE 1989
Explanation: The percentage of females in the population with at least 3 years of formal schooling in 1989.

PRIMF84   PERCENT FEMALE IN PRIMARY 84
Explanation: The percentage of females aged 5 to 12 enrolled in primary school in the country in 1984.

SECFEM65   PERCENT FEMALE IN SECONDARY 65
Explanation: The percentage of females aged 13 to 18 enrolled in secondary school in the country in 1965.

SECFEM84   PERCENT FEMALE IN SECONDARY 84
Explanation: The percentage of females aged 13 To 18 enrolled in school in the country in 1984.

GDP80   GDP PER CAPITA 1980
Explanation: The country's gross domestic product per capita in 1980 in US$ adjusted for inflation.

GDP85   GDP PER CAPITA 1985
Explanation: The country's gross domestic product per capita in 1985 in US$ adjusted for inflation.

GNP83   GNP PER CAPITA 1983
Explanation: The country's gross national product per capita in 1983 in US$ adjusted for inflation.

GNP89   GNP PER CAPITA 1989
Explanation: The country's gross national product per capita in 1989 in US$ adjusted for inflation.

LGDP80   LOG GDP PER CAPITA 1980
Explanation: The natural log of the country's GDP in 1980.

LGDP85   LOG GDP 1985
Explanation: The natural log of the country's GDP in 1985.

LGDP87   LOG GDP 1987
Explanation: The natural log of the country's GDP in 1987.

INCMRANK   WORLD BANK INCOME RANKING 1985
Explanation: The ordinal ranking of the country's per-capita income by the World Bank in 1985. Range 1–99.

INFANT83   INFANT MORTALITY RATE 1983
Explanation: Number of deaths per 1000 live births.

INFANT93   INFANT MORTALITY RATE 1993
Explanation: Number of deaths per 1000 live births.

LIFEXP80   LIFE EXPECTANCY AT BIRTH 1980

LIFEXP94   LIFE EXPECTANCY AT BIRTH 1994

MFGADD80   MANUFACTURING VALUE ADDED 1980

Explanation: The value in U.S.$ added by the manufacturing sector of the economy in 1980.

MFGADD83   MANUFACTURING VALUE ADDED 1983
Explanation: The value in U.S.$ added by the manufacturing sector of the economy in 1983.

MFGADD89   MANUFACTURING VALUE ADDED 1989
Explanation: The value in U.S.$ added by the manufacturing sector of the economy in 1989.

URBAN83   PERCENT OF URBAN POP 1983
Explanation: The percentage of the country's population living in urban areas in 1983.

URBAN89   PERCENT OF URBAN POP 1989
Explanation: The percentage of the country's population living in urban areas in 1989.

TFR84   TOTAL FERTILITY RATE 1984
Explanation: The total fertility rate of the country in 1984.

TFR89   TOTAL FERTILITY RATE 1989
Explanation: The number of live births per 1000 women in the country in 1989.

TFR90   TOTAL FERTILITY RATE 1990
Explanation: The number of live births per 1000 women in the country in 1990.

CHGPREV   CHANGE IN CONTRACEPTIVE PREVALENCE FROM 1980 TO 1990
Explanation: Percentage change (+ or −) in use of contraceptives by sexually active women.

PREVL83   PERCENT OF CONTRACEPTIVE PREVALENCE 1983
Explanation: The percentage of sexually active women using modern contraceptives in 1983.

PREVL89   PERCENT OF CONTRACEPTIVE PREVALENCE 1989
Explanation: The percentage of sexually active women using modern contraceptives in 1989.

PRCNTDRP   DROP IN CRUDE BIRTHRATE 1985 TO 1995
Explanation: The percentage drop in the country's crude birthrate from 1985 to 1995.

SEDINDX   OVERALL INDEX OF ECONOMIC DEVELOPMENT 1984
Explanation: An index of overall socioeconomic development that includes GDP per capita, life expectancy, and education. Range 9–93.

Codebook for File CULTURE

CNUM   COUNTRY NUMBER

1 AUSTRIA	2 BELGIUM	3 BRAZIL
4 CANADA	5 CHINA	6 DENMARK
7 FINLAND	8 FRANCE	9 GERMANY
10 INDIA	11 IRELAND	12 ITALY
13 JAPAN	14 KOREA	15 MEXICO
16 NETHERLA	17 NIGERIA	18 NORWAY
19 SOUTHAFR	20 SPAIN	21 SWEDEN
22 SWITZERL	23 TURKEY	24 UK
25 USA		

CNAME   COUNTRY NAME
Explanation: This is a string variable and is not available in Micro-Crunch files.

GROW6089   CHANGE IN GROSS DOMESTIC PRODUCT FROM 1960 TO 1989, in U.S.$ adjusted for inflation.

GDP1960   GROSS DOMESTIC PRODUCT IN 1960, in U.S.$ adjusted for inflation.

PRISCH60   PERCENT OF THE SCHOOL CHILDREN OF PRIMARY SCHOOL AGE ENROLLED IN 1960

SECSCH60   PERCENT OF THE SCHOOL CHILDREN OF SECONDARY SCHOOL AGE ENROLLED IN 1960 *Note:* Can exceed 100% because some enrollees may be above primary-school age.

ACHIEVE   SCORE ON ACHIEVEMENT MOTIVATION
Explanation: The difference between % of respondents choosing "autonomous and achievement values" as important and the % choosing "conformity to traditional norms and values"

POSTMAT   SCORE ON POSTMATERIALISM
Explanation: Based on the scale devised by Inglehart. See Jim Granato, Ronald Inglehart, and David Leblang, "The Effects of Cultural Values on Economic Development." *American Journal of Political Science* 40(1996).

Codebook for File HRIGHTS

COUNTRY
Explanation: The standard Country Code Number plus name.

YEAR   NUMERIC YEAR

NAMELONG   NAME: LONG VERSION
Explanation: This is a string variable and is not available in Micro-Crunch files.

PCGNP   PER-CAPITA GNP IN THOUSANDS OF US$ DOLLARS adjusted for inflation.

LEFT   LEFTIST REGIME

   0 Regime not leftist   1 Leftist regime

AINEW   ORDINAL HUMAN RIGHTS SCALE
Explanation: A scale from Amnesty International.

   1 Least violations, rule of law

   2 Limited political imprisonment

   3 Moderate political imprisonment

   4 Extensive political imprisonment

   5 Extensive political imprisonment and executions

SDNEW   HUMAN RIGHTS SCALE
Explanation: A scale gathered from U.S. State Department data.

   1 Least violations

   2 Limited political imprisonment

   3 Moderate political imprisonment

   4 Extensive political imprisonment

   5 Human rights disaster

MILCTR2   GOVERNMENT CONTROLLED BY MILITARY

   0 Civilian control

   1 Military control or mixed military-civilian control

BRITINFL   FORMER MEMBER OF BRITISH EMPIRE

   0 Never a part of the British Empire

   1 Once a part of the British Empire

LPOP   POPULATION (LOGGED)

IWAR   INTERNATIONAL WAR

   0 No ongoing international war

   1 Ongoing international war

CWAR　　　CIVIL WAR

0 No ongoing civil war during the year

1 Ongoing civil war during the year

DEMOCRA　ORDINAL MEASURE OF DEMOCRACY

1 Least democratic to 7 Most democratic

NOTES

[1] Jeffrey A. Segal, Lee Epstein, Charles M. Cameron, and Harold J. Spaeth, "Ideological Values and the Votes of U.S. Supreme Court Justices Revisited," *Journal of Politics* 57 (1995), pp. 812–823.

[2] Ibid.

[3] Ibid.

[4] Sidney Ulmer, "Are Social Background Models Timebound?" *American Political Science Review* 80 (1986), pp. 957–967.

[5] C. Neal Tate and Roger Handberg, "Time Binding and Theory Building in Personal Attribute Models of Supreme Court Justice Voting Behavior, 1916–1988," *American Journal of Political Science* 35 (1991), pp. 460–480.

[6] Segal, Epstein, et al., "Ideological Values."

Glossary

Administrative Tribunal. A special court outside the judicial system that decides conflicts in a particular area such as tax or labor issues.

Agenda Setting. The stage of the policy-making process in which political decision makers decide which issues will become subjects for possible government action.

Alternate Hypothesis. The hypothesis that an observed association between **variables** did not occur by chance.

Anarchy. A community or society that functions without the apparatus of a state.

Antithesis. A concept in Marxist thought that contradicts a **thesis** to generate a new **synthesis**. The struggle between the thesis and antithesis is the driving engine of history in Marxist ideology.

Association (statistical). The regular occurrence together of two variables, which represents a necessary but not sufficient step in establishing causation; for example, lightning and thunder are associated.

Authoritarian Government. A nonconstitutional type of government that involves rule by the few. Types of authoritarian governments include civilian and military dictators, single-party regimes in which the party does not lose elections, and governments that limit political participation to a minority of citizens. Authoritarian governments rarely have a well-defined ideology.

Autumn of the People. The autumn of 1989 when many of the eastern European communist states fell to anticommunist forces.

Bourgeoisie. The capitalist class; those who own the means of production.

By-product. A **collective good** supplied by a group.

Cabinet Responsibility. The institutional condition in which the Government in a parliamentary system must have the confidence of parliament. Should one member of the cabinet lose the confidence of the legislature, then the entire cabinet may be forced to resign.

Campaign Activity. Political participation designed to influence electoral outcomes. Among the actions included in this category are donating money to elections, helping to register voters, and working in a candidate's campaign office.

[...]dual unit of analysis in an empirical

Charismatic Leader. A leader with a recognized gift for leadership. The leader leads not because of any particular trait or quality other than this recognition.

Chi-Square Statistic. A statistic that evaluates the probability that a distribution observed in a contingency table could have occurred by chance.

Class Consciousness. An individual's group identity based on whether that person is a capitalist or a worker.

Coalition Government. A condition in a parliamentary system in which two or more parties form The Government.

Collective Dilemma. A situation created when people pursuing their rational self-interest all end up in a worse position than they would experience if they were to cooperate.

Collective Good. A good that one person in a set can enjoy only if all members of the set enjoy it. National defense and clean air are two examples.

Communal Activity. Political activity aimed at achieving a collective benefit for one's community.

Communitarian. Someone who believes that a sense of community is a necessary part of a good society and who recognizes the obligations that come with membership in the community.

Consensual State. A society that structures decision making so that the government must achieve a consensus or supermajority of votes to make a major policy decision. To accomplish this, the constitution often divides power through federalism, separation of powers, and multiple chambers of the legislature.

Constituency Service. Work by legislators on behalf of a member or members of their constituency. For example, ensuring that a government pension check comes to an eligible constituent.

Constitutionalism. Belief in a set of political institutions that guarantees individual rights and limits government power.

Core (North). The more industrialized countries of Western Europe, North America, Japan, Australia, and New Zealand.

Corporatist State. A country in which a few broad interest organizations called **peak associations** organize and collaborate with elected leaders to determine policies. The state recognizes peak associations as the official representatives of legitimate interests in the society, and only one peak association represents each major economic interest.

Correlation. A measure of common occurrence. This text uses Pearson's r to measure association between two variables. That score, the **correlation coefficient**, can range from -1.0 if the two variables are perfectly associated in a negative relationship to $+1.0$ if the variables are perfectly associated in a positive relationship. A correlation coefficient of 0.0 indicates that two variables are not associated.

Critical Value. The level of probability at which a researcher chooses to reject the null hypothesis and accept the alternate hypothesis.

Delegate Representation. The conception of political representation in which the representative is expected to vote and wield influence according to the wishes and instructions of constituents.

Democratic Socialist. An ideological position advocated by a group of writers who proposed a series of social and economic institutions that they believed would alleviate the suffering caused by capitalism. They did not want a revolution to create a socialist state but rather a gradual evolution of institutions that would increase economic equality.

Dependency Theory. A model of international economics and politics based on the proposition that the economies of less industrialized countries (LICs) are exploited by more industrialized countries (MICs). The LICs depend upon the MICs for capital, technology, and manufactured goods. The MICs exploit this dependence and prevent the LICs from developing competitive economies.

Dependent Variable. A variable that is affected by other variables, according to the researcher's hypothesis.

Dialectic. The struggle between the **thesis** and **antithesis** that creates a new **synthesis**. For both Marx and Hegel, the dialectic was the form of struggle that allowed history to evolve.

Difference Principle. The principle of John Rawls that the only acceptable inequalities in a just society are those that ultimately benefit the least advantaged members in the society.

Direct Democracy. (See Participatory Democracy.)

Dummy Variable. A variable constructed from a nominal variable in which there are only two values. One value is assigned a value of 0 and the other value is assigned a value of 1. For example, the variable sex might have a value of 0 for female and 1 for male.

Duty/Entertainment Model. The model of voting behavior that suggests that citizens vote not to influence the outcome of the election, but to do their citizen duty and to participate in the greatest pageant of democracy, elections.

Economic (Historical) Determinism. Marx's theory that human history evolves through stages characterized by different modes of production. The dialectical struggle between **thesis** and **antithesis** moves humans from one stage to another.

Efficacy. The perception of an individual that personal activities can effect change. Political efficacy is the perception that the individual can influence political events.

Embeddedness. The idea that people are partially defined by their cultures and their places within those cultures. Therefore, morality must be defined, at least in part, by social context.

Empirical Statements. Claims of fact that depend on observation derived from experience or experiments.

Explained Variation. The name given to the total variation in x accounted for by variation in y in a regression equation.

Externalities. Positive or negative effects (benefits or costs) of actions by a person or persons that unavoidably fall on others.

Falsifiable Hypothesis. A researcher's statement of a possible causal relationship that indicates the circumstances that would invalidate the proposition. Only a falsifiable empirical proposition or hypothesis is meaningful in science.

Forces of Production. The physical elements (raw materials, human labor, capital equipment, tools, and land) that combine to make goods and services.

Formulation. That stage of the policy-making process in which political decision makers consider and choose among alternative methods for dealing with a political issue.

Free Rider. An individual who consumes a **collective good** but does not help pay for it.

General Will. The outcome chosen by the people in a society through the procedures of direct democracy when every individual seeks to promote the best interests of all of society rather than a personal self-interest.

Genocide. The systematic killing of a racial, ethnic, or tribal group.

Government. The institutions of the state responsible for making and implementing laws and for adjudicating disputes that arise under those laws. "**The Government**" in a parliamentary system is the portion of the executive branch made up of the prime minister, cabinet ministers, and important advisors.

Hypothesis. A potentially **falsifiable, empirical statement** of a researcher's expectation. A hypothesis is usually derived from a more encompassing theory or model.

Idealist. The foreign policy perspective that national leaders should act in the interests of all the nations in the world and that the **realists'** perspective (that nations are greedy and power-seeking) is a self-fulfilling prophesy caused by its own assumptions.

Ideology. An internally consistent set of propositions that makes demands on human behavior. All ideologies have implications for (1) criteria for ethically good and bad actions, (2) the rights and duties of citizens, (3) the distribution of resources, and (4) the appropriate locations of power.*

Implementation. The stage of the policy-making process that carries out the laws and rules chosen and legitimated by government.

Imperialism. The effort by one nation-state to dominate the politics, economics, or culture of another nation.

Import Substitution. A proposed solution to the problem of dependence by less industrialized countries on more industrialized countries for capital, technology, and manufactured goods. Import substitution is a deliberate effort by an LIC government to replace major consumer imports by protecting domestic industries through tariffs and quotas.

Independent Variable. A variable that the researcher postulates causes change in other variables.

Informed Voter Model. That model of voting that hypothesizes that individuals obtain sufficient information about political candidates to identify their preferred candidate and the benefits they will experience should that candidate win the election. The potential voter then multiplies these benefits by the probability that a single vote will determine the electoral outcome. If the result is greater than the costs of registering and voting, then an individual will vote.

Institution. A set of related patterns of behavior that persist over time.

Institutional Structure. The conceptions of participants in institutions of their own roles and their expectations about the roles of others within those institutions. For example, in the institution of the family, a mother will have a set of exceptions concerning the behaviors not only of herself, but also of the father and children.

Interaction Effect. A nonadditive effect of two variables on a third variable.

Interval Measure. Rank ordering of values of a variable to reflect greater or lesser amounts of some quality with equal amounts of that quality between each unit of the measure.

Invisible Hand. Adam Smith's name for the workings of supply and demand in a free-market society.

Isolationism. The foreign policy priority of staying out of the political affairs of other countries and focusing efforts mainly on events at home.

Judicial Review (concrete, abstract, and administrative). The ability of the courts to overrule decisions of other branches of government because those decisions do not meet constitutional requirements as determined by the courts.

Laissez-Faire. An economy where government does not attempt to influence economic outcomes and regulates transactions as little as possible.

Legal Realist. A researcher of the judicial process who argues that the personal values and political considerations of judges influence their decisions.

Legislative Competence. The actions that are within the theoretical scope of a legislature. These are often spelled out in a country's constitution.

---

and Michael C. Munger, *Ideology and the Theory of Political Choice* (Ann Arbor: University of Michigan
11.

Legislative Process. The institutional arrangements in a country's legislature that lead to the making of laws.

Legitimation. The institutionally prescribed procedures for making rules and laws by governments.

Leviathan. The name of the all-powerful ruler advocated by Thomas Hobbes.

Libertarian. An ideology that opposes most government intervention into both the economy and social issues.

Logrolling. A situation in which members of a legislature agree in advance to support each other's bills. For example, a legislator in Arizona might support a bill that helps Iowa farmers in return for the votes of Iowa legislators on a bill to supply a water project in Arizona.

Majoritarian State. A country in which political institutions allow the majority of the voters to decide issues and prevent any minority from blocking the majority's decision. Majoritarian societies tend to concentrate power in the political executive, and the political parties identify positions along a simple left-right economic dimension. Interest groups attach themselves to parties according to this same left-right economic dimension. Examples of such countries include Australia, Great Britain, New Zealand, Norway, and Sweden.

Mechanical Conception of the Judicial Process. The perception that judges use their expert knowledge to decide cases using only the facts and the existing law. The judge's personal beliefs do not enter into the decision process.

Merit Good. A good for which the government subsidizes consumption in order to produce positive externalities for the society at large. Common examples are immunization and education.

Minority Government. A condition in a parliamentary system in which one or more parties form The Government without controlling a majority of votes in the legislature.

Multinational Corporation. A business enterprise owned and managed by a single entity that reaches beyond the border of a single country. Some multinational corporations have total budgets larger than some of the nations in which they do business.

Nation. A large group of people who perceive that they share a common ethnicity, history, culture, and language.

Natural Law. Law based on reason that preceded any written law. According to those who advocate natural law, it imposes higher requirements than laws made by humans, and all people can discover it by applying their own reason.

Natural Right. A right that all humans can claim. Such a right stems from natural law, and government may not legitimately deprive citizens of the right except as a punishment. For Locke, natural rights included life, liberty, property, and equality before the law.

Negative Externality. The detrimental effect to society produced when an action taken without cost by one or more individuals harms others who did not participate in the decision to take the action. Pollution and second-hand cigarette smoke are common examples.

New International Economic Order. The solution proposed by supporters of the **World Systems Theory** to the problem of LIC dependency. The countries of the **core** would provide substantial aid to the countries of the **periphery**. The core countries would also grant more favorable terms of trade to the countries in the periphery to promote their economic growth.

Nominal Classification. A measurement scheme that separates variables as alike and different when their values cannot be placed in a definite rank order.

Normative Statement. A proposition that indicates a preferable situation, procedure, society, or outcome as compared to other alternatives.

Null Hypothesis. The proposition that two variables have no true, causal relationship and that any observed association between them occurred by chance.

Operationalize. To define the terms in a hypothesis in a way that clarifies how a researcher will measure variables.

Ordinal Measure. A scheme for rank ordering the values of a variable to indicate greater or lesser amounts of some quality.

Original Position. A concept in the theory of John Rawls in which people decide on laws and distributions of resources before they know their own positions in society.

Parliamentary System. A system of government in which the elected members of the executive branch, including the prime minister, are also members of the legislature (parliament). The cabinet is responsible to the legislature.

Participatory (Direct) Democracy. A political system in which the people rule immediately and directly by making government decisions themselves rather than selecting representatives to make decisions.

Particularized Contacting. Political behavior aimed at achieving a private benefit for the person or group making the contact.

Peak Association. An interest group that includes multiple, smaller organizations in the same economic sector. For example, the American Federation of Labor–Congress of Industrial Organizations (AFL-CIO) unifies over 130 labor unions.

Periphery (South). The less industrialized countries in Africa, Asia, and Latin America.

Pluralism. A normative theory that argues for equal opportunities for all interests within the polity to organize and influence decision makers. Political decisions emerge from this struggle that reflect both the number of members in a group and the intensity of their preferences. Advocates of pluralism argue that this arrangement is more fair than elections because elections cannot easily measure intensity of opinion. Also, an empirical theory that something approximating the normative theory actually occurs in many Western democracies.

Pluralist State. A country in which numerous groups organize around relatively narrow interests and lobby all branches and levels of government. For example, several national and many regional organizations purport to represent farmers. Rather than a single major labor union for industrial workers, a separate union may represent workers in each industry.

Political Behavior. Actions and purposeful nonactions taken to influence government policy outcomes. Also, the subfield of political science that studies political attitudes, values, and behavior.

Political Philosophy. The method of studying politics that deals largely with normative questions. This in~ ~Socrates when he asked, "How ~?" and "What forms of govern~ ~age them to live this type of life?"

Political philosophy deals with both normative and empirical statements.

Political Science. The scientific study of politics.

Political Socialization. The process of developing appropriate views and orientations about politics, political life, and the state.

Politics. The social process that selects government leaders and allocates resources and values within a polity.

Popular Sovereignty. The claim that citizens are the ultimate source of power and authority in a society.

Postmaterialism. An ideology that focuses on the liberal positions on social issues such as environmental protection and self-expression.

Pragmatism. The philosophical school that argues that the criterion for judging the value or truth of an idea or action is determined by its usefulness to society.

Presidential System. A system of government in which the head of government (the president) is directly elected and does not serve in the legislature. The laws are made by a separate legislative branch of government.

Probability. The likelihood that something will occur. In statistics, the probability value states the likelihood that a particular observed association between two variables occurred by chance.

Progressive Tax. A government levy for which the rate of taxation increases with the taxpayer's income or personal wealth. For example, a progressive income tax would tax higher incomes at higher rates than lower incomes.

Proletariat. The working class in Marxist theory.

Proportional Representation. The institutional arrangement of elections that selects more than one legislator in each district. The system allocates the seats to political parties based on the percentage of the total vote each party receives in the district.

Public Choice. A subfield of political science that develops formal models similar to those used in economics.

Public Interest. The social choice that represents the best outcome for society as a whole rather than for some subset of the population.

Publius. The pseudonym under which Alexander Hamilton, James Madison, and John Jay wrote the *Federalist Papers*.

Rationale. The theoretical explanation for why two variables occur together.

Realism. The foreign policy perspective that a statesman should act to promote the national interest, so that a country's foreign policy will increase its international power base.

Regression Analysis. A statistical method that measures the impact of independent variables on a dependent variable. **Multiple regression** analyzes more than one independent variable to break down the total effect into the individual effect of each independent variable and to estimate the total effect of all variables in the regression equation.

Regressive Tax. A government levy for which the rate of taxation decreases with the taxpayer's income or personal wealth. For example, sales taxes on basic goods such as food and clothing tax higher proportions of the incomes of poor people than the incomes of rich people. Regressive taxes tend to increase income inequality in a society.

Relations of Production (Superstructure). In Marxist theory the complex relationships among people that enable them to perform their various roles producing and distributing goods and services. Relations of production include the law and the institutions that make and enforce the law.

Representative Democracy. A system of government in which citizens choose leaders who will make government decisions and attend to matters of state.

Scatterplot. A two-dimensional plot in which the researcher charts the values of one variable along the horizontal axis and the values of another variable along the vertical axis. The chart identifies where the two dimensions intersect for each case.

Selective Incentive. A material benefit received when someone joins a group and from which nonmembers can be excluded. Examples include group publications, insurance plans, and discounts for consumer goods.

Separation of Powers. The constitutional division of powers into executive, legislative, and judicial branches of government. Each branch has its own powers and independent base of support.

Single-Member District. An institutional arrangement of elections that selects only one representative from each legislative district.

Slope. A value that describes the effect of x on y in a linear equation with the form $y = a + bx$ where b is the slope. A larger slope indicates that a greater change in y is associated with a 1-unit change in x.

Social Contract. A philosophical device used by Hobbes, Locke, Rousseau, and Rawls to present the imagined agreement through which people agree to leave the state of nature and form a constitutional government.

Social Democratic Party. A leftist party that argues for a more equal distribution of income, more generous social welfare programs, and greater power to trade unions.

Social Insurance Program. A state-funded benefit program such as unemployment compensation, aid to the poor, old-age pensions, and guaranteed medical care.

Solidary Benefit. A social or psychological benefit of group membership.

Sovereignty. The power to make political decisions that no other political body can overrule.

Spurious Association. A false association between two variables caused by the separate association of each a third variable. When a researcher applies statistical control for the value of the third variable, the association between the first pair of variables disappears.

Standard Operating Procedure. An institutionalized action that a bureaucracy uses to deal with a regularly occurring issue.

Stare Decisis. A legal term meaning that judges should follow the precedents decided by other judges in similar cases. It is an important component of English common law.

State. The institutions that formalize and institutionalize politics. It includes citizens, their political rights and duties, and the institutions of government.

State of Nature. The situation in which people lived prior to the formation of government.

Statistical Significance. The probability that an observed association between two variables could have occurred by chance.

Statistics. The study of probabilities combined with collection and analysis of data.

Student's *t*. The probability table for correlation and regression coefficients.

Synthesis. The product of the dialectical struggle between **thesis** and **antithesis.** This synthesis becomes the new thesis in the evolutionary process.

Thesis. In Marxist theory, the existing mode of production in society and the ideological superstructure that accompanies it.

Time Priority. A relationship in the occurrence together of two variables in which one regularly precedes the other. This is a necessary but not sufficient step in establishing causation. For example, heating water to 100 degrees centigrade has time priority over the water changing from a liquid to a gas.

Triadic Conflict Resolution. The intervention of a third party to help resolve a dispute between two parties.

Trial Court. A court that hears arguments in the first formal trials of disputes between parties or accusations that defendants have violated the law.

Trustee Representation. The principle in **representative democracy** that requires elected representatives to vote and otherwise influence policy according to their personal beliefs about the best interests of the polity. (See also **Delegate Representation**).

Unit of Analysis. An object of research. Each individual unit is a **case.** For example, if you were studying the expenditure patterns of cities, the units of analysis would be cities and the cases would be individual cities.

Utilitarianism. The political philosophy developed by Jeremy Bentham that argues that the best society is the one that generates the greatest happiness for the largest number of people. Therefore, government actions must be judged by their outcomes for pleasure and pain, not by their intentions or some conception of natural law.

Variable. A classification that divides research **cases** into two or more mutually exclusive and totally inclusive categories. Examples include sex, temperature, region, and height.

Veil of Ignorance. The situation that prevents individuals in Rawls' **original position** from knowing their eventual positions in society as they decide what form of government and society to choose.

Vote of Confidence. A vote taken in a parliamentary or mixed presidential-parliamentary system to indicate whether or not The Government continues to command the support of a majority of members in parliament. If The Government loses this vote, formation of a new Government or a call for new elections often results.

Voters' Paradox. The inability of any policy choice to command majority support when voters rank different preferences in different orders among three or more policy options.

Welfare State. A political and economic system in which the state maintains **social insurance programs** to provide economic security for citizens.

World Systems Theory. A more radical version of **dependency theory** that hypothesizes that elites in both more industrialized countries and less industrialized countries conspire with the leaders of multinational corporations to prevent development in the LICs. The MICs (the **core** or the **North**) force unequal exchanges on the LICs (the **periphery** or **South**).

Index

Abel and Cain, in Bible, 49
Abstract judicial review, 281
Achievement Motivation index, 359
Activism/restraint, by courts, 290, 291
Administrative judicial review, 281
Administrative structure, of U.S.
    government, 256
Administrative tribunals, courts as,
    275–276
Adults, economic roles of, 197
Affirmative action, racism and, 202
Africa
    authoritarian regimes in, 121
    democratic regimes in, 323
    governments and economies in, 312
    industrial development in, 313
    policy making and implementation in,
      245–246
African Americans
    ethnic violence and, 382
    voting by, 153
Age, spending and, 354. See also Elderly
Agenda setting, 243
    in democratic regimes, 247–248
    in nondemocratic regimes, 244–247
Aggregation
    of citizen demands, 186
    demand, 173–174
Aggression, 378. See also Wars and
    warfare
    Lorenz on, 378–379
Aging
    economic inequality and, 349
    of U.S. population, 338, 339, 340
AIDS (auto-immune deficiency
    syndrome), as world problem, 375
Ali, Muhammad, 373
Allende, Salvador, 124n
Almond, Gabriel, 352
Alternate hypothesis, 157
American Political Science Association,
    report on political parties, 182
American Revolution, 77–78, 82
Ames, Barry, 200
Amnesty International, 394
Analysis
    chi-square statistic and, 161–163
    control variables and, 233–237
    correlation analysis, 260–268
    of explanation and spurious
      association, 204–209
    of global human rights, 392–396
    multiple regression an, 326–333
    normative and empirical, 911
    of political culture and economic
      growth, 358–360
    probability, statistical significance,
      and, 156–170
    regression, 293–297
    of tables, 126–132
Anarchy, 16
Anarchy, State, and Utopia (Nozick),
    62–63
Antithesis, 87
Appeals, 277–278
    and courts of appeals, 283–285
Appellate courts. See Appeals
Aquinas, Thomas. See Thomas Aquinas

Arbitrator, courts as, 272
Arena legislatures, 247
Arguments, normative and empirical, 911
Aristotle, 7, 48
    on political socialization, 30
    on virtue, 81
Arms, proliferation of, 375
Arrow, Kenneth, 184n
Articles, of U.S. Constitution. See
    Constitution of the United States
Aryans, in Nazi Germany, 108
Asia
    authoritarian regimes in, 121
    democratic regimes in, 323
    democratization in, 119
    governments and economies in, 312
Assembly, in Athens, 66
Assistance programs, economic costs of,
    347
Associations
    between events, 96–97
    nonspurious, 206–207
    spurious, 204–209
Assumptions, for empirical research, 97
Atatürk, 116
Athens, democracy and, 66
Attitudes. See also Ideology
    and economic development, 308–309
    voter research and, 145
Augustine (Saint), 399
Authoritarianism, 105, 114–119, 178–182
    and economic development, 318
    flaws of, 125
    military rule as, 115–117
    single-party civilian regimes as,
      117–118
    single-party government and, 322–323
Authoritarian ruler, government by, 245
Authority, in legislature, 222–223
Autumn of the People, The, 119

Baksheesh, 314
Balkans, violence in, 382
Barber, James David, 82n
Behavior, political, 67
Behemoth (Neumann), 108n
Belief systems, and political ideologies,
    177
Bellah, Robert, 84
Benefits. See Negative externalities
Bentham, Jeremy, 51
    and utilitarianism, 56–58
Bible
    Abel and Cain in, 49
    Job in, 47
Bicameral legislatures, 220–221. See also
    Legislatures
Bills. See Legislative process
Bipolar system, 381
Birthrate, and economic development, 305
Black, Duncan, 184n
Blackstone, William, 34
Bodin, Jean, 35
Bounded competition theory, 380
Bourgeoisie, capitalists as, 90
Bribery, 314–315
Britain (England)

civil war in, 45
common law in, 34
economic inequalities in, 348
Fabian Society in, 93
Head of State in, 215
legislative process in, 225
monarchy in, 45–47
parliamentary system in, 214–232
political parties in, 187
representative democracy in, 67
Brown v. Board of Education, 278, 287
Bundestag (Germany), 219
Bureaucracy, 242. See also Democratic
    government; Nondemocratic
    governments
    managing, 255–257
    organization and decision making—
      principles of, 252–253
    and policy implementation, 251–257
    problems with, 254–255
Bureaucracy: What Government Agencies
    Do and Why They Do It (Wilson), 254
Burke, Edmund, 229
Burundi, ethnic violence in, 382
Bush, George, as pragmatist, 374
Business, economic goals and, 355–356
By-products, of interest groups, 147

Cabinet, responsibility of, 218–219
Calles, Plutarco Elias, 118
Calvin, John, 44
Calvinism, 28
Cambodia. See Kampuchea
Campaign activity, 139
Canada, NAFTA and, 119. See also
    Supreme courts
Capitalism. See also Economics; Labor
    government intervention and, 28
    imperialism and, 379
    as mechanism for peace, 379
    Smith on, 52
Capitalist class, in MICs, 306–307
Capitalist society, contradictions in, 88–90
Carmines, Edward, 202
Carter, Jimmy, 373
Case, in tables, 126
Case law, 34
Categorical imperative, 175–176
Causal relationships, between culture and
    social environment, 311
Central America. See Latin America
Centrally planned economy, 312–313
    difficulties of implementing, 313
Chai, 314
Chamber of Deputies (France), 223
Chamber of Deputies (Italy), 221, 224
Chambers, legislative, 220–221. See also
    Chamber of Deputies (France); Chamber
    of Deputies (Italy); Legislatures
Charismatic leadership
    economic development and, 319–321
    Hitler and, 109
    and single-party, noncommunist
      regimes, 323
Charles I (England), 45, 47
Charles II (England), 45, 47
Checks and balances, 68

Chief executive, 215–216, 350
  as Head of Government or Head of
    State, 242
  legislative oversight and control of,
    231
  prime minister as, 223
Chile, Allende in, 124n
China
  democratization and, 121
  economic development in, 309
  policy making and implementation in,
    246–247
  totalitarian government and economic
    growth in, 318
Chi-square statistic, 161
Choices, 4. *See also* Conservatives and
    conservatism; Liberalism
  general will and, 80
  political, 5–6
  public, 7
  voting as, 140–146
Christianity, natural rights and, 48. *See
    also* Religion
Cigarettes, as negative externalities, 22
Citizens and citizenship. *See also*
    Democracy
  aggregation of demands, 186
  elections and, 201
  and government, 173–210
  rights and duties of, 15–30
Civic Culture, The (Almond and Verba),
    352
Civic duty, and joining groups, 149
Civil rights, and courts, 290
Class conflict, 89
Class consciousness, 90
Classes. *See also* Laboring class
  Malthus on, 53–54
  unearned rents and, 55, 56
  world systems theory and, 307
Classical economists, Marx and, 88
Classical liberalism, 43–52
Class struggle, between LICs and MICs,
    306–307
Clinton, Bill
  interest groups and, 193–195
  legislature and, 248n
  political ideology of, 181–182
  as pragmatist, 374
Coalition Government, and minority
    governments, 217–218
Codebooks, for data sets, 431–449
Code law, decision making with, 279
Code of Hammurabi, 33
Codification, of laws, 33
Coefficient, correlation, 264–265
Cold War, 377
  ethnic conflicts after, 381
Collective action, 140. *See also* Political
    participation
  testing model of, 148–149
Collective dilemmas, 17–21
  defined, 17
  ... ma and, 17–18
  ... d, 18–19

  ... ing groups, 147,

and collective dilemmas, 16–21
  defined, 16
  reasons for joining groups and, 198
Common Cause, 98–99
Common law, 34
Commons. *See* Collective dilemmas
Commonwealth. *See* Government
Communal activities, 139
Communism and communists. *See also*
    Socialism
  and democratization in Eastern
    Europe, 119–121
  as leftist parties, 351
  life under, 91
  Marx on, 90–92
  policy making and implementation by,
    246–247
  and totalitarianism, 110–111
Communist Party, economic growth and,
    318
Communitarianism
  feminist critique of, 95–96
  modern, 84–86
  policy implications of, 85–86
  Rousseau and, 77–84
Community, 84. *See also*
    Communitarianism
Community standards, effects of changing,
    24–25
Comparative advantage
  dependency theory and, 306
  law of, 304–305
  LICs and, 303
Competition, 54
  capitalist, 89
  political, 350
Compromise, by president and Congress,
    250n
Computer software. *See also* Analysis
  Micro-Crunch as, 404–415
  SPSS 6.1 for Windows, 416–430
Concentration camps
  human rights and, 385
  in Nazi Germany, 110
Concrete judicial review, 281
*Condition of the Working Class in
    England, The* (Engels), 86n
Condorcet, Marquis de (Marie-Jean
    Caritat), 184n
Conflict. *See also* Wars and warfare
  class, 89
  political, 82–83
Conflict resolution, by courts, 272
Confucian culture, economic development
    and, 309, 310
Congress (United States)
  deliberation in, 226–227
  legislative process in, 225
  presidential system and, 214–232
Consensual governments, 351–352, 355
Consensus, in communitarian society, 85
Conservative Party (Britain), 187
Conservatives and conservatism, 350. *See
    also* Rightist
  interest groups and, 190
  use of term, 62
*Considerations on Representative
    Government* (Mill), 59

Consistency, of voter opinions, 177
Constituency service, of legislature,
    231–232
Constitutional courts, 280
Constitutional government, 65
Constitutionalism, 64–69
  principles and development of, 65–66
Constitution of the United States, 65
  Article I of, 219–220
  checks on majority rule in, 68–69
  Federalist Papers and, 75–77
Constitutions, written, 65
Constructive vote of confidence, in
    Germany, 219
Contingency tables, 127–129, 169–170
Control variables, 233–237
Converse, Philip, 177
Core (more industrialized countries), 306
Corporatism
  leftist political party and, 356
  in MICs, 353
Corpus Juris Civilis (Justinian), 34
Correlation, 260
  and probability, 265–266
Correlation coefficient, 264–265
  calculating, 267–268
Corruption, governmental, 314–315, 316
Costs, of war, 376–377
Council of 500, in Athens, 66
Counterrevolutionaries, totalitarian
    governments and, 111–112
County courts (England), 282
Coups d'état, 315
  in LICs, 321
Courts
  activism/restraint by, 290
  of appeals, 283–285
  civil rights, liberties issues, and, 290
  defined, 273
  economic issues and, 290–291
  of first instance (trial courts), 282–283
  hierarchies of, 281–286
  and judicial policy making, 271–298
  judicial review by, 280–281
  lawmaking and, 276
  mechanical conception of, 272
  social control by, 274–275
  triadic conflict resolution by, 272
  weakness of, 287
Crepaz, Markus, 355
Crime and criminals, 349
  courts and, 274–275
  Locke on, 49
  victimless, 29
Criminal case, 283
Critical values, and statistical significance,
    163
Cromwell, Oliver, 45
Cross tabulations. *See* Statistics
Crown courts (England), 282
C-scale issues, 293
Cuba, economic development in, 318
Cultural explanations, 325
  of industrial development, 308–311
  of "modern" and "traditional" peoples,
    310
  and social environment, 309–311
Cultural Revolution (China), 309

Cultures. *See also* Cultural explanations
  economic development and, 358–360
  traditional, 308
Czechoslovakia, division of, 123

Darwin, Charles, 51
Das Kapital (Marx), 28n, 51, 86
Data sets, codebooks for, 431–449
Deal-making, political, 199–200
Debt. *See* Foreign debt
Decision making
  bureaucratic, 252–253
  with code law, 279
  by courts, 280
Declaration of Independence
  individual rights and duties in, 22
  Locke's impact on, 50
Degree of freedom, 164
Delegate, legislative representative as, 229–230
Deliberation stage, of legislative process, 226–227
Demand aggregation, 173–174
Demand and supply, 52
Demands, transmission of, 198–199
Democracy. *See also* Communitarianism
  communitarian, 77–84
  dangerous issues facing, 201–202
  direct, 66
  economic slowdowns and, 348
  human rights violation and, 388
  institutions and, 175
  relationship with war, 380
  representative, 66–67
  Rousseau on, 81–83
  use of term, 76
Democratic government
  agenda setting, formulation, and legitimation by, 247–250
  and economic development, 323–325
  policy evaluation by, 257
  policy implementation by, 253
  separation of powers in, 249
Democratic Kampuchea. *See* Kampuchea
Democratic Party
  ideology of, 183
  interest groups and, 190–191
  political ideology of, 181
Democratic socialism, 92–94
  Fabian socialists and, 92–93
Democratization, 119–123
  in Eastern Europe, 119–123
  elite support for, 123–124
  religious, ethnic, nationalistic conflicts and, 123
  success of, 122–123
DE model. *See* Duty/Entertainment (DE) model
Demographics
  political ideology and, 181
  of political participation, 153–154
  social welfare spending and, 354
Dependency theory
  and economic development, 305–307
  recommendations for LICs, 306–307
  world systems theory variation of, 306–307

Dependent variables, 127
  and economic development, 309–310
Depth, of court's decision making, 280
Desegregation, courts and, 287
Determinism, economic, 88
Deterministic laws, 157
Development, industrial. *See* Underdevelopment
Dialectic, of Hegel, 87–88
Dialectical materialism, 88
Dickens, Charles, 53
Dictators. *See also* Authoritarianism; Totalitarianism
  Atatürk (Kemal) as, 116
  judiciary and, 289
  Somoza as, 116
Diederich, Bernard, 116
Diet (Japan), 221
Difference principle, 63
Direct democracy, 66, 76
  Locke on, 50
  modern technology for, 82
  Rousseau and, 83
Discretion, judicial, 279
Distribution, economic laws and, 60
Distribution of power, country behavior and, 380
Divine right, 28, 35, 44, 115
Division of labor, 52
  of bureaucracy, 253
Dogan, Mattei, 346–347
Dole, Robert, political ideology of, 181, 182
Doves, in Vietnam War, 185
Drug addiction, 349
Dummy variables, 331–332
Duty
  of citizens, 22–23
  ideology and, 176
  of individual, 15–30
Duty/Entertainment (DE) model, of voting, 142, 143

Eastern Europe, democratization in, 119–123. *See also* Communism and communists; Soviet Union
East Germany, democratization in, 120
Economic classes. *See* Classes
Economic determinism, 88
Economic development
  analysis of, 358–360
  and costs of goods and services, 313–314
  cultural explanations for, 308–311
  culture and, 308–311
  dependency theory of, 305–307
  human capital theory of, 305
  indicators of, 303
  in MICs, 346–349, 355–357
  multiple regression analysis of, 326–333
  neoliberal theory of, 303–305
  in NICs, 307
  political explanations for, 311–317
  private-property rights and, 357
  regime types and, 317–325
  in Singapore, Taiwan, and South Korea, 325

  welfare state and, 345–346
Economic efficiency, 26–27, 59–60
Economic inequalities, 348–349
Economic rights, 385
Economics. *See also* Liberalism
  and courts, 291
  and LIC underdevelopment, 302–307
  natural law of, 51–52
  roles of adults and organizations, 197
  social welfare spending and, 354
Economy. *See also* Socialism
  Fabians on, 93
  government control of, 312–314
  government intervention in, 27–28
Education
  voter involvement and, 153–154
  as world problem, 375
Edward III (England), 67
Efficiency
  economic, 26–27, 59–60
  Smith on, 52
Eisenhower, Dwight D., 286
Elderly, economic inequality and, 349
Elections, 152. *See also* General elections; Political participation; Primary elections
  cabinets, parliament, and, 218–219
  as linkages, 200–201
Electronic democracy, 82
Elites
  democratic rule and, 324
  in LICs, 305, 313
  recruitment of political, 232
  support for democracy by, 123–124
Elizabeth II (England), 215
El Salvador, human rights abuses in, 389
Embeddedness, 95
Empirical statements, 5
  Mill and, 71–72
  and normative statements, 9–11, 96–102
Employment, welfare state and, 344. *See also* Unemployment
Enactment stage, of legislative process, 227–228
Ends, and means, 370
Engels, Friedrich, 86. *See also* Marxian socialism
England. *See* Britain (England)
Entitlement programs, 346–347
Environment. *See also* Community standards
  social, 94, 309–310
  as world problem, 375
Environmental Action, as interest group, 191
Environmental groups, joining, 149
Epstein, Richard, 70–71
Equal access, by political groups, 195–198
Equality, Rousseau on, 81. *See also* Social justice
Equation
  misspecified, 332
  regression, 294
Errors, by courts, 277–278
E-scale issues, 298
Essay on the Principle of Population as It Affects the Future Improvement of Society, An (Malthus), 53

Ethnic cleansing, 382
Ethnic conflicts, democracy and, 123
Ethnicity
 issue of, 201–202
 and voting rights, 153
Ethnic violence, 382
 as world problem, 375
Etzioni, Amitai, 84
Eulau, Heinz, 230
Europe
 democratization in, 119
 support for rights in, 122
Evaluation
 of policy, 244, 257–258
Examples, for operationalizing a hypothesis, 100–102
Executive. *See* Chief executive
Expertise, of judge, 273
Explained variation, 328
Explanations
 analysis of, 204–209
 for operationalizing a hypothesis, 100–102
Expropriation, 315
Externalities
 negative, 21–22
 positive, 27

Fabian socialism, 92–93
Fabius Maximus, 93
Factions, 192
Falsifications, 100
Family
 dissolution of, 349
 middle-class, 348
 working-class, 348
Fatalism, in "modern" cultures, 310
Federalism, 68–69
Federalist Papers, The
 and Constitution, 75–77
 on majority rule, 68
 No. 10, 77
 No. 49 (Madison), 30
Federal Reserve Board, economic growth and, 355
Feedback, about policy, 244
Feminism, 403
 critique of liberalism and communitarianism by, 95–96
First-world countries. *See* More industrialized countries (MICs)
First World War. *See* World War I
Fiscal policy, 355
Floor leader, 222
Flu epidemic, welfare state and, 344
Folk (Germany), 108
Forces of production, 88
Ford, Henry, 51
Foreign debt, 341
 IMF and, 301
 ... policy, 369. *See also* Policy
 ... on, 389
 ...
 ... nternational
 ... tics

Forsythe, David, 385
Fourier, Charles, 92
France
 bills introduced in, 224–226
 constitutions of, 65
Freedom. *See also* Liberty
 meanings of, 58
 Mill on, 61
Free enterprise, as cause of LIC poverty, 305
Free markets
 as detriment to South, 307
 LICs and, 303, 307
Free ride, 17, 198
Free trade, as mechanism for peace, 379
French Revolution, 77, 82
Freud, Sigmund, human aggression and, 378
Fuehrer, Hitler as, 108
Future Shock (Toffler), 366–368

Game theory, 7
Gandhi, Mohandas, 319
Gender, voting and, 153
General Agreement on Tariffs and Trade (GATT), 371
General elections, voter turnout in, 144
Generality, and specificity, 99–100
General will, Rousseau on, 79
Geneva Convention, 385
Genocide, 382
Germany. *See also* Nazi Germany
 Bundestag in, 219
 Constitutional Court in, 280
 democratization in, 120
 economic inequalities in, 348
 neo-Nazis in, 123
Ghana, corruption in, 317
 Nkrumah in, 319
Global politics, 365–398
Glorious Revolution (England), 47
Go-between, courts as, 272
Goods
 collective, 16–21
 merit, 27
Gorbachev, Mikhail, 119, 121
Gosnell, Harold, 143
Government. *See also* Authoritarianism; Conservatives and conservatism; Constitutionalism; Liberalism; Regimes; Totalitarianism
 administrative structure of U.S., 256
 Bentham on, 57–58
 citizens and, 173–210
 coalition and minority, 217–218
 constitutionalism and, 64–69
 control over economy by, 312–314
 corruption of, 314–315
 defined, 35–36, 215
 in Democratic Kampuchea, 112–113
 development of law and, 33–35
 economic efficiency, spending, and, 26–27
 economic goals and, 355–356
 economic intervention by, 27–28
 in England, 67
 formation and dissolution of, 216–217

functions of, 399–403
goals of, 23
instability of, 315–317
justifications for, 15–39
 as law enforcement agency, 33–34
 as law maker, 34–35
 limited, 47–50
 limiting through participation, 66–67
 and luck, 70–71
 majoritarian and consensual states, 351
 Mill on, 58–61
 minimal, 15–16
 as moral force, 28–29
 origins of, 30–33
 parliamentary system of, 213–238
 political socialization by, 29–30
 presidential system of, 213–238
 process of, 241–269
 protection and order by, 16
 role of, 23
 social intervention by, 26–27
 social justice and, 23–26
 social services of, 26
 welfare state and, 344–345
Governmental Process, The (Truman), 195
Grabosky, Peter, 349
Graft, governmental, 314–315
Granato, Jim, 358
Graphing, of statistical relationships, 166–167
Great Britain. *See* Britain (England)
Great Depression, welfare state and, 344–345
Gross national product (GNP), public programs and, 347
Groups, reasons for joining, 146–148, 198
Growth rates, decline in MICs, 346–349
Gulf War, technology and, 368
Gurr, Ted, 349

Habits of the Heart (Bellah and others), 84
Hamilton, Alexander, as Publius, 68n, 75
Hammurabi, 33
Happiness, Bentham on, 56–57
Hardin, Garrett, 18–19
Harmful actions, negative externalities and, 21–22
Harrington, James, 65–66
Hawks, in Vietnam War, 185
Head of Government, 215–216
 president as, 215–216
Head of State, 215
 president as, 216
Health care, as world problem, 375
Heclo, Hugh, 343, 345
Hegel, Georg Wilhelm Friedrich, 87–88
Heilbroner, Robert, 51, 58
Hekman, Susan, 95–96
Helms, Jesse, 223
Heredity monarchy, 33
Hierarchies
 of bureaucracy, 253
 of courts, 281–286
High Court (Australia), 285
High Court of Justice (England), 282
Hinich, Melvin, 175
Hirschmann, Nancy, 403

Historical materialism, 88
Hitler, Adolf, 107–110, 382
Hobbes, Thomas, 369
    social contract and, 45–47
Hobson, J. A., 379
House of Commons (England), 67, 223
    bills introduced in, 224
House of Lords (England), 67
House of Representatives (United States), 222
Hula, Richard, 349
Human capital theory, and economic advancement, 305
Human nature
    Hobbes on, 369
    Locke vs. Hobbes on, 48
    neorealists, idealists, and pragmatists on, 373–374
    war and, 378–379
Human rights, 375
    analysis of, 392–396
    economic and social, 385
    global abuses of, 386–387
    growing concern for, 383
    improvements in, 390–391
    personal integrity, 383–384
    reasons for abuses of, 385–389
    study of, 383–389
Hypotheses, 97, 98
    alternate, 157
    defined, 9
    empirically testable, 100–102
    for interaction, 236–237
    null, 157–163
    operationalizing, 99–100
    of pluralism, 195–199
    for spurious association, 208

Idealists
    realist criticisms by, 372–374
    and world politics, 372
Ideological superstructure, 88
Ideology, 175–182
    dimensions of, 178–182
    of interest groups, 189–191
    in MICs, 350–353
    political parties and, 182–189, 350–351
    of totalitarian regime, 113
    violence and, 382–383
    voter turnout and, 145–146
    in Western Europe, 181
Ideology and the Theory of Political Choice (Hinich and Munger), 175
IGO. *See* International governmental organization (IGO)
Illegal political activity, 150–151
IMF. *See* International Monetary Fund (IMF)
Impartiality, of judge, 273
Imperialism, 379
Implementation of policy, 244
    bureaucracy and, 251–257
Import substitution, 306
Inalienable rights, concept of, 44
Income
    redistribution of, 57–58

spending and, 354
    voter involvement and, 153–154
Independence
    of judge, 273
    of LICs, 312
Independence movements, charismatic leaders in, 319
Independent variables, 127
    combining, 329
    in economic development, 309
India. *See also* Supreme courts
    Gandhi in, 319
    Supreme Court of, 281, 286
Individualism, socialists and, 94
Individual rights, 72. *See also* Liberalism
    government and, 15–30
    Locke on, 48–50
Individuals. *See also* Communitarianism
    importance in international politics, 373
    wars and, 378–379
Industrial development, in LICs, 312–313. *See also* Less industrialized countries (LICs); Underdevelopment
Inequalities
    economic, 348–349
    in MICs, 353–355
Inflation, in MICs, 355–357
Information
    ideology and, 176
    from interest groups, 191
Informed Voter (IV) model, 142–146, 177
Inglehart, Ronald, 178, 308–309, 358
INGOs. *See* International nongovernmental organizations (INGOs)
Initiation stage, of legislative process, 224–225
Initiative, 82
Inquiry into the Nature and Causes of the Wealth of Nations, An. See Wealth of Nations, The (Smith)
Instability, governmental, 315–317
Institutionalized Revolutionary Party (PRI), economic development and, 322
Institutional structures, 174
Institutions, 174–175
    and democracy, 175
    liberal and constitutional, 75–95
    in MICs, 350–353
Insurance programs, welfare state and, 343–344
Interaction
    measuring, 234, 236
    among variables, 234–236
Intercept, 295
Interest groups
    demands transmitted by, 198–199
    linkages provided by, 189–200
    in parliamentary and presidential systems, 226
    pluralism and, 195–199
    problems of, 192–195
    reasons for joining, 146–148
    Rousseau on, 81
    and unearned rents, 192–195
International governmental organization (IGO), 385
International law, 384

International market, as cause of LIC poverty, 305
International Monetary Fund (IMF), 301
International nongovernmental organizations (INGOs), 372, 373
International relations. *See also* World politics
    political realism and, 369–370
    war and, 378
Interstate war, 377–378
Interval scale, 261
Intervention, in economy, 27–28
Investment, economic growth and, 356–357
Invisible hand, 28, 51
    criticisms of, 53
    Ricardo on, 306
Iran, corruption in, 314–315
Israel, political parties in, 188
Issue Evolution: Race and the Transformation of American Politics (Carmines and Stimson), 202
Issues. *See* Political issues; issues by name
Italy
    Chamber of Deputies in, 221
    legislative committees in, 224
    multiparty system in, 187
    totalitarianism in, 106
Item veto, 192n
IV model. *See* Informed Voter (IV) model

Jackson, Andrew, 286
James II (England), 47
Janowitz, Morris, 321
Japan
    culture of, 325
    Diet in, 221
Japanese Americans, ethnic violence and, 382
Jarulzelski, Wojciech, 120
Jay, John, as Publius, 68n, 75n
Jefferson, Thomas, 377
Jewish people
    Hitler and, 382
    in Nazi Germany, 110
Job (biblical), 47
Joining. *See* Groups; Voting
Judges. *See also* Courts
    administrative duties of, 275–276
    as authoritative party, 273
    expertise of, 277
Judicial decisions, "wrong," 277–278
Judicial discretion, and lawmaking, 279
Judicial policy making, courts and, 271–278
Judicial power
    and attitudes of judicial policy makers, 289
    global expansion of, 288–289
Judicial process
    mechanical conception of, 272, 276–277, 278
    precedent in, 278–279
Judicial review, 69, 280–281
    administrative, 281
Juries, 283
Justice, social, 23–26
Justinian, code of, 34

Kampuchea (Cambodia), 114
  cultural change in, 309
  totalitarianism in, 111–113
  violence in, 383
Kant, Immanuel, 380
  categorical imperative of, 175
  on democracy and foreign relations, 380
KANU. *See* Kenyan African National Union (KANU)
Kautsky, Karl, 379
Kegley, Charles, 377
Kemal, Mustafa. *See* Atatürk
Kennedy, John F., 286
Kenya, single-party authoritarian regime in, 118
Kenyan African National Union (KANU), 118
Kenyatta, Jomo, 118
Keohane, Robert, 372
Keynes, John Maynard, 344
Keynesian economics, welfare state and, 344
Khmer Rouge, 112–113
  cultural change and, 309
Killing Fields, The (movie), 383
King's Council (England), 67
Kissinger, Henry, 369
Kurdish people, 30
  concept of nation and, 37

Labor. *See also* Laboring class; Population
  division of, 52
  economic goals and, 355–356
  Locke on, 49, 51
  Marxist socialism on, 89
  population and, 53–54
  as proletariat, 90
Laboring class
  Malthus on, 53–54
  Ricardo on, 53–56
Labour Party (Britain), 93, 187
Laissez-faire, 52
Land. *See also* Property
  expropriation of, 315
  rents on, 55
  wealth and, 56
Latin America
  authoritarian regimes in, 121
  culture and underdevelopment in, 309
  democratization in, 119
  presidential system in, 250
  support for rights in, 122
Law(s). *See also* Lawmaking
  code, 279
  codification of, 33
  courts and, 274–275
  development of, 33–35
  enforcement of, 33–34
  international, 384
  legislative process stages and,
so Law(s)
  judicial discretion and, 279
  and "wrong" judicial decisions, 277–278
Law of Population (Smith), 53
Leadership
  charismatic, 319–321
  in legislature, 222–223
  in Nazi Germany, 109
League of Nations, 385
Leblang, David, 357, 358
Left (ideological)
  corporatist government and, 356
  party ideology and, 350–351
Leftist, 179–182
Legal policy making, importance of, 286–288
Legal realists, 278
Legislation, evaluating, 230–231
Legislative competence, 219–220
Legislative districts, single-member, 187
Legislative performance
  constituency service and, 231–232
  evaluating legislation and public policy, 230–231
  executive oversight and control and, 231
  recruitment of political elites and, 232
  representation and, 228–229
Legislative process, 214, 224–228
  deliberation stage, 225–226
  enactment stage, 227–228
  initiation stage, 224–225
Legislators, evaluation of, 230
Legislatures, 214. *See also* Legislative performance; Legislative process
  arena, 247
  authority and leadership structure in, 222–223
  chambers of, 220–221
  committee systems in, 223–224
  institutional framework of, 219–224
  rules of procedure in, 221
  transformative, 247
Legitimacy, of governments, 324–325
Legitimation
  in democratic regimes, 247–250
  in nondemocratic regimes, 244–247
  of policy, 244
Lenin, V. I., 379
Less industrialized countries (LICs), 301–335
  cultural explanations for underdevelopment, 308–311
  democratic regimes among, 323–325
  economic explanations for underdevelopment, 303–307
  government control of economy in, 312–314
  government instability in, 315–317
  military regimes in, 321–322
  political explanations for underdevelopment, 311–317
  regime types and development, 317–325
Leviathan (Hobbes), 45
  character of, 46–47
Lex (law), 34
Liberal, 350, 351. *See also* Leftist
  social insurance programs and, 343–344
Liberalism
  Bentham and, 56–58
  classical western tradition of, 43–52
  communitarians and, 85–86
  contemporary, 62–64
  feminist critique of, 95–96
  Mill and, 58–61
  pluralist systems and, 352
  reform, 53–61
  use of term, 44, 62
Liberalism against Populism (Riker), 201
Libertarians, 178–182
  interest groups as, 189–190
Liberty. *See also* Freedom; Rights
  and courts, 290
  democracy and, 76
  Mill and, 60–61
LICs. *See* Less industrialized countries (LICs)
Lifestyle, in communist society, 91
Lijphart, Arend, 351–352, 355
Limited government, Locke on, 47–50
Linkages
  elections as, 200–201
  by interest groups, 189–200
  by political parties, 188–189
Litigants, 283, 285
Locke, John, on limited government, 47–50
Loewenberg, Gerhard, 232
Logic of Collective Action, The (Olson), 140, 146, 198
Logrolling, 199
Lon Nol, 111
Lopez Portillo (Mexico), 119, 314
Lords of Appeal in Ordinary (Britain), 285, 286
Lorenz, Konrad, 378–379
Louis XIV (France), 44
Lower house, of bicameral legislature, 220
Luther, Martin, 44

MacIntyre, Alasdair, 96
Madison, James
  on development of law, 33
  on Montesquieu, 68
  on political socialization, 30
  as Publius, 68n, 75
  on special interests, 192
Majoritarian states, 351–352
  democracies as, 355
Majorities
  defeat by organized minorities, 199–200
  representation of, 229
Majority leader, 222
Majority rule
  and Athenian Assembly, 66
  checks on, 68–69
  Locke on, 50
  in multiparty political systems, 186–188
  Rousseau on, 81
  with two-party system, 183–184
  voters' paradox and, 184–185
Majority vote, Locke on, 50

Malthus, Thomas, 51, 53
    on role of population, 53–54
Management, of bureaucracy, 255–257
Mao. *See* China
Marbury v. *Madison,* 69, 280
Marcos, Ferdinand, corruption of, 315, 316
Market, invisible hand in, 51. *See also* Free
  markets
Marshall, John, 69
Marx, Karl, 28, 51, 86. *See also*
  Communism and communists; Marxian
  socialism; Marxism-Leninism
    on capitalist society, 88–90
Marxian socialism, 86–92
    communist revolution and, 90–92
    theory of, 88–92
Marxism-Leninism, 43
    Locke and, 51
Mass production, 51
Material goods, and joining groups, 147
Materialism, dialectical (historical), 88
McCormick, Robert, 353
Mean (statistical), 327
Mearsheimer, John, 381
Measures, nominal and ordinal, 260–261
Mechanical conception, of judicial process,
  272, 276–277, 278
Mediator, courts as, 272
Mein Kampf (Hitler), 107
Meny, Yves, 132
Merit, and bureaucracy, 253
Merit good, 27
Merit system, 91
Mexico
    bribery and graft in, 315
    concept of state in, 36
    single-party regime in, 118–119, 322
Micro-Crunch, 161, 404–415
MICs. *See* More industrialized countries
  (MICs)
Middle-class families, taxation and, 348
Middle East, violence in, 382
Military. *See also* Arms
    in Chile, 124n
    elite use of, 124
    expenditures on, 376–377
    intervention to support elite, 124
Military dictators, 115
Military regime
    as authoritarian government, 115–117
    and economic development, 321–322
Mill, John Stuart, 51, 58–61, 85–86, 232
    empirical and normative arguments of,
    71–72
    social insurance and, 343
Minorities, defeat of majorities by, 199–200
Minority governments, coalitions and,
  217–218
Minority leader, 222
Minority rule, and Athenian Assembly, 66
Misspecified equation, 332
MNCs. *See* Multinational corporations
Mobuto Sese Seko, corruption of, 316
Model Parliament (England), 67
Models, of voting, 140–146
Modern societies, 310. *See also* Cultural
  explanations
    military contributions to, 321–322

Monarch and monarchy, 33, 43–44, 115.
  See also Britain (England)
    as Head of State, 215
    limited, 47–48
    Locke on, 50
Monopolistic control, by totalitarian
  regime, 113–114
Montesquieu, 68
Morality
    government and, 28–29
    social context of, 95
Mordida, La, 314
More industrialized countries (MICs)
    aging of populations in, 338–339, 340
    alternative political systems in,
    353–357
    challenges facing, 338–341
    economic slowdown in, 346–349
    institutional differences in, 351–353
    institutional similarities in, 350–351
    and LICs, 303
    politics in, 337–362
    social problems in, 349
    as welfare states, 343–346
Morgenthau, Hans J., 370
Mosaic Code, 33n
MPs (Members of Parliament). *See*
  Parliament (Britain)
Mueller, John, 377
Muller, Edward, 150, 158
Multinational corporations (MNCs), 305
    economic power of, 372–373
Multiparty system
    majority rule in, 186–188
    party labels in, 188
Multiple regression, 326–333
    for cultural and economic variables, 360
    defined, 329
Munger, Michael, 175
Muslims. *See* Middle East
Mussolini, Benito, 106

NAFTA. *See* North American Free Trade
  Agreement (NAFTA)
National defense, payment for, 21
National interest, 370
Nationalism
    issue of, 201–202
    Marx and Engels on, 90–92
    Rousseau and, 83–84
Nationalistic conflicts, democracy and, 123
National sovereignty. *See* Sovereignty
Nation-state, 38. *See also* Government;
  Law
    defined, 37
    sovereignty of, 35
    war and, 378, 379–380
Native Americans, ethnic violence and,
  382
Natural laws. *See also* Economics
    economic, 51–52, 59
    Locke on, 48
    and reform liberalism, 53–61
Natural rights
    Bentham on, 57
    Locke on, 48–50
Nature, Rousseau on, 77–78

Nazi Germany
    government of, 110
    totalitarianism in, 106–110
Nazi party, 108
    doctrine of, 108–109
Negative externalities, 21–22
Negative relationship, 263–264
Negative rights, 383
Neoliberal theory, of LIC development,
  303–305
Neo-Nazis, in Germany, 348
Neorealists, 371
    realist criticisms by, 372–374
Neumann, Franz, 108n
New international economic order, 307
Newly industrialized countries (NICs), 307
New York City, bureaucracy in, 254–255
Nicaragua, Somoza in, 116
NICs. *See* Newly industrialized countries
  (NICs)
Nixon, Richard, 369
Nkrumah, Kwame, 246, 319
Nobel Peace Prize, 373
Nominal measure, 260
Noncommunist regimes, single-party,
  322–323
Nonconstitutional regimes, 105–106
    authoritarianism, 114–119
    communism and totalitarianism as,
    106–113
    democratization and, 119–124
    problems with, 125
Nondemocratic governments, agenda
  setting, formulation, and legitimation by,
  244–247
Nonspurious association, 206–207
Nordström, Hakan, 347
Normative statements, 5
    and empirical statements, 9–11, 96–102
    Mill and, 71–72
North (industrialized countries), 306–307
North, Douglass, 357
North American Free Trade Agreement
  (NAFTA), 371, 373
    Mexican government and, 119
Nozick, Robert, 62–63, 72, 176
Nuclear-arms proliferation, 375
Null hypothesis, 157–163
Nuremberg War Crimes Tribunal, 107

Observation, defined, 9n
Occupation, voter involvement and,
  153–154
Occupation zones, in Germany, 110
Oceana (Harrington), 65–66
Oceans, overfishing of, 21
Oil prices, 340
Oligarchy, Locke on, 50
Oliver Twist (Dickens), 53
Olson, Mancur, Jr., 115, 140, 146–147,
  148–149, 198, 347–348
    on origins of government, 31–32
One-tail tests, of significance, 266
On Liberty (Mill), 59, 61
Operationalization, 98. *See also*
  Hypotheses
    of political terms, 371

Opinions
    consistency of, 177
    voter research and, 145
Opportunities, government and, 23–26
Order, by government, 16
Ordinal measure, 260–261
Organization
    bureaucratic, 252–253
    ease of, 198
    economic roles of, 197
    membership in, 196
    power of, 199–200
Organization of Petroleum Exporting
    Countries (OPEC), oil prices and, 340
Original position, Rawls on, 63–64
Origin of Species (Darwin), 51
Origin of the Family, The (Engels), 86
Oversight, of executive, 231
Owen, Robert, 92

Pacifism, 379. *See also* Wars and warfare
Palmer, Monte, 308, 319
Parliament (Britain), 67
    deliberation in, 227
    dissolution of, 218–219
    legislative competence of, 219–220
    legislative process in, 225
    parliamentary system and, 214–232
    question hour in, 219
Parliamentary democracies, system failure
    for, 259
Parliamentary government
    composition of, 217
    in Nazi Germany, 108
Parliamentary system, 213–238
Partial slope, 330
Participatory government, 66–67
    Rousseau and, 83
Particularized contacting, 139
Parties. *See* Political parties
Party manifestos, 190
Patriotism
    Marx and Engels on, 90–92
    Rousseau on, 83
Patterson, Samuel C., 232
Peace, capitalism and, 379. *See also* Wars
    and warfare
Peak associations, 353
Pearson, Karl, 295, 327
Pensions, economic costs of, 347
Percentagizing, 127
Performance
    appraising, 91
    of legislative functions, 228–232
Periphery (less industrialized countries),
    306–307
Perot, Ross, 82
Personal computer industry, labor, profits,
    and, 89
Personal computers. *See* Computer
    [...]

Philippines, policy making by Supreme
    Court, 287, 288
Planned economy, investment in, 356
Platforms, of political parties, 190–191
Plato, 6
Plessy v. *Ferguson,* 278–279
Pluralism
    equal access and participation
        hypothesis of, 195–198
    and interest groups, 195–199
    in MICs, 352–353
    organization of interests hypothesis of,
        198
    social benefits from interest groups
        hypothesis of, 198–199
Pluralist theory, 146
Poe, Steven C., 392
Poland, democratization in, 119–120
Police, and courts, 274–275
Policy. *See* Foreign policy; Policy making;
    Public policy
Policy makers, judicial, 289
Policy making, 243–244. *See also* Public
    policy
    in democratic regimes, 247–250
    judicial, 271–298
    legal, 286–288
    in nondemocratic regimes, 244–247
Politburo, 246
Political behavior, 6–7
Political competition, in MICs, 350
Political culture, analysis of, 358–360
Political elites, legislative recruitment of,
    232
Political equality, 81
Political explanations
    corruption as, 314–315
    government control of economy and,
        312–314
    government corruption and, 314–315
    government instability as, 315–317
    of industrial development, 311–317
    regime types and development,
        317–325
Political ideology. *See* Ideology
Political issues, 1, 6–7
Political participation, 137–171
    categories of, 139–140
    characteristics of participators,
        152–154
    defined, 138–140
    demographics of, 153–154
    forms of, 139
    in interest groups, 146–148
    paradox of, 152
    pluralism and, 195–198
    rationality of, 151–152
    unlawful, 150–151
    voting as, 140–146
Political parties, 182–189
    charismatic leader creation of, 320
    ideology of, 350–351
    impact of weak, nonideological, 200
    and interest groups, 190–191
    legislative committee membership
        and, 223
    nonideological functions of, 188

    platforms of, 190–191
    voter linkages through, 188–189
    whips of, 223
Political philosophy, defined, 6
Political prisoners, in Nazi Germany, 110
Political realism. *See* Realism
Political science
    choice and, 5–6
    defined, 4
Political socialization, 29–30
    by Hitler, 110
Political systems, alternative, in MICs,
    353–357
Politics
    choices in, 34
    deal-making in, 199–200
    defined, 2
    global, 365–398
    idealists in, 372
    in more industrialized countries
        (MICs), 337–362
    normative and empirical statements in,
        5
    realism in, 368–374
    science of, 4–5
Pol Pot, 111, 112, 114
Popular government, use of term, 76
Popular selection, of government, 50
Popular sovereignty, 81
Population. *See also* Demographics
    aging of, 338, 339
    economic role of, 53–54
    growth of, 375
Positive externalities, 27
Positive relationship, 263
Postmaterialist ideology, on social issues,
    178
Potter, Beatrix, 93
Poverty
    in MICs, 353–355
    public assistance and, 26
    as world problem, 375
Powell, Bingham, 145, 154
Power
    of elites, 305
    as national goal, 369
Pragmatism, in U.S. politics, 250
Pragmatists, 373–374
Preamble to the Constitution, 65
Prebisch, Raul, 306
Precedent, 278–279
    in law, 34
Prediction, with regression analysis, 294.
    See also Multiple regression
Prejudice, vs. ideology, 202
President, 215–216
    as Head of Government, 215–216
Presidential government
    composition of, 217
    system failure for, 259
Presidential system, 213–238
PRI (Institutionalized Party of the
    Revolution), 118
Price, Robert, 316
Prieswork, Roy, 373
Primary elections, voter turnout in, 144.
    See also Elections

Prime minister, and Parliament, 223. *See also* Chief executive
Principles of Political Economy (Mill), 59
Prisoner's dilemma, 17–18
Private Member's Bills, in Parliament, 226
Private property. *See* Property
Probabilistic relationships, 157
Probability, 127, 156–161
    correlation and, 265–266
    statistics and, 156–170
Problems, worldwide, 374–390
Procedures, in legislature, 221
Production
    demand, supply, and, 52
    economic laws and, 60
    Marx on, 88
Productivity, population and, 54
Profits, Marx on, 89. *See also* Capitalism
Progressive-Conservative Party, in Canada, 201
Progressive taxes, 348
Proletariat, 90
Property
    Bentham on, 57
    conservatives on, 63
    Locke vs. Hobbes on, 48–49
    Marx on, 90
    private, 90
    protection of, 357
    utilitarians on, 61
Proportional representation, 187
Protection, 194
    in first-world countries, 307
    by government, 16
Protest behavior, as unlawful participation, 150–151
Protest participation, 139–140
Provincial superior courts (Canada), 282
Przeworski, Adam, 121, 124, 355–356
Przeworski-Wallerstein model, 355–356
Public assistance, 26
Public choice, 7
Public dilemmas, overfishing of oceans, 21
Public education, economic costs of, 347
Public good, voluntary contributions to, 16–17, 18–19. *See also* Collective goods
Public interest
    groups, 198
    Rousseau on, 79
Public policy. *See also* Policy making
    agenda setting and, 244–251
    bureaucracy and implementation of, 251–257
    as citizen-government link, 173–174
    evaluating, 230–231, 257–258
    implementation in democratic regimes, 253
    policy-making process and, 242–244
    process of government and, 241–269
Publius, 68, 75–77
Puritans and Puritanism, 28
    in England, 45
Pygmalion (Shaw), 93n

Quebec, concept of nation and, 37

Queen, as Head of State, 215
Question hour, 219

Rabin, Yitzhak, 373
Race and racism
    democracy and, 123
    as issue, 202
    and voting rights, 153
Rational choice, 7
Rationale, of good explanation, 205–206
Rationality
    Hobbes on, 46
    and ideological consistency, 177
    Locke on, 49
    of nation-states, 369
    of political participation, 151–152
    Rawls on, 64
Rational self-interest
    group membership and, 198
    society and, 16
Rawls, John, 6, 62–64, 70, 71, 95, 176
    Realism, 369
    critics of, 371–372
    failures of, 372–374
    in world politics, 368–374
Reason, liberal tradition and, 44–45. *See also* Rationality
Rebellion, as unlawful participation, 150–151
Recall, 82
Recruitment, of political elites, 232
Redistribution of income, 57–58
Referendum, 82
Reform Act of 1832 (England), 67
Reform liberalism, natural law and, 53–61
Regimes. *See also* Government
    authoritarian, 318–319
    charismatic leadership in, 319–321
    democratic, 323–325
    and economic development, 317–325
    military, 321–322
    single-party, noncommunist, 322–323
    totalitarian, 318
Regression analysis, 293–297. *See also* Multiple regression
    success in predicting reality, 297
Regression equation, 294
Regression line, 295
    slope of, 330
Regressive taxes, 348
Reign of Terror (France), 83
Rein, Martin, 349
Relationships
    deterministic and probabilistic, 157
    graphing statistical, 166–167
    positive and negative, 263–264
    of production, 88
    statistical, 156–170
    among variables, 235
Religion. *See also* Jewish people
    Christianity, 48
    government and, 28–29
    issue of, 201–202
    laws and, 28–29
    liberal tradition and, 44–45
    and superstition, 310, 311

violence and, 382
    and voting rights, 153
Religious conflicts
    democracy and, 123
    as world problem, 375
Rents
    interest groups and, 192–195
    unearned, 55, 56, 192–195
Rent seeking, by interest groups, 192–195
Representation
    as legislative function, 228–230
    of majority, 229
Representative government, 66–67, 76
    Mill on, 59
    Rousseau on, 81
Republic, use of term, 76
Republican Party
    ideology of, 183
    interest groups and, 191
    political ideology of, 181
Republic of Chad, economy of, 313
Research, empirical, 97
Revolutionary War in America. *See* American Revolution
Revolutions, 77–78, 82
Rheinische Zeitung, 86
Ricardo, David, 51, 53, 54
    comparative advantage and, 304–305
    on interest groups, 192
    on Smith's theories, 306
Riding, Alan, 315
Right (ideological), party ideology and, 350, 351
Rightist, 179–182
Rights. *See also* Human rights
    in Central America, 122
    of citizens, 22–23
    economic and social, 385
    in Europe and Moscow, 122
    inalienable, 44
    of individuals, 15–30
    natural, 48–50
    to property, 48–49
Rights-based society, vs. communitarianism, 85–86
Riker, William, 201, 230
Robert's Rules of Order, 221
Robespierre, 83
Roman law, 34
Rondinelli, Dennis, 313
Rousseau, Jean-Jacques
    and communitarian democracy, 77–84
    on democracy, 81–83
    and totalitarianism, 83–84
Rulers, 44
    authoritarian, 115
    divine right of, 35
    government origins and, 31–32
    Locke on, 49
Rules of procedure, in legislature, 221
Rules of the game, in legislatures, 221
Russett, Bruce, 380
Russia
    as sovereign state, 36
    support for rights in, 122
Rustow, Dankwart, 116
Rwanda, ethnic violence in, 382

Saint-Simon (Claude-Henri de Rouvroy), 92
Scatterplot, 261–263
    multiple regression and, 327, 328
    for regression, 296
Schattschneider, E. E., 197–198
School desegregation, courts and, 287
Scope, of court's decision making, 280
Second Treatise of Civlil Government (Locke), 50, 51
Second World War. *See* World War II
Security, as national goal, 369
Security forces, of charismatic leaders, 320
Selective incentives, for joining groups, 147
Senate (United States), 222
Separation of powers, 68
    in presidential system, 249
    Rousseau on, 81
Shah of Iran, corruption of, 314–315
Shaw, George Bernard, 93
Short-term problems, 337
Shrinking-world phenomenon, 368
Significance, tests of, 266
Simpson, O. J., trial of, 291
Singapore, 325
Single-member legislative districts, 187
Single-party, noncommunist regimes, economic development and, 322–323
Single-party civilian regimes, 117–118
Sivard, Ruth Leger, 376, 378
Slope, 266
    of regression line, 295
Smeeding, Timothy, 349
Smith, Adam, 28, 51–52
    on Law of Population, 53
    Ricardo on, 306
Social choice, 7
Social classes. *See* Classes
Social contract, 45–47
    Rousseau on, 78
Social control, by courts, 274–275
Social democrats, 351
Social environment, culture and, 309–311
Social institutions, 30
Social insurance programs, welfare state and, 343
Socialism
    contemporary, 94
    democratic, 92–94
    Fabian, 92–93
    government intervention and, 28
    Marxian, 86–92
    Mill and, 58–61
Socialism: Scientific and Utopian (Engels), 86
Social issues
    drug addiction, family dissolution, crime, and, 349
    economic inequalities and, 349
    postmaterialist ideology on, 178
    ms and, 344
    tandards and,
    26

Social rights, 385
Social services, 26
Social tasks, of cultures, 308
Social welfare, spending on, 354
Society. *See also* Government
    Bentham on, 56–58
    government economic intervention in, 26–27
    government intervention in, 23–26
    government intervention in morality of, 28–29
    individual rational self-interest and, 16
    Mill on, 60–61
    political socialization and, 29–30
    Rousseau on, 77–78
    stateless, 92
Software. *See* Computer software
Solidarity benefits, of joining groups, 148, 149
Solidarity labor movement, 120
Somoza family
    Anastasio, 116–117
    Anastasio, Jr., 117
    corruption of, 314
SOPs. *See* Standard operating procedures (SOPs)
South (less industrialized countries), 306–307
South Africa, 323
South America. *See* Latin America
South Korea, 325
Sovereign state, 35
Sovereignty, 35
    human rights and, 389–390
    popular, 81
    Rousseau on, 81
Soviet Union
    democratization in, 119–122, 123
    economic development in, 318
    industrialization in, 312–313
    policy making and implementation in, 246
    as sovereign state, 36
Spain, economic development in, 325
Speaker of the House, 223
Special interests. *See* Interest groups
Specialization, 52
    of bureaucracy, 253
Specificity, generality and, 99–100
Spending
    by government, 26–27
    for social purposes, 344–345
    on social welfare, 354
Spirit of the Laws, The (Montesquieu), 68
Spurious association, analysis of, 204–209
Stages, of legislative process, 224–228
Standard error, 266
Standard operating procedures (SOPs), of bureaucracies, 253
Stare decisis, 34, 278
Starr, Harvey, 380
State
    defined, 36
    Fabians on, 93
    in Nazi Germany, 108
Stateless society, 92
State of nature, 45
    Locke on, 49

Rousseau on, 77–78
State terror, instruments of, 113
Stationary bandits concept, 31–32
Statistical significance, critical values and, 163
Statistics
    multiple regression analysis and, 326–333
    probability and, 156–170
    regression analysis and, 293–297
Stimson, James, 202
Stoicism, 48
Student's *t*, 266–267
Subsidies
    in first-world countries, 307
    interest groups and, 199
Suffrage
    in England, 67
    universal, 220
Superstition, 311
    in "modern" cultures, 310
Supply. *See* Demand and supply
Supreme Court (United States), 281
    judicial review and, 69
    regression analysis applied to, 293–297
    voting by, 261–263
Supreme courts, 281
    as final arbiters, 285–286
Surplus value, 89
Synthesis, 87–88
System of Logic (Mill), 59
Systems theory. *See* World systems

Tables
    analysis of, 126–132
    contingency, 127–129, 169–170
Taiwan, 325
Tariffs, interest groups and, 193–195
Tate, C. Neal, 279n, 392
Taxation
    progressive, 348
    regressive, 348
Tax collection, bureaucracy and, 252
Technology, 52
    for direct democracy, 82
    labor and, 89
    population and, 54
    world politics and, 367–368
Ten Commandments, 33n
Terror instruments, of totalitarian regimes, 113
Tests, of significance, 266
Theories, scientific, 97–98
Theory of Justice, A (Rawls), 63
Thesis, 87
Third-world countries. *See* Less industrialized countries (LICs)
Thomas Aquinas, 48
Thucydides, 7
    on political realism, 369
Tiananmen Square, demonstration in, 121
Toffler, Alvin, 366
Tollison, Robert, 353
Torrey, Barbara, 349
Totalitarianism, 83–84, 105, 106
    communism and, 110–111

counterrevolutionaries and, 111–112
defined, 113–114
and economic development, 318
flaws of, 125
ideology of, 113
in Kampuchea (Cambodia), 111–113
monopolistic control by, 113–114
in Nazi Germany, 106–110
policy evaluation by, 257
policy making and implementation under, 246–247
terror instruments of, 113
Total sum of squares, 327n
Total variation, 327
Traditional cultures, 308, 310. *See also* Cultural explanations; Underdevelopment
"Tragedy of the Commons" (Hardin), 18–19
Transformative legislatures, 247
Triadic conflict resolution, 272
Trial courts (courts of first instance), 282–283
Trials, 283
Tribunals (Italy), 282
Truman, David, 195, 198
Trustee, legislative representative as, 229
Truth, The, in Democratic Kampuchea, 113, 114
t-score, 266–267
Turkey, Atatürk in, 116
Two-party system, majority rule by, 183–184
Two-tail tests, of significance, 266
Tyson, Laura, 193

Udall, Morris, 199
Underdevelopment
cultural explanations for, 308–311
economic explanations for, 302–307
modern values and, 308
multiple regression analysis of, 326–333
political explanations for, 311–317
regime types and, 317–325
Unearned rents, 55, 56
interest groups and, 192–195
Unemployment
in MICs, 355–357
welfare state and, 344
Unemployment compensation, economic costs of, 347
Unemployment insurance, 343
Unexplained variation, 327
Unicameral legislature, 220
United Nations, 384
Declaration of Human Rights, 385
United States
administrative structure of government, 256
Constitution of, 65
differences from other presidential democracies, 249–250
economic inequalities in, 348
government assistance in, 26
legislative process in, 225
NAFTA and, 119
political ideology in, 181

presidential system in, 214–232
United States Congress. *See* Congress (United States)
United States Constitution. *See* Constitution of the United States
U.S. International Trade Commission, 193
U.S. State Department, human rights reports by, 394
Unit of analysis, 126
Universal suffrage, 220
Unwritten rules, in legislature, 221
Upper chamber, of bicameral legislature, 220
Utilitarianism, 56–58, 61
Utilitarianism (Mill), 59
Utopian vision, in Kampuchea, 112–113

Vallinder, Torbjorn, 279n
Value, surplus, 89
Value-free statements, 9
Values
of courts, 290
and economic development, 308–309
Variables, 98, 127. *See also* Cultural explanations; Economic development; Independent variables; Political explanations
control, 233–237
dummy, 331–332
independent, 329
Variance, 327
Veil of ignorance, Rawls on, 63
Verba, Sidney, 352
Victimless crimes, 29
Vietnam, Cambodian invasion by, 113
Vietnamese, ethnic violence and, 382
Vietnam War, 185, 186
Kampuchean totalitarianism and, 111
Violence
by democratic nations, 380
human rights violations and, 382–390
as world problem, 375
Virtue, 81
Voluntary associations, 352
Voluntary contributions, 16–17, 18–19
voting as, 140
Vote of confidence, in Parliament, 218–219
Voters' paradox, 184–185
and Vietnam War, 185, 186
Voting
interest groups and, 190–191
models of, 140–146
as political participation, 140–146
political participation beyond, 146–152
reasons for, 146–147
by Supreme Court, 261–263
Voting rights. *See also* Suffrage
restrictions on, 153
universal suffrage and, 220
Voting Rights Act (1965), 153

Wages, Marxist socialism and, 89
Wallerstein, Michael, 355–356
Waltz, Kenneth, 378

Walzer, Michael, 95
Wars and warfare, 375
costs of, 376–377
human rights violations and, 382–390
interstate, 377–378
reasons for, 378–381
relationship with democracy, 380
trends in, 377–378
Wealth
economic inequalities and, 348–349
Fabians on, 93
of landowners, 56
Wealth of Nations, The (Smith), 28n, 52
Weapons
costs of, 376–377
proliferation of, 375
Webb, Sidney, 93
Weber, Max, 319
Weede, Erich, 347
Welfare, collective good, negative externalities, and, 23
Welfare state
communitarians and, 85
development of, 343–346
MICs as, 343–346
Mill and, 60
Welfare systems, expenditures on, 353–355
Western Europe, political ideology in, 181
Whips, in Congress, 223
Wilensky, Harold, 354
William and Mary (England), 47–48
Wilson, James Q., 148, 254
Wilson, Woodrow, as idealist, 372
Wittkopf, Eugene, 377
Women
in LICs, 308
suffrage of, 220
Workers. *See also* Labor
Marx on, 89–90
as proletariat, 90
Working-class families, taxation and, 348
World Court, 384
Worldly Philosophers, The (Heilbroner), 58
World politics
game of, 367
human rights and, 382–390, 392–396
positive development in, 390–391
realism in, 368–374
technology and, 367–368
war and, 376–381, 382–390
world problems and, 374–390
World systems, 366
NICs and, 307
theory of, 306–307
warfare and, 380–381
World War I, welfare state and, 344
World War II, 106
human rights activities after, 385
welfare state and, 345

Yugoslavia, breakup of, 123

Zaire, corruption in, 316
Zeigler, Harmon, 309, 314, 316, 325
Zeno, 48